Lecture Notes in Computer Science 14300

Formal Methods

Subline of Lecture Notes in Computer Science

More information about this series at https://link.springer.com/bookseries/558

Paula Herber · Anton Wijs
Editors

Integrated Formal Methods

18th International Conference, IFM 2023
Leiden, The Netherlands, November 13–15, 2023
Proceedings

 Springer

Editors
Paula Herber 🄳
Embedded Systems Group
University of Münster
Münster, Germany

Anton Wijs 🄳
Eindhoven University of Technology
Eindhoven, The Netherlands

ISSN 0302-9743   ISSN 1611-3349 (electronic)
Lecture Notes in Computer Science
ISBN 978-3-031-47704-1   ISBN 978-3-031-47705-8 (eBook)
https://doi.org/10.1007/978-3-031-47705-8

This Springer imprint is published by the registered company Springer Nature Switzerland AG
The registered company address is: Gewerbestrasse 11, 6330 Cham, Switzerland

Paper in this product is recyclable.

Preface

This volume contains the papers presented at the 18th International Conference on integrated Formal Methods (iFM 2023), held in the charming city of Leiden, The Netherlands, and hosted by the Leiden Institute of Advanced Computer Science of Leiden University. These proceedings also contain three papers selected by the Program Committee of the PhD Symposium (PhD-iFM 2023), chaired by Crystal Chang Din and Gidon Ernst.

In recent years, we have witnessed a proliferation of approaches that integrate several modeling, verification, and simulation techniques, facilitating more versatile and efficient analysis of software-intensive systems. These approaches provide powerful support for the analysis of different functional and non-functional properties of the systems, and the complex interaction of components of different natures, as well as validation of diverse aspects of system behavior. The iFM conference series is a forum for discussing recent research advances in the development of integrated approaches to formal modeling and analysis. The conference series covers all aspects of the design of integrated techniques, including language design, verification and validation, automated tool support, and the use of such techniques in software engineering practice.

The iFM 2023 conference solicited high-quality papers reporting research results and/or experience reports related to the overall theme of formal methods integration. The Program Committee (PC) received a total of 51 paper submissions from authors in 17 different countries: 43 regular papers and 8 short papers. All submissions were rigorously reviewed by three PC members, with the help of many external reviewers, after which the reviewers had a short but intense discussion. The decision to accept or reject a submission was based on both the review reports with their scores and the outcomes of these in-depth discussions.

Ultimately, the PC of iFM 2023 selected 18 papers for presentation during the conference and inclusion in these proceedings: 16 regular papers and 2 short papers. This amounts to an overall acceptance rate of 35.3% (37% for regular papers and 25% for short papers). The PC of PhD-iFM 2023 received 12 submissions and selected 7 submissions for presentation at the symposium and 3 of those submissions for inclusion in these proceedings.

This edition of iFM continued the use of the EAPLS artifact badging scheme, which was introduced at iFM 2022, to credit tool developers and stimulate reproducibility of the reported results. The Artifact Evaluation Committee, chaired by Anna-Lena Lamprecht and Muhammad Osama, received 8 submissions and intensively tested the quality of the artifacts. All artifacts achieved the available and the functional badges, while 6 artifacts additionally were awarded the reusable badge.

The iFM 2023 conference featured keynotes by the following speakers:

- Erika Ábrahám (RWTH Aachen University, Germany);
- Barbara Jobstmann (EPFL and Cadence Design Systems, Switzerland);
- K. Rustan M. Leino (Amazon Web Services, USA).

The first speaker was an invited speaker for both iFM 2023 and the colocated Fifth Workshop on Formal Methods for Autonomous Systems. We heartily thank these invited speakers for accepting our invitation and sharing their research results and views with the iFM 2023 audience.

We thank everybody involved in iFM 2023. First of all, all PC members and external reviewers for their in-depth and timely reviewing, all authors for submitting their work, and all attendees for participating. We also thank the chairs and committees for the Artifact Evaluation and the PhD Symposium, listed on the following pages, and the excellent local organization team, including the Publicity Chair Alfons Laarman and the General Chair Marcello M. Bonsangue.

We are very grateful to the organizations that sponsored iFM 2023, namely the Leiden Institute of Advanced Computer Science, Springer, and the European Association for Programming Languages and Systems (EAPLS).

Finally, we thank Springer for publishing these proceedings in their FM subline, and we gratefully acknowledge the support from EasyChair in assisting us in managing the complete process from submissions to the proceedings.

We hope you enjoyed the conference!

September 2023

Paula Herber
Anton Wijs

The original version of the book has been revised. The main and subtitle was not correct. This was corrected. A correction to this book can be found at https://doi.org/10.1007/978-3-031-47705-8_23

Organization

General Chair

Marcello M. Bonsangue   Leiden University, The Netherlands

Program Committee Chairs

Paula Herber   University of Münster, Germany
Anton Wijs   Eindhoven University of Technology, The Netherlands

Publicity Chair

Alfons Laarman   Leiden University, The Netherlands

Artifact Evaluation Committee Chairs

Anna-Lena Lamprecht   University of Potsdam, Germany
Muhammad Osama   Eindhoven University of Technology, The Netherlands

PhD Symposium Chairs

Crystal Chang Din   University of Bergen, Norway
Gidon Ernst   Ludwig Maximilian University of Munich, Germany

Steering Committee

Erika Ábrahám   RWTH Aachen University, Germany
Wolfgang Ahrendt   Chalmers University of Technology, Sweden
Ferruccio Damiani   University of Turin, Italy
John Derrick   University of Sheffield, UK
Carlo A. Furia   Università della Svizzera italiana, Switzerland
Marieke Huisman   University of Twente, The Netherlands
Einar Broch Johnsen   University of Oslo, Norway
Luigia Petre   Åbo Akademi University, Finland
Nadia Polikarpova   University of California, USA
Steve Schneider   University of Surrey, UK
Emil Sekerinski   McMaster University, Canada
Silvia Lizeth Tapia Tarifa   University of Oslo, Norway
Helen Treharne   University of Surrey, UK
Heike Wehrheim   University of Oldenburg, Germany
Kirsten Winter   University of Queensland, Australia

Program Committee

Wolfgang Ahrendt	Chalmers University of Technology, Sweden
Maurice ter Beek	ISTI-CNR, Italy
Petra van den Bos	University of Twente, The Netherlands
Alessandro Cimatti	Fondazione Bruno Kessler, Italy
Pedro R. D'Argenio	Universidad Nacional de Córdoba, Argentina
Richard DeFrancisco	Augusta University, USA
John Derrick	University of Sheffield, UK
Claire Dross	AdaCore, France
Karine Even-Mendoza	King's College London, UK
Marie Farrell	University of Manchester, UK
Carlo A. Furia	Università della Svizzera Italiana, Italy
Dilian Gurov	KTH Royal Institute of Technology, Sweden
Marieke Huisman	University of Twente, The Netherlands
Einar Broch Johnsen	University of Oslo, Norway
Sebastian Junges	Radboud University, The Netherlands
Nikolai Kosmatov	CEA List, France
Alfons Laarman	Leiden University, The Netherlands
Martin Leucker	University of Lübeck, Germany
Rosemary Monahan	Maynooth University, Ireland
Thomas Neele	Eindhoven University of Technology, The Netherlands
Wytse Oortwijn	TNO, The Netherlands
Jun Pang	University of Luxembourg, Luxembourg
Luigia Petre	Åbo Akademi University, Finland
Giles Reger	Amazon Web Services and University of Manchester, UK
Anne Remke	University of Münster, Germany
David Šafránek	Masaryk University, Czech Republic
Thomas Santen	Formal Assurance, Germany
Ina Schäfer	Karlsruhe Institute of Technology, Germany
Ana Sokolova	University of Salzburg, Austria
Silvia Lizeth Tapia Tarifa	University of Oslo, Norway
Heike Wehrheim	University of Oldenburg, Germany
Kirsten Winter	University of Queensland, Australia
Naijun Zhan	Institute of Software, Chinese Academy of Sciences, China

Artifact Evaluation Committee

Sharar Ahmadi	University of Surrey, UK
Davide Basile	ISTI-CNR, Italy
César Cornejo	Universidad Nacional de Rio Cuarto, Argentina
Mathias Fleury	University of Freiburg, Germany
Mario Frank	University of Potsdam, Germany
Lars B. van den Haak	Eindhoven University of Technology, The Netherlands

Emilio Incerto	IMT School for Advanced Studies Lucca, Italy
Maurice Laveaux	Eindhoven University of Technology, The Netherlands
Yong Li	Institute of Software, Chinese Academy of Sciences, China
Anik Momtaz	Michigan State University, USA
Andres Noetzli	Cubist, Inc., USA
Danilo Pianini	University of Bologna, Italy
Cedric Richter	Carl von Ossietzky University of Oldenburg, Germany
Mouhammad Sakr	University of Luxembourg, Luxembourg
Dimitrios Thanos	Leiden University, The Netherlands

PhD Symposium Program Committee

Elvira Albert	Complutense University of Madrid, Spain
Eduard Kamburjan	University of Oslo, Norway
Ondrej Lengal	Brno University of Information Technology, Czech Republic
Anna Lukina	Technical University of Delft, The Netherlands
Andrei Paskevich	Paris-Saclay University, France
Chris Poskitt	Singapore Management University, Singapore
José Proença	CISTER Lab, ISEP, Portugal
Elvinia Riccobene	Università degli Studi di Milano, Italy
Dominic Steinhöfel	CISPA Helmholtz Center for Information Security, Germany

Additional Reviewers

Yehia Abd Alrahman	Alistair Finn Hackett
Jesper Amilon	Jan Haltermann
Luís Soares Barbosa	Nils Jansen
Lara Bargmann	Hannes Kallwies
Davide Basile	Eduard Kamburjan
Lukas Birkemeyer	Karam Kharraz
Sandrine Blazy	Paul Kobialka
Giovanna Broccia	Thierry Lecomte
Zhenbang Chen	Christian Lidström
Tim Coopmans	Frédéric Loulergue
Joanna Delicaris	Guillaume Melquiond
Ramiro Demasi	Mathis Niehage
Luca Di Stefano	Federico Olmedo
Adel Djoudi	Anurudh Peduri
Catherine Dubois	Cedric Richter
Tom Franken	Tobias Runge

Martin Sachenbacher   Marck van der Vegt
Rudolf Schlatte   Shuling Wang
Samuel Teuber   Xiong Xu
Nicola Thoben   Lina Ye
Daniel Thoma   Hengjun Zhao

Sponsors

Leiden Institute of Advanced Computer Science (LIACS)

European Association for Programming Languages and Systems (EAPLS)

Springer

Abstract of Invited Talks

Formal Signoff Flows

Barbara Jobstmann

EPFL and Cadence Design Systems, Switzerland
barbara.jobstmann@epfl.ch

Abstract. Verification sign-off flows aims to answer the question of when to stop the verification effort, i.e., when the design is good enough for tape-out (manufacturing). Classical functional verification sign-off flows are based on simulation coverage metrics, which allow one to track the performed verification effort. With the rise of formal verification in industry, formal verification sign-off flows are becoming more and more critical. In this talk, we will first discuss coverage models and metrics used in formal verification in the industry. These metrics allow analysis of a verification setup from two different angles: (1) From a controllability angle, to answer questions like does the verification setup exercise all parts of the design? Did I over-constrain my design? (2) From the observability angle, to know if the set of checks is sufficient to catch potential faults in the design. To be meaningful, the metrics need to be tailored to a design. Therefore, we will next discuss methods to ensure coverage is measured in the context of design-specific scenarios. Finally, we will discuss dedicated techniques like bound aggregation and bug hunting to increase the coverage numbers.

Industrial Experience with a Verification-Aware Programming Language

K. Rustan M. Leino ⓘ

Amazon Web Services, USA
leino@amazon.com

Abstract. The programming language Dafny was designed to support specifications and formal verification in a modern software-engineering setting. As a language, it blends imperative and functional features with specifications and proof authoring. The Dafny ecosystem includes not just compilers, but also, conspicuously, an automated program verifier. Following a decade of use in teaching and in research projects, the language and its verifier now also have several years of industrial use. In this talk, I reflect on some of the lessons learned from working with engineers to write and maintain verified software and how this has impacted the language and its tooling.

Contents

Hardware and Memory Verification

Verification and Learning

Temporal Logics

Autonomous Systems

Invited Presentations

SMT: Something You Must Try

Erika Ábrahám[1], József Kovács[1], and Anne Remke[2]($\boxtimes$)

[1] RWTH Aachen University, Aachen, Germany
{abraham,kovacs}@cs.rwth-aachen.de
[2] Westfälische Wilhelms-Universität, Münster, Germany
anne.remke@uni-muenster.de

Abstract. SMT (Satisfiability Modulo Theories) solving is a technology for the fully automated solution of logical formulas. Due to their impressive efficiency, SMT solvers are nowadays frequently used in a wide variety of applications. These tools are general purpose and as off-the-shelf solvers, their usage is truly integrated. A typical application (i) encodes real-world problems as logical formulas, (ii) check these formulas for satisfiability with the help of SMT solvers, and - in case of satisfiability - (iii) decodes their solutions back to solutions of the original real-world problem.

In this extended abstract we give some insights into the working mechanisms of SMT solving, discuss a few areas of application, and present a novel application from the domain of simulation.

1 Introduction

Satisfiability checking [2] is a relatively young research area, aiming at the development of fully automated methods for checking the satisfiability of logical formulas. While there are interesting new developments to handle quantified formulas, our focus in this paper will be on *quantifier-free* formulas.

Starting with *SAT solving* for propositional logic, satisfiability checking algorithms have been developed also for numerous first-order-logic theories. The implementation of these technologies in *SMT (SAT Modulo Theories) solvers* [6] turned out to be extremely powerful. This success is due to several key enabling factors. From the practical side, there has been a strong community support, agreeing on a standard input language SMT-LIB, providing a large collection of SMT-LIB benchmarks [5], and organizing annual competitions [1]. From the theoretical side, algorithms from mathematical logic and symbolic computation have been adapted and integrated into satisfiability checking methods, guided by a heuristic and strategic view from the computer science perspective, and resulting in elegant and innovative algorithms with nice synergies between the two disciplines.

Besides some well-known SMT solvers APROVE [13], cvc5 [4], MathSAT5 [8], veriT [7], Yices2 [12] and Z3 [18], we mention our C++ programming library named *SMT Real-Algebraic Toolbox (SMT-RAT)* [9], whose characteristics is a clean modular structure allowing to combine different decision procedures into strategic SMT solving, with the main focus on solving real-algebraic problems.

P. Herber and A. Wijs (Eds.): iFM 2023, LNCS 14300, pp. 3–18, 2024.
https://doi.org/10.1007/978-3-031-47705-8_1

These and a number of further SMT solvers are available as off-the-shelf tools. That means, they can be used in a black-box style as depicted in Fig. 1: feed them with a logical description of a problem to be solved using the

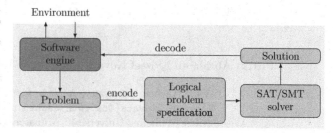

Fig. 1. Embedding SMT solvers in applications

SMT-LIB syntax and, if the problem is satisfiable, get a solution from the SMT solver and extract from it a solution for the original problem.

However, unsurprisingly, also SMT solvers have bounded scalability. The way how a real-world problem is encoded logically has a major influence on the effectiveness of SMT solving. Thus, despite their off-the-shelf nature, for the users of SMT solvers it might be helpful to have an idea about the internal working mechanisms of the underlying algorithms.

Therefore, our objectives in this paper are (1) to give an intuition about how SMT solvers work and (2) to provide some examples that demonstrate how SMT solvers can be integrated in different algorithms for solving suitable sub-problems. In the following, we

- give some basic insights into the algorithmic background of SMT solving in Sect. 2,
- discuss some example application domains in Sect. 3,
- present a new application to integrate SMT solving in the simulation of hybrid Petri nets in Sect. 4, and
- conclude the paper with some remarks in Sect. 5.

2   Satisfiability Checking

2.1   SAT Solving

SAT solvers are designed to check the satisfiability of *propositional logic* formulas, which are Boolean combinations of Boolean variables called *propositions*.

The input first needs to be transformed into *conjunctive normal form (CNF)*, being a conjunction of *clauses*, each clause being the disjunction of *literals*, and each literal being either a proposition or the negation of a proposition. This transformation can be done with the method of Tseitin [25] in polynomial time and space on the cost of additional variables, yielding for each propositional logic formula a satisfiability-equivalent formula in CNF.

SAT solvers have got really impactful since the discovery of an elegant combination of *exploration, (Boolean constraint) propagation*, and *(Boolean conflict) resolution* [11,17]. Instead of a formal description of a state-of-the-art SAT algorithm, we give an illustrative example.

– Assume an input CNF formula $(a \lor b) \land (a \lor \neg b)$, where a and b are propositions.
– Exploration might decide to check the existence of a solution if a is assigned *false*.
– Propagation detects that, if a is *false*, then the only chance to satisfy the first clause is assigning *true* to b.
– However, now the second clause is violated, because all of its literals are false. Boolean resolution[1], applied to the clause in conflict (i.e. the second clause) and the clause which implied the value for the last literal in the conflict clause (i.e. the first clause) yields the new clause (a).
– We backtrack by undoing assignments in reverse chronological order until the new clause is not violated anymore; in this example we undo all assignments.
– Propagation in the new clause detects that a needs to be *true*.
– Exploration can now choose any value for b, which will result in a full satisfying assignment.

2.2 SMT Solving

SMT solving typically extends SAT solving to be able to handle (quantifier-free) first-order-logic formulas over some theories. There are three different techniques which we describe in the following; their structures are illustrated in Fig. 2.

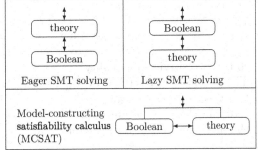

Fig. 2. The structure of SMT solving

Eager SMT Solving. For some theories, it is possible to transform their formulas to satisfiability-equivalent propositional logic formulas and use SAT solvers for their solution. This is the approach of *eager* SMT solving, where "eager" refers to the fact that the theory constraints are handled "eagerly", before handling the Boolean structure. Again, we avoid formal descriptions and illustrate the idea on an example for equality logic; similar approaches are available for e.g. uninterpreted functions and bit-vector arithmetic ("bit-blasting").

– Assume the formula $\varphi^E := x_1 = x_2 \land x_2 = x_3 \land x_1 \neq x_3$ from equality logic, where the variables x_1, x_2 and x_3 can take values from some arbitrary but "large enough" domain.
– We first replace each equation with a fresh proposition, encoding whether the given equation holds or not. This yields a *Boolean abstraction*, e.g. for our example $\varphi^{abs} := e_1 \land e_2 \land \neg e_3$.

---

[1] Given two clauses $(C_1 \lor b)$ and $(C_2 \lor \neg b)$ such that C_1 and C_2 are disjunctions of literals not referring to b, Boolean resolution on a proposition b can be used to derive the clause $(C_1 \lor C_2)$.

– The Boolean abstraction is yet an over-approximation, i.e. it has more solutions that the input formula. We need to encode also the *transitivity* of equality by stating $\varphi^{tra} := (e_1 \wedge e_2) \rightarrow e_3$.
– Now $\varphi^{abs} \wedge \varphi^{tra}$ is equi-satisfiable to φ^E, i.e. checking the former for satisfiability(with a SAT solver) will answer also the satisfiability question for the latter.

(Less) Lazy SMT Solving. In contrast to eager SMT solving, *lazy* SMT solving handles the Boolean structure first, before "lazily" considering the semantics of theory constraints. This approach first builds the over-approximative Boolean abstraction of the input problem and checks it for satisfiability using a SAT solver. If the Boolean abstraction is unsatisfiable, then also the input formula is unsatisfiable. Otherwise, given a solution for the Boolean abstraction, one or more theory solver(s) are asked to check the consistency of the Boolean solution in the theory.

– Consider again $\varphi^E := x_1 = x_2 \wedge x_2 = x_3 \wedge x_1 \neq x_3$ and its Boolean abstraction $\varphi^{abs} := e_1 \wedge e_2 \wedge \neg e_3$.
– φ^{abs} is satisfiable by making e_1 and e_2 *true*, and e_3 *false*.
– A suitable theory solver for equations is asked whether the constraints $x_1 = x_2$, $x_2 = x_3$ and $x_1 \neq x_3$ are together satisfiable, which is not the case (due to the transitivity of equality).
– The theory solver returns an *explanation* in the form of a theory lemma, in this case $(e_1 \wedge e_2) \rightarrow e_3$.
– Refining the abstraction with this information makes it unsatisfiable. Thus the input formula is unsatisfiable.

Model Constructing Satisfiability Calculus (MCSAT). [20] avoids master-slave structures and lets the SAT and the theory search evolve hand in hand in a consistent fashion. It does so by introducing exploration, propagation and conflict resolution also for the theory search, dually to the Boolean search.

– Assume again $\varphi^E := x_1 = x_2 \wedge x_2 = x_3 \wedge x_1 \neq x_3$ over the real domain.
– To explore in the theory, we guess a value for x_1, e.g. 0.
– The Boolean search detects that $x_1 = x_2$ needs to hold. Theory propagation yields $x_2 = 0$.
– The Boolean search detects that $x_2 = x_3$ and $x_1 \neq x_3$ needs to hold. However, they have no common solution with $x_1 = x_2 = 0$.
– Thus our guess $x_1 = 0$ was wrong. We can generalize such a wrong gues by e.g. quantifier elimination. In this case, the guess can be generalized to the whole real domain, i.e. the formula cannot be satisfied for any value of x_1. Thus φ^E is unsatisfiable.

3   Applications

At the 2022 edition of the Computer-Aided Verification (CAV) conference, Neha Rungta from Amazon suggested in her keynote titled *A billion SMT queries a day*

[23] that innovations at Amazon have "ushered in the golden age of automated reasoning".

Whereas in those applications, Amazon exploits SMT solving mainly for correctness reasoning, SAT and SMT solvers enjoy frequent usage in a diverse spectrum of further application domains. The aim of this section is to give an impression and a few examples about where and how SMT solvers can be employed to solve real-world problems.

3.1   A Toy Encoding Example

Let us start with a toy example to illustrate how a simple combinatorial problem can be encoded in linear real arithmetic. Assume that, after the Covid lockdown times, Eve is eager to make in 2023 scientific visits again.

– She has 100 travel wishes $A_1, \ldots, A_{100}$.
– She is allowed to make only 5 travels.
– She wants to be physically at $A_1 = iFM'23$.
– To coordinate a project, she needs to visit either A_2 or A_3.
– Travel A_i costs C_i EUR.
– Eve can spend up to C EUR.
– Travel A_i takes T_i days.
– Eve wants to travel at least T days.

The following linear real arithmetic formula encodes the solutions to the above problem. Besides the constants used in the problem specification, it uses for each $i \in \{1, \ldots, 100\}$ variables (i) $a_i \in \{0, 1\}$ to encode whether Eve chooses travel A_i ($x_i = 1$) or not ($x_i = 0$) and (ii) c_i and t_i for the costs and time for travel A_i, which are 0 if A_i is not chosen:

$$\left(\bigwedge_{i=1}^{100} \left((a_i = 0 \wedge c_i = 0 \wedge t_i = 0) \vee (a_i = 1 \wedge c_i = C_i \wedge t_i = T_i) \right) \right)$$

$$\wedge \left(\sum_{i=1}^{100} a_i \leq 5 \right) \wedge (a_1 = 1) \wedge (a_2 = 1 \vee a_3 = 1) \wedge \left(\sum_{i=1}^{100} c_i \leq C \right) \wedge \left(\sum_{i=1}^{100} t_i \geq T \right)$$

3.2   Planning with Optimization Modulo Theories

With the advent of Industry 4.0, increasing automation in production processes poses new challenges on production management. The RoboCup Logistics League (RCLL) [21] has been proposed to study these challenges at a comprehensible and manageable scale.

In an RCLL application, two teams of robots share a work space, as illustrated in Fig. 3. Each team consists of three robots and owns a set of machines (e.g. BS, RS1, RS2 or CS2) which they can use to produce certain products. Orders for products are announced dynamically during runtime. The production of each ordered product requires certain material and certain production

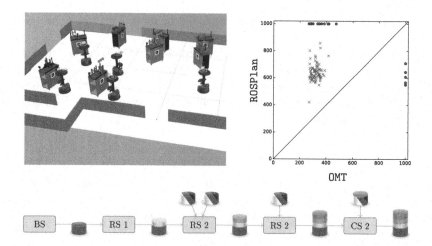

Fig. 3. Planning with optimization modulo theories. Source: E. Ábrahám, G. Lakemeyer, F. Leofante, T. D. Niemüller, A. Tacchella: PhD Leofante, publications in IJCAI'20, Information Systems Frontiers 2019, ECMS'19, AAAI'18, iFM'18, ICAPS'17, PlanRob'17, IRI'17.

steps to be executed under some partial order on certain machines with some required functionalities. The teams get rewards for each completed (or even partially completed) ordered product. The aim is to plan the production steps within a team in a collaborative manner to maximize the received rewards.

The complexity of the corresponding planning problem, due to e.g. temporal aspects, numerical quantities and the collaboration between the robots, makes its solution challenging. In a row of works, see e.g. [16], we proposed several ways to encode different sub-problems logically, and used SMT solvers for satisfiability checking as well as for optimization to solve those logically encoded sub-problems efficiently. Our methodology won the first place in the 2018 Planning and Execution Competition for Logistics Robots in Simulation, held at the International Conference on Automated Planning and Scheduling.

3.3 Reachability Analysis for Hybrid Systems with HyPro

Hybrid systems are systems with mixed discrete-continuous behavior. Typical examples are physical systems that are controlled by discrete controllers, like often present e.g. in the safety-critical automotive domain. *Formal methods* play an important role to assure the safety of such hybrid systems.

To enable the usage of formal methods, hybrid systems need to be formalized in a suitable modeling language, like e.g. hybrid automata. Furthermore, we need algorithms to compute, for a given formal model and a given set of initial states, all the states that can be reached during the evolution of the system model. Since the reachability problem for hybrid systems is undecidable, most algorithms side-step to over-approximative computations. Once we know (an over-approximation

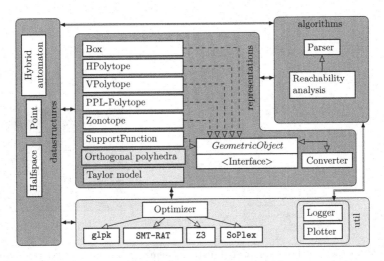

Fig. 4. The structure of the HyPro tool for computing reachability in hybrid systems. Source: S. Schupp, E. Ábrahám, I. Ben Makhlouf, S. Kowalewski. HyPro: A C++ library of state set representations for hybrid systems reachability analysis. In Proc. of NFM'17.

of) the set of all reachable states, we can check whether it includes any unwanted (dangerous or unsafe) states.

For the automation of these computations, we need *data structures* to represent state sets, along with all the operations on them which are needed for the reachability analysis, like e.g. the linear transformation of a state set, or the union, intersection or the Minkowski sum of two state sets. There are different state set representations are in use, which differ in their precision and efficiency. The HyPro C++ programming library [24] offers implementations for the most popular state set representations, and reachability algorithms using those representations.

The structure of HyPro is depicted in Fig. 4. To implement the different set operations on the representations, we often need to solve arithmetic sub-problems. Some of the available options to solve these sub-problems is to delegate them to some dedicated SMT solvers. Note that most SMT solvers accept command-line input in the SMT-LIB format, but their *application programming interface (API)* is not standardized (yet), such that adding a new SMT solver back-end requires a new wrapper around its API to fit the reachability analysis calls.

Besides HyPro, also other analysis tools for hybrid systems reachability employ SMT solvers. Here we mention only dReach [15] with its dedicated SMT engine named dReal.

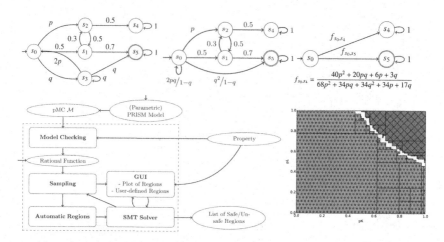

Fig. 5. Parameter synthesis for probabilistic systems. Source: C. Dehnert, S. Junges, N. Jansen, F. Corzilius, M. Volk, H. Bruintjes, J.-P. Katoen, E. Ábrahám. PROPhESY: A probabilistic parameter synthesis tool. In Proc. of CAV'15.

3.4   Parameter Synthesis for Probabilistic Systems

Discrete-time Markov chains (DTMCs) are a popular modeling formalism to describe systems whose behavior involves probabilistic behavior or whose behavior is influenced by uncertainties that can be quantified by probabilistic distributions. When the involved distributions are parameterized we talk about *parametric DTMCs*. Figure 5 depicts an example model on the top left. The circles are the system states; the state s_0 with the incoming arrow without a source state is the initial state. For each state, its outgoing transitions are labeled with probabilities, which should sum up to 1. If parametric expressions are involved, the valid domains for the parameters are such that the transition probabilities build valid probability distributions.

The PROPhESY tool has been developed to determine regions in the valid parameter domain, for which certain reachability probability bounds are provably satisfied or provably violated. For the example in Fig. 5, the probability to reach the state s_4 from s_0 satisfies some fixed upper bound in the green areas, this bound is violated in the red areas, whereas no guarantees can be given for the white areas.

To compute such regions, first the reachability probability in question is computed symbolically (using state elimination, the result shown on the top right in the figure). Then an SMT solver is used to check whether all values in the parameter domain satisfy, respectively violate the probability bound. If it is the case then we can "color" the domain green respectively red, otherwise the domain is split into smaller sets for which the check is done recursively. The main challenge here is that for relevant systems, the expression that denotes the symbolic reachability probability can get extremely large with complex high-degree polynomial expressions involved.

4   Hybrid Petri Nets and Rate Adaption

In the previous section we reported on some existing SMT solver embeddings in a few domains. In this section, we propose a novel application of SMT solving in the area of modeling and simulation for hybrid Petri nets.

4.1   Hybrid Petri Nets

A *Petri net* $\mathcal{D} = (\mathcal{P}^d, \mathcal{T}^d, \mathcal{A}^d, \mathbf{m_0})$ as defined by [22], consist of a set of (discrete) *places* $\mathcal{P}^d$, a set of *transitions* $\mathcal{T}^d$, and a set of directed *arcs* $\mathcal{A}^d$, connecting places and transitions and vice versa.

A place $p_i \in \mathcal{P}^d$ contains a discrete number of *tokens* $m_i \in \mathbb{N}$. The *marking* of a Petri net is given as a vector $\mathbf{m} = \{m_1, \ldots, m_{|\mathcal{P}^d|}\}$ indicating the number of tokens currently contained in each place. The initial marking is given by $\mathbf{m_0}$.

Directed arcs are defined by $\mathcal{A}^d \subseteq (\mathcal{P}^d \times \mathcal{T}^d) \cup (\mathcal{T}^d \times \mathcal{P}^d)$. Transitions change the marking of connected places upon firing as follows: A transition $t \in \mathcal{T}^d$ removes a predefined number of tokens from every *input* place p that is connected via an arc (p, t), hence directed towards t. Correspondingly, it adds a number of tokens to every *output* place p that is connected via an arc (t, p) pointing away from t. A transition can only fire if it is *enabled*, i.e., if the marking has a sufficient number of tokens in every input place. To ease notation, here we assume that each transition removes exactly one token from each of its input places and adds exactly one token to each of its output places. Enabled transitions may fire independently and in an arbitrary order in the original definition of Petri nets.

Hybrid Petri nets, as introduced in [3] extend a Petri net $\mathcal{D}$ with time and *continuous* places, transitions and arcs. A hybrid Petri net is defined by the tuple $\mathcal{H} = (\mathcal{P}, \mathcal{T}, \mathcal{A}, \mathbf{m_0}, \mathbf{x_0}, \Phi)$, which adds an initial continuous marking $\mathbf{x_0}$ and a parameter function Φ to the sets of places $\mathcal{P}$, transitions $\mathcal{T}$ and arcs $\mathcal{A}$ and the initial discrete marking $\mathbf{m_0}$.

The parameter function specifies additional values for places, transitions and arcs $\Phi = (\phi_c^{\mathcal{P}}, \phi_d^{\mathcal{T}}, \phi_c^{\mathcal{T}}, \phi_s^{\mathcal{A}}, \phi_p^{\mathcal{A}})$, which will be formalised below.

The set of places $\mathcal{P} = \mathcal{P}^d \cup \mathcal{P}^c$ is composed from disjoint finite sets of discrete and continuous places. Continuous places $p_i^c \in \mathcal{P}^c$ have a continuous marking $x_i \in \mathbb{R}_0^+$, which is referred to as *fluid* and is lower bounded by 0. The parameter function $\phi_c^{\mathcal{P}} : \mathcal{P}^c \to (\mathbb{Q}_{\geq 0} \cup \{\infty\})$ assigns a *capacity* to every continuous place. We say that a place is *empty* if there is no fluid in it and *full* if the amount of fluid in it equals its capacity. In contrast, discrete places $p_i^d \in \mathcal{P}^d$ contain a discrete marking $m_i \in \mathbb{N}_0$ and have an unbounded (infinite) capacity.

The finite set of transitions $\mathcal{T} = \mathcal{T}^d \cup \mathcal{T}^c$ is composed from discrete transitions $\mathcal{T}^d$ which change the discrete marking and continuous transitions $\mathcal{T}^c$ which change the continuous marking.

Discrete transitions have a deterministic firing time, specified by the parameter function $\phi_d^{\mathcal{T}} : \mathcal{T}^d \to \mathbb{R}^+$. Every deterministic transition t_i^d is associated with a clock c_i, which if enabled evolves with $dc_i/dt = 1$, otherwise $dc_i/dt = 0$.

Note that upon disabling, the clock value is preserved. A deterministic transition $t_i^d \in \mathcal{T}^d$ fires when c_i reaches the predefined transitions firing time. Discrete transitions with firing time zero are denoted as *immediate transitions* and fire as soon as they are enabled. If multiple immediate or deterministic transitions are supposed to fire at the same time, this so-called *conflict* is resolved using priorities and weights, which results in a probabilistic decision. For details on *conflict resolution* we refer to [3].

When enabled, continuous transitions $t^c \in \mathcal{T}^c$ fire continuously with a constant nominal flow rate assigned by $\Phi_c^{\mathcal{T}} : \mathcal{T}^c \to \mathbb{R}^+$. We refer to [10] for a detailed discussion of the concept of *enabling*.

Transitions and places are connected via the finite set of arcs $\mathcal{A}$. Discrete arcs $\mathcal{A}^d$ connect discrete places and transitions, while continuous arcs $\mathcal{A}^c$ connect continuous places and continuous transitions, respectively. Note that for simplicity, we omit guard and inhibitor arcs, as well as arc multiplicity and arc weights. Given a discrete marking $\mathbf{m}$, the above simplification leads to the marking $\mathbf{m}'$ after firing a discrete transition $t^d \in \mathcal{T}^d$, where

$$
m_i' = \begin{cases}
m_i - 1 & \text{iff } (p_i^d, t^d) \in \mathcal{A}^d \wedge (t^d, p_i^d) \notin \mathcal{A}^d, \\
m_i + 1 & \text{iff } (t^d, p_i^d) \in \mathcal{A}^d \wedge (p_i^d, t^d) \notin \mathcal{A}^d, \\
m_i & \text{otherwise.}
\end{cases}
$$

In addition to the firing of discrete transitions, the state of a hybrid Petri net changes continuously with time if at least one continuous transition is enabled. Again for simplicity, we restrict continuous transition t^c to have at most one *source* and one *target*, defined as follows:

- *source* : $\mathcal{T}^c \to (\mathcal{P}^c \cup \{\bot\})$: for all $t^c \in \mathcal{T}^c$, if there is a place p^c that is connected via an arc (p^c, t^c) then $source(t^c) = p^c$, otherwise $source(t^c) = \bot$,
- *target* : $\mathcal{T}^c \to \mathcal{P}^c \cup \{\bot\}$: for all $t^c \in \mathcal{T}^c$, if there is a place p^c that is connected via an arc (t^c, p^c), then $target(t^c) = p^c$, otherwise $target(t^c) = \bot$.

The *input bag* $I(p^c)$ and *output bag* $O(p^c)$ of a continuous place p^c are defined as follows:

- $I : \mathcal{P}^c \to 2^{\mathcal{T}^c}$: for all $p^c \in \mathcal{P}^c$, $I(p^c) = \{t \in \mathcal{T}^c \mid target(t^c) = p^c\}$ is the set of all transitions with target p^c.
- $O : \mathcal{P}^c \to 2^{\mathcal{T}^c}$: for all $p^c \in \mathcal{P}^c$, $I(p^c) = \{t \in \mathcal{T}^c \mid source(t^c) = p^c\}$ is the set of all transitions with source p^c.

A continuous transition can be disabled if a connected source place is empty or a connected target place is full. In order to model realistic physical behavior, the semantics of hybrid Petri nets *adapts* the nominal flow rate of transitions that are in the input bag of a full continuous place, as well as the nominal flow rate of transitions that are in the output bag of a an empty continuous place. Initially, all continuous transitions fire with their nominal rate, after *rate adaption* as described in Sect. 4.2 has taken place, the so-called actual flow rate $\theta(t^c)$ for $t^c \in \mathcal{P}^c$ may be smaller than the assigned nominal rate.

During time evolution, the continuous marking changes continuously with the *drift* specified for each continuous place as

$$d(p^c) = \sum_{t^c \in I(p^c)} \theta(t^c) - \sum_{t^c \in O(p^c)} \theta(t^c),$$

as the difference of the actual flow rates of the transitions to which p^c is connected as target or source.

4.2   Rate Adaption

If the fluid of a continuous place reaches one of its boundaries, i.e. zero or its upper-bounding capacity, *rate adaption* reduces the actual flow rates of the affected continuous transitions based on the share $\phi_s^{\mathcal{A}}$ and priority $\phi_p^{\mathcal{A}}$ of the corresponding continuous arcs to prevent under- or overflow of that place.

Rate adaption is introduced in [3] as fixed-point iteration. The change of the actual flow rate of a continuous transition potentially modifies the drifts of continuous places, which in turn can trigger rate adaption for further continuous transitions. Hence, the algorithm needs to iteratively check all continuous places that are at either boundary.

In every iteration, for all continuous places at their upper capacity with a positive drift, the inflow is reduced to match the outflow and at all continuous places at the lower boundary with a negative drift, the outflow is reduced to match the inflow.

More specifically, the algorithm iterates over the continuous places that are at a boundary and per place computes the amount of *available fluid*. In case of a place at the lower boundary, the available fluid is given by the sum of the actual flow rates of the connected input transitions, which is then redistributed over the connected output transitions according to their priority and share. The case for full places is analogous, but with a reduction of the input transitions' rates.

The iteration terminates when all fluid places at the upper boundaries have a drift that is smaller or equal to zero and all fluid places at the lower boundaries have a drift that is greater or equal to zero.

As described in [14], the adaption of the actual flow rates can be challenging, depending on the structure of the Petri net at hand. If each continuous transition is involved in at most one conflict, the rate adaption proposed in [10] always terminates with a unique result. In the general case, Algorithm 5.7 from [10] applies an additional partitioning and ordering which assures termination with a unique result. However, different orderings might yield different results, which does not necessarily truly model real physical behavior.

As an example, consider the hybrid Petri net shown in Fig. 6. Continuous places are drawn as double circles and continuous transitions as double rectangles, full continuous places are filled black, empty places are white. The nominal flows are shown besides the transitions. Note that this example contains no discrete components and that transition t_3 is involved in two conflicts, namely at p_1 and at p_2.

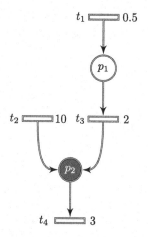

Fig. 6. Hybrid Petri net, where a transitions participates in two conflicts

If the conflict at p_2 is adapted first, its input transitions (t_2 and t_3) are reduced to match the outflow. Assuming equal priority and share, the actual flow rates are set to $\theta(t_2) = 2.5$ and $\theta(t_3) = 0.5$. With these actual flow rates rate adaption terminates, as the conflict at p_1 has been resolved "by chance".

However, if p_1 is processed first, it's outflow is reduced to match the inflow. The actual flow rate of t_3 is then set to $\theta(t_3) = 0.5$. As p_2 is still conflicted, it's incoming flow needs to be reduced by a factor of $2/7$ to achieve the new rates $\theta(t_2) = 10 \cdot 2/7 = 20/7$ and $\theta(t_3) = 0.5 \cdot 2/7 = 1/7$, i.e. an inflow of 3 and thus a drift of 0. For this order, the outflow of p_1 is reduced stronger than needed and results in a positive drift at p_1. However, without an explicit control, in reality the drift would be always adapted to zero.

4.3 Formulation as an SMT Problem

Hence, while the ordering applied for rate adaption ensures termination with a unique result, it clearly influences the resulting actual flow rates and does not always yield results that are physically meaningful.

We propose to change the rate adaption mechanism from an iterative fixed-point search to an SMT-based approach: instead of iteratively adapting places, we suggest to use a logical formulation of the smallest fixed-points, and use an SMT solver for finding the required rates.

The advantages are the following: Firstly, out method always terminates, without any restrictions on the shape of the hybrid Petri net. Secondly, we design the formulation to assure not only satisfiability but also a unique solution. Thirdly, this unique solution truly reflects the natural physical behavior, keeping all rate adaptions minimal, i.e. just as small as needed to resolve conflicts.

To emphasize the key ideas, we assume equal priorities and share. Intuitively, for each empty place p in conflict (i.e. with a negative drift) we consider its output bag and reduce the contained transitions with the same factor. However, some transitions from its output bag may be reduced by other places by more than what would be needed to bring the drift of p to zero according to the fixed-point.

In the SMT-based approach, this problem of mutual reduction is circumvented by introducing the concept of *ownership*. We call the place which implies a strongest reduction on a transition its *owner*. Each place then only reduces the

$$(1) \quad \left(\bigwedge_{p \in P} 0 \leq \texttt{factor}_p \leq 1 \right) \wedge \left(\bigwedge_{t \in T_a} 0 \leq \texttt{factor}_t \leq 1 \right) \wedge$$

$$(2) \quad \left(\bigwedge_{t \in T_a} ((\texttt{owner}_t = source(t) \wedge \texttt{owner}_t \in P_e) \vee (\texttt{owner}_t = target(t) \wedge \texttt{owner}_t \in P_f)) \right) \wedge$$

$$(3) \quad \Big(\bigwedge_{p \in P} \texttt{in}_p = (\textstyle\sum_{t \in I(p) \cap T_a} \texttt{factor}_t \cdot \Phi_c^T(t)) + (\textstyle\sum_{t \in I(p) \cap T_{na}} \Phi_c^T(t)) \wedge$$

$$\texttt{out}_p = (\textstyle\sum_{t \in O(p) \cap T_a} \texttt{factor}_t \cdot \Phi_c^T(t)) + (\textstyle\sum_{t \in O(p) \cap T_{na}} \Phi_c^T(t)) \quad \Big) \wedge$$

$$(4) \quad \Big[\bigwedge_{p \in P_e} \Big((\texttt{factor}_p = 1 \vee \bigvee_{t \in O(p)} \texttt{owner}_t = p) \wedge$$

$$(\bigwedge_{t \in O(p)} (\texttt{owner}_t = p \to \texttt{factor}_t = \texttt{factor}_p) \wedge$$

$$(\texttt{owner}_t \neq p \to \texttt{factor}_t < \texttt{factor}_p) \quad) \wedge$$

$$\texttt{in}_p \geq \texttt{out}_p \wedge (\texttt{factor}_p < 1 \to \texttt{in}_p = \texttt{out}_p) \quad) \Big] \wedge$$

$$(5) \quad \Big[\bigwedge_{p \in P_f} \Big((\texttt{factor}_p = 1 \vee \bigvee_{t \in I(p)} \texttt{owner}_t = p) \wedge$$

$$(\bigwedge_{t \in I(p)} (\texttt{owner}_t = p \to \texttt{factor}_t = \texttt{factor}_p) \wedge$$

$$(\texttt{owner}_t \neq p \to \texttt{factor}_t \leq \texttt{factor}_p) \quad) \wedge$$

$$\texttt{in}_p \leq \texttt{out}_p \wedge (\texttt{factor}_p < 1 \to \texttt{in}_p = \texttt{out}_p) \quad) \Big]$$

Fig. 7. SMT encoding for the novel rate adaption mechanism

rates of the transitions it owns by the same factor, namely by a maximal factor that just assures zero drift for p.

Recall that the capacity of a place $p \in \mathcal{P}^c$ is given $\Phi_c^{\mathcal{P}}(p)$, while the current amount of fluid for all continuous places is stored in the continuous marking $\mathbf{x}$, where $\mathbf{x}(p_i) = x_i$ for $p_i \in \mathcal{P}^c$.

For readability we introduce some relevant sets of continuous places and continuous transitions for rate adaption. Since we focus on the continuous part of a hybrid Petri net, we omit the superindex c for readability in the newly defined sets.

- P_e: the set of continuous places that are empty, i.e. all $p \in \mathcal{P}^c$ with $\mathbf{x}(p) = 0$.
- P_f: the set of continuous places that are full, i.e. all $p \in \mathcal{P}^c$ with $\mathbf{x}(p) = \phi_c^{\mathcal{P}}(p)$.
- $P = P_e \cup P_f$.
- T: the set of all transitions $t \in \mathcal{T}^c$ that are connected to at least one place from P, i.e. $\{source(t), target(t)\} \cap P \neq \emptyset$.
- T_a: the set of all potentially *adaptable* transitions $t \in T$ either with empty source or with full target, i.e., $\mathbf{x}(source(t)) = 0 \vee \mathbf{x}(target(t)) = \phi_c^{\mathcal{P}}(target(t))$.
- $T_{na} = T \setminus T_a$: the set of all *non-adaptable* transitions from T.

Our encoding, shown in Fig. 7, makes use of the following variables:

- For all $p \in P$, the variables $\mathtt{in}_p$ and $\mathtt{out}_p$, both with domain $\mathbb{Q}_{\geq 0}$, encode p's inflow resp. outflow after rate adaption: $\mathtt{in}_p = \sum_{t \in I(p)} \theta(t)$ and $\mathtt{out}_p = \sum_{t \in O(p)} \theta(t)$.
- For all $t \in T_a$, $\mathtt{owner}_t$ with domain P denotes the owner place of transition t.
- For all $p \in P$, by $\mathtt{factor}_p$ with domain $[0,1] \subset \mathbb{Q}$ we encode the reduction factor for the rates of all transitions owned by p. All other transitions from p's output resp. input bag need to be reduced by other places by a factor at most $\mathtt{factor}_p$ (i.e. at least as strongly reduced as p's reduction factor).
- For all $t \in T_a$, we encode by $\mathtt{factor}_t$ with domain $[0,1] \subset \mathbb{Q}$ the rate reduction factor for transitions t, i.e. the reduction factor of its owner place.

The encoding consists of 6 main components:

(1) All rate adaption factors *reduce* the nominal rates and do not change their signs.
(2) The owner of each adaptable transition is either its source place or its target place.
(3) The inflow of a place p accumulates the actual flow rate of all transitions from p's input bag, i.e. the transition's rate adaption factor multiplied by its nominal rate. The case for the outflow of a place is analogous.
(4) A reducing *empty* place p must own some transitions from its *output* bag (or otherwise the place is not reducing, i.e. it has reduction factor 1). All transitions owned by p are reduced with the same factor, namely the place's reduction factor. All other transitions from the output bag must be reduced by other places by a smaller factor (i.e. stronger). Finally, the last line in part (4) assures that the rate reduction resolve all conflicts, but it poses only as much restrictions as needed.
(5) The case for *full* places p is analogous but argues about rate reductions for the transitions in p's *input* bag.

5   Some Final Remarks

After providing a general overview of satifiability checking, the paper showcased its usefulness and applicability on three examples. First a toy example was presented, before applications in (i) planning with optimization modulo theories and (ii) reachability analysis for hybrid systems were given. Summarizing, one of the main advantages of SMT solvers is their use as black box, which entails that the rapid development of SMT solvers automatically improves these applications. This is witnessed by the wide rage of applications [19], such as optimization, proof and certificate generation, as well as satisfiability checking of quantified formulas.

The remainder of the paper illustrated an additional use-case for SMT solving in more detail: the analysis and simulation of hybrid Petri nets require a so-called rate adaption algorithm, which is traditionally implemented as fixed-point algorithm which converges to a unique result under very specific constraints. This paper proposes a more elegant approach, by formalising rate adaption as SMT problem, which can then be solved by state-of-the-art SMT solvers. Future work will introduce an additional iterative algorithm which is guaranteed to converge to a unique solution. Furthermore, we will proof that this unique solution equals the solution of the SMT encoding, presented here.

References

1. https://smt-comp.github.io/2023/
2. Biere, A., Heule, M., Van Maaren, H., Walsh, T. (eds.): Handbook of Satisfiability. Frontiers in Artificial Intelligence and Applications, vol. 185. IOS Press (2009)
3. Alla, H., David, R.: Continuous and hybrid Petri nets. J. Circ. Syst. Comput. 8(01), 159–188 (1998)
4. Barbosa, H., et al.: cvc5: a versatile and industrial-strength SMT solver. In: TACAS 2022. LNCS, vol. 13243, pp. 415–442. Springer, Cham (2022). https://doi.org/10.1007/978-3-030-99524-9_24
5. Barrett, C., Fontaine, P., Tinelli, C.: The Satisfiability Modulo Theories Library (SMT-LIB) (2016). www.SMT-LIB.org
6. Barrett, C., Sebastiani, R., Seshia, S.A., Tinelli, C.: Satisfiability modulo theories, chap. 26. In: Handbook of Satisfiability. Frontiers in Artificial Intelligence and Applications, vol. 185, pp. 825–885. IOS Press (2009)
7. Bouton, T., Caminha B. de Oliveira, D., Déharbe, D., Fontaine, P.: veriT: an open, trustable and efficient SMT-solver. In: Schmidt, R.A. (ed.) CADE 2009. LNCS (LNAI), vol. 5663, pp. 151–156. Springer, Heidelberg (2009). https://doi.org/10.1007/978-3-642-02959-2_12
8. Cimatti, A., Griggio, A., Schaafsma, B.J., Sebastiani, R.: The MathSAT5 SMT solver. In: Piterman, N., Smolka, S.A. (eds.) TACAS 2013. LNCS, vol. 7795, pp. 93–107. Springer, Heidelberg (2013). https://doi.org/10.1007/978-3-642-36742-7_7
9. Corzilius, F., Kremer, G., Junges, S., Schupp, S., Ábrahám, E.: SMT-RAT: an open source C++ toolbox for strategic and parallel SMT solving. In: Heule, M., Weaver, S. (eds.) SAT 2015. LNCS, vol. 9340, pp. 360–368. Springer, Cham (2015). https://doi.org/10.1007/978-3-319-24318-4_26
10. David, R., Alla, H.: Discrete, Continuous, and Hybrid Petri Nets, vol. 1. Springer, Heidelberg (2010). https://doi.org/10.1007/978-3-642-10669-9
11. Davis, M., Putnam, H.: A computing procedure for quantification theory. J. ACM 7(3), 201–215 (1960). https://doi.org/10.1145/321033.321034
12. Dutertre, B.: Yices 2.2. In: Biere, A., Bloem, R. (eds.) CAV 2014. LNCS, vol. 8559, pp. 737–744. Springer, Cham (2014). https://doi.org/10.1007/978-3-319-08867-9_49
13. Giesl, J., et al.: Proving termination of programs automatically with AProVE. In: Demri, S., Kapur, D., Weidenbach, C. (eds.) IJCAR 2014. LNCS (LNAI), vol. 8562, pp. 184–191. Springer, Cham (2014). https://doi.org/10.1007/978-3-319-08587-6_13
14. Gribaudo, M., Remke, A.: Hybrid Petri nets with general one-shot transitions. Perform. Eval. 105, 22–50 (2016)
15. Kong, S., Gao, S., Chen, W., Clarke, E.: dReach: δ-reachability analysis for hybrid systems. In: Baier, C., Tinelli, C. (eds.) TACAS 2015. LNCS, vol. 9035, pp. 200–205. Springer, Heidelberg (2015). https://doi.org/10.1007/978-3-662-46681-0_15
16. Leofante, F.: Optimal Planning Modulo Theories. Ph.D. thesis, RWTH Aachen University, Germany (2020)

17. Marques-Silva, J.P., Sakallah, K.A.: GRASP: a search algorithm for propositional satisfiability. IEEE Trans. Comput. **48**, 506–521 (1999)
18. de Moura, L., Bjørner, N.: Z3: an efficient SMT solver. In: Ramakrishnan, C.R., Rehof, J. (eds.) TACAS 2008. LNCS, vol. 4963, pp. 337–340. Springer, Heidelberg (2008). https://doi.org/10.1007/978-3-540-78800-3_24
19. de Moura, L., Dutertre, B., Shankar, N.: A tutorial on satisfiability modulo theories. In: Damm, W., Hermanns, H. (eds.) CAV 2007. LNCS, vol. 4590, pp. 20–36. Springer, Heidelberg (2007). https://doi.org/10.1007/978-3-540-73368-3_5
20. de Moura, L., Jovanović, D.: A model-constructing satisfiability calculus. In: Giacobazzi, R., Berdine, J., Mastroeni, I. (eds.) VMCAI 2013. LNCS, vol. 7737, pp. 1–12. Springer, Heidelberg (2013). https://doi.org/10.1007/978-3-642-35873-9_1
21. Niemueller, T., Lakemeyer, G., Ferrein, A.: The RoboCup Logistics League as a benchmark for planning in robotics. In: Proceedings of the PlanRob@ICAPS 2015 (2015)
22. Petri, C.: Kommunikation mit Automaten. Ph.D. thesis, TU Darmstadt (1962)
23. Rungta, N.: A billion SMT queries a day (invited paper). In: Shoham, S., Vizel, Y. (eds.) Computer Aided Verification, CAV 2022. LNCS, vol. 13371, pp. 3–18. Springer, Cham (2022). https://doi.org/10.1007/978-3-031-13185-1_1
24. Schupp, S., Ábrahám, E., Makhlouf, I.B., Kowalewski, S.: HyPro: a C++ library of state set representations for hybrid systems reachability analysis. In: Barrett, C., Davies, M., Kahsai, T. (eds.) NFM 2017. LNCS, vol. 10227, pp. 288–294. Springer, Cham (2017). https://doi.org/10.1007/978-3-319-57288-8_20
25. Tseitin, G.S.: On the complexity of derivation in propositional calculus. In: Siekmann, J.H., Wrightson, G. (eds.) Automation of Reasoning. Symbolic Computation. Springer, Heidelberg (1983). https://doi.org/10.1007/978-3-642-81955-1_28

Analysis and Verification

Automated Sensitivity Analysis
for Probabilistic Loops

Marcel Moosbrugger$^{(\boxtimes)}$ (iD), Julian Müllner(iD), and Laura Kovács(iD)

TU Wien, Vienna, Austria
`marcel.moosbrugger@tuwien.ac.at`

Abstract. We present an exact approach to analyze and quantify the sensitivity of higher moments of probabilistic loops with symbolic parameters, polynomial arithmetic and potentially uncountable state spaces. Our approach integrates methods from symbolic computation, probability theory, and static analysis in order to automatically capture sensitivity information about probabilistic loops. Sensitivity information allows us to formally establish how value distributions of probabilistic loop variables influence the functional behavior of loops, which can in particular be helpful when choosing values of loop variables in order to ensure efficient/expected computations. Our work uses algebraic techniques to model higher moments of loop variables via linear recurrence equations and introduce the notion of *sensitivity recurrences*. We show that sensitivity recurrences precisely model loop sensitivities, even in cases where the moments of loop variables do not satisfy a system of linear recurrences. As such, we enlarge the class of probabilistic loops for which sensitivity analysis was so far feasible. We demonstrate the success of our approach while analyzing the sensitivities of probabilistic loops.

Keywords: Probabilistic Programs · Sensitivity Analysis · Recurrences

1 Introduction

Probabilistic programs are imperative programs enriched with the capability to draw from probability distributions. By supporting native primitives to model uncertainty, probabilistic programming provides a powerful framework to model stochastic systems from many different areas, such as machine learning [19], biology [2], cyber-physical systems [15,31], cryptography [5], privacy [7], and randomized algorithms [28].

A challenging task in the analysis of probabilistic programs comes from the fact that values, or even value distributions, of symbolic parameters used within program expressions over probabilistic program variables are often unknown. Sensitivity analysis aims to quantify how small changes in such parameters influence computation results [1,4]. Sensitivity analysis thus provides additional information about the probabilistic program executions, even if some parameters are (partially) unknown. This sensitivity information can further be used, among

© The Author(s), under exclusive license to Springer Nature Switzerland AG 2024
P. Herber and A. Wijs (Eds.): iFM 2023, LNCS 14300, pp. 21–39, 2024.
https://doi.org/10.1007/978-3-031-47705-8_2

others, in code optimization: sensitivity information quantifies the influence of parameters on the program variables, allowing to derive cost-effective estimates and optimize expected runtimes of probabilistic loops.

The sensitivity analysis of probabilistic programs is however hard due to their intrinsic randomness: program variables are no longer assigned single values but rather hold probability distributions [6]. Uncountably infinite state spaces and non-linear assignments are further obstacles to the formal analysis of probabilistic programs. In recent years, several frameworks to *manually* reason about the sensitivity of probabilistic programs were proposed [1,4,33]. However, the state-of-the-art in *automated* sensitivity analysis mainly focuses on loop-free programs such as *Bayesian networks* [9,13,14,32] and statically-bounded loops [21]. The technique presented in [34] supports loops with variable-dependent termination times, but can only verify that the sensitivities obey certain bounds. To the best of our knowledge, up to now, there is no automated and exact method supporting the sensitivity analysis of (potentially) unbounded probabilistic loops.

In this paper, we propose a fully automatic technique for the sensitivity analysis of unbounded probabilistic loops. The crux of our approach lies within the integration of methods from symbolic computation, probability theory and static analysis in order to automatically capture sensitivity information about probabilistic loops. Such an integrated framework allows us to also characterize a class of loops for which our technique is sound and complete.

Our Framework for Algebraic Sensitivity Analysis. We advocate the use of algebraic recurrences to model the behavior of probabilistic loops. We combine and adjust techniques from symbolic summation, partial derivatives, and probability theory to provide a step towards the exact and automated sensitivity analysis of probabilistic loops, even in the presence of uncountable state spaces and polynomial assignments. Figure 1 shows two probabilistic loops for which our work automatically computes the sensitivities of program variables with respect to different parameters. For example, Fig. 1a depicts a probabilistic program, modelling the incidence of a disease within a population. More precisely, it models the probability `infected_prob` that a single organism within the population is infected, in dependence on symbolic parameters that model the amount of social interaction (`contac_param`), the frequency of vaccinations (`vax_param`) and effect of a vaccination weakening over time (`decline`). Sensitivity analysis helps to reason about the influence of these parameters on the disease infection process, answering for example the question "How will an increase in the rate of vaccinations `vax_param` influence the probability `infected_prob` of an infection?". Our work provides an algebraic approach to answering such and similar questions.

In a nutshell, our technique computes exact closed-form solutions for the sensitivities of (higher) moments of program variables for all, possibly infinitely many, loop iterations. Higher moments are necessary to recover/estimate the value distributions of probabilistic loop variables and hence these moments help in inferring valuable sensitivity information for the variance or skewness. In our work, we utilize algebraic techniques in probabilistic loop analysis to model moments of program variables with linear recurrences, so-called *moment*

```
infected_prob = 0
efficiency   = 0
while ★:
    contact = Bernoulli(contact_param)
    if contact == 1:
        infected_prob = 1-efficiency
    else
        infected_prob = 0
    end

    vax = Bernoulli(vax_param)
    if vax == 1:
        efficiency = Uniform(0.5, 1)
    else
        efficiency = decline*efficiency
    end
end
```

$$\partial_{vp}\mathbb{E}(\mathit{infected\_prob}_n) =$$
$$\frac{3 \cdot cp \cdot (d-1)}{4\,(1+d\cdot vp - d)^2} + 3 \cdot cp\,(d\,(1-vp))^n \cdot$$
$$\frac{1 - vp \cdot n + d\,(1+vp)\,(n\cdot vp - vp - 1)}{4\,(vp-1)^2\, d\,(1+d\cdot vp - d)^2}$$

(a)

```
u,w,x,y,z = 0,1,2,3,4
while ★:
    z = z + p² {1/2} z + p
    y = y - 5*p*z
    w = 5*w + x²
    x = 5 + w + x
    u = x + p*z*y
end
```

$$\partial_p\mathbb{E}(u_n) = \frac{n}{4}\left(-15p^5 + 25p^4 - 90p^3 - 42p^2 - 628p\right) +$$
$$\frac{n^2}{4}\left(-30p^5 - 260p^3 - 180p^2\right) +$$
$$\frac{n^3}{4}\left(-15p^5 - 25p^4 - 10p^3\right) + 12$$

(b)

Fig. 1. Two examples of parameterized probabilistic loops, where our approach automatically derives loop sensitivities ∂_p as polynomial expressions depending on the loop counter n and other parameters; for example `infected_prob` with respect to `vax_param` (Fig. 1a) or that of `u` with respect to `p` (Fig. 1b). Using these results, our work shows that, when assuming `decline`=0.9, `contact_param`=0.7, after $n = 10$ time steps and currently having `vax_param`=0.1, then a small change ε in `vax_param` will decrease `infected_prob` by approximately 1.7ε in the next time step of Fig. 1a.

recurrences [8,27]. However, moment recurrences do not support loops with intricate polynomial arithmetic, such as the loop in Fig. 1b. To overcome this limitation, we propose the notion of *sensitivity recurrences*, which shortcut computing closed-forms for variable moments and directly model sensitivities via linear recurrence equations. In Fig. 1b, the program variable w is independent of the parameter p. By exploiting the independence of program variables from parameters, *sensitivity recurrences* enable the exact sensitivity analysis for loops such as Fig. 1b. We characterize a class of probabilistic loops for which we prove *sensitivity analysis via sensitivity recurrences* to be sound and complete.

Our Contributions. We integrate symbolic computation, in particular symbolic summation and partial derivation, in combination with methods from probability theory into the landscape of probabilistic program reasoning. In particular, we argue that recurrence-based loop analysis yields a fully automated and precise way to derive sensitivity information over unknown symbolic parameters in probabilistic loops. As such, our paper brings the following main contributions:

- We propose a fully automated approach for the sensitivity analysis of probabilistic loops based on *moment recurrences* (Sect. 3.1).
- We introduce *sensitivity recurrences* and an algorithm for sensitivity analysis going beyond *moment recurrences* (Sect. 3.2, Algorithm 1).

– We provide a precise characterization of the class of probabilistic loops for which *sensitivity recurrences* are provably sound and complete (Theorem 2).
– We describe an experimental evaluation demonstrating the feasibility of our techniques on many interesting probabilistic programs (Sect. 4).

2   Preliminaries

We write $\mathbb{N}$ for the natural numbers, $\mathbb{R}$ for the reals, $\overline{\mathbb{Q}}$ for the algebraic numbers, and $\mathbb{K}[x_1, \ldots, x_k]$ for the polynomial ring with coefficients in the field $\mathbb{K}$. A polynomial consisting of a single monic term is a *monomial*. The expected value operator is denoted as $\mathbb{E}$.

2.1   Syntax and Semantics of Probabilistic Loops

Syntax. In this paper, we focus on unbounded probabilistic while-loops, as illustrated by the two examples of Fig. 1 and introduced in [27]. Our programming model considers non-nested while-loops preceded by a variable initialization part, with the loop body being a sequence of (nested) if-statements and variable assignments. Unbounded probabilistic loops occur frequently when modeling dynamical systems. Guarded loops `while G: body` can be analyzed by considering the limiting behavior of unbounded loops of the form `while true: if G: body`.

The right-hand side of every variable assignment is either a probability distribution with existing moments (e.g. Normal or Uniform) and constant parameters, or a probabilistic choice of polynomials in program variables, that is $x = poly_1\{p_1\} \ldots poly_k\{p_k\}$, where x is assigned to $poly_i$ with probability p_i. Further, programs can be parameterized by symbolic constants which represent arbitrary real numbers. For further details, we refer to Appendix (A) [26].

Throughout this paper, we refer to programs from our programming model simply by (probabilistic) loops or (probabilistic) programs. For a program $\mathcal{P}$ we denote the set of program variables by $\mathrm{Vars}(\mathcal{P})$ and the set of symbolic parameters by $\mathrm{Params}(\mathcal{P})$.

Dependencies between program variables is a syntactical notion introduced next, representing a central part in our work.

Definition 1 (Variable Dependency). *Let $\mathcal{P}$ be a probabilistic loop and $x, y \in \mathrm{Vars}(\mathcal{P})$. We say that x depends directly on y, and write $x \to y$, if y appears in an assignment of x or an assignment of x occurs in an if-statement where y appears in the if-condition. Furthermore, we say that the dependency is non-linear, denoted as $x \xrightarrow{N} y$, if y appears non-linearly in an assignment of x.*

By $\twoheadrightarrow$ we denote the transitive closure of $\to$. Regarding non-linearity, we write $x \xrightarrow{N} y$, if at least one of the direct dependencies from x to y is non-linear.

Example 1. In Fig. 1b, we have (among others) $y \to z$, $w \xrightarrow{N} x$, $u \xrightarrow{N} w$, and $w \xrightarrow{N} u$. To illustrate the influence of if-conditions, in Fig. 1a, note that *efficiency* $\to$ *vax* and *infected_prob* $\twoheadrightarrow$ *vax*.

Semantics. Operationally, every probabilistic loop models an infinite-state Markov chain, which in turn induces a canonical probability space. Due to brevity, we omit the straightforward but rather technical construction of the Markov chains associated to probabilistic loops. For more details, we refer the interested reader to [16,27]. For an arithmetic expression *Expr* in program variables, we denote by $Expr_n$ the stochastic process evaluating *Expr* after the nth loop iteration.

2.2   C-finite Recurrences

We recall notions from algebraic recurrences [17,23], adjusted to our work.

A *sequence* of algebraic numbers is a function $u \colon \mathbb{N} \to \overline{\mathbb{Q}}$, succinctly denoted by $\langle u(n) \rangle_{n=0}^{\infty}$ or $\langle u(n) \rangle_n$. A *recurrence* for the sequence u of order $\ell \in \mathbb{N}$ is specified by a function $f : \mathbb{R}^{\ell+1} \to \mathbb{R}$ and given by the equation $u(n+\ell) = f(u(n+\ell-1), \dots, u(n+1), u(n), n)$. The *solutions* of a recurrence are the sequences satisfying the recurrence equation. Of particular relevance to our work is the class of *linear recurrences with constant coefficients* or more shortly, *C-finite recurrences*. The sequence u satisfies a C-finite recurrence if $u(n+\ell) = c_{\ell-1}u(n+\ell-1) + c_{\ell-2}u(n+\ell-2) + \cdots + c_0 u(n)$ holds, where $c_0, \dots, c_{\ell-1} \in \overline{\mathbb{Q}}$ are constants and $c_0 \neq 0$. Every C-finite recurrence is associated with its *characteristic polynomial* $x^n - c_{\ell-1}x^{\ell-1} - \cdots - c_1 x - c_0$. The solutions of C-finite recurrences can always be computed [23] and written in closed-form as *exponential polynomials*. More precisely, if $\langle u(n) \rangle_n$ is the solution to a C-finite recurrence, then $u(n) = \sum_{k=1}^{r} P_k(n)\lambda_k^n$ where $P_k(n) \in \overline{\mathbb{Q}}[n]$ and $\lambda_1, \dots, \lambda_r$ are the roots of the characteristic polynomial. The properties of C-finite recurrences also hold for systems of C-finite recurrences (systems of linear recurrence equations with constant coefficients, specifying multiple sequences).

2.3   Higher Moment Analysis Using Recurrences

For a random variable x, its higher moments are defined as $\mathbb{E}(x^k)$ for $k \in \mathbb{N}$. More generally, mixed moments for a set of random variables S are expected values of monomials in S. Recent works in probabilistic program analysis [10,27] introduced techniques and tools based on C-finite recurrences to compute higher moments of program variables for probabilistic loops. For example, for a probabilistic loop, $k \in \mathbb{N}$ and a program variable x, a closed-form solution for the kth higher moment of x parameterized by the loop iteration n, that is $\mathbb{E}(x_n^k)$, is computed in [27] using the `Polar` tool. This is achieved by first normalizing the program to eliminate if-statements and ensure every variable is only assigned once in the loop body. Then, a system of C-finite recurrences is constructed that models expected values of monomials in program variables. More precisely, for a monomial M in program variables, the work of [27] constructs a linear recurrence equation, relating the expected value of M in iteration $n+1$ to the expected values of program variable monomials in iteration n. The linear recurrence for the expected value of M in iteration $n+1$ is constructed by starting with the expression $\mathbb{E}(M_{n+1})$ and replacing variables contained in the expression by their assignments bottom-up as they appear in the loop body. Throughout, the linearity of expectation is used to convert expected values of polynomials into expected values of monomials (cf. Appendix (C) [26]).

We adopt the setting of [10,27] and refer by *moment recurrences* to the recurrence equations these techniques construct for moments of program variables.

Definition 2 (Moment Recurrence). *Let $\mathcal{P}$ be a probabilistic loop and M a monomial in Vars($\mathcal{P}$). A moment recurrence for M is an equation $\mathbb{E}(M_{n+1}) = \sum_{i=1}^{r} c_i \cdot \mathbb{E}(W_n^{(i)})$ where $c_i \in \overline{\mathbb{Q}}$ and all $W^{(i)}$ are monomials in Vars($\mathcal{P}$).*

In order to compute a closed-form solution for $\mathbb{E}(x_n^k)$, we employ [27] to first compute a moment recurrence R for the monomial x^k. Next, we derive moment recurrences for all monomials $W^{(i)}$ in R (cf. Definition 2) to construct a system of C-finite recurrences.

Example 2. Consider the program from Fig. 1a. For a more succinct representation, we abbreviate the symbolic parameters as $cp := contact\_$param; $vp := vax\_$param and $d := decline$. The first moments of the program variables are modeled through the following system of C-finite recurrences [27]:

$$\mathbb{E}(infected\_prob_{n+1}) = cp - cp \cdot \mathbb{E}(efficiency_n)$$

$$\mathbb{E}(efficiency_{n+1}) = (d - d \cdot vp) \cdot \mathbb{E}(efficiency_n) + \frac{3}{4} \cdot vp$$

The initial values of $\mathbb{E}(infected\_prob_n)$ and $\mathbb{E}(efficiency_n)$ are both 0. The system can be automatically solved [23] to obtain closed-form solutions, which are, when expanded, exponential polynomials, e.g. for $\mathbb{E}(infected\_prob_n)$:

$$\mathbb{E}(infected\_prob_n) = cp + \frac{3 \cdot vp \cdot cp \cdot \left((d - d \cdot vp)^{n-1} - 1\right)}{4\,(d \cdot vp - d + 1)}$$

We note that moment recurrences do not always exist. Moreover, termination is not guaranteed when recursively inferring the moment recurrences for all monomials $W^{(i)}$ in Definition 2 in order to construct a C-finite system.

Example 3. To illustrate that the approach based on moment recurrences does not work unconditionally, consider the loop from Fig. 1b and construct the moment recurrence $\mathbb{E}(w_{n+1}) = 5 \cdot \mathbb{E}(w_n) + \mathbb{E}(x_n^2)$. Since the recurrence contains $\mathbb{E}(x_n^2)$, we require the moment recurrence $\mathbb{E}(x_{n+1}^2) = \mathbb{E}((5 + w_{n+1} + x_n)^2) = \mathbb{E}(w_{n+1}^2) + \dots$ which requires the recurrence for $\mathbb{E}(w_n^2)$. This in turn necessitates a recurrence for $\mathbb{E}(x_n^4)$, which necessitates the recurrence for $\mathbb{E}(w_n^4)$ and so on. This process will repeatedly require recurrences for increasing moments of x_n and w_n, implying that this process will not terminate.

To circumvent variable dependencies and compute closed-forms of moment recurrences, we note that the following two conditions on the probabilistic loops ensure existence and computability of higher order moments.

Definition 3 (Admissible Loop). *A loop is* admissible *if*

1. *all variables in branching conditions only assume values in a finite set (i.e. they are* finite valued*), and*
2. *no variable x is non-linearly self-dependent $(x \not\xrightarrow{N} x)$[1].*

Example 4. The probabilistic loop in Fig. 1a is admissible. However, the program in Fig. 1b is not admissible. It does not satisfy condition 2: the variable x depends linearly on w and w depends quadratically on x; therefore, x is non-linearly self-dependent.

Admissible probabilistic loops are *moment-computable* [27], that is, higher moments of program variables admit computable closed-forms as exponential polynomials. The restriction on finite valued variables in branching conditions is necessary to guarantee computability and completeness: a single branching statement involving an unbounded variable renders the program model Turing-complete [27].

3 Sensitivity Analysis

In this section, we study the sensitivity of program variable moments with respect to symbolic parameters. We present two exact and fully automatic methods to answer the question of how small changes in symbolic parameters influence the moments of program variables. As such, we exploit the fact that closed-forms for variable moments in admissible loops are computable (Sect. 3.1). We further go beyond the admissible loop setting (Sect. 3.2) and devise a sensitivity analysis technique applicable to some non-admissible loops, such as the program in Fig. 1b.

Definition 4 (Sensitivity). *Let $\mathcal{P}$ be a probabilistic loop, $x \in Vars(\mathcal{P})$ and $p \in Params(\mathcal{P})$. The* sensitivity *of the kth moment of x with respect to p, denoted as $\partial_p \mathbb{E}(x_n^k)$, is defined as the partial derivative of $\mathbb{E}(x_n^k)$ with respect to p, and parameterized by loop counter n. For monomials M of variables, the sensitivity $\partial_p \mathbb{E}(M_n)$ is defined analogously.*

Similar to *moment computability* [27], we define a program to be *sensitivity computable* if the sensitivities of all the variables' expected values are expressible in closed-form.

Definition 5 (Sensitivity Computability). *Let $\mathcal{P}$ be a probabilistic program and $p \in Params(\mathcal{P})$. $\mathcal{P}$ is* sensitivity computable *with respect to p, if for every variable $x \in Vars(\mathcal{P})$ the sensitivity $\partial_p \mathbb{E}(x_n)$ has an exponential polynomial closed-form that is computable.*

---

[1] While [27] allows arbitrary dependencies among finite valued variables, our work omits this generalization for simplicity. Nevertheless, our results also apply to admissible loops with arbitrary dependencies among finite valued variables.

3.1   Sensitivity Analysis for Admissible Loops

As mentioned in Sect. 2, for admissible loops, any moment of every program variable admits a closed-form solution as an exponential polynomial which is computable. That is, for a program variable x and $k \in \mathbb{N}$, the kth moment of x can be written as $\mathbb{E}(x_n^k) = \sum_{j=0}^{r} P_j(n) \lambda_j^n$, where $P_j \in \overline{\mathbb{Q}}[n]$ and $\lambda_j \in \overline{\mathbb{Q}}$ may contain symbolic parameters. We next show that based on the closed-forms of variable moments, we can compute exponential polynomials representing the sensitivities of moments on parameters.

Theorem 1 (Admissible Sensitivities). *Let $\mathcal{P}$ be an admissible program, $x \in Vars(\mathcal{P})$, $p \in Params(\mathcal{P})$, and $k \in \mathbb{N}$. Then, the sensitivity $\partial_p \mathbb{E}(x_n^k)$ has an exponential polynomial closed-form that is computable.*

Proof. Because $\mathcal{P}$ is admissible, $\mathbb{E}(x_n^k)$ can be expressed as an exponential polynomial. We show that the sensitivity can be expressed as an exponential polynomial by expanding $\mathbb{E}(x_n^k)$ into a sum of exponential monomials: $\mathbb{E}(x_n^k) = \sum_{j=0}^{r} P_j(n) \lambda_j^n = \sum_{j=0}^{r} \sum_{i=0}^{m_j} M_{ij}(n) \lambda_j^n$, where m_j is the number of monomials in P_j and every M_{ij} is a monomial. Note that every M_{ij} and λ_j may depend on the symbolic constant p. The derivative of the exponential monomials can then be obtained by applying the product rule for derivatives:

$$\partial_p \mathbb{E}(x_n^k) = \sum_{j=0}^{r} \sum_{i=0}^{m_j} (\partial_p M_{ij}(n)) \lambda_j^n + M_{ij}(n) \cdot n \cdot (\partial_p \lambda_j) \cdot \lambda_j^{n-1}$$

$$= \sum_{j=0}^{r} (\partial_p P_j(n) + P_j(n) \cdot n \cdot \partial_p \lambda_j \cdot \frac{1}{\lambda_j}) \lambda_j^n$$

It is left to show that the exponential polynomial $\partial_p \mathbb{E}(x_n^k)$ is computable. Because $\mathcal{P}$ is admissible, an exponential polynomial for $\mathbb{E}(x_n^k)$ is computable. Now, the second claim follows from the fact that exponential polynomials are elementary and that the derivative of any elementary function is computable.   □

As a corollary, admissible loops are sensitivity computable. Although *sensitivity computability* only refers to first moments, Theorem 1 shows that for admissible loops, sensitivities of *all* higher moments of program variables admit a computable closed-form.

Example 5. Consider Fig. 1a. In Example 2 we stated the closed-form solutions of $\mathbb{E}(infected\_prob_n)$. The sensitivities of the respective expected values can be computed by symbolic differentiation and, by Theorem 1, can be expanded to exponential polynomials. For example, the following expression describes the sensitivity of $\mathbb{E}(infected\_prob_n)$ with respect to the parameter vp:

$$\partial_{vp} \mathbb{E}(infected\_prob_n) = \frac{3 \cdot cp \left(1 - vp \cdot n + d \left(1 + vp\right) \left(n \cdot vp - vp - 1\right)\right) \left(d \left(1 - vp\right)\right)^n}{4 \left(vp - 1\right)^2 d \left(1 + d \cdot vp - d\right)^2}$$
$$+ \frac{3 \cdot cp \cdot \left(d - 1\right)}{4 \left(1 + d \cdot vp - d\right)^2}$$

3.2   Sensitivity Analysis for Non-admissible Loops

In general, moments of program variables of non-admissible loops do not satisfy linear recurrences. Therefore, we cannot utilize closed-forms of the moments for sensitivity analysis. Nevertheless, sensitivity analysis is feasible even for some non-admissible loops. In this section, we propose a novel sensitivity analysis approach applicable to non-admissible loops. Moreover, we characterize the class of (non-admissible) loops for which our method is sound and complete.

For admissible loops, linear recurrences describing variable moments can be used as an intermediary step to compute sensitivities. The core of our approach towards handling non-admissible loops is to shortcut moment recurrences and devise recurrences directly for sensitivities. Due to independence with respect to the sensitivity parameter, sensitivities of program variables can follow a linear recurrence even though their moments do not. We illustrate the idea of our new method on the non-admissible loop from Fig. 1b.

Example 6. Consider the non-admissible program from Fig. 1b. The moment recurrences for all program variables are:

$$\mathbb{E}(z_{n+1}) = \mathbb{E}(z_n) + 0.5 \cdot (p + p^2) \qquad \mathbb{E}(y_{n+1}) = \mathbb{E}(y_n) - 5p \cdot \mathbb{E}(z_{n+1})$$
$$\mathbb{E}(w_{n+1}) = 5 \cdot \mathbb{E}(w_n) + \mathbb{E}(x_n^2) \qquad \mathbb{E}(x_{n+1}) = 5 + \mathbb{E}(w_{n+1}) + \mathbb{E}(x_n)$$
$$\mathbb{E}(u_{n+1}) = \mathbb{E}(x_{n+1}) + p \cdot \mathbb{E}(zy_{n+1})$$

As illustrated in Example 3, we cannot complete the recurrences to a C-finite system because both w and x are non-linearly self-dependent. Therefore, we cannot compute closed-form solutions for $\mathbb{E}(w_n)$ and $\mathbb{E}(x_n)$. However, we can shortcut solving for $\mathbb{E}(w_n)$ and $\mathbb{E}(x_n)$ by differentiating the moment recurrences with respect to p and establish recurrences directly for the sensitivities:

$$\partial_p\mathbb{E}(z_{n+1}) = \partial_p\mathbb{E}(z_n) + 0.5 \cdot (1 + 2p)$$
$$\partial_p\mathbb{E}(y_{n+1}) = \partial_p\mathbb{E}(y_n) - 5p \cdot \partial_p\mathbb{E}(z_{n+1}) - 5 \cdot \mathbb{E}(z_{n+1})$$
$$\partial_p\mathbb{E}(w_{n+1}) = 5 \cdot \partial_p\mathbb{E}(w_n) + \partial_p\mathbb{E}(x_n^2)$$
$$\partial_p\mathbb{E}(x_{n+1}) = \partial_p\mathbb{E}(w_{n+1}) + \partial_p\mathbb{E}(x_n)$$
$$\partial_p\mathbb{E}(u_{n+1}) = \partial_p\mathbb{E}(x_{n+1}) + \mathbb{E}(zy_{n+1}) + p \cdot \partial_p\mathbb{E}(zy_{n+1})$$

Now, because the variables w and x do not depend on the parameter p, we conclude that $\partial_p\mathbb{E}(w_n) \equiv \partial_p\mathbb{E}(x_n) \equiv 0$. The sensitivity recurrences thus simplify:

$$\partial_p\mathbb{E}(z_{n+1}) = \partial_p\mathbb{E}(z_n) + \frac{1 + 2p}{2}$$
$$\partial_p\mathbb{E}(y_{n+1}) = \partial_p\mathbb{E}(y_n) - 5p \cdot \partial_p\mathbb{E}(z_{n+1}) - 5 \cdot \mathbb{E}(z_{n+1})$$
$$\partial_p\mathbb{E}(u_{n+1}) = \mathbb{E}(zy_{n+1}) + p \cdot \partial_p\mathbb{E}(zy_{n+1})$$

We can interpret sensitivities such as $\partial_p\mathbb{E}(z_n)$ or $\partial_p\mathbb{E}(u_n)$ as atomic recurrence variables. In the resulting recurrences, all variables with non-linear self-dependencies vanished. Therefore, the recurrences can be completed to a C-finite system and solved by existing techniques, even though $\mathbb{E}(w_n)$ and $\mathbb{E}(x_n)$ are not C-finite. The resulting system of recurrences consists of all recurrences for sensitivities and moments that appear on the right-hand side of another recurrence. That is, the system of recurrences consists of the sensitivity recurrences for $\partial_p\mathbb{E}(z)$, $\partial_p\mathbb{E}(y)$, $\partial_p\mathbb{E}(u)$, $\partial_p\mathbb{E}(yz)$, $\partial_p\mathbb{E}(z^2)$ and the moment recurrences for $\mathbb{E}(z)$, $\mathbb{E}(y)$, $\mathbb{E}(yz)$, $\mathbb{E}(z^2)$.

Motivated by Example 6, we introduce the notion of *sensitivity recurrences*.

Definition 6 (Sensitivity Recurrence). *Let $\mathcal{P}$ be a program, $p \in Params(\mathcal{P})$ a symbolic parameter, M a monomial in $Vars(\mathcal{P})$ and let $\mathbb{E}(M_{n+1}) = \sum_{i=1}^{r} c_i \cdot \mathbb{E}(W_n^{(i)})$ be the moment-recurrence of M. Then the* sensitivity recurrence *of M with respect to p is defined as*

$$\boxed{\partial_p\mathbb{E}(M_{n+1})} := \frac{\partial\mathbb{E}(M_{n+1})}{\partial p} = \frac{\partial}{\partial p}\left(\sum_{i=1}^{r} c_i \cdot \mathbb{E}\left(W_n^{(i)}\right)\right)$$
$$\boxed{= \sum_{i=1}^{r}\left(\frac{\partial}{\partial p}c_i\right) \cdot \mathbb{E}\left(W_n^{(i)}\right) + c_i \cdot \partial_p\mathbb{E}\left(W_n^{(i)}\right)} \tag{1}$$

The sensitivity recurrence of M equates the sensitivity of M at iteration $n+1$ to moments *and* sensitivities at iteration n. Along the ideas in Example 6, we provide with Algorithm 1 a procedure for sensitivity analysis also applicable to non-admissible loops. The idea of Algorithm 1 is to determine $\partial_p\mathbb{E}(M_n)$ by constructing a C-finite system consisting of all necessary recurrence equations for the moments and sensitivities of program variables. As illustrated in Example 6, we can exploit the independence of variables from the sensitivity parameter p to simplify the problem: if a monomial W' is independent from p then $\partial_p\mathbb{E}(W_n') \equiv 0$. Moreover, if p does not appear in the constant c_i of Equation (1), then $(\partial/\partial p)c_i = 0$, and hence the moment recurrence of W' does not need to be constructed (lines 8–9 of Algorithm 1). This is essential if the *expected value* of W' does not admit a closed-form. Algorithm 1 is sound by construction, however, termination is non-trivial. In the remainder of this section, we formalize the notion of parameter (in)dependence and give a characterization of the class of non-admissible loops for which Algorithm 1 terminates. As a consequence of Algorithm 1, we show that sensitivity recurrences yield an exact and complete technique for sensitivity analysis (Theorem 2).

Definition 7 (p-Dependent Variable). *Let $\mathcal{P}$ be a program with parameter $p \in Params(\mathcal{P})$. A variable $x \in Vars(\mathcal{P})$ is p-dependent, if (1) p appears in an assignment of x, (2) x depends on some $y \in Vars(\mathcal{P})$ ($x \twoheadrightarrow y$) and y is p-dependent or (3) an assignment of x occurs in an if-statement where p appears in the if-condition. A variable is p-independent if it is not p-dependent. A monomial M in program variables is p-dependent if M contains at least one p-dependent variable, otherwise it is p-independent.*

Algorithm 1. Computing Sensitivities via Sensitivity Recurrences

---

Input: program $\mathcal{P}$, monomial M in $\mathrm{Vars}(\mathcal{P})$, $p \in \mathrm{Params}(\mathcal{P})$
Output: closed-form for $\partial_p \mathbb{E}(M_n)$
  1: **if** M is p-independent **then**
  2:     **return** 0
  3: **end if**
  4: $Eqs \leftarrow \emptyset$; $Mom \leftarrow \emptyset$; $Sens \leftarrow \{M\}$
  5: **while** $Sens \neq \emptyset$ **do**   ▷ Add all necessary sensitivity recurrences
  6:     pick $W \in Sens$; $Sens \leftarrow Sens \setminus \{W\}$
  7:     $SRec \leftarrow$ sensitivity recurrence of W
  8:     Replace every $\partial_p \mathbb{E}(W'_n)$ in $SRec$ by 0 if W' is p-independent
  9:     Replace every $(\partial/\partial_p c) \mathbb{E}(W'_n)$ in $SRec$ by 0 if $(\partial/\partial_p c) = 0$
 10:     $Eqs \leftarrow Eqs \cup \{SRec\}$
 11:     Add to $Sens$ all monomials W' s.t. $\partial_p \mathbb{E}(W'_n)$ in $SRec$
 12:     $\hookrightarrow$ and the sensitivity recurrence of $W' \notin Eqs$
 13:     Add to Mom all monomials W' s.t. $\mathbb{E}(W'_n)$ in $SRec$
 14: **end while**
 15: **while** $Mom \neq \emptyset$ **do**   ▷ Add all necessary moment recurrences
 16:     pick $W \in Mom$; $Mom \leftarrow Mom \setminus \{W\}$
 17:     $MRec \leftarrow$ moment recurrence of W
 18:     $Eqs \leftarrow Eqs \cup \{MRec\}$
 19:     Add to Mom all monomials W' s.t. $\mathbb{E}(W'_n)$ in $MRec$
 20:     $\hookrightarrow$ and the moment recurrence of $W' \notin Eqs$
 21: **end while**
 22: $S \leftarrow$ solve system of C-finite recurrences Eqs
 23: **return** closed-form of $\partial_p \mathbb{E}(M_n)$ from S

For any p-independent monomial M in program variables, the corresponding sensitivity $\partial_p \mathbb{E}(M_n)$ is zero (by using induction on n and applying Definition 7).

Lemma 1. *Let $\mathcal{P}$ be a program, $p \in Params(\mathcal{P})$ a symbolic parameter and M a p-independent monomial in $Vars(\mathcal{P})$, then it holds that the sensitivity variable of M is zero, i.e., $\forall n \geq 0 : \partial_p \mathbb{E}(M_n) = 0$.*

In Example 6, the moments $\mathbb{E}(w_n)$ and $\mathbb{E}(x_n)$ do not admit closed-forms. We resolved this issue by differentiating all moment recurrences and working directly with the sensitivity recurrences, where the moment recurrences for w and x vanished. Crucial for this phenomenon is the fact that the variables w and x are independent of the sensitivity parameter p.

However, a second fact is necessary to guarantee that the moment recurrences of w and x do not appear in the resulting system of recurrences: Assume some new variable v depends on x and has the moment recurrence $\mathbb{E}(v_{n+1}) = \mathbb{E}(v_n) + p \cdot \mathbb{E}(x_n)$. Then the sensitivity recurrence for v is given by $\partial_p \mathbb{E}(v_{n+1}) = \partial_p \mathbb{E}(v_n) + \mathbb{E}(x_n) + p \cdot \partial_p \mathbb{E}(x_n)$. Even though x itself is p-independent, $\mathbb{E}(x_n)$ remains in the sensitivity recurrence of v because the coefficient of $\mathbb{E}(x_n)$ contains the parameter p. A similar effect occurs if the moment recurrence for v was $\mathbb{E}(v_{n+1}) = \mathbb{E}(v_n) + \mathbb{E}(z_n x_n)$, because z is p-dependent.

Our goal is to characterize the class of probabilistic loops for which sensitivity recurrences yield a sound and complete method for sensitivity analysis. Hence, we need to capture the notion that some dependencies between variables are free of multiplicative factors involving the sensitivity parameter. We do this in the following definition by refining our dependency relation $\twoheadrightarrow$.

Definition 8 (p-Influenced Dependency). *Let $\mathcal{P}$ be a program with parameter $p \in Params(\mathcal{P})$ and $x, y \in Vars(\mathcal{P})$ with $x \to y$. Then, the direct dependency between x and y is p-influenced, written as $x \to_p y$, if at least one of the following conditions hold:*

- *An assignment of x contains y and occurs in an if-statement with the if-condition involving p or a p-dependent variable.*
- *An assignment of x contains y and is a probabilistic choice with some probability of the choice depending on p.*
- *An assignment of x contains a term $c \cdot M \cdot y$ where c is constant and M is a monomial in program variables (possibly containing y). Moreover, either c contains p or M contains a p-dependent variable.*

If $x \twoheadrightarrow y$, we write $x \twoheadrightarrow_p y$ if some dependency from x to y is p-influenced. If $x \twoheadrightarrow y$ and $x \not\twoheadrightarrow_p y$ we call the dependency between x and y p-free.

Definition 8 covers all cases in the construction of moment recurrences that introduce multiplicative factors depending on the sensitivity parameter p [27]. We provide details on the construction of moment recurrences in Appendix (C) [26].

More concretely, assume $\mathcal{P}$ to be a program and $x \in Vars(\mathcal{P})$. The moment recurrence of x contains expected values of monomials M of program variables. Additionally, the moment recurrences of any M will again contain expected values of monomials of program variables and so on. We capture all of these monomials with the notion of *descendant monomials* in Definition 9. Intuitively, to construct a system of moment recurrences for $\mathbb{E}(x_n)$ one needs to include the moment recurrences of all descendants of x.

Definition 9 (Descendant Monomial). *Let $\mathcal{P}$ be a program, $x \in Vars(\mathcal{P})$, and M a monomial in program variables. The monomial M is a descendant of the variable x if (1) $M = x$, or (2) M occurs in the moment recurrence of a monomial W and W is a descendant of x. The variable x is an ancestor of M.*

There is a dependency between x and any variable of any descendant of x, which means $x \twoheadrightarrow y$ for every descendant M of x and every variable y in M. Our dependency relation from Definition 8 allows us to pinpoint the variables in the moment recurrence of any descendant of x (Definition 9) with a multiplicative factor involving the sensitivity parameter. Definitions 8 and 9 together with the procedure constructing moment recurrences (Appendix (C) [26]) yield:

Lemma 2 (p-Influenced Moment Recurrence). *Let $\mathcal{P}$ be a program, $x \in Vars(\mathcal{P})$, and $p \in Params(\mathcal{P})$. Assume M is a monomial in program variables* *descending from* x. *Let* W *be a monomial in* M's *moment recurrence with non-zero coefficient* c. *If the parameter* p *occurs in* c, *then for all variables* y *in* W *we have* $x \twoheadrightarrow_p y$. *Moreover, if some variable* z *in* W *is* p-*dependent, then for all variables* y *in* W *different from* z *we have* $x \twoheadrightarrow_p y$.

We now state our main result (Theorem 2) describing the class of probabilistic loops for which Algorithm 1 terminates and, hence, sensitivity recurrences are sound and complete. We characterize the class of loops in terms of our dependency relations as well as variables with non-linear self-dependencies, which we refer to as *defective* variables.

Definition 10 (Defective Variables). *Let* $\mathcal{P}$ *be a program and* $x \in \mathit{Vars}(\mathcal{P})$, *then* x *is* defective *if* $x \overset{N}{\twoheadrightarrow} x$. *Otherwise,* x *is* effective.

Theorem 2 (Non-admissible Sensitivities). *Let* $\mathcal{P}$ *be a probabilistic program,* $p \in \mathit{Params}(\mathcal{P})$, $x \in \mathit{Vars}(\mathcal{P})$, *and assume all the following conditions:*

1. *All variables occurring in branching conditions are finite.*
2. *All defective variables are* p-*independent.*
3. *All dependencies on defective variables are* p-*free.*

Then, for every monomial M *in program variables descending from* x, *Algorithm 1 terminates on input* $\mathcal{P}$, M *and* p.

Proof (Sketch). Algorithm 1 does not terminate iff infinitely many monomials are added to the set *Sens* one line 11 or to the set *Mom* on lines 13 or 19. However, every monomial added to these sets decreases with respect to some well-founded ordering. Hence, only finitely many monomials are added and Algorithm 1 terminates. This holds by using a well-founded ordering for monomials of effective variables and showing that all monomials added to *Sens* or *Mom* do *not* contain defective variables. Assuming then that some monomial added to the sets *Sens* or *Mom* contains defective variables leads to contradictions using conditions 2 and 3, and Lemma 2. See Appendix (D) [26] for more details.   □

Theorem 2 characterizes the class of probabilistic loops for which sensitivity recurrences provide a sound and complete method for sensitivity analysis. As an immediate corollary, this class of loops is sensitivity computable because every variable is a descendant of itself. Note that all conditions of Theorem 2 are statically checkable: the concepts of defective variables, p-independent variables, and p-free dependencies are purely syntactic notions. Moreover, program variables occurring in branching conditions only admitting finitely many values can be verified using standard techniques based on *abstract interpretation*.

Theorem 2 also applies to sensitivity analysis for higher moments: let $v \in \mathit{Vars}(\mathcal{P})$ and $k \in \mathbb{N}$, then Theorem 2 covers the sensitivity of v's kth moment if v^k is a descendant of some variable. Otherwise, v^k can be dealt with by introducing a fresh variable w and appending the assignment $w := v^k$ to $\mathcal{P}$'s loop body.

The proof of Theorem 2 provides an alternative argument for admissible loops being sensitivity computable (Theorem 1); as admissible loops do not contain defective variables by definition (Definition 3), the class of loops characterized by Theorem 2 subsumes the class of admissible loops.

4   Experiments and Evaluation

We evaluate our methods for sensitivity analysis for admissible loops (Sect. 3.1) and non-admissible loops (Sect. 3.2). Our techniques for sensitivity analysis extend the Polar framework [27], which is publicly available at https://github.com/probing-lab/polar. For admissible loops, we use the existing functionality of the Polar framework to compute closed-forms for the moments of program variables.

Experimental Setup. We split our evaluation into two parts. First, we compute the sensitivities of (higher) moments of program variables for admissible loops by automatically differentiating the closed-forms of the variables' moments (Table 1). In the second part, we consider our method using sensitivity recurrences, which is also applicable to non-admissible loops (Table 2). To the best of our knowledge, our work provides the first exact and fully automatic tool to compute the sensitivities of (higher) moments of program variables for probabilistic loops. All our experiments have been executed on a machine with a 2.6 GHz Intel i7 (Gen 10) processor and 32 GB of RAM with a timeout (TO) of 120 s.

Differentiating Closed-Forms. Table 1 shows the evaluation of our sensitivity analysis technique for admissible loops (Sect. 3) on 11 benchmarks. The benchmarks consist of the running example from Fig. 1a and parameterized probabilistic loops from the benchmarks in [27], coming from literature on probabilistic program analysis [3,9,12,20]. All the benchmarks contain at least one symbolic parameter with respect to which the sensitivities are computed. Table 1 shows that our approach is capable of computing the sensitivities of higher moments of program variables for challenging loops with various characteristics, such as discrete and continuous state spaces as well as drawing from common distributions.

Sensitivity Recurrences. Table 2 shows the evaluation of our sensitivity analysis technique from Algorithm 1 using *sensitivity recurrences*. The benchmarks consist of four non-admissible loops and six admissible loops from Table 1. Non-admissible loops are known to be notoriously hard to analyze automatically [2]. Table 2 shows that *sensitivity recurrences* are capable of computing the sensitivities for admissible as well as non-admissible loops.

Experimental Summary. When comparing both approaches on admissible loops, the differentiation-based approach typically performs better, e.g., on the benchmarks "Gambler's Ruin" or "Vaccination". This is not surprising, as the main complexity in both approaches lies in solving the system of recurrences and when using sensitivity recurrences, the number of recurrences tends to be higher. However, the exact number of recurrences depends on the program structure, and as such, there are cases where the approach using sensitivity recurrences performs equally well, such as in the "Randomized-Response" benchmark. Nevertheless,

Table 1. Evaluation of the sensitivity computation for 11 admissible loops by differentiating closed-forms of variable moments. REC: size of the recurrence system to compute the variables' moments; RT: runtime in seconds; TO: timeout.

Benchmark	Sensitivity	Rec, RT	Sensitivity	Rec, RT
50-Coin-Flips	$\partial_p \mathbb{E}(total)$	51, 1.56	$\partial_p \mathbb{E}(total^2)$	TO, TO
Bimodal	$\partial_p \mathbb{E}(x)$	3, 0.40	$\partial_p \mathbb{E}(x^2)$	5, 0.72
Component-Health	$\partial_{p1} \mathbb{E}(obs)$,	2, 0.61	$\partial_{p1} \mathbb{E}(obs^2)$,	2, 0.62
Umbrella	$\partial_{u1} \mathbb{E}(umbrella)$	2, 0.97	$\partial_{u1} \mathbb{E}(umbrella^2)$	2, 0.98
Gambler's Ruin	$\partial_p \mathbb{E}(money)$	4, 11.2	$\partial_p \mathbb{E}(money^2)$	10, 64.6
Hawk-Dove	$\partial_v \mathbb{E}(p1bal)$	1, 0.34	$\partial_v \mathbb{E}(p1bal^2)$	2, 0.67
Las-Vegas-Search	$\partial_p \mathbb{E}(attempts)$	2, 0.57	$\partial_p \mathbb{E}(attempts^2)$	4, 7.31
1D-Random-Walk	$\partial_p \mathbb{E}(x)$	1, 0.27	$\partial_p \mathbb{E}(x^2)$	2, 0.39
2D-Random-Walk	$\partial_{p\_right} \mathbb{E}(x)$	1, 0.28	$\partial_{p\_right} \mathbb{E}(x^2)$	2, 0.41
Randomized-Response	$\partial_p \mathbb{E}(p1)$	1, 0.29	$\partial_p \mathbb{E}(p1^2)$	2, 0.42
Vaccination (Fig. 1a)	$\partial_{vp} \mathbb{E}(infected)$	2, 1.25	$\partial_{vp} \mathbb{E}(infected^2)$	2, 1.19

for the class of loops characterized in Sect. 3.2, the differentiation-based approach fails, whereas sensitivity recurrences still deliver exact results in a fully automated manner.

Our experiments demonstrate that our novel techniques for sensitivity analysis can compute the sensitivities for a rich class of probabilistic loops with discrete and continuous state spaces, drawing from probability distributions, and including polynomial arithmetic. Moreover, the technique based on our new

Table 2. Evaluation of the sensitivity computation for 10 loops (4 are non-admissible) using sensitivity recurrences. REC: size of the recurrence system to compute the variables' sensitivities; RT: runtime in seconds; TO: timeout.

Benchmark	Sensitivity	Rec, RT	Sensitivity	Rec, RT
Non-Admissible (Fig. 1b)	$\partial_p \mathbb{E}(u)$	9, 1.40	$\partial_p \mathbb{E}(y^2)$	9, 1.75
Non-Admissible-2	$\partial_{par} \mathbb{E}(y)$	5, 6.56	$\partial_{par} \mathbb{E}(xz)$	4, 3.67
Non-Admissible-3	$\partial_p \mathbb{E}(total)$	6, 12.6	$\partial_p \mathbb{E}(z1^2)$	12, 56.5
Non-Admissible-4	$\partial_{p1} \mathbb{E}(z)$	4, 0.48	$\partial_{p1} \mathbb{E}(cnt^2)$	3, 0.39
Bimodal	$\partial_{var} \mathbb{E}(x)$	3, 0.28	$\partial_{var} \mathbb{E}(x^2)$	5, 0.42
Component-Health	$\partial_{p1} \mathbb{E}(obs)$	3, 0.74	$\partial_{p1} \mathbb{E}(obs^2)$	3, 0.73
Gambler's Ruin	$\partial_p \mathbb{E}(money)$	7, 66.9	$\partial_p \mathbb{E}(money^2)$	TO, TO
Las-Vegas-Search	$\partial_p \mathbb{E}(attempts)$	3, 0.81	$\partial_p \mathbb{E}(attempts^2)$	7, 13.3
Randomized-Response	$\partial_p \mathbb{E}(p1)$	1, 0.30	$\partial_p \mathbb{E}(p1^2)$	3, 0.40
Vaccination (Fig. 1a)	$\partial_{vp} \mathbb{E}(infected)$	3, 8.26	$\partial_{vp} \mathbb{E}(infected^2)$	3, 7.85

notion of *sensitivity recurrences* can compute sensitivities for probabilistic loops for which closed-forms of the variables' moments do not exist.

5   Related Work

Sensitivity and Probabilistic Programs. Bayesian networks can be seen as special loop-free probabilistic programs. The sensitivity of Bayesian networks with discrete probability distribution was studied in [13,14]. The works of [9,32] provide a framework to analyze properties (sensitivity among others) of *Prob-solvable Bayesian networks*. In contrast, our work focuses on probabilistic loops with more complex control flow and supports continuous distributions. In recent years, techniques emerged to manually reason about sensitivities of probabilistic programs, such as program calculi [1], custom logics [4], or type systems [33]. Although applicable to general probabilistic programs, these techniques require manual reasoning or user guidance, while our work focuses on full automation.

A fully-automatic and exact sensitivity analyzer for probabilistic programs with statically bounded loops was proposed in [21]. In comparison, our work focuses on potentially unbounded loops. The authors of [34] introduce an automatable approach for expected sensitivity based on martingales. Their technique proves that a given program is Lipschitz-continuous for *some* Lipschitz constant. In contrast, our work produces *exact* sensitivities for unbounded loops and we characterize a class of loops for which our technique is complete.

Recurrences in Program Analysis. Recurrence equations are a common tool in program analysis. The work of [29,30] first introduced the idea of using linear recurrences and Gröbner basis computation to synthesize loop invariants. This line of work has been further generalized in [22,25] to support more general recurrences. In [18,24] the authors apply linear recurrences to more complex programs and combine it with over-approximation techniques. The work [11] combines recurrence techniques with template-based methods to analyze recursive procedures. Recurrence equations were first used for the analysis of probabilistic loops in [8] to synthesize so-called *moment-based invariants*. This approach was further generalized by [27]. Our technique of *sensitivity recurrences* is applicable to loops whose variables' moments do not satisfy linear recurrences. The recent work [2] studies the synthesis of invariants for such loops, but does not address sensitivity analysis.

6   Conclusion

We establish a fully automatic and exact technique to compute the sensitivities of higher moments of program variables for probabilistic loops. Our method is applicable to probabilistic loops with potentially uncountable state spaces, complex control flow, polynomial assignments, and drawing from common probability distributions. For admissible loops, we utilize closed-forms of the variables' moments obtained through linear recurrences. Moreover, we propose the notion of *sensitivity recurrences* enabling the sensitivity analysis for probabilistic loops whose moments do not admit closed-forms. We characterize a class of loops for which we prove *sensitivity recurrences* to be sound and complete. Our experiments demonstrate the feasibility of our techniques on challenging benchmarks.

Acknowledgements. This research was supported by the Vienna Science and Technology Fund WWTF 10.47379/ICT19018 grant ProbInG, the ERC Consolidator Grant ARTIST 101002685, the Austrian FWF SFB project SpyCoDe F8504, and the SecInt Doctoral College funded by TU Wien.

References

1. Aguirre, A., Barthe, G., Hsu, J., Kaminski, B.L., Katoen, J., Matheja, C.: A pre-expectation calculus for probabilistic sensitivity. In: Proceedings of the POPL (2021). https://doi.org/10.1145/3434333
2. Amrollahi, D., Bartocci, E., Kenison, G., Kovács, L., Moosbrugger, M., Stankovic, M.: Solving invariant generation for unsolvable loops. In: Proceedings of the SAS (2022). https://doi.org/10.1007/978-3-031-22308-2_3
3. Barthe, G., Espitau, T., Ferrer Fioriti, L.M., Hsu, J.: Synthesizing probabilistic invariants via Doob's decomposition. In: Chaudhuri, S., Farzan, A. (eds.) CAV 2016. LNCS, vol. 9779, pp. 43–61. Springer, Cham (2016). https://doi.org/10.1007/978-3-319-41528-4_3
4. Barthe, G., Espitau, T., Grégoire, B., Hsu, J., Strub, P.: Proving expected sensitivity of probabilistic programs. In: Proceedings of the POPL (2018). https://doi.org/10.1145/3158145
5. Barthe, G., Grégoire, B., Zanella Béguelin, S.: Probabilistic relational Hoare logics for computer-aided security proofs. In: Gibbons, J., Nogueira, P. (eds.) MPC 2012. LNCS, vol. 7342, pp. 1–6. Springer, Heidelberg (2012). https://doi.org/10.1007/978-3-642-31113-0_1
6. Barthe, G., Katoen, J.P., Silva, A.: Foundations of Probabilistic Programming. Cambridge University Press (2020). https://doi.org/10.1017/9781108770750
7. Barthe, G., Köpf, B., Olmedo, F., Béguelin, S.Z.: Probabilistic relational reasoning for differential privacy. In: Proceedings of the POPL (2012). https://doi.org/10.1145/2103656.2103670
8. Bartocci, E., Kovács, L., Stanković, M.: Automatic generation of moment-based invariants for prob-solvable loops. In: Chen, Y.-F., Cheng, C.-H., Esparza, J. (eds.) ATVA 2019. LNCS, vol. 11781, pp. 255–276. Springer, Cham (2019). https://doi.org/10.1007/978-3-030-31784-3_15
9. Bartocci, E., Kovács, L., Stanković, M.: Analysis of Bayesian networks via prob-solvable loops. In: Pun, V.K.I., Stolz, V., Simao, A. (eds.) ICTAC 2020. LNCS, vol. 12545, pp. 221–241. Springer, Cham (2020). https://doi.org/10.1007/978-3-030-64276-1_12
10. Bartocci, E., Kovács, L., Stanković, M.: MORA - automatic generation of moment-based invariants. In: TACAS 2020. LNCS, vol. 12078, pp. 492–498. Springer, Cham (2020). https://doi.org/10.1007/978-3-030-45190-5_28
11. Breck, J., Cyphert, J., Kincaid, Z., Reps, T.W.: Templates and recurrences: better together. In: Proceedings of the PLDI (2020). https://doi.org/10.1145/3385412.3386035

12. Chakarov, A., Sankaranarayanan, S.: Expectation invariants for probabilistic program loops as fixed points. In: Müller-Olm, M., Seidl, H. (eds.) SAS 2014. LNCS, vol. 8723, pp. 85–100. Springer, Cham (2014). https://doi.org/10.1007/978-3-319-10936-7_6

13. Chan, H., Darwiche, A.: When do numbers really matter? J. Artif. Intell. Res. (2002). https://doi.org/10.1613/jair.967

14. Chan, H., Darwiche, A.: Sensitivity analysis in Bayesian networks: from single to multiple parameters. In: Proceedings of the UAI (2004)

15. Chou, Y., Yoon, H., Sankaranarayanan, S.: Predictive runtime monitoring of vehicle models using Bayesian estimation and reachability analysis. In: Proceedings of the IROS (2020). https://doi.org/10.1109/IROS45743.2020.9340755

16. Durrett, R.: Probability: Theory and Examples. Cambridge University Press (2019). https://doi.org/10.1017/9781108591034

17. Everest, G., van der Poorten, A., Shparlinski, I., Ward, T.: Recurrence Sequences. Mathematical Surveys and Monographs, vol. 104. American Mathematical Society, Providence, RI (2003)

18. Farzan, A., Kincaid, Z.: Compositional recurrence analysis. In: Proceedings of the FMCAD (2015)

19. Ghahramani, Z.: Probabilistic machine learning and artificial intelligence. Nature (2015). https://doi.org/10.1038/nature14541

20. Gretz, F., Katoen, J.-P., McIver, A.: PRINSYS—on a quest for probabilistic loop invariants. In: Joshi, K., Siegle, M., Stoelinga, M., D'Argenio, P.R. (eds.) QEST 2013. LNCS, vol. 8054, pp. 193–208. Springer, Heidelberg (2013). https://doi.org/10.1007/978-3-642-40196-1_17

21. Huang, Z., Wang, Z., Misailovic, S.: PSense: automatic sensitivity analysis for probabilistic programs. In: Lahiri, S.K., Wang, C. (eds.) ATVA 2018. LNCS, vol. 11138, pp. 387–403. Springer, Cham (2018). https://doi.org/10.1007/978-3-030-01090-4_23

22. Humenberger, A., Jaroschek, M., Kovács, L.: Invariant generation for multi-path loops with polynomial assignments. In: VMCAI 2018. LNCS, vol. 10747, pp. 226–246. Springer, Cham (2018). https://doi.org/10.1007/978-3-319-73721-8_11

23. Kauers, M., Paule, P.: The Concrete Tetrahedron. Symbolic Sums, Recurrence Equations, Generating Functions, Asymptotic Estimates. Springer, Vienna (2011). https://doi.org/10.1007/978-3-7091-0445-3

24. Kincaid, Z., Cyphert, J., Breck, J., Reps, T.W.: Non-linear reasoning for invariant synthesis. In: Proceedings of the POPL (2018). https://doi.org/10.1145/3158142

25. Kovács, L.: Reasoning algebraically about P-solvable loops. In: Ramakrishnan, C.R., Rehof, J. (eds.) TACAS 2008. LNCS, vol. 4963, pp. 249–264. Springer, Heidelberg (2008). https://doi.org/10.1007/978-3-540-78800-3_18

26. Moosbrugger, M., Müllner, J., Kovács, L.: Automated sensitivity analysis for probabilistic loops (2023). https://arxiv.org/abs/2305.15259

27. Moosbrugger, M., Stankovic, M., Bartocci, E., Kovács, L.: This is the moment for probabilistic loops. In: Proceedings of the ACM on Programming Languages (OOPSLA2) (2022). https://doi.org/10.1145/3563341

28. Motwani, R., Raghavan, P.: Randomized Algorithms. Cambridge University Press (1995). https://doi.org/10.1017/cbo9780511814075

29. Rodríguez-Carbonell, E., Kapur, D.: Automatic generation of polynomial loop invariants: algebraic foundations. In: Gutierrez, J. (ed.) Proceedings of the ISSAC (2004). https://doi.org/10.1145/1005285.1005324

30. Rodríguez-Carbonell, E., Kapur, D.: Generating all polynomial invariants in simple loops. J. Symb. Comput. (2007). https://doi.org/10.1016/j.jsc.2007.01.002

31. Selyunin, K., Ratasich, D., Bartocci, E., Islam, M.A., Smolka, S.A., Grosu, R.: Neural programming: towards adaptive control in cyber-physical systems. In: Proceedings of the CDC (2015). https://doi.org/10.1109/CDC.2015.7403319

32. Stankovic, M., Bartocci, E., Kovács, L.: Moment-based analysis of Bayesian network properties. Theor. Comput. Sci. (2022). https://doi.org/10.1016/j.tcs.2021.12.021

33. Vasilenko, E., Vazou, N., Barthe, G.: Safe couplings: coupled refinement types. In: Proceedings of the ICFP (2022). https://doi.org/10.1145/3547643

34. Wang, P., Fu, H., Chatterjee, K., Deng, Y., Xu, M.: Proving expected sensitivity of probabilistic programs with randomized variable-dependent termination time. In: Proceedings of the POPL (2020). https://doi.org/10.1145/3371093

DIFFDP: Using Data Dependencies and Properties in Difference Verification with Conditions

Marie-Christine Jakobs[1,2]([✉]) [ORCID] and Tim Pollandt[1] [ORCID]

[1] Technical University of Darmstadt, Computer Science, Darmstadt, Germany
[2] LMU Munich, Munich, Germany
M.Jakobs@lmu.de

Abstract. To deal with frequent software changes, as e.g., caused by agile software development processes, software verification tools must be incremental. While many existing incremental verification approaches are tailored to and coupled with a specific verifier, Beyer et al. recently introduced a verifier agnostic approach. The underlying idea of their approach is to (1) detect an overapproximation of those paths in the modified software that may cause regression bugs (i.e., property violations that do not exist in the original, unmodified software), (2) encode the detected paths in a condition, and (3) apply conditional model checking to restrict the verifier's exploration to the detected paths. So far, only a simple, syntax-based difference detector exists. In this paper, we propose a more complicated difference detector DIFFDP, which amongst others takes data dependencies and correctness properties (more concretely, (un)reachability properties) into account to determine which changes may cause regression bugs where. Our extensive evaluation confirms that for all considered conditional model checkers our proposed difference detector improves the effectiveness and efficiency of difference verification with condition on several tasks.

1 Introduction

Software plays a major role in our lives. Often, it must or we at least expect it to function reliably. At the same time, software is modified frequently, e.g., to fix bugs, to integrate new or to adapt existing features, but each modification bears the risk to introduce new bugs and, thus, to decrease the software's reliability.

Software verification [13,25] is one means to prove the absence or detect the existence of software bugs. However, fully verifying a software after each modification is often too costly and rarely necessary. A modification typically does not affect the complete software behavior, in particular, it will not introduce bugs in all parts of the software. Many incremental software verification techniques

This work was funded by the Hessian LOEWE initiative within the Software-Factory 4.0 project and by the Deutsche Forschungsgemeinschaft (DFG, German Research Foundation) - 496852682.

P. Herber and A. Wijs (Eds.): iFM 2023, LNCS 14300, pp. 40–61, 2024.
https://doi.org/10.1007/978-3-031-47705-8_3

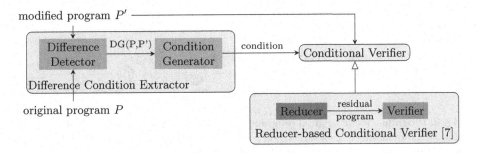

Fig. 1. Construction of a difference verifier

make use of this insight to speed up the reverification of a modified software. For example, they adjust previously computed fixpoints [2, 36, 40] or state space representations [18, 28, 39], reuse intermediate results [1, 9, 16, 20, 37, 43, 48], or do not reanalyze unchanged behavior [6, 12, 29, 30, 35, 38, 45, 46]. Despite a few exceptions [6, 20, 43], existing approaches are mostly tailored to and coupled with one specific verification approach while often requiring an initial full verification.

To overcome these problems, Beyer et al. proposed difference verification with conditions [6], which uses a difference verifier to look for new bugs in changed program execution paths only. A difference verifier (see Fig. 1) is based on an arbitrary (conditional) verifier and starts with a difference condition extractor, which overapproximates the execution paths of the modified program that may cause a regression bug, i.e., execution paths that may violate the property but whose inputs may not cause a property violation in the original program. The extractor encodes the determined paths into a condition, an automata-based exchange format known from conditional model checking [5]. Finally, the condition guides a conditional verifier to analyze the paths determined by the extractor. As conditional verifier, we may use an existing one or construct a reducer-based conditional verifier from an arbitrary verifier [7] as shown in Fig. 1.

So far, only one difference condition extractor has existed, which is purely syntax-based and which extracts all paths that syntactically changed, i.e., all syntactical paths of the modified program that do not occur in the original program. However, not all these paths may cause regression bugs. For example, fixing the computation of the negated absolute value of x in Fig. 2 by deleting the minus sign (shown in red) in the first statement does not affect the assertion. Therefore in this paper, we propose a new, more complex difference condition extractor, which also considers data dependencies and programs' correctness properties, and only extracts those changed paths that may affect the modified program's property. We show that our new difference condition extractor is sound. The detailed proofs can be found in our technical report [21]. In addition, we study performance of our new difference condition extractor in various difference verifiers using thousands of benchmark tasks. Our experimental results reveal that difference verification with our new extractor often improves on difference verification with the previous extractor.

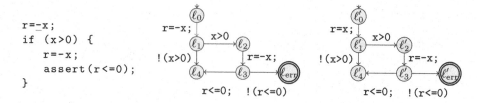

```
r=-x;
if (x>0) {
    r=-x;
    assert(r<=0);
}
```

Fig. 2. Program code of original program (left) as well as the CFA of original program (middle) and modified program (right). The modified program is derived from the original program by deleting the underlined parts in red.

2 Foundations of Difference Verification with Conditions

We start with the formal definition of programs. To simplify our presentation, we consider imperative programs that operate on assume operations and assignments from a set Ops. Also, we restrict our properties to the unreachability of certain program locations.[1] Formally, we use *control-flow automata* to model the syntax of original and modified programs and their properties.

Definition 1. *A* control-flow automaton *(CFA)* $P = (L, \ell_0, G, \ell_{err})$ *consists of a set L of program locations, initial location $\ell_0 \in L$, error location $\ell_{err} \in L$ indicating a property violation, and a set $G \subseteq L \times Ops \times L$ of control-flow edges.*
P *is* deterministic *if for all control-flow edges* $(\ell, op_1, \ell_1), (\ell, op_2, \ell_2) \in G$ *either* $op_1 = op_2 \wedge \ell_1 = \ell_2$ *or* op_1 *and* op_2 *are assume operations with* $op_1 \equiv \neg op_2$.

Consider a program that should compute the negated absolute value $-|x|$ of variable x. Figure 2 shows the code and CFA of an incorrect implementation, which mistakenly negates x in the first line, as well as the CFA for the modified program fixing the bug. The CFAs contain one edge per assignment, two edges for the condition in the if statement and the assertion (one for each condition evaluation), and any violation of the assertion leads to the error location.

For the program semantics, we consider a standard operational semantics that defines the executable program paths of a CFA $P = (L, \ell_0, G, \ell_{err})$. A program state is a pair of a program location $\ell \in L$ and a concrete data state c that assigns to each variable a concrete value. An *executable program path* $\pi = (\ell_0, c_0) \xrightarrow{g_1} (\ell_1, c_1) \xrightarrow{g_2} \dots \xrightarrow{g_n} (\ell_n, c_n)$ starts in the initial location ℓ_0 and an arbitrary concrete data state. From there, it may perform a number $n \geq 0$ of transition steps. Thereby, it ensures that each step i with $1 \leq i \leq n$ meets the control-flow, i.e., $g_i = (\ell_{i-1}, \cdot, \ell_i)$, as well as the operation's semantics, i.e., (a) in case of assume operations, $c_{i-1} \models op_i$ and $c_{i-1} = c_i$ or (b) in case of assignments, $c_i = SP_{op_i}(c_{i-1})$, where SP is the strongest-post operator of the semantics. Furthermore, set $wrt(op)$ describes all variables whose value may be changed by operation op and $rd(op)$ contains all variables required to

---

[1] Note that our implementation supports C programs and many safety properties can be encoded by the unreachability of an error location.

perform the operation op, i.e., if two data states c, c' agree on the values of the variables $rd(op)$, then in case of assume operations $c \models op \Leftrightarrow c' \models op$ and for assignments, $SP_{op}(c)$ and $SP_{op}(c')$ agree on the values of the variables in $wrt(op)$.

Above program paths that reach the error location, i.e., $\exists 0 \leq i \leq n : \ell_i = \ell_{\mathrm{err}}$, violate the program's property and are part of set $paths^{\mathrm{err}}(P)$. We use them to define all paths of the modified program $P' = (L', \ell_0', G', \ell_{\mathrm{err}}')$ that cause regression bugs, i.e., paths from $paths^{\mathrm{err}}(P')$ whose initial concrete data state c_0' does not trigger a property violation in the the original program $P = (L, \ell_0, G, \ell_{\mathrm{err}})$. Formally, a path $\pi' = (\ell_0', c_0') \xrightarrow{g_1'} (\ell_1', c_1') \xrightarrow{g_2'} \ldots \xrightarrow{g_n'} (\ell_n', c_n') \in paths^{\mathrm{err}}(P')$ causes a regression bug if $\neg \exists \pi = (\ell_0, c_0) \xrightarrow{g_1} (\ell_1, c_1) \xrightarrow{g_2} \ldots \xrightarrow{g_m} (\ell_m, c_m) \in paths^{\mathrm{err}}(P) :$ $c_0' = c_0$. From now on, set $paths^{\mathrm{rb}}(P, P')$ describes all *paths with regression bugs*.

Typically, one cannot precisely determine $paths^{\mathrm{rb}}(P, P')$. Instead one over-approximates the set and analyzes the paths in the overapproximation. As explained before, difference verification with condition relies on the idea of conditional model checking (CMC) [5,7] for describing and analyzing such overapproximations. CMC employs a conditional verifier (see right of Fig. 1) and uses a condition to steer the verification of a (modified) program to those paths that are not covered by the condition. Following CMC [5,7], we represent a condition by an automaton and use accepting states to identify covered paths.

Definition 2. *A condition $A = (Q, \delta, q_0, F)$ consists of a finite set Q of states, an initial state $q_0 \in Q$, a set $F \subseteq Q$ of accepting states, and a transition relation $\delta \subseteq Q \times G \times Q^2$ ensuring $\forall (q, op, q') \in \delta : q \notin F$.*

CMC analyzes at least all paths that are not covered by the condition. Formally, a condition covers a path if the condition accepts any prefix of the path.

Definition 3. *A condition $A = (Q, \delta, q_0, F)$ covers an executable program path $\pi = (\ell_0, c_0) \xrightarrow{g_1} (\ell_1, c_1) \xrightarrow{g_2} \ldots \xrightarrow{g_n} (\ell_n, c_n)$, i.e., $\pi \in cover(A)$, if there exists a run $\rho = q_0 \xrightarrow{g_1} q_1 \xrightarrow{g_2} \ldots \xrightarrow{g_k} q_k, 0 \leq k \leq n$, in A, s.t. $q_k \in F$.*

To apply CMC in difference verification with conditions, the difference verifier (see Fig. 1) first generates an appropriate condition. To this end, it uses a difference condition extractor that analyzes the original and modified program to generate a condition that only accepts paths that are not in $paths^{\mathrm{rb}}(P, P')$. Following the procedure of the existing syntax-based extractor [6], we assume the difference condition extractor computes the condition in two steps (see Fig. 1).

First, a *difference detector* explores the modified program together with the original program to determine an overapproximation of $paths^{\mathrm{rb}}(P, P')$, which is described by a *difference graph* $DG(P, P')$. Paths in the difference graph relate to program paths of the modified program. Thereby, paths in the difference graph that reach nodes from a set Δ of regression bug indicator nodes characterize program paths that may cause regression bugs (like paths in $paths^{\mathrm{rb}}(P, P')$) and should be analyzed. The set Δ is determined by the difference detector (see

---

[2] In general [5,7], the transition relation of a condition also specifies assumptions on the program states, which we omit because they are irrelevant in difference verification.

Algorithm 1. Condition generator extracting condition from difference graph

---

Input: difference graph DG(P,P') $= (N, E, n_0, \Delta)$
Output: extracted condition
1: $Q = \{n_0\} \cup \Delta$; waitlist $= \{n_0\} \cup \Delta$;
2: **while** (waitlist $\neq \emptyset$) **do**
3:    pop n_s from waitlist
4:    **for** each $(n_p, (\ell, op, \ell'), n_s) \in E$ with $n_p \notin Q$ **do**
5:      $Q = Q \cup \{n_p\}$; waitlist $=$ waitlist $\cup \{n_p\}$;
6: F $= \{n_s \mid \exists (n_p, g, n_s) \in E \wedge n_p \in Q \wedge n_s \notin Q\}$;
7: **return** $(Q \cup F, E \cap (Q \times G' \times (Q \cup F)), n_0, F)$;

---

e.g., Sect. 3). To ensure the relation to program paths and to avoid that paths in the difference graph are misclassified after reaching a node from Δ, a difference graph guarantees that all of its paths p that relate to (a prefix of) a path with a regression bug must be extendable to a path p' in the difference graph that ends in a node from Δ. Formally, we model difference graphs $DG(P, P')$ as follows.

Definition 4. *A* $DG(P, P') = (N, E, n_0, \Delta)$ *for original CFA* $P = (L, \ell_0, G, \ell_{\mathrm{err}})$ *and modified CFA* $P' = (L', \ell'_0, G', \ell'_{\mathrm{err}})$ *consists of a set* N *of nodes including the initial node* $n_0 \in N$ *as well as the set* $\Delta \subseteq N$ *of regression bug indicator nodes, and edges* $E \subseteq N \times G' \times N$. *It must ensure the soundness property*

$$\forall \pi' = (\ell'_0, c'_0) \xrightarrow{g'_1} (\ell'_1, c'_1) \xrightarrow{g'_2} \ldots \xrightarrow{g'_n} (\ell'_n, c'_n) \in paths^{\mathrm{rb}}(P, P'), 0 \leq k \leq n,$$
$$n_0 \xrightarrow{g'_1} n_1 \xrightarrow{g'_2} \ldots \xrightarrow{g'_k} n_k \in DG(P, P') : \exists n_k \xrightarrow{\cdot} \ldots \xrightarrow{\cdot} n_{k+m} : n_{k+m} \in \Delta \ .$$

Second, the *condition generator* converts the difference graph constructed in the previous step into a condition. Algorithm 1 shows that conversion. Its idea is to build a condition that accepts a path as soon as a prefix has been seen for which it is known that no extension of a related path in the difference graph can reach a node from Δ, i.e., due to the assumption on a difference graph the prefix cannot be extended to a path from $paths^{\mathrm{rb}}(P, P')$. Hence, the relevant paths in the difference graph start in n_0, end in a node that cannot reach a node from Δ and all other nodes on the paths may reach a node from Δ. To generate a condition from the relevant paths, Algorithm 1 performs a backward search from Δ to the initial node n_0 (lines 1-5) to determine the non-accepting condition states (intermediate nodes of the paths, which may reach a node from Δ). Then, it adds the accepting states (line 6), the end nodes of these paths, and copies all edges of the difference graph induced by the accepting and non-accepting states.

To ensure that difference verifiers using difference condition extractors following the above two step process analyze all paths with regression bugs, we need to show that the generated condition A does not accept paths causing regression bugs, i.e., $cover(A) \cap paths^{\mathrm{rb}}(P, P') = \emptyset$.

Theorem 1. *Let P and P' be two CFAs. Difference condition extractors that sequentially compose a difference detector with Algorithm 1 compute conditions A that do not cover paths that cause regression bugs, i.e., $cover(A) \cap paths^{rb}(P, P') = \emptyset$.*

Proof. Available in our technical report [21].

Beyer et al. [6] apply the above principle in their syntax-based difference condition extractor. Their difference detector explores a parallel composition of original and modified program that stops path exploration in a node from Δ when the modified program path syntactically differs from the original program path. Next, we present a difference detector that goes beyond syntactical differences.

3   Dependency and Property Aware Difference Detection

Key to difference verification with conditions is the restriction of the verification to a (small) overapproximation of the paths with regression bugs $paths^{rb}(P, P')$. Next, we present a new difference detector DIFFDP that utilizes data dependencies and error locations to compute a more precise overapproximation of $paths^{rb}(P, P')$ than the existing, syntax-based difference detector [6].

The coarsest overapproximation of $paths^{rb}(P, P')$ encompasses all execution paths of the modified program. More precise overapproximations may exclude paths that do not violate a property or paths for which one can show that the violation already exists in the original program. To exclude a path π' of the latter category, one needs to provide a witness path, a path of the original program that starts with the same input as π' and also violates a property. The syntax-based difference detector [6] only considers witness paths that are identical to π' except for location naming. Our difference detector DIFFDP relies on witness paths that have a similar branching structure as π', i.e., execute a similar sequence of assume operations, and violate properties no later than π'. In particular, DIFFDP may also use witness paths of the syntax-based detector.

Instead of detecting witness paths individually per execution path, which is not feasible, DIFFDP considers all paths following the same control-flow at once. More concretely, for each syntactical path p' of the modified program, i.e., each path in the respective CFA that starts at the initial location, DIFFDP tries to detect a syntactic (witness) path p in the original program that (1) has a similar branching structure, that (2) is executable for all inputs for which p' is executable (thus, ensuring executability of path p for all inputs of interest), and (3) in which an error location does not occur later than in p. For instance for the syntactical path $\ell_0' \xrightarrow{r=x;} \ell_1' \xrightarrow{x>0} \ell_2' \xrightarrow{r=-x;} \ell_3' \xrightarrow{!(r<=0)} \ell_{err}'$ of our modified program in Fig. 2, DIFFDP detects the syntactic witness path $\ell_0 \xrightarrow{r=-x;} \ell_1 \xrightarrow{x>0} \ell_2 \xrightarrow{r=-x;} \ell_3 \xrightarrow{!(r<=0)} \ell_{err}$. Note that condition (2) is met because there does not exist a data dependency between the change of variable r in the first operation and the two assume operations $x > 0$ and $!(r <= 0)$.

Algorithm 2. Difference detector DIFFDP (P, P')

Input: deterministic CFAs $P = (L, \ell_0, G, \ell_{err})$, $P' = (L', \ell_0', G', \ell_{err}')$
Output: difference graph $DG(P, P')$
1: $waitlist := \{(\ell_0, \ell_0')\}$; $N_l := \{(\ell_0, \ell_0')\}$; $E_l := \emptyset$; $\Delta := \emptyset$; $V_\delta := \lambda((\ell_1, \ell_1')).\emptyset$;
2: **while** $waitlist \neq \emptyset$ **do**
3:     pop (ℓ_1, ℓ_1') from $waitlist$
4:     **for each** $g' = (\ell_1', op', \ell_2') \in G'$ **do**
5:         **if** op' is assignment **then**
6:             **if** $\exists (\ell_1, op', \ell_2) \in G$ **then**
7:                 **if** $V_\delta((\ell_1, \ell_1')) \cap rd(op') \neq \emptyset$ **then** $V_{\text{diff}} := V_\delta((\ell_1, \ell_1')) \cup wrt(op')$;
8:                 **else** $V_{\text{diff}} := V_\delta((\ell_1, \ell_1')) \setminus wrt(op')$;
9:                 PROCESS$(((\ell_1, \ell_1'), g', (\ell_2, \ell_2')), V_{\text{diff}})$
10:            **else** PROCESS$(((\ell_1, \ell_1'), g', (\ell_1, \ell_2')), V_\delta((\ell_1, \ell_1')) \cup wrt(op'))$
11:        **else**   // op' assume
12:            $\ell_p := \ell_1$; $V_{\text{diff}} := V_\delta((\ell_1, \ell_1'))$;
13:            **while** $\ell_p \neq \ell_{err} \wedge \exists (\ell_p, op_a, \ell_s) \in G : op_a$ is assignment **do**
14:                $\ell_p := \ell_s$; $V_{\text{diff}} := V_{\text{diff}} \cup wrt(op_a)$;
15:            **if** $\ell_p \neq \ell_{err} \wedge (\exists (\ell_p, op, \ell_2) \in G : op = op' \vee ((op' \Rightarrow op) \wedge op' \not\equiv false))$ **then**
16:                **if** $V_{\text{diff}} \cap (rd(op) \cup rd(op')) \neq \emptyset$ **then** PROCESS$(((\ell_1, \ell_1'), g', \ell_2'), \emptyset)$
17:                **else** PROCESS$(((\ell_1, \ell_1'), g', (\ell_2, \ell_2')), V_{\text{diff}})$
18:            **else** PROCESS$(((\ell_1, \ell_1'), g', (\ell_p, \ell_2')), V_{\text{diff}})$
19: **if** $\ell_0' \in \Delta \vee (\ell_0' = \ell_{err}' \wedge \ell_0 \neq \ell_{err})$ **then return** $(\{\ell_0'\}, \emptyset, \ell_0', \{\ell_0'\})$
20: $E := \{(n, g', n') \in N_l \times G' \times (N_l \cup \Delta) \mid (n, g, n') \in E_l \vee (n' \in \Delta \wedge \exists (n, g, (\cdot, n')) \in E_l)\}$;
21: **return** $(N_l \cup \Delta, E, (\ell_0, \ell_0'), \Delta)$

22: PROCESS$((pred, g', succ), V_{\text{diff}})$
23: **if** $succ \in L'$ **then**
24:     $\Delta := \Delta \cup \{succ\}$; $E_l := E_l \cup \{(pred, g', succ)\}$;
25:     $N_l := N_l \setminus \{(\cdot, succ) \in N_l\}$; $waitlist := waitlist \setminus \{(\cdot, succ) \in waitlist\}$;
26: **else**
27:     **if** $succ \in (L \setminus \{\ell_{err}\}) \times \{\ell_{err}'\}$ **then** PROCESS$((pred, g', \ell_{err}'), \emptyset)$
28:     **else**
29:         **if** $succ \notin L \times \Delta \wedge succ \notin \{\ell_{err}\} \times L' \wedge (succ \notin N_l \vee V_{\text{diff}} \not\subseteq V_\delta(succ))$ **then**
30:             $waitlist := waitlist \cup \{succ\}$;
31:         **if** $succ \notin L \times \Delta$ **then**
32:             $N_l := N_l \cup \{succ\}$; $V_\delta(succ) := V_\delta(succ) \cup V_{\text{diff}}$;
33:         $E_l := E_l \cup \{(pred, g', succ)\}$;

Algorithm 2 shows our DIFFDP implementation. It gets two deterministic CFAs P and P' (original and modified program) and outputs its computed overapproximation of $paths^{\text{rb}}(P, P')$ as a difference graph, which provides a witness path for each path excluded from the coarsest overapproximation.

The main part of Algorithm 2 (outer while loop) detects and records syntactic witness paths p for the syntactic paths p' of the modified program. To this end, it uses data structure $waitlist$ to explore the paths of the modified program step-by-step in combination with the paths of the original program. Thereby, Algorithm 2 uses pairs $(\ell, \ell') \in L \times L'$ of program locations to describe where p and p' align and records this information by storing aligned locations in N_l and their connection in E_l. If an aligned witness path p cannot be extended to the next step of a path p' in the modified program, Algorithm 2 stops the exploration of p' and stores its next location in Δ, the set of regression bug indicator nodes of the difference graph, which characterize paths of the over-approximation. To detect (dis)agreements on executability between paths and witness path extensions, data structure V_δ tracks for all aligned locations (ℓ, ℓ') the change affected variables, i.e., those variables which may have different values at alignment point (ℓ, ℓ').

After detecting and recording witness paths, Algorithm 2 constructs the difference graph in lines 19–21. If ℓ'_0 is contained in Δ or ℓ'_0 is a new error location, the alignment of the initial locations failed. In this case, any path may cause regression bugs. To reflect this, the difference graph returned in line 19 consists of a single regression bug indicator node. Otherwise, Algorithm 2 uses the data structures N_l, Δ and E_l, which record the alignment of paths and their witness paths as well as whether no witness path could be detected for a path, to generate the difference graph describing the overapproximation of $paths^{\mathrm{rb}}(P, P')$. The basic idea is to copy the information of paths with and without witness paths into the difference graph. Hence, set Δ becomes the regression bug indicator nodes. The graph's nodes are the union of the determined aligned locations N_l and the regression bug indicator nodes Δ. The graph edges are derived from the connection between determined aligned locations and regression bug indicator nodes, thereby considering that aligned locations may be replaced by regression bug indicator nodes, which are not explored, i.e., they must not have successors.

Next, let us have a closer look at the combined step-by-step exploration of paths. It starts in line 1 with the programs' initial location (initial alignment point of any path and its witness path) and no connections ($E_l := \emptyset$;). Since no program modification has been seen yet, nothing is known about paths for which no witness path can be detected ($\Delta := \emptyset$) nor about change affected variables (i.e., V_δ does not track any change affected variable). Thereafter, each iteration of the outer while loop explores one aligned pair (ℓ_1, ℓ'_1) that has not yet been explored or whose change affected variables altered. Each iteration computes one successor per outgoing CFA edge g' in the modified program. The successor and the update of its change affected variables depend on g''s operation.

In case of an assignment (lines 5–10), we do not need to consider executability (assignments are always executable) and, thus, only check whether an outgoing edge with an identical assignment exists in the original program. If an identical edge exists, we explore in lock-step and similar to slicing [44] update the change affected variables according to the data dependencies. For example, when exploring $(\ell_2, r = -x;, \ell_3)$ for aligned pair (ℓ_2, ℓ'_2), Algorithm 2 detects the matching edge $(\ell_2, r = -x;, \ell_3)$, aligns (ℓ_3, ℓ'_3), and propagates that variable r is no longer affected by a modification. If no identical edge exists, we detect a modification. Since it is non-trivial to detect a good alignment of original and modified program [33], we decided to (a) always handle the modification like a new assignment (i.e., no step in the original program and all variables $wrt(op')$ become change affected), which is simpler to handle than alternatively presuming deletion of statements, and (b) if this assumption was wrong to postpone resynchronization to the beginning of assume operations.[3] For example, when exploring $(\ell'_0, r = x;, \ell'_1)$ for aligned pair (ℓ_0, ℓ'_0), Algorithm 2 detects a modification, thus, aligns (ℓ_0, ℓ'_1), and propagates that variable r is affected by the modification. In both cases, procedure PROCESS updates the data structures based on the suggested alignment and determined change affected variables.

In case of an assume operation (lines 11–18), we first try to resynchronize (lines 12–14). Thereby, we explore all assignments in the original program until we hit the next assume operation or an error location (i.e., no regression bug possible). Explored assignments are treated like modifications, i.e., we add their modified variables to the changed affected variables V_{diff} of the alignment. Then, line 15 checks whether both programs provide matching assume operations (either identical or the original assume is more general[4]) and if this is the case whether the assume operations are affected by the modification (line 16). If the matching check fails, we consider the assume as a new operation, which may restrict the executability of the modified path and, thus, the relevant inputs, but does not restrict the executability of the witness path on relevant inputs. Hence, only if matching assumes are affected by the modification (line 16), we can no longer deduce that the potential witness path is executable on all inputs of the explored modified program path and stop the alignment. To this end, we let the alignment end in the location of the modified path, which describes a regression bug indicator node and for which change affected variables are irrelevant. In all other cases (lines 17 and 18), we align original and modified program accordingly and since assume operations do not change the data state, forward the already determined change affected variables V_{diff}. Finally, procedure PROCESS updates the data structures. For example, when exploring $(\ell'_1, x > 0, \ell'_2)$ for aligned pair (ℓ_0, ℓ'_1) with $V_\delta((\ell_0, \ell'_1)) = \{r\}$, Algorithm 2 first resynchronizes, thereby exploring edge $(\ell_0, r = -x;, \ell_1)$ and adding r to the change affected variables V_{diff}. Then, it detects the matching assume edges $(\ell_1, x > 0, \ell_2)$ in the original program. Since the assume operation of original and modified program do not consider any change affected variables ($V_{\text{diff}} = \{r\}$), Algorithm 2 aligns (ℓ_2, ℓ'_2) and propagates V_{diff}.

Procedure PROCESS updates the data structures based on the proposed successor (edge) and the determined change affected variables. In case the witness path extension failed (lines 22–24), we stop exploration, add the successor to Δ, add the successor edge, and remove any aligned locations considering the successor's location from N_l and *waitlist*. The edges are adapted later in line 19. In case of a proposed alignment (extension) (lines 26–32), we need to properly handle violations of the modified program. If only a violation in the modified program

---

[3] To be more precise, our implementation also keeps the alignment if an assignment exists that changes the same variables (left out for simplicity of Algorithm 2).

[4] To get deterministic difference graphs for our proofs, op' must be satisfiable, too.

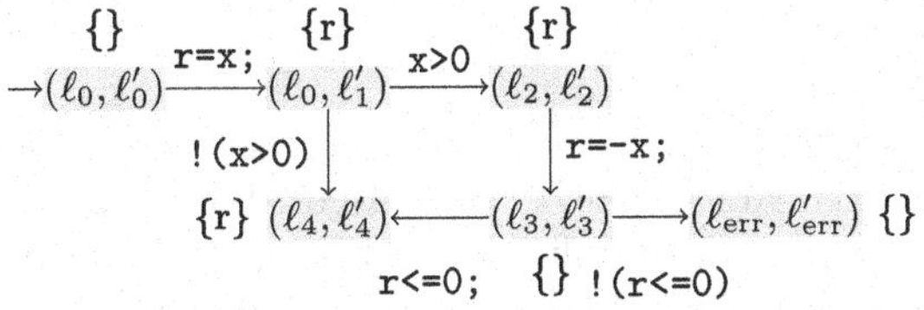

$$
\begin{array}{ccc}
\{\} & \{r\} & \{r\} \\
\rightarrow(\ell_0, \ell_0') \xrightarrow{\ \ \texttt{r=x;}\ \ } (\ell_0, \ell_1') \xrightarrow{\ \ \texttt{x>0}\ \ } (\ell_2, \ell_2') \\
\texttt{!(x>0)} \downarrow & & \downarrow \texttt{r=-x;} \\
\{r\}\ (\ell_4, \ell_4') \longleftarrow (\ell_3, \ell_3') \longrightarrow (\ell_{\mathrm{err}}, \ell_{\mathrm{err}}')\ \{\} \\
\texttt{r<=0;}\quad \{\}\ \texttt{!(r<=0)}
\end{array}
$$

Fig. 3. Difference graph of Algorithm 2 for original and modified CFA from Fig. 2

is present, we recursively call PROCESS, but now exchanging the alignment with the location of the modified path, a regression bug indicator node.[5] Otherwise, line 28–29 mark the successor for (re)exploration if we neither end in a regression bug indicator node (difference already established), nor align with an error location of the original program (regression bug impossible), nor the successor and all change affected variables are known (information already considered for exploration). If we do not end in a regression bug indicator node, we need to ensure that successor information and the detected change affected variables are available for exploration and graph construction. Hence, lines 30–31 add them to N_l and V_δ. Finally, line 32 adds the corresponding edge to E_l.

Figure 3 shows the difference graph computed for our example (Fig. 2). Algorithm 2 starts with the pair of initial locations (ℓ_0, ℓ_0') and no change affected variables. Next, it considers the modified assignment, only moves forward in the modified program, and remembers that variable r is affected. Thereafter, Algorithm 2 considers the first two assume operations of the modified program. To resynchronize, it passes over the first assignment of the original program resulting in changed affected variables $V_{\mathrm{diff}} = \{r\}$. Then, it detects the identical assume operations in the original program, propagates the changed affected variables $\{r\}$, and continues exploration because the assume operations are not affected by the modification. Afterwards, it explores the second assignment of the modified program, for which an identical assignment in the original program exists. The propagated change affected variables become $\{\}$ because r is redefined and no longer affected. Finally, Algorithm 2 explores the assume operations resulting from the assertion. For both there exists an identical assume operation in the original program, which is not affected by the modification. Thus, the assumptions are explored in lockstep and the change affected variables are forwarded.

To use Algorithm 2 as a difference detector, we must show that it constructs proper difference graphs. Theorem 2, which is proven in the appendix, claims this.

Theorem 2. *Algorithm 2 returns a difference graph.*

Proof. Available in our technical report [21].

---

[5] To further exclude non-regression bugs, our implementation first searches for an error location of the original program in its follow-up sequence of assignments.

4   Evaluation

The goal of our evaluation is to compare difference verification with our difference condition extractor (DIFFDP plus Algorithm 1) against a full verification and against difference verification with the previously existing difference condition extractor (i.e., the syntax-based difference condition extractor DIFFCOND from [6]).

4.1   Experimental Setup

Verification Tasks. All tasks consist of pairs of original and modified program and consider the property function `reach_error()` is never executed. To ensure that verification and difference verification can only find regression bugs, either the original program, the modified program, or none of them executes `reach_error()`. More concretely, we have tasks that were originally correct and introduce new bugs into the modified program. To solve them correctly, a (newly introduced) bug must be found. Also, there exist tasks in which the modified program fixes the bugs of the original program and tasks in which the modified program remains correct. To correctly solve these tasks, the absence of (regression) bugs needs to be shown. We use two sets of tasks. Our first set contains the 10 426 combination tasks previously used for evaluating difference verification with conditions [6]. Its tasks are organized in five categories (1) `eca05+token`, (2) `gcd+newton`, (3) `pals+eca12`, (4) `sfifo+token`, (5) `square+softflt`. For the second set, we consider the set of programs that Beyer et al. [9] derived from revisions of 62 Linux device drivers. Each program relates to one revision of a device driver and checks one of six API usage rules (encoded s.t. upon rule violation `reach_error()` is called). From these programs, we pair all those that ensure that they verify the same rule, the modified program relates to the next revision available, and the ground truth for the modified program is known. The resulting task set contains 3 936 so-called regression tasks.

Verifiers. We consider three verifiers, which we may transform into difference verifiers. Based on the performance of the SV-COMP 2022 participants in the categories `SoftwareSystems-DeviceDriversLinux64-ReachSafety` and `ReachSafety-Combinations`, the categories closest to our tasks, we select two off-the-shelf verifiers, namely the best tool CPACHECKER 2.1 and ESBMC, the next best tool that uses a different verification platform. CPACHECKER 2.1 applies strategy selection [4] based on program features to choose from different sequential analysis combinations, which e.g., may use bounded, explicit, or predicate model checking as well as k-induction. ESBMC [14] uses k-induction enhanced with invariants. Since both verifiers are not conditional[6], we also choose PREDICATE, a native conditional verifier [5] that applies predicate model checking with adjustable block-encoding [8], abstracts at loop heads and computes predicates via counterexample-guided abstraction refinement with lazy refinement [17].

---

[6] Their difference verifiers will need to use reducer-based conditional verifiers [7].

Table 1. Number of correct proofs (✓), of correct alarms (✗), and of incorrectly solved tasks (⚡) detected by each verifier and their related difference verifiers

	eca05+token (2 340+1 300)			gcd+newton (1 352+572)			pals+eca12 (1 700+1 050)			sfifo+token (1 206+663)			square+softflt (165+75)			regression (3 936+0)		
	✓	✗	⚡	✓	✗	⚡	✓	✗	⚡	✓	✗	⚡	✓	✗	⚡	✓	✗	⚡
PREDICATE	912	**1040**	0	0	520	0	0	50	0	558	**507**	0	22	51	0	2595	0	0
PREDICATE$^{\Delta_{\mathrm{syn}}^{\mathrm{nat}}}$	1395	987	0	48	520	0	10	52	0	589	481	0	61	**75**	0	2599	0	0
PREDICATE$^{\Delta_{\mathrm{DP}}^{\mathrm{nat}}}$	**1400**	985	0	156	520	0	**125**	75	0	594	488	0	115	**75**	0	2663	0	0
PREDICATE$^{\Delta_{\mathrm{syn}}^{\mathrm{red}}}$	1394	975	0	48	474	0	10	**95**	0	642	468	0	81	45	0	2639	0	0
PREDICATE$^{\Delta_{\mathrm{DP}}^{\mathrm{red}}}$	1390	955	0	156	572	0	**125**	50	0	639	456	0	**135**	60	0	**2685**	0	0
CPACHECKER	633	**1296**	0	0	494	0	0	100	0	434	510	0	0	75	0	**3931**	0	0
CPACHECKER$^{\Delta_{\mathrm{syn}}^{\mathrm{red}}}$	1000	1282	0	48	469	0	41	140	0	480	**663**	0	61	45	0	3906	0	0
CPACHECKER$^{\Delta_{\mathrm{DP}}^{\mathrm{red}}}$	1119	1252	0	156	520	0	671	500	0	480	638	0	117	60	0	3618	0	0
ESBMC	0	1125	0	570	572	0	198	530	0	0	**663**	0	**165**	**75**	0	0	0	0
ESBMC$^{\Delta_{\mathrm{syn}}^{\mathrm{red}}}$	0	0	0	333	572	0	0	0	0	0	78	0	105	**75**	0	0	0	0
ESBMC$^{\Delta_{\mathrm{DP}}^{\mathrm{red}}}$	0	900	0	**880**	572	0	0	70	10	101	618	0	156	**75**	0	0	0	0

We use all three verifiers V standalone, i.e., they verify the complete modified program, and as verifier component in difference verifiers. For the difference verifiers, we use reducer-based CMC [7] to combine every verifier V with the syntax-based difference condition extractor DIFFCOND from [6] ($V^{\Delta_{\mathrm{syn}}^{\mathrm{red}}}$) and our difference condition extractor ($V^{\Delta_{\mathrm{DP}}^{\mathrm{red}}}$). Also, we natively combine conditional verifier PREDICATE with the syntax-based extractor DIFFCOND (PREDICATE$^{\Delta_{\mathrm{syn}}^{\mathrm{nat}}}$) and our extractor (PREDICATE$^{\Delta_{\mathrm{DP}}^{\mathrm{nat}}}$). For the two off-the-shelf verifiers, we use their SV-COMP 2022 [3] version, while for PREDICATE, the reducer, and the two difference condition extractors we use the later CPAchecker version 40843.

Computing Environment. For our experiments, we use machines with an Intel Xeon E3-1230 v5 CPU (frequency of 3.4 GHz, 8 processing units) and 33 GB of memory that run an Ubuntu 20.04 (Linux kernel 5.4.0). In addition, we use BENCHEXEC [10] version 3.11 to limit each verifier run to 4 processing units, 15 min of CPU time, and 15 GB of memory.

4.2 Experimental Results

RQ 1 Is Difference Verification with Our Extractor Better Than a Full Verification? Beyer et al. [6] showed that difference verification with the syntax-based difference condition extractor DIFFCOND may be more effective and is more efficient for a significant number of tasks. This research question studies whether these findings still hold despite using our difference condition extractor.

First, let us look at effectiveness. Table 1 shows for each verifier and its difference verifiers the number of correctly proved tasks (✓) and disproved (✗) tasks as well as the number of incorrectly solved tasks (⚡)[7] in each task category. The number of tasks with and without property violations are shown at the top.

---

[7] All incorrectly solved tasks are false proofs. No false alarms were detected.

The difference between the number of tasks and the number of tasks solved by a (difference) verifier represents the number of tasks for which the (difference) verifier does not produce a result, e.g., times out, gives up, etc.

Comparing the results of the verifiers and their respective difference verifiers that use our difference condition extractor (Δ_{DP}), we observe that for all three verifiers there exist categories for which the difference verifier (highlighted in yellow) correctly detects more proofs and often there exist categories in which the difference verifier correctly detects more alarms (i.e., property violations). One reason is that the difference verifier still succeeds when the full analysis runs out of resources. Also, the difference detector excludes paths with program features unsupported by the respective analysis. Thus, difference verification with our difference condition extractor can be more effective than a full verification. Even if it is more effective, often there exist a few tasks that the verifier can solve but the difference verifier cannot. Also, the difference verifier is not always more effective. While for PREDICATE and CPACHECKER our difference verification approach is rarely less, but often more effective, for ESBMC the difference verifier only sometimes performs better and even misses 10 bugs[8] (column ↯ of category pals+eca12 in Table 1). One major reason is the residual program constructed and verified by the reducer-based conditional verifier. Residual programs change the structure, e.g., use deeply nested branching structures that regularly exceeded the maximum bracket nesting level of the ESBMC parser and heavily use goto statements, but no while or for loop constructs, which makes loop detection more difficult for ESBMC. The issues with the residual program are orthogonal to difference verification and were already observed previously [6].

After we examined effectiveness, we now study the efficiency in terms of runtime. Figure 4a shows a scatter plot that compares for all verifiers the CPU time the verifier takes to check task t (x-axis) with the CPU time a corresponding difference verifier, which applies our difference condition extractor, takes to inspect task t (y-axis). Note that the scatter plot uses the maximum CPU time of 900 s if a task is not solved and excludes times in case the reported result of the (difference) verifier is incorrect. For a significant number of task-verifier pairs (38%), the data points are below the diagonal but not on the right border, i.e., the difference verification and the full verification succeed while the difference verification is faster than full verification. In even more cases (63%), the conditional verifier is faster than full verification, but the time saved is not enough to compensate the runtime of the difference condition extractor. Whether the costs of the extractor can be compensated depends on the verifier and the tasks. To demonstrate this, let us examine the speedup of difference verification over the full verification. For each category, Fig. 4b shows the distribution of the speed up. The order of the categories is the same as in Table 1. We observe that tasks in category square+softflt often achieve a (significant) speedup (median 3.44 and mean 7.95) while for tasks from the pals+eca12 the difference verifier typically slows down (median speedup 0.63 and mean speed up 0.91). The median and mean speed up in all other categories are between 0.63-3.44 and 0.91-7.95.

---

[8] CPACHECKER$^{\Delta_{\mathrm{DP}}^{\mathrm{red}}}$ correctly detected those 10 bugs. Likely, it is an issue of ESBMC.

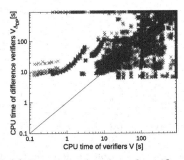

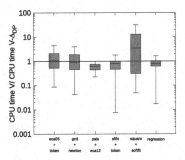

(a) Per pair of task and verifier, comparison of CPU time for verification (x-axis) vs. CPU time for difference verification with our extractor (y-axis)

(b) Per category, distribution of speedup of difference verification over verification

Fig. 4. Comparison of CPU time for verification vs. CPU time for difference verification with our extractor

The findings of Beyer et al. carry over. Also, difference verification with our condition extractor may be more effective and efficient than full verification.

RQ 2 Do DIFFCONDand Our Difference Condition Extractor Differ?
So far, we have shown that difference verification with our extractor can be beneficial. One reason could be that the syntax-based extractor DIFFCOND [6] and our extractor do not differ. In the following, we investigate this hypothesis.

Difference condition extractors differ if they (a) generate different conditions or (b) differ in performance. Since all our difference verifiers unroll the program along the condition and, thus, their verification changes when given a structurally different conditions, we compare the condition structure to investigate (a). For each task except for 286 regression tasks for which our condition extractor failed (mostly due to time out), Fig. 5a compares the number of states in the condition generated by $\mathrm{DIFFCOND}(\Delta_{\mathrm{syn}}$, x-axis) with the number of states in the condition produced by our difference condition extractor (Δ_{DP}, y-axis). Most data points in Fig. 5a are above or below the diagonal, i.e., the conditions differ in the number of states. Only for 317 tasks (<5% of all tasks) the condition size is the same. While for 82% of the combination tasks (blue data points) and for 55% of the regression tasks (orange data points) our extractor generates larger conditions, which may be larger by several orders of magnitude, there exist 1 676 data points on the x-axis for which our difference condition extractor generates conditions consisting of a single accepting state, i.e., our extractor proved the absence of regression bugs. The syntax-based difference verification extractor only proves the absence of regression bugs for 121 tasks, for which our extractor succeeds too. We argue that our extractor produces more precise conditions than DIFFCOND.

To study the performance difference (b), we compare the CPU times of both difference condition extractors. Figure 5b shows a scatter plot that compares for

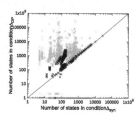 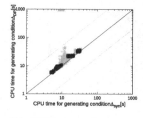 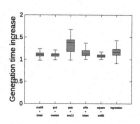

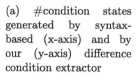

(a) #condition states generated by syntax-based (x-axis) and by our (y-axis) difference condition extractor

(b) CPU time of syntax-based difference condition extractor (x-axis) and of our difference condition extractor (y-axis)

(c) Per category, distribution of slow down of our difference condition extractor over the syntax-based difference condition extractor

Fig. 5. Several comparisons involving our difference condition extractor

each task the CPU time required by DIFFCOND (Δ_{syn}, x-axis) with the CPU time required by our extractor (Δ_{DP}, y-axis) while Fig. 5c shows the distribution of the ratio of the CPU time required by our extractor (Δ_{DP}) and the CPU time required by DIFFCOND (Δ_{syn}). We observe that most of the data points (99%) in Fig. 5b are above the diagonal, i.e., our extractor takes (up to 5-times) longer and even times out for 285 regression tasks. Looking at Fig. 5c, which compares the ratio of the times, we see that the ratio is typically above one, but rarely larger than 1.5, i.e., our extractor takes longer but often less than 50% more time. Indeed median and mean increase per category is between 8% and 40%. The observed runtime increase is likely caused by the more precise condition generation. Still, our difference condition extractor typically uses a small fraction (less than 10%) of the complete verification time (900 s).

> In summary, the two difference condition extractors differ. Our extractor computes more precise conditions and takes longer.

RQ 3 Does Difference Verification with Our Extractor Improve over Difference Verification with Extractor DIFFCOND? Based on the previous results, we can expect a performance difference, but not necessarily an improvement. This is what we investigate next.

Again, let us first look at effectiveness. To this end, we compare those pairs of difference verifiers in Table 1 that only differ in the difference condition extractors (Δ_{syn}^{red} vs. Δ_{DP}^{red} or Δ_{syn}^{nat} vs. Δ_{DP}^{nat}). Table 1 highlights difference verifiers with our extractor in yellow. Looking at the native approach for difference verification with PREDICATE, difference verification with our difference condition extractor (PREDICATE$^{\Delta_{DP}^{nat}}$) is mostly better than difference verification with the syntax-based extractor DIFFCOND (PREDICATE$^{\Delta_{syn}^{nat}}$). Often, our approach, which computes a more precise overapproximation of the paths with regression bugs, enables the difference verifier to solve additional tasks and only for the regression tasks there exist several hundred tasks solvable by PREDICATE$^{\Delta_{\mathrm{syn}}^{\mathrm{nat}}}$ for which PREDICATE$^{\Delta_{\mathrm{DP}}^{\mathrm{nat}}}$ fails due to timeout in the extractor. When using the reducer-based approach for PREDICATE, results are more diverse. For some categories, difference verification with our extractor (PREDICATE$^{\Delta_{\mathrm{DP}}^{\mathrm{red}}}$) detects significantly fewer alarms and sometimes also a slightly smaller number of proofs, which PREDICATE$^{\Delta_{\mathrm{syn}}^{\mathrm{red}}}$ detects close to timeout. Since most of these alarms are detected by PREDICATE$^{\Delta_{\mathrm{DP}}^{\mathrm{nat}}}$, we think the structure of the residual program is the cause and not our extractor. Still, there exist categories like `gcd+newton` and `square+softflt` in which our extractor enables the difference verifier to improve and solve all tasks solved by PREDICATE$^{\Delta_{\mathrm{syn}}^{\mathrm{red}}}$ plus some additional tasks. Likewise, CPACHECKER$^{\Delta_{\mathrm{DP}}^{\mathrm{red}}}$ typically detects additional proofs, but sometimes detects fewer alarms than CPACHECKER$^{\Delta_{\mathrm{syn}}^{\mathrm{red}}}$. While the decrease in category `regression` is caused by the timeout of our extractor, a decrease of detected alarms occurs only in categories for which PREDICATE$^{\Delta_{\mathrm{DP}}^{\mathrm{red}}}$ also performs worse, and is, thus, likely caused by the residual program. For ESBMC, difference verification with our extractor (ESBMC$^{\Delta_{\mathrm{DP}}^{\mathrm{red}}}$) always improves over ESBMC$^{\Delta_{\mathrm{syn}}^{\mathrm{red}}}$, typically solving the same plus some additional tasks, but it does not solve more regression tasks because their entry function is not main and, thus, not supported by ESBMC.

After comparing effectiveness, we continue to compare efficiency in terms of CPU time. For each category (column in Table 1) and for all pairs $(V^{\Delta_{\mathrm{syn}}}, V^{\Delta_{\mathrm{DP}}})$ of difference verifiers that only vary in the difference condition extractor, the three scatter plots in Fig. 6 compare the CPU times $V^{\Delta_{\mathrm{syn}}}$ (x-axis) and $V^{\Delta_{\mathrm{DP}}}$ (y-axis) take to solve a task. Again, we use the maximum CPU time of 900 s if a task is not solved and exclude times in case the reported result of the difference verifier is incorrect. Looking at the three scatter plots, we observe that for each category there exist data points in the lower right half, i.e., the difference verifier $V^{\Delta_{\mathrm{DP}}}$ with our extractor is more efficient. For categories `eca05+token` and `sfifo+token` (scatter plot on the top left), the extra effort of our extractor rarely pays off. More concretely, only for 23% of the tasks that belong to these two categories and that are solved by both difference verifiers the difference verifier using our extractor is faster. For categories `regression` and `gcd+newton` (scatter plot on the top right), the extra effort invested by our difference condition extractor sometimes (48%) pays off. While for `gcd+newton` in particular native PREDICATE and ESBMC profit from our more precise extractor, for `regression` all verifiers benefit for some tasks. Similarly, all verifiers often (64%) benefit from our extractor in the categories `square+softflt` and `pals+eca12` (scatter plot on the bottom left). Looking at the distribution of the speedup shown at the bottom right of Fig. 6, we also observe that for categories `eca05+token` and `sfifo+token` (first and fourth box) there is hardly any difference between the difference verifiers. The median and mean speed up are between 0.99 and 1.05. In contrast, for categories `square+softflt` and `pals+eca12` the median speedup is 1.14 and 1.48, respectively.

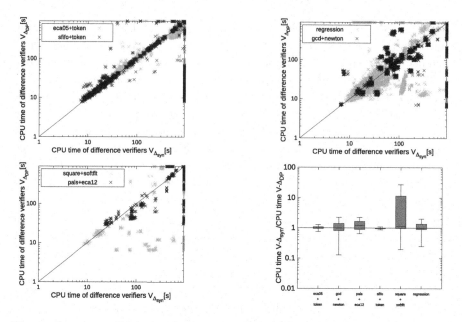

Fig. 6. Comparing CPU times of difference verifiers with syntax-based condition extractor (x-axis) and with our condition extractor (y-axis)

> We conclude that while difference verification with our extractor is not always better, there exist several tasks for which it is more effective or efficient.

Threats to Validity. All combination tasks were artificially constructed by Beyer et al. [6] to evaluate difference verification with conditions and the regression tasks only focus on Linux device drivers. While our results may not apply to arbitrary programs, we have shown that difference verification may be beneficial on real world tasks. Also, our observations may not carry over to different verifiers and extractors. Nevertheless, we confirmed the finding of Beyer et al. [6] for our new extractor. Furthermore, the verifier may have benefited from the (structure of the) residual program instead of the condition extractors. First, we also observe positive effects when using a native conditional verifier. Second, our observation from the past and this paper is that residual programs are often more difficult to verify. Finally, bugs in one of the extractors, the residual program generator, or the verifiers may threaten the validity of our results. We would expect that bugs in extractors or residual program generator result in (many) false proofs. However, only ESBMC reported false results for ten tasks, for which another verifier succeeds and the verifiers themselves participate in SV-COMP, therefore aiming to reduce the number of false results. Hence, we expect that implementation bugs have little impact on our results.

5   Related Work

Several approaches protect modified programs against regression bugs. They range from regression testing [47] over (dis)proving functional equivalence between original and modified program, e.g., [15,19,23,26,41], to incremental verification approaches that (a) adapt previous analysis results like fixed points [2,36,40] or the explored state space [18,28,39], (b) reuse intermediate results like constraint solutions [1,43], abstraction details [9,20,37], or annotations [16,48], or (c) like our approach do not reanalyze unchanged behavior [6,12,29,30,35,38,45,46].

We enhance difference verification with conditions [6], which combines a difference condition extractor with conditional model checking [5] to skip reverification of program parts in which the property is not affected by the modification. Several other approaches also skip verification of unaffected code parts. RMC [45] stops DFS exploration and Memoise [46] stops symbolic execution of states that cannot reach any modification. Memoise also disables constraint solving on unchanged paths. iCoq [12] only reverifies Coq proofs affected by the modification and Dafny [30] only reverifies methods affected by the modification, thereby reusing unaffected verification conditions, while regression property selection (RPS) [29] restricts runtime verification to properties connected to classes affected by the modification. Similarly, DiSE [35,38] directs symbolic execution towards program statements that are affected by the modification.

Although there exist several approaches that use abstract interpretation [27, 32] or symbolic execution [11,31,34,42] to determine those inputs and, thus, the paths for which the behavior of original and modified programs differ functionally, the above approaches use more lightweight techniques to determine the affected program paths or proof parts that must be reverified. Dafny [30] relies on checksums and iCoq [12] relies on timestamps and checksums to determine affected components. The proof-of-concept implementation of difference verification with conditions [6], Memoise [46], and RMC [45] assume that all paths that changed syntactically may be affected. RPS [29] uses class dependencies to determine affected classes, while DiSE [35,38] uses control and data dependencies to detect program statements affected by the modification, while Jana et al. [24] consider those dependencies to determine which properties the modification affects at which locations. In contrast, our enhanced difference verification with conditions mainly relies on data dependencies to determine the paths on which the modification may threaten the validity of a previously satisfied property.

6   Conclusion

Software changes frequently and each change may introduce new, so called regression bugs. Thus, when applied to accomplish software reliability, software verifiers should keep up with the changes. Since fully verifying nearly identical software repeatedly is most often too costly, verifiers must be incremental and exploit that changes do not introduce regression bugs everywhere in the software.

Difference verification with conditions is an approach to build incremental verification tools from arbitrary verifiers. Its idea is to steer the verifier to only reverify program parts in which new bugs may occur due to the change. While the change analysis (i.e., the difference detector) that identifies the program paths relevant for reverification is exchangeable, before this paper only a syntax-based difference detector has been used. In this paper, we propose a more complex difference detector that also considers data dependencies and program properties and prove its soundness. Our experiments show for a couple of verifiers that this new difference detector improves the effectiveness and efficiency of difference verification with condition on several tasks.

Data Availability Statement. All experimental data is made publicly available in a replication package [22].

References

1. Aquino, A., Bianchi, F.A., Chen, M., Denaro, G., Pezzè, M.: Reusing constraint proofs in program analysis. In: Proceedings of ISSTA, pp. 305–315. ACM (2015). https://doi.org/10.1145/2771783.2771802
2. Arzt, S., Bodden, E.: Reviser: Efficiently updating IDE-/IFDS-based data-flow analyses in response to incremental program changes. In: Proceedings of ICSE, pp. 288–298. ACM (2014). https://doi.org/10.1145/2568225.2568243
3. Beyer, D.: Progress on software verification: SV-COMP 2022. In: Fisman, D., Rosu, G. (eds.) TACAS 2022. LNCS, vol. 13244. Springer, Cham (2022). https://doi.org/10.1007/978-3-030-99527-0_20
4. Beyer, D., Dangl, M.: Strategy selection for software verification based on boolean features. In: Margaria, T., Steffen, B. (eds.) ISoLA 2018. LNCS, vol. 11245, pp. 144–159. Springer, Cham (2018). https://doi.org/10.1007/978-3-030-03421-4_11
5. Beyer, D., Henzinger, T.A., Keremoglu, M.E., Wendler, P.: Conditional model checking: A technique to pass information between verifiers. In: Proceedings of FSE, p. 57. ACM (2012). https://doi.org/10.1145/2393596.2393664
6. Beyer, D., Jakobs, M.-C., Lemberger, T.: Difference verification with conditions. In: de Boer, F., Cerone, A. (eds.) SEFM 2020. LNCS, vol. 12310, pp. 133–154. Springer, Cham (2020). https://doi.org/10.1007/978-3-030-58768-0_8
7. Beyer, D., Jakobs, M., Lemberger, T., Wehrheim, H.: Reducer-based construction of conditional verifiers. In: Proceedings of ICSE, pp. 1182–1193. ACM (2018). https://doi.org/10.1145/3180155.3180259
8. Beyer, D., Keremoglu, M.E., Wendler, P.: Predicate abstraction with adjustable-block encoding. In: Proceedings of FMCAD, pp. 189–197. IEEE (2010). https://ieeexplore.ieee.org/document/5770949/
9. Beyer, D., Löwe, S., Novikov, E., Stahlbauer, A., Wendler, P.: Precision reuse for efficient regression verification. In: Proceedings of FSE, pp. 389–399. ACM (2013), https://doi.org/10.1145/2491411.2491429
10. Beyer, D., Löwe, S., Wendler, P.: Reliable benchmarking: Requirements and solutions. Int. J. Softw. Tools Technol. Transfer **21**(1), 1–29 (2017). https://doi.org/10.1007/s10009-017-0469-y
11. Böhme, M., d. S. Oliveira, B.C., Roychoudhury, A.: Partition-based regression verification. In: Proceedings of ICSE, pp. 302–311. IEEE (2013). https://doi.org/10.1109/ICSE.2013.6606576

12. Çelik, A., Palmskog, K., Gligoric, M.: iCoq: Regression proof selection for large-scale verification projects. In: Proceedings of ASE, pp. 171–182. IEEE (2017). https://doi.org/10.1109/ASE.2017.8115630

13. D'Silva, V.V., Kroening, D., Weissenbacher, G.: A survey of automated techniques for formal software verification. IEEE TCAD **27**(7), 1165–1178 (2008). https://doi.org/10.1109/TCAD.2008.923410

14. Gadelha, M.R., Monteiro, F., Cordeiro, L., Nicole, D.: ESBMC v6.0: Verifying C programs using k-induction and invariant inference. In: Beyer, D., Huisman, M., Kordon, F., Steffen, B. (eds.) TACAS 2019. LNCS, vol. 11429, pp. 209–213. Springer, Cham (2019). https://doi.org/10.1007/978-3-030-17502-3_15

15. Godlin, B., Strichman, O.: Regression verification. In: Proceedings of DAC, pp. 466–471. ACM (2009), https://doi.org/10.1145/1629911.1630034

16. He, F., Yu, Q., Cai, L.: Efficient summary reuse for software regression verification. TSE **48**(4), 1417–1431 (2022). https://doi.org/10.1109/TSE.2020.3021477

17. Henzinger, T.A., Jhala, R., Majumdar, R., Sutre, G.: Lazy abstraction. In: Proceedings of POPL, pp. 58–70. ACM (2002). https://doi.org/10.1145/503272.503279

18. Henzinger, T.A., Jhala, R., Majumdar, R., Sanvido, M.A.A.: Extreme model checking. In: Dershowitz, N. (ed.) Verification: Theory and Practice. LNCS, vol. 2772, pp. 332–358. Springer, Heidelberg (2003). https://doi.org/10.1007/978-3-540-39910-0_16

19. Jakobs, M.: PEQcheck: Localized and context-aware checking of functional equivalence. In: Proceedings of FormaliSE, pp. 130–140. IEEE (2021). https://doi.org/10.1109/FormaliSE52586.2021.00019

20. Jakobs, M.: Reusing predicate precision in value analysis. In: ter Beek, M.H., Monahan, R. (eds.) IFM 2022. LNCS, vol. 13274. Springer, Cham (2022). https://doi.org/10.1007/978-3-031-07727-2_5

21. Jakobs, M.C., Pollandt, T.: Incorporating data dependencies and properties in difference verification with conditions (technical report). https://doi.org/10.48550/arXiv.2309.01585 CoRR abs/ arXiv: 2309.01585 (2023)

22. Jakobs, M.C., Pollandt, T.: Replication package for article 'diffDP: using data dependencies and properties in difference verification with conditions. In: Proceedings of iFM 2023, Zenodo (2023). https://doi.org/10.5281/zenodo.8272913

23. Jakobs, M.-C., Wiesner, M.: PEQtest: Testing functional equivalence. In: Johnsen, E.B., Wimmer, M. (eds.) FASE 2022. LNCS, vol. 13241. Springer, Cham (2022). https://doi.org/10.1007/978-3-030-99429-7_11

24. Jana, A., Khadsare, A., Chimdyalwar, B., Kumar, S., Ghime, V., Venkatesh, R.: Fast change-based alarm reporting for evolving software systems. In: Proceedings of ISSRE, pp. 546–556. IEEE (2021). https://doi.org/10.1109/ISSRE52982.2021.00062

25. Jhala, R., Majumdar, R.: Software model checking. ACM CSUR **41**(4), 21:1–21:54 (2009). https://doi.org/10.1145/1592434.1592438

26. Jin, W., Orso, A., Xie, T.: Automated behavioral regression testing. In: Proceedings of ICST, pp. 137–146. IEEE (2010). https://doi.org/10.1109/ICST.2010.64

27. Kawaguchi, M., Lahiri, S.K., Rebelo, H.: Conditional equivalence. Tech. Rep. MSR-TR-2010-119, Microsoft Research (2010). https://www.microsoft.com/en-us/research/publication/conditional-equivalence/

28. Lauterburg, S., Sobeih, A., Marinov, D., Viswanathan, M.: Incremental state-space exploration for programs with dynamically allocated data. In: Proceedings of ICSE, pp. 291–300. ACM (2008), https://doi.org/10.1145/1368088.1368128

29. Legunsen, O., Zhang, Y., Hadzi-Tanovic, M., Rosu, G., Marinov, D.: Techniques for evolution-aware runtime verification. In: Proceedingd of ICST, pp. 300–311. IEEE (2019). https://doi.org/10.1109/ICST.2019.00037

30. Leino, K.R.M., Wüstholz, V.: Fine-grained caching of verification results. In: Kroening, D., Păsăreanu, C.S. (eds.) CAV 2015. LNCS, vol. 9206, pp. 380–397. Springer, Cham (2015). https://doi.org/10.1007/978-3-319-21690-4_22

31. Palikareva, H., Kuchta, T., Cadar, C.: Shadow of a doubt: Testing for divergences between software versions. In: Proceedings of ICSE, pp. 1181–1192. ACM (2016). https://doi.org/10.1145/2884781.2884845

32. Partush, N., Yahav, E.: Abstract semantic differencing for numerical programs. In: Logozzo, F., Fähndrich, M. (eds.) SAS 2013. LNCS, vol. 7935, pp. 238–258. Springer, Heidelberg (2013). https://doi.org/10.1007/978-3-642-38856-9_14

33. Partush, N., Yahav, E.: Abstract semantic differencing via speculative correlation. In: Proceedings of OOPSLA, pp. 811–828. ACM (2014). https://doi.org/10.1145/2660193.2660245

34. Person, S., Dwyer, M.B., Elbaum, S.G., Pasareanu, C.S.: Differential symbolic execution. In: Proceedings of FSE, pp. 226–237. ACM (2008). https://doi.org/10.1145/1453101.1453131

35. Person, S., Yang, G., Rungta, N., Khurshid, S.: Directed incremental symbolic execution. In: Proceedings of PLDI, pp. 504–515. ACM (2011). https://doi.org/10.1145/1993498.1993558

36. der Plas, J.V., Stiévenart, Q., Es, N.V., Roover, C.D.: Incremental flow analysis through computational dependency reification. In: Proceedings of SCAM, pp. 25–36. IEEE (2020). https://doi.org/10.1109/SCAM51674.2020.00008

37. Rothenberg, B.-C., Dietsch, D., Heizmann, M.: Incremental verification using trace abstraction. In: Podelski, A. (ed.) SAS 2018. LNCS, vol. 11002, pp. 364–382. Springer, Cham (2018). https://doi.org/10.1007/978-3-319-99725-4_22

38. Rungta, N., Person, S., Branchaud, J.: A change impact analysis to characterize evolving program behaviors. In: Proceedings of ICSM, pp. 109–118. IEEE (2012). https://doi.org/10.1109/ICSM.2012.6405261

39. Sery, O., Fedyukovich, G., Sharygina, N.: Incremental upgrade checking by means of interpolation-based function summaries. In: Proceedings of FMCAD, pp. 114–121. IEEE (2012). http://ieeexplore.ieee.org/document/6462563/

40. Szabó, T., Erdweg, S., Voelter, M.: IncA: A DSL for the definition of incremental program analyses. In: Proceedings of ASE, pp. 320–331. ACM (2016). https://doi.org/10.1145/2970276.2970298

41. Taneja, K., Xie, T., Tillmann, N., de Halleux, J.: eXpress: Guided path exploration for efficient regression test generation. In: Proceedings of ISSTA, pp. 1–11. ACM (2011). https://doi.org/10.1145/2001420.2001422

42. Trostanetski, A., Grumberg, O., Kroening, D.: Modular demand-driven analysis of semantic difference for program versions. In: Ranzato, F. (ed.) SAS 2017. LNCS, vol. 10422, pp. 405–427. Springer, Cham (2017). https://doi.org/10.1007/978-3-319-66706-5_20

43. Visser, W., Geldenhuys, J., Dwyer, M.B.: Green: Reducing, reusing, and recycling constraints in program analysis. In: Proceedings of FSE, pp. 58:1–58:11. ACM (2012). https://doi.org/10.1145/2393596.2393665

44. Weiser, M.: Program slicing. TSE SE 10(4), 352–357 (1984). https://doi.org/10.1109/TSE.1984.5010248

45. Yang, G., Dwyer, M.B., Rothermel, G.: Regression model checking. In: Proceedings of ICSM, pp. 115–124. IEEE (2009). https://doi.org/10.1109/ICSM.2009.5306334

46. Yang, G., Păsăreanu, C.S., Khurshid, S.: Memoized symbolic execution. In: Proceedings of ISSTA, pp. 144–154. ACM (2012). https://doi.org/10.1145/2338965.2336771

47. Yoo, S., Harman, M.: Regression testing minimization, selection and prioritization: A survey. STVR **22**(2), 67–120 (2012). https://doi.org/10.1002/stvr.430

48. Yu, Q., He, F., Wang, B.: Incremental predicate analysis for regression verification. TOPLAS **4**(OOPSLA), 184:1–184:25 (2020). https://doi.org/10.1145/3428252

CHC Model Validation with Proof Guarantees

Rodrigo Otoni[1]([⊠]), Martin Blicha[1,2], Patrick Eugster[1],
and Natasha Sharygina[1]

[1] Università della Svizzera italiana, Lugano, Switzerland
{otonir,blichm,eugstp,sharygin}@usi.ch
[2] Charles University, Prague, Czech Republic

Abstract. Formal verification tooling increasingly relies on logic solvers as automated reasoning engines. A point of commonality among these solvers is the high complexity of their codebases, which makes bug occurrence disturbingly frequent. Tool competitions have showcased many examples of state-of-the-art solvers disagreeing on the satisfiability of logic formulas, be them solvers for Boolean satisfiability (SAT), satisfiability modulo theories (SMT), or constrained Horn clauses (CHC). The validation of solvers' results is thus of paramount importance, in order to increase the confidence not only in the solvers themselves, but also in the tooling which they underpin. Among the formalisms commonly used by modern verification tools, CHC is one that has seen, at the same time, extensive practical usage and very little efforts in result validation. As one of the initial steps in addressing this issue, we propose and evaluate a two-layered validation approach for witnesses of CHC satisfiability. Our approach relies, first, on a proof producing SMT solver to validate a CHC model via a series of SMT queries, and, second, on a proof checker to validate the SMT solver's results. We developed a modular evaluation framework and assessed the approach's viability via large scale experimentation, comparing three CHC solvers, five SMT solvers, and four proof checkers. Our results indicate that the approach is feasible, with potential to be incorporated into CHC-based tooling, and also confirm the need for validation, with nine bugs being found in the tools used.

Keywords: validation · constrained Horn clauses · SMT proofs

1 Introduction

First-order logic (FOL) is a formalism capable of representing many interesting verification problems, ranging from simple integer overflow to elaborate safety and liveness properties. Different fragments of FOL are suitable to aid in specific verification tasks, with one fragment of particular practical interest being constrained Horn clauses (CHC) [28]. The CHC fragment has been shown to be a match for Hoare logic [33] with practical uses [12], aiding in reasoning about the

P. Herber and A. Wijs (Eds.): iFM 2023, LNCS 14300, pp. 62–81, 2024.
https://doi.org/10.1007/978-3-031-47705-8_4

behaviour of procedural [12] and functional [27] programs, as well as concurrent systems [35] and smart contracts [46], to name a few examples.

To enable the automated reasoning of FOL formulas different logic solvers can be used, depending on the fragment selected. The most common categories of such tools are arguably Boolean satisfiability (SAT) and satisfiability modulo theories (SMT) solvers [40], which respectively solve formulas in the propositional fragment of FOL and in extensions of it with theories such as arithmetics, arrays, and bit vectors. CHC solvers are also available, e.g., ELDARICA [36], GOLEM [14], and SPACER [39], serving, for instance, as the back-end reasoning engines of verification tools targeting programs written in C/C++ [29], Java [38], Rust [43], and Solidity [1], as well as Android applications [18].

Despite their extensive usage in verification, logic solvers are themselves not immune to bugs. To illustrate this point, in the 2022 edition of the annual SMT competition there were 18 benchmarks in which at least two state-of-the-art solvers disagreed on the results [7][1]. In light of this, having guarantees about solvers' results is of paramount importance. One approach to achieve this goal is to formally verify the solvers' code, as has been done for read-eval-print loop (REPL) [41] and garbage collector [49] implementations. Despite the strong guarantees provided, this approach incurs a high cost to verify the existing codebase and any future modifications to it, as well as potentially preventing many code optimizations to be made, which are essential for solver performance. Another, less invasive, approach, is to validate solvers' outputs, rather than verifying the solvers themselves. This requires a solver, in addition to producing its standard output, to also produce a witness that can be used by an independent tool to validate the given result. Currently, the community is moving towards the second approach, with many witness formats being proposed to validate the outputs of SAT [4,20,30,32,51,54] and SMT [34,44,45,50,52] solvers, and both the annual SAT and SMT competitions now following this approach[2]. Codebase verification can still be applied, however, targeting instead the validation tools [31,42], which are much less complex and easier to maintain.

When it comes to CHC solvers, the annual CHC competition, CHC-COMP, encountered similar issues to its SAT and SMT counterparts, with competing solvers disagreeing on certain benchmarks, and its organizers having the validation of results as a goal [21]. The input of a CHC solver, detailed in Sect. 2, is a conjunction of logical implications containing uninterpreted predicates, with the task of the solver being to decide if *false* can be derived or not. If it can the input is considered unsatisfiable, UNSAT for short, and if it cannot the input is considered satisfiable, SAT for short, not to be confused with Boolean satisfiability. A witness for an UNSAT result, called an UNSAT proof, should contain an explanation of how *false* can be derived, while a witness for a SAT result,

---

[1] This is down from 274 benchmarks in the 2021 edition, showcasing the attention given by competitors to addressing unsound results found.

[2] The SAT competition requires its competitors to produce witnesses since its 2013 edition, while the SMT competition started an exhibition track for this, still separate from the main tracks, in its 2022 edition.

called a SAT model, should contain interpretations for all the predicates in such a way that all clauses evaluate to *true*, entailing that *false* cannot be derived; for the remainder of the paper UNSAT proofs and SAT models will be referred to simply as proofs and models.

The production of witnesses is a common feature of modern CHC solvers, but efforts in witnesses validation are limited at present. The validation of models is done via SMT queries, and is currently supported only by an ad hoc validator tied to the SMT solver Z3 [22][3]. Unlike the case for models, however, the proofs produced cannot be validated with available tooling, given that, to the best of our knowledge, no proof checking approach currently exists.

Since CHC model validation is underpinned by SMT solving, the same concern regarding the correctness of CHC solvers' results is put on the validation itself, i.e., on the

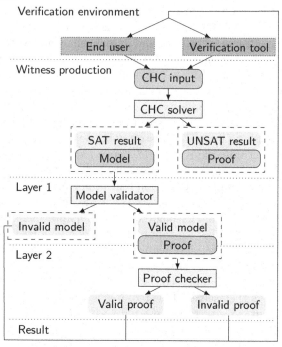

Fig. 1. Overview of our two-layered validation approach for CHC models. Although capable of being produced, CHC proofs cannot be checked currently.

correctness of SMT solvers' results. To address this, we propose a two-layered validation approach to provide additional guarantees about the results obtained, illustrated in Fig. 1. The first layer, consisting of the SMT queries responsible for model validation, is enhanced by a second layer, consisting of the production and checking of SMT proofs, with the result obtained being forwarded to the user or tool interacting with the CHC solver. The approach is generic w.r.t. FOL theories and solvers, and is also very modular, enabling different SMT solvers to be used in the validation, further increasing assurances.

To asses the viability of practical model validation we developed a modular evaluation framework, called ATHENA, capable of catering to different combinations of state-of-the-art CHC and SMT solvers, and conducted a large scale evaluation. Concretely, we used our framework to validate the models produced by three CHC solvers, ELDARICA [36], GOLEM [14], and SPACER [39], with each

---

[3] See https://github.com/chc-comp/chc-tools/blob/master/chctools/chcmodel.py.

model produced being separately validated, in Layer 1, by five proof producing SMT solvers, CVC5 [5], OPENSMT [37], SMTINTERPOL [19], VERIT [16], and Z3 [22]. In addition, we checked, in Layer 2, all the proofs produced in the proof formats currently supported by automated proof checkers, by using the checkers CARCARA [2], LFSC checker [52], SMTINTERPOL checker [34], and TSWC [45].

To have a focused evaluation we conducted our experiments on benchmarks from one specific FOL theory, namely the linear integer arithmetic (LIA) theory. We used all 955 LIA benchmarks from CHC-COMP 2022 in our evaluation, 499 containing only linear Horn clauses, i.e., implications with a single uninterpreted predicate in the implicant, and 456 containing nonlinear Horn clauses, i.e., implications with multiple uninterpreted predicates in the implicant. The benchmarks used led to 91626 SMT instances and 385303 SMT proofs being produced as part of the validation process.

Three observations can be made from the results obtained. First, the proof-backed model validation approach proposed is viable in practice, with the majority of the models being validated with available tooling. This means that any CHC-based tool, e.g., the SEAHORN [29] and SOLCMC [1] model checkers, can in principle benefit from the guarantees provided by model validation. Second, model and proof sizes, which were in the order of hundreds of megabytes in our experiments and can potentially require gigabytes of storage, are a concern and a potential limitation to the practical use of validation. Producing compact models and proofs is thus an important goal, with compression, recently investigated in the context of unsatisfiability proofs for SAT solvers [47], being a potential complementary goal. Lastly, model validation provides a useful way to generate new and interesting SMT instances. Our evaluation uncovered bugs not only in the selected CHC solvers, which are our main focus, but also in two SMT solvers and two proof checkers for SMT proofs. The bugs found, listed in Table 1, range from parsing errors to invalid models being produced. They were all acknowledged by the developers and are detailed in Sect. 5. In addition to aiding in tool development, these bugs confirm the need for additional guarantees to be provided to modern verification tooling.

Table 1. Brief descriptions of the bugs found during the evaluation.

		Bug Effect
CHC solvers	ELDARICA	Invalid model produced (see footnote 8)
	SPACER	Invalid model produced (see footnote 10)
	GOLEM	Syntactically malformed model produced (see footnote 7)
	GOLEM	Crash during model production (see footnote 6)
SMT solvers	CVC5	Invalid proof produced (see footnote 13)
	CVC5	Crash during proof production (see footnote 12)
	OPENSMT	Crash during sort inference (see footnote 11)
Proof checkers	CARCARA	Parsing error due to unknown attribute (see footnote 14)
	LFSC checker	Crash during type inference (see footnote 15)

To summarise, our contributions are the following:

1. Proposal of a two-layered validation approach for CHC models;
2. Development of an evaluation framework, ATHENA, to assess the approach;
3. Staging of a large scale evaluation to determine the viability of the approach.

The remainder of the paper is structured as follows: the necessary background is given in Sect. 2, the two layers of our validation approach are presented in Sect. 3, ATHENA is detailed in Sect. 4, the evaluation is discussed in Sect. 5, and, finally, our conclusions are laid out in Sect. 6.

2   Background

The constrained Horn clauses formalism has been proposed as a unified, purely logic-based, intermediate language for reasoning about verification tasks [27]. It builds upon the success achieved with SAT and SMT, using logical constraints to capture various verification tasks, including safety, termination, and loop invariant computation, from a variety of domains. In this section the necessary CHC background is presented, followed by an overview of related witness validation approaches. We refer readers to [40] for details on SAT and SMT.

2.1   Constrained Horn Clauses

Following standard SMT terminology [9], we assume a first-order theory T and a set of uninterpreted predicates P disjoint from the signature of T. A constrained Horn clause is a formula $\varphi \land P_1 \land \ldots \land P_n \implies H$, where φ is an interpreted formula in the language of T, each P_i is an application of a symbol $p \in P$ to terms of T, H is either an application of a symbol $p \in P$ to terms of T or $false$, and all variables in the formula are implicitly universally quantified. Commonly, the antecedent and the consequent of the implication are denoted as the $body$ and the $head$ of the Horn clause, and φ is referred to as its $constraint$.

Given a set of constrained Horn clauses S over the uninterpreted predicates P and theory T, we say that S is satisfiable if there exists a model M of T extended with an interpretation for all the uninterpreted predicates P such that all the clauses evaluate to $true$ in M, i.e., every clause evaluate to $true$ in M for all possible instantiations of the universally quantified variables. In practice, we are interested in interpretations that are definable in the language of T, i.e., we want a mapping of the predicates to a set of formulas in the language of T such that each clause from S is valid in T after the uninterpreted predicates are replaced by their interpretations. This is called $syntactic\ solvability$, as opposed to the more general $semantic\ solvability$ [48]. The interpretations of the predicates from the discovered model serve as witnesses for the satisfiability answer. An unsatisfiability answer, on the other hand, needs to be witnessed by a derivation of $false$ from the original clauses, likely via universal instantiation and resolution.

2.2   Related Witness Validation Approaches

As logic solvers became more powerful they were quickly adopted as the back-end reasoning engines of many verification tools. The need to validate the answers from these solvers arose soon after, with the complexity of the validation increasing hand-in-hand with the expressiveness of the underlying formalism.

In line with its relative simplicity, witness validation in the context of Boolean satisfiability was the first to be investigated. Validating a satisfying model is an easy task: one simply substitutes the variables of the formula with their values from the model and checks if the resulting Boolean expression over constants *true* and *false* simplifies to *true*. The validation of unsatisfiability proofs, however, is far from trivial, even in such a restricted domain. Many proof formats have been proposed, offering different trade-offs between proof compactness and checking efficiency. Initial formats were based on resolution [51] and clausal proofs [30], with resolution asymmetric tautology (RAT) [32] being a base for many recent developments, e.g., deletion RAT (DRAT) [54], linear RAT (LRAT) [20], and flexible RAT (FRAT) [4]. The production of proofs in the DRAT format has been a requirement in the SAT competition since its 2014 edition, with DRAT-TRIM [54] being the standard proof checker for proofs following this format.

In regards to satisfiability modulo theories, witness validation is complicated by the presence of theories and quantifiers. No standard way of representing SMT models currently exists, with a consistent push by the SMT competition organizers having been made in recent years for the adoption of a unified format in line with the SMT-LIB standard [8]. A separate, experimental, model validation track has been established and has seen a steady increase in the SMT-LIB logics supported, with PySMT [26] and DOLMEN [17] used as validating tools. Despite recent advances, model validation is still restricted to quantifier-free formulas. For unsatisfiability proofs, different formats, often attached to a specific solver, have been proposed. The ALETHE format [50] was initially supported by VERIT, but has since also being integrated into cvc5's proof production. cvc5 also caters for proofs based on the logical framework with side conditions (LFSC) [52], with LFSC support preceding ALETHE's integration and dating back to the CVC3 version of the tool. SMTINTERPOL [34], OPENSMT [45], and Z3 [44] also support their own, unnamed, proof formats. Each format has one or more associate tools that can consume the proofs produced, with said tools being either interactive or automated. In the interactive side, proof assistants discharge some verification conditions to external logic solvers as a way to increase their level of automation, with the proofs produced providing new theorems to be checked by the proof assistant's internal engine, as it has been done with CoQ [3,23] and ISABELLE/HOL [6,13,15,25]. When it comes to automated checkers, their goal is mainly to serve as independent lightweight validators, with potential to be integrated into tools such as model checkers. Automated checkers are available for a variety of formats [2,34,45,52,54]. As of the time of writing, no proof format is enforced by the SMT competition, with an experimental track being available as a way to showcase the strengths of existing formats.

In addition to logic solving, witness validation is also pursued in other contexts. A good example of this is the use of validation in the annual competition on software verification [10]. Software verification witnesses are different from those used by logic solvers, being categorizes as either correctness or violation witnesses, with their own formats[4] and limitations [11]. The tool that maybe best illustrates usage of witness is Korn [24], a participant in the software verification competition that relies on Horn solvers as its back-end and produces witnesses for its reasoning about C programs' properties from the witnesses produced by the underlying solvers.

3   Validation of CHC Models

A CHC solver is a complex piece of software, often implementing sophisticated algorithms relying on decision and interpolation procedures, which allows for subtle bugs to occur and lead to incorrect answers. In addition to providing much needed stronger guarantees in regards to SAT or UNSAT results, model validation also ensures the correctness of the models themselves, which are commonly relied upon by verification tools to, for instance, establish inductive invariants of programs. Model validation is therefore critical for assurance not only of solvers' results, but also of all structures derived from models presented to end users.

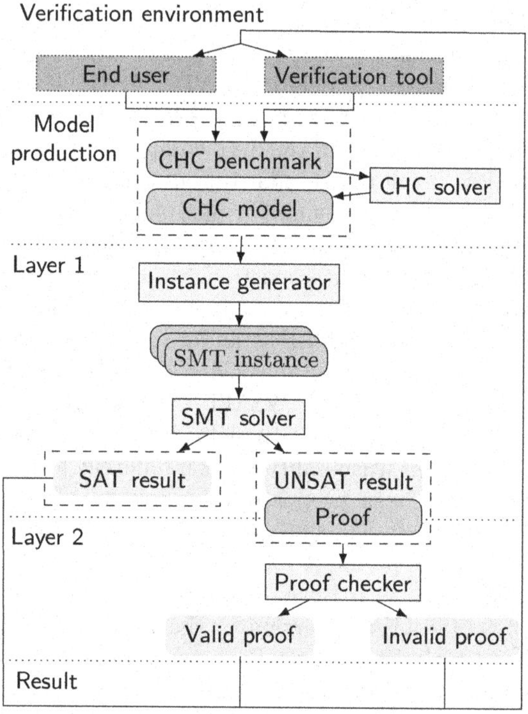

Fig. 2. Breakdown of our two-layered validation approach for CHC models. A valid model will have all the SMT instances generated from it yield an UNSAT result backed by a valid SMT proof.

We propose a two-layered validation approach for CHC models, detailed in Fig. 2; since our focus is on models, the illustration assumes the benchmark is satisfiable. The first of the two layers in the approach handles model validation via SMT solving. Following the CHC model definition laid out in Sect. 2.1, model validation can be done via a number of SMT queries

---

[4] See https://gitlab.com/sosy-lab/benchmarking/sv-witnesses.

which is linear w.r.t. to the number of Horn clauses present in the input. Each such query checks if a specific Horn clause is logically valid in the theory $\mathcal{T}$ after its uninterpreted predicates are substituted by their interpretations given by the model. This is done by checking if the negation of the Horn clause, augmented with the interpretations, is satisfiable, i.e., if a satisfying assignment for $\varphi \wedge P_1 \wedge \ldots \wedge P_n \wedge \neg H$ exists. This check is well suited for SMT solving, with a valid model leading to all queries being unsatisfiable. An important note is that, depending on the theory $\mathcal{T}$, the query checking might be intractable for existing SMT solvers, and in some cases even undecidable.

As an example, consider the following CHC system, consisting of three Horn clauses and a single uninterpreted predicate Inv:

$$x \leq 0 \implies Inv(x)$$
$$Inv(x) \wedge x < 5 \wedge x' = x + 1 \implies Inv(x')$$
$$Inv(x) \wedge \neg(x < 10) \implies false$$

This system is satisfiable with a potential model being one that contains the interpretation $Inv(x) \equiv x \leq 5$. To validate this model we need to establish that the following three formulas are logically valid in the LIA theory:

$$x \leq 0 \implies x \leq 5$$
$$x \leq 5 \wedge x < 5 \wedge x' = x + 1 \implies x' \leq 5$$
$$x \leq 5 \wedge \neg(x < 10) \implies false$$

The validation can be done by showing that the three formulas below are unsatisfiable, which can be trivially seen for this small example:

$$x \leq 0 \wedge \neg(x \leq 5)$$
$$x \leq 5 \wedge x < 5 \wedge x' = x + 1 \wedge \neg(x' \leq 5)$$
$$x \leq 5 \wedge \neg(x < 10) \wedge \neg false$$

While it can be easy to validate models such as the one above, this is far from the case when dealing with real world examples. As a consequence, SMT solvers are, like their CHC counterparts, very complex tools that are susceptible to bugs. The second layer in the approach we propose tackles this issue via the validation of SMT solvers' results. A number of SMT solvers produce unsatisfiability proofs that can be independently checked. These proofs provide much needed guarantees regarding unsatiafiability results, which are at the core of the validation done in Layer 1. By relying on the currently untapped power of SMT proofs we provide additional correctness guarantees for CHC model validation.

Our approach is theory independent and can be applied to any CHC, with the only requirement being that a proof producing SMT solver and a proof checker are available for the theory in question. In addition to validating direct end user usage of CHC solvers, our approach can also be embedded into CHC-based verification tools, enhancing their own guarantees.

4   Implementation

To enable the practical use of our approach, with the immediate goal of ascertaining the capabilities of state-of-the-art CHC and SMT solvers, we developed the modulAr consTrained Horn clauses modEl validatioN frAmework, ATHENA for short. Our framework is capable of validating CHC models via SMT solving while using different solver combinations. ATHENA also handles the production and checking of SMT proofs, for the SMT solvers with proof production capabilities. In addition, metrics such as model and proof sizes can be gathered and analysed. The framework consists of 2535 lines of shell and Python code in total, is fully automated, and uses GNU PARALLEL [53] to achieve a large degree of parallelisation in order to better tackle the high computation cost. ATHENA is open-source[5], enabling third-parties to make full use of it, with one of our goals being to provide the groundwork for model validation at CHC-COMP.

5   Evaluation

We first describe the benchmarks and tools used, in Sect. 5.1, and then discuss the results obtained related to CHC model validation, in Sect. 5.2, and SMT proof checking, in Sect. 5.3. We used a machine with 64 AMD EPYC 7452 processors and 256 GB of memory for the evaluation. All individual tool executions had a timeout of 60 s and a memory limit of 5 gigabytes.

5.1   Benchmarks and Tools

We used the benchmarks of the two LIA tracks of CHC-COMP 2022 [21], the LIA-lin track, consisting of benchmarks containing only linear Horn clauses, and the LIA-nonlin track, consisting of benchmarks containing nonlinear Horn clauses. We decided to use LIA benchmarks for two reasons: first, the LIA tracks are the most traditional in CHC-COMP, being present in every edition of the competition and having the most competing solvers, and second, the LIA theory is covered by all proof producing SMT solvers available, even if for some only in its quantifier-free fragment.

For model production we chose the current three best performing CHC solvers in the LIA tracks for comparison, which are, in alphabetical order, ELDARICA [36], GOLEM [14], and SPACER [39]. For model validation we used all SMT solvers that competed in the proof exhibition track of the 2022 SMT competition, which are, in alphabetical order, CVC5 [5], OPENSMT [37], SMTINTERPOL [19], and VERIT [16], as well as Z3 [22], which can produce proofs but did not compete in the track. To check the SMT proofs we used the fully automated checkers CARCARA [2], for ALETHE proofs produced by CVC5 and VERIT, LFSC checker [52], for LFSC proofs produced by CVC5, SMTINTERPOL checker [34], for proofs produced by SMTINTERPOL, and TSWC [45], for proofs produced by OPENSMT; to the best of our knowledge there is currently no independent automated checker for proofs produced by Z3.

---

[5] Available at https://github.com/usi-verification-and-security/athena.

5.2   Model Validation Results

To produce the CHC models we executed the selected CHC solvers with all benchmarks; the results are summarised in Table 2. All tools were executed with their default engine configurations. The performance of the tools is in line with the CHC-COMP results, with SPACER solving the most benchmarks overall, followed by GOLEM and ELDARICA. Only one execution, with SPACER, yielded an unknown result, meaning that the solver terminated within the allocated time frame but was not able to decide if the benchmark was satisfiable or not. A number of errors, i.e., tool crashes, were observed with GOLEM while testing our framework[6], as well as syntactically malformed models being produced by it[7], with the underlying causes of both issues being addressed before the full-scale evaluation. Regarding the models' sizes, ELDARICA's models tended to be the most compact, followed by GOLEM's, with SPACER producing most of the larger models, as can be seen in Fig. 3; the single largest model is an outlier produced by GOLEM, with a size exceeding 100 MB. The last point of note is that all models

Table 2. Results for solving the CHC benchmarks of the two LIA tracks.

		SAT	UNSAT	Unknown	Timeout	Memout	Error
	ELDARICA	141	51	0	307	0	0
LIA-lin	GOLEM	165	80	0	254	0	0
(499 benchmarks)	SPACER	182	89	0	212	16	0
	ELDARICA	117	56	0	283	0	0
LIA-nonlin	GOLEM	209	118	0	129	0	0
(456 benchmarks)	SPACER	244	130	1	74	7	0

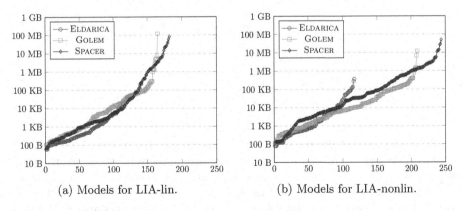

(a) Models for LIA-lin.   (b) Models for LIA-nonlin.

Fig. 3. Sizes of the CHC models. The models are ordered according to their size, the x-axis indicates their position in the order and the y-axis indicates their size.

---

[6] See https://github.com/usi-verification-and-security/golem/issues/29.

[7] See https://github.com/usi-verification-and-security/golem/issues/27.

produced by GOLEM are quantifier-free, while ELDARICA produced 1 quantified model, for 1 nonlinear benchmark, and SPACER produced 281 quantified models in total, 90 from linear benchmarks and 191 from nonlinear benchmarks.

To validate each model we executed the SMT instances generated from it with the selected SMT solvers; in this section all the reported SMT solvers' executions were done with proof production disabled. One SMT instance is generated for each Horn clause in the CHC benchmark for which the model was produced, thus many SMT instances, sometimes hundreds, can be generated for a single model. We consider the SMT instances generated for the models produced by each CHC solver, by track, as separate instance sets, thus we have three instance sets per track. The results for the LIA-lin and LIA-nonlin instance sets can be seen in Tables 3 and 4, respectively; the number of SMT instances generated for each CHC solver is related to the amount of models it produced.

Table 3. Results for solving the SMT instances generated from the LIA-lin models. Due to the space limitation, unknown, timeout, memout, and error are shortened to UNK, TO, MO, and ERR. UNS stands for unsupported, meaning that the SMT solver is not equipped to handle some features of the instance.

		SAT	UNSAT	UNK	TO	MO	ERR	UNS
	CVC5	0	5041	0	0	0	9	0
LIA-lin	OPENSMT	0	4970	0	0	0	80	0
ELDARICA	SMTINTERPOL	0	5041	0	0	0	9	0
(5050 instances)	VERIT	0	4986	0	0	0	9	55
	Z3	3	5047	0	0	0	0	0
	CVC5	0	5268	0	0	0	0	0
LIA-lin	OPENSMT	0	5268	0	0	0	0	0
GOLEM	SMTINTERPOL	0	5265	0	3	0	0	0
(5268 instances)	VERIT	0	5216	0	0	0	0	52
	Z3	0	5268	0	0	0	0	0
	CVC5	695	15464	0	73	0	0	0
LIA-lin	OPENSMT	7	700	0	0	0	912	14613
SPACER	SMTINTERPOL	105	11909	28	4190	0	0	0
(16232 instances)	VERIT	19	1543	0	0	0	0	14670
	Z3	690	15026	0	516	0	0	0

The validation results provide a useful insight into the quality of the models produced by each CHC solver. The models produced by GOLEM are the only ones for which no invalid result, i.e., a SAT output, was observed. Both ELDARICA and SPACER produced invalid models, although the latter to a significantly higher degree. ELDARICA's invalid models are due to the embedding of Boolean

Table 4. Results for solving the SMT instances generated from the LIA-nonlin models. Due to the space limitation, unknown, timeout, memout, and error are shortened to UNK, TO, MO, and ERR. UNS stands for unsupported, meaning that the SMT solver is not equipped to handle some features of the instance.

		SAT	UNSAT	UNK	TO	MO	ERR	UNS
	CVC5	0	6216	0	0	0	0	0
LIA-nonlin	OPENSMT	0	2493	0	0	0	3706	17
ELDARICA	SMTINTERPOL	0	6216	0	0	0	0	0
(6216 instances)	VERIT	0	6195	2	0	0	0	19
	Z3	0	6216	0	0	0	0	0
	CVC5	0	22458	0	0	0	0	0
LIA-nonlin	OPENSMT	0	22458	0	0	0	0	0
GOLEM	SMTINTERPOL	0	22458	0	0	0	0	0
(22458 instances)	VERIT	0	22449	0	0	0	0	9
	Z3	0	22458	0	0	0	0	0
	CVC5	147	36254	0	1	0	0	0
LIA-nonlin	OPENSMT	0	961	0	0	0	1326	34115
SPACER	SMTINTERPOL	97	34095	764	1446	0	0	0
(36402 instances)	VERIT	0	2286	0	0	0	0	34116
	Z3	147	36230	0	25	0	0	0

values into arithmetic operations[8], which leads to an error in most SMT solvers, but can be solved by Z3 via unit propagation[9]. SPACER's invalid models are due to problematic internal transformations[10]. Another aspect of model quality is the presence of quantifiers, which can make solving harder and is unsupported by both OPENSMT and VERIT. Two last points of note are the high number of OPENSMT errors, i.e., crashes, when handling instances generated from ELDARICA and SPACER models, which is due to a limitation in scoping in the presence of different sorts[11], and the small, but consistent, number of instances unsupported by VERIT. After a manual inspection, it was discovered that the lack of support observed with VERIT is due to the LIA tracks containing some benchmarks that, although semantically belonging to the LIA fragment of FOL, use operators reserved for the nonlinear integer arithmetic (NIA) logic of the SMT-LIB standard; the competition organizers were informed of this finding.

5.3   Proof Checking Results

To validate the UNSAT results given by the SMT solvers we rely on the proofs produced by them. For each SMT instance generated from a CHC model we executed the selected SMT solvers in proof production mode. The number of proofs produced by each SMT solver can be seen in Table 5. Since proof production adds an overhead to solver execution, the number of proofs produced is expected to be lower than the amount of UNSAT results reported in Tables 3

---

[8] See https://github.com/uuverifiers/eldarica/issues/51.
[9] See https://github.com/Z3Prover/z3/issues/6719.
[10] See https://github.com/Z3Prover/z3/issues/6716.
[11] See https://github.com/usi-verification-and-security/opensmt/issues/613.

and 4. Concretely, the combined percentage of proofs produced in relation to the previous UNSAT results, for the six instance sets, is: 95.59% for CVC5-ALETHE, 99.27% for CVC5-LFSC, 100% for OPENSMT, 96.05% for SMTINTERPOL, 0% for VERIT, and 99.76% for Z3. The reduction in performance is overall small, with OPENSMT showing no performance degradation and CVC5-LFSC and Z3

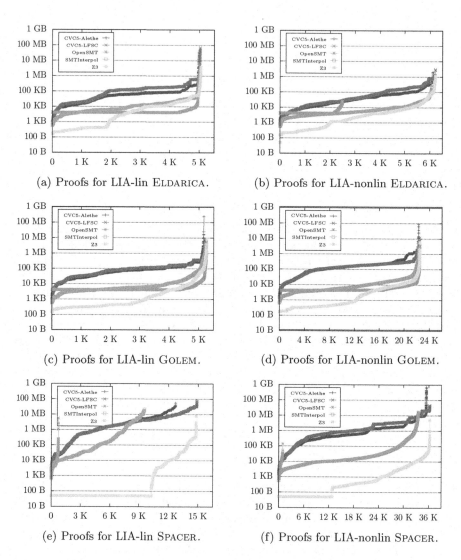

(a) Proofs for LIA-lin ELDARICA.

(b) Proofs for LIA-nonlin ELDARICA.

(c) Proofs for LIA-lin GOLEM.

(d) Proofs for LIA-nonlin GOLEM.

(e) Proofs for LIA-lin SPACER.

(f) Proofs for LIA-nonlin SPACER.

Fig. 4. Sizes of the SMT proofs. The proofs are ordered according to their size, the x-axis indicates their position in the order and the y-axis indicates their size; the scale of the x-axis changes between the plots, due to the high variation on the number of proofs produced.

having less than 1% reduction. Two points of note are that ALETHE proofs led to more than six times the overhead than LFSC proofs in CVC5, and that VERIT was not able to produce any proofs. The reason for the behaviour observed with VERIT is that the `define_fun` construct of the SMT-LIB standard, present in the models produced by all CHC solvers, is supported by VERIT in its default configuration, but not in its proof production mode. In addition, 117 new errors were observed with CVC5, which only happened in proof production mode, due to an unexpected free assumption leading to a fatal failure[12].

Table 5. Number of proofs produced by the selected SMT solvers; CVC5 has separate results for its two proof formats. Each column shows the amount of proofs produced from a given instance set, with the total amount of instances in each set shown below the CHC solver that produced the models for it.

| | Proofs Produced | | | | | |
| | LIA-lin | | | LIA-nonlin | | |
	ELDARICA (5050)	GOLEM (5268)	SPACER (16232)	ELDARICA (6216)	GOLEM (22458)	SPACER (36402)
CVC5-ALETHE	4992	5169	12719	6116	22282	35419
CVC5-LFSC	5028	5226	14873	6216	22454	36234
OPENSMT	4970	5268	700	2493	22458	961
SMTINTERPOL	5010	5222	9548	6062	22299	33486
VERIT	0	0	0	0	0	0
Z3	5047	5268	14807	6216	22458	36230

The proof formats used by each SMT solver can be quite different, not only in shape, but also in the amount of information stored, with the choice of finer or coarser proofs potentially having a significant effect on proof size. The sizes of all proofs produced in our evaluation can be seen in Fig. 4. Overall, CVC5 produced the largest proofs, in both of its proof formats, in some cases with an order of magnitude difference with the proofs produced by the solver with the third largest proofs. The ranking between OPENSMT, SMTINTERPOL, and Z3 depends on which CHC solver's models the instances are generated from. A large number of Z3 proofs, all with a size of 50 B, consisted simply of `(proof (asserted false))`, showcasing how coarse proofs can be; although very compact, these extreme examples make checking essentially degenerate into solving the instance again. Regarding the CHC solvers themselves, ELDARICA's models led to the majority of the largest proofs for LIA-lin instances and SPACER's models led to the majority of the largest proofs for LIA-nonlin instances. The single largest proof produced, by CVC5-ALETHE from an instance generated from a SPACER LIA-nonlin model, had a size of 699 MB, which is a good illustration of the need of compact proofs.

To check the proofs we used the available automated checkers suitable for each proof format, namely CARCARA and TSWC for the proofs produced by CVC5-ALETHE and OPENSMT, and the LFSC and SMTINTERPOL checkers

---

[12] See https://github.com/cvc5/cvc5/issues/9770.

Table 6. Results for checking the proofs produced by solving the SMT instances generated for the LIA-lin benchmarks; LFSC and SMTINTERPOL stand for their respective checkers. In addition to the raw number of proofs verified, the percentage relation to the total number of proofs is presented in parentheses.

		Valid	Invalid	Timeout	Memout	Error
LIA-lin ELDARICA	CARCARA	4992 (100%)	0	0	0	0
	LFSC	5026 (99.9%)	0	2	0	0
	SMTINTERPOL	5010 (100%)	0	0	0	0
	TSWC	4970 (100%)	0	0	0	0
LIA-lin GOLEM	CARCARA	5038 (97.4%)	131	0	0	0
	LFSC	5214 (99.7%)	0	7	3	2
	SMTINTERPOL	5222 (100%)	0	0	0	0
	TSWC	5268 (100%)	0	0	0	0
LIA-lin SPACER	CARCARA	1478 (11.6%)	109	0	0	11132
	LFSC	11295 (75.9%)	0	7	3570	1
	SMTINTERPOL	9542 (99.9%)	0	6	0	0
	TSWC	700 (100%)	0	0	0	0

for the proofs produced by CVC5-LFSC and SMTINTERPOL. The results for the proofs produced for the LIA-lin and LIA-nonlin instance sets can be seen in Tables 6 and 7, respectively. Overall, the four checkers were able to validate most of the proofs produced, with the LFSC checker being the only tool to be significantly affected by the resource constraints, specifically the memory limit of 5 gigabytes. An important discovery is that CVC5-ALETHE produced 562 invalid proofs, due to incorrect proof steps[13]. While not implying that the UNSAT results the proofs are supposed to validate are incorrect, since the problem can be in the proof production itself, this is a serious issue. Still in regards to ALETHE proofs, CARCARA had 44282 number of errors when checking proofs produced for SMT instances generated from SPACER models, due to the presence of attribute annotations in models containing quantifiers[14]. Lastly, 3 errors were also observed with the LFSC checker, due to a type mismatch[15].

6   Conclusions

We presented a novel two-layered approach for CHC model validation that relies on SMT proofs to provide additional correctness guarantees. The approach is supported by a modular evaluation framework, ATHENA, that enables models to be validated by many different SMT solvers and the SMT solving results to be validated by available proof checkers. A large scale evaluation was conducted using all LIA benchmarks from CHC-COMP 2022 to compare three CHC solvers, five SMT solvers, and four proof checkers. The results indicate that the approach is feasible in practice, with potential to benefit CHC-based verification tools, and also highlight model and proof sizes as a crucial practicality factor.

---

[13] See https://github.com/cvc5/cvc5/issues/9760.

[14] See https://github.com/ufmg-smite/carcara/issues/12.

[15] See https://github.com/cvc5/LFSC/issues/87.

Table 7. Results for checking the proofs produced by solving the SMT instances generated for the LIA-nonlin benchmarks; LFSC and SMTINTERPOL stand for their respective checkers. In addition to the raw number of proofs verified, the percentage relation to the total number of proofs is presented in parentheses.

		Valid	Invalid	Timeout	Memout	Error
LIA-nonlin ELDARICA	CARCARA	6115 (99.9%)	1	0	0	0
	LFSC	6216 (100%)	0	0	0	0
	SMTINTERPOL	6062 (100%)	0	0	0	0
	TSWC	2493 (100%)	0	0	0	0
LIA-nonlin GOLEM	CARCARA	21999 (98.7%)	283	0	0	0
	LFSC	22453 (99.9%)	0	1	0	0
	SMTINTERPOL	22299 (100%)	0	0	0	0
	TSWC	22458 (100%)	0	0	0	0
LIA-nonlin SPACER	CARCARA	2231 (6.2%)	38	0	0	33150
	LFSC	36222 (99.9%)	0	3	9	0
	SMTINTERPOL	33468 (99.9%)	0	18	0	0
	TSWC	961 (100%)	0	0	0	0

A final important point is that many bugs were found in the tools compared, including invalid models being produced by two state-of-the-art CHC solvers, which confirms the need to provide modern verification tooling with additional correctness guarantees.

Directions for future work include (i) evaluating the approach with other FOL theories, (ii) embedding the approach into CHC-based verification tooling, and (iii) designing a complementary approach to validate CHC proofs. For the first direction, enhancements can be made to the framework's implementation to cater to theories other than LIA, with a point of interest being the checker support for SMT proofs not involving arithmetics. For the second direction, the use of proof-backed model validation in CHC-based model checkers is a direct application. For the third direction, one possibility is to use the ALETHE format to represent and check CHC proofs, since it is rich enough to describe the necessary proof steps. An important unknown regarding potential ALETHE CHC proofs is the correct level of granularity, as it is unclear if coarse proofs can be efficiently checked, either by CARCARA or any future checker, or if additional burden needs to be put on the solvers to produce fine-grained proofs.

Acknowledgements. Rodrigo Otoni's work was supported by the Swiss National Science Foundation, via grant 200021_197353. Martin Blicha's work was supported by the Czech Science Foundation, via grant 23-06506S. The authors thank Fedor Gromov for his assistance in preparing the SMT instance generator.

References

1. Alt, L., Blicha, M., Hyvärinen, A.E.J., Sharygina, N.: SolCMC: solidity compiler's model checker. In: Proceedings of the 34th International Conference on Computer Aided Verification, pp. 325–338 (2022)
2. Andreotti, B., Lachnitt, H., Barbosa, H.: Carcara: an efficient proof checker and elaborator for SMT proofs in the alethe format. In: Proceedings of the 29th International Conference on Tools and Algorithms for the Construction and Analysis of Systems, pp. 367–386 (2023)
3. Armand, M., Faure, G., Grégoire, B., Keller, C., Théry, L., Werner, B.: A modular integration of SAT/SMT solvers to COQ through proof witnesses. In: Proceedings of the 1st International Conference on Certified Programs and Proofs, pp. 135–150 (2011)
4. Baek, S., Carneiro, M., Heule, M.J.H.: A flexible proof format for SAT solver-elaborator communication. In: Proceedings of the 27th International Conference on Tools and Algorithms for the Construction and Analysis of Systems, pp. 59–75 (2021)
5. Barbosa, H., et al.: CVC5: a versatile and industrial-strength SMT solver. In: Proceedings of the 28th International Conference on Tools and Algorithms for the Construction and Analysis of Systems, pp. 415–442 (2022)
6. Barbosa, H., Blanchette, J.C., Fleury, M., Fontaine, P.: Scalable fine-grained proofs for formula processing. J. Autom. Reason. **64**(3), 485–510 (2020)
7. Barbosa, H., Hoenicke, J., Bobot, F.: SMT-COMP 2022: Competition Report (2022). https://smt-comp.github.io/2022/slides-smtworkshop.pdf
8. Barrett, C., Fontaine, P., Tinelli, C.: The SMT-LIB Standard: Version 2.6 (2021). https://smtlib.cs.uiowa.edu/papers/smt-lib-reference-v2.6-r2021-05-12.pdf
9. Barrett, C., Sebastiani, R., Seshia, S., Tinelli, C.: Satisfiability modulo theories. In: Biere, A., Heule, M.J.H., van Maaren, H., Walsh, T. (eds.) Handbook of Satisfiability. IOS Press (2021)
10. Beyer, D.: Competition on software verification and witness validation: SV-COMP 2023. In: Proceedings of the 29th International Conference on Tools and Algorithms for the Construction and Analysis of Systems, pp. 495–522 (2023)
11. Beyer, D., Strejček, J.: Case study on verification-witness validators: where we are and where we go. In: Proceedings of the 29th International Symposium on Static Analysis, pp. 160–174 (2022)
12. Bjørner, N., Gurfinkel, A., McMillan, K., Rybalchenko, A.: Horn clause solvers for program verification. In: Beklemishev, L.D., Blass, A., Dershowitz, N., Finkbeiner, B., Schulte, W. (eds.) Fields of Logic and Computation II. LNCS, vol. 9300, pp. 24–51. Springer, Cham (2015). https://doi.org/10.1007/978-3-319-23534-9_2
13. Blanchette, J.C., Böhme, S., Fleury, M., Smolka, S.J., Steckermeier, A.: Semi-intelligible ISAR proofs from machine-generated proofs. J. Autom. Reason. **56**(2), 155–200 (2016)
14. Blicha, M., Britikov, K., Sharygina, N.: The golem horn solver. In: Proceedings of the 35th International Conference on Computer Aided Verification, pp. 209–223 (2023). https://doi.org/10.1007/978-3-031-37703-7_10

15. Böhme, S., Weber, T.: Fast LCF-style proof reconstruction for Z3. In: Proceedings of the 1st International Conference on Interactive Theorem Proving, pp. 179–194 (2010)

16. Bouton, T., Caminha, B., de Oliveira, D., Déharbe, D., Fontaine, P.: veriT: an open, trustable and efficient SMT-solver. In: Proceedings of the 22nd International Conference on Automated Deduction, pp. 151–156 (2009)

17. Bury, G.: Dolmen: a validator for SMT-LIB and much more. In: Proceedings of the 19th International Workshop on Satisfiability Modulo Theories, pp. 32–39 (2021)

18. Calzavara, S., Grishchenko, I., Maffei, M.: HornDroid: practical and sound static analysis of android applications by SMT solving. In: Proceedings of the 1st IEEE European Symposium on Security and Privacy, pp. 47–62 (2016)

19. Christ, J., Hoenicke, J., Nutz, A.: SMTInterpol: an interpolating SMT solver. In: Proceedings of the 19th International SPIN Workshop, pp. 248–254 (2012)

20. Cruz-Filipe, L., Heule, M.J.H., Hunt, W.A., Kaufmann, M., Schneider-Kamp, P.: Efficient certified RAT verification. In: Proceedings of the 26th International Conference on Automated Deduction, pp. 220–236 (2017)

21. De Angelis, E., Govind, V.K.H.: CHC-COMP 2022: competition report. In: Proceedings of the 9th Workshop on Horn Clauses for Verification and Synthesis, pp. 44–62 (2022)

22. De Moura, L., Bjørner, N.: Z3: an efficient SMT solver. In: Proceedings of the 14th International Conference on Tools and Algorithms for the Construction and Analysis of Systems, pp. 337–340 (2008)

23. Ekici, B., et al.: SMTCoq: a plug-in for integrating SMT solvers into COQ. In: Proceedings of the 29th International Conference on Computer Aided Verification, pp. 126–133 (2017)

24. Ernst, G.: Korn - software verification with horn clauses (competition contribution). In: Proceedings of the 29th International Conference on Tools and Algorithms for the Construction and Analysis of Systems, pp. 559–564 (2023)

25. Fontaine, P., Marion, J.Y., Merz, S., Nieto, L.P., Tiu, A.: Expressiveness + automation + soundness: towards combining SMT solvers and interactive proof assistants. In: Proceedings of the 12th International Conference on Tools and Algorithms for the Construction and Analysis of Systems, pp. 167–181 (2006)

26. Gario, M., Micheli, A.: PySMT: a solver-agnostic library for fast prototyping of SMT-based algorithms. In: Proceedings of the 13th International Workshop on Satisfiability Modulo Theories, pp. 1–10 (2015)

27. Grebenshchikov, S., Lopes, N.P., Popeea, C., Rybalchenko, A.: Synthesizing software verifiers from proof rules. In: Proceedings of the 33rd ACM SIGPLAN Conference on Programming Language Design and Implementation, pp. 405–416 (2012)

28. Gurfinkel, A., Bjørner, N.: The science, art, and magic of constrained horn clauses. In: Proceedings of the 21st International Symposium on Symbolic and Numeric Algorithms for Scientific Computing, pp. 6–10 (2019)

29. Gurfinkel, A., Kahsai, T., Komuravelli, A., Navas, J.A.: The SeaHorn verification framework. In: Proceedings of the 27th International Conference on Computer Aided Verification, pp. 343–361 (2015)

30. Heule, M.J.H., Hunt, W.A., Wetzler, N.: Trimming while checking clausal proofs. In: Proceedings of the 13th Conference on Formal Methods in Computer-Aided Design, pp. 181–188 (2013)
31. Heule, M., Hunt, W., Kaufmann, M., Wetzler, N.: Efficient, verified checking of propositional proofs. In: Proceedings of the 8th International Conference on Interactive Theorem Proving, pp. 269–284 (2017)
32. Heule, M.J.H., Hunt, W.A., Wetzler, N.: Verifying refutations with extended resolution. In: Proceedings of the 24th International Conference on Automated Deduction, pp. 345–359 (2013)
33. Hoare, C.A.R.: An axiomatic basis for computer programming. Commun. ACM **12**(10), 576–580 (1969)
34. Hoenicke, J., Schindler, T.: A simple proof format for SMT. In: Proceedings of the 20th International Workshop on Satisfiability Modulo Theories, pp. 54–70 (2022)
35. Hojjat, H., Rümmer, P., Subotic, P., Yi, W.: Horn clauses for communicating timed systems. In: Proceedings of the 1st Workshop on Horn Clauses for Verification and Synthesis, pp. 39–52 (2014)
36. Hojjat, H., Rümmer, P.: The Eldarica Horn solver. In: Proceedings of the 18th Conference on Formal Methods in Computer-Aided Design, pp. 1–7 (2018)
37. Hyvärinen, A.E.J., Marescotti, M., Alt, L., Sharygina, N.: OpenSMT2: an SMT solver for multi-core and cloud computing. In: Proceedings of the 19th International Conference on Theory and Applications of Satisfiability Testing, pp. 547–553 (2016)
38. Kahsai, T., Rümmer, P., Sanchez, H., Schäf, M.: JayHorn: a framework for verifying java programs. In: Proceedings of the 28th International Conference on Computer Aided Verification, pp. 352–358 (2016)
39. Komuravelli, A., Gurfinkel, A., Chaki, S.: SMT-based model checking for recursive programs. Formal Method. Syst. Design **48**(3), 175–205 (2016)
40. Kroening, D., Strichman, O.: Decision Procedures - An Algorithmic Point of View, 2nd edn. Springer, Heidelberg (2016)
41. Kumar, R., Myreen, M.O., Norrish, M., Owens, S.: CakeML: a verified implementation of ML. In: Proceedings of the 41st ACM SIGPLAN-SIGACT Symposium on Principles of Programming Languages, pp. 179–191 (2014)
42. Lammich, P.: Efficient verified (UN)SAT certificate checking. J. Autom. Reason. **64**(3), 513–532 (2020)
43. Matsushita, Y., Tsukada, T., Kobayashi, N.: RustHorn: CHC-based verification for rust programs. ACM Trans. Program. Lang. Syst. **43**(4), 1–54 (2021)
44. de Moura, L., Bjørner, N.: Proofs and refutations, and Z3. In: Proceedings of the 7th International Workshop on the Implementation of Logics, pp. 123–132 (2008)
45. Otoni, R., Blicha, M., Eugster, P., Hyvärinen, A.E.J., Sharygina, N.: Theory-specific proof steps witnessing correctness of SMT executions. In: Proceedings of the 58th ACM/IEEE Design Automation Conference, pp. 541–546 (2021)
46. Otoni, R., Marescotti, M., Alt, L., Eugster, P., Hyvärinen, A., Sharygina, N.: A solicitous approach to smart contract verification. ACM Trans. Privacy Secur. **26**(2), 1–28 (2023)
47. Reeves, J.E., Kiesl-Reiter, B., Heule, M.J.H.: Propositional proof skeletons. In: Proceedings of the 29th International Conference on Tools and Algorithms for the Construction and Analysis of Systems, pp. 329–347 (2023)
48. Rümmer, P., Hojjat, H., Kuncak, V.: On recursion-free Horn causes and Craig interpolation. Formal Method. Syst. Design **47**(1), 1–25 (2015)
49. Sandberg Ericsson, A., Myreen, M.O., Åman Pohjola, J.: A verified generational garbage collector for CakeML. In: Proceedings of the 8th International Conference on Interactive Theorem Proving, pp. 444–461 (2017)

50. Schurr, H.J., Fleury, M., Barbosa, H., Fontaine, P.: Alethe: towards a generic SMT proof format. In: Proceedings of the 7th Workshop on Proof eXchange for Theorem Proving, pp. 49–54 (2021)
51. Sinz, C., Biere, A.: Extended resolution proofs for conjoining BDDs. In: Proceedings of the 1st International Symposium on Computer Science in Russia, pp. 600–611 (2006)
52. Stump, A., Oe, D., Reynolds, A., Hadarean, L., Tinelli, C.: SMT proof checking using a logical framework. Formal Method. Syst. Design $42(1)$, 91–118 (2013)
53. Tange, O.: GNU parallel - the command-line power tool; login. The USENIX Magaz. $36(1)$, 42–47 (2011)
54. Wetzler, N., Heule, M.J.H., Hunt, W.A.: DRAT-trim: efficient checking and trimming using expressive clausal proofs. In: Proceedings of the 17th International Conference on Theory and Applications of Satisfiability Testing, pp. 422–429 (2014)

Verify This: Memcached—A Practical Long-Term Challenge for the Integration of Formal Methods

Gidon Ernst[1]($\boxtimes$) and Alexander Weigl[2]

[1] Ludwig Maximilian University, Munich, Germany
`gidon.ernst@lmu.de`
[2] Karlsruhe Institute of Technology, Karlsruhe, Germany
`weigl@kit.edu`

Abstract. Challenging benchmarks are a major driver for sharpening our tools and theories. This paper introduces the second VerifyThis long-term challenge: The specification and verification of a remote key-value cache, inspired by and acting as compatible drop-in replacement of the `memcached` software package, which is widely used in industry. We identify open gaps in the formal specification and verification of systems. Goal of the challenge is therefore to foster collaboration in order to advance the capabilities of current methods and also to verify a realistic and industrially-relevant software application. This challenge has it all: high-level modeling of communication protocols, intricate algorithms and data structure, code level verification, safety and liveness properties as well as security challenges. It emphasizes the opportunity and need to integrate approaches and tools across the entire spectrum of formal methods.
Website: https://verifythis.github.io/
Mailing List: https://www.lists.kit.edu/sympa/info/verifythis-ltc
Reference System: http://memcached.org/

1 Introduction

Software and systems verification is an established research area that involves many approaches and tools for a variety of types of verification problems across multiple dimensions such as scalability of proof automation, expressiveness of specifications, and degree of abstraction. One point on the spectrum consists of fully automated approaches at a high degree of abstraction, such as model checking of systems with respect to safety and liveness properties [8], with many applications, e.g., embedded system controllers or security protocols. Another point on the spectrum are approaches for code-level static analysis and SMT-based software verification, targeting generic properties like memory safety and termination. A well-known and widely-used benchmark set of C programs is associated with the international competitions of Software Verification (SV-COMP [2])

© The Author(s), under exclusive license to Springer Nature Switzerland AG 2024
P. Herber and A. Wijs (Eds.): iFM 2023, LNCS 14300, pp. 82–89, 2024.
https://doi.org/10.1007/978-3-031-47705-8_5

and Testing (Test-Comp [3]). Tools like those participating at these two competitions are being successfully adopted by industry [6,11]. Deductive verification in comparison can tackle highly complex, application-specific requirements but typically requires a significant human effort to formulate specifications and to give proof hints. State-of-the-art deductive tools are compared and evaluated in competitions such as VerifyThis [12] and VSComp [15,18]. Two famous hallmark verification projects among many impressive efforts are seL4 [19] and CompCert [21].

In this paper, we propose a practical verification challenge that calls for a collaborative long term effort to be solved. The goal is to demonstrate that program verification can produce relevant results for real systems with acceptable effort and to identify insufficient areas in our theories and tools for further research. We aim to bring together researchers for a focused exchange of ideas, techniques, insights, and experiences. The developments will serve to evaluate and improve the effectiveness and maturity of verification tools, with an emphasis on conceptual and technical *integration* of approaches.

Verification Target: As subject of this challenge we suggest to specify and verify memcached, an open-source in-memory key-value cache, respectively to develop feature-compatible replacements of parts or the whole system. This software is a backbone for fast response in cloud-native applications and deployed widely at major companies. The intuitive understanding of memcached, described in detail in Sect. 2, is that of a mapping from keys to values, subject to some specific details of the cache lifecycle. Despite a simple interface, however, possible implementations of a memcached-like system can embrace intricate data structures, algorithms, and other types of complexity to achieve a high performance and memory efficiency. Similarly, going beyond safety and functional correctness to liveness and security aspects connects the perspectives mentioned above— from a high-level systems view via expressive requirements down to the code level. The challenge can therefore be scaled in many dimensions, and while it is *easy to get started*, there is plenty of ground for scientifically and practically meaningful results as well as for collaboration.

Goals of the Challenge: The overarching goals and research directions of this long-term challenge, further elaborated in Sect. 3, are as follows:

- *Verified Software*: Contribute a fully specified and verified software as a drop-in replacement for memcached to demonstrate practical use of formal methods.
- *Improved Methods*: Identify and improve on current difficulties of formal developments, such as writing specifications, automating proofs (including inference of proof hints), and dealing with scale and change.
- *Collaboration & Integration*: Foster opportunities to exchange formal artifacts of varying degrees of abstraction, across different theoretical settings and between tools (a long-standing issue), and integration with unverified code.

Contribution of this Paper: The first contribution of this paper is to map out a behavioral understanding of the system in terms of a functional specification (Sect. 2). The second contribution is to describe the practical and scientific challenges in this case study and how these are tied to unsolved issues and open problems in the area of formal methods, and what the potential impact of solving these could be (Sect. 3).

Call for Participation: We call for contributions to this challenge, which will be coordinated via a mailing list, informal community meetings, and joint publication efforts (cf. Sect. 4).

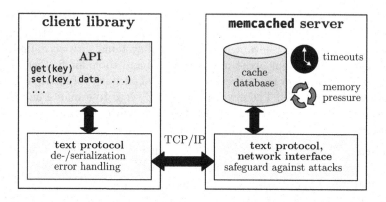

Fig. 1. The architecture of `memcached`

2   System Description

The `memcached` server is an in-memory key-value store that acts as a cache. It offers operations to enter keys into the cache data structure with associated values. In contrast to traditional databases, entries may implicitly be deleted by `memcached`, either when the optional per-entry expiry time is passed, in which case the entry becomes invalid, or in case of memory pressure, in which case `memcached` prefers to evict less-recently accessed entries.

The architecture of the `memcached`, shown in Fig. 1, is a client/server distributed system. The interface between the client and server side is a simple text and line-based protocol over TCP with a small set of commands. These encompass adding key-value pairs, looking up entries by key, and various methods of updating or replacing existing entries. `memcached` also offers a large number of diagnostic commands but these are targeted at interactive use rather than to be processed by an application. Typically, applications use `memcached` via a client library interface, which abstracts this textual interface by a high-level API. Such libraries exist for many mainstream programming languages and some can load-balance internally with respect to multiple `memcached` instances.

Behavioral Model: The state of the server can be represented by a partial map *cache*, mapping keys to entries. Valid *Keys* in `memcached` are sequences of bytes with a length at most 250 bytes, and without control or whitespace characters (extended ASCII range 33–152, as a regular expression /[!-ÿ]{1,250}/).

var *cache*: *Map⟨Key ↦ Entry⟩*   **var** *used-uniques*: *Set⟨ℕ⟩*   **var** *clock*: 𝕋
data *Entry* = (*flags*: ℕ, *expiry*: 𝕋, *unique* : ℕ, *data*: *Value*)

Entries track information associated to the keys, where *Values* are sequences of arbitrary bytes, of length at most 1M in `memcached`. There is a user-supplied set of flags, which is opaque to the server and represented as (the bits of an) unsigned number of 32 bits, and an expiry time for the cache (where 𝕋 is some representation for moments in time), and a version counter that uniquely identifies this entry. This unique number is picked afresh (*unique* ∉ *used-uniques*) with every modification to *entries* for the affected entry, and can therefore be used by clients for a lightweight compare and swap synchronization (operation `cas`). Note, in order to make sense of the *expiry* time-stamps, the model includes a global *clock* that implicitly advances in some appropriate way.

All main system operations of `memcached` can be realized in terms of the abstract state shown above, namely: `get`, `gets`, `gat`, `gats`, `set`, `cas`, `touch`, `delete`, `incr`, `decr`, `prepend`, and `append`. There are many additional operations and features for logging and diagnostics that go beyond the scope of this summary. More information is available in the official documentation [1] the challenge proposal [13], and two prototypical implementations in that style (Python and Java, available through the challenge website).

Text Protocol: The actual interface offered by `memcached` is not in terms of abstract data types but in terms of a protocol between the client and server. Messages are passed as textual information and binary data, corresponding to either *commands* (lowercase), denoting the invocation of an operation, or *responses* (uppercase) encoding the respective return values. An example exchange is shown in Fig. 2, where for a key `year` the value 2023 of length 4 is stored with *flags* = 0 and *expiry* = 0 (no expiry). At the protocol level, expiry times of entries are denoted in seconds, and values smaller or equal to 2592000 (seconds in 30 d) are considered relatively to the current time, otherwise they represent the absolute UNIX timestamp (seconds since 00:00:00 UTC on 1 January 1970). Apart from operation-specific responses, there

```
set year 0 0 4
2023

get year
VALUE year 0 4
2023
END

incr year 1
2024
```

Fig. 2. Example protocol exchange

are two generic ones for client-side errors (e.g. malformed message) and internal server errors.

Implementation Details: `memcached` is written in C. We describe some of the ways it achieves high performance, but emphasize that challenge contributions should investigate their own design. The cache database in Fig. 1 encompasses

---

[1] https://github.com/memcached/memcached/blob/master/doc/.

a dynamically sized hash table which chains keys with the same hash in linked lists. The entries themselves are organized by a SLAB allocator, which partitions them into classes of exponentially increasing sizes.

Entries are removed from the cache data structure in two situations: Explicitly after their expiration time (by a background thread that scans the cache) and implicitly when memory pressure is encountered. memcached can be configured to use one of two eviction strategies, an older one based on intrusive LRU lists, and a newer one that maintains three sets of HOT, WARM, and COLD entries, whereas the latter are candidates for eviction only.

In memcached each client is served by a separate thread, and there is internal concurrency with maintenance threads, too, using an per-item locking scheme. memcached supports SSL to encrypt connections and it has support for basic authentication of clients.

3   Challenge Goals

Verified Software: As a practical goal, this effort aims to contribute a fully specified and verified software as a potential drop-in alternative to memcached. This effort can target the cache server as well as the client library. Solutions to the challenge should aim to be not just abstract behavioral models but executable software packages; albeit we deem it out of scope to actually replace memcached in production—the original system has been developed for 20 years now. As such, we encourage participants to develop specifications that are not just faithful to the reference system but also capture a wide range of potential requirements as well as to take documentation seriously (e.g. for installation and use).

Requirements come in many flavors, not just functional correctness. The abstract model given above, for example, exhibits a non-deterministic behavior with respect to dropping entries from the cache due to absense of a notion of capacity of storage or precedence entries related to their access pattern. Formalizing such requirements at a suitable degree of abstraction suggests specifications that are not typical for traditional deductive tools, such as the (angelic) existence of an execution that *can* return any mapping entered despite the general possibility nondeterministic eviction. Other properties of interest are a global characterization of the cache expiry protocol as LTL or CTL formulas, runtime and space complexity bounds, and resilience against attacks such as denial of service. Therefore, memcached, despite its simple behavioral description, is rich in characteristics of a good benchmark for further substantiating the long-standing ambition of formal methods to be applicable to "real-world" systems.

Improved Methods: Identify and improve on current difficulties of formal developments, such as writing specifications, automating proofs, and dealing with scale and change. An important topic discussed in the VerifyThis community is the question how specification paradigms can be bridged [1]. Looking at the requirements outlined above, memcached offers many opportunities to further develop approaches like [17,23,24], which link code-level deductive verification to global system properties. However, such techniques are yet to be developed to the maturity of those for functional correctness.

Inference of proof hints, including data invariants, loop invariants, procedure summaries, and coupling relations, is necessarily heuristic; we lack good methods and those that exist (e.g. abstract interpretation over numeric domains) are rarely integrated into deductive tools that support expressive logics. We therefore propose to use this challenge as an opportunity to try out how for example recent advances [14,20] can be incorporated into a full system verification. It is similarly still an expert task to debug failed proof attempts. While some tools provide insight into such situations, e.g., with concrete counterexamples, this research goal perhaps needs some more attention by the community. We do have to acknowledge the trade-off that comes with streamlined "push-button" verification technology in contrast to highly interactive proof assistants, whereas the latter typically provide much more insight. A related issue is dealing with changing models, requirements, and code [7,22] and the potential regressions introduced by such changes. Overall, while the research community still struggles to get a hold on automating verification at both scale and expressivity at the same time, this challenge provides grounds for evaluating existing approaches and improving on these.

Collaboration and Integration: Foster opportunities to exchange formal artifacts of varying degrees of abstraction, across different theoretical settings and between tools (a long-standing issue), and integration with unverified code. Following the excellent analysis of [16], we want to emphasize how opportunities for collaboration can be driven by this challenge.

The landscape of approaches to tackle the challenge as outlined in this paper is diverse. As mentioned in the introduction, there are multiple perspectives, high-level model checking, deductive verification, and code-level static and dynamic analysis. It seems that key to integrating their respective strengths and capabilities for a whole system verification is to make explicit the conceptual and technical interfaces between the different worlds: What kind of artifacts and results can be transferred—possibly manually—so that collaboration can be achieved? For example, the SV-COMP community has developed exchange formats for invariants, written as C expressions, which has lead to approaches that compose existing tools in a black-box manner [4]. No such exchange format has been established for deductive tools, despite being a topic for discussions for long-time [10].

A major reason for this lack of lingua franca is that verification methodologies and specification languages are tailored towards certain use cases and problems—it is not straight forward to translate for example a Separation Logic based specification from VerCors [5] into JML [9]. In recent discussions [1], it has become clearer that it is perhaps possible to achieve integration at abstraction boundaries. As an example, the model from Sect. 2 is a representation of behavior that is completely independent of implementation data structures and details, an can insofar easily be communicated regardless of how correspondence down to code or to higher-level requirements is established. Therefore we will attempt to base joint work for this challenge on a primary shared model that is developed by and adhered to by all participants. This will also clarify the technical issues of mapping it between the respective tools and approaches.

4 Participation, Time Schedule, Conclusion

The challenge has been announced officially at ETAPS 2023. A first in-person informal meeting is intended to take place at the iFM in Leiden in 2023 and a second meeting at the ETAPS in April 2024, perhaps complemented by online discussions similar to those for the first challenge. We intend to close the challenge with a track at ISoLA in autumn 2024.

We invite all members of the formal methods community to participate in the memcached challenge. Please register on the VerifyThis LTC Mailing List (see abstract), and announce your participation by sending a short E-Mail.

Acknowledgement. We thank the anonymous reviewers for their feedback.

References

1. Ahrendt, W., Herber, P., Huisman, M., Ulbrich, M.: SpecifyThis - bridging gaps between program specification paradigms. In: ISoLA (1). LNCS, vol. 13701, pp. 3–6. Springer (2022). https://doi.org/10.1007/978-3-031-19849-6_1

2. Beyer, D.: Competition on software verification and witness validation: SV-COMP 2023. In: TACAS (2). LNCS, vol. 13994, pp. 495–522. Springer (2023). https://doi.org/10.1007/978-3-031-30820-8_29

3. Beyer, D.: Software testing: 5th comparative evaluation: Test-Comp 2023. In: FASE. LNCS, vol. 13991, pp. 309–323. Springer (2023). https://doi.org/10.1007/978-3-031-30826-0_17

4. Beyer, D., Wehrheim, H.: Verification artifacts in cooperative verification: survey and unifying component framework. In: Margaria, T., Steffen, B. (eds.) ISoLA 2020. LNCS, vol. 12476, pp. 143–167. Springer, Cham (2020). https://doi.org/10.1007/978-3-030-61362-4_8

5. Blom, S., Darabi, S., Huisman, M., Oortwijn, W.: The VerCors tool set: verification of parallel and concurrent software. In: Polikarpova, N., Schneider, S. (eds.) IFM 2017. LNCS, vol. 10510, pp. 102–110. Springer, Cham (2017). https://doi.org/10.1007/978-3-319-66845-1_7

6. Chong, N., et al.: Code-level model checking in the software development workflow at Amazon Web Services. Softw. Pract. Exp. **51**(4), 772–797 (2021)

7. Chudnov, A., et al.: Continuous formal verification of amazon s2n. In: Chockler, H., Weissenbacher, G. (eds.) CAV 2018. LNCS, vol. 10982, pp. 430–446. Springer, Cham (2018). https://doi.org/10.1007/978-3-319-96142-2_26

8. Clarke, E.M., Grumberg, O., Kroening, D., Peled, D.A., Veith, H.: Model checking, 2nd edn. MIT Press (2018)

9. Cok, D.R.: JML and OpenJML for Java 16. In: Proceedings of the 23rd ACM International Workshop on Formal Techniques for Java-like Programs, pp. 65–67 (2021)

10. Cruanes, S., Hamon, G., Owre, S., Shankar, N.: Tool integration with the evidential tool bus. In: Giacobazzi, R., Berdine, J., Mastroeni, I. (eds.) VMCAI 2013. LNCS, vol. 7737, pp. 275–294. Springer, Heidelberg (2013). https://doi.org/10.1007/978-3-642-35873-9_18

11. Distefano, D., Fähndrich, M., Logozzo, F., O'Hearn, P.W.: Scaling static analyses at Facebook. Commun. ACM **62**(8), 62–70 (2019)

12. Ernst, G., Huisman, M., Mostowski, W., Ulbrich, M.: VerifyThis – verification competition with a human factor. In: Beyer, D., Huisman, M., Kordon, F., Steffen, B. (eds.) TACAS 2019. LNCS, vol. 11429, pp. 176–195. Springer, Cham (2019). https://doi.org/10.1007/978-3-030-17502-3_12

13. Ernst, G., Weigl, A.: VerifyThis Long-term Challenge: Specifying and Verifying a Real-life Remote Key-Value Cache (memcached) (2023). https://verifythis.github.io/03memcached/challenge.pdf

14. Fedyukovich, G., Rümmer, P.: Competition report: CHC-COMP-21. arXiv preprint arXiv:2109.04635 (2021)

15. Filliâtre, J., Paskevich, A., Stump, A.: The 2nd verified software competition: experience report. In: Klebanov, V., Beckert, B., Biere, A., Sutcliffe, G. (eds.) Proceedings of the 1st International Workshop on Comparative Empirical Evaluation of Reasoning Systems, Manchester, United Kingdom, 30 June 2012. CEUR Workshop Proceedings, vol. 873, pp. 36–49. CEUR-WS.org (2012)

16. Hähnle, R., Huisman, M.: Deductive software verification: from pen-and-paper proofs to industrial tools. In: Computing and Software Science: State of the Art and Perspectives, pp. 345–373 (2019)

17. Jacobs, B.: Modular verification of liveness properties of the I/O behavior of imperative programs. In: Margaria, T., Steffen, B. (eds.) ISoLA 2020. LNCS, vol. 12476, pp. 509–524. Springer, Cham (2020). https://doi.org/10.1007/978-3-030-61362-4_29

18. Klebanov, V., et al.: The 1st verified software competition: experience report. In: Butler, M., Schulte, W. (eds.) FM 2011. LNCS, vol. 6664, pp. 154–168. Springer, Heidelberg (2011). https://doi.org/10.1007/978-3-642-21437-0_14

19. Klein, G., et al.: seL4: formal verification of an operating-system kernel. Commun. ACM **53**(6), 107–115 (2010)

20. Koenig, J.R., Padon, O., Shoham, S., Aiken, A.: Inferring invariants with quantifier alternations: taming the search space explosion. In: TACAS 2022. LNCS, vol. 13243, pp. 338–356. Springer, Cham (2022). https://doi.org/10.1007/978-3-030-99524-9_18

21. Leroy, X.: Formal verification of a realistic compiler. Commun. ACM **52**(7), 107–115 (2009)

22. O'Hearn, P.W.: Continuous reasoning: scaling the impact of formal methods. In: Proceedings of the 33rd annual ACM/IEEE Symposium on Logic in Computer Science, pp. 13–25 (2018)

23. Oortwijn, W., Gurov, D., Huisman, M.: An abstraction technique for verifying shared-memory concurrency. Appl. Sci. **10**(11), 3928 (2020)

24. Sprenger, C., et al.: Igloo: soundly linking compositional refinement and separation logic for distributed system verification. In: Proceedings of the ACM on Programming Languages 4(OOPSLA), pp. 1–31 (2020)

Deductive Verification

Towards Formal Verification of a TPM Software Stack

Yani Ziani[1,2] , Nikolai Kosmatov[1]([⊠]) , Frédéric Loulergue[2] ,
Daniel Gracia Pérez[1] , and Téo Bernier[1]

[1] Thales Research & Technology, Palaiseau, France
{yani.ziani,nikolai.kosmatov,daniel.gracia-perez,
teo.bernier}@thalesgroup.com
[2] Univ. Orléans, INSA Centre Val de Loire, LIFO EA 4022, Orléans, France
frederic.loulergue@univ-orleans.fr

Abstract. The Trusted Platform Module (TPM) is a cryptoprocessor designed to protect integrity and security of modern computers. Communications with the TPM go through the TPM Software Stack (TSS), a popular implementation of which is the open-source library *tpm2-tss*. Vulnerabilities in its code could allow attackers to recover sensitive information and take control of the system. This paper describes a case study on formal verification of tpm2-tss using the FRAMA-C verification platform. Heavily based on linked lists and complex data structures, the library code appears to be highly challenging for the verification tool. We present several issues and limitations we faced, illustrate them with examples and present solutions that allowed us to verify functional properties and the absence of runtime errors for a representative subset of functions. We describe verification results and desired tool improvements necessary to achieve a full formal verification of the target code.

1 Introduction

The *Trusted Platform Module* (TPM) [20] has become a key security component in modern computers. The TPM is a cryptoprocessor designed to protect integrity of the architecture and ensure security of encryption keys stored in it. The operating system and applications communicate with the TPM through a set of APIs called *TPM Software Stack* (TSS). A popular implementation of the TSS is the open-source library *tpm2-tss*. It is highly critical: vulnerabilities in its code could allow attackers to recover sensitive information and take control of the system. Hence, it is important to formally verify that the library respects its specification and does not contain runtime errors, often leading to security vulnerabilities, for instance, exploiting buffer overflows or invalid pointer accesses. Formal verification of this library is the main motivation of this work. This target is new and highly ambitious for deductive verification: the library code is very large for a formal verification project (over 120,000 lines of C code). It is also highly complex, heavily based on complex data structures (with multiple levels of nested structures and unions), low-level code, calls to external (e.g. cryptography) libraries, linked lists and dynamic memory allocation.

In this paper we present a first case study on formal verification of tpm2-tss using the FRAMA-C verification platform [15]. We focus on a subset of functions involved in storing an encryption key in the TPM, one of the most critical features of the TSS. We verify both functional properties and the absence of runtime errors. The functions are annotated in the ACSL specification language [2]. Their verification with FRAMA-C currently faces several limitations of the tool, such as its capacity to reason about complex data structures, dynamic memory allocation, linked lists and their separation from other data. We have managed to overcome these limitations after minor simplifications and adaptations of the code. In particular, we replace dynamic allocation with `calloc` by another allocator (attributing preallocated memory cells) that we implement, specify and verify. We adapt a recent work on verification of linked lists [4] to our case study, add new lemmas and prove them in the COQ proof assistant [19]. We identify some deficiencies in the new FRAMA-C–COQ extraction for lists (modified since [4]), adapt it for the proof and suggest improvements. We illustrate all issues and solutions on a simple illustrative example while the (slightly adapted) real-life functions annotated in ACSL and fully proved in FRAMA-C are available online as a companion artifact[1]. Finally, we identify desired extensions and improvements of the verification tool.

Contributions. The contributions of this paper include the following:

- specification and formal verification in FRAMA-C of a representative subset of functions of the tpm2-tss library (slightly adapted for verification);
- presentation of main issues we faced during their verification with an illustrative example, and description of solutions and workarounds we found;
- proof in COQ of all necessary lemmas (including some new ones) related to linked lists, realized for the new version of FRAMA-C–COQ extraction;
- a list of necessary enhancements of FRAMA-C to achieve a complete formal verification of the tpm2-tss library.

Outline. The paper is organized as follows. Section 2 presents FRAMA-C. Section 3 introduces the TPM, its software stack and the tpm2-tss library. Sections 4 and 5 present issues and solutions related, resp., to memory allocation and memory management. Necessary lemmas are discussed in Sect. 6. Section 7 describes our verification results. Finally, Sects. 8 and 9 present related work and a conclusion with necessary tool improvements.

2   FRAMA-C Verification Platform

FRAMA-C [15] is an open-source verification platform for C code, which contains various plugins built around a kernel providing basic services for source-code analysis. It offers ACSL (ANSI/ISO C Specification Language) [2], a formal

---

[1] Available (with the illustrative example, all necessary lemmas and their proofs) on https://doi.org/10.5281/zenodo.8273295.

specification language for C, that allows users to specify functional properties of programs in the form of *annotations*, such as assertions or function contracts. A function contract basically consists of pre- and postconditions (stated, resp., by `requires` and `ensures` clauses) expressing properties that must hold, resp., before and after a call to the function. It also includes an `assigns` clause listing (non-local) variables and memory locations that *can* be modified by the function. While useful built-in predicates and logic functions are provided to handle properties such as pointer validity or memory separation for example, ACSL also supplies the user with different ways to define predicates and logic functions.

FRAMA-C offers WP, a plugin for deductive verification. Given a C program annotated in ACSL, WP generates the corresponding proof obligations (also called verification conditions) that can be proved either by WP or, via the WHY3 platform [13], by SMT solvers or an interactive proof assistant like COQ [19]. To ensure the absence of runtime errors (RTE), WP can automatically add necessary assertions via a dedicated option, and try to prove them as well.

Our choice to use FRAMA-C/WP is due to its capacity to perform deductive verification of industrial C code with successful verification case studies [7] and the fact that it is currently the only tool for C source code verification recognized by ANSSI, the French Common Criteria certification body, as an acceptable formal verification technique for the highest certification levels EAL6–EAL7 [8].

3   The TPM Software Stack and the tpm2-tss Library

This section briefly presents the Trusted Platform Module (TPM), its software stack and the implementation we chose to study: the tpm2-tss library. Readers can refer to the TPM specification [20] and reference books as [1] for more detail.

TPM Software Stack. The TPM is a standard conceived by the Trusted Computing Group (TCG)[2] for a passive secure cryptoprocessor designed to protect secure hardware from software-based threats. At its base, a TPM is implemented as a discrete cryptoprocessor chip, attached to the main processor chip and designed to perform cryptographic operations. However, it can also be implemented as part of the firmware of a regular processor or a software component.

Nowadays, the TPM is well known for its usage in regular PCs to ensure integrity and to provide a secure storage for the keys used to encrypt the disk with *Bitlocker* and *dm-crypt*. However, it can be (and is actually) used to provide other cryptographic services to the Operating System (OS) or applications. For that purpose, the TCG defines the TPM Software Stack (TSS), a set of specifications to provide standard APIs to access the functionalities and commands of the TPM, regardless of the hardware, OS, or environment used.

The TSS APIs provide different levels of complexity, from the Feature API (FAPI) for simple and common cryptographic services to the System API (SAPI) for a one-to-one mapping to the TPM services and commands providing greater flexibility but complexifying its usage. In between lies the Enhanced System API

---

[2] https://trustedcomputinggroup.org/.

(ESAPI) providing SAPI-like functionalities but with slightly limited flexibility. Other TSS APIs complete the previous ones for common operations like data formatting and connection with the software or hardware TPM.

The TSS APIs, as any software component or the TPM itself, can have vulnerabilities[3] that attackers can exploit to recover sensitive data communicated with the TPM or take control of the system. We study the verification of one of the implementations of the TSS, tpm2-tss, starting more precisely with its implementation of the ESAPI.

ESAPI Layer of tpm2-tss. The ESAPI layer provides functions for decryption and encryption, managing session data and policies, thus playing an essential role in the TSS. It is very large (over 50,000 lines of C) and is mainly split into two parts: the API part containing functions in a one-to-one correspondence with TPM commands (for instance, the `Esys_Create` function of the TSS will correspond to—and call—the `TPM2_Create` command of the TPM), and the back-end containing the core of that layer's functionalities. Each API function will call several functions of the back-end to carry out various operations on command parameters, before invoking the lower layers and finally the TPM.

The ESAPI layer relies on a notion of context (`ESYS_CONTEXT`) containing all data the layer needs to store between calls, so it does not need to maintain a global state. Defined for external applications as an opaque structure, the context includes, according to the documentation, data needed to communicate to the TPM, metadata for each TPM resource, and state information. The specification, however, does not impose any precise data structure: it is up to the developer to provide a suitable definition. Our target implementation uses complex data structures and linked lists.

4   Dynamic Memory Allocation

Example Overview. We illustrate our verification case study with a simplified version of some library functions manipulating linked lists. The illustrative example is split into Fig. 1–6 that will be explained below step-by-step. Its full code being available in the companion artifact, we omit in this paper some less significant definitions and assertions which are not mandatory to understand the paper (but we preserve line numbering of the full example for convenience of the reader). This example is heavily simplified to fit the paper, yet it is representative for most issues we faced (except the complexity of data structures). It contains a main list manipulation function, getNode (`esys_GetResourceObject` in the real code), used to search for a resource in the list of resources and return it if it is found, or to create and add it using function createNode (`esys_CreateResourceObject` in the real code) if not.

Figure 1 provides the linked list structure as well as logic definitions used to handle logic lists in specifications. Our custom allocator (used by createNode) is

---

[3] Like CVE-2023-22745 and CVE-2020-24455, documented on www.cve.org.

defined in Fig. 2. Figure 3 defines a (simplified) context and additional logic definitions to handle pointer separation and memory freshness. The search function is shown in Fig. 4 and 5. As it is often done, some ACSL notation (e.g. \forall, integer, ==>, <=, !=) is pretty-printed (resp., as ∀, ℤ, ⇒, ≤, ≠). In this section, we detail Figs. 1, 2 and 3.

```
...
11  typedef struct NODE_T {
12    uint32_t      handle;    // the handle used as reference
13    RESOURCE      rsrc;      // the metadata for this rsrc
14    struct NODE_T * next;    // next node in the list
15  } NODE_T; // linked list of resource

25  /*@
26    predicate ptr_sep_from_list{L}(NODE_T* e, \list<NODE_T*> ll) =
27      ∀ ℤ n; 0 ≤ n < \length(ll) ⇒ \separated(e, \nth(ll, n));
28    predicate dptr_sep_from_list{L}(NODE_T** e, \list<NODE_T*> ll) =
29      ∀ ℤ n; 0 ≤ n < \length(ll) ⇒ \separated(e, \nth(ll, n));
30    predicate in_list{L}(NODE_T* e, \list<NODE_T*> ll) =
31      ∃ ℤ n; 0 ≤ n < \length(ll) ∧ \nth(ll, n) == e;
32    predicate in_list_handle{L}(uint32_t out_handle, \list<NODE_T*> ll) =
33      ∃ ℤ n; 0 ≤ n < \length(ll) ∧ \nth(ll, n)->handle == out_handle;
34    inductive linked_ll{L}(NODE_T *bl, NODE_T *el, \list<NODE_T*> ll) {
35      case linked_ll_nil{L}: ∀ NODE_T *el; linked_ll{L}(el, el, \Nil);
36      case linked_ll_cons{L}: ∀ NODE_T *bl, *el, \list<NODE_T*> tail;
37        (\separated(bl, el) ∧ \valid(bl) ∧ linked_ll{L}(bl->next, el, tail) ∧
38        ptr_sep_from_list(bl, tail)) ⇒
39          linked_ll{L}(bl, el, \Cons(bl, tail));
40    }
41    predicate unchanged_ll{L1, L2}(\list<NODE_T*> ll) =
42      ∀ ℤ n; 0 ≤ n < \length(ll) ⇒
43        \valid{L1}(\nth(ll,n)) ∧ \valid{L2}(\nth(ll,n)) ∧
44        \at((\nth(ll,n))->next, L1) == \at((\nth(ll,n))->next, L2);
...
48    axiomatic Node_To_ll {
49      logic \list<NODE_T*> to_ll{L}(NODE_T* beg, NODE_T* end)
50        reads {node->next | NODE_T* node; \valid(node) ∧
51                            in_list(node, to_ll(beg, end))};
52      axiom to_ll_nil{L}: ∀ NODE_T *node; to_ll{L}(node, node) == \Nil;
53      axiom to_ll_cons{L}: ∀ NODE_T *beg, *end;
54        (\separated(beg, end) ∧ \valid{L}(beg) ∧
55        ptr_sep_from_list{L}(beg, to_ll{L}(beg->next, end))) ⇒
56          to_ll{L}(beg, end) == \Cons(beg, to_ll{L}(beg->next, end));
57    }
58  */
59
60  #include "lemmas_node_t.h"
```

Fig. 1. Linked list and logic definitions.

Lists of Resources. Lines 11–15 of Fig. 1 show a simplified definition of the linked list of resources used in the ESAPI layer of the library. Each node of the list consists of a structure containing a handle used as a reference for this node, a resource to be stored inside, and a pointer to the next element. The handle is supposed to be unique[4]. In our example, a resource structure (omitted in Fig. 1) is assumed to contain only a few fields of relatively simple types. The real

---

[4] This uniqueness is currently not yet specified in the ACSL contracts.

code uses a more extensive and complex definition (with several levels of nested structures and unions), covering all possible types of TPM resources. While it does add some complexity to prove certain properties (as some of them may require to completely unfold all resource substructures), it does not introduce new pointers that may affect memory separation properties, so our example remains representative of the real code regarding linked lists and separation properties.

In particular, we need to ensure that the resource list is well-formed—that is, it is not circular, and does not contain any overlap between nodes—and stays that way throughout the layer. To accomplish that, we use and adapt the logic definitions from [4], given on lines 26–44, 48–57 of Fig. 1. To prove the code, we need to manipulate linked lists and segments of linked lists. Lines 48–57 define the *translating function* to_ll that translates a C list defined by a NODE_T pointer into the corresponding ACSL logic list of (pointers to) its nodes. By convention, the last element end is not included into the resulting logic list. It can be either NULL for a full linked list, or a non-null pointer to a node for a *linked list segment* which stops just before that node. Lines 34–40 show the *linking predicate* linked_ll establishing the equivalence between a C linked list and an ACSL logic list. This inductive definition includes memory separation between nodes, validity of access for each node, as well as the notion of reachability in linked lists. In ACSL, given two pointers p and q, \valid(p) states that *p can be safely read and written, while \separated(p,q) states that the referred memory locations *p and *q do not overlap (i.e. all their bytes are disjoint).

Lines 26–29 provide predicates to handle separation between a list pointer (or double pointer) and a full list. \nth(l,n) and \length(l) denote, resp., the n-th element of logic list l and the length of l. The predicate unchanged_ll in lines 41–44 states that between two labels (i.e. program points) L1 and L2, all list elements in a logic list refer to a valid memory location at both points, and that their respective next fields retain the same value. It is used to maintain the structure of the list throughout the code. Line 60 includes lemmas necessary to conduct the proof, further discussed in Sect. 6.

Lack of Support for Dynamic Memory Allocation. As mentioned above, per the TSS specifications, the ESAPI layer does not maintain a global state between calls to TPM commands. The library code uses contexts with linked lists of TPM resources, so list nodes need to be dynamically allocated at runtime. The ACSL language provides clauses to handle memory allocations: in particular, \allocable{L}(p) states that a pointer p refers to the base address of an unallocated memory block, and \fresh{L1,L2}(p, n) indicates that p refers to the base address of an unallocated block at label L1, and to an allocated memory block of size n at label L2. Unfortunately, while the FRAMA-C/WP memory model[5] is able to handle dynamic allocation (used internally to manage local variables), these clauses are not currently supported. Without allocability and

---

[5] that is, intuitively, the way in which program variables and memory locations are internally represented and manipulated by the tool.

freshness, proving goals involving validity or separation between a newly allocated node and any other pointer is impossible.

Static Memory Allocator. To circumvent that issue, we define in Fig. 2 a bank-based static allocator `calloc_NODE_T` that replaces calls to `calloc` used in the real-life code. It attributes preallocated cells, following some existing implementations (like the memb module of Contiki [17]). Line 63 defines a node bank, that is, a static array of nodes of size `_alloc_max`. Line 64 introduces an allocation index we use to track the next allocable node and to determine whether an allocation is possible. Predicate `valid_rsrc_mem_bank` on line 66 states a validity condition for the bank: `_alloc_idx` must always be between 0 and `_alloc_max`. It is equal to the upper bound if all nodes have been allocated. Predicates lines 67–73 specify separation between a logic list of nodes (resp., a pointer or a double pointer to a node) and the allocable part of the heap, and is used later on to simulate memory freshness.

Lines 76–99 show a part of the function contract for the allocator defined on lines 100–111. The validity of the bank should be true before and after the function execution (lines 77, 79). Line 78 specifies the variables the function is allowed to modify. The contract is specified using several cases (called *behaviors*). Typically, a behavior considers a subset of possible input states (respecting its **assumes** clause) and defines specific postconditions that must be respected for this subset of inputs. In our case, the provided behaviors are complete (i.e. cover all states allowed by the function precondition) and their corresponding subsets are disjoint (line 98). We show only one behavior (lines 89–97) describing a successful allocation (when an allocable node exists, as stated on line 90). Postconditions on lines 92–93 ensure the tracking index is incremented by one, and that the returned pointer points to the first allocable block. While this fact is sufficient to deduce the validity clause on line 94, we keep the latter as well (and it is actually expected for any allocator). In the same way, lines 96–97 specify that the nodes of the bank other than the newly allocated block have not been modified[6].

Currently, FRAMA-C/WP does not offer a memory model able to handle byte-level assignments in C objects. To represent as closely as possible the fact that allocated memory is initialized to zero by a call to `calloc` in the real-life code, we initialize each field of the allocated node to zero (see the C code on lines 104–106 and the postcondition on line 95).

Contexts, Separation Predicates and Freshness. In the target library (and in our illustrative example), pointers to nodes are not passed directly as function arguments, but stored in a context variable, and a pointer to the context is passed as a function argument. Lines 113–116 of Fig. 3 define a simplified context structure, comprised of an **int** and a **NODE_T** pointer to the head of a linked list of resources.

---

[6] This property is partly redundant with the assigns clause on line 78 but its presence facilitates the verification.

```
62  #define _alloc_max 100
63  static NODE_T _rsrc_bank[_alloc_max];   // bank used by the static allocator
64  static int _alloc_idx = 0;   // index of the next rsrc node to be allocated
65  /*@
66    predicate valid_rsrc_mem_bank{L} = 0 ≤ _alloc_idx ≤ _alloc_max;
67    predicate list_sep_from_allocables{L}(\list<NODE_T*> ll) =
68      ∀ int i; _alloc_idx ≤ i < _alloc_max ⇒
69                       ptr_sep_from_list{L}(&_rsrc_bank[i], ll);
70    predicate ptr_sep_from_allocables{L}(NODE_T* node) =
71      ∀ int i; _alloc_idx ≤ i < _alloc_max ⇒ \separated(node, &_rsrc_bank[i]);
72    predicate dptr_sep_from_allocables{L}(NODE_T** p_node) =
73      ∀ int i; _alloc_idx ≤ i < _alloc_max ⇒ \separated(p_node, &_rsrc_bank[i]);
74  */

76  /*@
77    requires valid_rsrc_mem_bank;
78    assigns _alloc_idx, _rsrc_bank[\old(_alloc_idx)];
79    ensures valid_rsrc_mem_bank;

89    behavior allocable:
90      assumes 0 ≤ _alloc_idx < _alloc_max;
91
92      ensures _alloc_idx == \old(_alloc_idx) + 1;
93      ensures \result == &(_rsrc_bank[ _alloc_idx - 1]);
94      ensures \valid(\result);
95      ensures zero_rsrc_node_t( *(\result) );
96      ensures ∀ int i; 0 ≤ i < _alloc_max ∧ i ≠ \old(_alloc_idx) ⇒
97              _rsrc_bank[i] == \old(_rsrc_bank[i]);
98    disjoint behaviors; complete behaviors;
99  */
100 NODE_T *calloc_NODE_T()
101 {
102   static const RESOURCE empty_RESOURCE;
103   if(_alloc_idx < _alloc_max) {
104     _rsrc_bank[_alloc_idx].handle = (uint32_t) 0;
105     _rsrc_bank[_alloc_idx].rsrc = empty_RESOURCE;
106     _rsrc_bank[_alloc_idx].next = NULL;
107     _alloc_idx += 1;
108     return &_rsrc_bank[_alloc_idx - 1];
109   }
110   return NULL;
111 }
```

Fig. 2. Allocation bank and static allocator.

Additional predicates to handle memory separation and memory freshness are defined on lines 118–132. In particular, the `ctx_sep_from_list` predicate on lines 118–119 specifies memory separation between a CONTEXT pointer and a logic list of nodes. Lines 120–121 define separation between such a pointer and allocables nodes in the bank.

In C, a successful dynamic allocation of a memory block implies its *freshness*, that is, the separation between the newly allocated block (typically located on the heap) and all pre-existing memory locations (on the heap, stack or static storages). As this notion of freshness is currently not supported by FRAMA-C/WP, we have to simulate it in another way. Our allocator returns a cell in a static array, so other global variables—as well as local variables declared within the scope of a function—will be separated from the node bank. To obtain a complete freshness within the scope of a function, we need to maintain separation between the allocable part of the bank and other memory locations accessible

```
113 typedef struct CONTEXT {
114   int placeholder_int;
115   NODE_T *rsrc_list;
116 } CONTEXT;
117 /*@
118   predicate ctx_sep_from_list(CONTEXT *ctx, \list<NODE_T*> ll) =
119     ∀ ℤ i; 0 ≤ i < \length(ll) ⇒ \separated(\nth(ll, i), ctx);
120   predicate ctx_sep_from_allocables(CONTEXT *ctx) =
121     ∀ int i; _alloc_idx ≤ i < _alloc_max ⇒ \separated(ctx, &_rsrc_bank[i]);
122
123   predicate freshness(CONTEXT * ctx, NODE_T ** node) =
124     ctx_sep_from_allocables(ctx)
125     ∧ list_sep_from_allocables(to_ll(ctx->rsrc_list, NULL))
126     ∧ ptr_sep_from_allocables(ctx->rsrc_list)
127     ∧ ptr_sep_from_allocables(*node)
128     ∧ dptr_sep_from_allocables(node);
129
130   predicate sep_from_list{L}(CONTEXT * ctx, NODE_T ** node) =
131     ctx_sep_from_list(ctx, to_ll{L}(ctx->rsrc_list, NULL))
132     ∧ dptr_sep_from_list(node, to_ll{L}(ctx->rsrc_list, NULL));
133 */
```

Fig. 3. Context and predicates to handle separation from a list and memory freshness.

through pointers. In our illustrative example, pointers come from arguments including a pointer to a CONTEXT object (and pointers accessible from it) and a double pointer to a NODE_T node. This allows us to define a predicate to handle freshness in both function contracts.

The **freshness** predicate on lines 123–128 of Fig. 3 specifies memory separation between known pointers within the scope of our functions and the allocable part of the bank, using separation predicates previously defined on lines 120–121, and on lines 67–73 of Fig. 2. This predicate will become unnecessary as soon as dynamic allocation is fully supported by FRAMA-C/WP.

In the meanwhile, a static allocator with an additional separation predicate simulating freshness provides a reasonable solution to verify the target library. Since no specific constraint is assumed in our contracts on the position of previously allocated list nodes already added to the list, the verification uses a specific position in the bank only for the newly allocated node. The fact that the newly allocated node does not become valid during the allocation (technically, being part of the bank, it was valid in the sense of ACSL already before) is compensated in our contracts by the freshness predicate stating that the new node— as one the allocable nodes—was not used in the list before the allocation (cf. line 310 in Fig. 4). We expect that the migration from our specific allocator to a real-life dynamic allocator—with a more general contract—will be very easy to perform, as soon as necessary features are supported by FRAMA-C.

Similarly, the **sep_from_list** predicate on lines 130–132 specifies separation between the context's linked list and known pointers, using predicates on lines 118–119, and on lines 28–29 of Fig. 1.

5   Memory Management

This section presents how we use the definitions introduced in Sect. 4 to prove selected ESAPI functions involving linked lists. We also identify separation issues related to limitations of the Typed memory model of WP, as well as a way to manage memory to overcome such issues. In this section, we detail Fig. 4–6.

The Search Function. Figure 4 provides the search operation getNode with a partial contract illustrating functional and memory safety properties we aim to verify and judge necessary for the proof at a larger scale. Some proof-guiding annotations (assertions, loop contracts) have been skipped for readability, but the code is preserved (mostly with the same line numbers). The arguments include a context, a handle to search and a double pointer for the returned node.

Lines 380–416 perform the search of a node by its handle: variable temp_node iterates over the nodes of the resource list, and the node is returned if its handle is equal to the searched one (in which case, the function returns 616 for success).

Lines 420–430 convert the resource handle to a TPM one, call the creation function to allocate a new node and add it to the list as its new head with the given handle if the allocation was successful (and return 833 if not). The new node is returned by createNode in temp_node_2 (again via a double pointer).

Lines 435–462 perform some modifications on the content of the newly allocated node, without affecting the structure of the list. An error code is returned in case of a failure, and 1611 (with the allocated node in *node) otherwise. Lines 450–451, 453–454 and 461 provide some assertions to propagate information to the last return clause of the function, attained in case of the successful addition of the new element to the list.

Compared to the real-life code, we have introduced anonymous blocks on lines 380–416 and 422–452 (which are not semantically necessary and were not present in the original code), as well as two local variables tmp_node and tmp_node2 instead of only one. We explain these code adaptations below.

Contract of the Search Function. Lines 309–375 of Fig. 4 provide a partial function contract, illustrating two behaviors of getNode: if the element was found by its handle in the list (cf. lines 325–326), and if the element was not found at first, but was then successfully allocated and added (cf. lines 355–359), for each of them specific postconditions are stated. For instance, for the latter behavior, lines 369–370 ensure that if a new node was successfully allocated and added to the list, the old head becomes the second element of the list, while line 372 ensures the separation of known pointers from the new list. We specify that the complete list of provided behaviors must be complete and disjoint (line 374).

As global preconditions, we notably require for the list to be well-formed (through the use of the linking predicate, cf. line 313), and the validity of our bank and freshness of allocable nodes with respect to function arguments and global variables (cf. line 310). Line 317 requires memory separation of known

```
309  /*@
310    requires valid_rsrc_mem_bank{Pre} ∧ freshness(ctx, node);
313    requires linked_ll(ctx->rsrc_list, NULL, to_ll(ctx->rsrc_list, NULL));
317    requires sep_from_list(ctx, node) ∧ \separated(node, ctx);
     ...
321    ensures valid_rsrc_mem_bank ∧ freshness(ctx, node);
     ...
325    behavior handle_in_list:
326      assumes in_list_handle(rsrc_handle, to_ll(ctx->rsrc_list, NULL));
     ...
332      ensures unchanged_ll{Pre, Post}(to_ll(ctx->rsrc_list, NULL));
333      ensures \result == 616;
     ...
355    behavior handle_not_in_list_and_node_allocated:
356      assumes !(in_list_handle(rsrc_handle, to_ll(ctx->rsrc_list, NULL)));
357      assumes rsrc_handle ≤ 31U ∨ (rsrc_handle \in {0x10AU, 0x10BU})
358              ∨ (0x120U ≤ rsrc_handle ≤ 0x12FU);
359      assumes 0 ≤ _alloc_idx < _alloc_max;
     ...
369      ensures \old(ctx->rsrc_list) ≠ NULL ⇒
370              \nth(to_ll(ctx->rsrc_list, NULL), 1) == \old(ctx->rsrc_list);
371      ensures linked_ll(ctx->rsrc_list, NULL, to_ll(ctx->rsrc_list, NULL));
372      ensures sep_from_list(ctx, node);
373      ensures \result == 1611;
374    disjoint behaviors; complete behaviors;
375  */
376  int getNode(PSEUDO_CONTEXT *ctx, uint32_t rsrc_handle, NODE_T ** node) {
377    /*@ assert linked_ll(ctx->rsrc_list, NULL, to_ll(ctx->rsrc_list, NULL));*/
378    int r;
379    uint32_t tpm_handle;
380    { /* Block added to circumvent issues with the WP memory model */
381      NODE_T *tmp_node;
401      for (tmp_node = ctx->rsrc_list; tmp_node ≠ NULL;
402           tmp_node = tmp_node->next) {
405        if (tmp_node->handle == rsrc_handle){*node = tmp_node; return 616;}
415      }
416    }
420    r = iesys_handle_to_tpm_handle(rsrc_handle, &tpm_handle);
422    { /* Block added to circumvent issues with the WP memory model */
423      NODE_T *tmp_node_2 = NULL;
428      r = createNode(ctx, rsrc_handle, &tmp_node_2);
429      /*@ assert sep_from_list(ctx, node);*/
430      if (r == 833) {return r;};
435      tmp_node_2->rsrc.handle = tpm_handle;
436      tmp_node_2->rsrc.rsrcType = 0;
437      size_t offset = 0;
440      r = uint32_Marshal(tpm_handle, &tmp_node_2->rsrc.name.name[0],
441                          sizeof(tmp_node_2->rsrc.name.name),&offset);
443      if (r ≠0) {return r;};
444      tmp_node_2->rsrc.name.size = offset;
449      *node = tmp_node_2;
450      /*@ assert unchanged_ll{Pre, Here}(
451              to_ll{Pre}(\at(ctx->rsrc_list, Pre), NULL));*/
452    }
453    /*@ assert unchanged_ll{Pre, Here}(
454            to_ll{Pre}(\at(ctx->rsrc_list, Pre), NULL));*/
461    /*@ assert sep_from_list(ctx, node);*/
462    return 1611;
463  }
```

Fig. 4. The (slightly rewritten) search function, where some annotations are removed.

pointers from the list of resources using the `sep_from_list` predicate, and separation among known pointers using the `\separated` predicate.

As a global postcondition, we require that our bank stays valid, and that freshness of the (remaining) allocable nodes relatively to function arguments and global variables is maintained (cf. line 321). However, properties regarding the list itself—such as the preservation of the list when it is not modified (line 332), or ensuring it remains well-formed after being modified (line 371)—have to be issued to ACSL behaviors to be proved, due to the way how local variables are handled in the memory model of WP. The logic list properties are much more difficult for solvers to manipulate in global behaviors.

Memory Model Limitation: An Uprovable Property. Consider the assertion on line 377 of Fig. 4. Despite the presence of the same property as a precondition of the function (line 313), currently this assertion cannot be proved by WP at the entry point for the real-life version of the function. Basically, the real-life version can be obtained[7] from Fig. 4 by removing the curly braces on lines 380, 416, 422, 452. This issue is due to a limitation of the WP memory model.

Indeed, for such an assertion (as in general for any annotation to be proved), WP generates a proof obligation, to be proved by either WP itself or by external provers via the WHY3 platform [13]. Such an obligation includes a representation of the current state of the program memory. In particular, pointers such as the resource list `ctx->rsrc_list` (and by extension, any reachable node of the list) will be considered part of the heap. To handle the existence of a variable in memory—should it be the heap, the stack or the static segments—WP uses an allocation table to express when memory blocks are used or freed, which is where the issue lies. For instance, on line 428 of Fig. 4, the `temp_node_2` pointer has its address taken, and is considered as used locally due to `requires` involving it in our function contract for `createNode`. It is consequently transferred to the memory model, where it has to be allocated.

Currently, the memory model of WP does not provide separated allocation tables for the heap, stack and static segments. Using `temp_node_2` the way it is used on line 428 changes the modification status of the allocation table, which is then considered as modified as a whole. This affects the status of other "allocated" (relatively to the memory model) variables as well, including (but not limited to) any reachable node of the list.

Therefore, the call to `createNode` line 428 of Fig. 4 in the real-life code that uses the address of a local pointer as a third argument is sufficient to affect the status of the resource list on the scale of the entire function. As a result, the assertion on line 377 is not proved.

A Workaround. As a workaround (found thanks to an indication of the WP team) to the aforementioned issue, we use additional blocks and variable declarations. Figure 5 presents those minor rewrites (with line numbers in alphabetical

---

[7] another difference—removing variable `tmp_node2` declared on line 423 and using `tmp_node` instead—can be ignored in this context.

style to avoid confusion with the illustrative example). The left side illustrates the structure of the original C code, where the address of `tmp_node` is taken and used in the `createNode` call on line j, and the same pointer is used to iterate on the list. On the right, we add additional blocks and a new pointer `temp_node_2`, initialized to NULL to match the previous iteration over the list. Each block defines a new scope, outside of which the pointer used by `createNode` will not exist and side-effect-prone allocations will not happen. It solves the issue.

```
a int getNode(..., NODE_T ** node){        a int getNode(..., NODE_T ** node){
b   // list properties unprovable          b   // list properties proved
c   int r;                                 c   int r;
d                                          d   {
e   NODE_T *tmp_node;                       e       NODE_T *tmp_node;
f   ... // iterate over the list            f       ... // iterate over the list
g                                          g   }
h                                          h   {
i                                          i       NODE_T *tmp_node_2 = NULL;
j   r = createNode(..., &tmp_node);         j       r = createNode(..., &tmp_node_2);
k   ...                                    k       ...
l   *node = tmp_node;                       l       *node = tmp_node_2;
m                                          m   }
n   return 1611;                            n   return 1611;
o }                                        o }
```

Fig. 5. Comparison of the real-life code of `getNode` (on the left) and its rewriting with additional blocks (on the right) for proving list properties.

Additional Proof-Guiding Annotations. Additional annotations (mostly omitted in Fig. 4) include, as usual, loop contracts and a few assertions. Assertions can help the tool to establish necessary intermediate properties or activate the application of relevant lemmas. For instance, assertions of lines 450–451 and 453–454 help propagate information over the structure of the linked list (by its logic list representation) outside of each block, and finally to postconditions. Assertions on lines 429 and 461 help propagate separations from the list through the function and its anonymous blocks. Some other intermediate assertions are needed to prove the unchanged nature of the list. Such additional assertions can be tricky to find in some cases and need some experience.

Handling Pointer Casts. Another memory manipulation issue we have encountered comes from the function call on line 440 in `getNode`: after having been added to the resource list, the newly allocated node must have its name (or more precisely, the name of its resource) set from its TPM handle `tpm_handle` (derived from the handle of the node by the function call on line 420). This is done through marshaling using the `uint32_Marshal` function, partially shown on lines 298–306 of Fig. 6, whose role is to store a 4-byte unsigned int (in this case, our TPM handle) in a flexible array of bytes (the name of the resource). The function calls `memcpy` on (commented) line 302, which is the source of our issue (a correct endianness being ensured by a previous byte swap in `in`).

```
271  /*@
272    requires \valid(src) ∧ \valid(dest + (0 .. sizeof(*src)-1));
       ⋯
279  */
280  void memcpy_custom(uint8_t *dest, uint32_t *src) {
281    dest[3] = (uint8_t)(*src & 0xFF);
282    dest[2] = (uint8_t)((*src >> 8) & 0xFF);
283    dest[1] = (uint8_t)((*src >> 16) & 0xFF);
284    dest[0] = (uint8_t)((*src >> 24) & 0xFF);
285  }
       ⋯
298  int uint32_Marshal(uint32_t in,uint8_t buff[],size_t buff_size,size_t *offset){
299    size_t  local_offset = 0;
       ⋯
302    // memcpy(&buff[local_offset], &in, sizeof (in));
303    memcpy_custom(&buff[local_offset], &in);
       ⋯
306  }
```

Fig. 6. Definition for `memcpy` replacement in marshal.

For most functions of the standard libraries, FRAMA-C provides basic ACSL contracts to handle their use. However, for memory manipulation functions like `memcpy`, such contracts rely on pointer casts, whose support in WP is currently limited. To circumvent this issue, we define our own memory copy function on lines 280–285: instead of directly copying the 4-byte unsigned int pointed by `src` byte per byte using pointer casts using `memcpy`, we extract one-byte chunks using byte shifts and bitmasks (cf. lines 281–284, 303) without casts. Line 272 requires that both source and destination locations are valid, also without casts. This version is fully handled by WP. Current contracts are sufficient for the currently considered functional properties and the absence of runtime errors (and we expect they will be easy to extend for more precise properties if needed).

6 Lemmas

When SMT solvers become inefficient (e.g. for inductive definitions), it can be necessary to add lemmas to facilitate the proof. These lemmas can then be directly instantiated by solvers, but proving them often requires to reason by induction, with an interactive proof assistant.

The previous work using logic lists [4] defined and proved several lemmas using the COQ proof assistant. We have added two new useful lemmas (defined in Fig. 7) and used twelve of the previous ones to verify both the illustrative example and the subset of real-life functions. However, because the formalization of the memory models and various aspects of ACSL changed between the version of FRAMA-C used in the previous work and the one we use, we could not reuse the proofs of these lemmas. While older FRAMA-C versions directly generated COQ specifications, more recent FRAMA-C versions let WHY3 generate them. Even if the new translation is close to the previous one, the way logic lists are handled was modified significantly.

In the past, FRAMA-C logic lists were translated into the lists COQ offers in its standard library: an inductively defined type as usually found in functional

```
lemma in_next_not_bound_in{L}: ∀ NODE_T *bl, *el, *item, \list<NODE_T*> ll;
  linked_ll(bl, el, ll) ⇒ in_list(item, ll) ⇒ item->next ≠ el ⇒
    in_list(item->next, ll);
lemma linked_ll_split_variant{L}:
  ∀ NODE_T *bl, *bound, *el, \list<NODE_T*> l1, l2;
  linked_ll(bl, el, l1 ^ l2) ⇒ l2 ≠ \Nil ⇒
  bound == \nth(l1 ^ l2, \length(l1 ^ l2) - \length(l2)) ⇒
    linked_ll(bl, bound, l1) ∧ linked_ll(bound, el, l2);
```

Fig. 7. New lemmas proved in our verification work (in addition to those in [4]).

programming languages such as OCaml and Haskell. Such types come with an induction principle that allows to reason by induction. Without reasoning inductively, it also offers the possibility to reason by case on lists: a list is defined either as empty, or as built with the cons constructor. In recent versions of FRAMA-C, ACSL logic lists are axiomatized as follows: two functions nil and cons are declared, as well as a few other functions on lists, including the length of a list (length), the concatenation of two lists (concat), and getting an element from a list given its position (nth). However, there is no induction principle to reason by induction on lists, and because nil and cons are not constructors, it is not possible to reason by case on lists in this formalization. It is possible to test if a list is empty, but if not, we do not know that it is built with cons. Writing new recursive functions on such lists is also very difficult. Indeed, we only have nth to observe a list, while the usual way to program functions on lists uses the head and the tail of a list for writing the recursive case.

Interestingly, when the hypotheses of our lemmas include a fact expressed using linked_ll, it is still possible to reason by case, because this inductive predicate is translated into COQ as an inductive predicate. Consequently, there are only two possible cases for the logic list: either it is empty, or it is built with constail. When such a hypothesis is missing, we axiomatized a tail function, and a decomposition principle stating that a list is either nil or cons. These axioms are quite classic and can be implemented using a list type defined by induction. We did not need an inductive principle on logic lists as either the lemmas did not require a proof by induction, or we reasoned inductively on the inductive predicate linked_ll. However, we proved such an induction principle using only the axioms we added. It is thus available to prove some other lemmas provided in [4]—not needed yet in our current work—that were proved by induction on lists.

Because of these changes, to prove all lemmas we need, we had to adapt all previous proof scripts, and in a few cases significantly. The largest proof scripts are about 100 lines long excluding our axioms, and the shortest takes a dozen lines. We suggest that the next versions of FRAMA-C come back to a concrete representation of lists. Thanks to our approach, we expect that the required changes in our proofs of lemmas will remain minimal: we will only have to prove the axioms introduced on tail and our decomposition principle.

7   Verification Results

Proof results, presented in Fig. 8, were obtained by running FRAMA-C 26.1 (Iron) on a desktop computer running Ubuntu 20.04.4 LTS, with an Intel(R) Core(TM) i5-6600 CPU @ 3.30 GHz, featuring 4 cores and 4 threads, with 16 GB RAM. We ran FRAMA-C with options `-wp-par 3` and `-wp-timeout 30`. We used the Alt-Ergo v2.4.3 and CVC4 v1.8 solvers, via WHY3 v1.5.1. Both functional properties and the absence of runtime errors (RTE) were proved. Assertions to ensure the absence of runtime errors are automatically generated by the RTE plugin of FRAMA-C (using the `-wp-rte` option). Functional properties include usual properties such as the fact that the well-formedness of the list is preserved, that a new resource has been successfully added to the resource list, that the searched element is correctly found if present, etc.

Code subset	Prover	User-provided ACSL #Goals	RTE #Goals	Total #Goals	Time
Illustrative example	Qed	105	18	123 (43.62%)	
	Script	1	0	1 (0.35%)	
	SMT	137	21	158 (56.03%)	
	All	243 (86.17%)	39 (13.83%)	**282**	**5m13s**
Library code subset	Qed	274	38	312 (47.34%)	
	Script	5	0	5 (0.76%)	
	SMT	311	31	342 (51.90%)	
	All	590 (89.53%)	69 (10.47%)	**659**	**18m07s**

Fig. 8. Proof results for the illustrative example and the real-life code.

In our illustrative example, 282 goals were proved in a total time of 5min13s with 56% proved by SMT solvers, and the rest by the internal simplifier engine Qed of WP and one WP script. The maximum time to prove a goal was 20 s.

Solutions to memory manipulation problems presented in this paper were used on a larger verification study over 10 different functions of the target library (excluding macro functions, and interfaces without code whose behaviors needed to be modeled in ACSL), related to linked-list manipulations and some internal ESAPI feasibility checks and operations (cryptographic operations excluded). Over 659 goals proved in a total of 18 m 07 s, 52% were proved by SMT solvers and 47% by Qed. Only 5 WP proof scripts were used, when automatic proof either failed or was too slow. This shows a high level of automation achieved in our project, in particular, thanks to carefully chosen predicates and lemmas (which are usually tricky to find for the first time and can be useful in other similar projects). The maximum time to prove a goal was 1 min 50 s.

We also used smoke-tests to detect unexpected dead code or possible inconsistencies in the specification, and manually checked that no unexpected cases of those were detected.

As for the 14 lemmas we used, 11 are proved by COQ using our scripts, and the remaining 3 directly by Alt-Ergo. Their proof takes 6 s in our configuration, with the maximum time to prove a goal being 650 ms.

8   Related Work

TPM Related Safety and Security. Various case studies centered around TPM uses have emerged over the last decade, often focusing on use cases relying on functionalities of the TPM itself. A recent formal analysis of the key exchange primitive of TPM 2.0 [22] provides a security model to capture TPM protections on keys and protocols. Authors of [21] propose a security model for the cryptographic support commands in TPM 2.0, proved using the CryptoVerif tool. A model of TPM commands was used to formalize the session-based HMAC authorization and encryption mechanisms [18]. Such works focus on the TPM itself, but to the best of our knowledge, none of the previously published works aim at verifying the tpm2-tss library or any implementation of the TSS.

Linked Lists and Recursive Data Structures. We use logical definitions from [4] to formalize and manipulate C linked lists as ACSL logic lists in our effort, while another approach [3] relies on a parallel view of a linked list via a companion ghost array. Both approaches were tested on the linked list module of the Contiki OS [12], which relies on static allocations and simple structures. In this work we used a logic list based approach rather than a ghost code based approach following the conclusions in [4]. Realized in SPARK, a deductive verification tool for a subset of the Ada language and also the name of this subset, the approach to the verification of black-red trees [11] is related to the verification of linked lists in FRAMA-C using ghost arrays including the auto-verification aspects [5]. However, the trees themselves were implemented using arrays as pointers have only been recently introduced in SPARK [10]. Programs with pointers in SPARK are based on an ownership policy enforcing non-aliasing which makes their verification closer to Rust programs than C programs.

Formal Verification for Real-Life Code. Deductive verification on real-life code has been spreading in the last decades, with various verification case studies where bugs were often found by annotating and verifying the code [14]. Such studies include [9], providing feedback on the authors' experience of using ACSL and FRAMA-C on a real-world example. Authors of [7] managed a large scale formal verification of global security properties on the C code of the JavaCard Virtual Machine. SPARK was used in the verification of a TCP Stack [6]. Authors of [16] highlight some issues specific to the verification of the Hyper-V hypervisor, and how they can be solved with VCC, a deductive verification tool for C.

9   Conclusion and Future Work

This paper presents a first case study on formal verification of the tpm2-tss library, a popular implementation of the TPM Software Stack. Making the bridge between the TPM and applications, this library is highly critical: to take advantage of security guarantees of the TPM, its deductive verification is highly desired. The library code is very complex and challenging for verification tools.

We have presented our verification results for a subset of 10 functions of the ESAPI layer of the library that we verified with FRAMA-C. We have described current limitations of the verification tool and temporary solutions we used to address them. We have proved all necessary lemmas (extending those of a previous case study for linked lists [4]) in COQ using the most recent version of the FRAMA-C–COQ translation and identified some necessary improvements in handling logic lists. Finally, we identified desired tool improvements to achieve a full formal verification of the library: support of dynamic allocations and basic ACSL clauses to handle them, a memory model that works at byte level, and clearer separation of modification statuses of variables between the heap, the stack, and static segments. The real-life code was slightly simplified for verification, but the logical behavior was preserved in the verified version. While the current real-life code cannot be verified without adaptations, we expect that it will become provable as soon as those improvements of the tool are implemented[8].

This work opens the way towards a full verification of the tpm2-tss library. Future work includes the verification of a larger subset of functions, including lower-level layers and operations. Specification and verification of specific security properties is another future work direction. Maintaining proofs for changing versions of tools and axiomatizations is also an interesting research direction. Finally, combining formally verified modules with modules which undergo a partial verification (e.g. limited to the absence of runtime errors, or runtime assertion checking of expected specifications on large test suites) can be another promising work direction to increase confidence in the security of the library.

Acknowledgment. Part of this work was supported by ANR (grants ANR-22-CE39-0014, ANR-22-CE25-0018) and French Ministry of Defense via a PhD grant of Yani Ziani. We thank Allan Blanchard, Laurent Corbin and Loïc Correnson for useful discussions, and the anonymous referees for helpful comments.

References

1. Arthur, W., Challener, D.: A Practical Guide to TPM 2.0: Using the Trusted Platform Module in the New Age of Security, 1st edn. Apress, Berkeley (2015)
2. Baudin, P., et al.: ACSL: ANSI/ISO C Specification Language. https://frama-c.com/acsl.html
3. Blanchard, A., Kosmatov, N., Loulergue, F.: Ghosts for lists: a critical module of Contiki verified in Frama-C. In: Dutle, A., Muñoz, C., Narkawicz, A. (eds.) NFM 2018. LNCS, vol. 10811, pp. 37–53. Springer, Cham (2018). https://doi.org/10.1007/978-3-319-77935-5_3
4. Blanchard, A., Kosmatov, N., Loulergue, F.: Logic against ghosts: comparison of two proof approaches for a list module. In: Proceedings of the 34th Annual ACM/SIGAPP Symposium on Applied Computing, Software Verification and Testing Track (SAC-SVT 2019), pp. 2186–2195. ACM (2019)

---

[8] Detailed discussions of limitations and ongoing extensions of FRAMA-C can be found at https://git.frama-c.com/pub/frama-c/.

5. Blanchard, A., Loulergue, F., Kosmatov, N.: Towards full proof automation in Frama-C using auto-active verification. In: Badger, J.M., Rozier, K.Y. (eds.) NFM 2019. LNCS, vol. 11460, pp. 88–105. Springer, Cham (2019). https://doi.org/10.1007/978-3-030-20652-9_6

6. Cluzel, G., Georgiou, K., Moy, Y., Zeller, C.: Layered formal verification of a TCP stack. In: Proceedings of the IEEE Secure Development Conference (SecDev 2021), pp. 86–93. IEEE (2021)

7. Djoudi, A., Hána, M., Kosmatov, N.: Formal verification of a JavaCard virtual machine with Frama-C. In: Huisman, M., Păsăreanu, C., Zhan, N. (eds.) FM 2021. LNCS, vol. 13047, pp. 427–444. Springer, Cham (2021). https://doi.org/10.1007/978-3-030-90870-6_23

8. Djoudi, A., et al.: A bottom-up formal verification approach for common criteria certification: application to JavaCard virtual machine. In: Proceedings of the 11th European Congress on Embedded Real-Time Systems (ERTS 2022), June 2022

9. Dordowsky, F.: An experimental study using ACSL and Frama-C to formulate and verify low-level requirements from a DO-178C compliant avionics project. Electron. Proc. Theor. Comput. Sci. **187**, 28–41 (2015)

10. Dross, C., Kanig, J.: Recursive data structures in SPARK. In: Lahiri, S.K., Wang, C. (eds.) CAV 2020. LNCS, vol. 12225, pp. 178–189. Springer, Cham (2020). https://doi.org/10.1007/978-3-030-53291-8_11

11. Dross, C., Moy, Y.: Auto-active proof of red-black trees in SPARK. In: Barrett, C., Davies, M., Kahsai, T. (eds.) NFM 2017. LNCS, vol. 10227, pp. 68–83. Springer, Cham (2017). https://doi.org/10.1007/978-3-319-57288-8_5

12. Dunkels, A., Grönvall, B., Voigt, T.: Contiki - a lightweight and flexible operating system for tiny networked sensors. In: Proceedings of the 29th Annual IEEE Conference on Local Computer Networks (LCN 2004), pp. 455–462. IEEE Computer Society (2004)

13. Filliâtre, J.-C., Paskevich, A.: Why3—where programs meet provers. In: Felleisen, M., Gardner, P. (eds.) ESOP 2013. LNCS, vol. 7792, pp. 125–128. Springer, Heidelberg (2013). https://doi.org/10.1007/978-3-642-37036-6_8

14. Hähnle, R., Huisman, M.: Deductive software verification: from pen-and-paper proofs to industrial tools. In: Steffen, B., Woeginger, G. (eds.) Computing and Software Science. LNCS, vol. 10000, pp. 345–373. Springer, Cham (2019). https://doi.org/10.1007/978-3-319-91908-9_18

15. Kirchner, F., Kosmatov, N., Prevosto, V., Signoles, J., Yakobowski, B.: Frama-C: a software analysis perspective. Formal Asp. Comput. **27**(3), 573–609 (2015)

16. Leinenbach, D., Santen, T.: Verifying the Microsoft Hyper-V hypervisor with VCC. In: Cavalcanti, A., Dams, D.R. (eds.) FM 2009. LNCS, vol. 5850, pp. 806–809. Springer, Heidelberg (2009). https://doi.org/10.1007/978-3-642-05089-3_51

17. Mangano, F., Duquennoy, S., Kosmatov, N.: Formal verification of a memory allocation module of Contiki with FRAMA-C: a case study. In: Cuppens, F., Cuppens, N., Lanet, J.-L., Legay, A. (eds.) CRiSIS 2016. LNCS, vol. 10158, pp. 114–120. Springer, Cham (2017). https://doi.org/10.1007/978-3-319-54876-0_9

18. Shao, J., Qin, Y., Feng, D.: Formal analysis of HMAC authorisation in the TPM2.0 specification. IET Inf. Secur. **12**(2), 133–140 (2018)

19. The Coq Development Team: The Coq proof assistant. https://coq.inria.fr

20. Trusted Computing Group: Trusted Platform Module Library Specification, Family "2.0", Level 00, Revision 01.59, November 2019. https://trustedcomputinggroup.org/work-groups/trusted-platform-module/. Accessed May 2023

21. Wang, W., Qin, Yu., Yang, B., Zhang, Y., Feng, D.: Automated security proof of cryptographic support commands in TPM 2.0. In: Lam, K.-Y., Chi, C.-H., Qing, S. (eds.) ICICS 2016. LNCS, vol. 9977, pp. 431–441. Springer, Cham (2016). https://doi.org/10.1007/978-3-319-50011-9_33
22. Zhang, Q., Zhao, S.: A comprehensive formal security analysis and revision of the two-phase key exchange primitive of TPM 2.0. Comput. Netw. **179**, 107369 (2020)

Reasoning About Exceptional Behavior
at the Level of Java Bytecode

Marco Paganoni$^{(\boxtimes)}$ and Carlo A. Furia

Software Institute, USI Università della Svizzera italiana, Lugano, Switzerland
marco.paganoni@usi.ch
https://bugcounting.net

Abstract. A program's exceptional behavior can substantially complicate its control flow, and hence accurately reasoning about the program's correctness. On the other hand, formally verifying realistic programs is likely to involve exceptions—a ubiquitous feature in modern programming languages.

In this paper, we present a novel approach to verify the exceptional behavior of Java programs, which extends our previous work on BYTE-BACK. BYTEBACK works on a program's bytecode, while providing means to specify the intended behavior at the source-code level; this approach sets BYTEBACK apart from most state-of-the-art verifiers that target source code. To explicitly model a program's exceptional behavior in a way that is amenable to formal reasoning, we introduce Vimp: a high-level bytecode representation that extends the Soot framework's Grimp with verification-oriented features, thus serving as an intermediate layer between bytecode and the Boogie intermediate verification language. Working on bytecode through this intermediate layer brings flexibility and adaptability to new language versions and variants: as our experiments demonstrate, BYTEBACK can verify programs involving exceptional behavior in all versions of Java, as well as in Scala and Kotlin (two other popular JVM languages).

1 Introduction

Nearly every modern programming language supports exceptions as a mechanism to signal and handle unusual runtime conditions (so-called *exceptional behavior*) separately from the main control flow (the program's *normal* behavior). Exceptions are usually preferable to lower-level ad hoc solutions (such as error codes and defensive programming), because deploying them does not pollute the source code's structured control flow. However, by introducing extra, often implicit execution paths, exceptions may also complicate reasoning about all possible program behavior—and thus, ultimately, about program correctness.

In this paper, we introduce a novel approach to perform deductive verification of Java programs involving exceptional behavior. Exceptions were baked into the Java programming language since its inception, where they remain widely

Work partially supported by SNF grant 200021-207919 (LastMile).

used [13, 15, 17]; nevertheless, as the example of Sect. 2 demonstrates, they can be somewhat of a challenge to reason about formally. To model together normal and exceptional control flow paths, and to seamlessly support any exception-related language features, our verification approach crucially targets a program's *byte-code* intermediate representation—instead of the source code analyzed by state-of-the-art verifiers such as KeY [1] and OpenJML [6]. We introduced the idea of performing formal verification at the level of bytecode in previous work [20]. In this paper, we build on those results and implement support for exceptions in the BYTEBACK deductive verifier.

The key idea of our BYTEBACK approach (pictured in Fig. 1) is using JVM bytecode solely as a convenient intermediate representation; users of BYTEBACK still annotate program source code in a very similar way as if they were working with a source-level verifier. To this end, we extend the specification library introduced with BYTEBACK (called BBlib) with features to specify exceptional behavior (for example, conditions under which a method terminates normally or exceptionally) using custom Java expressions; thus, such specifications remain available in bytecode after compiling an annotated program using a standard Java compiler. BYTEBACK analyzes the bytecode and encodes the program's semantics, its specification, and other information necessary for verification into Boogie [3]—a widely-used intermediate language for verification; then, verifying the Boogie translation is equivalent to verifying the original Java program against its specification.

As we demonstrate with experiments in Sect. 4, performing verification on bytecode offers several advantages: *i) Robustness* to source-language changes: while Java evolves rapidly, frequently introducing new features (also for exceptional behavior), bytecode is generally stable; thus, our verification technique continues to work with the latest Java versions. *ii) Multi-language* support: BYTEBACK and its BBlib specification library are designed so that they can be applied, in principle, to specify programs in any language that is bytecode-compatible; while the bulk of our examples are in Java, we will demonstrate verifying exceptional behavior in Scala and Kotlin—two modern languages for the JVM. *iii) Flexibility* of modeling: since exceptional behavior becomes explicit in bytecode, the BYTEBACK approach extensively and seamlessly deals with any intricate exceptional behavior (such as implicit or suppressed exceptions).

Contributions and Positioning. In summary, the paper makes the following contributions: *i)* Specification features to specify exceptional behavior of JVM languages. *ii)* A verification technique that encodes bytecode exceptional behavior into Boogie. *iii)* An implementation of the specification features and the verification technique that extend the BBlib library and BYTEBACK verifier. *iv)* Vimp: a high-level bytecode format suitable to reason about functional correctness, built on top of Soot's Grimp format [11, 26]. *v)* An experimental evaluation with 37 programs involving exceptional behavior in Java, Scala, and Kotlin. *vi)* For reproducibility, BYTEBACK and all experimental artifacts are available in a replication package [19]. While we build upon BBlib and BYTEBACK, introduced in previous work of ours [20], this paper's contributions substantially extend them

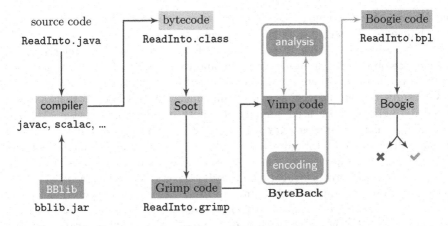

Fig. 1. An overview of BYTEBACK's verification workflow.

with support for exceptional behavior, as well as other Java related features (see Sect. 3). For simplicity, henceforth "BBlib" and "BYTEBACK" denote their current versions, equipped with the novel contributions described in the rest of the paper.

2   Motivating Example

Exceptions can significantly complicate the control flow of even seemingly simple code; consequently, correctly reasoning about exceptional behavior can be chal-

```
1 @Require(r = null ∨ ¬r.closed)
2 @Raise(NullPointerException, a = null ∨ r =
     null)
3 @Return(a ≠ null ∧ a.length = 0)
4 @Ensure(r = null ∨ r.closed)
5 static void into(final Resource r, final
     int[] a) {
6   try (r) {
7     int i = 0;
8     while (true) { invariant(0 ≤ i ≤ a.
     length);
9       a[i] = r.read(); ++i;
10    }
11  } catch (IndexOutOfBoundsException
12         | NoSuchElementException e) {
       return; }
13 }
```

```
class Resource implements
    AutoCloseable {

  boolean closed;
  boolean hasNext;

  @Raise(IllegalStateException,
    closed)
  @Raise(NoSuchElementException, ¬
    hasNext)
  @Return(¬closed ∧ hasNext)
  int read()
  { /* ... */ }

  // ...
}
```

(a) Method into copies r's content into array a. It is annotated with normal and exceptional pre- and postconditions using a simplified BBlib syntax.

(b) An outline of class Resouce's interface with Boolean attributes closed and hasNext, and method read.

Fig. 2. Annotated Java method into and class Resource, which demonstrate some pitfalls of specifying and reasoning about exceptional behavior.

lenging even for a language like Java—whose exception-handling features have not changed significantly since the language's origins.

To demonstrate, consider Fig. 2a's method `into`, which inputs a reference r to a `Resource` object and an integer array a, and copies values from r into a—until either a is filled up or there are no more values in r to read. Figure 2b shows the key features of class `Resource`—which implements Java's `AutoCloseable` interface, and hence can be used similarly to most standard I/O classes. Method `into`'s implementation uses a **try**-with-resources block to ensure that r is closed whenever the method terminates—normally or exceptionally. The **while** loop terminates as soon as any of the following conditions holds: *i*) r or a is **null**; *ii*) k reaches a.`length` (array a is full); *iii*) r.`read()` throws a `NoSuchElementException` (r has no more elements). Method `into` returns with an (propagated) exception only in case *i*); case *ii*)'s `IndexOutOfBounds` and case *iii*)'s `NoSuchElement` exceptions are caught by the **catch** block that *suppresses* them with a **return**—so that `into` can return normally.

Figure 2a's annotations, which use a simplified syntax for `BBlib`—Byte-Back's specification library—specify part of `into`'s expected behavior. Precondition `@Require` expresses the constraint that object r must be open (or **null**) for `into` to work as intended. Annotation `@Raise` declares that `into` terminates with a `NullPointer` exception if r or a are **null**; conversely, `@Return` says that `into` returns *normally* if a is a non-**null** empty array. Finally, postcondition `@Ensure` says that, if it's not **null**, r will be closed when `into` terminates—regardless of whether it does so normally or exceptionally. The combination of language features and numerous forking control-flow paths complicate reasoning about—and even specifying—`into`'s behavior. While exception handling has been part of Java since version 1, try-with-resources and multi-catch (both used in Fig. 2a) were introduced in Java 7; thus, even a state-of-the-art verifier like KeY [1] lacks support for them. OpenJML [6] can reason about all exception features up to Java 7; however, the try-with-resources using an existing **final** variable became available only in Java 9. [28] Furthermore, OpenJML implicitly checks that verified code does not throw any implicit exceptions (such as `NullPointer` or `IndexOutOfBound` exceptions)—thus disallowing code such as Fig. 2a's, where implicitly throwing exceptions is part of the expected behavior. These observations are best thought of as design choices—rather than limitations—of these powerful Java verification tools: after all, features such as multi-catch are syntactic sugar that makes programs more concise but does not affect expressiveness; and propagating uncaught implicit exceptions can be considered an anti-pattern [29] [14, 27]. However, they also speak volumes to the difficulty of fully supporting all cases of exceptional behavior in a feature-laden language like Java.

As we detail in the rest of the paper, ByteBack's approach offers advantages in such scenarios. Crucially, the implicit control flow of exception-handling code becomes explicit when compiled to bytecode, which eases analyzing it consistently and disentangling the various specification elements. For instance, the **while** loop's several exceptional exit points become apparent in `into`'s bytecode translation, and ByteBack can check that the declared invariant holds in all of them, and that postcondition @Ensure holds in all matching method return points. Furthermore, bytecode is more stable than Java—thus, a verifier like BYTEBACK is more robust to source language evolution. Thanks to these capabilities, BYTEBACK can verify the behavior of Fig. 2's example.

3 Specifying and Verifying Exceptional Behavior

This section describes the new features of BYTEBACK to specify and verify exceptional behavior. Figure 1 shows BYTEBACK's workflow, which we revisited to support these new features. Users of BYTEBACK—just like with every deductive verifier—have to annotate the source code to be verified with a specification and other annotations. To this end, BYTEBACK offers BBlib: an annotation library that is usable with any language that is bytecode compatible. Section 3.1 describes the new BBlib features to specify exceptional behavior. Then, users compile the annotated source code with the language's bytecode compiler. BYTE-BACK relies on the Soot static analysis framework to analyze bytecode; precisely, Soot offers Grimp: a higher-level alternative bytecode representation. BYTEBACK processes Grimp and translates it to Vimp: a verification-oriented extension of Grimp that we introduced in the latest BYTEBACK version and is described in Sect. 3.2. As we discuss in Sect. 3.3, BYTEBACK transforms Grimp to Vimp in steps, each taking care of a different aspect (expressions, types, control flow, and so on). Once the transformation is complete, BYTEBACK encodes the Vimp program into the Boogie intermediate verification language [3]; thanks to Vimp's custom design, the Boogie encoding is mostly straightforward. Finally, the Boogie tool verifies the generated Boogie program, and reports success or any verification failures (which can be manually traced back to source-code specifications that could not be verified).

3.1 Specifying Exceptional Behavior

Users of BYTEBACK add behavioral specifications to a program's source using BBlib: BYTEBACK's standalone Java library, offering annotation tags and static methods suitable to specify functional behavior. Since BBlib uses only basic language constructs, it is compatible with most JVM languages (as we demonstrate in Sect. 4); and all the information added as BBlib annotations is preserved at the bytecode level. This section first summarizes the core characteristics of BBlib (to make the paper self contained), and then describes the features we introduced to specify exceptional behavior.

Specification Expressions. Expressions used in BYTEBACK specifications must be *aggregable*, that is pure (they can be evaluated without side effects) and branchless (they can be evaluated without branching instructions). These are common requirements to ensure that specification expressions are well-formed [24]—hence, equivalently expressible as purely *logic expressions*. Correspondingly, BBlib forbids impure expressions, and offers aggregable replacements for the many Java operators that introduce branches in the bytecode, such as the standard Boolean operators (&&, ||, ...) and comparison operators (==, <, ...). Table 1 shows several of BBlib's aggregable operators, including some that have no immediately equivalent Java expression (such as the quantifiers). Using only BBlib's operators in a specification ensures that it remains in a form that BYTE-BACK can process after the source program has been compiled to bytecode [20]. Thus, BBlib operators map to Vimp logic operators (Sect. 3.2), which directly translate to Boogie operators with matching semantics (Sect. 3.4).

Table 1. BBlib's aggregable operators, used instead of Java's impure or branching operators in specification expressions.

	IN JAVA/LOGIC	IN BBlib
comparison	x < y, x <= y, x == y	lt(x, y), lte(x, y), eq(x, y)
	x != y, x >= y, x > y	neq(x, y), gte(x, y), gt(x, y)
conditionals	c ? t : e	conditional(c, t, e)
propositional	!a, a && b, a $\implies$ b	not(a), a & b, a | b, implies(a, b)
quantifiers	$\forall$x: T • P(x)	T x = Binding.T(); **forall**(x, P(x))
	$\exists$x: T • P(x)	T x = Binding.T(); **exists**(x, P(x))

Method Specifications. To specify the input/output behavior of methods, BBlib offers annotations @Require and @Ensure to express a method's pre- and postconditions. For example, @Require(p) @Ensure(q) t m(args) specifies that p and q are method m's pre- and postcondition; both p and q denote names of *predicate* methods, which are methods marked with annotation @Predicate. As part of the verification process, BYTEBACK checks that every such predicate method p is well-formed: i) p returns a **boolean**; ii) p's signature is the same as m's or, if p is used in m's postcondition and m's return type is not **void**, it also includes an additional argument that denotes m's returned value; iii) p's body returns a single aggregable expression; iv) if p's body calls other methods, they must also be aggregable. For example, the postcondition q of a method **int** fun(**int** x) that always returns a value greater than the input x is expressible in BBlib as @Predicate **boolean** q(**int** x, **int** result) {**return** gt(result, x);}. Postcondition predicates may also refer to a method's pre-state by means of **old**(a) expressions, which evaluates to a's value in the method's pre-state.

For simplicity of presentation, we henceforth abuse the notation and use an identifier to denote a predicate method's *name*, the *declaration* of the predicate method, and the *expression* that the predicate method returns. Consider, for instance, Fig. 2a's precondition; in BBlib syntax, it can be declared as @Require("null_or_open"), where "null_or_open" is the name of a method null_or_open, whose body returns expression eq(r, **null**) | not(r.closed), which is into's actual precondition.

```
27 class C {
28
29    int x = 0;
30
31    @Ensure("x_eq_y")    // x = y when m terminates normally or
          exceptionally
32    @Ensure("x_pos")     // if x > 0 then m throws an exception
33    @Ensure("y_neg")     // if y ≤ 0 then m terminates normally
34    void m(int y) { x = y; if (x > 0) throw new PosXExc(); }
35
36    @Predicate public boolean y_neg(int y, Throwable e)
37    { return implies(lte(y, 0), isVoid(e)); }
38
39    @Predicate public boolean x_pos(int y, Throwable e)
40    { return implies(gt(x, 0), e instanceof PosXExc); }
41
42    @Predicate public boolean x_eq_y(int y)
43    { return eq(x, y); }
44
45 }
```

Fig. 3. Examples of exceptional postconditions in BBlib.

Table 2. BBlib's @Raise and @Return and annotation shorthands.

SHORTHAND	EQUIVALENT POSTCONDITION
@Raise(exception = E.class, when = p)	@Ensure(implies(**old**(p), e **instanceof** E))
@Return(when = p)	@Ensure(implies(**old**(p), isVoid(e)))
@Return	@Return(when = **true**)

Exceptional Postconditions. Predicate methods specified with @Ensure are evaluated on a method's post-state regardless of whether the method terminated normally or with an exception; for example, predicate x_eq_y in Fig. 3 says that attribute x always equals argument y when method m terminates. To specify exceptional behavior, a method's postcondition predicate may include an additional argument e of type Throwable, which denotes the thrown exception if the method terminated with an exception or satisfies BBlib's predicate isVoid(e) if the method terminated normally. Predicate x_pos in Fig. 3 is an example of exceptional behavior, as it says that m throws an exception of type PosXExc when attribute x is greater than zero upon termination; conversely, predicate y_neg specifies that m terminates normally when argument y is negative or zero.

Shorthands. For convenience, BBlib offers annotation shorthands @Raise and @Return to specify when a method terminates exceptionally or normally. Table 2 shows the semantics of these shorthands by translating them into equivalent postconditions. The `when` argument refers to a method's pre-state through the `old` expression, since it is common to relate a method's exceptional behavior to its inputs. Thus, Table 3's postcondition y_neg is equivalent to `@Return(lte(y, 0))`, since m does not change y's value; conversely, `@Raise(PosXExc.class, gt(x, 0))` is *not* equivalent to x_pos because m sets x to y's value.

Intermediate Specification. `BBlib` also supports the usual intra-method specification elements: assertions, assumptions, and loop invariants. Given an aggregable expression e, `assertion`(e) specifies that e must hold whenever execution reaches it; `assumption`(e) restricts verification from this point on to only executions where e holds; and `invariant`(e) declares that e is an invariant of the loop within whose body it is declared. As we have seen in Fig. 2a's running example, loop invariants hold, in particular, at all exit points of a loop—including exceptional ones.

3.2 The Vimp Intermediate Representation

In our previous work [20], BYTEBACK works directly on Grimp—a high-level bytecode representation provided by the Soot static analysis framework [11,26]. Compared to raw bytecode, Grimp conveniently retains information such as types and expressions, which eases BYTEBACK's encoding of the program under verification into Boogie [3]. However, Grimp remains a form of bytecode, and hence it represents well executable instructions, but lacks support for encoding logic expressions and specification constructs. These limitations become especially inconvenient when reasoning about exceptional behavior, which often involves logic conditions that depend on the types and values of exceptional objects. Rather than reconstructing this information during the translation from Grimp to Boogie, we found it more effective to extend Grimp into Vimp, which fully supports logic and specification expressions.

Our bespoke Vimp bytecode representation can encode all the information relevant for verification. This brings several advantages: *i*) it decouples the input program's static analysis from the generation of Boogie code, achieving more flexibility at either ends of the toolchain; *ii*) it makes the generation of Boogie code straightforward (mostly one-to-one); *iii*) BYTEBACK's transformation from Grimp to Vimp becomes naturally *modular*: it composes several simpler transformations, each taking care of a different aspect and incorporating a different kind of information. The rest of this section presents Vimp's key features, and how they are used by BYTEBACK's Grimp-to-Vimp transformation $\mathcal{V}$.[1] As detailed in Sect. 3.4, $\mathcal{V}$ composes the following feature-specific transformations: $\mathcal{V}_{exc}$ makes the exceptional control flow explicit; $\mathcal{V}_{agg}$ aggregates Grimp expressions into compound Vimp expressions; $\mathcal{V}_{inst}$ translates Grimp instructions (by

---

[1] In the following, we occasionally take some liberties with Grimp and Vimp code, using a readable syntax that mixes bytecode instruction and Java statement syntax; for example, m() represents an invocation of method m that corresponds to a suitable variant of bytecode's `invoke`.

applying transformation $\mathcal{V}_{stm}$ to statements, transformation $\mathcal{V}_{exp}$ to expressions within statements, and $\mathcal{V}_{types}$ to expression types); $\mathcal{V}_{loop}$ handles loop invariants.

Expression Aggregation. Transformation $\mathcal{V}_{agg}$ *aggregates* specification expressions (see Sect. 3.1), so that each corresponds to a single Vimp pure and branchless expression. In a nutshell, $\mathcal{V}_{agg}(s)$ takes a piece s of aggregable Grimp code, converts it into static-single assignment form, and then recursively replaces each variable's single usage with its unique definition. For example, consider Fig. 2a's loop invariant: it corresponds to `a := lte(0, i); b := lte(i, a.length); c := a & b` in Grimp, and becomes `c := lte(0, i) & lte(i, a.length)` in Vimp.

Expected Types. Transformation $\mathcal{V}_{type}$ reconstructs the *expected type* of expressions when translating them to Vimp. An expression e's expected type depends on the context where e is used; in general, it differs from e's type in Grimp, since Soot's type inference may not distinguish between Boolean and integer expressions—which both use the **int** bytecode type.

Boolean Expressions. Another consequence of bytecode's lack of a proper **boolean** representation is that Grimp uses integer operators also as Boolean operators (for example the unary minus - for "not"). In contrast, Vimp supports the usual Boolean operators $\neg$, $\wedge$, $\vee$, $\implies$, and constants `true` and `false`. Transformation $\mathcal{V}_{exp}$ uses them to translate Vimp expressions e whose expected type $\mathcal{V}_{type}(e)$ is **boolean**; this includes specification expressions (which use BBlib's replacement operators), but also regular Boolean expressions in the executable code. For example, $\mathcal{V}_{exp}(\text{-a}) = \neg\mathcal{V}_{exp}(a)$, $\mathcal{V}_{exp}(k) = \text{true}$ for every constant $k \geq 1$, and $\mathcal{V}_{exp}(h) = \text{false}$ for every constant $h < 1$.

Transformation $\mathcal{V}_{exp}(e)$ also identifies quantified expressions—expressed using a combination of BBlib's `Contract` and `Binding`—after aggregating them, and renders them using Vimp's quantifier syntax:

$$\mathcal{V}_{exp}(\text{Contract.forall(Binding.T(),}e)) = \forall\, \mathcal{V}_{type}(\text{Binding.T()})\, v\, ::\, \mathcal{V}_{exp}(e)$$
$$\mathcal{V}_{exp}(\text{Contract.exists(Binding.T(),}e)) = \exists\, \mathcal{V}_{type}(\text{Binding.T()})\, v\, ::\, \mathcal{V}_{exp}(e)$$

Assertion Instructions. Vimp includes instructions **assert**, **assume**, and **invariant**, which transformation $\mathcal{V}_{stm}$ introduces for each corresponding instance of BBlib assertions, assumptions, and loop invariants. Transformation $\mathcal{V}_{loop}$ relies on Soot's loop analysis capabilities to identify loops in Vimp's unstructured control flow; then, it expresses their invariants by means of assertions and assumptions. As shown in Fig. 4, $\mathcal{V}_{loop}$ checks that the invariant holds upon loop entry (label *head*), at the end of each iteration (*head* again), and at every exit point (label *exit*).

```
k = 0;                          k := 0;                      k := 0;
while (k < 10) {                head:                        head:  assert k ≤ 10 ∧ k
   invariant(lte(k, 10) & lte(     if k ≥ 10 goto exit;                 ≤ X;
      k, X));                      invariant k ≤ 10 ∧ k        if k ≥ 10 goto exit;
   k++;                                ≤ X;                    assume k ≤ 10 ∧ k ≤ X;
   if (k ≥ X) break;               k := k + 1;                 k := k + 1;
}                                  if k ≥ X goto exit;          if k ≥ X goto exit;
return k;                       back: goto head;             back: goto head;
                                exit:                        exit:  assert k ≤ 10 ∧ k
                                   return k;                            ≤ X;
                                                                return k;
```

Fig. 4. A loop in Java (left), its unstructured representation in Vimp (middle), and the transformation $\mathcal{V}_{\mathsf{loop}}$ of its invariant into assertions and assumptions (right).

```
try {                       ℓ₁: x := o.size();          ℓ₁: x := o.size();
   x = o.size();                                            if @thrown = void goto skip₂;
   if (x = 0)                                               Vexc(throw @thrown;)
      throw new E();        ℓ₂: if x != 0 goto ℓ₅       skip₂: ℓ₂: if x ≠ 0 goto ℓ₅;
} catch (E e) {                 ;                         ℓ₃: e := new E();
   x = 1;                   ℓ₃: e := new E();            ℓ₄: @thrown := e;
}                           ℓ₄: throw e;                     if ¬(@thrown instanceof E)
                                                                goto skip₅;
                                                             goto hE;
                            ℓ₅: goto ℓ₆;                 skip₅: ℓ₅: goto ℓ₆;
                            hE:                          hE:
                               e := @caught;               e := @thrown; @thrown := void;
                               x := 1;                      x := 1;
                            ℓ₆: ...                       ℓ₆: ...
```

Fig. 5. A try-catch block in Java (left), its unstructured representation as a trap in Grimp (middle, empty lines are for readability), and its transformation $\mathcal{V}_{\mathsf{exc}}$ in Vimp with explicit exceptional control flow (right).

3.3 Modeling Exceptional Control Flow

Bytecode stores a block's exceptional behavior in a data structure called the *exception table*. [30] Soot represents each table entry as a *trap*, which renders a try-catch block in Grimp bytecode. Precisely, a trap t is defined by: *i*) a block of instructions B_t that may throw exceptions; *ii*) the type E_t of the handled exceptions; *iii*) a label h_t to the handler instructions (which terminates with a jump back to the end of B_t). When executing B_t throws an exception whose type conforms to E_t, control jumps to h_t. At the beginning of the handler code, Grimp introduces e := @caught, which stores into a local variable e of the handler a reference @caught to the thrown exception object. Figure 5 shows an example of try-catch block in Java (left) and the corresponding trap in Grimp (middle): $\ell_1, \ldots, \ell_5$ is the instruction block, E is the exception type, and hE is handler's entry label. The rest of this section describes BYTEBACK's transformation $\mathcal{V}_{\mathsf{exc}}$, which transforms the implicit exceptional control flow of Grimp traps into explicit control flow in Vimp.

Explicit Exceptional Control-Flow. Grimp's variable @caught is called @thrown in Vimp. While @caught is read-only in Grimp—where it only refers to the currently handled exception—@thrown can be assigned to in Vimp. This is how BYTEBACK makes exceptional control flow explicit: assigning to `@thrown` an exception object e signals that e has been thrown; and setting `@thrown` to void marks the current execution as normal. Thus, BYTEBACK's Vimp encoding sets `@thrown := void` at the beginning of a program's execution, and then manipulates the special variable to reflect the bytecode semantics of exceptions as we outline in the following. With this approach, the Vimp encoding of a **try** block simply results from encoding each of the block's instructions explicitly according to their potentially exceptional behavior.

Throw Instructions. Transformation $\mathcal{V}_{\text{exc}}$ desugars **throw** instructions into explicit assignments to `@thrown` and jumps to the suitable handler. A **throw** e instruction within the blocks of n traps $t_1, \ldots, t_n$—handling exceptions of types $E_1, \ldots, E_n$ with handlers at labels $h_1, \ldots, h_n$—is transformed into:

$$\mathcal{V}_{\text{exc}}(\textbf{throw e}) = \begin{pmatrix} & \texttt{@thrown := e;} \\ & \textbf{if } \neg(\texttt{@thrown instanceof } E_1) \textbf{ goto } \underline{skip_1}; \\ & \textbf{goto } h_1; \\ \underline{skip_1}: & \textbf{if } \neg(\texttt{@thrown instanceof } E_2) \textbf{ goto } \underline{skip_2}; \\ & \textbf{goto } h_2; \\ \underline{skip_2}: & \textbf{if } \neg(\texttt{@thrown instanceof } E_3) \textbf{ goto } \underline{skip_3}; \\ & \vdots \\ \underline{skip_{n-1}}: & \textbf{if } \neg(\texttt{@thrown instanceof } E_n) \textbf{ goto } \underline{skip_n}; \\ & \textbf{goto } h_n; \\ \underline{skip_n}: & \textbf{return}; \text{ // propagate exception to caller} \end{pmatrix}$$

The assignment to `@thrown` stores a reference to the thrown exception object e; then, a series of checks determine if e has type that conforms to any of the handled exception types; if it does, execution jumps to the corresponding handler.

Transformation $\mathcal{V}_{\text{exc}}$ also replaces the assignment `e := @caught` that Grimp puts at the beginning of every handler with `e := @thrown; @thrown := void`, signaling that the current exception is handled, and thus the program will resume normal execution.

Exceptions in Method Calls. A called method may throw an exception, which the caller should propagate or handle. Accordingly, transformation $\mathcal{V}_{\text{exc}}$ adds after every method call instructions to check whether the caller set variable `@thrown` and, if it did, to handle the exception within the caller as if it had been directly thrown by it.

$$\mathcal{V}_{\text{exc}}(\textbf{m}(a_1, \ldots, a_m)) = \begin{pmatrix} & \texttt{m}(a_1, \ldots, a_m); \\ & \textbf{if } (\texttt{@thrown} = \text{void}) \textbf{ goto } \underline{skip}; \\ & \mathcal{V}_{\text{exc}}(\textbf{throw @thrown}) \\ \underline{skip}: & \text{/* code after call */} \end{pmatrix}$$

Potentially Excepting Instructions. Some bytecode instructions may implicitly throw exceptions when they cannot execute normally. In Fig. 2a's running example, `r.read()` throws a NullPointer exception if r is **null**; and the assignment to a[i] throws an IndexOutOfBounds exception if i is not between 0 and a.length - 1. Transformation $\mathcal{V}_{\text{exc}}$ recognizes such potentially excepting instructions and adds explicit checks that capture their implicit exceptional behavior. Let op be an instruction that throws an exception of type E_{op} when condition F_{op} holds; $\mathcal{V}_{\text{exc}}$ transforms op as follows.

$$\mathcal{V}_{\text{exc}}(\text{op}) = \begin{pmatrix} \textbf{if } \neg F_{\text{op}} \textbf{ goto } \underline{normal}; \\ \mathcal{V}_{\text{exc}} \begin{pmatrix} \text{e} := \textbf{new } E_{\text{op}}(); \\ \textbf{throw } \text{e}; \end{pmatrix} \\ \underline{normal}: \text{ op} \end{pmatrix}$$

By chaining multiple checks, transformation $\mathcal{V}_{\text{exc}}$ handles instructions that may throw multiple implicit exceptions. For example, here is how it encodes the potentially excepting semantics of array lookup a[i], which fails if a is **null** or i is out of bounds.

$$\mathcal{V}_{\text{exc}}(\text{res} := \text{a[i]}) = \begin{pmatrix} \textbf{if } \neg(\text{a} = \text{null}) \textbf{ goto } \underline{normal}_1; \\ \mathcal{V}_{\text{exc}} \begin{pmatrix} \text{e}_1 := \textbf{new } \text{NullPointerException}(); \\ \textbf{throw } \text{e}_1; \end{pmatrix} \\ \underline{normal}_1: \textbf{if } \neg(0 \leq \text{i} \wedge \text{i} < \text{a.length}) \textbf{ goto } \underline{normal}_2; \\ \mathcal{V}_{\text{exc}} \begin{pmatrix} \text{e}_2 := \textbf{new } \text{IndexOutOfBoundsException}(); \\ \textbf{throw } \text{e}_2; \end{pmatrix} \\ \underline{normal}_2: \text{ res} := \text{a[i]}; \end{pmatrix}$$

3.4 Transformation Order and Boogie Code Generation

ByteBack applies the transformations $\mathcal{V}$ from Grimp to Vimp in a precise order that incrementally encodes the full program semantics respecting dependencies.

$$\boxed{\text{Grimp} \rightarrow \underbrace{\mathcal{V}_{\text{exc}} \longrightarrow \mathcal{V}_{\text{agg}} \longrightarrow \mathcal{V}_{\text{inst}} \longrightarrow \mathcal{V}_{\text{loop}} \longrightarrow \text{Vimp}}_{\text{ByteBack}} \rightarrow \mathcal{B} \rightarrow \text{Boogie}}$$

Like raw bytecode, the source Grimp representation on which ByteBack operates is a form of three-address code, where each instruction performs exactly one operation (a call, a dereferencing, or a unary or binary arithmetic operation). *i*) ByteBack first applies $\mathcal{V}_{\text{exc}}$ to make the exceptional control flow explicit. *ii*) Then, it aggregates expressions using $\mathcal{V}_{\text{agg}}$. *iii*) Transformation $\mathcal{V}_{\text{inst}}$ is applied next to every instruction; in turn, $\mathcal{V}_{\text{inst}}$ relies on transformations $\mathcal{V}_{\text{exp}}$, $\mathcal{V}_{\text{stm}}$, and $\mathcal{V}_{\text{type}}$ (presented in Sect. 3.2) to process the expressions and types manipulated by the instructions (the instructions themselves do not change, and hence $\mathcal{V}_{\text{inst}}$'s definition is straightforward). *iv*) Finally, it applies $\mathcal{V}_{\text{loop}}$ to encode loop invariants as intermediate assertions; since this transformation is applied after $\mathcal{V}_{\text{exc}}$, the loop invariants can be checked at all loop exit points—normal and exceptional.

The very last step $\mathcal{B}$ of ByteBack's pipeline takes the fully transformed Vimp program and encodes it as a Boogie program. Thanks to Vimp's design, and to the transformation $\mathcal{V}$ applied to Grimp, the Vimp-to-Boogie translation is straightforward. In addition, ByteBack also generates a detailed Boogie axiomatization of all logic functions used to model various parts of JVM

execution—which we described in greater detail in previous work [20]. One important addition is an axiomatization of subtype relations among exception types, used by Boogie's `instanceof` function to mirror the semantics of the homonymous Java operator. Consider the whole tree T of exception types used in the program:[2] each node is a type, and its children are its direct subtypes. For every node C in the tree, BYTEBACK produces one axiom asserting that every child X of C is a subtype of C ($X \preceq C$), and one axiom for every pair X, Y of C's children asserting that any descendant types x of X and y of Y are *not* related by subtyping (in other words, the subtrees rooted in X and Y are disjoint):
$$\forall x, y \colon \mathsf{Type} \bullet x \preceq X \wedge y \preceq Y \implies x \not\preceq y \wedge y \not\preceq x.$$

3.5 Implementation Details

BBlib as Specification Language. We are aware that BBlib's syntax and conventions may be inconvenient at times; they were designed to deal with the fundamental constraints that any specification must be expressible in the source code and still be fully available for analysis in bytecode after compilation. This rules out the more practical approaches (e.g., comments) adopted by source-level verifiers. More user-friendly notations could be introduced on top of BBlib—but doing so is outside the present paper's scope.

Attaching Annotations. As customary in deductive verification, BYTEBACK models calls using the modular semantics, whereby every called method needs a meaningful specification of its effects within the caller. To support more realistic programs that call to Java's standard library methods, BBlib supports the `@Attach` annotation: a class S annotated with `@Attach(I.class)` declares that any specification of any method in S serves as specification of any method with the same signature in I. We used this mechanism to model the fundamental behavior of widely used methods in Java's, Scala's, and Kotlin's standard libraries. As a concrete example, we specified that the constructors of common exception classes do not themselves raise exceptions.

Implicit Exceptions. Section 3.3 describes how BYTEBACK models potentially excepting instructions. The mechanism is extensible, and the current implementation supports the ubiquitous `NullPointer` and `IndexOutOfBounds` exceptions, as shown in Table 3. Users can selectively enable or disable these checks for implicitly thrown exceptions either for each individual method, or globally for the whole program.

Dependencies. BYTEBACK is implemented as a command-line tool that takes as input a classpath and a set E of class files within that path. The analysis

---

[2] Since the root of all exception types in Java is *class* `Throwable`—a concrete class—an exception type cannot be a subtype of multiple exception classes, and hence T is strictly a tree.

Table 3. Potentially excepting instructions currently supported by BYTEBACK.

EXCEPTING INSTRUCTIONS	EXCEPTION	CONDITION
dereferencing `o._`, `o[i]`	`NullPointerException`	`o = null`
array access `a[i]`	`IndexOutOfBoundsException`	$\neg$ `(0 ≤ i && i < a.length)`

collects all classes on which the entry classes in E recursively depend—where "A depends on B" means that A inherits from or is a client of B. After collecting all dependencies, BYTEBACK feeds them through its verification toolchain (Fig. 1) that translates them to Boogie. In practice, BYTEBACK is configured with a list of *system packages*—such as `java.lang`—that are treated differently: their implementations are ignored (i.e., not translated to Boogie for verification), but their interfaces and any specifications are retained to reason about their clients. This makes the verification process more lightweight,

Features and Limitations. The main limitations of BYTEBACK's previous version [20] were a lack of support for exception handling and `invokedynamic`. As discussed in the rest of the paper, BYTEBACK now fully supports reasoning about exceptional behavior. We also added a, still limited, support for `invokedynamic`: any instance of `invokedynamic` is conservatively treated as a call whose effects are unspecified; furthermore, we introduced ad hoc support to reason about concatenation and comparison of string literal—which are implemented using `invokedynamic` since Java 9.[3] A full support of `invokedynamic` still belongs to future work.

Other remaining limitations of BYTEBACK's current implementation are a limited support of string objects, and no modeling of numerical errors such as overflow (i.e., numeric types are encoded with infinite precision). Adding support for all of these features is possible by extending BYTEBACK's current approach.

4   Experiments

We demonstrated BYTEBACK's capabilities by running its implementation on a collection of annotated programs involving exceptional behavior in Java, Scala, and Kotlin.

4.1   Programs

Table 4 lists the 37 programs that we prepared for these experiments; all of them involve *some* exceptional behavior in different contexts.[4] More than half of the

---

[3] https://docs.oracle.com/javase/9/docs/api/java/lang/invoke/StringConcatFactory.html.

[4] We focus on these exception-related programs, but the latest version of BYTEBACK also verifies correctly the 35 other programs we introduced in previous work to demonstrate its fundamental verification capabilities.

programs (20/37) are in Java: 17 only use language features that have been available since Java 8, and another 3 rely on more recent features available since Java 17. To demonstrate how targeting bytecode makes BYTEBACK capable of verifying, at least in part, other JVM languages, we also included 9 programs written in Scala (version 2 of the language), and 8 programs written in Kotlin (version 1.8.0). Each program/experiment consists of one or more classes with their dependencies, which we annotated with BBlib to specify exceptional and normal behavior, as well as other assertions needed for verification (such as loop invariants). The examples total 7 810 lines of code and annotations, with hundreds of annotations and 1 070 methods (including BBlib specification methods) involved in the verification process. According to their features, the experiments can be classified into two groups: feature experiments and algorithmic experiments.

Feature Experiments. Java 8 programs 1–7, Java 17 program 18, Scala programs 21–25, and Kotlin programs 30–33 are *feature* experiments: each of them exercises a small set of exception-related language features; correspondingly, their specifications check that BYTEBACK's verification process correctly captures the source language's semantics of those features. For example, experiments 4, 24, and 32 feature different combinations of try-catch blocks and throw statements that can be written in Java, Scala, and Kotlin, and test whether BYTEBACK correctly reconstructs all possible exceptional and normal execution paths that can arise. A more specialized example is experiment 5, which verifies the behavior of loops with both normal and exceptional exit points.

Algorithmic Experiments. Java 8 programs 8–17, Java 17 programs 19–20, Scala programs 26–29, and Kotlin programs 34–37 are *algorithmic* experiments: they implement classic algorithm that also use exceptions to signal when their inputs are invalid. The main difference between feature and algorithmic experiments is specification: algorithmic experiments usually have more complex pre- and postconditions than feature experiments, which they complement with specifications of exceptional behavior on the corner cases. For example, experiments 8, 26, and 34 implement array reversal algorithms; their postconditions specify that the input array is correctly reversed; and other parts of their specification say that they result in an exception if the input array is null. Experiment 20 is an extension of Fig. 2's running example, where the algorithm is a simple stream-to-array copy implemented in a way that may give rise to various kinds of exceptional behavior.

Experiments 16 and 17 are the most complex programs in our experiments: they include a subset of the complete implementations of Java's ArrayList and LinkedList standard library classes, [31] part of which we annotated with basic postconditions and a specification of their exceptional behavior (as described in their official documentation). In particular, ArrayList's exceptional specification focuses on possible failures of the class constructor (for example, when given a negative number as initial capacity); LinkedList's specification focuses on possible failures of some of the read methods (for example, when trying to get elements from an empty list). Thanks to BBlib's features (including the @Attach mechanism described in Sect. 3.5), we could add annotations without modifying the implementation of these classes. Note, however, that we verified relatively simple specifications, focusing on exceptional behavior; a dedicated support for complex data structure functional specifications [9,22] exceeds BBlib's current capabilities and belongs to future work.

Implicit Exceptions. As explained in Sect. 3.5, users of BYTEBACK can enable or disable checking of implicitly thrown exceptions. Experiments 2, 20, 22, and 31 check implicit **null**-pointer exceptions; experiments 1, 20, 21, and 30 check implicit out-of-bounds exceptions; all other experiments do not use any implicitly thrown exceptions, and hence we disabled the corresponding checks.

4.2 Results

All experiments ran on a Fedora 36 GNU/Linux machine with an Intel Core i9-12950HX CPU (4.9GHz), running Boogie 2.15.8.0, Z3 4.11.2.0, and Soot 4.3.0. To account for measurement noise, we repeated the execution of each experiment five times and report the average wall-clock running time of each experiment, split into BYTEBACK bytecode-to-Boogie encoding and Boogie verification of the generated Boogie program. We ran Boogie with default options except for experiment 19, which uses the /infer:j option (needed to derive the loop invariant of the enhanced **for** loop, whose index variable is implicit in the source code).

All of the experiments verified successfully. To sanity-check that the axiomatization or any other parts of the encoding introduced by BYTEBACK are consistent, we also ran Boogie's so-called smoke test on the experiments;[5] these tests inject **assert false** in reachable parts of a Boogie program, and check that none of them pass verification.

As you can see in Table 4, BYTEBACK's running time is usually below 1.5 s; and so is Boogie's verification time. Unsurprisingly, programs 16 and 17 are outliers, since they are made of larger classes with many dependencies; these slow down both BYTEBACK's encoding process and Boogie's verification, which have to deal with many annotations and procedures to analyze and verify.

Only about 11% of the time listed under Table 4's column ENCODING is taken by BYTEBACK's actual encoding; the rest is spent to perform class resolution (Sect. 3.5) and to initialize Soot's analysis—which dominate BYTEBACK's overall running time.

5   Related Work

The state-of-the-art deductive verifiers for Java include OpenJML [6], KeY [1], and Krakatoa [7]; they all process the source language directly, and use variants

---

[5] Smoke tests provide no absolute guarantee of consistency, but are often practically effective.

Table 4. Verification experiments with exceptional behavior used to demonstrate BYTEBACK's capabilities. Each row reports: a numeric identifier # and a short description of the EXPERIMENT; the source programming LANGuage (Java 8, Java 17, Scala 2, Kotlin 1.8); the wall-clock time (in seconds) taken for ENCODING bytecode into Boogie, and for the VERIFICATION of the Boogie program; the size (in non-empty lines of code) of the SOURCE program with its annotations, and of the generated BOOGIE program; the number of METhods that make up the program and its BBlib specification; and the number of ANNOTATIONS introduced for verification, among: specification predicates P (@Predicate), pre- and postconditions S (@Require, @Ensure), and exception annotations E (@Raise, @Return).

#	EXPERIMENT	LANG	ENCODING TIME [s]	VERIFICATION	SOURCE SIZE [LOC]	BOOGIE	MET	ANNOTATIONS P	S	E
1	Implicit Index Out of Bounds	J 8	1.2	1.0	87	366	16	5	2	8
2	Implicit Null Dereference	J 8	1.0	1.0	84	429	26	4	0	10
3	Multi-Catch	J 8	1.2	0.9	67	311	10	1	1	4
4	Throw-Catch	J 8	1.1	1.1	164	504	46	10	0	17
5	Throw-Catch in Loop	J 8	1.1	1.0	97	398	11	1	0	9
6	Try-Finally	J 8	1.0	1.0	125	386	15	2	4	6
7	Try-With-Resources	J 8	1.3	1.2	199	1 635	26	3	4	13
8	Array Reverse	J 8	1.1	1.1	72	221	9	5	3	2
9	Binary Search	J 8	1.2	0.8	52	169	6	4	4	1
10	GCD	J 8	1.1	0.8	50	200	6	3	1	1
11	Linear Search	J 8	1.2	0.8	62	193	9	6	6	2
12	Selection Sort (**double**)	J 8	1.2	1.9	110	234	16	9	9	3
13	Selection Sort (**int**)	J 8	1.1	3.2	110	234	16	9	9	3
14	Square of Sorted Array	J 8	1.1	0.8	61	187	7	4	1	1
15	Sum	J 8	1.1	0.8	45	175	5	2	1	1
16	ArrayList	J 8	5.7	5.7	2 653	7 160	294	14	0	24
17	LinkedList	J 8	2.1	2.9	2 472	3 041	366	8	2	17
18	Try-With-Resources on Local	J 17	1.0	0.9	44	220	6	1	1	1
19	Summary	J 17	0.9	0.8	48	171	5	2	2	1
20	Read Resource	J 17	1.1	0.8	117	447	14	12	6	7
21	Implicit Index Out of Bounds	S 2	1.2	0.8	44	231	7	2	1	4
22	Implicit Null Dereference	S 2	1.0	0.9	43	275	6	1	0	6
23	Multi-Catch	S 2	1.2	0.9	45	297	7	1	1	2
24	Throw-Catch	S 2	1.1	1.1	121	460	22	7	1	12
25	Try-Finally	S 2	1.3	1.0	117	455	15	2	4	3
26	Array Reverse	S 2	1.1	1.2	62	221	8	4	2	2
27	Counter	S 2	1.2	0.8	48	183	8	3	3	4
28	GCD	S 2	1.1	0.8	51	203	5	2	1	1
29	Linear Search	S 2	1.0	0.8	46	155	6	4	3	1
30	Implicit Index Out of Bounds	K 1.8	1.2	0.8	45 ·	279	7	2	4	4
31	Implicit Null Dereference	K 1.8	1.2	0.9	41	309	6	1	0	6
32	Throw-Catch	K 1.8	1.2	1.1	121	442	22	7	0	12
33	Try-Finally	K 1.8	1.3	1.0	108	409	15	2	4	3
34	Array Reverse	K 1.8	1.2	1.0	60	226	8	4	2	2
35	Counter	K 1.8	1.2	0.9	46	177	8	3	3	4
36	GCD	K 1.8	1.1	0.8	50	202	5	2	1	1
37	Linear Search	K 1.8	1.3	0.8	43	193	6	4	3	1
	total		47.8	44.0	7 810	21 398	1 070	156	89	199
	average		1.3	1.2	211	578	29	4	2	5

of JML specification language—which offers support for specifying exceptional behavior.

Exceptional Behavior Specifications. Unlike BBlib, where postconditions can refer to both exceptional and normal behavior, JML clearly separates between the two, using `ensures` and `signals` clauses (as demonstrated in Fig. 6). These JML features are supported by OpenJML, KeY, and Krakatoa according to their intended semantics.

```
//@ ensures this.a == a;
//@ signals (Throwable) this.a == a;
public void m(int a)
{ this.a = a; if (ε) throw new
    RuntimeException(); }
```

```
@Ensure(this.a = a)
public void m(int a)
{ this.a = a;
  if (ε) throw new
    RuntimeException(); }
```

Fig. 6. Equivalent exceptional specifications in JML (left) and BBlib (right).

Implicit Exceptional Behavior. Implicitly thrown exceptions, such as those occurring when accessing an array with an out-of-bounds index, may be handled in different ways by a verifier: *i*) ignore such exceptions; *ii*) implicitly check that such exceptions never occur; *iii*) allow users to specify these exceptions like explicit ones. OpenJML and Krakatoa [12] follow strategy *ii*), which is sound but loses some precision since it won't verify some programs (such as Sect. 2's example); KeY offers options to select any of these strategies, which gives the most flexibility; BYTEBACK offers options *i*) and *iii*), so that users can decide how thorough the analysis of exceptional behavior should be.

Java Exception Features. OpenJML, KeY, and Krakatoa [7] all support try-catch-finally blocks, which have been part of Java since its very first version. The first significant extension to exceptional feature occurred with Java 7, which introduced multi-catch and try-with-resources blocks. [32] KeY and Krakatoa support earlier versions of Java, and hence they cannot handle either feature. OpenJML supports many features of Java up to version 8, and hence can verify programs using multi-catch or try-with-resources—with the exception of try-with-resources using an existing **final** variable, a feature introduced only in Java 9. As usual, our point here is not to criticize these state-of-the-art verification tools, but to point out how handling the proliferation of Java language features becomes considerably easier when targeting bytecode following BYTE-BACK's approach.

Intermediate Representation Verifiers. A different class of verifiers — including JayHorn [10,25], SeaHorn [8], and SMACK [23]—target intermediate representations (JVM bytecode for JayHorn, and LLVM bitcode for SeaHorn and SMACK). Besides this similarity, these tools' capabilities are quite different from BYTEBACK's: they implement analyses based on model-checking (with verification conditions expressible as constrained Horn clauses, or other specialized logics), which provide a high degree of automation (e.g., they do not require loop invariants) to verify simpler, lower-level properties (e.g., reachability). Implicitly thrown exceptions are within the purview of tools like JayHorn, which injects checks before each instruction that may dereference a null pointer, access an index out of bounds, or perform an invalid cast. In terms of usage, this is more similar to a specialized static analysis tool that checks the absence of certain runtime errors [2,4,21] than to fully flexible, but onerous to use, deductive verifiers like BYTEBACK.

BML [5] is a specification language for bytecode; since it is based on JML, it is primarily used as a way of expressing a high-level Java behavioral specification at the bytecode level. This is useful for approaches to proof-carrying code [18] and proof transformations [16], where one verifies a program's source-code and then certifies its bytecode compilation by directly transforming the proof steps.

6   Conclusions

Reasoning about exceptional behavior at the level of Java bytecode facilitates handling exception-related features in any version of Java, as well as in other JVM languages like Scala and Kotlin. More generally, the BYTEBACK approach that we extended in this paper can complement the core work in source-level deductive verification and make it readily available to the latest languages and features.

References

1. Ahrendt, W., et al.: The KeY platform for verification and analysis of java programs. In: Giannakopoulou, D., Kroening, D. (eds.) VSTTE 2014. LNCS, vol. 8471, pp. 55–71. Springer, Cham (2014). https://doi.org/10.1007/978-3-319-12154-3_4
2. Banerjee, S., Clapp, L., Sridharan, M.: NullAway: practical type-based null safety for Java. In: Dumas, M., Pfahl, D., Apel, S., Russo, A. (eds.) Proceedings of the ACM Joint Meeting on European Software Engineering Conference and Symposium on the Foundations of Software Engineering, ESEC/SIGSOFT FSE 2019, Tallinn, Estonia, 26–30 August 2019, pp. 740–750. ACM (2019). https://doi.org/10.1145/3338906.3338919
3. Barnett, M., Chang, B.-Y.E., DeLine, R., Jacobs, B., Leino, K.R.M.: Boogie: a modular reusable verifier for object-oriented programs. In: de Boer, F.S., Bonsangue, M.M., Graf, S., de Roever, W.-P. (eds.) FMCO 2005. LNCS, vol. 4111, pp. 364–387. Springer, Heidelberg (2006). https://doi.org/10.1007/11804192_17
4. Calcagno, C., et al.: Moving fast with software verification. In: Havelund, K., Holzmann, G., Joshi, R. (eds.) NFM 2015. LNCS, vol. 9058, pp. 3–11. Springer, Cham (2015). https://doi.org/10.1007/978-3-319-17524-9_1
5. Chrząszcz, J., Huisman, M., Schubert, A.: BML and related tools. In: de Boer, F.S., Bonsangue, M.M., Madelaine, E. (eds.) FMCO 2008. LNCS, vol. 5751, pp. 278–297. Springer, Heidelberg (2009). https://doi.org/10.1007/978-3-642-04167-9_14
6. Cok, D.R.: OpenJML: Software verification for Java 7 using JML, OpenJDK, and Eclipse. In: Dubois, C., Giannakopoulou, D., Méry, D. (eds.) Proceedings 1st Workshop on Formal Integrated Development Environment, F-IDE 2014, Grenoble, 6 April 2014. EPTCS, 149, pp. 79–92 (2014). https://doi.org/10.4204/EPTCS.149.8

7. Filliâtre, J.-C., Marché, C.: The Why/Krakatoa/Caduceus platform for deductive program verification. In: Damm, W., Hermanns, H. (eds.) CAV 2007. LNCS, vol. 4590, pp. 173–177. Springer, Heidelberg (2007). https://doi.org/10.1007/978-3-540-73368-3_21

8. Gurfinkel, A., Kahsai, T., Komuravelli, A., Navas, J.A.: The SeaHorn verification framework. In: Kroening, D., Păsăreanu, C.S. (eds.) CAV 2015. LNCS, vol. 9206, pp. 343–361. Springer, Cham (2015). https://doi.org/10.1007/978-3-319-21690-4_20

9. Hiep, H.A., Maathuis, O., Bian, J., de Boer, F.S., de Gouw, S.: Verifying OpenJDK's LinkedList using KeY (extended paper). Int. J. Softw. Tools Technol. Transf. 24(5), 783–802 (2022). https://doi.org/10.1007/s10009-022-00679-7

10. Kahsai, T., Rümmer, P., Sanchez, H., Schäf, M.: JayHorn: a framework for verifying Java programs. In: Chaudhuri, S., Farzan, A. (eds.) CAV 2016. LNCS, vol. 9779, pp. 352–358. Springer, Cham (2016). https://doi.org/10.1007/978-3-319-41528-4_19

11. Lam, P., Bodden, E., Lhoták, O., Hendren, L.: The Soot framework for Java program analysis: a retrospective. In: Cetus Users and Compiler Infrastructure Workshop (CETUS 2011) (2011). https://www.bodden.de/pubs/lblh11soot.pdf

12. Marché, C., Paulin-Mohring, C., Urbain, X.: The KRAKATOA tool for certification of JAVA/JAVACARD programs annotated in JML. J. Log. Algeb. Methods Prog. 58(1–2), 89–106 (2004). https://doi.org/10.1016/j.jlap.2003.07.006

13. Marcilio, D., Furia, C.A.: How Java programmers test exceptional behavior. In: Proceedings of the 18th Mining Software Repositories Conference (MSR), pp. 207–218. IEEE (2021)

14. Marcilio, D., Furia, C.A.: What is thrown? Lightweight precise automatic extraction of exception preconditions in Java methods. In: Proceedings of the 38th IEEE International Conference on Software Maintenance and Evolution (ICSME), pp. 340–351. IEEE Computer Society (2022)

15. Melo, H., Coelho, R., Treude, C.: Unveiling exception handling guidelines adopted by Java developers. In: SANER. IEEE (2019)

16. Müller, P., Nordio, M.: Proof-transforming compilation of programs with abrupt termination. In: Proceedings of SAVCBS, pp. 39–46. ACM (2007). https://doi.org/10.1145/1292316.1292321

17. Nakshatri, S., Hegde, M., Thandra, S.: Analysis of exception handling patterns in Java projects: An empirical study. IEEE/ACM MSR (2016)

18. Necula, G.C.: Proof-carrying code. In: Lee, P., Henglein, F., Jones, N.D. (eds.) POPL, pp. 106–119. ACM Press (1997). https://doi.org/10.1145/263699.263712

19. Paganoni, M., Furia, C.A.: ByteBack iFM 2023 Replication Package (2023). https://doi.org/10.5281/zenodo.8335240

20. Paganoni, M., Furia, C.A.: Verifying functional correctness properties at the level of Java bytecode. In: Chechik, M., Katoen, J.P., Leucker, M. (eds.) Proceedings of the 25th International Symposium on Formal Methods (FM). LNCS, vol. 14000, pp. 343–363. Springer, Cham (2023). https://doi.org/10.1007/978-3-031-27481-7_20

21. Papi, M.M., Ali, M., Jr., T.L.C., Perkins, J.H., Ernst, M.D.: Practical pluggable types for Java. In: Ryder, B.G., Zeller, A. (eds.) Proceedings of the ACM/SIGSOFT International Symposium on Software Testing and Analysis, ISSTA 2008, Seattle, 20–24 July 2008, pp. 201–212. ACM (2008). https://doi.org/10.1145/1390630.1390656

22. Polikarpova, N., Tschannen, J., Furia, C.A.: A fully verified container library. Formal Aspects Comput. 30(5), 495–523 (2018)

23. Rakamarić, Z., Emmi, M.: SMACK: decoupling source language details from verifier implementations. In: Biere, A., Bloem, R. (eds.) CAV 2014. LNCS, vol. 8559, pp. 106–113. Springer, Cham (2014). https://doi.org/10.1007/978-3-319-08867-9_7

24. Rudich, A., Darvas, Á., Müller, P.: Checking well-formedness of pure-method specifications. In: Cuellar, J., Maibaum, T., Sere, K. (eds.) FM 2008. LNCS, vol. 5014, pp. 68–83. Springer, Heidelberg (2008). https://doi.org/10.1007/978-3-540-68237-0_7

25. Rümmer, P.: JayHorn: a Java model checker. In: Murray, T., Ernst, G. (eds.) Proceedings of the 21st Workshop on Formal Techniques for Java-like Programs, FTfJP@ECOOP 2019, London, 15 July 2019, p. 1:1. ACM (2019). https://doi.org/10.1145/3340672.3341113

26. Vallée-Rai, R., Co, P., Gagnon, E., Hendren, L.J., Lam, P., Sundaresan, V.: Soot - a Java bytecode optimization framework. In: MacKay, S.A., Johnson, J.H. (eds.) Proceedings of the 1999 Conference of the Centre for Advanced Studies on Collaborative Research, 8–11 November 1999, Mississauga, p. 13. IBM (1999). https://dl.acm.org/citation.cfm?id=782008

27. Weimer, W., Necula, G.C.: Finding and preventing run-time error handling mistakes. In: Proceedings of the 19th Annual ACM SIGPLAN Conference on Object-Oriented Programming, Systems, Languages, and Applications, OOPSLA 2004 (October), pp. 24–28, 2004. Vancouver, BC, Canada, pp. 419–431. ACM (2004). https://doi.org/10.1145/1028976.1029011

URL References

28. https://jcp.org/en/jsr/detail?id=334
29. https://docs.oracle.com/javase/tutorial/essential/exceptions/runtime.html
30. https://docs.oracle.com/javase/specs/jvms/se7/html/jvms-2.html#jvms-2.10
31. https://docs.oracle.com/javase/8/docs/api/java/util/package-summary.html
32. https://www.oracle.com/java/technologies/javase/jdk7-relnotes.html

Analysis and Formal Specification of OpenJDK's `BitSet`

Andy S. Tatman[1]([✉])[iD], Hans-Dieter A. Hiep[1,2][iD], and Stijn de Gouw[3][iD]

[1] Leiden Institute of Advanced Computer Science (LIACS), Leiden, The Netherlands
tatmanandys@gmail.com, hdh@cwi.nl
[2] Centrum Wiskunde and Informatica, Amsterdam, The Netherlands
[3] Open Universiteit, Heerlen, The Netherlands
sdg@ou.nl

Abstract. This paper uses a combination of formal specification and testing, to analyse OpenJDK's `BitSet` class. This class represents a vector of bits that grows as required. During our analysis, we uncovered a number of bugs. We propose and compare various solutions, supported by our formal specification. While a full mechanical verification of the `BitSet` class is not yet possible due to limited support for bitwise operations in the KeY theorem prover, we show initial steps taken to formally verify the challenging `get(int,int)` method, and discuss some required extensions to the theorem prover.

Keywords: Formal specification · Testing · Java/OpenJDK · KeY · JML

1 Introduction

Formal specification and verification are extremely powerful techniques to inspect program code and determine either its correctness or find errors that can be missed by traditional testing techniques. These formal methods may uncover bugs that have laid dormant in code for years. However, applying formal methods can also be extremely time-consuming: even a small section of code can require a large proof to verify it. As such, formal verification is generally directed to essential and frequently used code, such as standard libraries. Previous examples of such an effort include the verification of OpenJDK's `LinkedList` class [12] and OpenJDK's sorting implementation [10]. In this paper, we discuss and analyse another of Java's standard library classes, specifically the OpenJDK's `BitSet` class. The original goal was to formally verify the correctness of an essential part of the `BitSet` class using the KeY theorem prover. However, when using techniques such as formal specification and testing, we encountered a number of issues that appear to have existed in the code since the original push on OpenJDK's public repository back in 2007[1].

---

[1] https://github.com/openjdk/jdk/blob/319a3b994703aac84df7bcde272adfcb3cdbbb
f0/jdk/src/share/classes/java/util/BitSet.java.

P. Herber and A. Wijs (Eds.): iFM 2023, LNCS 14300, pp. 134–152, 2024.
https://doi.org/10.1007/978-3-031-47705-8_8

We first identified an overflow bug in `BitSet`'s `get(int,int)` method. Later, we also encountered issues with the `valueOf(...)` methods that under certain conditions leaves (an instance of) bitset in an unexpected state, causing erratic behaviour in the other methods of the class. We have chosen to use the KeY theorem prover because it most accurately models Java semantics, including, for example, integer overflows. Unlike other available verification tools, KeY allows to load the unaltered `BitSet` class. And even then, we need to extend KeY with additional proof rules before we are able to perform a full verification. However, a full verification of the `BitSet` class is not yet possible, since the issues we encountered are not yet resolved by the Java developers and so the specification and implementation is not settled yet.

Related Work. To the best of our knowledge, this is the first paper presenting a formal analysis of Java's `BitSet` class, but there is related work in two directions. On the one hand, in recent years there have been several case studies in formal verification [2,6,13] and model checking [3,9] of various Java libraries. However, these libraries did not substantially use bitwise operations. At most a few bit-shifts were present and shifts can be covered purely arithmetically in a fairly straightforward manner by multiplying or dividing with a power of two.

In another direction, there are numerous works that focus on (mechanisation of) logical theories for bit vectors, not necessarily tied to Java. The SMT solver Z3 [15] has a theory for fixed-width bit vectors. It works roughly by flattening (also known as bit-blasting) a given arithmetic formula of interest that involves bit vectors into an equisatisfiable propositional formula and then solving the resulting propositional formula with SAT-solving techniques. An extension of the CVC4 SMT-solver [11] also supports bit vectors using bit-blasting and, recently, a more advanced technique called int-blasting [17]. Isabelle/HOL is a proof assistant that supports bit vectors [7], building on the work in Z3. The Coq proof assistant also includes a theory for bit vectors [5] which has been applied to a (self-written) library for finite sets, represented by bit vectors. There is also a tool-supported approach for verifying LTL properties (a common temporal logic) of programs involving bit vectors.

While none of these solvers and proof assistants directly support the full-fledged Java semantics required to load and analyse the unaltered `BitSet` class with the formal JML specifications, they could potentially serve as back-ends to solve proof obligations that arise during verification with KeY. This requires developing a translator for proof obligations from KeY into e.g. SMT-LIB. KeY already supports translating standard arithmetic formulas into SMT-LIB (and then using e.g. Z3 as a back-end) but the translation of bitwise operations is limited and would have to be enhanced: most bitwise operations are currently translated as uninterpreted function symbols.

Outline. In Sect. 2 we explain the structure and inner workings of the `BitSet` class. Section 3 then discusses our formal specification that captures the expected behaviour of the class. Section 4 discusses the issues that we discovered while analysing the correctness of the class, and Sect. 4.3 offers various solution directions. Finally, Sect. 5 covers a proof sketch of the formal verification of the `get(int,int)` method, as well as extensions that are required to the KeY theorem prover in order to complete the proof.

Listing 1. The fields and methods of the `BitSet` class relevant for this paper. See also the Javadoc of `BitSet` [1] for a full description of all its methods.

```java
package java.util;

public class BitSet {
    // The internal field storing the bits.
    private long[] words;
    // The number of words in the logical size of this BitSet.
    private transient int wordsInUse = 0;

    /** Creates a new bit set. */
    public BitSet() { ... }
    /** Creates a bit set whose initial size is large enough to
        explicitly represent bits with indices in the range 0 through
        nbits-1. */
    public BitSet(int nbits) { ... }
    /** Returns a new bit set containing all the bits in the given long
        array. */
    public static BitSet valueOf(long[] longs) { ... }

    /** Sets the bit at the specified index to true. */
    public void set(int bitIndex) { ... }
    /** Returns the value of the bit with the specified index. */
    public boolean get(int bitIndex) { ... }
    /** Sets the bit specified by the index to false. */
    public void clear(int bitIndex) { ... }
    /** Returns a new BitSet composed of bits from this BitSet from
        fromIndex (inclusive) to toIndex (exclusive). */
    public BitSet get(int fromIndex, int toIndex) { ... }

    /** Returns the "logical size" of this BitSet: the index of the
        highest set bit in the BitSet plus one. */
    public int length() { ... }
}
```

2   The BitSet Class

The `BitSet` class is part of Java's standard library in the open-source Java Development Kit (OpenJDK). Listing 1 shows the fields and methods of the class relevant for this paper. The class allows users to store bits (or primitive Booleans) as a bit vector and packs these bits efficiently as an array of elements of primitive type **long**, where each long element stores (and occupies, on mainstream architectures) 64 bits. This is typically far more efficient memory-wise than storing an unpacked array of individual primitive Booleans. In arrays, all elements must be directly addressable, and so, on byte-aligned memory architectures, every single bit in an array of primitive Booleans would use 8 bits.

The class has methods to set, clear or get the value of one bit, as well as methods to do the same for sequences of consecutive bits. These methods operate on Booleans, and internally perform packing and unpacking of the bit vector. We shall simply speak of bit values 1 and 0, instead of true and false, respectively.

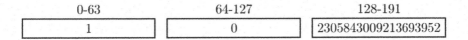

Fig. 1. A representation of the words array. Each individual word is depicted by a decimal number inside a box. The third box contains the decimal number 2^{61}, which has exactly 1 bit set to 1. wordsInUse is 3, as the words array has 3 elements and the last word has bits set.

0	1	2		189	190	191
1	0	0	...	1	0	0

Fig. 2. The logical representation of the same bitset as depicted in Fig. 1. Each bit is stored separately. Every bit between the dots is set to 0. The bit in 189 is set to 1, because it is the bit set in 2^{61} in the third element of words.

The field words contains the array of (64-bit) long elements. Each word packs bits, also making use of the sign bit. Index 0 of a bitset is the least significant bit in the first word, index 63 is the most significant bit of the first word (the sign bit), and index 64 is the least significant bit of the second word.

Figure 1 shows the words array of a bitset instance, while Fig. 2 shows the logical representation of that same array as a sequence of bits. The class also maintains an integer field wordsInUse that keeps track of the last word that contains at least one set bit. The wordsInUse field is used to approximate the logical size of the bitset instance. In fact, the *logical size* of the BitSet is the position of the most significant bit that is set to 1, and therefore is closely related to wordsInUse. If no bits are set in a bitset instance, then the logical size is 0. If the first bit (at index 0) is the most significant bit that is set to 1, the logical size is 1. In the example above, the logical size is 190, as index 189 is the last bit that is set to 1.

Initially every bit in a bitset instance is set to 0. If a user tries to retrieve the value of a bit outside of the logical size of a bitset, then this value is by default 0. This allows the class to handle access to any bit at a non-negative index, even if the corresponding index would fall outside the bounds of the words array. When setting a bit at an index outside of the words array, the bitset expands dynamically by allocating a larger words array.

3 Formal Specification

We focused on a selection of methods that cover the main operations of the BitSet class: querying and modifying bitsets, shown in Listing 1, and the internal methods recalculateWordsInUse(), expandTo(int), ensureCapacity(int) that are explained later. Next, we formulate a specification of the class, in the form of a class invariant and contracts for methods in scope. We also introduce model methods (see below) to express method contracts at an abstraction level that corresponds more closely to our intuition of expected method behaviour.

We employ the Java Modelling Language (JML) [14] as the language in which we express our formal specification. The KeY tool automatically translates our given specifications into Java Dynamic Logic (JavaDL) [2] to be able to reason about the correctness of methods.

Method contracts describe what must be true in the state prior to the method being called (pre-condition) and what must be true in the state after the method terminates (post-condition). The pre-condition for a method is described in JML using the `requires` clause, while the post-condition is described using the `ensures` clause. A contract can also specify exactly what parts of the heap can be altered using the `assignable` clause. For example, `assigable \nothing` means that the fields of any pre-existing object must remain exactly the same, but the method is allowed to create new objects.

Further, we distinguish helper methods from normal methods. The contracts of normal methods implicitly includes the class invariant as part of the pre-condition and post-condition, while helper methods do not implicitly include the class invariant. We can use `\invariant_for(this)` to explicitly specify that the invariant *does* hold in the pre-condition or post-condition of a helper method. This is used, for example, in the helper method `recalculateWordsInUse()` that restores the class invariant of a bitset where the invariant did not hold in the pre-condition.

3.1   Class Invariant

Our starting point for defining the class invariant is the three assertions given in the `checkInvariants()` method. These are the following:

1. Either `wordsInUse` is zero or `words[wordsInUse-1]` is non-zero. The latter condition states that the word possibly indicated by `wordsInUse` has at least one bit that is set.
2. The value of `wordsInUse` is in the range of [0, `words.length`], inclusive.
3. Either `wordsInUse` equals the length of `words`, or the first word outside the meaningful part of the `words` array, i.e. `words[wordsInUse]`, has no set bits and so `words[wordsInUse] = 0`.

These conditions are indeed necessarily part of the class invariant, but these conditions alone are not sufficient: there are more conditions that remain invariant.

The `words` array is allocated and we know that `words` is never null. Further, the last condition suggests that *all* words after `words[wordsInUse-1]` should be equal to zero. In fact, the implementations of the in-scope methods guarantee this property. As an example, take the `recalculateWordsInUse` method. This helper method restores the class invariant by setting the `wordsInUse` variable to the proper value: when the method is called, it is assumed that all words after `words[wordsInUse-1]` equal zero, and the method moves the `wordsInUse` as much as is possible to the left to ensure that condition (1) above holds. By moving `wordsInUse` to the left when `words[wordsInUse]` is zero, we indeed have that all words after `wordsInUse` are equal to 0.

We formalise this intuition by the class invariant in Listing 2.

Listing 2. The first part of the class invariant, written in JML.

```
 1  /*@ invariant
 2    @ words != null &
 3    @ // The first three are from checkInvariants:
 4    @ (wordsInUse == 0 | words[wordsInUse - 1] != 0) &&
 5    @ (wordsInUse >= 0 && wordsInUse <= words.length) &&
 6    @ (wordsInUse == words.length || words[wordsInUse] == 0) &&
 7    @ // Our addition to the invariant:
 8    @ (wordsInUse < words.length ==> (\forall \bigint i; wordsInUse <= i
          < words.length; words[i] == 0) ) &&
 9    @ ...
10    @*/
```

Next, we look for upper bounds of words.length and wordsInUse. Bitsets that are generated by the public constructors (i.e. not by the valueOf(...) methods, see Sect. 4.2) will allocate a words array. When acting on bitsets using e.g. the set(...) method, the words array grows as required by the internal expandTo(int) and ensureCapacity(int) methods, while the wordsInUse variable is updated to reflect the largest word with a set bit. The largest addressable position of a bit is at position Integer.MAX_VALUE, which is stored in words[Integer.MAX_VALUE/64]. Hence, the upper bound of wordsInUse is Integer.MAX_VALUE/64 + 1.

The ensureCapacity(int wordsRequired) method grows the array if necessary, specifically if wordsRequired is larger than the current length of words. If the array should grow, this method allocates a new array of length Math.max(2 * words.length, wordsRequired), meaning that the array gets at least doubled every time words is expanded. The bound for the parameter wordsRequired is the same as for wordsInUse, namely Integer.MAX_VALUE/64 + 1. The largest word array that the public constructors create is also of length Integer.MAX_VALUE/64 + 1. For the upper bound of the length of words, we thus take double this value: 2 * (Integer.MAX_VALUE/64 + 1).

These bounds hold while using BitSet's methods to interact with specific bits, such as set(...) and clear(...). However, in Sect. 4.2, we will show that these bounds are violated when using the static valueOf(...) methods.

3.2 The wordsToSeq() Model Method

In order to express properties of the contents of a bitset, we use a sequence of Booleans as representation, such that position i in the sequence corresponds to the bit at position i in the bitset. We employ a *model method*, which is a method that is only used in our contracts and does not affect the (run-time) state of the object [8], shown in Listing 3.

Listing 3. Our wordsToSeq() model method.

```
 1  /*@ private model strictly_pure \seq wordsToSeq() {
 2    @ return (\seq_def \bigint i; 0; (\bigint)wordsInUse * (\bigint)
          BITS_PER_WORD; (words[i / BITS_PER_WORD] >>>
 3            (int)(i % BITS_PER_WORD)) & 1);
 4    @ }
 5    @*/
```

For each word in the **words** array, the sequence isolates each of the individual 64 bits and stores them as an element of the sequence returned by the model method. Note that, contrary to the logical size of a bitset, the length of our sequence of Booleans is a multiple of 64, the number of bits per word. As an example, consider that the **wordsToSeq()** model method converts the array as seen in Fig. 1 to the sequence as seen in Fig. 2.

As with the behaviour of the **BitSet** class itself, any bit at a position larger than the length of this sequence in the **words** array must equal 0.

It is now possible to give contracts for the methods **get(int)**, **set(int)**, and **clear(int)**. Namely, the value that is returned by **get(int)** is precisely the value of the Boolean of the **wordsToSeq** sequence at the right position, or zero if it falls outside. Similarly, for **set(int)** and **clear(int)** we can relate the **wordsToSeq** sequence in the pre-state and the post-state by expressing what bit values remain unchanged, and the new bit value at the changed position in the bit vector.

3.3   The **get(int,int)** Method

A more challenging method to specify is the **get(int fromIndex, int toIndex)** method. It returns a new **BitSet** instance that contains the bits from the given range. As we will show in Sect. 4, the **get(int,int)** method has a bug in it, not only in the current Java version (JDK 20, at the time of writing)[2] but also all the way back to the first release of OpenJDK and possibly even further back. Assuming that the bug will eventually be resolved, **get(int,int)** is still an interesting method to look at. It is one of the larger and more complex methods in the **BitSet** class, and its verification requires giving a non-trivial loop invariant.

The method returns a subsequence of the current bitset, containing all bits from the **fromIndex** up to but *not* including the **toIndex**. Both **fromIndex** and **toIndex** must be non-negative integers, and **fromIndex** must be less than or equal **toIndex**. Furthermore, the specification involves comparing two different Boolean sequences, namely the original sequence and the sequence associated to the new **BitSet** instance returned by the method.

The contract for this method can be seen in Listing 4.

Listing 4. The contract for the **get(int,int)** method.

```
1   /*@ normal_behaviour
2     @ requires fromIndex >= 0 && fromIndex <= toIndex;
3     @ ensures \result != this && \invariant_for(\result);
4     @ ensures (\forall \bigint i; 0 <= i < \result.wordsToSeq().length;
        (fromIndex + i < wordsToSeq().length ?
        wordsToSeq()[fromIndex + i] : 0) == \result.wordsToSeq()[i]);
5     @ ensures (\result.wordsToSeq().length < toIndex - fromIndex) ==>
        (\forall \bigint i; \result.wordsToSeq().length <= i < toIndex -
        fromIndex; (fromIndex + i < wordsToSeq().length ?
        wordsToSeq()[fromIndex + i] : 0) == 0);
```

---

[2] https://github.com/openjdk/jdk/blob/a52c4ede2f043b7d4a234c7d06f91871312e965 4/src/java.base/share/classes/java/util/BitSet.java.

```
6    @ assignable \nothing;
7    @*/
```

The pre-condition of the method states that $0 \leq$ fromIndex $\leq$ toIndex. For the post-condition of this method, we have, first of all, that the invariant must hold for the resulting bitset and that the resulting instance is different from this. Further, the last two ensures clauses express that the resulting bitset contains the expected bits. Every element in result.wordsToSeq() should match in value to the corresponding element in the original this.wordsToSeq(). If an element at position i is out of the bounds of one of the Boolean sequences, then that element should equal 0 in the other sequence. For example, assume the user calls get(0, 100) and the method returns a bitset with result.wordsToSeq().length = 64. This means that the bits at positions 64–99 in result are set to 0, and as such the corresponding bits in the original bitset should also all equal 0. Finally, the assignable \nothing clause expresses that the state of the current object is not changed in any way.

4   Issues in BitSet

Using formal specification and testing, we discovered several issues. These issues are outlined in this section, and we suggest solution directions. The two issues are orthogonal, but the issues do overlap in one aspect: an integer overflow of the logical size as returned by length().

4.1   A Bug in get(int,int) Caused by a Negative length()

The first issue occurs in the get(int fromIndex, int toIndex) method[3]. The beginning of the implementation of this method is visible in Listing 5.

Listing 5. Beginning of the get(int, int) method, where the first bug occurs.

```
1   public BitSet get(int fromIndex, int toIndex) {
2     checkRange(fromIndex, toIndex);
3     checkInvariants();
4     int len = length();
5     if (len <= fromIndex || fromIndex == toIndex)
6       return new BitSet(0); // If no set bits in range
7     if (toIndex > len)
8       toIndex = len; // An optimization
9     ...
```

The length() method should return the position of the most significant bit set, plus 1. For example, if the user sets the bit at position 200 in a previously empty bitset, then the length() method will return 201. However, if the user sets the bit at index Integer.MAX_VALUE, then the length() method will return the integer Integer.MAX_VALUE $+ 1$, which overflows to Integer.MIN_VALUE.

Listing 6. Example of how the bug can lead to unexpected results of get(int,int).

```
1   BitSet bset = new BitSet(0);
```

---

[3] This bug report has been accepted by Oracle, see JDK-8305734.

```
2   bset.set(Integer.MAX_VALUE);
3   bset.set(999);
4   BitSet result = bset.get(0,1000);
```

Listing 6 shows an example where this gives faulty behaviour. The expected behaviour would be that `result` is a bitset with logical size 1000 and which has bit 999 set. However, with the current implementation, the `result` has logical size 0 and has no bits set!

This is because `bset.length()` returns the negative `Integer.MIN_VALUE`. The expression `len <= fromIndex` on line 5 will always evaluate to true, since `Integer.MIN_VALUE` is smaller than or equal to all 32-bit signed integers, causing the `bset.get(0,1000)` to return the empty bitset.

4.2   Bugs Caused by `valueOf(...)` Corrupting `length()`

The next issue occurs in the `valueOf(...)` methods[4]. We focus on the method with a parameter of type `long[]` (Listing 7), but the same bug occurs in the overloaded methods with parameter types `LongBuffer`, `ByteBuffer` and `byte[]`.

Listing 7. The `valueOf(long[])` method and the private constructor it uses.

```
1    private BitSet(long[] words) {
2      this.words = words;
3      this.wordsInUse = words.length;
4      checkInvariants();
5    }
6    ...
7    public static BitSet valueOf(long[] longs) {
8      int n;
9      for (n = longs.length; n > 0 && longs[n - 1] == 0; n--);
10     return new BitSet(Arrays.copyOf(longs, n));
11   }
```

The `valueOf(long[])` method takes in an array, copies it, and stores it in the internal `words` field of a new bitset instance. The `valueOf(long[])` method does not specify any preconditions: any non-null array can thus be converted to a bitset. Issues arise when the user calls `valueOf(long[])` with an array that has a bit set beyond index `Integer.MAX_VALUE`. This is for example the case when `longs.length` is larger than 2^{25} and contains non-zero elements in that part: since longs are 64-bit, arrays with 2^{25} elements cover all $64 * 2^{25} = 2^{31}$ non-negative integer indices. Listing 8 shows an example how this can go wrong.

Listing 8. Example of how the bug can occur with `valueOf(long[])`.

```
1    final int MAX_WIU = Integer.MAX_VALUE/Long.SIZE + 1; // 2^25+1
2    BitSet normal = new BitSet();
3    normal.set(0);
4    long[] largeArray = new long[2*MAX_WIU + 1];
5    largeArray[largeArray.length - 1] = 1;
6    BitSet broken = BitSet.valueOf(largeArray);
7    broken.set(0);
```

The constant `MAX_WIU` equals $2^{25} + 1$ (the bound of `wordsInUse` as determined in Sect. 3.1). The `BitSet` class can only access elements of the array up to

---

[4] This bug report has been accepted by Oracle, see JDK-8311905.

largeArray[MAX_WIU-1]. As a result, the bit set at largeArray[2*MAX_WIU] is *not* accessible from the broken instance(!)

The equals(Object obj) method specifies that two bitsets are equal "if and only if ... for every non-negative int index k, ((BitSet)obj).get(k) == this.get(k) [is] true." [1] However, this is not the case here: the equals() method returns false when comparing normal to broken, yet normal.get(k) equals broken.get(k) for every non-negative integer k. Furthermore, the length() method says both objects have the same logical length 1.

Going back to the resulting value from length() of broken: in this case, the return value did not only overflow to Integer.MIN_VALUE, but has even gone back up to 1. So broken and normal have the same length as observed through length(). This problem is not limited to only this example. An array with length 4*MAX_WIU+1 for which the last word is set to 1 will result in the same length() value, but in this case the length() has wrapped around *twice*.

Listing 9. The length() method calculates its returned value using wordsInUse.

```
1  public /*@ strictly_pure @*/ int length() {
2    if (wordsInUse == 0) return 0;
3    return BITS_PER_WORD * (wordsInUse - 1) + (BITS_PER_WORD -
         Long.numberOfLeadingZeros(words[wordsInUse - 1]));
4  }
```

The issue with length() persists when interacting normally with the broken bitset: if the user sets a bit $i > 0$ using broken.set(i), then the expected behaviour would be that length() would return $i + 1$. Instead it remains at 1, as the value of wordsInUse was not changed due to wordsInUse already being higher than any value (MAX_WIU or lower) that BitSet would ever normally assign to it, which means that the calculated value of length() is not affected (see Listing 9). Note that in some methods that call length() such as clear(int,int) and previousSetBit(int) behaviour is not negatively affected, for the same reason, that wordsInUse is already higher than expected.

This issue in the valueOf(...) methods does not appear to be a mistake in its implementation. In fact, based on the specification of the methods, a user could use the class to for example convert a LongBuffer to a long array: the user uses the valueOf(LongBuffer) method to get a bitset based on the LongBuffer, and then uses BitSet's toLongArray() method to then convert to a long array. The current implementation of the methods allows for this, provided that the last element of the buffer has at least one bit set (and so is not 0).

But this issue nicely demonstrates the utility of formal specifications: using the methods in this way results in BitSet objects that break crucial internal class invariants, causing public methods to malfunction.

4.3   Solution Directions

We now discuss possible solutions to the issues raised above. To structure the discussion, we distinguish between two solution *directions*: permit using the bit with index Integer.MAX_VALUE, or forbid using that bit. We show which changes are required to the specification (method contracts and class invariant) and implementation to realise these solutions.

Permit Using `Integer.MAX_VALUE` *bit.* Many operations on `BitSet` work fine out-of-the-box for the full range of integers, even when the bit at index `Integer.MAX_VALUE` is used. We show how the methods `get(int,int)`, `length()` and `valueOf(...)` can be fixed while allowing to use that bit.

As stated in Sect. 4.1, `length()` returns the negative value `Integer.MIN_VALUE` if the bit at index `Integer.MAX_VALUE` is set. Note however that no information is lost by returning `Integer.MIN_VALUE`: clients can distinguish bitsets in which the bit at index `Integer.MAX_VALUE` *is* set (returning `Integer.MIN_VALUE`) from `BitSet`s where the bit is not set (returning a non-negative length). Hence, a simple fix is to add to the Javadoc specification that the `length()` method "returns `Integer.MIN_VALUE` if the bit at index `Integer.MAX_VALUE` is set." Effectively, this means the client can interpret the negative return value as an unsigned 32-bit integer.

Using the above solution for `length`, we now turn to the `get(int,int)` method. Listing 1 showed that for the `get` method, the upper bound, given by the second parameter **toIndex**, is *exclusive*, so the highest bit the method can access is at index `Integer.MAX_VALUE-1`. Hence, if the `length()` overflows, we can simply pretend it returned `Integer.MAX_VALUE`. This yields the solution show in Listing 10.

Listing 10. A possible solution of the bug in `get(int,int)`.

```
1   ...
2   int len = length();
3   if (len < 0)
4     len = Integer.MAX_VALUE;
5   if (len <= fromIndex || fromIndex == toIndex)
6     ...
```

This simple fix thus only requires a two-line code change in the internal implementation and does not affect the method specification, nor does it require changes to the class invariant.

For the `valueOf(...)` methods, the question arises what to do if an array is passed in that is too large (i.e. contains bits that are set beyond `Integer.MAX_VALUE`). An obvious fix is to simply prevent such arrays by throwing an `IllegalArgumentException`, along the lines of Listing 11. We also add the constant `MAX_WIU` to the `BitSet` class, initialising it with the value `Integer.MAX_VALUE/Long.SIZE + 1`.

Listing 11. A possible fix for `valueOf(long[] longs)` at the beginning of the method.

```
1   int len = longs.length;
2   if (len > MAX_WIU)
3     throw new IllegalArgumentException("Input array length " + len +
4                         " is larger than maximum");
```

More lenient approaches (not shown here) are also possible: one can allow larger arrays, as long as all bits above the `Integer.MAX_VALUE` index are set to

0, or ignore such bits and only copy the first `Integer.MAX_VALUE` bits. In all those cases, the specification must also be updated to reflect these changes.

Forbid Using the `Integer.MAX_VALUE` *bit.* The second solution direction is to systematically forbid access to the bit with index `Integer.MAX_VALUE`. This can be enforced in the code by throwing an exception in methods with index parameters, along the lines of Listing 12.

Listing 12. Preventing access to the `Integer.MAX_VALUE` bit.

```
1  if (bitIndex == Integer.MAX_VALUE)
2     throw new IndexOutOfBoundsException("bitIndex " + bitIndex +
3                    "must be smaller than " + Integer.MAX_VALUE);
4     ...
```

Now, the length cannot overflow, so the implementation of the `length()` method and `get(int,int)` method do not have to be changed. The `valueOf` method can be fixed along the lines of the above solution, but with an additional check to ensure that the `Integer.MAX_VALUE` bit is not set. Furthermore, it enables the methods with `fromIndex` (inclusive) and `toIndex` (exclusive) parameters, such as the `get(int,int)` method, to access all bits of a `BitSet`: since the highest bit has index `Integer.MAX_VALUE-1`, it can be accessed by taking `Integer.MAX_VALUE` for `toIndex`. The class invariant can also be strengthened to take into account that the `Integer.MAX_VALUE` bit cannot be used.

Discussion. We now briefly reflect and compare the two solution directions. The first direction enables using the full range of non-negative integer indices. It requires few and relatively small changes: the specification of `length()` is strengthened, the specification and implementation of `valueOf` is changed and the internal implementation of `get(int,int)` is fixed. This does not break existing clients that acted in good faith: `length` behaves the same, but its behaviour is now guaranteed in the Javadoc specification. The behaviour of `valueOf` is not changed when arrays are passed in with at most `Integer.MAX_VALUE` bits. But, bad faith clients that relied on the presence of these bugs (e.g. by passing an array to `valueOf` that is too large) cannot do so anymore. On the negative side, the methods with two index parameters where the upper bound is exclusive cannot access the `Integer.MAX_VALUE` bit.

The second solution direction forbids using the `Integer.MAX_VALUE` bit. It requires changing many implementations and specifications, except methods such as `get(int,int)`: all methods with a single index parameter are affected and may now throw an exception. This may break existing client code that relies on the full range of integer indices. On the positive side, the methods with two index parameters can now access the same set of bits in a `BitSet` as their single index parameter counterparts.[5]

---

[5] This solution direction was also considered in an issue from 2003 with `nextClearBit(..)`, see JDK-4816253, but the bugs we described above were not discovered.

5   Towards Formal Verification of the **BitSet** Class

One reason why formal verification of real-world software is costly is that software changes. We reported the above issues to the Java developers (including a suggested fix for the **get(int,int)** method)[6]. This discussion is ongoing at the time of writing and it is not yet clear how the **BitSet** class will be fixed. In particular, the specification and implementation of **BitSet** is not settled yet. Hence, this section is speculative, since the Java developers ultimately are responsible for choosing which solution direction to take to solve the issues mentioned above.

Instead, we will informally describe how the proof of **get(int,int)** can be carried out (Sect. 5.2), assuming that the issues described above are resolved in one particular way (discussed in Sect. 5.1). Moreover, we experienced some issues with the KeY theorem prover (see Sect. 5.3), which block us from completing the formal proof.

5.1   Background

As explained in Sect. 3, we write our formal specification in JML, which is translated into JavaDL by KeY. We add the bounds as described in Sect. 3.1 to the class invariant (see Listing 13). Furthermore, we add a condition that indicates to the KeY prover that each element in the **words** array is within the integer bounds of the primitive **long** type, and we use a KeY-specific extension of JML to do so, the so-called **\dl_** escape hatch [4]. To be able to apply various taclets that are sound only for primitive longs, we require the assumption that each array element of words satisfies the **inLong** predicate. However, we did not manage to automatically show this in KeY itself, even though the type information of the **words** array is known to KeY.

Listing 13. The last part of the class invariant, continuing Listing 2.

```
1    /*@ invariant
2      @ ... &&
3      @ (wordsInUse<=Integer.MAX_VALUE/BITS_PER_WORD+1) &&
4      @ (words.length<=2*(Integer.MAX_VALUE/BITS_PER_WORD+1)) &&
5      @ (\forall \bigint i; 0 <= i < words.length; \dl_inLong(words[i]));
6      @*/
```

We have used the KeY theorem prover version 2.10.0.

5.2   Proof Sketch of **get(int,int)**

In this exposition we will sketch out the proof of correctness of the **get(int,int)** method. For the purposes of this explanation, we assume the bug is fixed according to our suggested fix permitting the **Integer.MAX_VALUE** bit. The full method body is visible in Listing 14.

---

[6] See https://github.com/openjdk/jdk/pull/13388.

Listing 14. The full method body of the get(int,int) method, including our suggested fix and our loop invariant.

```
1   public BitSet get(int fromIndex, int toIndex) {
2       checkRange(fromIndex, toIndex);
3       checkInvariants();
4
5       int len = length();
6       if (len < 0) // Our proposed bug fix
7           len = Integer.MAX_VALUE;
8
9       // If no set bits in range return empty bitset
10      if (len <= fromIndex || fromIndex == toIndex)
11          return new BitSet(0);
12      if (toIndex > len) // An optimization
13          toIndex = len;
14
15      BitSet result = new BitSet(toIndex - fromIndex);
16      int targetWords = wordIndex(toIndex - fromIndex - 1) + 1;
17      int sourceIndex = wordIndex(fromIndex);
18      boolean wordAligned = ((fromIndex & BIT_INDEX_MASK) == 0);
19
20      // Process all words but the last word
21      /*@ // Adjusting wordsToSeq for result:
22      @ maintaining (\forall \bigint j;
23      @    0 <= j < ((\bigint)i*(\bigint)BITS_PER_WORD);
24      @      ( (result.words[j / BITS_PER_WORD]
25      @            >>> (int)(j % BITS_PER_WORD)) & 1 )
26      @ == (fromIndex + i < wordsToSeq().length
27      @       ? wordsToSeq()[fromIndex + i] : 0) );
28      @   // >>> is not defined for bigint.
29      @ maintaining i >= 0 & i <= targetWords - 1;
30      @ maintaining sourceIndex < wordsInUse;
31      @ maintaining (i < targetWords-1)
                ==> sourceIndex+1 < wordsInUse;
32      @ maintaining sourceIndex >= fromIndex / 64 &&
                     sourceIndex <= toIndex / 64;
33      @ maintaining (\forall \bigint j; 0 <= j < result.words.length;
              \dl_inLong(result.words[j]) );
34      @ assignable result.words[*];
35      @ decreasing targetWords - i;
36      @*/
37      for (int i = 0; i < targetWords - 1; i++, sourceIndex++)
38          result.words[i] = wordAligned ? words[sourceIndex] :
39              (words[sourceIndex] >>> fromIndex) |
40              (words[sourceIndex+1] << -fromIndex);
41
42      // Process the last word
43      long lastWordMask = WORD_MASK >>> -toIndex;
44      result.words[targetWords - 1] =
45          ((toIndex-1) & BIT_INDEX_MASK) < (fromIndex & BIT_INDEX_MASK)
46          ? /* straddles source words */
47          ((words[sourceIndex] >>> fromIndex) |
48           (words[sourceIndex+1] & lastWordMask) << -fromIndex)
49          :
50          ((words[sourceIndex] & lastWordMask) >>> fromIndex);
51
52      // Set wordsInUse correctly
53      result.wordsInUse = targetWords;
54      result.recalculateWordsInUse();
55      result.checkInvariants();
56
57      return result;
58  }
```

Initialising Local Variables. After input validation, the `get` method calls several small methods that do not modify any fields of pre-existing objects. These methods have all been given contracts, the main one being `wordIndex(i)`, which returns $i/64$ for non-negative i. Besides `length()`, these contracts have all been verified either automatically or with minimal human interaction in KeY.

Next, several local variables are initialised in lines 15-18. First, a bitset `result` is created through a public constructor, with a `words` array that can fit all the bits required, and `result.wordsInUse` is initialised to 0. The `words` array is filled directly. `result.wordsInUse` is only updated after it is filled completely. The integer `targetWords` is the number of words to copy to `results.words`, and has the same value as `results.words.length`. The `sourceIndex` variable indicates the starting index in `this.words` of the bits to copy. The boolean `wordAligned` indicates if the `result` bitset is aligned to the original bitset. If this is *not* the case, then copying the bits is made more complicated, as each element of `result.words` is spread across two elements of `this.words`.

Loop Invariant. The clause of the loop invariant on line 22 is an adjusted version of `wordsToSeq()`. As `result.wordsInUse` is 0 during the loop, we cannot use `wordsToSeq()` to track the copied bits in `result.words`, as it has a zero length when `wordsInUse` is zero. So, the loop counter i takes care of this.

To verify the statements from line 29 onwards, we use a number of lemmas. First, the number of words that the method copies (`targetWords`) is less than or equal to the number of logically defined elements of `words` (`wordsInUse`). The largest value `toIndex` can have is `wordsInUse`*64, as the `get(int,int)` method reduces `toIndex` so that it is within the logically significant length of the `BitSet`. Hence, the largest value `targetWords` can have is `wordsInUse`, in the case of $\frac{toIndex-fromIndex-1}{64} + 1 = \frac{wordsInUse*64-0-1}{64} + 1 \leq wordsInUse.$[7]

Using this bound for `targetWords`, we can verify that in the loop body, the expressions `this.words[sourceIndex]` and `this.words[sourceIndex+1]` have significant bits as bounded by `wordsInUse`. This is needed for establishing the relation between the resulting bitset and the current bitset, and for preventing an exception.

$$sourceIndex + targetWords - 1 < wordsInUse.$$

This can be rewritten to:[8]

$$\frac{fromIndex}{64} + \left(\frac{toIndex - fromIndex - 1}{64} + 1\right) - 1 < wordsInUse.$$

Next, consider division of *fromIndex* by 64: we can write $fromIndex = 64k + x$ with $k \geq 0$ and $0 \leq x < 64$. Plugging this in into the above equation we can derive that the left-hand side equals $(64k+x)/64+(toIndex-1-x-64k)/64$. By Java's integer division semantics (where non-negative results are rounded down),

---

[7] Rounded using Java rules.

[8] Note that both `sourceIndex` and `targetWords` are calculated using `wordIndex(...)`.

this equals $k + (toIndex - 1 - x)/64 - k = (toIndex - 1 - x)/64$. Clearly this is smaller or equal to $(toIndex - 1)/64$. This is smaller than `wordsInUse`, using the bound for `targetWords` proved before, so the desired inequality follows.

Finally, if `((toIndex-1) & BIT_INDEX_MASK) < (fromIndex & BIT_INDEX_MASK)` holds[9], then the boolean `wordAligned` must be false (as f `(fromIndex & BIT_INDEX_MASK)` must be larger than 0), and we know that the method uses `sourceIndex+1` to access the `this.words` array. To compensate for the +1, we set the bound of `sourceIndex+targetWords` to `wordsInUse-1`. The proof for this is similar to the previous inequality.

As KeY does not fully support binary AND operations (see Sect. 5.3), we replaced `n & 63` with `n % 64`. These are equivalent for non-negative `n`. With suitable lemmas, we expect the preservation of the loop invariant is provable.

End of the `get(int, int)` Method. Once all bits have been copied from the original bitset to `result`, the method calls the `recalculateWordsInUse()` method to establish the invariant in `result`. In our case, `wordsInUse == 0 || words[wordsInUse - 1] != 0` and `wordsInUse == words.length || words[wordsInUse] == 0` from the class invariant need not be true when the method starts (the method is in fact responsible for re-establishing these properties). In particular, `wordsInUse` may be too high, so `words[wordsInUse-1]` may be zero. All other clauses from the class invariant do hold initially. To restore the class invariant, the method lowers `wordsInUse` to the most significant element of `result.words` that is not zero (and to zero if there is none).

As can be seen above, a substantial part of both the (development of) the specification and the proof concerns dealing with Java's bounded integer semantics. We now reflect briefly on our approach, where we chose to deal with Java's bounded integer semantics right from the start. The question may arise whether a two-step approach would have been simpler, where as a first step, a proof of the `BitSet` class is given using ordinary mathematical integer semantics and in a second step, this proof is amended by using Java's bounded integer semantics. KeY supports both mathematical integer semantics and Java's bounded semantics so on first sight a two-step approach may sound promising.

But consider our bug fix in Listing 14, line 6. Without overflows, `length()` returns a positive integer, so the true-branch is dead code with mathematical integer semantics. In the bounded integer version it is not dead code and causes execution to proceed differently in the subsequent code. Formally, the program using bounded integer semantics is not a refinement of that 'same' program with mathematical integers: it satisfies different properties/contracts. Different specifications may have to be developed for the two different integer semantics, symbolic execution of the method proceeds rather differently as witnessed by the dead-code example above and consequently, different proof obligations are generated (which in turn requires different proofs). This complicates proof reuse between the two 'steps'. Practically, the division into two steps would thus amount to an extra step where one would investigate which specifications,

---

[9] BIT_INDEX_MASK is a constant integer equalling 63.

proofs etc. would be needed for the non-real-world version that uses mathematical integers. We chose to avoid such an extra step and deal with the Java's actual bounded integer semantics from the beginning.

5.3   Required Extensions to KeY

Bit shift operations, such as the >>> and << used in get(int,int), cause the so-called *Finish symbolic execution* macro to get stuck in a loop, endlessly applying rules on the shift term. There are workarounds, such as by hiding the shift terms, but this comes at the cost of more manual interactions.

More importantly, KeY currently lacks full support for bitwise operators, such as binaryOr and binaryAnd, which prevents a full mechanic verification of the class. Rules need to be added, or the terms could be translated to an SMT solver, which could then handle these bitwise operations. It may be possible to develop a general theory involving binaryOr and binaryAnd operators, but in our case this does not appear to be necessary. A large amount of the proof goals (not discussed here) are related to wordsToSeq(). An individual element of this sequence is a single bit. This knowledge can be used to make rules where one or both of the operators are a single bit, allowing us to add specific, but simple rules to KeY. Listing 15 shows an example of such a rule for the binaryOr operation.

Listing 15. Taclet rule for binaryOr.

```
1  // x | y = 0. This is true iff x = 0 and y = 0.
2  orLongZero {
3    \schemaVar \term int x, y;
4    \assumes(inLong(x), inLong(y) ==>)
5    \find(moduloLong(binaryOr(x, y)) = 0)
6    \sameUpdateLevel
7    \replacewith(x = 0 & y = 0)
8  };
```

This rule is necessary to close the proof of BitSet's set(int) method. In general, all specific rules we *need* should follow from a more general theory involving bitwise operators. But since the implementation and Javadoc specification are not settled yet, the precise rules that are needed are not known yet, so we left development of the proof rules as future work.

6   Conclusion

We discussed OpenJDK's BitSet class, formulated its formal specification and wrote tests. Using these formal analyses, we discovered bugs triggered by integer overflows and proposed several solution directions for resolving these issues. The integer overflow in length()'s return value when the Integer.MAX_VALUE bit is set is a relatively minor issue, as the method is still usable as long as the user takes this possibility into account. Meanwhile, the bug discovered in the get(int,int) method prevents the method from being properly functioning as long as the Integer.MAX_VALUE bit is set. The bug in the valueOf(..) methods allows the user to create objects which contain inaccessible bits. The length()

method is no longer reliable in these objects due to an integer overflow. Both of these bugs are significant, as they fundamentally break the (intended) specification of the `BitSet` class. Finally, we discussed initial steps towards verification of the `get(int,int)` method and illustrated remaining challenges. The artifact with formal specifications and proofs for several smaller methods is publicly available at [16].

References

1. BitSet (Java Platform SE 8). https://docs.oracle.com/javase/8/docs/api/java/util/BitSet.html. Accessed 12 May 2023
2. Ahrendt, W., Beckert, B., Bubel, R., Hähnle, R., Schmitt, P.H., Ulbrich, M. (eds.): Deductive Software Verification - The KeY Book - From Theory to Practice. LNCS, vol. 10001. Springer (2016). https://doi.org/10.1007/978-3-319-49812-6
3. Beckert, B., Kirsten, M., Klamroth, J., Ulbrich, M.: Modular verification of JML contracts using bounded model checking. In: Margaria, T., Steffen, B. (eds.) ISoLA 2020. LNCS, vol. 12476, pp. 60–80. Springer, Cham (2020). https://doi.org/10.1007/978-3-030-61362-4_4
4. Bian, J., Hiep, H.A., de Boer, F.S., de Gouw, S.: Integrating ADTs in KeY and their application to history-based reasoning about collection. Formal Methods in System Design, pp. 1–27 (2023). https://doi.org/10.1007/s10703-023-00426-x
5. Blot, A., Dagand, P.É., Lawall, J.: From sets to bits in Coq. In: Kiselyov, O., King, A. (eds.) FLOPS 2016. LNCS, vol. 9613, pp. 12–28. Springer, Cham (2016). https://doi.org/10.1007/978-3-319-29604-3_2
6. de Boer, M., de Gouw, S., Klamroth, J., Jung, C., Ulbrich, M., Weigl, A.: Formal Specification and Verification of JDK's Identity Hash Map Implementation. In: ter Beek, M.H., Monahan, R. (eds.) Integrated Formal Methods - 17th International Conference, IFM 2022, Lugano, Switzerland, June 7–10, 2022, Proceedings. LNCS, vol. 13274, pp. 45–62. Springer (2022). https://doi.org/10.1007/978-3-031-07727-2_4
7. Böhme, S., Fox, A.C.J., Sewell, T., Weber, T.: Reconstruction of Z3's bit-vector proofs in HOL4 and Isabelle/HOL. In: Jouannaud, J.-P., Shao, Z. (eds.) CPP 2011. LNCS, vol. 7086, pp. 183–198. Springer, Heidelberg (2011). https://doi.org/10.1007/978-3-642-25379-9_15
8. Cheon, Y., Leavens, G., Sitaraman, M., Edwards, S.: Model variables: cleanly supporting abstraction in design by contract: research articles. Softw. Pract. Exper. **35**(6), 583–599 (2005)
9. Cordeiro, L., Kesseli, P., Kroening, D., Schrammel, P., Trtik, M.: JBMC: a bounded model checking tool for verifying Java bytecode. In: Chockler, H., Weissenbacher, G. (eds.) CAV 2018. LNCS, vol. 10981, pp. 183–190. Springer, Cham (2018). https://doi.org/10.1007/978-3-319-96145-3_10
10. De Gouw, S., Rot, J., de Boer, F.S., Bubel, R., Hähnle, R.: OpenJDK's Java.utils.Collection.sort() Is Broken: The Good, the Bad and the Worst Case. In: Computer Aided Verification: 27th International Conference, CAV 2015, San Francisco, CA, USA, July 18–24, 2015, Proceedings, Part I 27. pp. 273–289. Springer (2015)
11. Hadarean, L., Barrett, C., Reynolds, A., Tinelli, C., Deters, M.: Fine grained SMT proofs for the theory of fixed-width bit-vectors. In: Davis, M., Fehnker, A., McIver, A., Voronkov, A. (eds.) LPAR 2015. LNCS, vol. 9450, pp. 340–355. Springer, Heidelberg (2015). https://doi.org/10.1007/978-3-662-48899-7_24

12. Hiep, H.-D.A., Bian, J., de Boer, F.S., de Gouw, S.: A tutorial on verifying LinkedList using KeY. In: Ahrendt, W., Beckert, B., Bubel, R., Hähnle, R., Ulbrich, M. (eds.) Deductive Software Verification: Future Perspectives. LNCS, vol. 12345, pp. 221–245. Springer, Cham (2020). https://doi.org/10.1007/978-3-030-64354-6_9

13. Hiep, H.A., Maathuis, O., Bian, J., de Boer, F.S., de Gouw, S.: Verifying Open-JDK's LinkedList using KeY (extended paper). Int. J. Softw. Tools Technol. Transf. **24**(5), 783–802 (2022). https://doi.org/10.1007/s10009-022-00679-7

14. Leavens, G.T., Baker, A.L., Ruby, C.: JML: A Notation for Detailed Design (1999). https://doi.org/10.1007/978-1-4615-5229-1_12

15. de Moura, L., Bjørner, N.: Z3: an efficient SMT solver. In: Ramakrishnan, C.R., Rehof, J. (eds.) TACAS 2008. LNCS, vol. 4963, pp. 337–340. Springer, Heidelberg (2008). https://doi.org/10.1007/978-3-540-78800-3_24

16. Tatman, A.S., Hiep, H.A., de Gouw, S.: Analysis and Formal Specification of Open-JDK's BitSet: Proof Files (2023). https://doi.org/10.5281/zenodo.8043379

17. Zohar, Y., Irfan, A., Mann, M., Niemetz, A., Nötzli, A., Preiner, M., Reynolds, A., Barrett, C., Tinelli, C.: Bit-precise reasoning via int-blasting. In: Finkbeiner, B., Wies, T. (eds.) VMCAI 2022. LNCS, vol. 13182, pp. 496–518. Springer, Cham (2022). https://doi.org/10.1007/978-3-030-94583-1_24

Joining Forces! Reusing Contracts for Deductive Verifiers Through Automatic Translation

Lukas Armborst(✉) , Sophie Lathouwers(✉) , and Marieke Huisman(✉)

University of Twente, Enschede, The Netherlands
{l.armborst,s.a.m.lathouwers,m.huisman}@utwente.nl

Abstract. Deductive verifiers can be used to prove the correctness of programs by specifying the program's intended behaviour using annotations such as pre- and postconditions. Unfortunately, most verifiers use their own unique specification language for those contract-based annotations. While many of them have similar concepts and syntax, there are numerous semantic differences and subtleties that make it very difficult to reuse specifications between verifiers. But reusing specifications could help overcome one of the bottlenecks of deductive verification, namely writing specifications. Therefore, we present the SPECIFICATION TRANSLATOR, a tool to automatically translate annotations for deductive verifiers. It currently supports Java programs annotated for OpenJML, Krakatoa and VerCors. Using the SPECIFICATION TRANSLATOR, we show that we can reuse 81% of the annotations, which would otherwise need to be manually translated. Moreover, it allows to reuse tools such as Daikon that generate annotations only in the syntax of one specific tool.

Keywords: Annotations · Specifications · Deductive verification · Translation · Tool interoperability

1 Introduction

Deductive verification is a powerful technique that can be used to improve the reliability of software. It can be used to reason about e.g. memory safety and functional correctness, even if the system has an infinite state space and concurrency. There exist many deductive verifiers, some of which are better suited to certain problems than others. Therefore, it is important that tools cooperate such that users can select the tool best suited to their problem. For example, some deductive verifiers support the use of different solvers for individual proof tasks (e.g. Why3 [18], Krakatoa [17]). However, tool interoperability for deductive verifiers is much harder when it comes to reusing specifications, because most tools use their own unique specification language. As a result, it is currently impossible to switch between tools without investing significant time and effort to manually translate the specifications.

This work was supported by the NWO VICI 639.023.710 Mercedes project.

P. Herber and A. Wijs (Eds.): iFM 2023, LNCS 14300, pp. 153–171, 2024.
https://doi.org/10.1007/978-3-031-47705-8_9

Finding and writing the specifications is considered to be one of the large bottlenecks in applying deductive verification in practice [3,22]. This is why we would like to reuse specifications where possible, such as for APIs (e.g. [2,5,7, 15,20,26]). Often the verification requires more lines of specification than lines of code. For example, one of the APIs [2] required four times as many lines of specification as lines of code. Unfortunately, with the current limited tool interoperability, it can be difficult for users to verify a program that uses one of these APIs. The user is either limited to using the same verifier for their program as was used for the library, or they need to spend significant effort to re-verify the library in their verifier of choice.

To enable the reuse of specifications, we propose the SPECIFICATION TRANSLATOR, a tool to automatically translate specifications between OpenJML [13], Krakatoa [17] and VerCors [6]. We specifically target deductive verifiers for Java programs. We chose to support OpenJML because it is one of the most well-known deductive verifiers for Java and it supports a large subset of Java Modeling Language (JML) [27]. Krakatoa has been included since it is no longer actively developed and thus it would be useful to port the specifications to another tool that is still being maintained. And, it is one of the few verifiers that supports using various solvers for individual proof tasks. VerCors has been included because it is based on separation logic, which showcases how to deal with extensions to standard JML. The SPECIFICATION TRANSLATOR makes it easier to share verified programs between these tools. Moreover, it can also be used to reuse results from other tools, such as specification generators like Daikon [16].

In this paper, we investigate to what extent specifications can be automatically translated to enable reuse between verifiers. To achieve this, we explore the semantic differences between verifiers. There are often commonalities between specification languages, as many Java-based deductive verifiers have a specification language inspired by JML. However, translating annotations is not as straightforward as it might seem since you need detailed knowledge about the specification languages and their semantic differences. For example, some of the things one needs to know when translating from tool X to Y, for example OpenJML to VerCors, include:

- Does tool X have any built-in assumptions? If so, do these correspond to the built-in assumptions of tool Y?
  - OpenJML assumes that variables are non-null by default whereas VerCors requires the user to write annotations to express this.
- Does tool Y support all the concepts used in the annotations for tool X? If not, does it have a similar concept?
  - OpenJML has `assignable` clauses to indicate whether you can write to a variable. VerCors does not have those, but it is built on permission-based separation logic and requires annotations indicating the amount of permissions for a specific memory location.
  - OpenJML supports `behavior` clauses, which can be used to make case distinctions in the specifications. VerCors does not support those, so one needs to rewrite pre- and postconditions with implications to indicate that something should hold only for a specific case.

- Even if Y supports a concept, does it have the same semantics as in tool X?
  - In OpenJML the term "predicate" refers to a boolean expression, whereas in VerCors it is a function that returns a boolean. As such, VerCors' predicates are more similar to model methods in OpenJML.

The SPECIFICATION TRANSLATOR handles most of these details automatically, reducing the manual effort for the user.

For the translation, the SPECIFICATION TRANSLATOR uses an intermediate representation which contains concepts supported by multiple tools, and makes many implicit assumptions explicit. This makes it easy to extend the SPECIFICATION TRANSLATOR with new input and output languages.

In our evaluation, we show that we can translate most annotations between the verifiers (81%), and we analyse whether the program can be verified after translation or how much effort is still required. Moreover, we show how we can use the SPECIFICATION TRANSLATOR combined with Daikon to generate specifications for VerCors. This used to be impossible without manual intervention.

Contributions. In short, this paper introduces the tool SPECIFICATION TRANSLATOR, which can translate specifications between Krakatoa, OpenJML and VerCors. With this tool, we enable tool interoperability, and thereby prevent users from spending a lot of time re-doing existing work, such as library verification, and instead allow them to build on top of it and focus on new research instead. Our evaluation shows for 30 programs and 2 larger case studies that more than 80% of the specifications can be reused when using the SPECIFICATION TRANSLATOR, highlighting its effectiveness in reducing the effort of integrating tool results. The SPECIFICATION TRANSLATOR also supports the integration of tools like Daikon, which supports one single specification language for Java, with other verifiers, maximising their impact. Moreover, the paper highlights the differences in semantics between Krakatoa, OpenJML and VerCors, as well as how to translate between them.

Outline of the Paper. In the next section, we will describe the design of the SPECIFICATION TRANSLATOR. Section 3 explains some of the more intricate translations and design choices. Then, Sect. 4 evaluates the tool, specifically how many annotations can be reused and reverified. We discuss related work in Sect. 5 and conclude in Sect. 6.

2   Design of the Specification Translator

This section gives an overview of how the SPECIFICATION TRANSLATOR works (see Fig. 1). We briefly explain which transformations are done on an example. Let us assume we have a file with OpenJML annotations that we want to translate into VerCors annotations. First, the file is converted into an OpenJML-specific syntax tree that resembles an *abstract syntax tree*. However, it is enriched with formatting information such as whitespace, which is normally left out of an AST. This allows all translations to remain as close as possible to the original

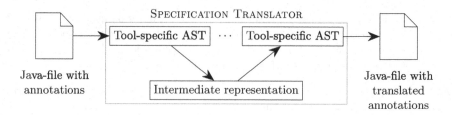

Fig. 1. Overview of how the SPECIFICATION TRANSLATOR works. Given an annotated Java-file, the input is first converted into a tool-specific AST. This is translated via a tool-independent intermediate representation into the tool-specific AST of the target tool. From there, the output file is generated.

file, including formatting. We will refer to these syntax trees as AST, despite the additional verbosity. Then, the OpenJML-specific AST is translated into the intermediate representation. OpenJML-specific annotations are commented if they are not supported by any other tool and thus cannot be translated. It will also desugar some expressions, such as making implicit assumptions explicit. Afterwards, the intermediate representation is translated into a VerCors-specific AST. This may again comment some annotations, if VerCors does not support them. Others may be rewritten, if they are not supported in the target specification language directly, but the intention can still be expressed. Using the VerCors-specific AST, we generate the output file with all translated annotations.

If there are annotations that are not translatable, the tool informs the user on the command line. In the file, instead of silently removing the problematic annotations, they are turned into comments. This ensures traceability, and helps the user in case manual intervention is needed.

Intermediate Representation. Given that many tools based their specification language on the Java Modeling Language (JML), the intermediate representation (IR) is also based on that standard. A few JML concepts were left out of the IR, most notably redundancy, such as `assignable_redundantly` or `example` definitions. This does not change the specifications' meaning, as redundant specifications do not constrain the program any more than the given non-redundant specifications. Concepts were left out if at most one tool supported them, taking into account tools whose support may be added in the future, such as KeY [1] and Verifast [25]. If several tools support a feature in some way, it is incorporated into the IR to facilitate translating between such tools without losing functionality. Currently, this mostly concerns memory access permissions for tools that are based on separation logic, such as VerCors and Verifast. The IR is defined in more detail with a grammar in the appendix[1].

---

[1] Due to publisher constraints, the appendix was moved online after peer review, to https://doi.org/10.4121/73361fbb-2633-4011-b615-cce19d8ac196.

Limitations. The SPECIFICATION TRANSLATOR translates as much as possible, however we cannot guarantee that the file will verify with the target tool. One possible reason is that a concept used in the original specification is not directly supported by the target tool, and the user has to find a different way to express the property. The tool rewrites specifications into a related concept wherever possible. Another reason for an unsuccessful verification after translation is that the target tool requires more extensive annotations. Where possible, the tool generates annotations for built-in assumptions, such as objects being non-null in OpenJML, but it does not generate completely new specifications.

We do not provide soundness guarantees for the translation. To do so, one needs to formalise the semantics of all tools involved, which is an effort out of scope for this work. Instead, we provide carefully considered translations and show their usefulness in practice. In the unlikely event that a substantial part of the specifications is dropped or altered semantically, we expect the user or target verifier to catch this during re-verification (see Sect. 4).

The SPECIFICATION TRANSLATOR only uses syntactic analysis to identify features and translate them, there is no semantic analysis such as name resolution or typing. While this limits the translation in a few cases, as mentioned in Sect. 3, it significantly reduces the complexity of the tool, and thereby the potential for errors. The evaluation in Sect. 4 shows that this analysis is sufficient to translate the annotations in the overwhelming majority of cases.

Extending the Tool. The SPECIFICATION TRANSLATOR has been designed keeping extendability in mind. By having an IR, a new language does not require a direct translation to every other language. Instead, to add a new input language, one only needs to add a parser and a translation into the IR. To add a new output language, one needs to add a translation from the IR into the new output language. The syntax trees for the different tools are based on a common underlying data structure, on which any new tool-specific AST can also build. This eliminates the need to redefine AST nodes from scratch if similar nodes exist in the other languages.

Artifact. The tool is available at https://doi.org/10.4121/21e79524-40c4-4dc1 -8108-94e7b6fc6d9f.

3   Translating Annotations

The SPECIFICATION TRANSLATOR currently supports the translation of annotations between OpenJML, Krakatoa and VerCors. This section discusses for each tool the choices that have been made in the translations to and from these tools.

3.1   OpenJML

OpenJML [13] is an open-source tool, which can verify Java programs that are annotated with JML specifications. Its annotation language closely adheres to the JML standard. As the IR is largely based on JML, the translation from OpenJML to the IR does not require many changes.

Non-null By Default. One notable exception is that OpenJML assumes by default that references are not null, for instance a method only returns non-null values. References that can be null need to be explicitly annotated as `nullable`. This is different from other tools like VerCors and the Java standard, where references are always nullable. Therefore, the SPECIFICATION TRANSLATOR annotates all classes as `nullable_by_default` when translating to OpenJML, disabling this implicit assumption of OpenJML. In turn, when translating from OpenJML to the IR, the SPECIFICATION TRANSLATOR generates `non_null` modifiers in cases such as parameters that are nullable in Java but implicitly non-null in OpenJML.

Access Permissions. When translating to OpenJML, the SPECIFICATION TRANSLATOR needs to deal with the extensions that the IR adds to JML. One example are access permissions which are used by tools built on separation logic.

Access permissions are used to indicate whether it is allowed to read from or write to a variable. The SPECIFICATION TRANSLATOR will therefore generate `assignable` clauses for all variables that occur in permission expressions in preconditions, and `loop_modifies` clauses for all permission expressions in loop invariants. Tools based on fractional permissions [8], such as VerCors, allow for more fine-grained control than these JML clauses and therefore the translation can be an over-approximation.

If the permission expression also contains the value at that location, such as the "x points to 5" ($x \mapsto 5$) of classical separation logic, then this is turned into a Boolean equality `x==5`. Other concepts of separation logic are also turned into Boolean versions, for instance the separating conjunction becomes a Boolean conjunction. This retains a significant part of the meaning, although additional annotations may be required before the program can be verified again, e.g. explicitly stating that two references are not aliases.

Privacy Modifiers. OpenJML takes privacy modifiers into account for its verification. For example, the contract of a public method usually cannot refer to private variables of the object. Other tools, like VerCors, do not have such a restriction, meaning everything is implicitly in the public scope. To mimic such behaviour, and avoid OpenJML giving many warnings about object visibility, the translation from the IR to OpenJML's AST marks all fields and methods, which are not already public, as `spec_public`.

Predicates. Both Krakatoa and VerCors have *predicates*, with slightly different meanings. In Krakatoa, they are boolean functions (see Listing 1.1 for an example), while in VerCors they can also contain access permissions. Additionally, VerCors treats them like abstract functions and does not automatically inspect and use their body; an explicit `unfold` statement is needed to do so (for more details, see [32]). OpenJML does not support predicates like that. The most similar construct in OpenJML is a model method, which is a method that only exists for the specification. We can translate the declaration of the predicate

Listing 1.1. Krakatoa predicate

```
1  /*@ predicate Sorted(int a[],
2         integer l, integer h)
3  @   = \forall integer i;
4  @      l<=i<h ==> a[i] <= a[i
          +1];
5  @*/
```

Listing 1.2. Translated predicate

```
/*@ ensures \result ==
@   (\forall int i;   l <= i < h
         ==> a[i] <= a[i+1]);
@ model boolean Sorted(int a[],
@    int l, int h);
@*/
```

into the declaration of a model method with a boolean return type and otherwise the same signature as the predicate. In Krakatoa and VerCors, predicates do not have contracts and instead their body is completely visible to the calling context (potentially after using unfold). To mimic that, the body is turned into a postcondition of the model method. We show a small example of a predicate translation from Krakatoa to OpenJML in Listings 1.1 and 1.2.

Data Types. Some tools have additional data types that can be used in ghost code, such as VerCors' multisets. Other tools often do not have an exactly equivalent type, so the SPECIFICATION TRANSLATOR comments out any explicit reference to data types that OpenJML does not support. However, as our syntactic analysis does not do type checking, it cannot identify all places where an object of such a type is used. As a result, the SPECIFICATION TRANSLATOR may only comment out some of the usages, and others may require manual intervention.

3.2 Krakatoa

Krakatoa was originally developed as a Java frontend for the Why platform [17]. Nowadays, it can still be used in combination with Why3 [18]. It can verify Java programs annotated with the Krakatoa Modeling Language (KML) [34]. KML is inspired by JML and ANSI/ISO C Specification Language (ACSL). We have used Krakatoa's documentation and the generated WhyML programs to determine the semantics of KML. Krakatoa is no longer actively developed and there are only a handful of examples available which seems to indicate limited use of the tool. As a result, it seems that there is little demand for translation to Krakatoa, therefore we have chosen to provide limited support for this.

Assumes in Behaviors. Method contracts in JML can have *behaviors*. These clauses can be used to split the specification into multiple cases, e.g. if an element is in the list or not. To distinguish which case applies, Krakatoa uses *assumes*-clauses instead of *requires*-clauses. For the translation of assumes clauses into the IR, we use the semantics as explained in Krakatoa's reference manual[2]. Namely, given an assumes-clause A and an ensures-clause E in a behavior, then \old $(A) \implies E$ should hold if the program terminates normally.

---

[2] https://krakatoa.lri.fr/krakatoa.html.

Inductive Predicates. Krakatoa supports inductive predicates. These inductive predicates consist of a predicate, possibly some parameters, and several case definitions. The case definitions describe when the predicate should evaluate to true. This should be a least fixpoint, meaning that only these cases should evaluate to true and no others. Other tools do not have a concept to express a least fixpoint and therefore the best we can do is to over-approximate for the IR. We define a (non-inductive) predicate and translate the case definitions into postconditions. We warn the user about this over-approximation.

Lemmas. Lemmas are typically used to assist the prover to determine whether the program adheres to the specification. They become part of the prover's implicit knowledge, and the prover can automatically use them where needed. We considered translating lemmas to ghost functions. However, that would require the user to call the ghost method explicitly, i.e. add additional annotations. Instead, we translate them into axioms in the IR which makes sure that the user does not need to add any annotations manually. Axioms are assumed to be correct, whereas lemmas generate proof obligations. The lemmas (should) have already been verified in Krakatoa originally, so simply assuming their correctness at this point should not introduce any unsoundness. Nevertheless, to be safe, we warn the user that these axioms should be proven separately.

3.3   VerCors

VerCors [6] is an open-source tool to verify concurrent programs, using JML-like annotations and permission-based separation logic as its foundation. While the specification language is JML-like, there are some notable deviations. In particular, many JML features are not supported, such as axioms, and instead there are new constructs to accommodate concepts from separation logic.

Permissions. VerCors does not support `assignable` or `accessible` clauses in method contracts, which can be used to indicate whether you can write to or read from a variable. In VerCors this can be expressed with write permission for the locations that are assignable, and at least read permission for those that are accessible. Thus each `assignable` or `accessible` clause can be represented with a pair of a pre- and a postcondition containing those access permissions. Likewise, `loop_modifies` clauses are turned into loop invariants with write permissions. This may be an over-approximation as `loop_modifies` can refer to local variables on the stack, while permissions can only refer to heap locations. However, the SPECIFICATION TRANSLATOR's lack of name resolution means that we cannot distinguish them, and the user needs to remove these permissions manually. In the examples in the evaluation (Sect. 4), this was not a frequent case, and was always a quick and straight-forward fix.

Bound Checks. A notable difference between VerCors and other tools are type bounds: VerCors only supports unbounded integers. In contrast, OpenJML checks at every assignment if the value is within the bounds of a machine integer, and warns about potential over- or underflows. This means that a program that verifies in VerCors may not verify in OpenJML. In the opposite direction, a verified OpenJML program will also verify in VerCors, as long as the specification does not explicitly rely on the boundedness guarantees. The SPECIFICATION TRANSLATOR could try to add explicit assertions about value bounds to every assignment to mimic OpenJML's behaviour. However, they would require information about the type of expressions to derive the right bounds, which the syntactic analysis of the SPECIFICATION TRANSLATOR cannot always provide. More importantly, they would clutter the program a lot, so we decided to not include those checks. Instead, the user has to manually add bound checks when translating to VerCors, if variable bounds are of interest. Moreover, they may have to provide additional annotations that ensure variable bounds after translating from VerCors to OpenJML, before the program verifies again, or disable the bound checks in OpenJML.

Behaviors. Unlike the IR, VerCors does not support `behavior`-clauses. In other tools, like OpenJML and Krakatoa, a method contract can specify multiple behaviours for the method, for example depending on the value of a parameter (Listing 1.3 gives an example). Whenever a `behavior`'s precondition is met, the method has to adhere to the specifications of that `behavior` block, such as guaranteeing its postconditions. When calling the method, at least one `behavior`'s precondition has to be met. In contrast, in VerCors all preconditions must be met at every call, and the postconditions are ensured unconditionally. However, a postcondition can be an implication, thereby explicitly containing a condition.

The SPECIFICATION TRANSLATOR uses this to turn a `behavior` into conditional postconditions: Each postcondition of a `behavior` is turned into an implication, using the conjunction of all preconditions of the `behavior` as a condition (see Lines 8–9 and 10–12 in Listing 1.4). If the `behavior` contains `accessible` and `assignable` clauses, they are treated similarly: They are turned into a pair of pre- and postcondition as described above, both of which are conditional on the `behavior`'s precondition (Lines 1–4). Additionally, the individual preconditions of the `behavior` are replaced with one single precondition of the form $\bigvee_{\text{behavior } b} \left(\bigwedge_{\text{precond. } p \text{ in } b} p \right)$, meaning a disjunction over all `behavior` blocks for the method, where each disjunct is a conjunction of the preconditions of that `behavior` (Lines 5–7). If the clause used the keyword `normal_behavior` or `exceptional_behavior`, then this clause implicitly assumes the postcondition `signals (Exception e) false` or `ensures false`, respectively. These implicit postconditions are made explicit in the translation, and also become conditional on the `behavior`'s preconditions (Line 13).

Invariants. In JML, one can define invariants, which an object has to satisfy at every observable execution point, such as the end of initialisation and before and after invoking any method which is not declared as `helper` [28, Ch. 8.2]. VerCors does not support invariants. Thus, invariants are turned into pre- and postconditions for every non-`helper` method, and postconditions for constructors.

Listing 1.3. OpenJML program with **behaviors**

```
1  /*@ behavior
2     requires inp > 0 || inp
          ==0;
3     requires inp > -1;
4     ensures \result;
5  also exceptional_behavior
6     requires inp < 0;
7     assignable errors;
8     signals(Exception e)
9        errors == \old(errors
           )+1;
10 @*/
11 boolean checkPos(int inp)
      {
12    ...
13 }
14
```

Listing 1.4. Translated contract

```
1  /*@ requires (inp<0)
2         ==> Perm(errors, write);
3     ensures \old(inp<0)
4         ==> Perm(errors, write);
5     requires ((inp>0 || inp==0)
6            && (inp>-1))
7         || (inp<0);
8     ensures \old((inp>0 || inp==0)
9            && (inp>-1)) ==> \result;
10    signals(Exception e)
11       \old(inp<0) ==>
12          (errors == \old(errors)+1);
13    ensures \old(inp<0) ==> false;
14 */
15    boolean checkPos(int inp) {...}
```

While this is a close approximation, it does not exactly replicate the meaning of **invariant**: Observable points also include any time when no method is ongoing. The authors of [28] note themselves that the definition is highly non-modular, and propose the same work-around we use, to allow modular verification. Note that in the concurrent setting of VerCors, a concurrent thread may observe more execution points than the ones mentioned above. Zaharieva-Stojanovski et al. [35] propose a more involved notion of class invariants for concurrency. However, this requires explicitly marking program segments where the class invariant may be broken. VerCors does not support these special annotations, yet, so we keep the original notion of observability.

Predicates. As mentioned in Sect. 3.1, VerCors supports predicates, which can contain both boolean expressions and access permissions. To use this content, the predicate has to be explicitly unfolded, and refolded back into a predicate afterwards. In the translation from VerCors to the IR, these **fold** and **unfold** statements are turned into assertions. This mimics the fact that VerCors actually checks that the predicate holds at that position. It can also serve as a guidance to provers, indicating that the knowledge of this predicate is needed here.

4   Evaluation

We evaluate how much the SPECIFICATION TRANSLATOR improves tool interoperability by showing (1) how many annotations can be reused between tools, and (2) how the SPECIFICATION TRANSLATOR allows the reuse of tools like Daikon.

4.1   Reuse of Specifications

In this section we focus on the question "How many annotations can be reused?". We have randomly selected 10 verifiable programs per tool (Krakatoa, OpenJML and VerCors) from the Java examples that are distributed with each tool, as well as 2 bigger case studies. We will first discuss the results for the smaller examples. This includes overviews per tool of how many annotations could be translated, a discussion on how much manual effort is needed after translation and a note on how many translations are trivial.

For each program, we measure how many lines were translated. This is determined by inspecting the specifications to see whether the intent of the specification before translation was preserved in the specification after translation. This could either be through a correct translation, or by omitting the specification if there is a corresponding default assumption in the target verifier. Aside from how many lines could be translated, we also measure how long the translation took, and whether the program could be verified after translation. If the verification was unsuccessful, the error message was manually inspected to determine the cause of the verification failure.

We distinguish between errors caused by the verifier (e.g. missing support for a Java construct used in the original file) and those caused by the translator (e.g. a method signature is no longer uniquely defined after translation). For the verification, we have used OpenJML v0.8.59 and VerCors v2.0.0 (beta). As mentioned in Sect. 3.2, support for translating to Krakatoa is limited, so we did not evaluate that direction. However, all Krakatoa examples were verified with Krakatoa v2.41 (with Why3 v0.88.3) before translating them. For the translation time, each translation was run five times, and the average is provided. The given time is CPU time, obtained with Python profiling tools. The time was recorded in the virtual machine which was provided for the iFM 2023 artifact evaluation (4 CPU cores, 8 GB of RAM, running Ubuntu 22.04).

The results can be seen in Tables 1, 2 and 3. The second column of the tables indicates the number of lines that have specifications. This includes lines of code that have specifications embedded, such as `void m(/*@nullable*/ int[] a)`, but does not include lines that have no meaningful specifications, such as the line `@*/`. Of the total of 991 lines analysed for this subsection, 806 were successfully translated or not needed in the target tool (81%).

Krakatoa Examples. The results of translating the Krakatoa examples to OpenJML and VerCors can be found in Table 1. The translation takes around three seconds for each example, which is significantly faster than any human could translate them. Several examples verify after translation without any manual intervention.

There are several examples (tagged 'I') that require additional annotations before they can be re-verified. For example, OpenJML checks for integer overflows while this was disabled in several Krakatoa examples. Therefore, OpenJML requires additional specifications about the bounds of variables. The `MyCosine` example only had annotations that used built-in functions from Krakatoa. These functions are not available in other tools and can therefore not be translated. Nonetheless, the translation to OpenJML contains some annotations as the tool adds privacy modifiers and ensures that objects are nullable as discussed in Sect. 3.1. The translation introduces an error in one case (`TreeMax`), which is a name clash between two originally polymorphic methods. This is a limitation of the SPECIFICATION TRANSLATOR as it does not do name resolution.

Table 1. Krakatoa examples and their translation into OpenJML and VerCors. In the result columns, 'I' indicates incomplete, i.e. more annotations are needed. 'E' indicates empty, i.e. the file does not contain any annotations that express the intent of the original annotations. 'T' indicates that the translation introduced an error. 'L' indicates failed verification due to a limitation of the target verifier.

Krakatoa		OpenJML				VerCors			
program	lines with annotations	lines successfully translated	lines with annotations	time in s	result	lines successfully translated	lines with annotations	time in s	result
ArrayMax	13	100%	12	2.67	✗(I)	85%	9	2.79	✗(I)
BankingExample	6	100%	8	2.12	✓	83%	7	2.16	✗(L)
Counter	5	40%	5	3.00	✗(I)	40%	2	2.19	✗(I)
Creation	20	95%	21	3.11	✗(I)	75%	7	2.16	✗(L)
MyCosine	9	0%	5	2.61	✓ (E)	0%	0	2.19	✗(L)
Negate	9	89%	10	2.98	✗(I)	78%	8	2.23	✗(L)
Purse	16	94%	19	2.66	✗(I)	88%	18	2.22	✗(I)
Sort2	38	11%	7	2.93	✗(I)	11%	4	2.63	✗(L)
Termination	6	83%	9	2.66	✓	83%	5	2.12	✓
TreeMax	24	33%	15	2.65	✗(T)	25%	5	2.40	✗(L)

Most of the issues we ran into when verifying programs with VerCors after the translation were caused by limitations of VerCors (tagged 'L'). Some were caused by minor bugs in VerCors, such as missed corner cases of the parser, that we expect to be fixed in the near future and thus we have not modified our tool. VerCors also has limited support for inheritance in Java and difficulties dealing with `Class.method()` calls. Similar to the previous examples, the user sometimes needs to add additional annotations (tagged 'I').

OpenJML Examples. Table 2 shows that all OpenJML examples could be translated to VerCors, with only a few lines not being translated. One such line had modifiers to disable integer bound checking that VerCors does not perform anyway, and one only contained a `nullable` modifier that is already the default in VerCors. Thus, the only line with an effect is a loop invariant that referred to the OpenJML built-in variable `\count` which does not exist in VerCors.

Like before, the translation time was negligible. Unfortunately, none of the examples verified after translation. This is to be expected, as VerCors requires the additional information of access permissions. While the SPECIFICATION TRANSLATOR tries to derive them from e.g. `assignable` clauses, none of the examples used those clauses. All the examples marked with 'I' were missing access permissions, and verified after manually adding those. Several examples failed because of limitations of VerCors, e.g. it does not support calls to standard library functions. Examples failing because of such limitations of VerCors are marked with 'L'. None of the verification failures are caused by the translator, instead they are caused by limitations of the verifiers.

VerCors Examples. The results of translating the VerCors is shown in Table 3. Some VerCors examples verified successfully in OpenJML. One example used a public class which did not match the file name, so OpenJML failed to verify it. This highlights the stronger visibility checks of OpenJML. Renaming the file made it verify. Several examples caused OpenJML to issue warnings about potential over- or underflows, but did otherwise verify. In some cases, constructs were not supported, such as data types, and additional annotations are required.

Table 2. OpenJML examples and their translation into VerCors. In the result columns, 'I' indicates incomplete, i.e. it needs more annotations to be verified. 'L' indicates that the program could not be verified due to a limitation of the verifier.

OpenJML		VerCors			
program	lines with annotations	lines successfully translated	lines with annotations	time in s	result
BinarySearchGood	12	100%	12	2.70	✗(L)
BubbleSort	10	100%	11	2.72	✗(I)
ChangeCase	8	100%	4	2.53	✗(L)
HeapSort	46	100%	47	3.80	✗(L)
InvertInjection	16	100%	16	3.49	✗(L)
MaxByElimination	7	100%	8	3.49	✗(I)
MergeSort	19	100%	21	3.01	✗(L)
SelectionSort	12	100%	12	2.75	✗(I)
SumMax	4	75%	4	2.73	✗(L)
TwoSum	18	84%	18	3.05	✗(L)

Effort to Verify. We also investigated how much manual effort is needed after the automatic translation, before the files verify successfully in the respective target tool. In some cases, the effort was negligible, for instance all files in Table 3 marked *overflow* verify if the overflow check is turned off by adding the modifiers code_bigint_math and spec_bigint_math to the respective class. Notice that turning off these checks actually makes the behaviour of OpenJML more faithful to the behaviour of VerCors. However, the translator keeps the checks by default, as this allows the user to leverage the additional capabilities of the target tool.

In other cases, only a little more effort is required. For Krakatoa, six of the translations to OpenJML required three or less changes, e.g. adding a bound check or redefining a simple predicate. Six translations from Krakatoa to VerCors also required some effort. For translations to VerCors, most examples required permissions to be added manually. For those small example files, an experienced VerCors user can determine the necessary permissions easily. However, in general this can be a non-trivial task, and research into permission inference is still ongoing (e.g. [14]). In such cases, one could use the SPECIFICATION TRANS-LATOR in a workflow pipeline, followed by invoking a dedicated inference tool. Another common task for VerCors was to add an existing precondition also as a postcondition or loop invariant. While the need for this may not always be obvious, an experienced user will quickly recognise and resolve the issue.

There were also five examples that required significant user intervention, such as redefining an intricate predicate. For the Krakatoa examples, these were Sort2 and TreeMax, which required significant effort to rewrite predicates. For the VerCors examples, in ListAppendASyncDefInline a VerCors-specific data type needed to be replaced, and RosterFixed required defining a JMLDataGroup to handle access restrictions. To resolve the issues for these VerCors examples, we also used a newer version of OpenJML (0.17.0-alpha-15). For the OpenJML examples, only MergeSort needed complex user intervention, namely providing a contract for a Java library function.

Table 3. VerCors examples and their translation into OpenJML.

VerCors		OpenJML			
program	lines with annotations	lines successfully translated	lines with annotations	time in s	result
BoogieTest	6	100%	7	2.39	✗(overflow)
Incr	6	100%	11	2.41	✗(overflow)
KnuthTabulate	8	100%	15	2.49	✗(incomplete)
LabeledWhile	19	63%	23	2.41	✓
ListAppend- ASyncDefInline	17	38%	9	2.53	✗(incomplete)
LoopInv	4	100%	5	2.34	✗(overflow)
PairInsertionSort	32	100%	42	2.87	✓
refute4	3	100%	6	2.25	(✓) (name)
RosterFixed	24	88%	32	2.61	✗(limitation)
SwapInteger	6	100%	11	2.25	✓

Some files could not be verified at all, because they relied on features not supported by the target tool. For example, VerCors does not support some Java features used by two Krakatoa examples and two OpenJML examples.

Trivial Translations. As many specification languages are based on JML, we also analysed how many of the translations were trivial, i.e. required no change at all for reuse. We compared the specifications generated by the SPECIFICATION TRANSLATOR with the original ones. We found that around 55% of the original specification lines needed changing in order to be reused, or were commented out because there was no direct translation. Thus, if translated manually without our tool, these 55% would require some user intervention. Since the SPECIFICATION TRANSLATOR was able to translate 81% of specification lines, we conclude that using it significantly reduces the amount of user intervention required.

Case Studies. Next, we demonstrate the SPECIFICATION TRANSLATOR on two bigger API verification case studies.

Firstly, we use a verification case study that used Krakatoa to verify a genetic algorithm [9]. The original file has 164 lines with specification. We have translated these specifications to OpenJML, resulting in 178 lines with specification. We were able to translate 89% of the original specification. Before OpenJML can analyse the file, some additional annotations are needed to resolve parsing issues. The original file contained several predicates that could not be translated, as they used labels, therefore the user will have to redefine these. The user will also need to add some **static** modifiers to several of these predicates. Finally, several \fresh expressions are used in preconditions. These should be removed as OpenJML does not allow \fresh expressions in preconditions.

Secondly, we use a verification case study where a version of Java's ArrayList was verified in VerCors[3]. The VerCors file has 258 lines with specifications. We used the SPECIFICATION TRANSLATOR to translate this to OpenJML, with the resulting file having 327 lines with specifications. All the lines could be translated. OpenJML could parse the translated file without manual intervention, and

---

[3] This was done by student Joost Sessink as part of a course.

already verified 17 out of 23 methods successfully. Some of the warnings resulted from two pure methods not being marked `pure`. Marking these methods as `pure` reduced the number of OpenJML warnings to 10. The majority concerned over- or underflows in arithmetic operations, which is to be expected when translating from VerCors. Another is related to inheritance, which is also not fully supported by VerCors. One method was a stub stand-in for a library, and used as a body `assume false`. OpenJML warned about that, but had no other complaints about that method. Finally, the anti-aliasing of VerCors' separation logic did not fully translate to OpenJML, causing some warnings.

To conclude, for the Krakatoa and VerCors case studies we were able to translate 89% and 100% respectively. This shows that using the SPECIFICATION TRANSLATOR allows us to reuse large parts of existing specifications for APIs, and significantly reduces the manual effort required for translation.

4.2 Reuse of Tools

Aside from reusing specifications, the SPECIFICATION TRANSLATOR also allows reusing tools that only support a limited number of specification languages. For example, Daikon [16] can generate specifications in JML, but does not support VerCors' specification language. With our tool, the JML specifications generated by Daikon can be translated to VerCors. This makes Daikon applicable for verifiers that do not support JML directly, without having to alter Daikon.

As an example, we use the `QueueAr.java` provided with Daikon. Running Daikon on the un-annotated file generates 127 lines with specifications. Many of those are JML-specific and not directly usable in VerCors, in particular class-level invariants and `assignable` clauses. After using the SPECIFICATION TRANS-LATOR, the file had 252 lines with annotations. 16 of those referred to the `owner` of JML's type system, which VerCors does not support, but the remaining 94% were valid VerCors specifications. Note that this means an increase by more than 100 usable specification lines. These mainly stem from adding class-level invariants as pre- and postconditions to all relevant methods. Without the SPECIFICA-TION TRANSLATOR, all these specifications would have to be written manually.

Note that while the specifications generated by Daikon were helpful, they were not sufficient for verification with OpenJML, nor with VerCors after the translation. However, our goal was to make Daikon-generated specifications usable for VerCors, regardless of the verification result. This was successful for nearly all specifications.

5   Related Work

To the best of our knowledge, this paper presents the first tool for translating annotations for deductive verification. We discuss three related research areas: (1) translations to/from JML, (2) common tool formats, and (3) tool interoperability.

Translating to/from JML. Many translations to and from JML have been proposed in earlier work. This includes translation from B machines to JML [10], OCL to/from JML [23], JML to executable Java [4], JML from Alloy expressions [21], from temporal properties [19], from VDM-SL [33] and from security automata [24]. However, none of these target the translation of annotations between different deductive verifiers. Also of note is Raghavan and Leavens [29], who simplify JML specifications by removing syntactic sugar, thus a JML-to-JML translation. While some of the transformations we do are similar, there is not a lot of overlap: Many of the syntactic sugar that they remove is already supported by the verifiers we looked at. Moreover, their translation left concepts that we needed to remove, such as `behavior` clauses when translating to VerCors.

Common Tool Formats. Many different common formats for tools have been proposed, such as the earlier mentioned JML (Java Modeling Language) [27]. Other formats include JIR (JML Intermediate Language) and JFSL (JForge Specification Language). JIR [31] aims to decouple front-ends and back-ends by introducing an intermediate representation. JFSL aims to address some shortcomings of JML by extending it with e.g. support for expressing the transitive closure [11]. These languages are not sufficient for our goals since they do not support constructs outside of JML such as permissions in VerCors. Moreover, we believe that a new language will not solve the problem because new techniques are still being developed that may require new types of specifications. Also, it would require all tool developers to modify their tool to support the new language. With the SPECIFICATION TRANSLATOR we can improve the tool interoperability between deductive verifiers without burdening the tool developers.

Tool Interoperability. Another related topic is tool interoperability. Christakis et al. [12] have proposed to extend the output of static verifiers to make implicit assumptions explicit, for instance about integer overflows. They then use other verifiers or test case generation to check these assumptions, creating a tool chain. During our translation, we similarly turn some implicit assumptions into explicit proof obligations. While we both address tool interoperability, they focus on the verification results and how these can be used in tool chains, whereas we focus on the reuse of specifications between verifiers as well as from inference tools such as Daikon. Aside from making assumptions explicit, our approach also supports the reuse of other specifications through translation. Consequently, our target verifier attempts to re-verify the properties proven by the original verifier, without reusing its results. Moreover, our approach does not require any modifications to the existing verifiers as is the case for the work of Christakis et al. For their approach, differences in the specification languages of tools can be a major hindrance, and a translation tool like ours can increase the applicability of their work.

Another idea that focuses on the reuse of existing artefacts is proof repair. The idea of proof repair is to automatically update proofs used by proof assistants. This can be used to fix a proof when a newer version of the same proof assistant has changes that are backward incompatible [30]. Instead of updating proofs, we focus on updating specifications between different deductive verifiers. We can extend the SPECIFICATION TRANSLATOR to support translating specifications between different versions of the same tool to achieve a similar goal for deductive verifiers.

6   Conclusion

We have presented the SPECIFICATION TRANSLATOR, the first tool for translating contract-based specifications between deductive verifiers for Java. Using the SPECIFICATION TRANSLATOR allows users to reuse existing tools and specifications, thereby minimising the burden of writing specifications and enhancing tool interoperability. We have shown that we could translate 81% of the specifications between tools, reducing the effort for the user significantly compared to having to translate them manually. Moreover, it allows us to use tools such as Daikon for new deductive verifiers without needing to modify these tools.

For future work, aside from supporting other tools like Verifast, we would like to exploit the new abilities for reuse. This includes building verified libraries based on verification efforts from other tools, and exploring tool integration like the Daikon example.

References

1. Ahrendt, W., Beckert, B., Bubel, R., Hähnle, R., Schmitt, P.H., Ulbrich, M.: Deductive Software Verification - The KeY Book - From Theory to Practice, Lecture Notes in Computer Science, vol. 10001. Springer, Cham (2016). https://doi.org/10.1007/978-3-319-49812-6, Tool website: https://www.key-project.org/
2. Armborst, L., Huisman, M.: Permission-based verification of red-black trees and their merging. In: 2021 IEEE/ACM 9th International Conference on Formal Methods in Software Engineering (FormaliSE), pp. 111–123 (2021). https://doi.org/10.1109/FormaliSE52586.2021.00017
3. Baumann, C., Beckert, B., Blasum, H., Bormer, T.: Lessons learned from microkernel verification—specification is the new bottleneck. Electron. Proc. Theor. Comput. Sci. **102**, 18–32 (2012). https://doi.org/10.4204/eptcs.102.4
4. Beckert, B., Kirsten, M., Klamroth, J., Ulbrich, M.: Modular verification of JML contracts using bounded model checking. In: Margaria, T., Steffen, B. (eds.) ISoLA 2020. LNCS, vol. 12476, pp. 60–80. Springer, Cham (2020). https://doi.org/10.1007/978-3-030-61362-4_4
5. Beckert, B., Schiffl, J., Schmitt, P.H., Ulbrich, M.: Proving JDK's dual pivot quicksort correct. In: Paskevich, A., Wies, T. (eds.) VSTTE 2017. LNCS, vol. 10712, pp. 35–48. Springer, Cham (2017). https://doi.org/10.1007/978-3-319-72308-2_3
6. Blom, S., Darabi, S., Huisman, M., Oortwijn, W.: The VerCors tool set: verification of parallel and concurrent software. In: Polikarpova, N., Schneider, S.A. (eds.) IFM 2017. LNCS, vol. 10510, pp. 102–110. Springer, Cham (2017). https://doi.org/10.1007/978-3-319-66845-1_7, Tool website: https://www.utwente.nl/vercors/

7. Boer, M.d., Gouw, S.d., Klamroth, J., Jung, C., Ulbrich, M., Weigl, A.: Formal specification and verification of JDK's identity hash map implementation. In: ter Beek, M.H., Monahan, R. (eds.) IFM 2022. LNCS, vol. 13274, pp. 45–62. Springer, Cham (2022). https://doi.org/10.1007/978-3-031-07727-2_4

8. Boyland, J.: Checking interference with fractional permissions. In: Cousot, R. (ed.) Static Analysis. LNCS, vol. 2694, pp. 55–72. Springer, Heidelberg (2003). https://doi.org/10.1007/3-540-44898-5_4

9. Brizhinev, D., Goré, R.: A case study in formal verification of a Java program. Computing Research Repository abs/1809.03162 (2018). http://arxiv.org/abs/1809.03162

10. Cataño, N., Wahls, T., Rueda, C., Rivera, V., Yu, D.: Translating B machines to JML specifications. In: Ossowski, S., Lecca, P. (eds.) Proceedings of the ACM Symposium on Applied Computing, SAC 2012, Riva, Trento, Italy, 26–30 March 2012, pp. 1271–1277. ACM (2012). https://doi.org/10.1145/2245276.2231978

11. Chicote, M., Ciolek, D., Galeotti, J.: Practical JFSL verification using TACO. Softw. Pract. Exp. **44**(3), 317–334 (2014). https://doi.org/10.1002/spe.2237, https://onlinelibrary.wiley.com/doi/abs/10.1002/spe.2237

12. Christakis, M., Müller, P., Wüstholz, V.: Collaborative verification and testing with explicit assumptions. In: Giannakopoulou, D., Méry, D. (eds.) FM 2012. LNCS, vol. 7436, pp. 132–146. Springer, Heidelberg (2012). https://doi.org/10.1007/978-3-642-32759-9_13

13. Cok, D.R.: OpenJML: JML for Java 7 by extending OpenJDK. In: Bobaru, M., Havelund, K., Holzmann, G.J., Joshi, R. (eds.) NFM 2011, vol. 6617, pp. 472–479. Springer, Heidelberg (2011). https://doi.org/10.1007/978-3-642-20398-5_35, Tool website: https://www.openjml.org/

14. Dohrau, J.: Automatic Inference of Permission Specifications. Ph.D. thesis, ETH Zurich (2022)

15. Efremov, D., Mandrykin, M., Khoroshilov, A.: Deductive verification of unmodified Linux kernel library functions. In: Margaria, T., Steffen, B. (eds.) ISoLA 2018. LNCS, vol. 11245, pp. 216–234. Springer, Cham (2018). https://doi.org/10.1007/978-3-030-03421-4_15

16. Ernst, M.D., et al.: The Daikon system for dynamic detection of likely invariants. Sci. Comput. Program. **69**(1–3), 35–45 (2007). https://doi.org/10.1016/j.scico.2007.01.015, Tool website: https://plse.cs.washington.edu/daikon/

17. Filliâtre, J., Marché, C.: The Why/Krakatoa/Caduceus platform for deductive program verification. In: Damm, W., Hermanns, H. (eds.) CAV 2007. LNCS, vol. 4590, pp. 173–177. Springer, Cham (2007). https://doi.org/10.1007/978-3-540-73368-3_21, Tool website: https://krakatoa.lri.fr/

18. Filliâtre, J.-C., Paskevich, A.: Why3—where programs meet provers. In: Felleisen, M., Gardner, P. (eds.) ESOP 2013. LNCS, vol. 7792, pp. 125–128. Springer, Heidelberg (2013). https://doi.org/10.1007/978-3-642-37036-6_8

19. Giorgetti, A., Groslambert, J.: JAG: JML Annotation Generation for verifying temporal properties. In: Baresi, L., Heckel, R. (eds.) FASE 2006. LNCS, vol. 3922, pp. 373–376. Springer, Heidelberg (2006). https://doi.org/10.1007/11693017_27

20. de Gouw, S., Rot, J., de Boer, F.S., Bubel, R., Hähnle, R.: OpenJDK's Java.utils.Collection.sort() is broken: the good, the bad and the worst case. In: Kroening, D., Păsăreanu, C.S. (eds.) CAV 2015. LNCS, vol. 9206, pp. 273–289. Springer, Cham (2015). https://doi.org/10.1007/978-3-319-21690-4_16

21. Grunwald, D., Gladisch, C., Liu, T., Taghdiri, M., Tyszberowicz, S.: Generating JML specifications from alloy expressions. In: Yahav, E. (ed.) HVC 2014. LNCS,

vol. 8855, pp. 99–115. Springer, Cham (2014). https://doi.org/10.1007/978-3-319-13338-6_9

22. Hähnle, R., Huisman, M.: Deductive software verification: from pen-and-paper proofs to industrial tools. In: Steffen, B., Woeginger, G. (eds.) Computing and Software Science. LNCS, vol. 10000, pp. 345–373. Springer, Cham (2019). https://doi.org/10.1007/978-3-319-91908-9_18

23. Hamie, A.: Translating the object constraint language into the Java modelling language. In: Proceedings of the 2004 ACM Symposium on Applied Computing. SAC '04, pp. 1531–1535. Association for Computing Machinery, New York, NY, USA (2004). https://doi.org/10.1145/967900.968206

24. Huisman, M., Tamalet, A.: A formal connection between security automata and JML annotations. In: Chechik, M., Wirsing, M. (eds.) FASE 2009. LNCS, vol. 5503, pp. 340–354. Springer, Heidelberg (2009). https://doi.org/10.1007/978-3-642-00593-0_23

25. Jacobs, B., Smans, J., Philippaerts, P., Vogels, F., Penninckx, W., Piessens, F.: VeriFast: a powerful, sound, predictable, fast verifier for C and Java. In: Bobaru, M., Havelund, K., Holzmann, G.J., Joshi, R. (eds.) NFM 2011. LNCS, vol. 6617, pp. 41–55. Springer, Heidelberg (2011). https://doi.org/10.1007/978-3-642-20398-5_4

26. Knüppel, A., Thüm, T., Pardylla, C., Schaefer, I.: Experience report on formally verifying parts of OpenJDK's API with KeY. Electron. Proc. Theor. Comput. Sci. **284**, 53–70 (2018). https://doi.org/10.4204/eptcs.284.5

27. Leavens, G.T., Baker, A.L., Ruby, C.: Preliminary design of JML: a behavioral interface specification language for Java. SIGSOFT Softw. Eng. Notes **31**(3), 1–38 (2006). https://doi.org/10.1145/1127878.1127884

28. Leavens, G.T., et al.: JML Reference Manual, Department of Computer Science, Iowa State University, May 2013. http://www.jmlspecs.org

29. Raghavan, A., Leavens, G.: Desugaring JML method specifications. Comput. Sci. Tech. Rep. **345** (2005). http://lib.dr.iastate.edu/cs_techreports/345

30. Ringer, T., Yazdani, N., Leo, J., Grossman, D.: Adapting proof automation to adapt proofs. In: Proceedings of the 7th ACM SIGPLAN International Conference on Certified Programs and Proofs. CPP 2018, pp. 115–129. Association for Computing Machinery, New York, NY, USA (2018). https://doi.org/10.1145/3167094

31. Robby, Chalin, P.: Preliminary design of a unified JML representation and software infrastructure. In: Proceedings of the 11th International Workshop on Formal Techniques for Java-like Programs. FTfJP '09. Association for Computing Machinery, New York, NY, USA (2009). https://doi.org/10.1145/1557898.1557903

32. Summers, A.J., Drossopoulou, S.: A formal semantics for isorecursive and equirecursive state abstractions. In: Castagna, G. (ed.) ECOOP 2013. LNCS, vol. 7920, pp. 129–153. Springer, Heidelberg (2013). https://doi.org/10.1007/978-3-642-39038-8_6

33. Tran-Jørgensen, P.W.V., Larsen, P.G., Leavens, G.T.: Automated translation of VDM to JML-annotated Java. Int. J. Softw. Tools Technol. Transf. **20**(2), 211–235 (2017). https://doi.org/10.1007/s10009-017-0448-3

34. Tushkanova, E., Giorgetti, A., Marché, C., Kouchnarenko, O.: Modular Specification of Java Programs. Research Report RR-7097, INRIA (2009). https://hal.inria.fr/inria-00434452

35. Zaharieva-Stojanovski, M., Huisman, M.: Verifying class invariants in concurrent programs. In: Gnesi, S., Rensink, A. (eds.) FASE 2014. LNCS, vol. 8411, pp. 230–245. Springer, Heidelberg (2014). https://doi.org/10.1007/978-3-642-54804-8_16

Hardware and Memory Verification

Lifting the Reasoning Level in Generic Weak Memory Verification

Lara Bargmann$^{(\boxtimes)}$ [iD] and Heike Wehrheim [iD]

Department of Computing Science, University of Oldenburg, Oldenburg, Germany
{lara.bargmann,heike.wehrheim}@uol.de

Abstract. Weak memory models specify the semantics of concurrent programs on multi-core architectures. Reasoning techniques for weak memory models are often specialized to one fixed model and verification results are hence not transferable to other memory models. A recent proposal of a *generic* verification technique based on *axioms* on program behaviour expressed via weakest preconditions aims at overcoming this specialization to dedicated models. Due to the usage of weakest preconditions, reasoning however takes place on a very low level requiring the application of numerous axioms for deriving program properties, even for a single statement.

In this paper, we lift reasoning in this generic verification approach to a more abstract level. Based on a view-based assertion language, we provide a number of novel *proof rules* for directly reasoning on the level of program constructs. We prove soundness of our proof rules and exemplify them on the write-to-read causality (WRC) litmus test. A comparison to the axiom-based low-level proof reveals a significant reduction in the number of required proof steps.

Keywords: Axiomatic Reasoning · Concurrency Verification · Weak Memory Models

1 Introduction

The behaviour of concurrent programs running on modern multi-core processors is influenced by the (weak) *memory model* of the processor. A memory model fixes how concurrent threads can access shared variables, in particular which values of shared variables a thread can read. The behaviour of weak memory models differs from the often assumed *sequential consistency* (SC) [22] in which an execution is simply an interleaving of sequential executions of threads following their program order.

As weak memory models deviate from sequential consistency, verification techniques for concurrent programs like rely-guarantee [29] or Owicki-Gries reasoning [25] become unsound on weak memory models. Consequently, past years

---

Bargmann and Wehrheim are supported by DFG-WE2290/14-1.

have seen the development of numerous reasoning approaches *specific* to a memory model (like, e.g., [5,10,11,21,26]). The drawback of all these techniques is that a correctness proof for a concurrent program running on one memory model is not directly transferable to other memory models.

To alleviate this problem, Doherty et al. [13] propose a *generic* reasoning technique for weak memory models provided these have a *view-based semantics* [14]. A view of a thread specifies which write events to shared variables a thread can observe (and hence read from). The core of the reasoning technique is the concept of threads being *view-maximal* and memory-model internal steps to not invalidate view-maximality. On top of such novel concepts, [13] simply builds on standard Owicki-Gries reasoning for concurrent programs [25]. So far, memory models SC, TSO [27], PSO [1] and C11 RAR [10] have been shown to fall into this category. Reasoning (about single program instructions) then proceeds by applying low-level axioms based on weakest preconditions. The result is a correctness proof of a concurrent program (a proof outline) which is sound for *every* memory model satisfying the axioms.

While providing a memory-model independent approach, the technique however suffers from the need to apply very low-level, detailed axioms combined with standard properties of weakest preconditions. Moreover, reasoning engines (like Isabelle, as used in [11]) might not record the axioms employed for a specific proof. This hinders transferability to memory models fulfilling only a *subset* of the axioms: we do not know anymore whether a proof is or is not valid on such a partially fitting model.

To improve on these shortcomings, we propose a lifting of the reasoning technique to a higher level. Starting from a view-based language for formulating assertions on concurrent programs, we develop several novel proof rules for program statements. We prove soundness of each of these rules via the low-level axioms. Moreover, together with every new rule we list the required axioms. This enables us to directly see whether a proof is transferable to a memory model which only partially fulfills the axiom set. We exemplify our new proof rules on the write-to-read causality litmus test (see, e.g., [6]) for which we provide both the low-level and the novel high-level reasoning steps. This demonstrates a significant reduction in the number of required proof steps.

2   Program Syntax

We start by introducing the syntax of concurrent programs. We define a concurrent program as a parallel composition of sequential programs. Each thread $t \in \mathsf{Tid}$ runs a sequential program Com and with the function $\Pi : \mathsf{Tid} \to Com$ we model a concurrent program over threads Tid. We let $\mathsf{Var_G}$ be the set of global variables and $\mathsf{Var_L}$ the set of local variables (or *registers*) with $\mathsf{Var_G} \cap \mathsf{Var_L} = \emptyset$ and $\mathsf{Var} = \mathsf{Var_G} \cup \mathsf{Var_L}$. We assume that initially all variables have the value 0.

For $x \in \mathsf{Var_G}$, $r \in \mathsf{Var_L}$ and value $v \in \mathsf{Val}$ the following grammar defines Com:

$$\{[x=0]_1 \cap [x=0]_2 \cap [y=0]_3 \cap r_1 = 0 \cap r_2 = 0\}$$

Thread 1	Thread 2	Thread 3
$\{P_{1,1} : [x=0]_1$	$\{P_{2,1} : [y \not\approx 1]_3 \cap r_2 \neq 1$	$\{P_{3,1} : r_1 \neq 1$
$\cap [x \not\approx 1]_2 \cap r_1 \neq 1\}$	$\cap ([x=0]_2 \cup \langle x=1 \rangle [x=1]_2)\}$	$\cup \langle y=1 \rangle^{\mathsf{S}} [x=1]_3\}$
$1 : x := 1;$	$2 : r_1 := x;$	$4 : r_2 :=^{\mathsf{RS}} y;$
$\{P_{1,2} : true\}$	$\{P_{2,2} : [y \not\approx 1]_3 \cap r_2 \neq 1$	$\{P_{3,2} : r_1 \neq 1$
	$\cap (r_1 \neq 1 \cup [x=1]_2)\}$	$\cup r_2 \neq 1 \cup [x=1]_3\}$
	$3 : y :=^{\mathsf{WS}} 1;$	$5 : r_3 := x;$
	$\{P_{2,3} : true\}$	$\{P_{3,3} : r_1 \neq 1$
		$\cup r_2 \neq 1 \cup r_3 = 1\}$

$$\{r_1 \neq 1 \cup r_2 \neq 1 \cup r_3 = 1\}$$

Fig. 1. Write-Read-Causality litmus test as proof outline

$$E ::= v \mid e$$

$$com ::= skip \mid fnc \mid r := E \mid r := x \mid r :=^{\mathsf{RS}} x \mid x := E \mid x :=^{\mathsf{WS}} E$$

$$Com ::= com \mid Com; Com \mid \text{if } b \text{ then } Com \text{ else } Com \mid \text{while } b \text{ do } Com$$

where $e \in Exp$ and $b \in BExp$ are expressions over local variables only, e arithmetic and b boolean, and fnc is a so-called *fence* (or barrier) instruction. The two annotations RS (read synchronized) and WS (write synchronized) provide ways of synchronizing a write with a read.

Example 1. In C11 [20], the annotation **Release** is a WS and **Acquire** an RS synchronization. In SC, reads and writes only occur in synchronized form (and thus the writes and reads without annotation behave like the ones with annotation). Such synchronizations guarantee causal consistency.

We let $\mathsf{Act} = \{rd(x,r,v), rd^{\mathsf{RS}}(x,r,v), wr(x,v), wr^{\mathsf{WS}}(x,v), fence \mid x \in \mathsf{Var_G}, r \in \mathsf{Var_L}, v \in \mathsf{Val}\}$ be the set of actions containing synchronized and unsynchronized reads and writes; $\mathsf{Act_{ext}} = \mathsf{Act} \cup \{r := v \mid r \in Var_L, v \in \mathsf{Val}\} \cup \{\tau\}$ (τ an internal action). For an action $a \in \mathsf{Act}$, $var(a) \in \mathsf{Var_G}$ describes the global variable of the action. For a (synchronized or unsynchronized) read action $rd(x,r,v)$, we let $rdval(a) = v \in \mathsf{Val}$, otherwise we set $rdval(a) = \bot \notin \mathsf{Val}$; $wrval(a)$ is similarly defined for write actions. With these functions we can define subsets of Act: $Rd = \{a \in \mathsf{Act} \mid wrval(a) = \bot, rdval(a) \neq \bot\}$ and $Wr = \{a \in \mathsf{Act} \mid rdval(a) = \bot, wrval(a) \neq \bot\}$. For a value v, we assume $Rd[v] = \{a \in Rd \mid rdval(a) = v\}$ and $Wr[v] = \{a \in Wr \mid wrval(a) = v\}$. We let $\mathsf{Act_{|x}}$ be the set of all actions a with $var(a) = x$. Hence $Rd_{|x}$ is the set of all reads in $\mathsf{Act_{|x}}$ and $Wr_{|x}$ the set of all writes.

Example 2. Figure 1 shows our running example, the Write-to-Read-Causality litmus test WRC (originally formulated by Boehm and Adve [6] and appearing here in the form of [24]). The program is a parallel composition of three threads, accessing global variables x and y plus using local registers r_1, r_2 and r_3. In between statements in the program, we see named assertions (in blue), making it a *proof outline*. The assertion $\{r_1 \neq 1 \cup r_2 \neq 1 \cup r_3 = 1\}$ at the end (the post-condition) states the expected outcome of the program: when both r_2 and r_1 take the value 1, then r_3 should also be 1. Such a behaviour holds for some but not all memory models, e.g., TSO, SC and C11 satisfy it, but, e.g., the memory model with a promise semantics in [28] does not.

The semantics of programs Com depends on the specific memory model a program runs on. In general, such semantics are typically defined in the following way (see, e.g., [13]): First, a semantics for the *local* part, i.e., the registers, is defined. As registers are not shared among threads, every thread directly writes to and reads from its registers. For shared variables, the local semantics simply assumes that any value can be read. In a next step, the local semantics is combined with a specific memory model semantics that details which values can actually be read by which threads in some given state. As we develop a generic reasoning approach here, we cannot further detail the semantics (we have no fixed memory model).

$$\Sigma = \mathsf{wlp}(R, \Sigma) \qquad \text{(Non-aborting)}$$
$$R' \subseteq R \wedge P \subseteq P' \Rightarrow \mathsf{wlp}(R, P) \subseteq \mathsf{wlp}(R', P') \qquad \text{((Anti)-Monotonicity)}$$
$$\mathsf{wlp}(R, \mathsf{wlp}(R', P)) = \mathsf{wlp}(R \,\mathring{\!;}\, R', P) \qquad \text{(Composition)}$$
$$R[\mathsf{wlp}(R, P)] \subseteq P \qquad \text{(Relation Application)}$$
$$\mathsf{wlp}(R, P) \cap \mathsf{wlp}(R, Q) = \mathsf{wlp}(R, P \cap Q) \qquad \text{(Conjunctivity)}$$
$$\mathsf{wlp}(R, P) \cup \mathsf{wlp}(R, Q) \subseteq \mathsf{wlp}(R, P \cup Q) \qquad \text{(Disjunctivity)}$$

Fig. 2. Properties of wlp $(P, Q \subseteq \Sigma, R, R' \subseteq \Sigma \times \Sigma)$

3   Axiomatic Reasoning

Instead of trying to provide separate correctness proofs for WRC for all memory models, we could employ the generic approach in [13] and construct *one* proof which is then valid for all memory models fulfilling the axioms employed *in this proof*. To this end, the generic reasoning technique abstracts from the semantics (and thus from a concrete memory model) and bases reasoning on *axioms*.

3.1   Axioms

The approach of [13] reasons about arbitrary transition systems $TS \,\hat{=}\, (\mathsf{Act}_{\mathsf{ext}}, \Sigma, I, T)$ where $\mathsf{Act}_{\mathsf{ext}}$ is the set of actions, Σ a set of states, $I \subseteq \Sigma$ a set of initial states and $T \in \mathsf{Tid} \times \mathsf{Act} \to 2^{\Sigma \times \Sigma}$ a set of transitions. The axiomatisation is build upon the *weakest liberal precondition transformer* (wlp) [12], which is used both as a basis for property specification and verification. For a relation R and set of states P (representing a predicate), we let $\mathsf{wlp} : 2^{\Sigma \times \Sigma} \times 2^{\Sigma} \to 2^{\Sigma}$ be

$$\mathsf{wlp}(R, P) \mathrel{\widehat{=}} \{\sigma \in \Sigma \mid \forall \sigma' : (\sigma, \sigma') \in R \implies \sigma' \in P\}$$

Figure 2 details some properties of wlp where $\mathbin{\mathring{,}}$ denotes relational composition and $R[\cdot]$ relational image. Here, R typically is the relation $T(t, a)$, $t \in \mathsf{Tid}$, $a \in \mathsf{Act_{ext}}$. We say R is *disabled* in a state σ iff $\sigma \in \mathsf{dis}(R)$ holds, where $\mathsf{dis}(R) \mathrel{\widehat{=}} \mathsf{wlp}(R, \emptyset)$. This will in particular be employed for read actions, to state that it is impossible for a thread t to read a certain value of a shared variable.

The core concept of reasoning is the idea of *views* of threads. In weak memory models, threads *observe* global variables to have certain values (namely the values of write actions); a thread might observe several different values at a time and different threads might have different such observations. This differs from sequential consistency in which all threads have the same observation and can only see one value at a time. We say that a thread is *view maximal*, $vmax(t, a)$ (on an action a operating on a variable $x \in \mathsf{Var_G}$), if it has the "most up-to-date" view on this variable. While non view maximal threads might be able to read older values of x, thread t reads the most up-to-date value.

Example 3. As an example, consider the WRC program after the execution of line 1 ($x := 1$). In SC, all threads observe x to be 1 (only). In TSO, in which written values are first placed in thread-local store buffers before being flushed to main memory, there is a state in which thread 1 observes x to be 1 while threads 2 and 3 still see x to be 0. In such a state, we, e.g., have $\mathsf{dis}(T(2, Rd_{|x}[1])$. In C11, there is even a state in which threads 2 and 3 can see $x = 1$ and $x = 0$ *at the same time*. In all these models, we have $vmax(1, rd(x, \cdot, \cdot))$ (thread 1 is view maximal on x) in that state.

A specific memory model will give rise to some concrete definition of $vmax$. For the axiomatisation it is only important to guarantee that memory model internal steps preserve view maximality in the sense of view-preserving simulations.

Definition 1. *For a transition system* $TS = (\mathsf{Act}, \Sigma, I, T)$, *a view-preserving simulation, denoted β, is the weakest relation R satisfying for all threads $t \in \mathsf{Tid}$ and all actions $a \in \mathsf{Act}$*

$$R \mathbin{\mathring{,}} T(t, a) \subseteq T(t, a) \mathbin{\mathring{,}} R \qquad \text{(semi-commutation)}$$
$$vmax(t, a) \subseteq \mathsf{wlp}(R, vmax(t, a)) \qquad \text{(view maximality)}$$

A view-preserving simulation keeps view maximality of threads and semi-commutes with the transition relation.

C1 : $\forall\, t \in \mathsf{Tid}, a \in \mathsf{Act} : I \subseteq vmax(t,a)$

C2 : $\forall\, \sigma, \sigma' \in \Sigma, t, t' \in \mathsf{Tid}, a \in \mathsf{Act} :$

$\quad \sigma \in vmax(t,a) \wedge (\sigma, \sigma') \in T(t,a) \Rightarrow \exists \tau \in \Sigma : (\sigma', \tau) \in \beta \wedge (\sigma, \tau) \in T(t',a) \,\mathring{,}\, \beta$

C3 : $\forall\, t \in \mathsf{Tid}, a \in \mathsf{Act} : T(t,a) \subseteq \beta \,\mathring{,}\, interf(t,a) \,\mathring{,}\, \beta$

C4 : $\forall\, t \in \mathsf{Tid}, a, b \in \mathsf{Act} : vmax(t,a) \subseteq \mathsf{wlp}(interf(t,b), vmax(t,a))$

Fig. 3. Core axioms

Example 4. A view-preserving simulation for SC is the identity relation. For TSO it is the flushing of contents of store buffers to main memory. For C11 in which all write events to the same variable x are ordered in some *modification order*, it is the advancement of a thread's observation on x (a write to x of a value) to another write which occurs later in modification order.

The concept of views is inherent to the axiomatic reasoning and hence is also employed for property specification. As threads might observe more than one value for a variable, the ordinary first-order logic assertions on program variables of Hoare-logic [16] need to be replaced by *view-based* assertions.

Definition 2. *For a thread t, a variable $x \in \mathsf{Var_G}$ and values $u, v \in \mathsf{Val}$ we define*

$$[x \not\approx v]_t \,\hat{=}\, \mathsf{dis}(T(t, Rd_{|x}[v])) \qquad \textit{(Impossible value)}$$
$$[x \equiv v]_t \,\hat{=}\, \bigcap\nolimits_{u \neq v}[x \not\approx u]_t \qquad \textit{(Definite value)}$$
$$x_{\uparrow t} \,\hat{=}\, \bigcap\nolimits_{a \in \mathsf{Act}_{|x}} vmax(t,a) \qquad \textit{(Maximal view)}$$
$$[x = v]_t \,\hat{=}\, [x \equiv v]_t \cap x_{\uparrow t} \qquad \textit{(Maximal value)}$$
$$\langle y = u \rangle^\mathsf{S}[x = v]_t \,\hat{=}\, \mathsf{wlp}(T(t, rd^\mathsf{RS}(y, \cdot, u)), [x = v]_t) \qquad \textit{(Synced conditional observation)}$$
$$\langle x = v \rangle[x = v]_t \,\hat{=}\, \mathsf{wlp}(T(t, rd(x, \cdot, v)), [x = v]_t) \qquad \textit{(Conditional observation)}$$

Example 5. Consider the state of WRC after executing lines 1, 2 and 3 (in this order). In SC, we then have $[x = 1]_t$ for all threads t (same for y). In TSO (when store buffer contents has not been flushed yet), we, e.g., have $[x = 1]_1$, $[y = 1]_2$ and $[x \not\approx 1]_3$ (thread 3 cannot read x to be 1). In C11, we might have $[y \approx 0]_3$ and $[y \approx 1]_3$ (thread 3 can read both 0 and 1). Moreover, the following synced conditional observation is valid in all three memory models: $\langle y = 1 \rangle^\mathsf{S}[x = 1]_3$ (by a synchronized read of y to be 1, thread 3 becomes view maximal on x and definitely observes the value 1 for x).

We let $\mathcal{G}$ be the set of (all logical combinations of) such *global* assertions. In our proof outlines (like in the one of WRC) we also allow for normal Hoare-like assertions on local registers (e.g. $(r_1 = 1) \in BExp$), and define the logical combinations of such *local* ($\mathcal{L}$) assertions and the global assertions to be the set $\mathcal{A}$ of all assertions.

Assertions define sets of states. Of particular interest are β-stable assertions.

SV1 : $\forall a, b \in \mathsf{Act}, t, t' \in \mathsf{Tid}$ s.t. $var(a) \neq var(b)$:
$$interf(t', b) \, \mathring{,} \, T(t, a) \subseteq T(t, a) \, \mathring{,} \, interf(t', b)$$

SV2 : $\forall a, b \in \mathsf{Act}, t, t' \in \mathsf{Tid}$ s.t. $var(a) \neq var(b)$:
$$vmax(t, a) \subseteq \mathsf{wlp}(interf(t', b), vmax(t, a))$$

RW1 : $\forall t, t' \in \mathsf{Tid}, x \in \mathsf{Var}_{\mathsf{G}}, a_r \in Rd_{|x}, a_w \in Wr_{|x}$ s.t. $rdval(a_r) \neq wrval(a_w)$:
$$interf(t', a_w) \, \mathring{,} \, T(t, a_r) \subseteq T(t, a_r) \, \mathring{,} \, interf(t', a_w)$$

RW2 : $\forall a \in \mathsf{Act}, t, t' \in \mathsf{Tid}, a_r \in Rd_{|var(a)}$:
$$interf(t', a_r) \, \mathring{,} \, T(t, a) \subseteq T(t, a) \, \mathring{,} \, interf(t', a_r)$$

RW3 : $\forall a \in \mathsf{Act}, t, t' \in \mathsf{Tid}, a_r \in Rd_{|var(a)}$:
$$vmax(t, a) \subseteq \mathsf{wlp}(interf(t', a_r), vmax(t, a))$$

RW4 : $\forall x \in \mathsf{Var}_{\mathsf{G}}, t \in \mathsf{Tid} : \Sigma \subseteq dom(T(t, Rd_{|x}))$

RW5 : $\forall x \in \mathsf{Var}_{\mathsf{G}}, a_w \in Wr_{|x}, v = wrval(a_w) : \Sigma \subseteq \mathsf{wlp}(T(t, a_w), dom(T(t, Rd_{|x}[v])))$

RW6 : $\forall x \in \mathsf{Var}_{\mathsf{G}}, t \in \mathsf{Tid} : x_{\uparrow t} \subseteq \bigcup_{v \in \mathsf{Val}} [x \equiv v]_t$

RW7 : $\forall x \in \mathsf{Var}_{\mathsf{G}}, a_w, a_r, a \in \mathsf{Act}_{|x}, t, t' \in \mathsf{Tid}$, s.t. $wrval(a_w) = rdval(a_r) \wedge t \neq t'$:
$$vmax(t, a_w) \cap \mathsf{dis}(T(t', a_r)) \subseteq \mathsf{wlp}(T(t, a_w), \mathsf{wlp}(T(t', a_r), vmax(t', a)))$$

Fig. 4. Axioms on shared variables

Definition 3. *Any predicate* $P \in 2^{\Sigma}$ *is* β-stable *iff* $P \subseteq \mathsf{wlp}(\beta, P)$.

All assertions in $\mathcal{G}$ are β-stable (see [13]). The axioms furthermore make use of an *interference relation* $interf \in \mathsf{Tid} \times \mathsf{Act} \to 2^{\Sigma \times \Sigma}$ which (together with β) provides an *overapproximation* of the transition relation $T(t, a)$ in order to abstract from details of the memory model and to regain standard properties of reasoning (like writes and reads on different variables commuting). Figure 3 gives all core axioms; Fig. 4 gives axioms concerning read and write actions on shared variables.

We only briefly explain the axioms; an example application of the axioms for reasoning about WRC is given below. Axiom **C1** states that initially all threads are view maximal w.r.t. all actions. Axiom **C2** describe the independence of actions w.r.t. thread identifiers (where additional β steps are required). Axiom **C3** states that $interf$ together with β *over-approximates* the behaviour of an action. Axiom **C4** states that the interference relation preserves every view-maximality property of the thread performing the interference (of the action).

Axiom **SV1** is a weakening of the commutation property present in SC. **SV2** states that a view-maximality property of any thread is stable under actions on any other variable. Axioms **RW1** and **RW2** capture semi-commutativity properties for writes and reads, respectively, and are analogous to **SV1**. Axiom **RW3** states that view-maximality on a variable is preserved by reading the variable. Axiom **RW4** states that it is always possible to read some value of a variable, and **RW5** states that a thread t writing some value can afterwards read it. **RW6** states that whenever t is view maximal on actions over variable

x, then t has a definite value assertion over *some* value for x (i.e., can only read one value for x). Axiom **RW7** considers a situation in which thread t is *vmax* on a variable x but t' cannot read a specific value for this variable. We then obtain view-maximality of t' on x after t has performed the write a_w and t' has read this write's value.

Finally, the axiom set contains one specific axiom for *fences* and one for *message passing*. Fence instructions are employed in weak memory models to make programs behave more like SC. The fence axiom given below states this by saying that a fence in a thread being view maximal on some action a makes all other threads view maximal on a as well.

FNC $\forall a \in \mathsf{Act}, t, t' \in \mathsf{Tid}$: $vmax(t, a) \subseteq \mathsf{wlp}(T(t, fence), vmax(t', a))$.
MP For $a_w, a_r, b \in \mathsf{Act}$ and $t, t' \in \mathsf{Tid}$ such that $(a_w, a_r) \in sync$, $var(a_w) = var(a_r)$, $wrval(a_w) = rdval(a_r)$, $var(b) \neq var(a_w)$, and $t \neq t'$, we have

$$vmax(t, b) \cap \mathsf{wlp}(T(t', a_r), vmax(t', b))$$
$$\subseteq \mathsf{wlp}(T(t, a_w), \mathsf{wlp}(T(t', a_r), vmax(t', b))).$$

The message passing axiom **MP** describes the *passing of knowledge on variable values* from one thread to another upon *synchronization*. Synchronization is incorporated here by requiring $(a_w, a_r) \in sync$ which is achieved when the write has a WS and the read an RS annotation. More specifically, it describes a situation where a thread t is maximal on some action b ($vmax(t, b)$) and thread t' upon executing action a_r would become view maximal on b as well. Then, writing the value to be read (i.e., $T(t, a_w)$) followed by reading this value ($T(t', a_r)$) makes thread t' view maximal on b.

As a first result, we restate two lemmas stating the stability of global assertions under fence and read actions.

Lemma 1 ([4]). *Assume the axioms C3, SV1 and SV2 hold. For all $P \in \mathcal{G}$ and threads t, $P \subseteq \mathsf{wlp}(T(t, fence), P)$.*

Lemma 2 ([13]). *Assume the axioms C3, SV1, SV2, RW2 and RW3 hold. For all $P \in \mathcal{G}$, threads t and $a_r \in \mathsf{Rd}$, $P \subseteq \mathsf{wlp}(T(t, a_r), P)$.*

Note that – contrary to [4,13] – we name the axioms required for the proof in the lemmata. This is of importance for dealing with memory models which only fulfill part of the axioms (so that we can see whether a generic proof is transferable to such a memory model).

3.2 Reasoning Example on Axiom Level

Next, we employ the axioms for showing one step in the correctness proof of WRC. Note that the proof of WRC in the generic framework has not appeared before. In general, such proofs involve proof steps of the form

$$P \subseteq \mathsf{wlp}(T(t, a), Q)$$

for actions a belonging to program instructions com_t, where $P \in \mathcal{A}$ is the pre-assertion before and $Q \in \mathcal{A}$ the post-assertion after the instruction. We also write these as Hoare-triples

$$\{P\} \, com_t \, \{Q\} \, .$$

Such steps need to be performed to show local and global correctness (as of Owicki-Gries' approach [25]).

Definition 4. *A thread t is* locally correct *in a proof outline if $\{P\}com_t\{Q\}$ holds for every program command com in t with pre-assertion P and post-assertion Q.*

A proof outline is globally correct *(interference-free) if for every pair of threads t, t', $\{R \cap P\}com_{t'}\{R\}$ holds for every assertion R in the proof outline of t and command com with pre-assertion P in thread t'.*

We exemplify one such proof step for the proof outline in Fig. 1, which is part of the local correctness of thread 3.

$$\{r_1 \neq 1 \cup \langle y = 1 \rangle^S [x = 1]_3\} \, r_2 :=_3^{RS} y \, \{r_1 \neq 1 \cup r_2 \neq 1 \cup [x = 1]_3\}$$

For this we have to prove for every $v \in \mathsf{Val}$

$$r_1 \neq 1 \cup \langle y = 1 \rangle^S [x = 1]_3 \subseteq \mathsf{wlp}(T(3, rd^{RS}(y, r_2, v)), r_1 \neq 1 \cup r_2 \neq 1 \cup [x = 1]_3)$$

Because of the disjunctivity of wlp (see Fig. 2), we can divide the proof in two parts

(i) $r_1 \neq 1 \subseteq \mathsf{wlp}(T(3, rd^{RS}(y, r_2, v)), r_1 \neq 1)$
(ii) $\langle y = 1 \rangle^S [x = 1]_3 \subseteq \mathsf{wlp}(T(3, rd^{RS}(y, r_2, v)), r_2 \neq 1 \cup [x = 1]_3)$

For reasoning about local registers, we employ a version of the standard technique of backward substitution from the rule of assignment of Hoare-logic[1], i.e.,

$$e[r := v] \subseteq \mathsf{wlp}(T(t, rd^{RS}(x, r, v))), e)$$

where $e \in Exp$ is an expression on local variables only and $[r := v]$ means replacing all occurrence of r by value v. For (i) we then have

$$(r_1 \neq 1) = (r_1 \neq 1[r_2 := v]) \subseteq \mathsf{wlp}(T(3, rd^{RS}(y, r_2, v)), r_1 \neq 1)$$

For (ii) we look at two cases. First, let $v = 1$. Using the monoticity of wlp we get

$$\langle y = 1 \rangle^S [x = 1]_3 = \mathsf{wlp}(T(3, rd^{RS}(y, r_2, 1)), [x = 1]_3)$$
$$\subseteq \mathsf{wlp}(T(3, rd^{RS}(y, r_2, v)), r_2 \neq 1 \cup [x = 1]_3)$$

In the case $v \neq 1$, we need Lemma 2 and therefore the axioms C3, SV1, SV2, RW2, and RW3 have to hold. Because of the disjunctivity of wlp we get

---

[1] Such backward substitution is sound here as it only considers local registers.

$$\langle y = 1 \rangle^S [x = 1]_3 \subseteq \Sigma$$

$$\overset{v \neq 1}{=} (r_2 \neq 1 [r_2 := v]) \cup [x = 1]_3$$

$$\subseteq \mathsf{wlp}(T(3, rd^{\mathsf{RS}}(y, r_2, v)), r_2 \neq 1 \cup [x = 1]_3)$$

Many steps of such correctness proofs are complex, time consuming and repetitive. In the next section we summarize multiple such steps into *proof rules* and thereby lift reasoning to the higher level of syntactic assertions, not employing weakest preconditions anymore.

$$\text{TRUE} \frac{}{\{P\} \ com_t \ \{true\}} \qquad \text{FALSE} \frac{}{\{false\} \ com_t \ \{P\}}$$

$$\text{MONO} \frac{P_1 \supseteq P_2 \quad Q_1 \subseteq Q_2 \quad \{P_1\} \ com_t \ \{Q_1\}}{\{P_2\} \ com_t \ \{Q_2\}}$$

$$\text{CONJ} \frac{\{P_1\} \ com_t \ \{Q_1\} \quad \{P_2\} \ com_t \ \{Q_2\}}{\{P_1 \cap P_2\} \ com_t \ \{Q_1 \cap Q_2\}}$$

$$\text{DISJ} \frac{\{P_1\} \ com_t \ \{Q_1\} \quad \{P_2\} \ com_t \ \{Q_2\}}{\{P_1 \cup P_2\} \ com_t \ \{Q_1 \cup Q_2\}}$$

Fig. 5. General rules

4   Rules

In this section we explain our novel proof rules for the axiomatic reasoning. Remember that for a program command com_t in a thread t, we prove $\{P\} \ com_t \ \{Q\}$ for assertions $P, Q \in \mathcal{A}$ by showing

$$P \subseteq \mathsf{wlp}(T(t, a), Q)$$

where a is the action in com_t. Some interim results of those proofs can be generalised and lifted to the higher level of syntactic assertions. We formalise them in the form of rules which then can be used to directly prove the correctness of a proof outline without the need of weakest preconditions.

We start by giving general rules (Fig. 5) which hold regardless of the validity of axioms. Those rules are all in the original Hoare-logic form [16] and are here translated to our setting. For the rules TRUE and FALSE note that the assertions $\{true\}$ and $\{false\}$ describe the set of states Σ and the empty set, respectively. With that in mind both rules follow directly from our definition of Hoare-triple. The intuitive idea of the MONO rule are that a Hoare-triple still holds if the pre-assertion becomes stronger or the post-assertion weaker. The first follows by definition and the second from the monotonicity of wlp (see Fig. 2). Analogously, the rules CONJ and DISJ formalise the conjunctivity and disjunctivity properties of Fig. 2. Hence we get the following Theorem.

Theorem 1. *The general proof rules in Fig. 5 are sound.*

The proof of the theorem can be found in the extended version [3]. Note that these rules can be used to combine different Hoare-triples from other rules.

$$\text{FENCE1(LEMMA 1)} \frac{P \in \mathcal{G} \quad C3 \quad SV1 \quad SV2}{\{P\} \; \mathit{fnq} \; \{P\}} \qquad \text{FENCE2} \frac{FNC}{\{x_{\uparrow t}\} \; \mathit{fnq} \; \{x_{\uparrow t'}\}}$$

$$\text{FENCE3} \frac{C2 \quad C3 \quad SV1 \quad SV2 \quad RW6 \quad FNC}{\{[x = v]_t\} \; \mathit{fnq} \; \{[x = v]_{t'}\}}$$

Fig. 6. Fence rules

Next we look at rules specific to a certain program command and start with fence actions. If we formalise the property given in Lemma 1, we get the first rule of Fig. 6: FENCE1. Note that with regard to showing global correctness, the rule implies the following lemma.

Lemma 3. *In every proof outline fence actions are globally correct for β-stable assertions, i.e., for every assertions $G \in \mathcal{G}$ and $P \in \mathcal{A}$: $\{G \cap P\} \; \mathit{fnc}_t \; \{G\}$.*

The **FNC** Axiom is formalised in FENCE2 and if we additionally assume the axioms **C2** and **RW6** we can not only pass view-maximality to a different thread, but also the value that can be read. In the extended version [3] we show the following theorem.

Theorem 2. *The fence proof rules in Fig. 6 are sound.*

$$\text{READ1(LEMMA 2)} \frac{P \in \mathcal{G} \quad C3 \quad SV1 \quad SV2 \quad RW2 \quad RW3}{\{P\} \; r :=_t x \; \{P\}}$$

$$\text{READ2} \frac{}{\{[x \not\approx v]_t\} \; r :=_t x \; \{r \neq v\}} \qquad \text{READ3} \frac{}{\{[x = v]_t\} \; r :=_t x \; \{r = v\}}$$

$$\text{CONREAD1} \frac{}{\{\langle x = v \rangle [x = v]_t\} \; r :=_t x \; \{r \neq v \cup [x = v]_t\}}$$

$$\text{CONREAD2} \frac{}{\{\langle x = v \rangle^S [y = u]_t\} \; r :=_t^{RS} x \; \{r \neq v \cup [y = u]_t\}}$$

$$\text{READREG} \frac{P \in \mathcal{L} \quad r \notin reg(P)}{\{P\} \; r :=_t x \; \{P\}} \qquad \text{LOCREAD} \frac{r \notin reg(P)}{\{P\} \; r :=_t E \; \{P\}}$$

Fig. 7. Read rules ($reg(P)$ being the local registers occurring in P)

For read actions (Fig. 7) we similarly formalise Lemma 2 in rule READ1 and get the following lemma.

Lemma 4. *In every proof outline read actions are globally correct for β-stable assertions, i.e., for every assertions $G \in \mathcal{G}$ and $P \in \mathcal{A}$: $\{G \cap P\}\ r :=_t v\ \{G\}$.*

The rules READ2, READ3, CONREAD1 and CONREAD2 describe how we replace different global assertions (containing x) by local ones (containing r) after reading the value of x to r. Here READ2 says that if thread t cannot read v for x, then after reading x to r, r cannot be v. Analogous in READ3 where t cannot read a value different from v for x and is view maximal (which means that t can read the most up-to-date value for x), after the read, r has to be equal to v. If we have a conditional observation assertion $\langle x = v \rangle [x = v]_t$ and read in the same thread from x, then either we do not read v or $[x = v]_t$ holds afterwards (CONREAD1). We get a similar rule for the synchronized read and the synced conditional observation (CONREAD2). READREG tells us that a local assertion remains unchanged after a read to a register which is not included in the assertion. In LOCREAD we describe that an assertion will not change, if we read a local expression to a register. In this case the register must not be included in the assertion. Note that by $reg(P)$ we mean the set of registers in P. Summarised we get

Theorem 3. *The read proof rules in Fig. 7 are sound.*

which we also proved in the extended version [3].

$$\text{WRITE1}\frac{x \neq y \quad C3 \quad SV1}{\{[y \not\approx u]_{t'}\}\ x :=_t E\ \{[y \not\approx u]_{t'}\}}$$

$$\text{WRITE2}\frac{x \neq y \quad C3 \quad SV1}{\{[y \equiv u]_{t'}\}\ x :=_t E\ \{[y \equiv u]_{t'}\}}$$

$$\text{WRITE3}\frac{x \neq y \quad C3 \quad SV2}{\{y_{\uparrow t'}\}\ x :=_t E\ \{y_{\uparrow t'}\}} \qquad \text{WRITE4}\frac{x \neq y \quad C3 \quad SV1 \quad SV2}{\{[y = u]_{t'}\}\ x :=_t E\ \{[y = u]_{t'}\}}$$

$$\text{WRITE5}\frac{C3 \quad C4}{\{x_{\uparrow t}\}\ x :=_t E\ \{x_{\uparrow t}\}} \qquad \text{WRITE6}\frac{[\![E]\!] = v \quad C3 \quad C4 \quad RW5 \quad RW6}{\{[x = u]_t\}\ x :=_t E\ \{[x = v]_t\}}$$

$$\text{CONWRITE1}\frac{[\![E]\!] = v \quad t \neq t' \quad C2 \quad C3 \quad C4}{SV1 \quad SV2 \quad RW2 \quad RW3 \quad RW5 \quad RW6 \quad RW7}{\{[x \not\approx v]_{t'} \cap [x = u]_t\}\ x :=_t E\ \{\langle x = v \rangle [x = v]_{t'}\}}$$

$$\text{CONWRITE2}\frac{[\![E]\!] = v \quad t \neq t' \quad x \neq y \quad C2 \quad C3}{SV1 \quad SV2 \quad RW2 \quad RW3 \quad RW6 \quad MP}{\{[x \not\approx v]_{t'} \cap [y = u]_t\}\ x :=_t^{\text{WS}} E\ \{\langle x = v \rangle^{\text{S}}[y = u]_{t'}\}}$$

$$\text{WRITEREG}\frac{P \in \mathcal{L}}{\{P\}\ x :=_t E\ \{P\}}$$

Fig. 8. Write rules

In Fig. 8 we formalised rules for write actions. There we differentiate between global assertions about the variable written to and about other variables. In both cases we need the **C3** axiom. This allows us to apply a hand full of axioms that describe properties of $interf$, e.g., **SV1** and **SV2**. For different variables we can pass readability of a value with the axiom **SV1** (see rules WRITE1 and WRITE2). If we want to pass view-maximality (WRITE3), we need **SV2**. The rule WRITE4 combines WRITE2 and WRITE3. In the case where the assertion contains the same variable as the write action, we can use the axiom **C4** to pass view-maximality (WRITE5). If we additionally assume **RW5** and **RW6**, we can update the value thread t can read (WRITE6). If we write a new value to x (which means that before the write, t and t' could not read v) in a view-maximal thread t, then if t' can read v, it also has to be view-maximal. This behaviour is decribed in rule CONWRITE1. We need to assume **RW7** to pass the conditional view-maximality to a different thread. The rule CONWRITE2 describes message passing. If t' can read v for x and t can read u for y and is view-maximal in t, then if we write v to x in t, $[y = u]_{t'}$ only holds if we can read v for x in t'. This behaviour only differs from CONWRITE1 by allowing different variables. Because of this, we cannot apply **RW7** and need **MP**. Hence this rule only holds for synchronised writes. The last rule of Fig. 8 (WRITEREG) formalises the fact that a write will not change the value of a register. In the extended version [3], we prove

Table 1. Rules employed for showing local correctness of the WRC proof outline

com_t	Hoare-Triples	Proof Rules	Axioms
$x :=_1 1$	$\{P_{1,1}\}\ x :=_1 1\ \{P_{1,2}\}$	TRUE	
$r_1 :=_2 x$	$\{P_{2,1}\}\ r_1 :=_2 x\ \{P_{2,2}\}$	READ1, READREG, READ3, CONREAD1	C3, SV1, SV2, RW2, RW3
$y :=_2^{\text{WS}} 1$	$\{P_{2,2}\}\ y :=_2 1\ \{P_{2,3}\}$	TRUE	
$r_2 :=_3^{\text{RS}} y$	$\{P_{3,1}\}\ r_2 :=_3 y\ \{P_{3,2}\}$	READREG, CONREAD2	
$r_3 :=_3 x$	$\{P_{3,2}\}\ r_3 :=_3 x\ \{P_{3,3}\}$	READREG, READ3	

Theorem 4. *The write proof rules in Fig. 8 are sound.*

With all these rules being sound, we can now prove correctness much easier and shorter. Also we then know exactly which axioms we need for a certain proof outline to be valid.

5   Correctness Proof of WRC via Proof Rules

In this section, we finally apply our rules to the correctness proof of the WRC example in Fig. 1.

Lemma 5. *The proof outline in Fig. 1 is valid under the axioms C2, C3, C4, SV1, SV2, RW2, RW3, RW5, RW6, RW7 and MP.*

Table 2. Rules employed for showing global correctness of the WRC proof outline

com_t	Hoare-Triples	Proof Rules	Axioms
$x :=_1 1$	$\{P_{1,1} \cap P_{2,1}\}\ x :=_1 1\ \{P_{2,1}\}$	WRITE1, WRITEREG, CONWRITE1	C2, C3, C4, SV1, SV2, RW2, RW3, RW5, RW6, RW7
	$\{P_{1,1} \cap P_{2,2}\}\ x :=_1 1\ \{P_{2,2}\}$	WRITE1, WRITEREG	C3, SV1
	$\{P_{1,1} \cap P_{2,3}\}\ x :=_1 1\ \{P_{2,3}\}$	TRUE	
	$\{P_{1,1} \cap P_{3,1}\}\ x :=_1 1\ \{P_{3,1}\}$	WRITEREG	
	$\{P_{1,1} \cap P_{3,2}\}\ x :=_1 1\ \{P_{3,2}\}$	WRITEREG	
	$\{P_{1,1} \cap P_{3,3}\}\ x :=_1 1\ \{P_{3,3}\}$	WRITEREG	
$r_1 :=_2 x$	$\{P_{2,1} \cap P_{1,1}\}\ r_1 :=_2 x\ \{P_{1,1}\}$	READ1, READ3	C3, SV1, SV2, RW2, RW3
	$\{P_{2,1} \cap P_{1,2}\}\ r_1 :=_2 x\ \{P_{1,2}\}$	TRUE	
	$\{P_{2,1} \cap P_{3,1}\}\ r_1 :=_2 x\ \{P_{3,1}\}$	READ1	C3, SV1, SV2, RW2, RW3
	$\{P_{2,1} \cap P_{3,2}\}\ r_1 :=_2 x\ \{P_{3,2}\}$	READREG	
	$\{P_{2,1} \cap P_{3,3}\}\ r_1 :=_2 x\ \{P_{3,3}\}$	READREG	
$y :=_2^{\mathsf{SW}} 1$	$\{P_{2,2} \cap P_{1,1}\}\ y :=_2 1\ \{P_{1,1}\}$	WRITE1, WRITE4, WRITEREG	C3, SV1, SV2
	$\{P_{2,2} \cap P_{1,2}\}\ y :=_2 1\ \{P_{1,2}\}$	TRUE	
	$\{P_{2,2} \cap P_{3,1}\}\ y :=_2 1\ \{P_{3,1}\}$	WRITEREG, CONWRITE2	C2, C3, SV1, SV2, RW2, RW3, RW6, MP
	$\{P_{2,2} \cap P_{3,2}\}\ y :=_2 1\ \{P_{3,2}\}$	WRITEREG	
	$\{P_{2,2} \cap P_{3,3}\}\ y :=_2 1\ \{P_{3,3}\}$	WRITEREG	
$r_2 :=_3^{\mathsf{SR}} y$	$\{P_{3,1} \cap P_{1,1}\}\ r_2 :=_3 y\ \{P_{1,1}\}$	READ1, READREG	C3, SV1, SV2, RW2, RW3
	$\{P_{3,1} \cap P_{1,2}\}\ r_2 :=_3 y\ \{P_{1,2}\}$	TRUE	
	$\{P_{3,1} \cap P_{2,1}\}\ r_2 :=_3 y\ \{P_{2,1}\}$	READ1, READ2	C3, SV1, SV2, RW2, RW3
	$\{P_{3,1} \cap P_{2,2}\}\ r_2 :=_3 y\ \{P_{2,2}\}$	READ1, READREG, READ2	C3, SV1, SV2, RW2, RW3
	$\{P_{3,1} \cap P_{2,3}\}\ r_2 :=_3 y\ \{P_{2,3}\}$	TRUE	
$r_3 :=_3 x$	$\{P_{3,1} \cap P_{1,1}\}\ r_3 :=_3 x\ \{P_{1,1}\}$	READ1, READREG	C3, SV1, SV2, RW2, RW3
	$\{P_{3,1} \cap P_{1,2}\}\ r_3 :=_3 x\ \{P_{1,2}\}$	TRUE	
	$\{P_{3,1} \cap P_{2,1}\}\ r_3 :=_3 x\ \{P_{2,1}\}$	READ1, READREG	C3, SV1, SV2, RW2, RW3
	$\{P_{3,1} \cap P_{2,2}\}\ r_3 :=_3 x\ \{P_{2,2}\}$	READ1, READREG	C3, SV1, SV2, RW2, RW3
	$\{P_{3,1} \cap P_{2,3}\}\ r_3 :=_3 x\ \{P_{2,3}\}$	TRUE	

This means that the proof outline holds for every memory model that satisfies the axioms named.

To prove this lemma, we have to check every Hoare-triple that we need for local and global correctness (see Definition 4). Starting with local correctness, Table 1 gives us an overview of every Hoare-triple we need to prove. In there we see which proofs require which rules and thus which axioms. For better readability, we have omitted the use of the rules MONO, CONJ and DISJ. One of the Hoare-triples is

$$\{r_1 \neq 1 \cup \langle y = 1\rangle^{\mathsf{S}}[x = 1]_3\}\ r_2 :=_3^{\mathsf{RS}} y\ \{r_1 \neq 1 \cup r_2 \neq 1 \cup [x = 1]_3\}$$

which we already proved at the end of Sect. 2. With our novel proof rules at hand we can show its validity with a fewer number of steps. As written in Table 1 we need the rules READREG and CONREAD2. The first one tells us

$$\{r_1 \neq 1\} \; r_2 :=_3^{\mathsf{RS}} y \; \{r_1 \neq 1\}$$

and with CONREAD2 we get

$$\{\langle y = 1 \rangle^{\mathsf{S}} [x = 1]_3\} \; r_2 :=_3^{\mathsf{RS}} y \; \{r_2 \neq 1 \cup [x = 1]_3\}$$

Applying the DISJ-rule we are done. Analogously we can now prove every Hoare-triple. In this way we need significantly fewer steps to prove one triple than we did in Sect. 2. Hence the entire correctness proof (which contains the proof of 31 Hoare-triple for Fig. 1) is easier and shorter to prove, simply by applying the abstract proof rules. An overview of all the rules used for global correctness is given in Table 2. Due to the non-interference condition in Owicki-Gries style proofs, there are still a number of proof steps to be done, however significantly fewer than on the level of axioms. The number of proof steps could furthermore be reduced by employing a compositional proof technique like rely-guarantee reasoning [29]. For this, the same proof rules are sound.

6   Related Work

There are a number of approaches which propose novel program logics for weak memory models. The view-based logic we employ here has first appeared in [10, 14] for C11 RAR and has then been generalized to the generic reasoning approach in [13]. The work in [5] uses (and extends) view-based assertions to persistent memory, but does not develop a memory model independent technique. Similarly, Lahav et al. [19] propose a new program logic for the strong-release-acquire model of [18] and employ rely-guarantee reasoning. While the rely-guarantee framework is independent of a concrete memory model, the program logic is not.

Besides that there are verification techniques which are applicable to several memory models. Alglave and Cousot [2] present an invariance proof method which shows that a given program is correct w.r.t. a given memory model and an invariant specification of that program. It does so by first proving that a so-called communication specification is sufficient for the program's invariant. If a memory model guarantees the communication, the program is correct under that model. Ponce de Leon et al. [23] and Gavrilenko et al. [15] present generic bounded model checkers which translate a given program under a given memory model into an SMT formula. They are generic because their input contains not only the program but also the memory model, formalised in CAT as a set of relations. Kokologiannakis et al. [17] developed a generic model checker that transforms a given program into an execution graph to check its correctness under a given memory model with an axiomatic semantics. Colvin [7] proposes a special sequential composition operator which mimics the reordering behaviour of many weak memory models. Coughlin et al. [8,9] discuss rely-guarantee reasoning for weak memory models in general and introduce a specific new verification condition called reordering-interference-freedom. This technique can be instantiated to memory models with a reordering semantics.

Our approach discussed here lifts the generic reasoning technique of [13] to the syntactic level, allowing to construct proof outlines operating on the level of program instructions and view-based assertions. Thereby, we avoid low-level reasoning about weakest preconditions while still preserving genericity.

7   Conclusion

In this paper, we have proposed high level proof rules lifting the generic reasoning principle of [13] to a more abstract level. Similar to standard Hoare-logic, our proof rules allow to reason on the syntactic level of assertions, departing from the semantic level of weakest preconditions. This significantly simplifies reasoning, and moreover allows us to directly see which axioms have been used in a proof. We have exemplified our proof technique by providing a generic correctness proof for the WRC litmus test. By the results of [13] (showing that SC, TSO and C11 RAR instantiate all axioms), this proof is valid for WRC running on a sequentially consistent as well as the TSO and C11 memory models.

References

1. Adve, S.V., Gharachorloo, K.: Shared memory consistency models: a tutorial. Computer **29**(12), 66–76 (1996). https://doi.org/10.1109/2.546611
2. Alglave, J., Cousot, P.: Ogre and pythia: an invariance proof method for weak consistency models. In: Castagna, G., Gordon, A.D. (eds.) POPL, pp. 3–18. ACM (2017). https://doi.org/10.1145/3009837.3009883
3. Bargmann, L., Wehrheim, H.: Lifting the reasoning level in generic weak memory verification (Extended Version). CoRR abs/2309.01433 (2023). https://doi.org/10.48550/arXiv.2309.01433
4. Bargmann, L., Wehrheim, H.: View-based axiomatic reasoning for PSO. In: TASE (2023). to appear
5. Bila, E.V., Dongol, B., Lahav, O., Raad, A., Wickerson, J.: View-based Owicki–Gries reasoning for persistent x86-TSO. In: ESOP 2022. LNCS, vol. 13240, pp. 234–261. Springer, Cham (2022). https://doi.org/10.1007/978-3-030-99336-8_9
6. Boehm, H., Adve, S.V.: Foundations of the C++ concurrency memory model. In: Gupta, R., Amarasinghe, S.P. (eds.) PLDI, pp. 68–78. ACM (2008). https://doi.org/10.1145/1375581.1375591
7. Colvin, R.J.: Parallelized sequential composition and hardware weak memory models. In: Calinescu, R., Păsăreanu, C.S. (eds.) SEFM 2021. LNCS, vol. 13085, pp. 201–221. Springer, Cham (2021). https://doi.org/10.1007/978-3-030-92124-8_12
8. Coughlin, N., Winter, K., Smith, G.: Rely/guarantee reasoning for multicopy atomic weak memory models. In: Huisman, M., Păsăreanu, C., Zhan, N. (eds.) FM 2021. LNCS, vol. 13047, pp. 292–310. Springer, Cham (2021). https://doi.org/10.1007/978-3-030-90870-6_16

9. Coughlin, N., Winter, K., Smith, G.: Compositional reasoning for non-multicopy atomic architectures. Form. Asp. Comput. (2022). https://doi.org/10.1145/3574137. just Accepted

10. Dalvandi, S., Doherty, S., Dongol, B., Wehrheim, H.: Owicki-Gries reasoning for C11 RAR. In: Hirschfeld, R., Pape, T. (eds.) ECOOP, pp. 11:1–11:26. LIPIcs, Schloss Dagstuhl - Leibniz-Zentrum für Informatik (2020). https://doi.org/10.4230/LIPIcs.ECOOP.2020.11

11. Dalvandi, S., Dongol, B., Doherty, S., Wehrheim, H.: Integrating Owicki-Gries for C11-style memory models into Isabelle/HOL. J. Autom. Reason. 66(1), 141–171 (2022). https://doi.org/10.1007/s10817-021-09610-2

12. Dijkstra, E.W.: A Discipline of Programming. Prentice-Hall, Upper Saddle river (1976). https://www.worldcat.org/oclc/01958445

13. Doherty, S., Dalvandi, S., Dongol, B., Wehrheim, H.: Unifying operational weak memory verification: an axiomatic approach. ACM Trans. Comput. Log. 23(4), 27:1–27:39 (2022). https://doi.org/10.1145/3545117

14. Doherty, S., Dongol, B., Wehrheim, H., Derrick, J.: Verifying C11 programs operationally. In: PPoPP, pp. 355–365 (2019). https://doi.org/10.1145/3293883.3295702

15. Gavrilenko, N., Ponce-de-León, H., Furbach, F., Heljanko, K., Meyer, R.: BMC for weak memory models: relation analysis for compact SMT encodings. In: Dillig, I., Tasiran, S. (eds.) CAV 2019. LNCS, vol. 11561, pp. 355–365. Springer, Cham (2019). https://doi.org/10.1007/978-3-030-25540-4_19

16. Hoare, C.A.R.: An axiomatic basis for computer programming. Commun. ACM 12(10), 576–580 (1969). https://doi.org/10.1145/363235.363259

17. Kokologiannakis, M., Raad, A., Vafeiadis, V.: Model checking for weakly consistent libraries. In: McKinley, K.S., Fisher, K. (eds.) PLDI, pp. 96–110. ACM (2019). https://doi.org/10.1145/3314221.3314609

18. Lahav, O., Boker, U.: What's decidable about causally consistent shared memory? ACM Trans. Program. Lang. Syst. 44(2), 8:1–8:55 (2022). https://doi.org/10.1145/3505273

19. Lahav, O., Dongol, B., Wehrheim, H.: Rely-guarantee reasoning for causally consistent shared memory. In: CAV (2023). to appear

20. Lahav, O., Giannarakis, N., Vafeiadis, V.: Taming release-acquire consistency. In: Bodík, R., Majumdar, R. (eds.) POPL, pp. 649–662. ACM (2016). https://doi.org/10.1145/2837614.2837643

21. Lahav, O., Vafeiadis, V.: Owicki-Gries reasoning for weak memory models. In: Halldórsson, M.M., Iwama, K., Kobayashi, N., Speckmann, B. (eds.) ICALP 2015. LNCS, vol. 9135, pp. 311–323. Springer, Heidelberg (2015). https://doi.org/10.1007/978-3-662-47666-6_25

22. Lamport, L.: How to make a multiprocessor computer that correctly executes multiprocess programs. IEEE Trans. Comput. 28(9), 690–691 (1979). https://doi.org/10.1109/TC.1979.1675439

23. de León, H.P., Furbach, F., Heljanko, K., Meyer, R.: BMC with memory models as modules. In: Bjørner, N.S., Gurfinkel, A. (eds.) FMCAD. pp. 1–9. IEEE (2018). https://doi.org/10.23919/FMCAD.2018.8603021

24. Maranget, L., Sarkar, S., Sewell, P.: A Tutorial Introduction to the ARM and POWER Relaxed Memory Models (2012). https://www.cl.cam.ac.uk/pes20/ppc-supplemental/test7.pdf. Accessed May 2022

25. Owicki, S.S., Gries, D.: An axiomatic proof technique for parallel programs I. Acta Inf. 6, 319–340 (1976). https://doi.org/10.1007/BF00268134

26. Ridge, T.: A rely-guarantee proof system for x86-TSO. In: Leavens, G.T., O'Hearn, P., Rajamani, S.K. (eds.) VSTTE 2010. LNCS, vol. 6217, pp. 55–70. Springer, Heidelberg (2010). https://doi.org/10.1007/978-3-642-15057-9_4

27. Sarkar, S., et al.: The semantics of x86-CC multiprocessor machine code. In: Shao, Z., Pierce, B.C. (eds.) POPL, pp. 379–391. ACM (2009). https://doi.org/10.1145/1480881.1480929

28. Wehrheim, H., Bargmann, L., Dongol, B.: Reasoning about promises in weak memory models with event structures. In: Chechik, M., Katoen, J., Leucker, M. (eds.) FM, Lecture Notes in Computer Science, vol. 14000, pp. 282–300. Springer, Heidelberg (2023). https://doi.org/10.1007/978-3-031-27481-7_17

29. Xu, Q., de Roever, W.P., He, J.: The rely-guarantee method for verifying shared variable concurrent programs. Formal Aspects Comput. **9**(2), 149–174 (1997). https://doi.org/10.1007/BF01211617

Automatic Formal Verification of RISC-V Pipelined Microprocessors with Fault Tolerance by Spatial Redundancy at a High Level of Abstraction

Miroslav N. Velev[(✉)] [iD]

Aries Design Automation, Chicago, IL, U.S.A.
mvelev@gmail.com
http://www.miroslav-velev.com

Abstract. Presented are abstraction techniques for efficient modeling of pipelined microprocessors of the RISC-V architecture, including designs with fault tolerance by spatial redundancy. This is done at a high-level of abstraction, allowing us to formally verify such processors extremely efficiently by using the property of Positive Equality. To the best of our knowledge, this is the first work on formal verification of RISC-V pipelined processors at a high level of abstraction, and the first work on formal verification of pipelined microprocessors with fault tolerance by spatial redundancy.

Keywords: Abstraction · Boolean Satisfiability (SAT) · Correspondence Checking · Fault Tolerance by Spatial Redundancy · Formal Verification · Logic of Equality with Uninterpreted Functions and Memories · Microprocessor Correctness · RISC-V · Positive Equality

1 Introduction

The RISC-V Instruction Set Architecture (ISA) [23] is a free open-source ISA that is extensively researched by thousands of scientists, e.g., [12, 22], and adopted by hundreds of companies worldwide, e.g., [4]. It is suitable for a wide range of applications from Internet of Things (IoT) to supercomputers. In contrast to all prior ISAs, RISC-V is free to use and free from the whims and fate of a single company, and instead is owned, defined, and maintained by a non-profit foundation. Because of these factors, RISC-V has already gained wide use.

Implementation and testing of a RISC-V processor for space applications is presented in [4]; however, the authors do not use formal methods. Darbari [10] used theorem proving and property checking on the RTL designs of the same or similar RISC-V processor

This research was partially funded by the U.S. Air Force under Contract FA864921P1648, and by NASA under Contract 80NSSC22PA949.

Approved for public release; distribution is unlimited. Public Affairs release approval # AFRL-2023-3256.

cores that we formally verify in this paper. Specifically, he formally verified properties of the 2-stage Ibex RISC-V processor core [22]. To formally verify just the Branch if Equal instruction, BEQ, his theorem-proving method required proving 70 properties, and over 900 invariants. To check such properties and invariants for all instructions, his theorem proving method required more than 2 hours of CPU time. Most importantly, his theorem proving method does not guarantee that enough properties have been proved to imply complete correctness. Wolf [54] used assertion based verification, combined with Bounded Model Checking (BMC) for a depth of 10 to 50 clock cycles. The method requires one check for each instruction in the ISA, and a number of consistency checks. However, BMC does not guarantee that a sufficient depth has been considered to detect all possible bugs that could affect an instruction. Thus, this method is also not exhaustive, and does not guarantee that enough properties have been proved to imply complete correctness.

In contrast to the above methods, we use formal verification at a high level of abstraction. Every time the design of computer systems has shifted to a higher level of abstraction, productivity has increased. The logic of Equality with Uninterpreted Functions and Memories (EUFM) [8] allows us to abstract functional units and memories, while completely modeling the control of a processor. In earlier work on applying EUFM to formal verification of pipelined and superscalar processors, some simple restrictions [27, 28] were imposed on the modeling style for defining processors, resulting in correctness formulas where most of the terms (abstracted word-level values) appear only in positive equations (equality comparisons) that are called p-equations. Such terms, called p-terms (for positive terms), can be treated as distinct constants [6], thus significantly pruning the solution space, and resulting in orders of magnitude speedup of the formal verification; this property is called *Positive Equality*. On the other hand, equations that appear in negative polarity, or in both positive and negative polarity, are called g-equations (for general equations), and their arguments g-terms. G-equations can be either *true* or *false*, and can be encoded with Boolean variables [13, 20, 34, 45] by accounting for the property of transitivity of equality [7], when translating an EUFM correctness formula to an equivalent Boolean formula.

The modeling restrictions and the resulting scalability, together with techniques to model multicycle functional units, exceptions, and branch prediction [29], allowed an earlier version of our tool flow based on Positive Equality to be used to formally verify a model of the M•CORE processor at Motorola, and detect three bugs [16]. This methodology was also applied to formally verify an out-of-order superscalar processor, where the reorder buffer could hold up to 1,500 instructions that are in various stages of execution, and the issue and retire logic could dispatch and complete, respectively, up to 128 instructions per clock cycle [32]. A VLIW processor imitating the Intel Itanium [15, 25] in many features, and that could have more than 200 RISC-like instructions in execution, was formally verified in [30, 44]. Techniques for automatic formal verification of pipelined processors with hardware mechanisms for soft-error tolerance [5, 11] were presented in [47], and with multithreaded execution in [50]. The Bahurupi polymorphic heterogeneous multicore architecture [21] was modeled and formally verified at a high level of abstraction in [52].

Our tool flow consists of: 1) a symbolic simulator, used to symbolically simulate a pipelined, or superscalar, or VLIW implementation processor and its non-pipelined specification, both described in the high-level hardware description language AbsHDL [44], and produce an EUFM correctness formula; 2) a decision procedure for the logic of EUFM that exploits Positive Equality and other optimizations to translate the EUFM correctness formula to a satisfiability-equivalent Boolean formula; and 3) an efficient Boolean Satisfiability (SAT) solver.

Significant improvements in the speed and capacity of SAT-solvers in the last two decades [14, 18, 19, 24]—see [17, 33] for comparative studies—accelerated dramatically the solving of Boolean formulas from formal verification of microprocessors. However, as found in [33], the new efficient SAT-solvers would not have scaled for solving these Boolean formulas if not for the property of Positive Equality that produces at least 5 orders of magnitude speedup when formally verifying complex dual-issue superscalar processors. Efficient translations of the EUFM correctness formula to a satisfiability-equivalent Boolean formula, and then to Conjunctive Normal Form (CNF), the most common input format of SAT-solvers, by using block-level translation [35, 36, 38 – 42], resulted in additional speedup of at least 2 orders of magnitude, and an order of magnitude reduction of the CNF formula size, thus producing an order of magnitude increase in scalability for SAT-solving of larger formulas.

In the last 22 years, SAT-solvers became faster by 6 – 7 orders of magnitude and scalable for 3 – 4 orders of magnitude larger problems, where at least 2 orders of magnitude speedup and at least one order of magnitude scalability were contributed by the author's block-level translation to CNF [35, 36, 38 – 42], while essentially all highly efficient academic and industrial SAT-solvers were developed on his collection of CNF formulas from formal verification of complex microprocessors [53].

The contribution of this paper is that it is the first work on formal verification of RISC-V pipelined processors at a high level of abstraction, as well as pipelined designs with fault tolerance by spatial redundancy that was implemented in two RISC-V pipelined processors. We present abstraction techniques that allow us to formally verify such processors extremely efficiently, as demonstrated in the results section.

2 Background on Using Positive Equality to Formally Verify Pipelined Processors

We use the method of *Correspondence Checking* to formally verify a pipelined implementation processor against a non-pipelined specification. The *safety property* (see Fig. 1) is expressed as a formula in the logic of Equality with Uninterpreted Functions and Memories (EUFM), and checks that one step of the implementation corresponds to between 0 and k steps of the specification, where k is the issue width of the implementation, i.e., the maximum number of instructions that the implementation can start executing per clock cycle.

In Fig. 1, F_{Impl} is the transition function of the implementation, and F_{Spec} is the transition function of the specification. The *abstraction function, Abs*, is used to map an implementation state to an equivalent specification state. We will refer to the sequence of first applying the abstraction function *Abs* and then k steps of F_{Spec} as the *specification side* of the diagram in Fig. 1, and to the sequence of first applying F_{Impl} and then the abstraction function *Abs* as the *implementation side*.

The safety property in Fig. 1 is the inductive step of a proof by induction, since the initial implementation state, Q_{Impl}, is completely arbitrary, as represented with fresh symbolic variables for the initial state of all architectural and pipeline state elements, possibly restricted by a set of invariant constraints. If the implementation is correct for all transitions that can be made for one step from an arbitrary initial state, then the implementation will be correct for one step from the next implementation state in the figure, Q'_{Impl}, since that state will be a special case of an arbitrary initial state, and so on for any number of steps.

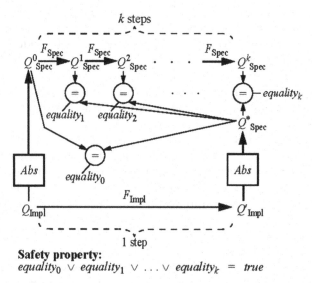

Fig. 1. Applying Correspondence Checking to prove the safety correctness property for an implementation processor with issue width k: one step of the implementation should correspond to between 0 and k steps of the specification, when the implementation starts from an arbitrary initial state Q_{Impl} that is possibly restricted by a set of invariant constraints.

For some processors, e.g., where the control logic is optimized by using unreachable states as don't-care conditions, we might have to impose a set of *invariant constraints* for the initial state, Q_{Impl}, in order to exclude unreachable states, because the correctness property may not hold for them. Then, we need to prove that those constraints will be satisfied in the implementation state after one step, Q'_{Impl}, so that the correctness will hold by induction for that state, and so on for all subsequent states. The reader is referred to [1, 2] for a discussion of correctness criteria, and to [46, 51] for debugging techniques for Correspondence Checking.

To illustrate the safety property in Fig. 1, let the implementation and specification have three architectural state elements—Program Counter (PC), Register File, and Data Memory. Let PC^i_{Spec}, $RegFile^i_{Spec}$, and $DMem^i_{Spec}$ be the state of the PC, Register File, and Data Memory, respectively, in specification state Q^i_{Spec} ($i = 0, ..., k$) along the specification side of the diagram. Let PC^*_{Spec}, $RegFile^*_{Spec}$, and $DMem^*_{Spec}$ be the state of the PC, Register File, and Data Memory in specification state Q^*_{Spec}, reached after the implementation side of the diagram. Then, each disjunct $equality_i$ ($i = 0, \ldots, k$) in the formula for the safety property is defined as:

$$equality_i \leftarrow pc_i \wedge rf_i \wedge dm_i,$$
where
$$pc_i \leftarrow (PC^i_{Spec} = PC^*_{Spec}),$$
$$rf_i \leftarrow (RegFile^i_{Spec} = RegFile^*_{Spec}),$$
$$dm_i \leftarrow (DMem^i_{Spec} = DMem^*_{Spec}).$$

That is, $equality_i$ is the conjunction of pair-wise equality comparisons for all architectural state elements, thus ensuring that the architectural state elements are updated in synchrony by the same number of instructions. In processors with more architectural state elements, an equality comparison is conjuncted for each additional state element. Hence, for this implementation processor, the safety property is:

$$pc_0 \wedge rf_0 \wedge dm_0 \ \vee \ pc_1 \wedge rf_1 \wedge dm_1 \ \vee \ \ldots \ \vee \ pc_k \wedge rf_k \wedge dm_k \ = \ true.$$

We can prove liveness similarly—by symbolically simulating the implementation for a finite number of steps, n, and proving that:

$$equality_1 \vee equality_2 \vee \ldots \vee equality_{n \times k} \ = \ true, \tag{1}$$

where k is the issue width of the implementation. The formula proves that n steps of the implementation match between 1 and $n \times k$ steps of the specification, when the implementation starts from an arbitrary initial state that may be restricted by invariant constraints. Note that (1) *guarantees that the implementation has made at least one step*, while the safety correctness criterion allows the implementation to stay in its initial state when formula $equality_0$ (checking whether the implementation matches the initial state of the specification) is *true*. The correctness formula is generated automatically in the same way as the formula for safety, except that the implementation and the specification are symbolically simulated for many steps, and formula $equality_0$ is not included. As in the formula for safety, every formula $equality_i$ is the conjunction of equations, each comparing corresponding states of the same architectural state element. That is, formula (1) consists of top-level positive equations that are conjuncted and disjuncted but not negated, allowing us to exploit Positive Equality when proving liveness. The minimum number of steps, n, to symbolically simulate the implementation, can be determined experimentally, by trial and error, or identified by the user after analyzing the processor. We will refer to the above approach as the *direct method for proving liveness*.

To avoid the validity checking of the monolithic liveness correctness formula (1), which becomes complex for designs with long pipelines and many features, we can prove liveness indirectly [37, 43]:

Theorem 1. *If after n implementation steps, $equality_0 = false$ under a maximally diverse interpretation of the p-terms, and the safety property is valid, then the liveness property is valid under any interpretation.*

Since $equality_0$ is the conjunction of the pair-wise equality comparisons for all architectural state elements, it suffices to prove that one of those equality comparisons is *false* under a maximally diverse interpretation of the p-terms. In particular, we can prove that $pc_0 = false$, where pc_0 is the equality comparison between the PC state after the implementation side of the diagram (see Fig. 1), and the PC that is part of the initial specification state. Note that choosing the Register File or the Data Memory instead would not work, since they are not updated by each instruction, and so there can be infinitely long instruction sequences that do not modify these state elements. Note that proving *forward progress—that the PC is updated at least once after n implementation steps*, i.e., proving $pc_0 = false$ under a maximally diverse interpretation of the p-terms—is done without the specification. However, the specification is used to prove safety, thus inductively the correctness for any number of steps. We will refer to the above approach as the *indirect method for proving liveness*. That is, we can prove liveness indirectly [37, 43]—by first proving safety, thus inductively the implementation correctness for any number of steps, and then using Positive Equality to prove that the implementation processor will make forward progress by analyzing only the updates of the PC.

In order to automatically compute the abstraction function *Abs* (see Fig. 1), we use *flushing* [8] of the implementation processor pipeline—feeding it with bubbles, while simulating it symbolically until all partially executed instructions get completed. The difference between a bubble and a nop instruction is that a bubble does not modify the architectural state, while a nop increments the PC. Hence, flushing uses the logic of the processor to compute an abstraction function, and avoids the need to manually reproduce any of that logic. Flushing requires the implementation processor to have a Flush signal that, if set to *true*, will disable the fetching of new instructions, and will feed the pipeline with bubbles. However, many processors already have a Valid_Fetch signal (possibly named differently in different designs), indicating whether the Instruction Memory is providing a valid instruction in the current clock cycle; if not, then the PC is not incremented, the pipeline is fed with a bubble, and the fetch is repeated. In such processors, we can override the original Valid_Fetch signal with the Flush signal, in order to force the processor to feed the pipeline with bubbles. Incorporating a Flush signal can be viewed as *design for formal verification*. Even if the implementation does not have a Valid_Fetch signal, incorporating a Flush signal will affect only a part of the logic in the Instruction Fetch stage, and so will require significantly less work than to manually define an abstraction function that completes all instructions in the processor pipeline. We will refer to flushing, defined above, as *regular flushing* in order to distinguish it from the variant described next.

Burch [9] proposed *controlled flushing*, where extra control signals are introduced, in addition to the Flush signal, in order to modify the instruction flow during flushing. He used the extra controls to override stalling signals until it was guaranteed that the original control logic for each stalling signal would produce value *false*, and thus a stalled instruction would advance if the extra controls let it go. Then, he allowed the first-in-program-order stalled instruction to continue, while stalling the rest, and so on. Thus, he eliminated the uncertainty in the instruction flow during flushing, and generated a simpler EUFM correctness formula that could be checked for validity much faster. Again, the introduction of the extra control signals can be viewed as *design for formal verification*.

The syntax of EUFM [8] includes *terms* and *formulas*. Terms are used to abstract word-level values, as well as the entire states of memory arrays, regardless of the actual number of bits in the abstracted value. The syntax for a term allows it to be an Uninterpreted Function (UF) applied to a list of argument terms, a term variable, or an *ITE* operator (where *ITE* stands for If-Then-Else) selecting between two argument terms based on a controlling formula, such that $ITE(formula, term_1, term_2)$ will evaluate to $term_1$ when $formula = true$, and to $term_2$ when $formula = false$. Formulas are used to model the control path of a processor, as well as to express a correctness condition. The syntax for a formula allows it to be an Uninterpreted Predicate (UP) applied to a list of argument terms, a Boolean variable, an *ITE* operator selecting between two argument formulas based on a controlling formula, or an equation (equality comparison) of two terms. Formulas can be negated and combined with Boolean connectives. We refer to both terms and formulas as *expressions*.

UFs are used to abstract combinational functional units that produce word-level values, and UPs those that produce bit-level values. In both cases, the functional unit is replaced with a "black box" that satisfies only the *functional consistency* property of the original functional unit, i.e., pair-wise equal combinations of input values applied to the inputs of the functional unit produce equal output values. If the formal verification goes through without any of the actual properties of the abstracted functional unit, then the implementation processor will be correct for any functionally consistent implementation of each abstracted functional unit. Note that the control logic of an implementation processor virtually never takes into account the actual functions computed by the functional units, but only the data and control dependencies between instructions. (If the control logic of a processor depends on specific properties of functional units abstracted with UFs or UPs, then these abstractions will result in a counterexample that will indicate the need for the abstracted property to be modeled.)

The property of functional consistency of UFs and UPs can be enforced by Ackermann constraints [3], or by nested *ITE*s [26], which is the method that we use—see [40] for the details of both methods. Techniques for abstraction of multicycle functional units are presented in [29]. We assume that the functional units are formally verified separately—the technology for that is very mature.

We model memory arrays in EUFM by means of functions *read* and *write* [8, 31]. Function *read* takes as arguments two terms that abstract the memory state and address, respectively, and returns a term for the data at that address in the given memory array. Function *write* takes three argument terms abstracting the memory state, address, and data, and returns a term for the new memory state. Functions *read* and *write* satisfy the *forwarding property of the memory semantics*, where $read(write(mem, waddr, wdata), raddr)$ is equivalent to $ITE((raddr = waddr), wdata, read(mem, raddr))$, i.e., a *read* operation after a *write* operation should return the data written by the *write* operation if the addresses of the two operations are equal, or otherwise the data read from the state of the memory before the *write* operation.

By applying the constructs of EUFM, we can define microprocessors where the control logic is fully implemented, while the functional units and memories are abstracted. We can also define a non-pipelined specification for the given Instruction Set Architecture by using the same UFs, UPs, and memory models to abstract the same functional units and memory arrays, respectively. Then, we can perform term-level symbolic simulation according to the correctness condition for safety in Fig. 1 in order to generate an EUFM correctness formula for the safety property.

Given an EUFM correctness formula, we refer to the equations (i.e., equality comparisons between terms) that appear negated as *g-equations* (for general equations), and as *p-equations* (for positive equations) otherwise. We classify all terms that appear as arguments of g-equations as *g-terms* (for general terms), and as *p-terms* (for positive terms) otherwise. We classify all applications of a given UF as g-terms if at least one application of that UF appears as a g-term, and as p-terms otherwise.

In previous work [27, 28], the style for modeling high-level processors was restricted in order to increase the number of terms that appear only in positive equations or as arguments to UFs and UPs, and reduce the number of terms that appear in both positive and negated equations. This was done without losing expressive power, i.e., we can still model the same microprocessors as before. Namely, equations between data operands, where the result appears in both positive and negated polarity—e.g., determining whether to take a branch-on-equal instruction—are abstracted with a new UP in both the implementation and the specification. Furthermore, the Data Memory is abstracted with a conservative model, where the interpreted functions *read* and *write* are replaced with new UFs, *DMem_read* and *DMem_write*, respectively, that do not satisfy the forwarding property. This property is not needed, if both the implementation and the specification execute the same sequence of memory operations (where each is a *read* or a *write*) that are not stalled based on conditions that depend on equations between addresses for that memory [31].

3 Efficient Modeling of the RISC-V Architecture at a High Level of Abstraction

We formally verified both safety and liveness of high-level models of the 2-stage RISC-V pipelined Ibex core [22], and the 4-stage RISC-V pipelined RI5CY core [22]. The two pipeline stages of the Ibex core are Instruction Fetch (IF), and a combined Instruction Decode and Execute (IDEX) stage. The four pipeline stages of the RI5CY core are Instruction Fetch (IF), Instruction Decode (ID), Execute (EX), and Write Back (WB). Both cores implement the RISC-V Base Integer ISA, RV32I. To formally verify them, we defined high-level models of these pipelined cores and their non-pipelined specifications, using the following techniques.

3.1 Abstraction of the Register File

The Register File in the RISC-V ISA has 32 registers, x0 through x31, such that register x0 is hardwired to 0. To model this in EUFM, we used the abstraction of the Register File shown in Fig. 2.

In the RISC-V Base Integer ISA, the Register File has to support two read operations, and one write operation per clock cycle. Thus, the Register File was abstracted with a memory model with two read ports, rport1 and rport2, and one write port, wport, as shown in Fig. 2. The first read port's input raddr1 accepts a term for the address to

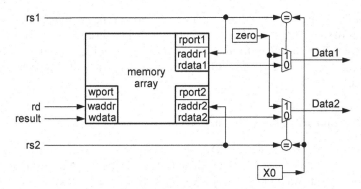

Fig. 2. Abstract model of the Register File in RISC-V.

read data from through that port, and its output rdata1 produces a term that abstracts the data at that address. Similarly, the second read port's input raddr2 accepts a term for the address to read data from through that port, and its output rdata2 produces a term that abstracts the data at that address. The write port's input waddr accepts a term for the address to write data to, and its input wdata accepts a term that abstracts the data to be written to that address.

In Fig. 2, the unique value of register id x0 is abstracted with a fresh term variable produced by a UF with no arguments, X0. The same fresh term variable will have to be used in all other instances where the register id x0 is used, if applicable. Similarly, the hardwired 0 for the value of x0 is abstracted with a fresh term variable produced by a UF with no arguments, zero. As can be seen in the figure, the fresh term variable zero is selected as the data read from a read port, if the term abstracting the register id for that read port, rs1 or rs2, respectively, is equal to the fresh term variable X0 abstracting register id x0, or else the term abstracting the data value read from the memory array at address equal to the register id for that port is used.

The same abstraction of the Register File is also used in the non-pipelined specification.

3.2 Abstraction of the Decoding Logic

The decoding logic of the 2-stage pipelined RISC-V core is in the IDEX stage, and of the 4-stage pipelined RISC-V core in the ID stage. In both designs, the instruction fetched from the instruction memory in the IF stage is abstracted with a term Instr that is passed through the pipeline latch between the IF stage and the second pipeline stage, where the decoding logic is abstracted with a collection of UFs and UPs, each of them having as an argument the term abstracting the instruction in the IDEX stage of the 2-stage pipeline, or the ID stage of the 4-stage pipeline, respectively.

For example, if IF_IDEX_Instr is the term abstracting the instruction in the IDEX stage of the 2-stage pipeline, then an UF Decoder_rd with input the term IF_IDEX_Instr is used to abstract the combinational logic that extracts the destination register rd from the instruction term IF_IDEX_Instr, while a UP Decoder_RegWrite with input the term IF_IDEX_Instr is used to abstract the combinational logic producing control signal RegWrite that indicates whether the instruction will write a value to the Register File. Similarly for the other control and word-level values produced by the decoding logic in the 2-stage pipeline, as well as for abstracting the decoding logic in the 4-stage pipeline.

3.3 Abstraction of the CSR Memory Array

The Control and Status Register (CSR) memory array was abstracted with a conservative model in the same way that the Data Memory was abstracted in previous work—see Sect. 2. Namely, that was done using new UFs, CSR_read and CSR_write, respectively, that do not satisfy the forwarding property of the memory semantics. This property is not needed, if both the implementation and the specification execute the same sequence of CSR memory operations that are not stalled based on conditions that depend on equations between addresses for that memory [31].

3.4 Non-Pipelined Specifications

The non-pipelined RISC-V specifications were defined to perform computations using the same UFs and UPs that were used to abstract functional units in the pipelined implementation processors, using instructions and data abstracted with terms, supplied by the same architectural state elements abstracted with memories or latches, but without the pipeline latches, and without the pipeline control logic that prevents data and control hazards in the pipelined implementations. Each non-pipelined specification fetches a symbolic instruction, decodes it, and completes it by making computations, if applicable, and updating architectural state elements in a single clock cycle.

3.5 Formal Verification of Liveness

Because of the relative simplicity of the two RISC-V pipelined cores under formal verification, we proved liveness directly. Specifically, the 2-stage pipelined core was symbolically simulated for 2 clock cycles, starting from an arbitrary initial state, followed by flushing of the pipeline. The resulting state of the architectural state elements—PC, Register File, CSR, and Data Memory—was proved to correspond to the state of the architectural state elements in the non-pipelined specification after either 1 or 2 cycles of symbolic execution of the specification that follows flushing from the initial state of the implementation (see Fig. 1).

Namely, if the symbolic instruction initially in the IDEX stage is a jump or a branch that is taken, then the instruction that is fetched in the IF stage in the same clock cycle will be squashed because there are no delayed branches in the RISC-V ISA, but the instruction that will be fetched during the next clock cycle, when the fetched instruction will be from the target address of the jump or the taken branch, will be guaranteed to be completed, because the second pipeline stage will be empty then, as the instruction there was squashed (invalidated) in the previous clock cycle, when that instruction was in the IF stage.

Similarly, the 4-stage RISC-V pipelined core was symbolically simulated for 4 clock cycles, starting from an arbitrary initial state, followed by flushing of the pipeline. This was to account for the worst-case delay when a jump or a branch that will be taken is initially in the pipeline latch between the IF and ID stages, and has a data dependency on a load that is initially in the pipeline latch between the ID and EX stages. Then that jump or branch to be taken will be stalled in the pipeline latch between the IF and ID stages for one clock cycle (when a bubble will be inserted in the ID stage), will then advance to the pipeline latch between the ID and EX stages on the second clock cycle, will update the PC with the target address of the jump or taken branch on the third clock cycle while squashing instructions that were fetched from subsequent addresses and that are in the first two pipeline stages, and will finally fetch a new instruction from the target address in the fourth clock cycle, such that this instruction will be guaranteed to be completed, as the pipeline stages ahead will be empty. Flushing the implementation state of the pipeline at that time should produce a resulting state of the architectural state elements that corresponds to either 1, or 2, or 3, or 4 instructions completed by the nonpipelined specification. That is, at least one instruction will be guaranteed to be completed, starting from an arbitrary implementation state.

3.6 Invariant Constraints Were Not Needed for the Correct Designs, but Were Proved for Debugging the 4-Stage Pipelined Processor

Initially we imposed and proved two invariant constraints for the instruction in the Execute stage of the 4-stage pipelined RISC-V processor core:

1) if that instruction is valid, then it cannot be simultaneously a branch and a load instruction; and
2) if that instruction is valid, then it cannot be simultaneously a jump and a load instruction.

That is, that instruction was not allowed to be of two of those instruction types simultaneously, which is the case for all instructions. To prove these two invariant constraints, we had to impose the same constraints for the outputs of the abstracted decoding logic in the Instruction Decode stage. Formally verifying the two invariant constraints took 0.005 sec on the computer listed in Sect. 5. After we completed the debugging of the 4-stage pipelined RISC-V processor core, we determined that invariant constraints are not needed for its formal verification. However, imposing and proving invariant constraints may ease the debugging, as the process eliminates possible reasons for incorrectness of the implementation.

4 Modeling of Spatial Redundancy in Pipelined Processors at a High Level of Abstraction for Formal Verification of Safety

In order to implement spatial redundancy for the functional units in the 2-stage pipelined RISC-V core, we created two copies of the UF ALU that abstracts the Arithmetic Logic Unit (ALU) in the combined Instruction Decode and Execute (IDEX) stage of the 2-stage pipelined RISC-V core. Similarly, we created two copies of the UP TakeBranchALU that abstracts the functional unit that determines whether to take a conditional branch. In the case of the 4-stage pipelined RISC-V core, we also created two copies of the other two UFs that abstract functional units in the Execute (EX) stage of that pipeline, namely the multiplier MULT and the adder PCAdder that increments the Program Counter (PC) of the currently executed instruction in that stage, ID_EX_PC, in order to compute the address of the consecutive instruction, to be written to the Register File by *Jump and Link*, jal, and *Jump and Link Register*, jalr, instructions.

Comparing the two copies of a computation produced by spatial redundancy requires the introduction of an equality comparator, as shown in Fig. 3.(a) for the results from the two copies of the ALU. The output of that equality comparator will be used in positive polarity if the two copies of the result are equal and there is no need for re-execution of the computation, but in negated polarity otherwise. This will turn the two terms for the ALU results from p-terns to g-terms, which will require the use of Boolean variables to encode their equality comparisons in the decision procedure for EUFM, reducing the efficiency from exploiting the property Positive Equality.

Abstraction Technique 1. In order to avoid the classification of the ALU results as g-terms, we abstracted their negated equality comparator with a UP, as shown in Fig. 3.(b). Furthermore, we added as an additional input of that UP the PC of the instruction in that stage, ID_EX_PC, resulting in partial functional non-consistency, i.e., functional consistency for the same instruction, as identified by its PC that is a p-term, but not among different instructions. This is a *conservative approximation*, i.e., an abstraction that makes the abstract model of the implementation processor more general than the original model, such that if the more general abstract model of the implementation is proven correct, the same will hold for the original implementation. However, an incorrect counterexample may result if any property discarded with the abstraction is needed for the formal verification; in that case, counterexamples should be analyzed to determine if a property discarded through the abstraction is needed for the formal verification, and if so the abstraction should not be used.

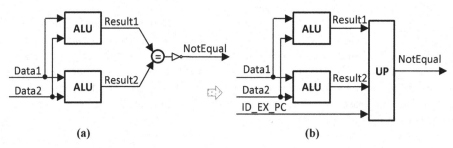

Fig. 3. (a) The equality comparator that compares for equality the results from the two spatially redundant copies of the ALU in the EX stage, combined with the inverter after that, is abstracted with (b) an UP that takes as an additional input the PC of the instruction in that stage, ID_EX_PC, resulting in partial functional non-consistency, i.e., functional consistency for the same instruction, as identified by its PC that is a p-term, but not among different instructions. This is a conservative approximation.

To increase the efficiency from this technique, for each pair of spatially redundant computations we used a different UP that takes as inputs the pair of spatially redundant computation results and the PC of the corresponding instruction in order to abstract the equality comparator between that pair. This is a further conservative approximation, where we are discarding the property that these UPs are the same, because they abstract the same functionality.

Thus, with this abstraction of the equality comparators discarded were the properties of symmetry, reflexivity, and transitivity of the original equality comparators. This abstraction turned the two copies of the ALU results, introduced for spatial redundancy, back into p-terms, since those terms were then used as arguments of only uninterpreted predicates, uninterpreted functions, and the positive equations in the EUFM correctness formula. For increased efficiency of the formal verification, a different UP can be used for abstracting the negated equality comparison of each pair of spatially redundant results in the described way, as was done for the experiments.

Abstraction Technique 2. A fresh symbolic value is used to abstract the result that is to be used by the processor, when a pair of spatially redundant results are determined to differ, as indicated by the UP introduced in Abstraction Technique 1 to abstract the negated equality comparator. For every pair of spatially redundant functional units that are abstracted with UFs, we use a new UF that has the same inputs as the UP that abstracts the negated equality comparator of the results of those two spatially redundant copies, and whose output is used instead of the original result when the UP introduced in Abstraction Technique 1 non-deterministically chooses that the two spatially redundant copies differ. This ensures that the original copy of the result (that might be correct) is not used incorrectly, when the two spatially redundant copies are determined to differ. This new UF should be different in the implementation and the specification, or should be used only in the implementation, so that we can detect if the implementation incorrectly uses the result when it is not to be used.

Similarly, for every pair of spatially redundant functional units that produce bit-level signals and are abstracted with UPs, we use a new UP that has the same inputs as the UP that abstracts the negated equality comparator of the results of those two spatially redundant copies, and whose output is used instead of the original result when the UP introduced in Abstraction Technique 1 non-deterministically chooses that the two spatially redundant copies differ. Again, this new UP should be different in the implementation and the specification, or should be used only in the implementation.

In order to use the presented abstraction techniques, it was necessary to enrich the non-pipelined specification processor with spatial redundancy, the same UPs introduced with Abstraction Technique 1, and the mechanism for re-executing an instruction for which a pair of spatially redundant results differ. If UFs and UPs are introduced in the non-pipelined specification processor based on Abstraction Technique 2, then they have to be different from those introduced in the pipelined implementation. This can be viewed as *design for formal verification.*

Let the *abstracted implementation* refer to the variant of the implementation processor where Abstraction Techniques 1 and 2 have been applied, i.e., uninterpreted predicates are used to abstract the negated equality comparators between pairs of spatially redundant results (based on Abstraction Technique 1), and a fresh symbolic value is used to abstract the result to be used by the processor when a pair of spatially redundant results are determined to differ (based on Abstraction Technique 2).

Note that after the specification is enriched in the above way, the output NotEqual of the UP that abstracts the negated equality comparator (see Fig. 3.(b)) for each pair of spatially redundant results in the implementation and the specification will be arbitrary, as it will be represented with a symbolic Boolean expression that will be functionally consistent for each instruction (identified by its PC that is a p-term) and each combination of data operands that are inputs to that UP (p-terms, except for the Boolean expressions for the outputs of the functional unit that computes the taken or not taken direction of conditional branches). Thus, there will be a 1-to-1 correspondence between the output NotEqual in the implementation and the specification for each instruction and each combination of data values for that instruction.

Theorem 2. *If the abstracted implementation is formally verified with respect to the enriched specification, and the enriched specification is equivalent to the original specification under the condition that the uninterpreted predicates introduced with Abstraction Technique 1 abstract negated equality comparators, then the original implementation is correct with respect to the original specification.*

Sketch of Proof: If the abstracted implementation is formally verified with respect to the enriched specification, then that result holds for any functionally consistent implementations of the introduced uninterpreted predicates, including those of negated equality comparators (that do not depend on the input for the PC of the instruction) that transform the abstracted implementation into the original implementation, and the enriched specification into a model equivalent to the original specification.   □

5 Results

The formal verification was done on a computer with a 3.0-GHz 16-core AMD EPYC 7302P processor, and 512 GB of 3,200-MHz memory, running Red Hat Enterprise Linux v8.6. However, each experiment used only a single thread of execution on a single core. We applied our formal verification tool, combined with a proprietary SAT-solver. Translation to CNF was done with block-level methods, where blocks of logic gates are translated to CNF without extra CNF variables for internal values [35, 36, 38 – 42].

Table 1 presents the experimental results from formal verification of safety of the 2-stage pipelined RISC-V core, and the 4-stage pipelined RISC-V core. For each of the two cores, we extended a base design without spatial redundancy to a version with spatial redundancy. As shown, proving safety took our tool flow less than a second for each of the variants, including the time for symbolic simulation by our symbolic simulator to produce an EUFM formula for the correctness criterion, the time for translating the EUFM correctness formula by our decision procedure to an equisatisfiable Boolean formula and then to an equivalent CNF formula, and the time to prove the CNF formula unsatisfiable by our SAT-solver, which indicated the absence of a counterexample for the correctness of the processor.

The total time to prove safety for the 2-stage pipelined RISC-V core was 0.008 sec, such that the CNF formula had 173 Boolean variables, 691 clauses, and 1,847 literals, with an average of 2.673 literals per clause. The total time to prove safety for the variant of the 2-stage pipelined RISC-V core with spatial redundancy was 0.01 sec, such that the CNF formula had 248 Boolean variables, 1,141 clauses, and 3,085 literals, with an average of 2.704 literals per clause.

Using regular flushing [8], the total time to prove safety for the 4-stage pipelined RISC-V core was 0.081 sec, such that the CNF formula had 2,689 Boolean variables, 23,933 clauses, and 67,589 literals, with an average of 2.824 literals per clause. In contrast, the total time to prove safety for the variant of the 4-stage pipelined RISC-V core with spatial redundancy increased to 0.139 sec, such that the CNF formula had

Table 1. Results from formal verification of safety.

| Comparison Criteria | 2-Stage Pipelined RISC-V Core | | 4-Stage Pipelined RISC-V Core | | | |
| | Regular Flushing | | Regular Flushing | | Controlled Flushing | |
	Base Design	Design with Spatial Redundancy	Base Design	Design with Spatial Redundancy	Base Design	Design with Spatial Redundancy
Time for symbolic simulation [sec]	0.003	0.003	0.003	0.004	0.003	0.003
Time to translate the EUFM correctness formula to equivalent CNF [sec]	0.003	0.004	0.027	0.056	0.009	0.017
Time for SAT-solving to prove CNF unsat [sec]	0.002	0.003	0.051	0.079	0.015	0.024
Total [sec]	0.008	0.010	0.081	0.139	0.027	0.044
CNF vars	173	248	2,689	5,508	728	1,174
CNF clauses	691	1,141	23,933	63,609	5,838	10,639
CNF literals	1,847	3,085	67,589	181,531	16,392	30,095
Average CNF literals per clause	2.673	2.704	2.824	2.854	2.808	2.829

5,508 Boolean variables (more than a 2× increase), 63,609 clauses (almost a 3× increase), and 181,531 literals (again almost a 3× increase), with an average of 2.854 literals per clause.

Controlled flushing [9] reduced the total time for proving safety of the 4-stage pipelined RISC-V core by 3× to 0.027 sec, while the number of Boolean variables, clauses, and literals in the CNF formula were reduced approximately 4× to 728 Boolean variables, 5,838 clauses, and 16,392 literals, with an average of 2.808 literals per clause. Controlled flushing also reduced the total time for proving safety of the variant of the 4-stage pipelined RISC-V core with spatial redundancy by more than 3× to 0.044 sec, such that the number of CNF variables were reduced by more than 4× to 1,174, while the number of clauses, and literals in the CNF formula were reduced approximately 6× to 10,639 clauses, and 30,095 literals, with an average of 2.829 literals per clause. (Controlled flushing is not applicable to the 2-stage pipelined RISC-V processor core, because it does not have stalling.)

Table 2 presents the experimental results from formal verification of liveness of the 2-stage RISC-V pipelined core, and the 4-stage RISC-V pipelined core. Using the direct method for proving liveness [37] for the 2-stage pipelined RISC-V core, combined with regular flushing, took 0.013 sec, while the CNF formula had 480 Boolean variables, 2,643 clauses, and 7,257 literals, with an average of 2.746 literals per clause. Using the direct method for proving liveness for the 4-stage pipelined RISC-V core, combined with regular flushing, took 5.241 sec, while the CNF formula had 24,285 Boolean variables, 295,992 clauses, and 847,014 literals, with an average of 2.862 literals per clause. This represents a significant increase relative to proving liveness of the 2-stage pipelined RISC-V core, or to proving safety of the 4-stage pipelined RISC-V core using regular flushing. Using the direct method for proving liveness for the 4-stage pipelined RISC-V core, combined with controlled flushing, reduced the formal verification time to 3.044 sec, and reduced the size of the CNF formula by more than 2× (Table 2).

The greatest speedup was achieved with the indirect method for proving liveness [37, 43] for the 4-stage pipelined RISC-V core, combined with controlled flushing, which required 0.047 sec, while the CNF formula had 4,074 Boolean variables, 31,428 clauses, and 88,144 literals, with an average of 2.805 literals per clause. The indirect method, combined with controlled flushing will result in even greater speedup for proving liveness of more complex RISC-V pipelined cores.

Table 2. Results from formal verification of liveness.

Comparison Criteria	2-stage Pipelined RISC-V Core	4-stage Pipelined RISC-V Core				
	Direct Method	Direct Method		Indirect Method		
	Regular Flushing	Regular Flushing	Controlled Flushing	Regular Flushing	Controlled Flushing	
Time for symbolic simulation [sec]	0.002	0.004	0.004	0.003	0.003	
Time to translate the EUFM correctness formula to equivalent CNF formula [sec]	0.006	0.225	0.097	0.084	0.027	
Time for SAT-solving to prove the CNF formula unsatisfiable [sec]	0.005	5.012	2.943	0.044	0.017	
Total time [sec]	0.013	5.241	3.044	0.131	0.047	
CNF variables	480	24,285	10,967	9,404	4,074	
CNF clauses	2,643	295,992	120,360	85,778	31,428	
CNF literals	7,257	847,014	342,992	242,360	88,144	
Average CNF literals per clause	2.746	2.862	2.850	2.825	2.805	

6 Conclusion

Presented were abstraction techniques for efficient modeling at a high-level of abstraction of pipelined microprocessors implementing the RISC-V architecture, including designs with fault tolerance by spatial redundancy, allowing us to formally verify such processors extremely efficiently by using the property Positive Equality. Specifically, suitable abstractions were used for the register file in the RISC-V ISA where register x0 is hardwired to 0, the CSR memory array, and the mechanism that compares for equality two spatially redundant results in order to determine whether they differ and so the instruction should be re-executed, among other features. Results showed that the presented techniques allowed the efficient formal verification of both safety and liveness of 2-stage and 4-stage pipelined implementations of the RISC-V ISA, based on corresponding designs from [22], as well as safety of variants of the two pipelined processors with fault tolerance of functional units by spatial redundancy. To the best of our knowledge, this is the first work on formal verification at a high level of abstraction of RISC-V pipelined processors, and of pipelined processors with fault tolerance by spatial redundancy.

References

1. Aagaard, M.D., Day, N.A., Lou, M.: Relating Multi-step and Single-Step Microprocessor Correctness Statements. In: Aagaard, M.D., O'Leary, J.W. (eds.) Formal Methods in Computer-Aided Design. FMCAD 2002. LNCS, vol. 2517, pp 123–141. Springer, Berlin (2002). https://doi.org/10.1007/3-540-36126-X_8

2. Aagaard, M.D., Cook, B., Day, N.A., Jones, R.B.: A framework for superscalar microprocessor correctness statements. Softw. Tools Technol. Transfer (STTT) 4(3), 298–312 (2003)

3. Ackermann, W.: Solvable Cases of the Decision Problem. North-Holland, Amsterdam (1954)

4. Agonoy, E., Hasbrouck, S., Udrea, B.: Implementation and test of a RISC-V microprocessor for space vehicle embedded computing. In: AIAA ASCEND, November 2021. https://doi.org/10.2514/6.2021-4085

5. Blaauw, D., Das, S.: CPU, heal thyself: a fault-monitoring microprocessor design can save power or allow overclocking. IEEE Spectrum 46(8), 40–56 (2009). http://spectrum.ieee.org/semiconductors/processors/cpu-heal-thyself/0

6. Bryant, R.E., German, S., Velev, M.N.: Processor verification using efficient reductions of the logic of uninterpreted functions to propositional logic. ACM Trans. Comput. Logic (TOCL) 2(1), 93–134 (2001)

7. Bryant, R.E., Velev, M.N.: Boolean satisfiability with transitivity constraints. ACM Trans. Comput. Logic (TOCL) 3(4), 604–627 (2002)

8. Burch, J.R., Dill, D.L.: Automatic verification of pipelined microprocessor control. In: Dill, D.L. (ed.) Computer Aided Verification. CAV 1994. LNCS, vol. 818. Springer, Berlin (1994). https://doi.org/10.1007/3-540-58179-0_44

9. Burch, J.R.: Techniques for verifying superscalar microprocessors. In: 33rd Design Automation Conference (DAC 1996), pp. 552–557, June 1996

10. Darbari, A.: Democratising Formal Verification of RISC-V Processors (2019). https://riscv.org/wp-content/uploads/2019/12/12.10-16.40-AXIOMISE__RISCV__Final__RISCV__Summit__2019.pdf

11. Das, S., et al.: RazorII. In situ error detection and correction for PVT and SER tolerance. IEEE J. Solid-State Circuits 44(1), 32–48 (2009)

12. Gautschi, M., et al.: Near-threshold RISC-V core with DSP extensions for scalable IoT endpoint devices. IEEE Trans. Very Large Scale Integr. (VLSI) Syst. 25(10), 2700–2713 (2017)

13. Goel, A., Sajid, K., Zhou, H., Aziz, A., Singhal, V.: BDD based procedures for a theory of equality with uninterpreted functions. Formal Methods Syst. Des. 22, 205–224 (2003)

14. Goldberg, E., Novikov, Y.: BerkMin: A fast and robust SAT-solver. In: Design, Automation, and Test in Europe (DATE 2002), pp. 465–478, March 2002

15. Intel Corporation, IA-64 Application Developer's Architecture Guide. May 1999. http://developer.intel.com/design/ia-64/architecture.htm

16. Lahiri, S., Pixley, C., Albin, K.: Experience with term level modeling and verification of the M•CORE™ microprocessor core. In: 6th Annual IEEE International Workshop on High Level Design, Validation and Test (HLDVT 2001), pp.109–114, November 2001

17. Le Berre, D., Simon, L.: Fifty-five solvers in Vancouver: the SAT 2004 competition. In: Hoos, H.H., Mitchell, D.G. (eds.) Theory and Applications of Satisfiability Testing. SAT 2004. LNCS, vol. 3542, pp. 321–344. Springer, Berlin (2005). https://doi.org/10.1007/115 27695_25

18. Moskewicz, M.W., Madigan, C.F., Zhao, Y., Zhang, L., Malik, S.: Chaff: engineering an efficient SAT-solver. In: 38th Design Automation Conference (DAC '01), pp. 530–535, June 2001

19. Pipatsrisawat, K., Darwiche, A.: A new clause learning scheme for efficient unsatisfiability proofs. In: AAAI Conference on Artificial Intelligence (AAAI 2008), pp. 1481–1484, July 2008

20. Pnueli, A., Rodeh, Y., Strichman, O., Siegel, M.: The small model property: how small can it be? J. Inf. Comput. **178**(1), 279–293 (2002)

21. Pricopi, M., Mitra, T.: Bahurupi: a polymorphic heterogeneous multi-core architecture. ACM Trans. Archit. Code Optim. **8**(4), 1–21 (2012)

22. PULP Platform, ETH Zurich. https://pulp-platform.org

23. RISC-V: The Free and Open RISC Instruction Set Architecture. https://riscv.org

24. Ryan, L.: Siege SAT-Solver v.4. http://www.cs.sfu.ca/~loryan/personal

25. Sharangpani, H., Arora, K.: Itanium processor microarchitecture. IEEE Micro **20**(5), 24–43 (2000)

26. Velev, M.N., Bryant, R.E.: Bit-level abstraction in the verification of pipelined microprocessors by correspondence checking. In: Gopalakrishnan, G., Windley, P. (eds.) Formal Methods in Computer-Aided Design. FMCAD 1998. LNCS, vol. 1522, pp. 18–35. Springer, Berlin (1998). https://doi.org/10.1007/3-540-49519-3_3

27. Velev, M.N., Bryant, R.E.: Exploiting positive equality and partial non-consistency in the formal verification of pipelined microprocessors. In: 36th Design Automation Conference (DAC 1999), pp. 397–401, June 1999

28. Velev, M.N., Bryant, R.E.: Superscalar processor verification using efficient reductions of the logic of equality with uninterpreted functions to propositional logic. In: Pierre, L., Kropf, T. (eds.) Correct Hardware Design and Verification Methods. CHARME 1999. LNCS, vol. 1703, pp. 37–53. Springer, Berlin, Heidelberg (1997). https://doi.org/10.1007/3-540-48153-2_5

29. Velev, M.N., Bryant, R.E.: Formal verification of superscalar microprocessors with multicycle functional units, exceptions, and branch prediction. In: 37th Design Automation Conference (DAC 2000), pp. 112–117, June 2000

30. Velev, M.N.: Formal verification of VLIW Microprocessors with Speculative Execution. In: Emerson, E.A., Sistla, A.P. (eds.), CAV 2000. LNCS ,vol. 1855, pp. 296–311. Springer, Berlin (2000). https://doi.org/10.1007/10722167_24

31. Velev, M.N.: Automatic abstraction of memories in the formal verification of superscalar microprocessors. In: Margaria, T., Yi, W. (eds.) TACAS 2001. LNCS, vol. 2031, pp. 252–267. Springer, Berlin (2001). https://doi.org/10.1007/3-540-45319-9_18

32. Velev, M.N.: Using rewriting rules and positive equality to formally verify wide-issue out-of-order microprocessors with a reorder buffer. In: Design, Automation and Test in Europe (DATE 2002), pp. 28–35, March 2002

33. Velev, M.N., Bryant, R.E.: Effective use of Boolean satisfiability procedures in the formal verification of superscalar and VLIW microprocessors. J. Symbolic Comput. (JSC) **35**(2), 73–106 (2003)

34. Velev, M.N. (2003). Automatic abstraction of equations in a logic of equality. In: Mayer, M.C., Pirri, F. (eds.) Automated reasoning with analytic tableaux and related methods. TABLEAUX

2003. LNCS, vol. 2796, pp. 196–213. Springer, Berlin (2003). https://doi.org/10.1007/978-3-540-45206-5_16

35. Velev, M.N.: Using automatic case splits and efficient CNF translation to guide a SAT-solver when formally verifying out-of-order processors. In: Artificial Intelligence and Mathematics (AI&MATH 2004), pp. 242–254, January 2004

36. Velev, M.N.: Efficient translation of Boolean formulas to CNF in formal verification of microprocessors. In: Asia and South Pacific Design Automation Conference (ASP-DAC 2004), pp. 310–315, January 2004

37. Velev, M.N.: Using positive equality to prove liveness for pipelined microprocessors. In: Asia and South Pacific Design Automation Conference (ASP-DAC 2004), pp. 316–321, January 2004

38. Velev, M.N.: Exploiting signal unobservability for efficient translation to CNF in formal verification of microprocessors. In: Design, Automation and Test in Europe (DATE 2004), pp. 266–271, February 2004

39. Velev, M.N.: Encoding global unobservability for efficient translation to SAT. In: 7th International Conference on Theory and Applications of Satisfiability Testing (SAT 2004), pp. 197–204, May 2004

40. Velev, M.N.: Formal verification of pipelined microprocessors by correspondence checking, Ph.D. thesis, Dept. of ECE, Carnegie Mellon University, May 2004

41. Velev, M.N.: Comparative study of strategies for formal verification of high-level processors. In: 22nd International Conference on Computer Design (ICCD 2004), pp. 119–124, October 2004

42. Velev, M.N.: Comparison of schemes for encoding unobservability in translation to SAT. In: Asia and South Pacific Design Automation Conference (ASP-DAC 2005), pp. 1056–1059, January 2005

43. Velev, M.N.: Automatic formal verification of liveness for pipelined processors with multicycle functional units. In: Borrione, D., Paul, W. (eds.) Correct Hardware Design and Verification Methods. CHARME 2005. LNCS, vol. 3725, pp. 97–113. Springer, Berlin (2005). https://doi.org/10.1007/11560548_10

44. Velev, M.N., Bryant, R.E.: TLSim and EVC: a term-level symbolic simulator and an efficient decision procedure for the logic of equality with uninterpreted functions and memories. Int. J. Embed. Syst. (IJES) 1(1/2), 134–149 (2005)

45. Velev, M.N., Gao, P.: Exploiting hierarchical encodings of equality to design independent strategies in parallel SMT decision procedures for a logic of equality. In: IEEE High Level Design Validation and Test Workshop (HLDVT 2009), pp. 8–13, November 2009

46. Velev, M.N., Gao, P.: A method for debugging of pipelined processors in formal verification by correspondence checking. In: 15th Asia and South Pacific Design Automation Conference (ASP-DAC 2010), pp. 619–624, January 2010

47. Velev, M.N., Gao, P.: Method for formal verification of soft-error tolerance mechanisms in pipelined microprocessors. In: Dong, J.S., Zhu, H. (eds.) ICFEM 2010. LNCS, vol. 6447, pp. 355–370. Springer, Berlin (2010). https://doi.org/10.1007/978-3-642-16901-4_24

48. Velev, M.N., Gao, P.: Automatic formal verification of reconfigurable DSPs. In: 16th Asia and South Pacific Design Automation Conference (ASP-DAC 2011), pp 293–296, January 2011

49. Velev, M.N., Gao, P.: Exploiting abstraction for efficient formal verification of DSPs with arrays of reconfigurable functional units. In: Qin, S., Qiu, Z. (eds.) ICFEM 2011. LNCS, vol. 6991, pp. 307–322. Springer, Berlin (2011). https://doi.org/10.1007/978-3-642-24559-6_22

50. Velev, M.N., Gao, P.: Automatic formal verification of multithreaded pipelined microprocessors. In: 30th IEEE/ACM International Conference on Computer-Aided Design (ICCAD 2011), pp. 679–686, November 2011

51. Velev, M.N., Gao, P.: Automated debugging of counterexamples in formal verification of pipelined microprocessors. In: 17th Asia and South Pacific Design Automation Conference (ASP-DAC 2012), January–February 2012, pp. 689–694
52. Velev, M.N., Gao, P.: Formal verification of safety of polymorphic heterogeneous multi-core architectures. In: 15th International Symposium on Quality Electronic Design (ISQED 2014), pp. 611–617, March 2014
53. Velev, M.N.: SAT Benchmarks. www.miroslav-velev.com/sat_benchmarks.html
54. Wolf, C.: Formal verification of RISC-V cores with riscv-formal (2018). https://riscv.org/wp-content/uploads/2018/12/13.30-Humbenberger-Wolf-Formal-Verification-of-RISC-V-processor-implementations.pdf

Refinement and Separation: Modular Verification of Wandering Trees

Gerhard Schellhorn⬤, Stefan Bodenmüller$^{(\boxtimes)}$⬤, and Wolfgang Reif⬤

Institute for Software and Systems Engineering, University of Augsburg,
Augsburg, Germany
{schellhorn,stefan.bodenmueller,reif}@informatik.uni-augsburg.de

Abstract. Flash memory does not allow in-place updates like conventional hard disks. Therefore all file systems must maintain an index that maps identifiers for files and directories to the address of their most recently written version. For efficiency, the index is typically implemented as a Wandering Search Tree. However, the verification of Wandering Trees is challenging since it has to deal with multiple aspects at once: the algorithmic complexity of search trees, trees in RAM that are partially loaded from snapshots on flash, where only modified parts are incrementally saved, and the efficient representation of trees as pointer structures. This paper proposes a modular solution that allows verifying each aspect separately. The solution has been mechanized in the theorem prover KIV.

Keywords: Wandering Trees · Refinement · Interactive Verification

1 Introduction

Flash memory has the constraint that it does not allow direct overwriting of data. It is organized in blocks that can only be written sequentially. Writing new data into a block is possible only after it has been erased as a whole. Therefore, file systems for flash memory (as well as flash translation layers used by SSDs, that mimic an ordinary hard disk that allows overwriting) have to manage an *index* that maps unique keys that identify elements of the file system to the physical address where their latest version can be found. The keys are usually based on *inode numbers* that uniquely identify files and directories, together with page numbers that identify data pages of a file.

An efficient implementation of the index is crucial for the efficiency of the file system. Of course, storing the index simply on flash memory itself is not an efficient solution since, again, incremental updates in place would not be possible. On the other hand, just keeping the index in RAM is not an option either since the index would be lost on a crash (e.g., a power loss). The standard

Supported by the Deutsche Forschungsgemeinschaft (DFG), "Correct translation of abstract specifications to C-Code (VeriCode)" (grant RE828/26-1).

P. Herber and A. Wijs (Eds.): iFM 2023, LNCS 14300, pp. 214–234, 2024.
https://doi.org/10.1007/978-3-031-47705-8_12

solution used nowadays in flash file systems is to use *Wandering Trees* [11] as an efficient solution. In Linux, for example, UBIFS [13] uses this solution.

We will explain Wandering Trees in Sect. 2. They present a challenge for verification as they combine algorithmic complexity, reasoning about pointer structures, and incremental caching.

The contribution of this paper is a mechanized verification of Wandering Trees using the theorem prover KIV, available online at [14]. The solution allows addressing these verification challenges in isolation using *components* without losing the efficiency of the overall solution. That pointer reasoning can be tackled in a small separate component is a generic aspect that should be reusable in other case studies.

We give some basic information on KIV's logic and specification concepts in Sect. 3 and discuss the concept of components and subcomponents, which are connected by refinement, in Sect. 4. The verification we present here is the last gap that was long open in the verification of Flashix, which is a fully verified file system for flash memory, see [1] for an overview.

Section 5 will give an overview of the modularization, and Sect. 6 gives the core concepts used in the verification. An interesting aspect of the verification is that we could make use of various operators of Separation Logic [19, 23]. In particular, we found Separation Logic and the use of the magic wand to be useful as a concept already when viewing the index abstractly as a map, generalizing its usual use for heaps (or other low-level resources). We also used the sharing separation operator to verify the correct representation of snapshots on flash memory.

Finally, Sect. 7 concludes.

2 Wandering Trees

Wandering Trees are used to implement an index, which maps keys that identify file system data to addresses on flash memory. Typically, they are organized as B^+-Trees. In this paper, we will use simple binary search trees since they are easier to explain, and rebalancing algorithms for trees are not the focus of this paper. Verification of B^+-Trees alone (without the aspects discussed here) has already been addressed in our paper [7], and we have also verified the rebalancing algorithms of Red-Black Trees in [24]. Several other papers have also discussed the verification of B^+-Trees in isolation, see [16, 17]. Concurrent search trees have also been verified in [15].

How Wandering Trees work is shown in Fig. 1. The system keeps a current version of the index stored as a search tree in RAM (top row), and an older snapshot is saved on Flash memory (bottom row). The two versions are called the *ram index* and the *flash index*. A new snapshot is saved when the *log* of the file system that sequentially saves changes (log entries record additions, modifications, and deletions) to the file system becomes full. Then the ram index is saved to the flash index in a *commit* operation, which also starts a new log (the old log becomes regular memory). A commit is also done when shutting down the file system, so on a reboot, a current flash index is available.

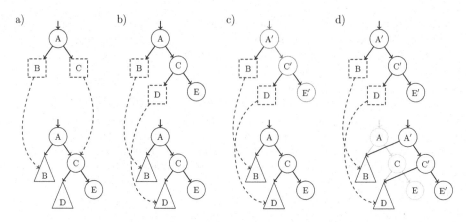

Fig. 1. Exemplary sequence of Wandering Tree operations with blue proxy nodes and red dirty nodes. RAM content shown on top, flash content below it. (Color figure online)

However, the flash index is not immediately loaded to the ram index, as this would be too expensive. Instead, just the root node A is loaded to RAM, as shown in Fig. 1 a). Its child nodes B, C are proxy nodes (shown in blue): these just store the address on flash memory of the actual nodes B, C.

Reading data from flash memory will need some part of the index to find their current version. Since files in the same directory and pages of the same file have similar keys, this will typically require accessing some nodes that are close together in some subtree of the flash index. In Fig. 1b), nodes C and E were required to find some content of flash memory. Accessing the nodes will load their actual content. To speed up following reads and writes to these files, they are replaced in the ram index with their actual content. A new proxy node for D is created.

Updating files and directories will modify some nodes of the ram index. Figure 1c) shows the changes caused by updating node E to point to a new version of some data. This will not just update the content of node E (to E') but it will also set a *dirty* flag in all nodes on the path from the root to E (here A, C, E). *Dirty nodes*, where the flag is set, are shown in red. Precisely the dirty nodes differ between ram index and flash index.

A commit operation, that saves the content of the flash index to the ram index will only save the dirty nodes, causing the flash index to wander (hence the name: Wandering Trees). The effect of a commit can be seen in Fig. 1d): only the dirty nodes A', C' and E' need to be saved on Flash memory, all nodes in the subtrees B and D still remain valid. In the ram index the dirty flag is cleared, since after the commit these nodes agree again with the flash index.

Wandering Trees are crash-safe since the ram index that, like all data in RAM, is lost on a power loss can be reconstructed: a reboot will find a non-empty log on flash memory. Starting with the flash index, a recovery routine will reconstruct the current ram index by replaying the entries of this log. Verification of crash safety is part of this case study, as is ensuring that hardware errors (all operations on flash can return errors) are handled correctly. We refer to [20] for the theory that results in additional proof obligations for each component, but this issue is out of scope for the remainder of the paper. We just note that for crash safety, it is essential that the commit operation has a final atomic step that both switches the ram index from Fig. 1c) to d) and the log to a new empty log. Technically this is realized by switching to a new superblock, see [5].

Verification of Wandering Trees as a monolithic implementation has to deal with three problems at the same time:

- the ram index has to correctly implement a search tree.
- the ram index implements a cache for the flash index. Replacing proxies with actual nodes, the mechanism of having dirty nodes, and committing these have to work correctly.
- Wandering Trees are pointer structures. It has to be verified that they correctly represent trees and that there are no space leaks.

Of course in theory, it is possible to consider all these aspects at once, but early experiments indicated that, at least in our theorem prover, the resulting complexity of invariants and abstraction relations becomes overwhelming.

Therefore, this paper's contribution is a modular structure, explained in the next section, that allows the decoupling of the three aspects and defines intuitive invariants and abstraction relations to make the individual verification tasks manageable.

3   Structured Specifications of Algebraic Data Types

To develop the necessary formal specifications and prove that our implementation follows them, we use the theorem prover KIV, which provides interactive verification using a sequent calculus with explicit proof trees. The basic logic of the specification language is higher order logic (HOL), recently extended from monomorphic to polymorphic types.

In KIV, structured algebraic specifications are used to build a hierarchy of data type definitions. Primitive data types may be generated freely or non-freely. Specifications can be augmented by additional functions and combined using standard structuring operations like enrichment, union, and renaming. It is also possible to specify parameterized data types that can be instantiated explicitly.

3.1   Algebraic Definitions

The standard approach for proving the correctness of algorithms using complex data structures is to specify the data structures algebraically. Binary trees can be defined as a polymorphic free data type $Bintree(\kappa, \alpha)$ with a Leaf constructor (which maps one key to a value) and a Node constructor. Our case study will use type $Bintree(Key, Elem)$ for search trees, where the Key type is assumed to be totally ordered. This allows to formulate a standard invariant isOrdered(bt) for search trees bt: for any node in the tree, the keys stored in its right (left) subtree are bigger (less or equal) than the keys stored in the node.

$$Bintree(\kappa, \alpha) = \text{Node}(.\text{key} : \kappa; .\text{left} : Bintree(\kappa, \alpha); .\text{right} : Bintree(\kappa, \alpha))$$
$$| \text{ Leaf}(.\text{key} : \kappa; .\text{val} : \alpha)$$

For a free data type specification, KIV generates all necessary axioms, as well as update functions (written e.g. $bt.\text{key} := newkey$), including their definitions. KIV attaches a *domain* to selector functions. When used in programs, this ensures that selecting a value from a Node or the left subtree from a Leaf will raise an exception. Therefore, proving the correct use of the data type in programs includes showing the absence of such exceptions, i.e., one has to prove that all operations are called with arguments within their respective domain.

3.2   Modeling the Heap and Separation Logic

Reasoning about destructive pointer algorithms requires modelling the heap, either implicitly as part of the semantics of formulas or explicitly as an algebraic data type. In KIV, the latter approach is realized: heaps that store objects of type ω are specified as a polymorphic non-free data type $Heap(\omega)$.

A heap can be considered a partial function (a "map") that maps a finite number of references to objects, where allocation of references is explicit and the reference type contains a distinguished element null that is never allocated (representing the null pointer). Since Separation Logic formulas can be defined (and will be useful for our case study) for maps in general, we define generic maps as a generic type $Map(\kappa, \nu)$ that maps arbitrary keys of type κ to arbitrary values of type ν. Heaps then map references of type $Ref(\omega)$ to objects of type ω, i.e., $Heap(\omega)$ abbreviates $Map(Ref(\omega), \omega)$.

The $Map(\kappa, \nu)$ data type is inductively generated by the empty map $\emptyset$, and an operator $m[k := v]$ that stores the value v under key k, either allocating the key if it is new or overwriting the old value stored previously. A predicate $k \in m$ checks whether a key is allocated in the map, i.e., is in its domain, and a function $m[k]$ is used to lookup the value stored under a key (for heaps this corresponds to dereferencing a pointer). Keys and their value can also be removed (deallocated) by the function $m -- k$. The union $m_1 \cup m_2$ of two maps is defined when they have disjoint domains (written $m_1 \perp m_2$). Similar to the selector functions of free data types, lookup $m[k]$ and removal $m -- k$ raise exceptions in programs when the key is not in the map ($\neg\, k \in m$).

In KIV, all parameters of procedures are explicit. Hence, when reasoning about pointer-based programs, the heap must be an explicit parameter of the program as well. To facilitate the verification of such programs, we built a simple library for Separation Logic (SL) in KIV. We give some information to explain the notation used in the following. SL formulas are encoded using predicates over maps P with type $Map(\kappa, \nu) \to Bool$, abbreviated as $MapPrd$. A map predicate P describes the structure of a map m. Predicate emp describes an empty map:

$$\text{emp}(m) \leftrightarrow m = \emptyset$$

The maplet $k \mapsto v$ describes a singleton map containing only one key k mapping to a value v. The infix operator $\mapsto$ therefore has type $\kappa \times \nu \to MapPrd$ and is defined as

$$(k \mapsto v)(m) \leftrightarrow m = \emptyset[k := v]$$

More complex maps can be described using the separating conjunction $P * Q$ asserting that the map consists of two disjoint parts, one satisfying P and one satisfying Q, respectively. Since it connects two heap predicates, it is defined as a function with type $MapPrd \times MapPrd \to MapPrd$:

$$(P * Q)(m) \leftrightarrow \exists\, m_1, m_2.\ m_1 \perp m_2 \wedge m = m_1 \cup m_2 \wedge P(m_1) \wedge Q(m_2)$$

Separating conjunction is useful to assert that a map (or specifically: the heap) stores a tree-shaped structure where the left and right subtree are disjoint.

For our case study we will also make use of two more operators of the same type defined as

$$(P \mathbin{-\!*} Q)(m) \leftrightarrow \forall\, m_1.\ m_1 \perp m \wedge P(m_1) \to Q(m \cup m_1)$$
$$(P \circledast Q)(m) \leftrightarrow \exists\, m_1, m_0, m_2.\ m_1 \perp m_0 \wedge m_0 \perp m_2 \wedge m_1 \perp m_2$$
$$\wedge\ m = m_1 \cup m_0 \cup m_2 \wedge P(m_1 \cup m_0) \wedge Q(m_0 \cup m_2)$$

The *magic wand* $P \mathbin{-\!*} Q$ asserts that adding any disjoint map m_1 that satisfies P to the current map m will result in a map that satisfies Q.

Overlapping conjunction [9,12] $P \circledast Q$ asserts that the map m can be split into three disjoint parts m_0, m_1, m_2 such that P holds for the union of m_0 and m_1, while the union of m_0 and m_2 satisfies Q. This is useful, when the map stores a tree-shaped structure where the left and right subtree may have a shared part m_0 (so the structure becomes a directed acyclic graph).

Finally, some of the lemmas that we define will use implication $P \Rightarrow Q$ lifted to map predicates defined as $\forall\, m.\ P(m) \to Q(m)$.

4   Modular Software Systems

For the development of complex software systems in KIV, we use the concept of hierarchical components combined with the contract approach to data refinement [4,26]. A component is an abstract data type $(ST, \mathtt{Init}, (\mathtt{Op}_j)_{j \in J})$ consisting of a set of states ST, a set of initial states $\mathtt{Init} \subseteq ST$, and a set of operations $\mathtt{Op}_j \subseteq In_j \times ST \times ST \times Out_j$. An operation $\mathtt{Op}_j$ takes inputs In_i and outputs Out_j and modifies the state of the component. Operations are specified with contracts using the operational approach of ASMs [2]: for an operation $\mathtt{Op}_j$, we give a precondition pre_j and a program α_j in the form of a procedure declaration $\mathbf{op}_j\#(in_j; st; out_j)$ **pre** pre_j $\{\alpha_j\}$. The program α_j is given in KIV's imperative programming language, which supports recursive procedures and nondeterminism (details on the syntax can be found in [25]), and establishes the postcondition of the operation. The arguments of a procedure $\mathbf{op}_j\#(in_j; st; out_j)$ are grouped into sequences of input, reference, and output parameters. KIV does not support global variables, these must be added explicitly as reference parameters.

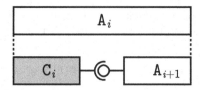

Fig. 2. Data refinement with subcomponents. Implementation C_i uses specification A_{i+1} as a subcomponent (depicted by —⊙—). Together they are a refinement of specification A_i (depicted by the dotted lines).

Instead of defining initial states directly, we also give a procedure declaration $\text{init}\#(in_{init}; st; out_{init})\ \{\alpha_{init}\}$.

Components are distinguished between specifications and implementations. The former are used to model the functional requirements of a (sub-)system and are typically kept as simple as possible by heavily utilizing algebraic functions and non-determinism. The approach is as general as specifying pre- and post-conditions since the program **choose** st', out' **with** $post(st', out')$ **in** $st, out :=$ st', out' can be used to establish any postcondition $post$ over state st and output out. Implementations are typically deterministic and only use constructs that allow generating executable Scala or C code from them with our code generator.

The functional correctness of implementation components is then proven by a data refinement of the corresponding specification components (we write $C \leq A$ if $C = (ST^C, \text{Init}^C, (Op_j^C)_{j \in J})$ is a refinement of $A = (ST^A, \text{Init}^A, (Op_j^A)_{j \in J})$ where C and A have the same set of operations J). Proofs for such a refinement are usually done by first showing strong enough *invariants* for each component (that are preserved by all operations) and then proving an abstraction relation $\text{abs} \subseteq ST^A \times ST^C$ to be a forward simulation. Proof obligations are based on a weakest precondition calculus for programs α that borrows notation from Dynamic Logic (DL) [10] and uses three modalities: $[\alpha]\varphi$ (corresponding to the weakest liberal precondition $wlp(\alpha, \varphi)$), $\langle\alpha\rangle\varphi$ (there is a terminating execution of α that establishes φ), and $\langle\!|\alpha|\!\rangle\,\varphi$ (corresponding to the weakest precondition $wp(\alpha, \varphi)$).

Proving a forward simulation correct requires to show the following proof obligation for each operation (i.e., $j \in J$) following the contract approach [4,26]:

$$\text{abs}(st^A, st^C) \wedge pre_j^A(st^A) \wedge inv^A(st^A) \wedge inv^C(st^C)$$
$$\rightarrow \langle\!|\mathbf{op}_j^C\#(in_j; st^C; out_j)|\!\rangle \langle\mathbf{op}_j^A\#(in_j; st^A; out'_j)\rangle(\text{abs}(st^A, st^C) \wedge out_j = out'_j)$$

The proof obligation assumes a pair of states st^A and st^C such that abs and the already established invariants hold and that the abstract precondition is true. It asserts that every concrete run terminates (in particular the concrete precondition must be satisfied) and has a corresponding abstract run with the same output, such that the abstraction relation holds for the resulting states (note that the postcondition refers to the final states of both programs). It is crucial that the calculus allows nested modalities (unlike Hoare calculus) to express the proof obligations. For information on symbolic execution and rewriting that are used for verification, see [25].

To facilitate the development of larger systems, we introduced a concept of modularization in the form of *subcomponents*. A component (usually an implementation) can use one or more subcomponents (usually specifications). The client component cannot access the state of its subcomponents directly but only via calls to the interface operations of the subcomponents. Using subcomponents, a refinement hierarchy is composed of multiple refinements like in Fig. 2. A specification component A_i is refined by an implementation C_i (dotted lines in Fig. 2) that uses a specification A_{i+1} as a subcomponent (—◎— in Fig. 2, we write $C_i(A_{i+1})$ for this subcomponent relation). Note that we visualize specification components as white boxes and implementation components as grey boxes throughout (cf. Figure 2).

This pattern then repeats in the sense that A_{i+1} is refined further by an implementation C_{i+1} that again uses a subcomponent A_{i+2} and so on. If it is not the top-level specification, A_i may also be used as a subcomponent of an implementation C_{i-1}. The complete implementation of the system then results from composing all individual implementation components $C_0(C_1(C_2(...)))$. In [6] we have shown that $C \leq A$ implies $M(C) \leq M(A)$ for a client component M which ensures that the composed implementation is a correct refinement of its top-level specification A_0, i.e., $C_0(C_1(C_2(...))) \leq A_0$. This allows us to divide a complex refinement task into multiple, more manageable ones, as demonstrated in the following sections for our Wandering Tree implementation.

5 Modularization

To specify and verify the different aspects of Wandering Trees separately, we employed the refinement hierarchy shown in Fig. 3. Starting from a concise and simple specification, multiple refinement steps are applied down to an efficient, pointer-based Wandering Tree implementation.

5.1 Specification of the Index

The top-level specification component **Index** completely abstracts from the tree data structure. Instead, the index is modeled as a map (i.e., a partial function) from index keys, which must be totally ordered, to values of an unspecified type *Elem*. The distinction between the cached and persisted version is realized by keeping two maps of type *Map(Key, Elem)*: the *ram index* (*ri*) representing the current state of the index and the *flash index* (*fi*) storing the latest *committed* state.

For the actual implementation, the *Elem* type is instantiated with a type *Adr* of flash addresses. However, as both index and data nodes are stored under these addresses in the file system, we keep the type abstract here to avoid confusion with addresses used for storing index data structures introduced with subsequent refinements.

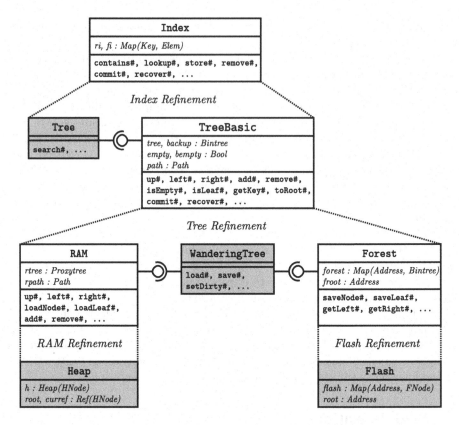

Fig. 3. The refinement hierarchy for Wandering Trees. Each component lists its state (first compartment) and its most important operations (second compartment). Together, the four refinements *Index Refinement*, *Tree Refinement*, *RAM Refinement*, and *Flash Refinement* guarantee correctness of the combined Wandering Tree implementation, i.e., Tree(WanderingTree(Heap, Flash)) ≤ Index.

Figure 4 lists the full Index specification. Initially, i.e., after formatting the file system, *ri* and *fi* are both empty (operation **init**#, lines 1–3). Modifications to the index are performed only on the ram index: **store**# adds a key/value pair to *ri* resp. updates the value stored under the respective key (lines 5–9), and **remove**# deletes an entry from the index (lines 11–15). Note that both operations return a flag *exists* signaling whether an entry for the requested *key* existed before the execution and, if so, the old value of the entry in *old* (otherwise, *old* is set to a random value ?). **contains**# checks whether a *key* is allocated in *ri* (lines 16–17), and **lookup**# additionally returns the value stored under *key* (lines 19–23). The flash index is altered only during a **commit**# (lines 25–26), where it is updated to the current version stored in *ri*. Conversely, recovery after a crash is specified as restoring *ri* from *fi* (lines 28–29).

```
1   init#()
2       initialization
3   { ri := ∅, fi := ∅ }
4
5   store#(key, v; ; old, exists) {
6       exists := key ∈ ri;
7       if exists then old := ri[key] else old := ?;
8       ri[key] := v;
9   }
10
11  remove#(key; ; old, exists) {
12      exists := key ∈ ri;
13      if exists then { old := ri[key]; ri -- key }
14      else old := ?;
15  }
```

```
16  contains#(key; ; exists)
17  { exists := key ∈ ri }
18
19  lookup#(key; ; exists, v) {
20      exists := key ∈ ri;
21      if exists then v := ri[key]
22      else v := ?
23  }
24
25  commit#()
26  { fi := ri }
27
28  recover#()
29  { ri := fi }
```

Fig. 4. Abstract representation of Wandering Trees: the component Index.

5.2 Index Refinement

In a first step, Index is refined by the component Tree using TreeBasic as a subcomponent (written Tree(TreeBasic) ≤ Index). This refinement addresses the realization of the index as a (binary) search tree. But instead of switching to a pointer representation directly, TreeBasic uses the *algebraic* trees $tree, backup : Bintree(Key, Adr)$ as state (cf. Sect. 3.1), representing the indices ri and fi, respectively. The state of TreeBasic also contains boolean flags *empty* and *bempty*, which are necessary to model that the respective tree is empty since *Bintree* only defines non-empty trees (consisting of at least a Leaf).

TreeBasic provides an interface for fine-grained manipulations of *tree* at a given location, like inserting a key/value pair in form of a Leaf with **add#** or reading the key of the current node with **getKey#**. These operations are used by the client component Tree to implement the interface of Index. For this, TreeBasic also has a state $path : Path$ describing the way from the root of the tree to the current location, where $Path$ is defined as a sequence of LEFT and RIGHT markers, i.e., $Path \equiv List(\text{LEFT} \mid \text{RIGHT})$. To navigate within the tree, Tree calls the operations **up#**, **left#**, and **right#** to extend or shorten *path*.

The models use several algebraic operations for accessing and updating the trees: the predicate $p \in t$ checks whether a path p is valid for a tree t, i.e., p points to a subtree within t, the function $t[p]$ selects the subtree of t that is reached when traversing t along p (if $p \in t$), and the function $t[p := t_0]$ yields the tree t where the subtree $t[p]$ is replaced with the tree t_0 (again, only defined for $p \in t$). These operations are defined recursively over the tree structure, for example, the following axioms are given for $t[p]$:[1]

$$t[[]] = t$$
$$\text{Node}(key, t_0, t_1)[\text{LEFT} + p] = t_0[p]$$
$$\text{Node}(key, t_0, t_1)[\text{RIGHT} + p] = t_1[p]$$

---

[1] [] denotes the empty path, $a + p$ denotes a path consisting of one leading element a and a remaining path p.

Using these axiomatized operations, the main part of the tree algorithms (and thus, their complexity) is placed in `Tree`, while the specification of `TreeBasic` is kept as simple as possible (most of the operations consist only of a single assignment). The verification of the `Tree` algorithms only needs to consider algebraic trees, abstracting from the more efficient but more complex tree representation used for the implementation of Wandering Trees.

```
 1   search#(key; ; exists) {
 2     let isEmpty = ? in {
 3       tree_basic_isEmpty#(; ; isEmpty); // isEmpty := empty
 4       if isEmpty then exists := false
 5       else let isLeaf = ?, key0 = ? in {
 6         tree_basic_toRoot#(); // path := []
 7         tree_basic_isLeaf#(; ; isLeaf); // isLeaf := tree[path].leaf?
 8         while ¬ isLeaf do {
 9           tree_basic_getKey#(; ; key0); // key0 := tree[path].key
10           if key0 < key then
11             tree_basic_right#(); // path := path + RIGHT
12           else
13             tree_basic_left#(); // path := path + LEFT;
14           tree_basic_isLeaf#(; ; isLeaf); // isLeaf := tree[path].leaf?
15         };
16         tree_basic_getKey#(; ; key0); // key0 := tree[path].key
17         exists := (key = key0);
18       }
19     }
20   }
```

Fig. 5. `Tree` auxiliary procedure for performing a binary search for an element *elem* within the tree.

Figure 5 shows how the interface of `TreeBasic` is used by `Tree` to implement a standard binary search. The auxiliary routine **search#** is used in most interface operations of `Tree` and searches for a *key*, returning a boolean flag whether a corresponding entry *exists* in the tree (set in lines 4 or 17, respectively). The comments in green show the implementation of the primitive operations of `TreeBasic`. For a non-empty tree (the state variable *empty* is set to true iff the tree does not contain any nodes), the tree is traversed by incrementally extending *path* with LEFT or RIGHT markers, depending on how the key key_0 of the current node compares to *key*, stopping when a leaf is reached (loop in lines 8–15). When **search#** has finished, *path* points to the location at which the actual modification (or lookup) of the respective `Tree` operation can be performed, e.g., adding/removing a node or reading the value.

At this level, **commit#** and **recovery#** are still modeled as simple atomic assignments of complete trees (*backup* := *tree* and *tree* := *backup*, respectively). Furthermore, *tree* always describes the complete index tree, so optimizations like lazy loading or caching modifications of individual nodes are not yet considered. These aspects are introduced with the next refinement step.

5.3   Tree Refinement

The refinement WanderingTree(RAM, Forest) ≤ TreeBasic introduces the concepts of multiple tree snapshots stored on flash memory and partially loaded trees in volatile memory. However, both aspects are again modeled using algebraic trees instead of pointer structures.

```
1    load#() {
2      let isProxy = ? in {
3        ram_isProxy#(; ; isProxy); // isProxy := rtree[rpath].proxy?
4        if isProxy then let adr = ?, key = ?, isLeaf = ? in {
5          ram_getAdr#(; ; adr); // adr := rtree[rpath].fadr
6          forest_getKey#(adr; ; key); // key := forest[adr].key
7          forest_isLeaf#(adr; ; isLeaf); // isLeaf := forest[adr].leaf?
8          if isLeaf then let v = ? in {
9            forest_getValue#(adr; ; v); // v := forest[adr].val
10           ram_loadLeaf#(key, v);
11           // rtree[rpath] := Leaf(key, rtree[rpath].fadr, v)
12         } else let ladr = ?, radr = ? in {
13           forest_getLeft#(adr; ; ladr);
14           // ladr with ladr ∈ forest ∧ forest[adr].left = forest[ladr]
15           forest_getRight#(adr; ; radr);
16           // radr with radr ∈ forest ∧ forest[adr].right = forest[radr]
17           ram_loadNode#(key, ladr, radr);
18           // rtree[rpath] := Node(key, rtree[rpath].fadr, Proxy(ladr), Proxy(radr))
19         }
20       }
21     }
22   }
```

Fig. 6. WanderingTree auxiliary procedure for instantiating a *proxy* node at the current path *rpath* by loading the node from flash.

The Forest component stores multiple binary trees in a map *forest* of type *ForestMap* ≡ *Map(Adr, Bintree(Key, Elem))*, where each entry represents a snapshot of the (full) tree created during a **commit#**. These snapshots are stored at an abstract *Adr* on flash, and *froot* stores the address of the most recent snapshot, which is crucial for **recover#**. Note that since all trees in *forest* are algebraic, the snapshots are completely disjoint and do not share any subtrees (in contrast to the final implementation, cf. situation d) in Fig. 1). Thus, verification on this level does not have to cope with the additional complexity of sharing/aliasing.

The RAM component introduces *proxy nodes*, using a *Proxytree(Key, Elem)* instead of a *Bintree* for the volatile version of the tree. The polymorphic data type *Proxytree(κ, α)* is specified analogously to *Bintree(κ, α)* but uses an additional constructor **Proxy** that represents not yet loaded subtrees and extends **Node** and **Leaf** nodes to also contain a field .fadr storing the address of the corresponding persisted tree on flash:

$$Proxytree(\kappa, \alpha) = \texttt{Node}(.\texttt{key} : \kappa; \ .\texttt{fadr} : Adr; \ .\texttt{left} : Proxytree(\kappa, \alpha);$$
$$.\texttt{right} : Proxytree(\kappa, \alpha))$$
$$| \ \texttt{Leaf}(.\texttt{key} : \kappa; \ .\texttt{fadr} : Adr; \ .\texttt{val} : \alpha) \ | \ \texttt{Proxy}(.\texttt{fadr} : Adr)$$

For *dirty* (sub)trees, i.e., trees that contain uncommitted modifications, there is no corresponding flash address. These utilize the invalid **null** address to signal their *dirty* state. Note that, for the concepts presented in this paper, a simple boolean flag instead of the .**fadr** field would be sufficient to distinguish between *dirty* and *clean* trees. We store the addresses to identify flash locations that become *garbage* during a commit, which must be freed during a *garbage collection* algorithm (cf. [5]). However, this mechanism is implemented on another level of the file system, so it is outside the scope of this paper.

To implement the functionality of **TreeBasic**, **WanderingTree** accesses **RAM** and **Forest**. Recall that this functionality comprises only fine-grained accesses to the tree at a single location. Analogously to **TreeBasic**, this location is determined by a path *rpath* as part of the state of **RAM**. Since *rtree* is usually not fully loaded, the operations of **WanderingTree** first check whether *rpath* points to a **Proxy** tree in **RAM** and load the node from **Forest** if necessary. This is done with the auxiliary routine **load#** listed in Fig. 6. Again, the comments in green show the implementation of the primitive operations of the subcomponents **RAM** and **Forest**, respectively. If *rtree*[*rpath*] is a **Proxy** node, its flash address is used to determine whether the node is a **Leaf** and to read its *key* from flash (lines 3–7). For a leaf node, its value *v* is read from flash, and the proxy tree in *rtree* is replaced with a **Leaf** storing the loaded key/value pair (lines 9–11).[2] For a non-leaf, the proxy tree is replaced by a **Node**, which in turn stores only **Proxy** trees for its children (containing their loaded flash addresses, lines 13–18). That way, the **RAM** tree is loaded only as far as the respective **Tree** operation requires.

```
1   setDirty#() {
2     let isRoot = ? in {
3       ram_isRoot#(; ; isRoot);
4       while ¬ isRoot do {
5         ram_up#();
6         ram_setAdr#(null);
7         ram_isRoot#(; ; isRoot);
8       }
9     }
10  }
```

```
1   setDirty#() {
2     let isRoot = ? in {
3       ram_isRoot#(; ; isRoot);
4       while ¬ isRoot do {
5         ram_up#();
6         ram_setAdr#(null);
7         ram_isRoot#(; ; isRoot);
8       }
9     }
10  }
```

Fig. 7. WanderingTree procedure for marking modified parts of the index dirty.

Fig. 8. WanderingTree procedure for committing the RAM index.

---

[2] The assignment *tree*[*path*] := t_0 is an abbreviation for *tree* := *tree*[*path* := t_0.].

The other important responsibility of WanderingTree is to cache index updates in RAM until they are committed to flash. To determine the parts of the index that have to be written to flash during a commit, the path between an updated location and the root must be marked *dirty*. Therefore, the auxiliary operation **setDirty**# (shown in Fig. 7) is called after each modification: starting from the current location in RAM (determined by *rpath*, which points to the just modified subtree), *rtree* is traversed bottom-up until the root is reached (lines 4–8), setting all .fadr fields to null (line 6).

```
1    save#(; ; adr) {
2      let isDirty = ? in {
3        ram_isDirty#(; ; isDirty); // isDirty := rtree[rpath].dirty?
4        if isDirty then let key = ?, isLeaf = ? in {
5          ram_isLeaf#(; ; isLeaf); // isLeaf := rtree[rpath].leaf?
6          ram_getKey#(; ; key); // key := rtree[rpath].key
7          if isLeaf then let v = ? in {
8            ram_getValue#(; ; v); // v := rtree[rpath].val
9            forest_saveLeaf#(key, v; ; adr);
10           // adr with ¬ adr ∈ forest ∧ adr ≠ null in forest[adr] := Leaf(key, v)
11         } else let ladr = ?, radr = ? in {
12           ram_left#(); // rpath := rpath + LEFT
13           save#(; ; ladr);
14           ram_up#(); // rpath := rpath.butlast
15           ram_right#(); // rpath := rpath + RIGHT
16           save#(; ; radr);
17           ram_up#(); // rpath := rpath.butlast
18           forest_saveNode#(key, ladr, radr; ; adr);
19           // adr with ¬ adr ∈ forest ∧ adr ≠ null in
20           //   forest[adr] := Node(key, forest[ladr], forest[radr])
21         };
22         ram_setAdr#(adr); // rtree[rpath].fadr := adr
23       } else {
24         ram_getAdr#(; ; adr); // adr := rtree[rpath].fadr
25       }
26     }
27   }
```

Fig. 9. WanderingTree auxiliary procedure for recursively saving all *dirty* parts of *rtree* to flash, starting from the node at the current path *rpath*.

The **commit**# operation (shown in Fig. 8) calls an auxiliary operation **save**# (line 6), which saves a new tree in *forest* for each *dirty* node in *rtree*[*rpath*], returning the new root address *adr* of the saved tree. Crucially, the root address *froot* of Forest is only updated at the very end of the operation (line 8), which ensures atomicity of the commit process w.r.t. crashes. In case of a crash during **commit**#, the RAM tree is initialized with the old *froot* address, under which the latest committed version of the index is still present.

The **save**# operation (listed in Fig. 9) has an interplay between RAM and Forest similar to **load**#: For a *dirty* Leaf in *rtree*, a corresponding Leaf is stored in *forest* (lines 8–10). For a *dirty* Node in *rtree*, the tree is traversed recursively (recursive calls in lines 13 and 16 for its left and right subtrees, respectively) before the corresponding Node is saved in *forest* with the flash addresses *ladr* and *radr* of its stored children (lines 18–20). In both cases, the tree is stored under a new address *adr* in *forest*. Finally, the flash addresses of committed nodes in *rtree* are also updated and thus marked *clean* (line 22).

5.4   Pointer Structures in the Heap and on Flash

Finally, the algebraic trees are implemented by pointer structures: *RAM Refinement* realizes the proxy tree of RAM by a structure of *HNodes* in the heap, which is explicitly given as state $h : Heap(HNode)$ with references $Ref(HNode)$, and *Flash Refinement* realizes the binary trees of Forest as structures of *FNodes* stored on flash memory, which is modeled as a map $flash : Map(Adr, FNode)$. In [24], we used a similar modularization and refinement methodology to verify an efficient Red-Black Tree implementation: we also utilized an algebraic tree as an intermediate representation to abstract from the complexity of pointer-based rotations for maintaining balance. In this work, we revisit the methodology but apply it to simplify reasoning over the lazy loading and caching mechanisms at the level of WanderingTree(RAM, Forest). For the refinements Heap $\leq$ RAM and Flash $\leq$ Forest, the only (real) remaining proof task is to show that the pointer structures form correct trees (matching their algebraic counterparts) and that navigation via paths can be realized by dereferencing pointers.

Since [24] covers the general concept of refining algebraic trees with pointer trees in detail, we just give a brief overview of the used tree data structures.

$$
\begin{aligned}
HNode \; = \; &\text{HNode}(.\texttt{key} : Key; \; .\texttt{fadr} : Adr; \; .\texttt{parent} : Ref(HNode); \\
&\qquad .\texttt{left} : Ref(HNode); \; .\texttt{right} : Ref(HNode)) \\
&\mid \text{HLeaf}(.\texttt{key} : Key; \; .\texttt{fadr} : Adr; \; .\texttt{parent} : Ref(HNode); \; .\texttt{val} : Elem) \\
&\mid \text{HProxy}(.\texttt{fadr} : Adr; \; .\texttt{parent} : Ref(HNode))
\end{aligned}
\tag{1}
$$

$$
\begin{aligned}
FNode \; = \; &\text{FNode}(.\texttt{key} : Key; \; .\texttt{left} : Adr; \; .\texttt{right} : Adr) \\
&\mid \text{FLeaf}(.\texttt{key} : Key; \; .\texttt{val} : Elem)
\end{aligned}
\tag{2}
$$

Analogously to *Proxytree*, the *heap node* data type *HNode* is defined with constructors for inner nodes (HNode), leaf nodes (HLeaf), and proxy nodes (HProxy). The in-memory tree structure is formed via .left/.right pointers of HNodes. Additionally, each node contains a pointer to its parent node, which is necessary to navigate efficiently within the tree, e.g., for implementing up#. All heap nodes store the address of their persistent counterpart, i.e., the corresponding *FNode* on flash, in the .fadr field (or null if the node is *dirty*).

The *flash node* data type *FNode* defines a standard pointer representation of binary trees with constructors for inner (FNode) and leaf nodes (FLeaf), but flash addresses are used instead of heap references to the left and right children. Parent pointers are omitted since the tree is traversed top-down only.

Note that the representation as a map in Flash is not the final representation of data in the full implementation of the Flashix file system. There, an *Adr* storing an *FNode* will be allocated in blocks of flash memory. Thus, in the actual integration into the full Flashix file system, the Flash component will call memory allocation from a subcomponent again instead of just choosing a new *Adr* when allocating. The interested reader can find information on these lower level components, which do caching and a mapping from logical to physical blocks, in [20, 21].

6 Verification

This section gives a rough overview of the verification of the individual refinements. For brevity, we only give the most important invariants of the components and the definitions of the abstraction relations needed to verify the individual refinements. This should enable the reader to understand the main ideas used in the proofs, which are available online [14]. Since the concepts for the refinement Heap $\leq$ RAM are basically the same as in [24], we skip them here, although the refinement is crucial for having an efficient implementation that is based on efficiently modifying pointer structures.

6.1 Correctness of the Tree Component

Verification of the top-level refinement Tree[TreeBasic] $\leq$ Index first has to prove total correctness of **search#** with precondition *empty* $\vee$ isOrdered(*tree*) and postcondition

$\neg$ *empty* $\rightarrow$ (*path* $\in$ *tree* $\wedge$ *tree*[*path*].isLeaf
  $\wedge$ (**neighbor**(LEFT, *path*) = [] $\vee$ *tree*[**neighbor**(LEFT, *path*).butlast].key < *key*)
  $\wedge$ (**neighbor**(RIGHT, *path*) = [] $\vee$ *key* $\leq$ *tree*[**neighbor**(RIGHT, *path*).butlast].key))

which asserts that the path found indeed points to the right node. In the formula **neighbor**(LEFT/RIGHT, *p*) computes the previous/next path of *p* in the tree. For the leftmost path (of the form LEFT*), the previous path is empty, and for $p = p_0$ RIGHT LEFT*, it is p_0 LEFT. *p*.butlast removes the last element from this path. The keys of the previous and next path are the relevant ones to verify that subsequent modifications of the tree at *path* preserve isOrdered. The loop invariant used is similar to the postcondition.

The main proof of refinement has to verify that the two abstract maps *fi*, *ri* : *Map*(*Key*, *Adr*) are correctly represented by the two trees *tree* and *backup* and the two boolean flags *empty* and *bempty* that indicate that the empty map needs no tree for representation. The definition of the abstraction relation[3]

$$(empty \supset \text{emp}; \text{absI}(tree))(ri) \wedge (bempty \supset \text{emp}; \text{absI}(backup))(fi)$$

uses predicate absI : *Bintree*(*Key*, *Adr*) $\rightarrow$ *MapPrd* defined as

$$\text{absI}(\text{Leaf}(key, v)) = key \mapsto v \qquad \text{absI}(\text{Node}(key, lt, rt)) = \text{absI}(lt) * \text{absI}(rt)$$

Note that separating conjunction is used here for the maps of the abstract specification; the common case is to use it to represent an abstract structure by a pointer structure as in the refinement Heap $\leq$ RAM. The refinement proofs use

---

[3] ($\varphi \supset e1; e2$) abbreviates **if** φ **then** *e1* **else** *e2*.

the magic wand to prove correctness of adding and removing an element. The main lemma needed is that for a valid path $p \in bt$ we have

$$\texttt{absI}(bt) \Rightarrow \texttt{absI}(bt[p]) * (\texttt{absI}(rt) \; \texttt{-*} \; \texttt{absI}(bt[p := rt]))$$

which says that the tree bt consists of two parts: the old subtree $bt[p]$ that is replaced in the operation by a new subtree rt, resulting in the new tree $bt[p := rt]$. For removal of a *key*, when $bt[p] = \texttt{Node}(key', \texttt{Leaf}(key, v), rt)$ we then have

$$
\begin{aligned}
&\texttt{absI}(\texttt{Node}(key', \texttt{Leaf}(key, v), rt)) * (\texttt{absI}(rt) \; \texttt{-*} \; \texttt{absI}(bt[p := rt])) \\
&= \texttt{absI}(\texttt{Leaf}(key, v)) * \texttt{absI}(rt) * (\texttt{absI}(rt) \; \texttt{-*} \; \texttt{absI}(bt[p := rt])) \\
&= (key \mapsto v) * \texttt{absI}(rt) * (\texttt{absI}(rt) \; \texttt{-*} \; \texttt{absI}(bt[p := rt])) \\
&\Rightarrow (key \mapsto v) * \texttt{absI}(bt[p := rt]))
\end{aligned}
$$

where the last step applies the standard modus ponens rule for magic wand. Removing the maplet $key \mapsto v$ from the map (with m -- key), we get that $\texttt{absI}(bt[p := rt])(m)$ holds, i.e., the new map is correctly represented by the updated tree. The proof for adding a key/value pair is similar.

6.2   Correctness of Wandering Trees

The refinement $\texttt{WanderingTree}(\texttt{RAM}, \texttt{Forest}) \leq \texttt{TreeBasic}$ is the most complex of the case study since it has the most complex algorithms. However, since it is purely based on recursive definitions over algebraic structures, the proofs of this refinement were best to automate. As a first step of the proof, all operations of the $\texttt{Forest}$ component have to maintain the critical invariant $\texttt{invForest}$ for the map *forest* that stores the flash index on this level. The invariant states that, whenever some $\texttt{Node}(lt, key, rt)$ is stored as a value in the map, its two children lt and rt are also stored under some address, i.e., the map is closed against subtrees. This guarantees that the operations $\textbf{getLeft}\#$ and $\textbf{getRight}\#$, which return the addresses of the children (see lines 13 and 15 in Fig. 6), are always successful. The invariant is preserved since the only operation modifying *forest* is $\textbf{save}\#$, which is called with a node which has its children saved already.

The main correctness argument for the refinement then uses a function $\texttt{merge} : Proxytree(Key, Adr) \times ForestMap \rightarrow Bintree(Key, Adr)$ defined as

$$
\begin{aligned}
&\texttt{merge}(\texttt{Leaf}(k, v, adr), forest) = \texttt{Leaf}(k, v) \\
&\texttt{merge}(\texttt{Node}(k, lt, rt, adr), forest) = \texttt{Node}(k, \texttt{merge}(lt, forest), \texttt{merge}(rt, forest)) \\
&\texttt{merge}(\texttt{Proxy}(adr), forest) = forest[adr]
\end{aligned}
$$

which replaces all proxies with the content stored in *forest*. This function is used in the main invariant $\texttt{invMerge}(rtree, forest)$ of component $\texttt{WanderingTree}$ which asserts that, for all clean nodes of *rtree* that store a non-$\texttt{null}$ address adr, the subtree below the node agrees with the tree stored at $forest[adr]$. The invariant is again defined recursively as

$$
\begin{aligned}
\texttt{invMerge}(t, forest) \leftrightarrow \; &(t.\texttt{fadr} \neq \texttt{null} \rightarrow forest[t.\texttt{fadr}] = \texttt{merge}(t, forest)) \\
&\wedge \; (t.\texttt{node?} \rightarrow \texttt{invMerge}(t.\texttt{left}, forest) \wedge \texttt{invMerge}(t.\texttt{right}, forest))
\end{aligned}
$$

It is preserved since new nodes are allocated dirty with $t.\mathtt{fadr} = \mathtt{null}$, so invMerge does not make an assertion for those. Again, only **save#** commits (the top-level node of a) tree t for which $t.\mathtt{fadr} \neq \mathtt{null}$, but for such a node the definition of merge directly computes $forest[t.\mathtt{fadr}]$.

The merge function is also used to define the abstraction relation

$$rpath = path \wedge (empty \leftrightarrow rtree = \mathtt{Proxy(null)})$$
$$\wedge (\neg\, empty \rightarrow tree = \mathtt{merge}(rtree, forest))$$
$$\wedge (bempty \leftrightarrow froot = \mathtt{null}) \wedge (\neg\, bempty \rightarrow backup = forest[froot])$$

which states that the abstract *tree* can be reconstructed by replacing proxies in *rtree*, and that the current flash index *backup* is stored under *froot*.

As one part of the refinement proof, the **load#** program has to be shown to be correct, which modifies the ram index *rtree* by replacing proxy nodes with real nodes (the transition from a) to b) in Fig. 1). Essentially this proof reduces to showing that the result of merge(*rtree*, *forest*) is unchanged by the operation. Similar lemmas have to be proved for the **setDirty#** from Fig. 7 and the **save#** program from Fig. 9, which do the main work in the transitions from b) to c) to d) in Fig. 1.

6.3   Correctness of Flash Representation

The refinement **Flash** $\leq$ **Forest** has to show that the abstract representation of flash memory as a *forest : ForestMap*, which stores whole trees under addresses, can be replaced with a node-based representation as *flash : Map(Adr, FNode)* (see (2) for the definition of type *FNode*). Since the various snapshots of the flash tree now share parts (as can be seen in Fig. 1 d)), we found it convenient to define the abstraction relation absF in terms of the sharing separation operator from Sect. 3.2.

$$\mathtt{absF(Leaf}(key, v), adr) = adr \mapsto \mathtt{FLeaf}(key, v) * \mathtt{true}$$
$$\mathtt{absF(Node}(key, lt, rt), adr) =$$
$$\exists\, ladr, radr.\, (adr \mapsto \mathtt{FNode}(key, ladr, radr)) \circledast \mathtt{absF}(lt, ladr) \circledast \mathtt{absF}(rt, radr)$$

Note that the base case has a "* true" clause that allows the representation to contain extra old data, e.g., the old node A in Fig. 1 d). The full abstraction relation states that the root is unchanged, both maps have the same domain (selected with **dom**) of addresses, and that any tree in *forest* can be reconstructed from the pointer representation:

$$froot = root \wedge \mathbf{dom}(flash) = \mathbf{dom}(forest)$$
$$\wedge \forall\, adr.\, adr \in \mathbf{dom}(forest) \rightarrow \mathtt{absF}(forest[adr], adr)(flash);$$

Since nodes are always added but never deleted on flash memory, using over-lapping conjunction made the proof of this refinement really simple.

7   Conclusion

In this paper we have presented a modular decomposition of the concept of Wandering Trees into 4 components, each consisting of an abstract specification and an implementation. The decomposition allows the verification of the three main verification problems in isolation: correctness of search trees, caching with proxies and dirty nodes, representation as pointer structures.

In particular, most of the problems could be addressed on the abstract level of algebraic trees, keeping verification effort manageable. Overall the effort for the case study was ca. one month to work out the concepts and ca. three months for verification. Our approach could be combined with one of the many techniques to further automate individual component proofs, e.g., [3,8,18,22,27].

Given that we could again (as in [24]) split away a small component that reasons about pointers from the main part, which addresses other correctness issues, increases our confidence that the component decomposition we employ should be usable in many other case studies that use pointer structures to represent abstract data types without having to compromise efficiency.

The final implementation, which composes all implementations (the grey parts of Fig. 3), is purely imperative and does not use any functional data structures like trees but pointer structures only. After inlining calls to subcomponents (as done by our code generator for Scala and C), the code is almost identical to and as efficient as a monolithically programmed version.

Acknowledgement. We would like to thank our student Felix Pribyl who has done a lot of the work presented in this paper as part of his Master thesis.

References

1. Bodenmüller, S., Schellhorn, G., Bitterlich, M., Reif, W.: Flashix: modular verification of a concurrent and crash-safe flash file system. In: Raschke, A., Riccobene, E., Schewe, K.-D. (eds.) Logic, Computation and Rigorous Methods. LNCS, vol. 12750, pp. 239–265. Springer, Cham (2021). https://doi.org/10.1007/978-3-030-76020-5_14

2. Börger, E., Stärk, R.F.: Abstract State Machines. A Method for High-Level System Design and Analysis. Springer, Heidelberg (2003). https://doi.org/10.1007/978-3-642-18216-7

3. Charguéraud, A.: Program verification through characteristic formulae. In: Proceedings of ACM SIGPLAN International Conference on Functional Programming (ICFP), pp. 321–332. Association for Computing Machinery (2010)

4. Derrick, J., Boiten, E.: Refinement in Z and in Object-Z: Foundations and Advanced Applications. FACIT. Springer, London (2001). Second, revised edition 2014

5. Ernst, G., Pfähler, J., Schellhorn, G., Reif, W.: Inside a verified flash file system: transactions and garbage collection. In: Gurfinkel, A., Seshia, S.A. (eds.) VSTTE 2015. LNCS, vol. 9593, pp. 73–93. Springer, Cham (2016). https://doi.org/10.1007/978-3-319-29613-5_5

6. Ernst, G., Pfähler, J., Schellhorn, G., Reif, W.: Modular, crash-safe refinement for ASMs with submachines. Sci. Comput. Program. **131**, 3–21 (2016). Abstract State Machines, Alloy, B, TLA, VDM and Z (ABZ 2014)

7. Ernst, G., Schellhorn, G., Reif, W.: Verification of B^+ trees: an experiment combining shape analysis and interactive theorem proving. In: Barthe, G., Pardo, A., Schneider, G. (eds.) SEFM 2011. LNCS, vol. 7041, pp. 188–203. Springer, Heidelberg (2011). https://doi.org/10.1007/978-3-642-24690-6_14

8. Faella, M., Parlato, G.: Reasoning about data trees using CHCs. In: Shoham, S., Vizel, Y. (eds.) CAV 2022. LNCS, vol. 13372, pp. 249–271. Springer, Cham (2022). https://doi.org/10.1007/978-3-031-13188-2_13

9. Gardner, P.A., Maffeis, S., Smith, G.D.: Towards a program logic for javascript. SIGPLAN Not. **47**(1), 31–44 (2012)

10. Harel, D., Tiuryn, J., Kozen, D.: Dynamic Logic. MIT Press, Cambridge (2000)

11. Havasi, F.: An improved B+ tree for flash file systems. In: Černá, I., et al. (eds.) SOFSEM 2011. LNCS, vol. 6543, pp. 297–307. Springer, Heidelberg (2011). https://doi.org/10.1007/978-3-642-18381-2_25

12. Hobor, A., Villard, J.: The ramifications of sharing in data structures. In: Proceedings of the POPL, New York, NY, USA, pp. 523–536. Association for Computing Machinery (2013)

13. Hunter, A.: A brief introduction to the design of UBIFS (2008). http://www.linux-mtd.infradead.org/doc/ubifs_whitepaper.pdf

14. KIV Proofs for the Correctness of Wandering Trees (2023). https://kiv.isse.de/projects/WanderingTrees.html

15. Krishna, S., Patel, N., Shasha, D., Wies, T.: Verifying concurrent search structure templates. In: Proceedings of the ACM SIGPLAN Conference on Programming Language Design and Implementation, PLDI 2020, pp. 181–196. ACM (2020)

16. Malecha, J.G., Morrisett, G., Shinnar, A., Wisnesky, R.: Toward a verified relational database management system. In: Proceedings POPL 2010, pp. 237–248. ACM (2010)

17. Mündler, N.N., Nipkow, T.: A verified implementation of B^+-trees in Isabelle/HOL. In: Seidl, H., Liu, Z., Pasareanu, C.S. (eds.) Theoretical Aspects of Computing - ICTAC 2022. LNCS, vol. 13572, pp. 324–341. Springer, Cham. (2022). https://doi.org/10.1007/978-3-031-17715-6_21

18. Nipkow, T.: Automatic functional correctness proofs for functional search trees. In: Blanchette, J.C., Merz, S. (eds.) ITP 2016. LNCS, vol. 9807, pp. 307–322. Springer, Cham (2016). https://doi.org/10.1007/978-3-319-43144-4_19

19. O'Hearn, P., Reynolds, J., Yang, H.: Local reasoning about programs that alter data structures. In: Computer Science Logic, 15th International Workshop, pp. 1–19, August 2001

20. Pfähler, J., Ernst, G., Bodenmüller, S., Schellhorn, G., Reif, W.: Modular verification of order-preserving write-back caches. In: Polikarpova, N., Schneider, S. (eds.) IFM 2017. LNCS, vol. 10510, pp. 375–390. Springer, Cham (2017). https://doi.org/10.1007/978-3-319-66845-1_25

21. Pfähler, J., Ernst, G., Schellhorn, G., Haneberg, D., Reif, W.: Formal specification of an erase block management layer for flash memory. In: Bertacco, V., Legay, A. (eds.) HVC 2013. LNCS, vol. 8244, pp. 214–229. Springer, Cham (2013). https://doi.org/10.1007/978-3-319-03077-7_15

22. Reynolds, A., Iosif, R., Serban, C., King, T.: A decision procedure for separation logic in SMT. In: Artho, C., Legay, A., Peled, D. (eds.) ATVA 2016. LNCS, vol. 9938, pp. 244–261. Springer, Cham (2016). https://doi.org/10.1007/978-3-319-46520-3_16

23. Reynolds, J.C.: Separation logic: a logic for shared mutable data structures. In: 17th Annual IEEE Symposium on Logic in Computer Science. Proceedings, pp. 55–74. IEEE (2002)

24. Schellhorn, G., Bodenmüller, S., Bitterlich, M., Reif, W.: Separating separation logic - modular verification of red-black trees. In: Lal, A., Tonetta, S. (eds.) Verified Software – Theories, Tools and Experiments. LNCS, vol. 13800, pp. 129–147. Springer, Cham (2022). https://doi.org/10.1007/978-3-031-25803-9_8

25. Schellhorn, G., Bodenmüller, S., Bitterlich, M., Reif, W.: Software & system verification with KIV. In: Ahrendt, W., Beckert, B., Bubel, R., Johnsen, E.B. (eds.) The Logic of Software: A Tasting Menu of Formal Methods. LNCS, vol. 13360, pp. 408–436. Springer, Cham (2022). https://doi.org/10.1007/978-3-031-08166-8_20

26. Woodcock, J.C.P., Davies, J.: Using Z: Specification, Proof and Refinement. Prentice Hall International Series in Computer Science, London (1996)

27. Zhan, B.: Efficient verification of imperative programs using Auto2. In: Beyer, D., Huisman, M. (eds.) TACAS 2018. LNCS, vol. 10805, pp. 23–40. Springer, Cham (2018). https://doi.org/10.1007/978-3-319-89960-2_2

Verification and Learning

Performance Fuzzing with Reinforcement-Learning and Well-Defined Constraints for the B Method

Jannik Dunkelau$^{(\boxtimes)}$ and Michael Leuschel

Institut Für Informatik, Heinrich-Heine-Universität Düsseldorf, Universitätsstraße 1,
40225 Düsseldorf, Germany
{jannik.dunkelau,michael.leuschel}@hhu.de

Abstract. The B method is a formal method supported by a variety of tools. Those tools, like any complex piece of software, may suffer from performance issues and vulnerabilities, especially for potentially undiscovered, pathological cases. To find such cases and assess their performance impacts within a single tool, we leverage the performance fuzzing algorithm BanditFuzz for the constraint solving backends of the PROB model checker. BanditFuzz utilises two multi-armed bandits to generate and mutate benchmark inputs for the PROB backends in a targeted manner. We describe how we adapted BanditFuzz for the B method, which differences exist to the original implementation for the SMT-LIB standard, and how we ensure well-definedness of the randomly generated benchmarks. Our experiments successfully uncovered performance issues in specific backends and even external tooling, providing valuable insights into areas which required improvement.

Keywords: B method · PROB · Constraint solving · Performance Fuzzing · Reinforcement Learning · Multi-armed bandits

1 Introduction

The B method is a formal method for software [1] and systems development [2] as well as data validation [9]. Specifications are written in the B language, which is rooted in predicate logic, arithmetic and set theory. The B method is based on a correct-by-construction approach and refinement calculus [5,6].

PROB [24,25] is a model checker, animator, and constraint solver for the B method. Its native constraint solver backend makes use of constraint logic programming over finite domains (CLP(FD)) [11], it provides other solver backends to SAT [32] and SMT [35,36]. While existing work already assessed strengths and weaknesses of these backends in a general scope [16], the proposed BanditFuzz approach by Scott et al. [38] for performance fuzzing promises a more targeted generation of examples where the backends' performances differ significantly.

P. Herber and A. Wijs (Eds.): iFM 2023, LNCS 14300, pp. 237–256, 2024.
https://doi.org/10.1007/978-3-031-47705-8_13

The original BanditFuzz [37] finds targeted benchmark examples within the SMT-LIB language [8], trying to increase the performance margin between two sets of solvers. It relies on two reinforcement learning agents which control a fuzzing-generator. This more targeted approach allows achieving pathological inputs for solvers which are concise yet cause significant performance issues and are valuable for finding and debugging edge-cases, as the BanditFuzz case study already proved [37].

In this work, we implement the BanditFuzz algorithms for the B method and apply it to a selection of PROB's constraint solving backends, namely the native CLP(FD) backend (with varying parameters), a translation to Z3 [35], as well as a natively implemented SMT backend based on CDCL(T) [36]. One particular difficulty of applying BanditFuzz to B as opposed to SMT-LIB is the notion of well-definedness, i.e. we have to take care that the fuzzer does not generate predicates whose logical meaning is not well-defined. Our contributions are

- a fuzzer generator for the B method which ensures well-definedness of the generated targets,
- a performance fuzzer based on BanditFuzz for the B method, and
- an evaluation of the applicability of the BanditFuzz algorithm outside the SMT-LIB domain.

The remainder of this paper is organised as follows. Section 2 provides an overview of PROB, performance fuzzing, and Thompson sampling. Section 3 then explains the general workings of the BanditFuzz algorithm while Sect. 4 describes the implementation of the algorithm for PROB and the resulting differences and challenges in contrast to the original SMT-LIB implementation. We summarise our experiments with the implemented performance fuzzer in Sect. 5. Section 6 explores related work concerned with performance fuzzing. We conclude the paper with a discussion of our results in Sects. 7 and 8.

2   Background

2.1   ProB and the B Method

PROB [24,25] is a model checker, animator, and constraint solver for the B method [1]. It is implemented in SICStus Prolog [10,12] and natively makes use of constraint logic programming over finite domains (CLP(FD)) [11]. This constraint solver lies at the heart of PROB. For instance, it is used during model checking for verification of machine invariants and thus responsible for finding specification violations as well as calculating the follow-up states (i.e., animation). The constraint solver is further utilised for symbolic verification, program synthesis [34], or test case generation [23].

The CLP(FD) based constraint solver, further referred to as PROB CLP(FD), works by setting up possible domains for any variable then propagating constraints modelling relationships between those variables, successively reducing said domains. If any domain becomes empty, no satisfying solution can be found.

Otherwise, when propagation terminates, satisfying solutions consist of simply assigning each variable to one of the remaining values within their respective domains.

PROB further provides a translation to the SMT-LIBv2 standard [8] with connection to the Z3 prover [15]. For the connection to Z3, two separate SMT-LIB translations are available. The initial implementation [19] matches B operators with their corresponding counterparts within SMT-LIB where possible. Constructs such as set comprehensions with no direct counterpart are translated as axiomatised formulae containing quantifiers, or are interpreted as forms of set comprehensions [36]. A new more constructive translation [36] uses Z3's lambda functions instead of quantifiers. PROB's Z3 backend runs both translations in parallel and reports the first found solution.

PROB also features a native implementation of conflict driven clause learning modulo theories [28], which we will refer to as PROB CDCL(T) [36]. This was implemented after observing the benefits of the Z3 integration in certain problem domains and solves problems regarding still untranslated or suboptimally translated constructs, as PROB CDCL(T) works natively with B as input languages.

2.2 Performance Fuzzing

Fuzzing was originally proposed by Miller et al. [29] who tested various Unix utility programs with randomly generated input and found inputs to crash 24% of the programs under test (PUT). Nowadays, fuzzing is a well-established technique to expose possible vulnerabilities and malfunctions of a PUT by constructing a fuzz generator that samples inputs which might not reside in the PUT's expected input space [26,27].

Fuzzing algorithms can be distinguished as blackbox or whitebox fuzzing [26]. Blackbox fuzzing considers the PUT as a blackbox and thus has only the observable outputs as feedback. Whitebox fuzzing on the other hand relies on knowledge of internals of the PUT, allowing the algorithm for instance to generate inputs that cover all possible execution paths. We can further differentiate between generation based or mutation based fuzzing [27]. In generation based fuzzing, the fuzzing algorithm randomly creates inputs based on a given model describing the form of expected inputs of the PUT. Mutation based fuzzing does not rely on such a model but rather takes a so called seed-input which it then subsequently mutates.

Performance fuzzing extends the application domain to finding pathological inputs over which the PUT loses performance [14]. While not focused on finding vulnerabilities, the acquisition of small inputs which produce large runtimes still allows to find performance bugs within the PUT [38].

2.3 Thompson Sampling

Thompson sampling [39] is an approach for choosing actions in the multi-armed bandit (MAB) problem [4,33]. In the MAB problem, a slot machine with N independent arms (corresponding to available actions) and time steps $t = 1, 2, 3, \ldots$ are given. Playing an arm at time step t yields a random reward R_t which is sampled from an unknown but fixed distribution. Within T time steps, the goal is to maximise the expected total reward

$$\mathbb{E}\left[\sum_{t=1}^{T} \mu_{i(t)}\right]$$

where $\mu_{i(t)}$ denotes the expected reward for arm i at step t based on previous observations [4]. For Bernoulli distributed rewards, Thompson sampling assumes priors are distributed by the Beta distribution, which has two shape parameters $\alpha > 0$ and $\beta > 0$. These priors are initialised for each arm to be Beta(1, 1), i.e. $\alpha = \beta = 1$ [4]. The algorithm samples N random numbers $\theta_1, \ldots, \theta_N$, one for each arm, from their respective distributions Beta(α_i, β_i) and selects $i(t) = \arg\max_i \theta_i$ as the arm to play next [13]. After observing the resulting reward, the chosen arm's prior distribution is updated in the following way: If the reward was positive, increment α_i, else increment β_i. See Algorithm 1 for a summary of the approach.

Algorithm 1: Thompson Sampling for Bernoulli bandits (adapted from [4,13]).

Require: Arms $i = 1, \ldots, N$ with priors $\alpha_i = 1, \beta_i = 1$
    for all $t \in 1, \ldots, T$ **do**
        For each arm i sample θ_i from Beta(α_i, β_i)
        Play arm $\hat{\imath} = \arg\max_i \theta_i$
        Observe reward $r_t \in \{0, 1\}$
        $\alpha_{\hat{\imath}} \leftarrow \alpha_{\hat{\imath}} + r_t,\ \beta_{\hat{\imath}} \leftarrow \beta_{\hat{\imath}} + (1 - r_t)$
    end for

---

3   The BanditFuzz Algorithm

BanditFuzz is a performance fuzzing algorithm for SMT solvers based on multi-agent reinforcement learning (RL) as proposed by Scott et al. [37,38]. The algorithm is composed of a fuzzing unit as well as two reinforcement learning agents based on Thompson sampling.

    BanditFuzz takes as input a set of target solvers and a set of reference solvers, and produces a new input (benchmark) which maximises the performance margin between the two sets of solvers. The performance margin is hereby measured as the runtime difference between the slowest reference solver and fastest target solver.

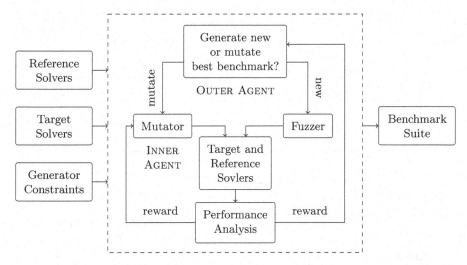

Fig. 1. Overview of the BanditFuzz architecture. Adapted from [38, Fig. 1]. The inner and outer RL agents to control whether to create a new input or how to mutate the current best input. Rewards are played back to the agents after performance analysis, based on whether the performance margin was increased.

BanditFuzz employs two Thompson sampling agents. The first agent (further referred to as inner agent) selects a mutation for the so far best found benchmark. In terms of MAB, the arms correspond to available grammatical language constructs which can be inserted into the given input to mutate it. The insertion happens by replacement of existing constructs to not continuously expand the benchmark's size. The second (outer) agent was introduced in an updated version of BanditFuzz [38] and prevents the inner agent from becoming stuck in local extrema. Its action set consists of either choosing to mutate the best benchmark or to sample a new input via fuzzing. Figure 1 visualises this double-agent architecture.

After selecting a new benchmark, it is passed to each solver from both the reference and the target sets. If the resulting performance margin is now greater than what the previously best benchmark produced, a new best benchmark was found and a positive reward is played back to the agents, otherwise the reward is negative. The implementation contains a hyperparameter $\gamma \in [0, 1]$ which influences the mean decay during reward playback. This changes the Thompson sampling algorithm slightly, as shown in Algorithm 2. Note that α_i and β_i are now starting at 0 and that the distribution formula is changed to Beta($\alpha_i + 1, \beta_i + 1$).

Algorithm 2: Thompson Sampling for Bernoulli bandits with mean decay.

Require: Arms $i = 1, \ldots, N$ with priors $\alpha_i = 0, \beta_i = 0$; decay factor γ
    for all $t \in 1, \ldots, T$ **do**
        For each arm i sample θ_i from $\text{Beta}(\alpha_i + 1, \beta_i + 1)$
        Play arm $\hat{\imath} = \arg\max_i \theta_i$
        Observe reward $r_t \in \{0, 1\}$
        $\alpha_i \leftarrow \gamma\alpha_i + r_t$
        $\beta_i \leftarrow \gamma\beta_i + (1 - r_t)$
    end for

```
(declare-const x Int)
(declare-const y Int)
(assert (= (+ x (* 4 y)) y))
(assert (>= (/ 1 x) 0))
(check-sat)
(get-value (x y))
```

```
x : INTEGER & y : INTEGER
& x + 4*y = y
& 1/x >= 0
```

(a) SMT-LIB   (b) Classical B

Fig. 2. Comparing SMT-LIB code to the respective Classical B formula for the constraint $x, y \in \mathbb{Z} \wedge x + 4y = y \wedge 1/x \geq 0$. The constraint is satisfied for $x = -3y \wedge x > 0$ and undefined for $x = y = 0$.

4   Adapting BanditFuzz for ProB

Implementing BanditFuzz for PROB results in major differences compared to the original implementation by Scott et al. [38]. The most obvious difference are the targeted formalisms, SMT-LIB [8] vs. Classical B [1]. This directly impacts the fuzz generator and mutator as these now have to account for valid B syntax. A direct result is the need to ensure well-definedness of the generated benchmarks as B implements well-definedness constraints over its operators [3,22]. A less apparent distinction is the choice of implementation language. While the original BanditFuzz implementation in Python, the application to PROB in our case renders the use of SICStus Prolog [10] most sensible. This is due to PROB being implemented in SICStus Prolog itself, allowing us to take advantage of already existing tooling such as encoded typing information of available B syntax nodes (encoded as Prolog facts within PROB), PROB's well-definedness checker [22], or direct access to the API of PROB's respective constraint solving backends.

In the following, we summarize our Prolog-based implementation and highlight arising differences to the original BanditFuzz, the entailed challenges, and our solutions in more detail.

4.1   Fuzzing for Classical B Instead of SMT-LIB

SMT-LIB [8] is a popular, standardised input language for SMT solvers and is supported by tools such as Z3 [15], CVC5 [7], Yices 2 [17], or Bitwuzla [30] among others. Syntactically, SMT-LIB has a Lisp-like syntax while B more closely resembles standard mathematical notation. For comparison, Fig. 2 shows the same constraint in both, SMT-LIB and Classical B. As Lisp-dialects already resemble their respective abstract syntax trees (ASTs) and tend to be homoiconic, generating SMT-LIB code can be done in a top-down fashion without much hassle. For achieving the same luxury, and given that PROB is implemented in SICStus Prolog, we opted to write the fuzz generation in Prolog as well. Hence, we fuzz B ASTs directly instead of their textual formula representations.

4.2   Targeted Fuzzing and Mutating

We generate ASTs of B formulae in a top-down manner. Hereby, we ensure that the ASTs are complete trees with respect to a fixed, user specified depth to ensure generation of compact benchmarks. This means each leaf in the tree is at the specified depth counted from the root node. Further, each generated AST's root node is ensured to form a predicate (contrary to an expression which simply evaluates to a single value) which will be sent to the solver sets.

Initially, a random predicate is generated from which the BanditFuzz loop is started. Subsequently, the outer agent selects whether the current benchmark is to be mutated or replaced entirely. On replacement, a random new predicate is generated (and any resulting feedback is only propagated to the outer agent). When the benchmark is to be mutated, the inner agent selects a syntax node which has to be incorporated into the new AST. As B is a strongly typed language, there are two possibilities. First, there exists at least one similarly typed node in the current benchmark already. In that case, one of these nodes is selected at random and replaced by the new one. If possible, sub-nodes are reused. For cases where the new node has a higher arity or demands sub-nodes of different types, new sub-nodes are generated by the fuzzer on demand.

Second, if there exists no node of similar type in the current benchmark, a new AST is fuzzed which is guaranteed to contain the demanded node by first generating a sub-AST with the demanded node as root of size less or equal to the user-specified maximum, then generating parents and siblings until the required maximum height is reached. This approach diverges from the original BanditFuzz which did not guarantee the node selected by the inner agent to be part of the newly generated benchmark in cases where replacement was not possible.

4.3   Well-Defined ASTs

Classical B implements the concept of well-definedness (WD) [3,22]. For instance, the B formula in Fig. 2b is not well-defined as division by zero is possible within the subformula 1/x >= 1. The B method consequently generates the

Table 1. Definition of the expression rewrites by η. Unlisted expressions are not rewritten but left as-is. E, E_1, E_2 are arbitrary expressions, f is an arbitrary function, P is an arbitrary predicate, and $\odot$ is an arbitrary binary operator that is defined over expressions $(+, -, *, \div, \cup, \cap, \ldots)$.

Expression ϕ	$\eta(\phi)$
$E_1 \odot E_2$	$\eta(E_1) \odot \eta(E_2)$
$f(E)$	$f(\eta(E))$
$\mathbb{P}(S)$	$\mathbb{P}(\eta(S))$
$\{x_1, \ldots, x_n \mid P\}$	$\{x_1, \ldots, x_n \mid \tau(P)\}$
$\lambda(x_1, \ldots, x_n).\,(P \mid E)$	$\lambda(x_1, \ldots, x_n).\,(\tau(P) \wedge \mathrm{WD}(\eta(E)) \mid \eta(E))$
$\sum(x_1, \ldots, x_n).\,(P \mid E)$	$\sum(x_1, \ldots, x_n).\,(\mathrm{WD}(\eta(E)) \wedge \tau(P) \mid \eta(E))$
$\prod(x_1, \ldots, x_n).\,(P \mid E)$	$\prod(x_1, \ldots, x_n).\,(\mathrm{WD}(\eta(E)) \wedge \tau(P) \mid \eta(E))$
$\bigcap(x_1, \ldots, x_n).\,(P \mid E)$	$\bigcap(x_1, \ldots, x_n).\,(\mathrm{WD}(\eta(E)) \wedge \tau(P) \mid \eta(E))$
$\bigcup(x_1, \ldots, x_n).\,(P \mid E)$	$\bigcup(x_1, \ldots, x_n).\,(\mathrm{WD}(\eta(E)) \wedge \tau(P) \mid \eta(E))$
IF P THEN E_1 ELSE E_2 END	IF $\tau(P)$ THEN $\eta(E_1)$ ELSE $\eta(E_2)$ END

WD proof obligation $\mathtt{x} \neq 0$. As this proof obligation cannot be discharged, the formula is not well-defined. This contrasts with SMT-LIB's approach of assuming all functions are total. As such, $1/0$ is an integer (but we don't know which one). Hence, for the SMT-LIB model in Fig. 2a, Z3 returns $\mathtt{x} = 0, \mathtt{y} = 0$ as solution. Consequently, when generating random B formulae, we need to account for any WD problems as well.

We ensure well-definedness for fuzzed predicates by introducing non-discharged WD proof obligations (like $\mathtt{x} \neq 0$ above) into the formula. This can be described formally by the means of functions $\tau(\cdot)$ and $\eta(\cdot)$. Hereby, τ is our rewrite operator for B predicates whereas η is the rewrite operator for B expressions. The distinction is important as τ concatenates any WD constraints as conjuncts into the original formula whereas η must not introduce new conjuncts as this would turn the input expression into a predicate which will break typing. Let $\mathrm{WD}(\cdot)$ denote the conjunction of non-discharged WD proof obligations of a predicate or B expression. We define $\eta(\cdot)$ as a function that takes a B expression and rewrites it recursively into well-defined expressions where applicable according to the rules listed in Table 1. This mostly involves expressions which have possibly non-WD predicates as operants. The final function $\tau(\cdot)$ can then be defined over the rewrite rules in Table 2. The helper function η^* hereby rewrites subexpressions within a predicate with η, for instance

$$\eta^*(\mathbb{N} = \{x \mid 1/x > 0\}) \equiv \mathbb{N} = \{x \mid x > 0 \wedge 1/x > 0\}.$$

For the calculation of $\mathrm{WD}(\cdot)$, PROB's internal WD prover is used [22].

During the BanditFuzz loop, we store the raw version of the best benchmark for further mutations, i.e. the version before ensuring well-definedness, while evaluation performances on the WD-enforced predicates. Thus, mutations do

Table 2. Definition of the WD-transformation τ. $P, P_1, \ldots, P_n$ are arbitrary predicates. E, E_1, E_2 are arbitrary expressions. S is an arbitrary set expression. $\Phi(\cdot)$ is an arbitrary predicate that takes an expression as argument. The function η^* rewrites every subexpression within a predicate P with η.

Formula ϕ	$\tau(\phi)$	Note
$\neg P$	$\neg\tau(P)$	
$P_1 \wedge \ldots \wedge P_n$	$\tau(P_1) \wedge \ldots \wedge \tau(P_n)$	
$P_1 \vee \ldots \vee P_n$	$\tau(P_1) \vee \ldots \vee \tau(P_n)$	
$P_1 \Rightarrow P_2$	$\tau(P_1) \Rightarrow \tau(P_2)$	
$P_1 \Leftrightarrow P_2$	$\tau(P_1) \Leftrightarrow \tau(P_2)$	
$\forall X.\,(P_1 \Rightarrow P_2)$	$\forall X.\,(\tau(P_1) \wedge \mathrm{WD}(\eta^*(P_2)) \Rightarrow \tau(P_2))$	X is a list of variables
$\exists X.\,P$	$\exists X.\,\tau(P)$	X is a list of variables
$E_1 = E_2$	$\mathrm{WD}(\eta(E_1)) \wedge \mathrm{WD}(\eta(E_2)) \wedge \eta(E_1) = \eta(E_2)$	$\neq, <, >\leq, \geq$ analogous
$E \in S$	$\mathrm{WD}(\eta(E)) \wedge \mathrm{WD}(\eta(S)) \wedge \eta(E) \in \eta(S)$	$\notin$ analogous
$E \subseteq S$	$\mathrm{WD}(\eta(E)) \wedge \mathrm{WD}(\eta(S)) \wedge \eta(E) \subseteq \eta(S)$	$\subsetneq, \not\subseteq, \not\subsetneq$ analogous

not take place within the WD-ensuring parts of the input and no unnecessary WD-ensuring parts are kept (e.g. when the respective syntax node was replaced).

5 Running the Performance Fuzzer

For evaluation of how well the BanditFuzz approach works for the B method and PROB, we applied our implementation to different combinations of target and reference solvers. These experiments can be split into four categories: fuzzing only, comparing the mentioned PROB backends with another, performance fuzzing different settings for PROB's native backend, and comparing the two existing SMT-LIB translations with Z3.

5.1 Fuzzing only

Employing the fuzzer alone already led to the discovery of multiple issues within the respective solvers. In the case of PROB this helped improve the robustness in the case of corner-cases of well-definedness, in particular involving infinite values and formulas using the new REAL datatype which PROB now supports. Findings include:

– A series of edge cases where PROB raised an internal error and failed to produce an answer:
– Cases where PROB raised a WD error because of missing or faulty treatments in the WD analyser (in particular for certain new REAL operators such as RPOW).
– Cases where PROB raised a WD error even though the input was WD already. This led to improvements in PROB's kernel, e.g., when partitioning a predicate into components and one component is false and an earlier one has a WD error.

We did not find any cases where PROB's default solver produced a wrong answer. Additionally, we were able to consistently generate inputs which caused segmentation faults within the Z3 prover in version 4.12.2.[1] As a consequence, we changed to the Z3 nightly builds henceforth which included the respective fix.

While this highlights the benefit of input fuzzing, it does not relate to the reinforcement learning approach of BanditFuzz. However, it is noteworthy that PROB already employed a fuzzer which was not able to locate these issues before, stressing the impact of using a secondary tool chain. As we implemented a new fuzzer from scratch in this work, we were now able to generate constructs which were apparently not generated before.

5.2   Performance Fuzzing Between ProB's Backends

In the experiments involving backends of PROB presented in Sect. 2.1, we used the following settings. Firstly, the fuzz generator was set to create predicates with 2–4 conjuncts. Each of these conjuncts had a fixed AST size of 3, meaning a path from root to leaf would contain three nodes. Secondly, while PROB has begun supporting reals the support is still experimental and not fully supported by all employed backends. Thus, we did not generate any constraints involving real-valued types during the performance fuzzing (note that reals were still employed during the fuzzing-only stage of our experiments in Sect. 5.1).

Thirdly, we measured the Par2 score for each solver's runtime. It is defined as

$$\text{Par2}(t, r) = \begin{cases} t, & \text{if } r \in \{\text{valid}, \text{invalid}\} \\ t + \delta, & \text{if } r \in \{\text{unknown}, \text{timeout}\} \end{cases}$$

where t is the measured runtime, r is the solver's response, and δ is a fixed timeout value. In all of our experiments, we used $\delta = 2.5$ s, which is PROB's default timeout.

Another point to mention is the use of the B compiler. While not a compiler in the sense of creating machine code, the B compiler transforms a B formula by inlining any variables that it depends upon. The B compiler is essential to create so called "closures" for symbolic B values. That is, given that the variable y has the value 2, the B compiler will translate $\{x \mid x > y + 1\}$ into $\{x \mid x > 3\}$, i.e., inlining the value of y and pre-computing static subexpressions. The result is a symbolic value that can be stored and evaluated without requiring the original state (of y). The B compiler is also used to pre-compute bodies of quantifiers and while loops, and it can be used as an additional pre-processing step before calling a solver. The B compiler is invoked by both, PROB CDCL(T) and the bridge to Z3, as a preprocessing step before the solving process starts. PROB CLP(FD) does, however, not invoke the B compiler by default. This led to the discovery of examples where PROB CDCL(T) seemed to perform better than PROB CLP(FD) solely due to the B compiler being able to reduce the input to

---

[1] Reported in https://github.com/Z3Prover/z3/issues/6734.

btrue (⊤) or bfalse (⊥), respectively. As this does not equate to instances in which the PROB CDCL(T) solver itself performs better, we opted to incorporate the B compiler as additional preprocessing step for PROB CLP(FD) in these experiments. We will refer to the version of PROB CLP(FD) with the B compiler preprocessing as PROB[Compile].

Figure 3 shows a subset of the results produced by the performance fuzzing. Given the timeout of 2.5 s, the Par2 score should be 5 at most per benchmark. We see this does not seem to hold true in Fig. 3a, where the final benchmarks had a Par2 score of around 20 for PROB CDCL(T). This looks like a bug where the timeout does not properly apply during solving, but closer investigation showed the issue to be related to the call_cleanup/2 predicate from the SICStus Prolog standard library.

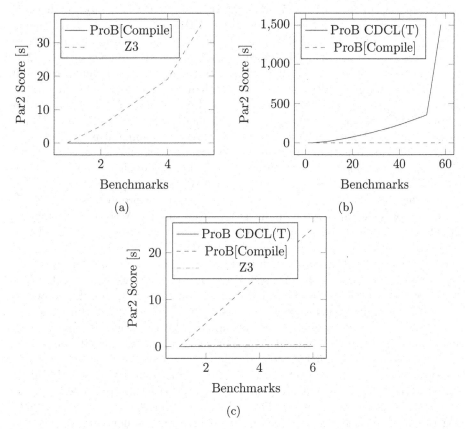

Fig. 3. Selection of performance fuzzing results between PROB[Compile], PROB CDCL(T), and Z3. All benchmarks were found within 18 h. The cactus plots show the accumulated Par2 scores up until the respective benchmarks.

Further findings include an unhandled case for the empty set, where the internal representation was not recognised, leading to a timeout for PROB CLP(FD) while PROB CDCL(T) found a solution in time. We also logged whether there were any contradictions within the solver's responses, namely if one solver reports a solution for a constraint and another saying there exists none. Such soundness bugs where found and fixed for PROB CDCL(T) and Z3. Results reported by PROB CLP(FD) were always found to be correct.

5.3   Performance Fuzzing Between ProB's Settings

While the constraint solving backends use different underlying algorithms, a comparison within one solver under different settings is testing the same algorithm, just with slightly altered behaviour in its processing steps.

We already presented PROB's default setting, PROB CLP(FD). Further settings we looked into are the addition of the CHR solver, and the SMT mode. CHR (constraint handling rules) should speed up the detection of unsolvable predicates at the price of slowing down the solving process in general. The SMT mode instructs PROB to give higher priority to choice points emanating from the logical structure of the formulas, rather than relying mainly on enumeration of data values. E.g., given the predicate $x \in A \land (x \in B \Rightarrow P)$ the enumeration would mainly be driven by $x \in A$ in regular mode, while in SMT mode, PROB would tend to make a case distinction on $\Rightarrow$ before enumerating $x \in A$. The PROB[SMT] mode is typically more suitable for symbolic model checking tasks, while the regular mode works well with animation and explicit model checking. We will refer to both as PROB[CHR] and PROB[SMT], respectively.

Further, PROB offers the option to run a clean-up preprocessing over the input, simplifying parts of the predicate for easier solving. Activating this option should desirably not reduce performance of the solving procedure. We refer to the solver with the enabled clean-up as PROB[CleanUp], which is not to be mistaken for PROB[Compile] which involves a different preprocessing step.

Figure 4 shows the Par2 scores of a selection of the settings experiments. Note the steep increase for PROB[CleanUp] in Fig. 4a from Benchmark 7 onwards where the aforementioned SICStus bug resulted in highly inflated runtimes once again. While we were capable of producing pathological inputs for almost each matchup, it remains to note that the reported benchmarks suffered from reproducibility issues. Rerunning the final benchmarks in a more isolated environment did often not mirror the expected runtime BanditFuzz reported. While this influenced to the SICStus bug, it might also indicate other clean-up problems within the solvers, as we were calling them all from within the same process, making room for shared state between them. If this state is not properly cleaned between calls, residues might accumulate, impacting subsequent performance. Further investigation is needed.

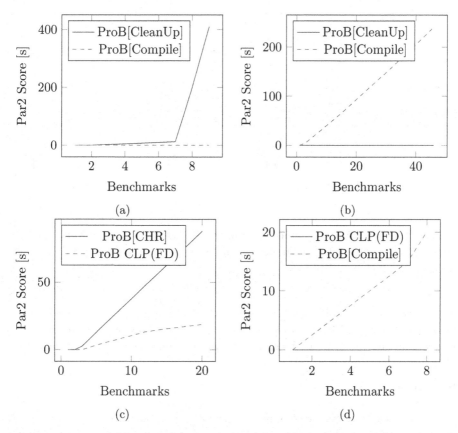

Fig. 4. Selection of performance fuzzing results between different PROB settings. The cactus plots show the accumulated Par2 scores up until the respective benchmarks.

5.4 Performance Fuzzing Between the SMT-LIB Translations

Finally, we applied the performance fuzzing to the two competing SMT-LIB translations described in Sect. 2.1. Recall that the former translation used an approach which translated the B predicates to axiomatised formulae with quantifiers, whereas the newer reimplementation reconstructs B operators by means of Z3's lambda functions. Hence, we will refer to these translations as Z3[Axm] and Z3[Cns], respectively. The solver from previous experiments in Sect. 5.2 simply labelled Z3 most notably made use of both translations in parallel, awaiting and propagating the faster solver's response.

Running this experiment, we quickly found a bug regarding the Z3 backend's clean-up handling during timeouts. As both, a timeout on Prolog side and a timeout within Z3, are employed, the Prolog timeout could end up interrupting

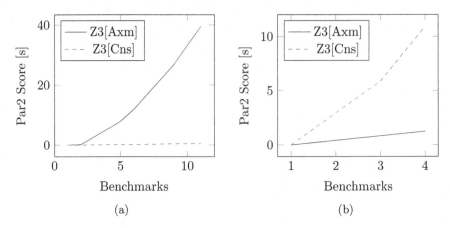

Fig. 5. Selection of performance fuzzing results between Z3[Axm] and Z3[Cns] The cactus plots show the accumulated Par2 scores up until the respective benchmarks.

Z3's internal timeout clean-up, polluting internal state and increasing runtime of subsequent calls. Figure 5 displays that after fixing this bug, we are still able to produce benchmarks in which either translation has the edge over the other.

6   Related Work

The area of performance fuzzing is comparably young but extends prior research of diagnosing performance issues and finding worst-case inputs and algorithmic complexity vulnerabilities in a static way. The first automated approaches were SLOWFUZZ [31] and PERFFUZZ [21], both of which used mutation-based fuzzing in an evolutionary algorithm context.

Other tools quickly made use of reinforcement learning, such as SAFFRON [20] and PySE [18]. SAFFRON takes a user-specified grammar as input and refines it first with respect to found inputs which are not part of the grammar but accepted by the PUT nonetheless. The following generation of pathological inputs over the synthetic grammar then assigns probabilities to the grammar's production rules which represent their likelihood to be chosen for input generation. The final choices are then done by tournament selection until an input with maximum depth is generated. If the input increases the measured performance complexity, the corresponding production rules' probabilities are updated accordingly.

PySE [18] is a tool for automatic worst-case test generation via symbolic execution of a Python program. Here, a Q-Learning [40] approach is utilised to learn a branching heuristic to navigate through the execution paths. This heuristic is gradually updated between subsequent runs of the search for a worst-case execution.

With regard to SMT solvers, one application of performance fuzzing (next to BanditFuzz, see Sect. 3) is SPRFinder [42]. SPRFinder targets solver performance regressions (SPRs) for SMT string solvers by using an adapted version of BanditFuzz which targets newer releases of a string solver and uses old releases as references. Adaptions to the original BanditFuzz include the use of a set of seed inputs instead of using a single one and an adaptive configuration per loop iteration (i.e. if no SPR was found within a number of iterations, the complexity of generated inputs is subsequently increased).

7   Discussion

In this work, we implemented and adapted the BanditFuzz algorithm by Scott et al. [38] to a performance fuzzing procedure for the B method and PROB specifically. In this section, we restate the findings of our performance experiments, talk about issues we experienced during implementation of the algorithm and experiments, and iterate over lessons learned as well as take-aways for future implementation and extensions, which are worth to consider for reimplementation for other tools and formalisms as well.

Performance Fuzzing Results. With the help of performance fuzzing as well as simple input fuzzing, we were able to find a set of performance bugs within PROB's default and alternative solver implementations, as well as more fundamental issues within external tooling these solvers build upon. We found cases in which internal exceptions within PROB were not captured accurately, missing value interpretations regarding empty sets causing timeouts where a solution was otherwise available, soundness issues in the PROB CDCL(T) and Z3 backends, segmentation faults within the Z3 prover itself, issues with state clean-up in the Z3 backend when a timeout fires, and a performance issue within the SICStus Prolog standard library which can inflate the post-cleanup runtime after solver calls in PROB CLP(FD) and PROB CDCL(T).

Size of Benchmarks. While the results make the performance fuzzing approach seem lucrative to employ, we ran into problems during implementation of the fuzz generator and reproduction capabilities of the reported results. Implementation wise, it is straight forward to create a valid B AST that PROB can technically work with, and the BanditFuzz approach promises small and concise, pathological benchmarks. Even though we restricted the size of the initially fuzzed predicates, the addition of the WD constraints in Sect. 4.3, inflated the constraints notably. In the future, a more involved fuzz generation which already accounts for the size of WD constraints during fuzzing might leverage the added complexity of produced benchmarks significantly. As discussed in Sect. 5.3, this can be caused by the found bug in SICStus Prolog regarding `call_cleanup/2` but might indicate another issue regarding subsequent calls to pathological inputs and improper clean-ups. This issue is still to be investigated, but made it harder for us to reliably produce valuable benchmarks.

Issues with Snapshotting and Repeated Benchmarks. Another problem were imprecisions on the millisecond scale. During fuzzing for different PROB settings, we often got results where one solver performed worse in our logs but during reproduction all solvers under test exhibited the same performances. This was due to all solvers varying in runtime over a multiple hundred milliseconds, and BanditFuzz snapshotting instances where the target solver happened to perform worse — even when we already took the mean runtime of three consecutive runs for each solver. A solution might consist of employing a minimal needed improvement over the last performance margin. This would also cancel a set of produced benchmarks which had the same Par2 scores ± 10 ms and only differed slightly while capturing the same underlying issues. This is a particular shortcoming in search for performance bugs: once one is found, due to the mutational nature of the algorithm, slightly varied inputs causing the same bug will be found as well.

Lessons Learned and Future Perspective. We found the BanditFuzz algorithm valuable for generating pathological inputs. In our implementation, we opted to link the performance fuzzer within PROB's source code instead of making it an external tool which uses the compiled executable. Having direct access to the internals of PROB allowed us to find bugs related to post-solving clean-up issues, such as for the Z3 backend or within SICStus Prolog. Any issues related to possibly shared state between two solver calls, i.e. subsequent queries of possibly distinct constraints, can only be caught if the program instance is the same. A draw-back is that the PROB source code is a direct dependency to the performance fuzzer. Hence, it is not possible to target different versions of the same solvers for performance regression testing as done by Zhang et al. [42]. Given that the SICStus Prolog bug we found was only reproducible for us in SICStus Prolog version 4.8.0 but not 4.7.0, the possibility of regression testing would have direct value for us as well and will be considered in the future. In retrospective, we would advise to use an external approach and keep regression testing as an easily implementable option. Implementing an API that allows the performance fuzzer to query the same solver instance subsequently should hereby still allow detection of problems with internal clean-up routines between calls.

The reported difficulty in finding reliable benchmarks targeting the different PROB settings might suggest that the fuzzed predicates were too small. For such cases, we advocate to incorporate an adaptive configuration into the algorithm, for instance as done by Zhang et al. [42]. The adaptive configuration would increase the predicate complexity until significant benchmarks are found, then should ideally aim to reduce the inflated complexity again while maintaining or increasing the performance margin.

While wallclock runtime and Par2 scores seem to be popular metrics for performance fuzzing [14,37,42], other performance related metrics should be accounted for as well [14]. For instance, targeting memory consumption, as done by Wen et al. [41], seems to be a valuable alternative we'd like to incorporate in future work as well.

8   Conclusions

We implemented a fuzzer for the B language which ensures well-definedness on the generated B formulae. We utilised said fuzzer within an adaption of the BanditFuzz performance fuzzing algorithm implemented within the PROB tool. Targeting different constraint solving backends and settings, our experiments successfully unveiled various performance bugs within our tooling as well as external tooling such as the Z3 prover and SICStus Prolog. Our results show that an adaption of BanditFuzz for other formalisms can become a powerful asset in debugging and fine-tuning respective tooling. The aggregated take-aways suggest benefits from implementing the performance fuzzer as an external tool which has no dependency on the version of the program under test, so as to allow regression tests over multiple releases of the program.

Acknowledgements. We want to thank our colleague Joshua Schmidt for his input and ideas regarding more targeted fuzz generation for the PROB CDCL(T) and Z3 backends. Computational support and infrastructure was provided by the "Centre for Information and Media Technology" (ZIM) at the University of Düsseldorf (Germany).

References

1. Abrial, J.R.: The B-book: assigning programs to meanings. Cambridge Univ. Press (1996). https://doi.org/10.1017/CBO9780511624162
2. Abrial, J.R.: Modeling in event-B: system and software engineering. Cambridge Univ. Press (2010). https://doi.org/10.1017/CBO9781139195881
3. Abrial, J.-R., Mussat, L.: On using conditional definitions in formal theories. In: Bert, D., Bowen, J.P., Henson, M.C., Robinson, K. (eds.) ZB 2002. LNCS, vol. 2272, pp. 242–269. Springer, Heidelberg (2002). https://doi.org/10.1007/3-540-45648-1_13
4. Agrawal, S., Goyal, N.: Analysis of Thompson sampling for the multi-armed bandit problem. In: Proceedings of the 25th Annual Conference on Learning Theory. Proceedings of Machine Learning Research, vol. 23, pp. 39.1-39.26. PMLR (2012)
5. Back, R.J.R.: On correct refinement of programs. J. Comput. Syst. Sci. **23**(1), 49–68 (1981). https://doi.org/10.1016/0022-0000(81)90005-2
6. Back, R.J., Wright, J.: Refinement calculus: a systematic introduction. Texts in Computer Science, Springer (2012). https://doi.org/10.1007/978-1-4612-1674-2
7. Barbosa, H., et al.: cvc5: a versatile and industrial-strength SMT solver. In: Fisman, D., Rosu, G. (eds.) Tools and Algorithms for the Construction and Analysis of Systems: 28th International Conference, TACAS 2022, Held as Part of the European Joint Conferences on Theory and Practice of Software, ETAPS 2022, Munich, Germany, April 2–7, 2022, Proceedings, Part I, pp. 415–442. Springer, Cham (2022). https://doi.org/10.1007/978-3-030-99524-9_24
8. Barrett, C., Stump, A., Tinelli, C.: The SMT-LIB standard: Version 2.0. In: Proceedings of the 8th International Workshop on Satisfiability Modulo Theories (Edinburgh, UK) (2010)
9. Butler, M., et al.: The first twenty-five years of industrial use of the B-method. In: ter Beek, M.H., Ničković, D. (eds.) FMICS 2020. LNCS, vol. 12327, pp. 189–209. Springer, Cham (2020). https://doi.org/10.1007/978-3-030-58298-2_8

10. Carlsson, M., Mildner, P.: SICStus prolog-the first 25 years. Theory Pract. Logic Program. **12**(1–2), 35–66 (2012). https://doi.org/10.1017/S1471068411000482
11. Carlsson, M., Ottosson, G., Carlson, B.: An open-ended finite domain constraint solver. In: Glaser, H., Hartel, P., Kuchen, H. (eds.) PLILP 1997. LNCS, vol. 1292, pp. 191–206. Springer, Heidelberg (1997). https://doi.org/10.1007/BFb0033845
12. Carlsson, M., Widen, J., Andersson, J., Andersson, S., Boortz, K., Nilsson, H., Sjöland, T.: SICStus Prolog user's manual, vol. 3. Swedish Institute of Computer Science, Kista, Sweden (1988)
13. Chapelle, O., Li, L.: An empirical evaluation of Thompson sampling. Adv. Neural. Inf. Process. Syst. **24**, 2249–2257 (2011)
14. Chen, Y., Bradbury, M., Suri, N.: Towards effective performance fuzzing. In: 2022 IEEE International Symposium on Software Reliability Engineering Workshops (ISSREW), pp. 128–129 (2022). https://doi.org/10.1109/ISSREW55968.2022.00055
15. de Moura, L., Bjørner, N.: Z3: an efficient SMT solver. In: Ramakrishnan, C.R., Rehof, J. (eds.) TACAS 2008. LNCS, vol. 4963, pp. 337–340. Springer, Heidelberg (2008). https://doi.org/10.1007/978-3-540-78800-3_24
16. Dunkelau, J., Schmidt, J., Leuschel, M.: Analysing PROB's constraint solving backends. In: Raschke, A., Méry, D., Houdek, F. (eds.) ABZ 2020. LNCS, vol. 12071, pp. 107–123. Springer, Cham (2020). https://doi.org/10.1007/978-3-030-48077-6_8
17. Dutertre, B.: Yices 2.2. In: Biere, A., Bloem, R. (eds.) CAV 2014. LNCS, vol. 8559, pp. 737–744. Springer, Cham (2014). https://doi.org/10.1007/978-3-319-08867-9_49
18. Koo, J., Saumya, C., Kulkarni, M., Bagchi, S.: PYSE: automatic worst-case test generation by reinforcement learning. In: 2019 12th IEEE Conference on Software Testing, Validation and Verification (ICST), pp. 136–147 (2019). https://doi.org/10.1109/ICST.2019.00023
19. Krings, S., Leuschel, M.: SMT solvers for validation of B and event-B models. In: Ábrahám, E., Huisman, M. (eds.) IFM 2016. LNCS, vol. 9681, pp. 361–375. Springer, Cham (2016). https://doi.org/10.1007/978-3-319-33693-0_23
20. Le, X.B.D., Pasareanu, C., Padhye, R., Lo, D., Visser, W., Sen, K.: Saffron: adaptive grammar-based fuzzing for worst-case analysis. SIGSOFT Softw. Eng. Notes **44**(4), 14 (2019). https://doi.org/10.1145/3364452.3364455
21. Lemieux, C., Padhye, R., Sen, K., Song, D.: Perffuzz: automatically generating pathological inputs. In: Proceedings of the 27th ACM SIGSOFT International Symposium on Software Testing and Analysis, pp. 254–265 (2018). https://doi.org/10.1145/3213846.3213861
22. Leuschel, M.: Fast and effective well-definedness checking. In: Dongol, B., Troubitsyna, E. (eds.) IFM 2020. LNCS, vol. 12546, pp. 63–81. Springer, Cham (2020). https://doi.org/10.1007/978-3-030-63461-2_4
23. Leuschel, M., Bendisposto, J., Dobrikov, I., Krings, S., Plagge, D.: From animation to data validation: the ProB constraint solver 10 years on. In: Formal Methods Applied to Complex Systems: Implementation of the B Method, chap. 14, pp. 427–446. Wiley ISTE (2014). https://doi.org/10.1002/9781119002727.ch14
24. Leuschel, M., Butler, M.: ProB: a model checker for B. In: Araki, K., Gnesi, S., Mandrioli, D. (eds.) FME 2003. LNCS, vol. 2805, pp. 855–874. Springer, Heidelberg (2003). https://doi.org/10.1007/978-3-540-45236-2_46
25. Leuschel, M., Butler, M.: ProB: an automated analysis toolset for the B method. Int. J. Softw. Tools Technol. Transfer **10**(2), 185–203 (2008). https://doi.org/10.1007/s10009-007-0063-9

26. Liang, H., Pei, X., Jia, X., Shen, W., Zhang, J.: Fuzzing: state of the art. IEEE Trans. Reliab. **67**(3), 1199–1218 (2018). https://doi.org/10.1109/TR.2018.2834476
27. Manès, V.J., Han, H., Han, C., Cha, S.K., Egele, M., Schwartz, E.J., Woo, M.: The art, science, and engineering of fuzzing: a survey. IEEE Trans. Software Eng. **47**(11), 2312–2331 (2021). https://doi.org/10.1109/TSE.2019.2946563
28. Marques-Silva, J., Lynce, I., Malik, S.: Conflict-driven clause learning SAT solvers. In: Handbook of Satisfiability, Frontiers in Artificial Intelligence and Applications, vol. 185, pp. 131–153. IOS press (2009). https://doi.org/10.3233/978-1-58603-929-5-131
29. Miller, B.P., Fredriksen, L., So, B.: An empirical study of the reliability of UNIX utilities. Commun. ACM **33**(12), 32–44 (1990). https://doi.org/10.1145/96267.96279
30. Niemetz, A., Preiner, M.: Bitwuzla at the SMT-COMP 2020. CoRR abs/2006.01621 (2020)
31. Petsios, T., Zhao, J., Keromytis, A.D., Jana, S.: Slowfuzz: automated domain-independent detection of algorithmic complexity vulnerabilities. In: Proceedings of the 2017 ACM SIGSAC Conference on Computer and Communications Security, pp. 2155–2168 (2017). https://doi.org/10.1145/3133956.3134073
32. Plagge, D., Leuschel, M.: Validating B,Z and TLA$^+$ using PROB and Kodkod. In: Giannakopoulou, D., Méry, D. (eds.) FM 2012. LNCS, vol. 7436, pp. 372–386. Springer, Heidelberg (2012). https://doi.org/10.1007/978-3-642-32759-9_31
33. Robbins, H.: Some aspects of the sequential design of experiments. Bull. Am. Math. Soc. **55**, 527–535 (1952)
34. Schmidt, J., Krings, S., Leuschel, M.: Repair and generation of formal models using synthesis. In: Furia, C.A., Winter, K. (eds.) IFM 2018. LNCS, vol. 11023, pp. 346–366. Springer, Cham (2018). https://doi.org/10.1007/978-3-319-98938-9_20
35. Schmidt, J., Leuschel, M.: Improving SMT solver integrations for the validation of B and Event-B Models. In: Lluch Lafuente, A., Mavridou, A. (eds.) FMICS 2021. LNCS, vol. 12863, pp. 107–125. Springer, Cham (2021). https://doi.org/10.1007/978-3-030-85248-1_7
36. Schmidt, J., Leuschel, M.: SMT solving for the validation of B and Event-B models. Int. J. Softw. Tools Technol. Transfer **24**, 1043–1077 (2022). https://doi.org/10.1007/s10009-022-00682-y
37. Scott, J., Mora, F., Ganesh, V.: BanditFuzz: a reinforcement-learning based performance fuzzer for SMT solvers. In: Christakis, M., Polikarpova, N., Duggirala, P.S., Schrammel, P. (eds.) NSV/VSTTE -2020. LNCS, vol. 12549, pp. 68–86. Springer, Cham (2020). https://doi.org/10.1007/978-3-030-63618-0_5
38. Scott, J., Sudula, T., Rehman, H., Mora, F., Ganesh, V.: BanditFuzz: fuzzing SMT solvers with multi-agent reinforcement learning. In: Huisman, M., Păsăreanu, C., Zhan, N. (eds.) FM 2021. LNCS, vol. 13047, pp. 103–121. Springer, Cham (2021). https://doi.org/10.1007/978-3-030-90870-6_6
39. Thompson, W.R.: On the likelihood that one unknown probability exceeds another in view of the evidence of two samples. Biometrika **25**(3–4), 285–294 (1933). https://doi.org/10.1093/biomet/25.3-4.285
40. Watkins, C.J., Dayan, P.: Q-learning. Machine Learn. **8**, 279–292 (1992). https://doi.org/10.1007/BF00992698

41. Wen, C., et al.: Memlock: memory usage guided fuzzing. In: Proceedings of the ACM/IEEE 42nd International Conference on Software Engineering, pp. 765–777. ICSE '20, Association for Computing Machinery (2020). https://doi.org/10.1145/3377811.3380396

42. Zhang, Y., et al.: Demystifying performance regressions in string solvers. IEEE Trans. Software Eng. **49**(3), 947–961 (2023). https://doi.org/10.1109/TSE.2022.3168373

Reinforcement Learning Under Partial Observability Guided by Learned Environment Models

Edi Muškardin[1,2(✉)] 🄳, Martin Tappler[1,2] 🄳, Bernhard K. Aichernig[2] 🄳,
and Ingo Pill[1] 🄳

[1] Silicon Austria Labs, TU Graz - SAL DES Lab, Graz, Austria
[2] Graz University of Technology, Institute of Software Technology, Graz, Austria
edi.muskardin@silicon-austria.com

Abstract. Reinforcement learning and planning under partial observability is notoriously difficult. In this setting, decision-making agents need to perform a sequence of actions with incomplete information about the underlying state of the system. As such, methods that can act in the presence of incomplete state information are of special interest to machine learning, planning, and control communities. In the scope of this paper, we consider environments that behave like a partially observable Markov decision process (POMDP) with known discrete actions, while assuming no knowledge about its structure or transition probabilities.

We propose an approach for reinforcement learning (RL) in such partially observable environments. Our approach combines Q-learning with IoAlergia, an automata learning method that can learn Markov decision processes (MDPs). By learning MDP models of the environment from the experiences of the RL agent, we enable RL in partially observable domains without explicit, additional memory to track previous interactions for dealing with ambiguities stemming from partial observability. We instead provide the RL agent with additional observations in the form of abstract environment states. By simulating new experiences on a learned model we extend the agent's internal state representation, which in turn enables better decision-making in the presence of partial observability. In our evaluation we report on the validity of our approach and its promising performance in comparison to six state-of-the-art deep RL techniques with recurrent neural networks and fixed memory.

Keywords: Reinforcement Learning · Automata Learning · Partially Observable Markov Decision Processes · Markov Decision Processes

1 Introduction

Reinforcement learning (RL) enables the automatic creation of controllers in stochastic environments through exploration guided by rewards. Partial observability presents a challenge to RL, which naturally arises in various control problems. Unreliable or inaccurate sensor readings may provide incomplete state

P. Herber and A. Wijs (Eds.): iFM 2023, LNCS 14300, pp. 257–276, 2024.
https://doi.org/10.1007/978-3-031-47705-8_14

information, e.g., static images provided by visual sensors do not capture the agent's movement trajectory and speed. Formally, partial observability occurs when observations of the environment do not allow to deduce the environment state directly. In such settings, optimal control based on observations only is generally impossible.

For this reason, RL methods often include some form of memory to cope with partial observability, such as the hidden state in recurrent neural networks [12] or fixed-size memory obtained by concatenating previous observations [21]. In this paper, we propose a method for RL in partially observable environments that combines Q-learning [28] with IoAlergia [18], a technique for learning deterministic labeled Markov decision processes (MDPs). With IoAlergia, we regularly learn and update MDPs based on the experiences of the RL agent. The learned MDPs approximate the dynamics of the partially observable Markov decision process (POMDP) underlying the environment and their states extend the observation space of Q-learning. To enable this extension, we trace every step of the RL agent on the most recently learned MDP and add the explored MDP state as an observation. Hence, we provide memory by tracking learned environmental states. With this approach, we follow the tradition of state estimation in RL under partial observability [8,19]. In comparison to earlier work, we overcome strict assumptions on the underlying POMDP, such as knowledge about the number of states, e.g., criticized by Singh et al. [25].

Our contributions comprise: (1) an approach for RL under partial observability aided by automata learning, which we term Q^A-learning. (2) This constitutes of a novel combination of classical RL algorithms with a formal automata inference technique, (3) an implementation of the approach in an environment conforming to the OpenAI gym interface [2], and (4) its evaluation against three baseline deep RL methods with fixed memory and three RL methods with LSTMs providing memory.

Structure. In Sect. 2, we introduce preliminaries like passive learning of stochastic automata. We present our method for reinforcement learning in partially observable environments in Sect. 3, followed by a corresponding evaluation in Sect. 4. After discussing related work in Sect. 5, we conclude by summarizing our findings and providing an outlook on future work in Sect. 6.

Demonstrating Example. In Fig. 1, we show on the left an example of a fully observable environment and a partially observable counterpart on the right. For both, the agent's aim is to navigate through the rooms and reach the cookie. In the fully observable variant, the agent is aware of its position in the form of a tuple (x, y) of coordinates, with the top left corner being the origin $(0, 0)$. From each position the agent can move in all four directions (top, right, down, left), and such a chosen action stochastically succeeds as expected or not. So the intuitive action sequence to reach the cookie in $(4, 3)$ from the initial position $(4, 1)$ would be the sequence ⟨left, left, left, down, down, down, right, right, right, up⟩. Since the agent, however, perceives its new position, this case can be seen as a fully observable MDP with a known structure but unknown (stochastic) transition

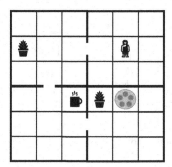 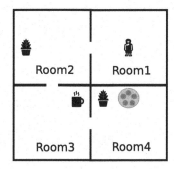

Fig. 1. Fully and partially observable slippery *OfficeWorld.* With full observations (left), the agent can observe *(x,y)* coordinates, while with the partial observability (right) it can observe only the room number. The agent may slip in some locations, changing the target position of a move.

probabilities. The agent can also always re-evaluate and re-plan, due to being aware of the exact position after each action. In the partially observable scenario on the right, the agent only knows in which room it is currently in (but not in which of the nine positions if compared to the other variant). Consequently, the agent can neither infer its exact position nor the appropriate action just from this observation. It could count, for example, though how often it moved in a certain direction in order to enable an educated guess (it would still be a guess due to the stochastic success of actions). In order to enable RL in such an environment, we propose to learn an abstract stochastic model for the environment, such as to capture unobservable state information.

2   Preliminaries

2.1   Models

In RL, we commonly assume that the environment behaves like an MDP (see Definition 1). An agent observes the environment's state and based on that reacts by choosing from a given set of actions—causing a probabilistic state transition.

Definition 1 (Markov decision processes (MDPs)). *A Markov decision process (MDP) is a tuple $\mathcal{M} = (S, s_0, A, \delta)$, where S is a finite set of states, $s_0 \in S$ is the initial state, A is a finite set of actions, $\delta : S \times A \to Dist(S)$ is a probabilistic transition function.*

Please note that for a simplified presentation, we assume MDPs to support all actions in all states, s.t. δ is total. In our work, we consider settings where the agent cannot observe the environment directly, but where it has only limited information—like a room's number, but not its position in the room (see Fig. 1) —and where we assume discrete states as well as finite action and state spaces. Such scenarios are commonly modeled as partially observable Markov decision processes (POMDPs) (Definition 2), see, e.g., Bork et al. [1]. Alternative POMDP definitions including probabilistic observation functions can also be handled [7].

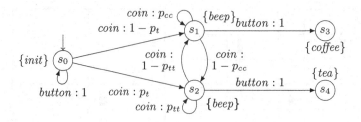

Fig. 2. A POMDP producing hot beverages.

Definition 2 (Partially observable Markov decision processes). *A partially observable Markov decision process (POMDP) is a triple* $(\mathcal{M}, Z, O)$, *where* $\mathcal{M} = (S, s_0, A, \delta)$ *is the underlying MDP,* Z *is a finite set of observations and* $O : S \to Z$ *is the observation function.*

Example 1 (Hot Beverage POMDP). Figure 2 shows a POMDP of a vending machine that, depending on parameterized probabilities, produces either tea or coffee. For the individual states s_i, we show the respective observation in curly braces. For each probabilistic transition reported (for brevity we ommit the transitions from s_3 and s_4, but they would loop back to s_0 for any action) we show a corresponding edge, labeled by the action and the transition's probability. While the parameterized probabilities will become more important later on, let us for now assume $p_t = 0.5$, $p_{cc} = 0.9$, and $p_{tt} = 0.1$. In the initial state s_0, for the action *coin*, we would now progress to *either* s_1 *or* s_2, but where the resulting observation would be *beep* for both. Pressing a *button*, we would then move to s_3 or s_4 receiving either a *coffee* or *tea*. Alternatively, we can add another *coin* to move to s_1 with a probability of 0.9 for increasing the chances to get a *coffee*.

Paths, Traces & Policies. The interaction of an agent with its environment can be described by a *path* that is defined by an alternating sequence of states and actions $s_0 \cdot a_1 \cdot s_1, \cdots, s_n$ starting in the initial state. We denote the set of paths in an MDP $\mathcal{M}$ by $Paths_{\mathcal{M}}$. For partially observable scenarios, *traces* basically replace the states in a path with the corresponding observations. We correspondingly lift observation functions O to paths, applying O on every state to derive trace $O(p) = O(s_0) \cdot a_1 \cdot O(s_1)$ from path $p = s_0 \cdot a_1 \cdot s_1$. An agent selects actions based on a *policy* that is a mapping from $Paths_{\mathcal{M}}$ to distributions over actions $Dist(A)$. If a policy σ depends only on the current state, we say that σ is memoryless. With policies relating to action choices, an MDP controlled by a policy defines a probability distribution over paths.

Rewards define the crucial feedback an agent needs during learning for judging whether the actions it chose were "good or bad". That is, the goal is to learn a policy that maximizes the reward. To this end, we consider a reward function $R : S \to \mathbb{R}$ that returns a real value[1]. For a path $p =$

---

[1] Alternative definitions including actions are possible as well.

$s_0 \cdot a_1 \cdot s_1, \cdots, s_n$, we can define a discounted cumulative reward at time step t as $Ret(p,t) = \sum_{i=0}^{n-t-1} \gamma^i R(s_{t+i+1})$, taking a (time) discount factor γ into account. For a memoryless policy σ, we can define a value function for a state s as $v_\sigma(s) = \mathbb{E}_\sigma [Ret(p,t) \mid s_t = s]$. To accommodate partial observability, we define reward-observation traces that extend traces with rewards, e.g., $rt = RO(p) = O(s_0) \cdot R(s_0) \cdot a_1 \cdot O(s_1) \cdot R(s_1), \cdots, O(s_n) \cdot R(s_n)$ for path $p = s_0 \cdot a_1 \cdot s_1, \cdots, s_n$.

Note that in RL, we usually consider memoryless policies—enabled by the assumption of a Markovian environment (modeled as MDP) which guarantees that there is an optimal, memoryless policy for maximizing the reward. With partial observability it is impossible to precisely identify the current state (consider the Hot Beverage example and $s1$ vs. $s2$), meaning that creating optimal policies for POMDPs entails taking the history of previous actions into account—rendering the problem non-Markovian. Alternatively, deriving policies under partial observability can be approached by creating belief-MDPs from POMDPs [6].

Belief-MDPs & Deterministic Labeled MDPs. Deterministic Labeled MDPs (DLMDPs) feature an observation function and adhere to a specific determinism property that guarantees that any possible (observation) trace reaches exactly one state. Belief MDPs (BMDPs) are special DLMDPs that represent the dynamics of a POMDP and are defined over so-called belief states. These belief states (beliefs for short) describe probability distributions over states in a POMDP, i.e., over those states that the paths relating to a trace would reach in the POMDP. That is, for any given trace, a BMDP progresses to a unique state that in turn defines a distribution over possible POMDP states.

Definition 3 (Deterministic Labeled MDPs). *A deterministic labeled MDP is a triple $(\mathcal{M}, Z, O)$, where $\mathcal{M} = (S, s_0, A, \delta)$ is the underlying MDP, Z is a set of observations, and O is an observation function, satisfying*

$$\forall s, s', s'' \in S, \forall a \in A: \delta(s,a,s') > 0 \wedge \delta(s,a,s'') > 0 \wedge O(s') = O(s'')$$
$$\implies s' = s''.$$

We introduce BMDPs with some auxiliary definitions: Let $P = (\mathcal{M}, Z, O)$ be a POMDP over an MDP $\mathcal{M} = (S, s_0, A, \delta)$. This defines the beliefs as the set $B = \{\mathbf{b} \in Dist(S) | \forall s, s' \in supp(\mathbf{b}) : O(s) = O(s')\}$, where $supp()$ returns the support of a probability distribution. Then the probability of observing $z \in Z$ after executing $a \in A$ in $s \in S$ is defined as $\mathbf{P}(s,a,z) = \sum_{s' \in S, O(s')=z} \delta(s,a,s')$ and in a belief (state) $\mathbf{b}$ it is $\mathbf{P}(\mathbf{b},a,z) = \sum_{s \in S} \mathbf{b}(s) \cdot \mathbf{P}(s,a,z)$. If $O(s') = z$, the subsequent belief update is defined as $[\![\mathbf{b}|a,z]\!](s') = \frac{\sum_{s \in S} \mathbf{b}(s) \cdot \delta(s,a,s')}{\mathbf{P}(\mathbf{b},a,z)}$.

Definition 4 (Belief MDPs). *The BMDP for a POMDP P as of Definition 2 is a DLMDP $(\mathcal{M}_B, Z, O_B)$ over an MDP $\mathcal{M}_B = (B, s_{0B}, A, \delta_B)$, with B as defined above, $s_{0B} = \{s_0 \mapsto 1\}$, $O_B(\mathbf{b}) = O(s)$ for an $s \in supp(\mathbf{b})$, and*

$$\delta_B(\mathbf{b}, a, \mathbf{b}') = \begin{cases} \mathbf{P}(\mathbf{b}, a, O(\mathbf{b}')) & \textit{if } \mathbf{b}' = [\![\mathbf{b}|a, O(\mathbf{b}')]\!], \\ 0 & \textit{otherwise.} \end{cases}$$

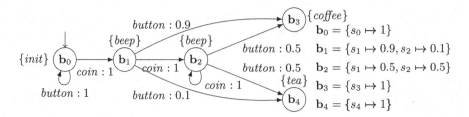

Fig. 3. A finite BMDP for the POMDP from Fig. 2 and parameters $p_t = 0.1$ and $p_{tt} = p_{cc} = 0.5$. For brevity reasons, we do not show transitions from b_3 and b_4.

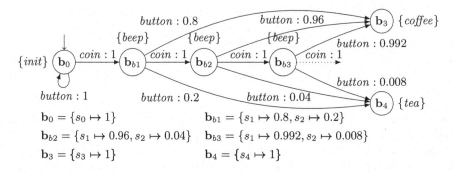

Fig. 4. An infinite BMDP for the POMDP from Fig. 2 for parameters $p_t = 0.2$, $p_{tt} = 0.2$, and $p_{cc} = 1$. For brevity reasons, we do not show transitions from b_3 and b_4.

BMDPs allow to synthesize policies under partial observability, i.e., it was shown that an optimal policy for a BMDP is optimal also for the corresponding POMDP [6]. Since they are Markovian, there are furthermore methods for synthesizing memoryless policies. Please note that while in principle there are finite BMDPs (e.g., Fig. 3), in general they are of infinite size [1] (see, e.g., Fig. 4).

Example 2 (Hot Beverage BMDPs). Let us consider again the POMDP from Fig. 2 and parameters $p_t = 0.1$ and $p_{tt} = p_{cc} = 0.5$. The corresponding finite BMDP is shown in Fig. 3. Now suppose that we get a reward for observing *tea*, i.e., when reaching b_4. The BMDP then supports a memoryless policy where we choose the actions *coin* in $\mathbf{b}_0$ and $\mathbf{b}_1$, and *button* in $\mathbf{b}_2$. That is, unless γ is very small (like 0) s.t. choosing *button* in $\mathbf{b}_1$ would be optimal for maximizing the immediate reward. A second, infinite BMDP for parameters $p_t = 0.2$, $p_{tt} = 0.2$ and $p_{cc} = 1$ is shown in Fig. 4.

2.2   Learning MDPs

We learn MDPs using the IoAlergia algorithm [18]. The algorithm has been originally proposed for the verification of reactive systems [17]. In our work we demonstrate its applicability for learning of RL environments.

IOALERGIA takes samples $\mathcal{T}$, which is a multiset of traces, and an ϵ_{AL} controlling the significance level of a statistical check as inputs and returns a deterministic labelled MDP.

The algorithm first creates an input/output frequency prefix tree acceptor (IOFPTA) from $\mathcal{T}$, a tree where common prefixes of traces are merged. Every node of the tree is labeled with an observation and every edge is labeled with input and a frequency. The frequency denotes the multiplicity of the trace prefix in $\mathcal{T}$ that corresponds to the path from the root node to the edge. After creating a tree, IOALERGIA creates an MDP by merging nodes that are *compatible* and promoting nodes to MDP states that are not compatible with other states. Initially, the root node is promoted to be the initial MDP state and labeled *red*. Then, the algorithm performs a loop comprising the following steps. All immediate successors of red states are labeled *blue*. A blue node b is selected and checked for compatibility with all red states. If there is a compatible red state r, b and r are merged and the subtree originating in b is folded into the currently created MDP. Otherwise, b is labeled red, thus being promoted to an MDP state. The loop terminates when there are only red states.

Nodes b and r are compatible if their observation labels are the same and the probability distributions of future observations conditioned on actions are not statistically different. The latter check is also performed recursively on all successors of b and r. The statistical difference is based on Hoeffding bounds [14], where a parameter ϵ_{AL} controls significance.

A data-dependent ϵ_{AL} guarantees convergence in the limit to an MDP isomorphic to the canonical MDP underlying the distribution of traces. For finite sample sizes, we can use ϵ_{AL} to influence the MDP size. For more information, we refer to Mao et al [18].

3 Q^A-Learning: RL Assisted by Automata Learning

In this section, we present Q^A-learning, an approach for reinforcement learning under partial observability. First, we describe the setting and the general intuition behind the approach. Then, we present the state space perceived by the learning agent, followed by a presentation of the complete approach.

3.1   Overview

Setting. We consider reinforcement learning in partially observable environments. That is, we assume that the environment behaves like a POMDP, where we cannot observe the state directly. Moreover, we do not assume to have a POMDP model of the environment. Initially we only know the available actions and as we learn, we learn more about the available observations and the environment dynamics and refine our policy.

Interface. We formalize the setting via an interface comprising two operations through which the RL agent interacts with the environment: (1) **reset** and (2) **step**. Following the conventions of OpenAI gym [2], the **reset** operation resets the environment into its initial state. The **step** operation takes an action as input, performs the actions, which changes the environment state, and returns the immediate reward, a Boolean flag *done*, and the observation in the new state. The flag *done* indicates whether a goal state was reached.

Execution & Traces. The agent learns in episodes, where it traverses a finite path in each episode. We want to note again that the agent cannot see the state that it visited. Each executed path yields a finite reward-observation trace rt consisting of observations, immediate rewards, and the performed actions. We store these reward-observation traces in a multiset $\mathcal{RT}$.

3.2   Extended State Space

The Q-table in Q-learning is a function $Q : S \times A \to \mathbb{R}$, where S are the observable states of the environment. Since we only observe observations from a set Z, we cannot use this function definition directly. As individual observations are insufficient to facilitate learning, we extend the observation space with states of a learned MDP leading to an extended state space. Suppose we are in episode i, we combine Z with the states of the last labeled MDP $(\mathcal{M}_i, Z, O_i)$, with $\mathcal{M}_i = (S_i, s_{0i}, A, \delta_i)$, learned via IOALERGIA. During training, we continuously simulate the observation traces perceived by the RL agent on the learned automaton and use the visited states from S_i as additional observations. Since a learned MDP may not define transitions for all action-observation pairs, we represent the current state of $\mathcal{M}_i$ as a pair $(s, d) \in S_i \times \{\top, \bot\}$, where the first element encodes the last visited state of $\mathcal{M}_i$ and the second element denotes whether the simulation encountered an undefined transition. To work with these state pairs, we define two functions, where for $a \in A$ and $o \in O$:

$$resetToInitial() = (s_{0i}, \top)$$

$$stepTo((s, d), a, o) = \begin{cases} (s', \top) & \text{if } d = \top \wedge \delta_i(s, a)(s') > 0 \wedge O_i(s') = o \\ (s, \bot) & \text{otherwise} \end{cases}$$

The extended state space uses these state pairs, i.e., the Q-function is defined as $Q : S_i^e \times A \to \mathbb{R}$ with $S_i^e = O \times S_i \times \{\top, \bot\}$. Due to $\mathcal{M}_i$ being deterministic, s' in the above definition is either uniquely defined or not defined at all, denoted by $\bot$. Once we reach undefined behavior, we remember the last visited state and leave it unchanged. The intuition is that when behavior is encountered after reaching some $(s, \bot)$ is important for RL performance, due to achieving high reward, this will be reflected in updates of the Q-function. As a result, learning will be directed towards s. This leads to more sampling in the vicinity of s s.t. subsequently learned MDPs are more accurate in this region. Consequently, previously undefined behavior will eventually become defined in the learned MDP.

Note that in the current version of the algorithm, rewards are not included in the observation space, as the Q-learning serves to keep track of future rewards, whereas IOALERGIA keeps track of the structure of the environment. This separation of concerns helps to keep the size of learned MDPs small. The learned

MDP states can be viewed as state estimators employed in other RL approaches in partially observable environments [3]. Carr et al. [3] rely on state estimation that yields belief supports, i.e., they estimate the currently possible environment states but abstract away the concrete state probabilities as they assume no knowledge about transition probabilities. In contrast to that, we learn transition probabilities and our discrete states include information on the probability of being in a particular environment state. However, these probabilities are only implicitly available to the RL agent, as the concrete states are not observable. To illustrate this, consider the BMDP shown in Fig. 4. IOALERGIA may learn an MDP with the six states shown in the figure. Hence, the agent can distinguish the states reached after one, two, and three *coin* input, respectively. A state estimator that solely estimates belief support would not be able to distinguish these states, since the beliefs $\mathbf{b}_{b1}$, $\mathbf{b}_{b2}$, and $\mathbf{b}_{b3}$ all have the same support.

3.3 Partially Observable Q-Learning

We apply tabular, ϵ-greedy Q-learning [28] combined with MDP learning. Deterministic labeled MDPs learned by IOALERGIA provide the Q-learning agent with additional information in order to make the learning problem Markovian despite partial observability.

We regularly learn new MDPs via IOALERGIA from the growing sample of reward-observation traces, where we discard the rewards, so that at each episode i there is an approximate MDP $\mathcal{M}_i$ with states S_i. To take information from $\mathcal{M}_i$ into account during RL, we extend the Q-table with observations corresponding to the states S_i. At every step performing action a and observing o during RL, we simulate the step in $\mathcal{M}_i$. This yields a unique state in S_i due to $\mathcal{M}_i$ being deterministic, which we feed to the RL agent as an additional observation.

We actually perform two stages of learning. First, we perform Q-learning while regularly updating $\mathcal{M}_i$. In the second stage, we fix the final MDP $\mathcal{M}_i$, referred to *freezing* below, and perform Q-learning without learning new MDPs with IOALERGIA. We term the resulting learning approach Q^A-learning.

Algorithm 1 implements this learning approach, i.e., training of a Q^A-learning agent. For a more detailed view of the training algorithm and agent parameterization, we point an interested reader to the implementation[2].

Algorithm 1 assumes that the Q^A-learning agent interacts with the environment *env* as described in Section. 3.1. The parameter *maxEp* defines the maximum number of training episodes. The other parameter *updateInterval* defines how often the agent recomputes the model, thus extending the state space perceived by the learning agent and the Q-table.

Lines 1-2 initialize the extended state space and set the actions of the agent to those of the environment. For the state-space initialization, we assume an initial approximate MDP to be given. In our implementation, we learn such an MDP from a small number of randomly generated traces. Alternatively, the extended state space S_E can be initialized to the observation space of the environment.

---

[2] https://github.com/DES-Lab/Q-learning-under-Partial-Observability.

Algorithm 1. Algorithm implementing Q^A-learning

Input: reinforcement learning environment *env*, fully configured partially observable agent *agent*, update interval *updateInterval*, number of training episodes *maxEp*

Output: trained *agent* implementing the policy for the *env*

1: $agent.S_E \leftarrow env.O \times agent.model.states \times \{\top, \bot\}$ ▷ Init. extended state space
2: $agent.A \leftarrow env.A$ ▷ Get action state space from *env*
3: $agent.Q(s,a) = 0, \forall s \in S_E, a \in A$ ▷ Initialize the Q-table
4: $\mathcal{RT} \leftarrow \{\}$ ▷ Multiset of traces
5: **for** $trainingEpisode \leftarrow 0$ **to** $maxExp$ **do**
6:     $initialObs, initialRew \leftarrow env.reset()$
7:     $rt \leftarrow \langle initialObs, initialRew \rangle$ ▷ Trace of a single episode
8:     $agentState \leftarrow agent.model.resetToInitial()$
9:     $epDone \leftarrow False$
10:     **while not** $epDone$ **do**
11:          ▷ Select an action using ϵ-greedy policy and extended state space
12:        $act \leftarrow agent.getAction(agent.state)$
13:          ▷ Record all observed (state, action,reward, newState) pairs
14:        $obs, reward, done, newObs \leftarrow env.step(act)$
15:        $agentState \leftarrow agent.model.stepTo(agentState, act, newObs)$
16:        $updateQValues(agent, obs, act, reward, newObs)$
17:        $rt \leftarrow rt \cdot \langle act, reward, newObs \rangle$
18:     $\mathcal{RT} \leftarrow \mathcal{RT} \uplus rt$
19:     **if** $trainingEpisode \geq agent.freezeAutomaton$ **then**   ▷ Freeze automaton
20:        **continue**
21:     **if** $trainingEpisode$ **mod** $updateInterval = 0$ **then**
22:        $agent.model \leftarrow runIOAlergia(\mathcal{RT})$ ▷ Learn the new environment model
23:        $agent.S_E \leftarrow agent.S_{Init} \times agent.model.states \times \{\top, \bot\}$
24:        $agent.Q(s,a) = 0, \forall s \in S_E, a \in A$ ▷ Reinitialize the extended Q-table
25:        **for** $episode \in \mathcal{RT}$ **do**
26:           $agentState \leftarrow agent.model.resetToInitial()$
27:           **for** $obs, action, reward, newObs \in episode$ **do**
28:              $agentState \leftarrow agent.model.stepTo(agentState, act, newObs)$
29:              $updateQValues(agent, obs, action, reward, newObs)$

30: **return** *agent*

It will in any case be extended as the algorithm progresses. Line 3 initializes the Q-table with the initial observation space and action space.

Training progresses until the maximum number of episodes is reached. In the implementation, we have added an early stopping criterion to end the training as soon as the agent achieves satisfactory performance on a predefined number of test episodes. Lines 5-17 show the steps taken in a single training episode. At the beginning of each episode, the environment and the agent's internal state are reset to their initial states (Lines 6 and 8). Until an episode terminates, either by reaching a goal or exceeding the maximum number of allowed steps, the Q^A-learning agent selects an action using an ϵ-greedy policy and executes it in the environment (Lines 12-14). Based on the selected action *act* and received observation *newObs*, the agent updates its current model state by tracing the pair *(act, newObs)* in the learned MDP (Line 15). cAfter performing a step, the agent updates the values in the Q-tables based on observations and received reward. Algorithm 2 describes the process of updating Q-values. It follows the same procedure as in standard Q-learning with the notable difference of using a state space extended with learned MDP states instead of the observation space of the environment. The extended state space is discussed in more detail in Sect. 3.2

In Line 19, we check whether the automaton should be *frozen*. Freezing of the automaton prevents further updates of the model and extensions of the state space. This way once the automaton is frozen, the Q-table will continue to be optimized with respect to the current extended state space. Automaton freezing operates under the assumption that once a model is computed that is "good enough", computing a new model in the next update interval is unnecessary and might even be detrimental to the performance of the agent (in the short term).

If the automaton freezing is not enabled or its episode threshold has not yet been reached, we proceed with the update of the model and the Q-table (Lines 22-24). This update happens every *updateInterval* episodes. IOALERGIA computes a new model that conforms to the sample $\mathcal{RT}$ with rewards discarded. In Line 23 we extend the state space with state identifiers of the learned model. After that, we recompute the Q-table by initializing it with the extended state space and action space (Line 24). To recompute the values in the extended Q-table we perform an experience replay [10] with all traces in $\mathcal{RT}$ (Lines 25-29).

Example. We use a simple *OfficeWorld* example to demonstrate state extension. In this example, an agent selects one of four actions: {*up, down, left, right*} to move into the given direction. The agent may also slip into a different direction with a location-specific probability.

Whereas [15,23] use *OfficeWorld* in a non-Markovian reward setting under full observability, we modify the *OfficeWorld* layout as shown in Fig. 1 to introduce partial observability. On the right-hand side of Fig. 1, abstraction is applied over the state space. The reinforcement learning agent can only observe in which room he is located, but not the x and y coordinates, which would truly identify a Markov state. Note that each observation, e.g. *Room1*, is shared by nine different POMDP states identified by their x, y coordinates, each with different future and stochastic behavior.

Table 1 shows a Q-table obtained from observations only. The Q-values indicate that the Q-learning agent is unable to find optimal actions due to partial observability. Table 2 shows an extended Q-table, but we do not include the definedness flag from {$\top, \bot$} for brevity. Each observation is extended with a learned MDP state as discussed in Sect. 3.2. We observe that each *(observation, state)* pair approximates the underlying BMDP to such an extend that every such pair has a clear optimal action defined by the Q-values. For example, in states *(Room1, s0)* and *(Room1, s1)* the agent needs to perform a *left* action,

Algorithm 2. Algorithm implementing update of Q-values of the agent.

Input: Q^A-learning *agent*, environment *state*, *reward*, reached environment *newState*
1: *extendedNewState ← agent.model.stepTo(action, newState)*
2: *oldValue ← agent.q(extendedState, action)*
3: *maxNextStateValue ← max(agent.Q(extendedNewState))*
4: *agent.Q(extendedState, action) ← (1 − α) * oldValue + α * (reward + γ * maxNextStateValue)*

---

whereas in state *(Room1, s3)* the agent needs to move *up*. We can also observe that the Q-values of the state *(Room2, s0)* are set to zero. This results from *s0* being unreachable while observing *Room2*.

3.4 Convergence

Q^A-learning learns an optimal policy in the limit, when the number of episodes tends to infinity, if the BMDP of the POMDP environment is finite, but when the BMDP is not finite and for finite sample sizes, we cannot guarantee convergence.

Finite BMDPs. Convergence for finite BMDPs follows from the convergence of IoALERGIA and Q-learning. We sample traces from a POMDP that, by assumption, is equivalent to a finite BMDP. The BMDP itself is a deterministic labeled MDP. IoALERGIA in the limit learns an MDP isomorphic to the canonical deterministic labeled MDP producing the traces when every action always has a non-zero probability to be executed, as has been shown by Mao et al. [18]. That is, every pair of belief-state and action would be explored infinitely often in the limit. This also ensures convergence of Q-learning in a Markovian environment [28]. The environment is Markovian once we learned the BMDP and add its current state to the observations of the Q-learning agent. Hence, we will learn an optimal policy for the BMDP and thus the POMDP in the limit.

Table 1. Non-extended Q-table.

State\Action	Up	Down	Left	Right
Room1	−0.35	−0.35	−0.45	−0.39
Room2	−0.67	−0.67	−0.32	−0.66
Room3	4.68	4.65	5.21	5.25
Room4	24.72	24.45	23.26	24.79

Table 2. Extended Q-table.

State\Action	Up	Down	Left	Right
(Room1, s0)	−0.35	−0.35	0.75	−0.39
(Room1, s1)	−0.33	−0.35	0.90	−0.36
(Room1, s2)	−0.31	−0.31	1.06	−0.30
(Room1, s3)	0.4	−0.41	0.06	−0.35
...				
(Room2, s0)	0	0	0	0
(Room2, s5)	−0.67	1.23	1.07	−0.66
(Room2, s6)	−0.67	1.42	0.4	−0.66
...				
(Room4, s10)	97.3	74.1	78.2	93.8
(Room4, s11)	97.9	74.7	78.8	92.1
(Room5, s12)	98.3	75.2	79.2	95.3
...				

Infinite BMDPs. We learn a finite-state approximation of the infinite BMDP. For instance, in the example shown in Fig. 4, we might learn the three belief states labeled with *beep*, but beyond that the probability of observing *tea* is likely too small to detect additional states. As we will demonstrate in the evaluation, such approximate MDPs encode sufficient information to aid reinforcement learning. The learned automaton and its states can be thought of as providing memory to the reinforcement learning agent.

3.5 Generalization and Limitations

The proposed state extension can be generalized to other reinforcement learning algorithms. To adapt Q^A-learning, or to be more precise it's state-extension method, to algorithms such as Actor-Critic, one would simply need to re-implement experience replay so that other algorithms can replay old traces and compute new state-action values.

The most notable limitation of the proposed approach is that, in its current form it, is only feasible with discrete observation space and action space. Continuous observation space would make IoAlergia infeasible as it would fail to learn meaningful models (without the number of actions/observations approaching infinity) due to the high cardinally of the output set. Current state-of-the-art automata learning algorithms cannot cope with continuous, or more generally high-dimensional inputs and output spaces. In such instances, it is advisable to use recurrent neural networks, most notably LSTMs to capture state-space information [12]. While LSTMs can encode state information for high dimensional input and output spaces, they reacquire substantially more data than automata learning approaches to achieve the same level of accuracy on discrete input/output observation sets.

4 Evaluation

To evaluate the proposed method we have implemented Q^A-learning in Python. The implementation uses AALpy's [22] IoAlergia implementation and it interfaces OpenAI *gym* [2]. The implementation can be used on all *gym* environments with discrete action and observation space. We have evaluated Q^A-learning by comparing its performance on four partially observable environments with multiple state-of-the-art RL algorithms implemented in OpenAI's stable-baselines [13], considering: *non-recurrent policies with a stacked history of observations* and *LSTM-based policies*.

Stacked History of Observations. In a first set of experiments, we have compared Q^A-learning with DQN [21], A2C [20], and ACKTR [29]. To aid those algorithms to cope with partial observablility, we encoded the history of observations as a stacked frame. Stacked observation frames encode an observation history by using the last n observations observed during training and evaluation. By using stacked observations, we extend the observation space from initially i

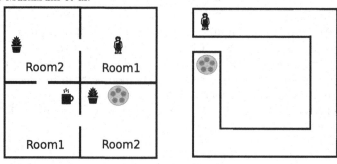

Fig. 5. *ConfusingOfficeWorld* (left) and partially observable *ThinMaze* (right).

observations to $(i + 1)^n$ observations[3]. For all experiments we have set the size of stacked frames to 5. A similar approach was, e.g., used in [21] as a method to encode movement in ATARI games.

Stacked History of Observation-Action Pairs. To further help previously mentioned algorithms to cope with partial observability, we also performed a set of experiments where history stack was extended not only by previous n observations, but with last n observation-action pairs, as done in [21]. This provides the RL algorithms with more state information, as the state implicitly encodes the actions which led to previously observed observations.

LSTM-Based Policies. Deep-recurrent Q-learning [12] has been used to solve ATARI games without stacking the history of observations. Hausknecht and Stone [12] show that recurrence is a viable alternative to frame stacking, and while no significant advantages were noticed during training of the agent, LSTM-based policies were more adaptable in the evaluation phase in the presence of previously unseen observations.

Setup. All experiments were conducted on a laptop with an Intel® Core™i7-11800H at 2.3 GHz, 32 GB RAM, and an NVIDIA RTX™3050 Ti graphics card using Python3.6. For all experiments we have set the maximum number of training episodes to 30,000 for all environments, except for *ThinMaze* where it was set to 50,000. A training episode ends if an agent reaches a goal or the maximum number of steps is exceeded. The training performance was periodically evaluated and training was halted when reaching satisfactory performance.

Hyperparameters. Q^A-learning combines IoALERGIA and Q-learning. The sole parameter of the IoALERGIA is the statistics confidence value ϵ_{AL}, used for state compatibility check, which we kept at 0.05. This is the default value presented in [18], and based on our experimentation different ϵ_{AL} do not significantly impact the model learning outcome. In Q-learning, the learning rate α is set to 0.1, while the discount factor γ is set to 0.9. The exploration rate ϵ linearly

---

[3] +1 due to the padding observation present in the first n steps of each training episode.

Table 3. Representative evaluation results.

Algorithm		OfficeWorld		Confusing OfficeWorld		GravityDomain		ThinMaze	
		# Steps to Goal	# Training Episodes	# Steps to Goal	# Training Episodes	# Steps to Goal	# Training Episodes	# Steps to Goal	# Training Episodes
Optimal Solution		12	–	12	–	18	–	20	–
Q^A-learning		12	3k	18	16k	18	3k	32	27k
Stacked observation	DQN	17	2k	✗	30k	75	30k	✗	50k
	A2C	24	12k	✗	30k	75	30k	✗	50k
	ACKTR	14	2k	✗	30k	75	30k	✗	30k
Stacked action observation	DQN	19	2k	12	3k	75	30k	✗	50k
	A2C	✗	30k	✗	30k	75	30k	✗	50k
	ACKTR	17	4k	✗	30k	✗	30k	✗	50k
LSTM-based policy	ACER	12	1k	✗	30k	75	30k	✗	50k
	A2C	12	1k	✗	30k	75	30k	✗	50k
	ACKTR	12	1k	✗	30k	75	30k	✗	50k

decreased during the algorithm execution, to provide more exploration at the beginning of the training. While the previous hyperparameters were intrinsic to Q^A-learning building blocs, we also define the freezing point and model update interval for Q^A-learning. Model update interval, that is number of episodes after which a new environment model is computed with IoAlergia was set to 1000 episodes. The freezing point was set on an environment basis, usually after 10,000 episodes. Freezing point is currently a hyperparameter, while in future work, we will develop heuristics for dynamic freezing, for example, freezing based on the dissimilarity of two consecutive learned models. For more details about the hyperparameter configuration, we refer to the official implementation.

Table 3 summarizes the results of the experiments. There are columns for each partially observable environment, where the first shows the average number of actions required to reach a dedicated goal with the best policy found by RL, and the second column shows the number of training episodes needed to learn a policy. The symbol ✗ denotes that no policy was found that reaches the goal within the allotted maximum number of steps. The rows correspond to: the optimal policy, the policy found by Q^A-learning, the three RL approaches with stacked observations, and the three approaches with LSTM-based policies. All experiments were repeated multiple times and we chose the best training run as a representative for each approach. As the agent performance was evaluated on 100 episodes, the average number of steps to reach a goal was rounded to the closest integer. In the remainder of this section, we will explain the partially observable environments on which the agents were trained and discuss the obtained results.

The *OfficeWorld* domain is depicted on the right of Fig. 1. Q^A-learning was able to find an optimal policy in this environment, but with a higher total number of training episodes compared to LSTM-based approaches. Stacked-frame based approaches also performed well, but were not able to find an optimal policy. This environment was solvable by all approaches despite its partial observability as each room has two actions which when executed repeatedly will lead the agent into the next room (e.g., in Room2 the agent needs to repeatedly perform down and right actions).

ConfusingOfficeWorld found on the left-hand side of Fig. 5 is a variation of the *OfficeWorld*. *ConfusingOfficeWorld* is harder to solve as the agent receives the same observations in the upper right and the lower left rooms, likewise in the upper left and the lower right rooms. The rooms labeled with *Room1* have two sets of opposite actions that need to be taken, depending on the actual agent location. The same holds for *Room2*. Q^A-learning was able to find a solution for this world in 16 thousand episodes, while other approaches except DQN with stacked action-observations pairs failed due to insufficient state differentiation.

GravityDomain was inspired by the environment discussed in [15]. In *GravityDomain*, gravity will pull the agent down in each state with 50% probability. By reaching a toggle indicated by a blue switch in Fig. 6, gravity is turned off and the environment becomes deterministic. We observed that both stacked-frame and LSTM-based approaches learned a policy, in which they repeatedly performed the *up* action, thus reaching the goal in only 50% of the test episodes within the maximum number of 100 steps. Q^A-learning was able to learn an optimal strategy in which it first reached the blue toggle and then proceeded to the goal, depicted by a cookie. Note that the approach presented in [15] is generally not able to solve the *GravityDomain*.

ThinMaze is depicted on the left-hand side of Fig. 5. In *ThinMaze*, the only observations are "cookie" and "wall", which signals that the agent performs an action that is blocked by a wall. Due to the lack of observations/state differentiation both stacked-frame and LSTM-based approaches failed to find a solution to *ThinMaze*. Q^A-learning was able to find a non-optimal solution in 27 thousand training episodes. This is due to the fact that IOALERGIA requires a high number of traces to approximate the underlying belief-MDP with sufficient accuracy.

Runtime and Model Size. We only briefly comment on runtime, considering *OfficeWorld* for a fair comparison, as all approaches found a decent policy. Other results might be skewed due to different training lengths. Stacked-frame DQN, A2C, and ACKTR, require $312s$, $373s$, and $48s$, respectively. Stopping after only $1k$ episodes, the LSTM-backed ACER, A2C, and ACKTR take $51s$, $74s$, and $80s$, respectively. Our approach is considerably faster, finishing after about $3s$. The reason is that we apply tabular Q-learning and IOALERGIA adds very little runtime overhead. The automata-learning technique has cubic worst-case runtime in the sample size, but has been reported to have linear runtime in practice [5]. Due to the small size and high degree of partial observability found in all used environments, IOALERGIA learns a relatively small MPD-approximations of underlying POMDPs. However, those models provide enough information to the Q^A-learning so that it may solve the RL tasks in all environments. Over multiple experiments, Q^A-learning learned 28 state model for the *OfficeWorld* and for the *ConfusingOfficeWorld*, 15 state model for *Gravity* and 26 state model for the *ThinMaze* environment.

Discussion About Scalability. All experiments were conducted in testing environments with a high degree of partial observability. To be more precise, in all considered environments each observation labeled many distinct neighboring Markov states that need to be distinguished by effective policies. Hence, we show that automata learning can effectively help to deal with incomplete information resulting from partial observability. To really focus on the aspect of partial observability, we limited experiments to relatively small, yet challenging environments, where we compare to state-of-the-art deep RL baselines. We argue that our approach can scale to high-dimensional environments with the help of feature extraction methods, like "image segmentation algorithms" assumed by DeepSynth [11], that enable automata learning over abstract observations corresponding to extracted features. In such a setting, IOALERGIA over abstract observations could be combined with deep RL methods working in large unstructured state spaces. Learned MDPs would benefit RL by providing insights into the abstract structure of the problem domain.

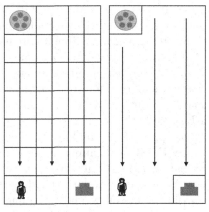

Note that our general approach could also work even more efficiently in environments with less uncertainty. In deterministic environments, we could learn DFAs to identify the hidden state structure, e.g., via RPNI [24]. There we would actually require less data for accurate learning since statistical compatibility checks are not necessary. If an environment can be modeled by a *finite* deterministic labeled MDP, i.e., it has finitely many belief states, IOALERGIA would converge to the true model. Yet such an environment may not be solvable by standard RL, since different states can have the same observation.

Fig. 6. Fully and partially observable gravity domain. Once the button in the lower right corner is reached, gravity is turned off. Please note that for conciseness, we show a width of three, while we used six states in our evaluation.

5   Related Work

In recent years, different forms of automata learning have been applied in combination with RL. Automata learning can aid RL by providing a stateful memory. This memory can be exploited either to further differentiate environment states or to capture steps required for non-Markovian rewards.

Early work closely related to our approach is [8,19]. Both techniques combine model learning and Q-learning for RL under partial observability, but they place stricter assumptions on the environment, like knowledge about the number of environmental states. More recently, Toro Icarte et al. [16] described optimization-based learning of finite-state models, called reward machines, to aid RL. However, they require a labeling function on observations that meets certain criteria and generally cannot handle changes in the transition probabilities, when observations stay the same. DeepSynth [11] follows a similar approach, but focuses on sparse rewards rather than partial observability. They learn automata via satisfiability checking to provide structure to complex tasks, where they also impose requirements on a labeling function.

Learning of reward machines has also been proposed to enable RL with non-Markovian rewards [23,30,31], where the gained rewards depend on the history of experiences rather than the current state and actions. In this context, different approaches to automata learning are applied to learn Mealy machines that keep track of previous experiences in an episode. Velasquez et al. [27] extend reward-machine learning to a setting with stochastic non-Markovian rewards. Our approach could be extended to non-Markovian rewards by adding rewards to the observations. Subgoal automata inferred by Furelos-Blanco et al. [9] through answer set programming serve a similar purpose as reward machines, by capturing interaction sequences that need to occur for the successful completion of a task. Brafman et al. [10] learn deterministic finite automata that also encode which interactions lead to a reward in RL with non-Markovian rewards. Similarly to our approach, the states of learned automata are used as additional observations.

Finally, we presented a combination of stochastic automata learning and reinforcement learning in previous work [26]. There, we abstract from complete observations to safety-relevant features such that learned MDPs provide information about safety-critical temporal aspects. In contrast, Q^A-learning extends RL states with automata states to optimize for cumulative rewards, thus our previous approach [26] and Q^A-learning are complementary; automata learning can make RL safer and improve RL performance. Carr et al. [3] propose an approach for safe RL in partially observable environments, where they apply state estimators in combination with shielding. In addition to helping RL agents cope with partial observability and providing a basis for shielding, learned environment models offer a way to analyze whether temporal properties hold in the given environment, potentially w.r.t. to some policy. Focusing on agent behavior, Carr et al. [4] propose a technique to extract finite-state controllers from recurrent neural networks that implement control policies for POMDPs. Hence, combining this technique with learning environment models would enable a thorough inspection of agent behavior in a partially observable environment.

6   Conclusion

We propose an approach for reinforcement learning under partial observability. For this purpose, we combine Q-learning with the automata learning technique IoALERGIA. With automata learning, we learn hidden information about the environment's state structure that provides additional observations to Q-learning, thus enabling this form of learning in POMDPs. We evaluate our approach in partially observable environments and show that it can outperform the baseline deep RL approach with LSTMs and fixed memory.

For future work, we plan to generalize our approach to other (deep) RL approaches by integrating explored learned MDP states as observations. Approaches already including experience replay naturally lend themselves to such extensions, since we merely need to change the replay mechanism and execute it after updating the learned MDP. To scale the proposed approach to larger environments, we intend to explore and develop automata-learning techniques that can model high-dimensional data.

Acknowledgments. This work has been supported by the"University SAL Labs" initiative of Silicon Austria Labs (SAL) and its Austrian partner universities for applied fundamental research for electronic based systems.

References

1. Bork, A., Junges, S., Katoen, J.-P., Quatmann, T.: Verification of indefinite-horizon POMDPs. In: Hung, D.V., Sokolsky, O. (eds.) ATVA 2020. LNCS, vol. 12302, pp. 288–304. Springer, Cham (2020). https://doi.org/10.1007/978-3-030-59152-6_16
2. Brockman, G., et al.: OpenAI gym. CoRR abs/1606.01540 (2016)
3. Carr, S., Jansen, N., Junges, S., Topcu, U.: Safe reinforcement learning via shielding under partial observability. In: Williams, B., Chen, Y., Neville, J. (eds.) Thirty-Seventh AAAI Conference on Artificial Intelligence, AAAI 2023, Thirty-Fifth Conference on Innovative Applications of Artificial Intelligence, IAAI 2023, Thirteenth Symposium on Educational Advances in Artificial Intelligence, EAAI 2023, Washington, DC, USA, 7–14 February 2023, pp. 14748–14756. AAAI Press (2023). https://doi.org/10.1609/aaai.v37i12.26723
4. Carr, S., Jansen, N., Topcu, U.: Task-aware verifiable RNN-based policies for partially observable markov decision processes. J. Artif. Intell. Res. **72**, 819–847 (2021). https://doi.org/10.1613/jair.1.12963
5. Carrasco, R.C., Oncina, J.: Learning stochastic regular grammars by means of a state merging method. In: Carrasco, R.C., Oncina, J. (eds.) ICGI 1994. LNCS, vol. 862, pp. 139–152. Springer, Heidelberg (1994). https://doi.org/10.1007/3-540-58473-0_144
6. Cassandra, A.R., Kaelbling, L.P., Littman, M.L.: Acting optimally in partially observable stochastic domains. In: AAAI (1994)
7. Chatterjee, K., Chmelik, M., Gupta, R., Kanodia, A.: Qualitative analysis of POMDPs with temporal logic specifications for robotics applications. In: 2015 IEEE International Conference on Robotics and Automation (ICRA) (2015)
8. Chrisman, L.: Reinforcement learning with perceptual aliasing: the perceptual distinctions approach. In: AAAI Conference on Artificial Intelligence (AAAI), pp. 183–188 (1992)
9. Furelos-Blanco, D., Law, M., Russo, A., Broda, K., Jonsson, A.: Induction of sub-goal automata for reinforcement learning. In: Proceedings of the AAAI Conference on Artificial Intelligence (AAAI) (2020)
10. Gaon, M., Brafman, R.I.: Reinforcement learning with non-Markovian rewards. In: Proceedings of the AAAI Conference on Artificial Intelligence (AAAI) (2020)
11. Hasanbeig, M., Jeppu, N.Y., Abate, A., Melham, T., Kroening, D.: DeepSynth: automata synthesis for automatic task segmentation in deep reinforcement learning. In: AAAI Conference on Artificial Intelligence (AAAI) (2021)
12. Hausknecht, M.J., Stone, P.: Deep recurrent Q-learning for partially observable MDPs. In: AAAI Conference on Artificial Intelligence (AAAI) (2015)
13. Hill, A., et al.: Stable baselines. https://github.com/hill-a/stable-baselines (2018)
14. Hoeffding, W.: Probability inequalities for sums of bounded random variables. J. Am. Stat. Assoc. **58**(301), 13–30 (1963)
15. Icarte, R.T., Klassen, T.Q., Valenzano, R.A., McIlraith, S.A.: Using reward machines for high-level task specification and decomposition in reinforcement learning. In: International Conference on Machine Learning (ICML) (2018)

16. Icarte, R.T., Waldie, E., Klassen, T.Q., Valenzano, R.A., Castro, M.P., McIlraith, S.A.: Learning reward machines for partially observable reinforcement learning. In: Advances in Neural Information Processing Systems (NeurIPS) (2019)

17. Mao, H., Chen, Y., Jaeger, M., Nielsen, T.D., Larsen, K.G., Nielsen, B.: Learning Markov decision processes for model checking. In: Quantities in Formal Methods (QFM) (2012)

18. Mao, H., Chen, Y., Jaeger, M., Nielsen, T.D., Larsen, K.G., Nielsen, B.: Learning deterministic probabilistic automata from a model checking perspective. Mach. Learn. **105**(2), 255–299 (2016). https://doi.org/10.1007/s10994-016-5565-9

19. McCallum, A.: Overcoming incomplete perception with utile distinction memory. In: International Conference on Machine Learning (ICML), pp. 190–196 (1993)

20. Mnih, V., et al.: Asynchronous methods for deep reinforcement learning. In: International Conference on Machine Learning (ICML) (2016)

21. Mnih, V., et al.: Playing Atari with deep reinforcement learning. CoRR abs/1312.5602 (2013)

22. Muškardin, E., Aichernig, B.K., Pill, I., Pferscher, A., Tappler, M.: AALpy: an active automata learning library. In: 19th International Symposium on Automated Technology for Verification and Analysis (ATVA) (2021)

23. Neider, D., Gaglione, J., Gavran, I., Topcu, U., Wu, B., Xu, Z.: Advice-guided reinforcement learning in a non-Markovian environment. In: Proceedings of the AAAI Conference on Artificial Intelligence (AAAI) (2021)

24. Oncina, J., Garcia, P.: Identifying regular languages in polynomial time. In: Advances in Structural and Syntactic Pattern Recognition. Machine Perception and Artificial Intelligence, vol. 5, pp. 99–108. World Scientific (1992). https://doi.org/10.1142/9789812797919_0007

25. Singh, S.P., Jaakkola, T.S., Jordan, M.I.: Learning without state-estimation in partially observable Markovian decision processes. In: International Conference on Machine Learning (ICML), pp. 284–292. Morgan Kaufmann (1994)

26. Tappler, M., Pranger, S., Könighofer, B., Muskardin, E., Bloem, R., Larsen, K.G.: Automata learning meets shielding. In: Margaria, T., Steffen, B. (eds.) Leveraging Applications of Formal Methods, Verification and Validation. Verification Principles – 11th International Symposium, ISoLA 2022, Rhodes, Greece, 22–30 October 2022, Proceedings, Part I. Lecture Notes in Computer Science, vol. 13701, pp. 335–359. Springer (2022). https://doi.org/10.1007/978-3-031-19849-6_20

27. Velasquez, A., Beckus, A., Dohmen, T., Trivedi, A., Topper, N., Atia, G.K.: Learning probabilistic reward machines from non-Markovian stochastic reward processes. CoRR abs/2107.04633 (2021)

28. Watkins, C.J.C.H., Dayan, P.: Q-learning. Mach. Learn. **8**(3), 279–292 (1992)

29. Wu, Y., Mansimov, E., Grosse, R.B., Liao, S., Ba, J.: Scalable trust-region method for deep reinforcement learning using Kronecker-factored approximation. In: Advances in Neural Information Processing Systems (NIPS) (2017)

30. Xu, Z., et al.: Joint inference of reward machines and policies for reinforcement learning. In: Proceedings of the International Conference on Automated Planning and Scheduling (ICAPS) (2020)

31. Xu, Z., Wu, B., Ojha, A., Neider, D., Topcu, U.: Active finite reward automaton inference and reinforcement learning using queries and counterexamples. In: Holzinger, A., Kieseberg, P., Tjoa, A.M., Weippl, E. (eds.) CD-MAKE 2021. LNCS, vol. 12844, pp. 115–135. Springer, Cham (2021). https://doi.org/10.1007/978-3-030-84060-0_8

Temporal Logics

Mission-Time LTL (MLTL) Formula Validation via Regular Expressions

Jenna Elwing[1], Laura Gamboa-Guzman[2], Jeremy Sorkin[3],
Chiara Travesset[4], Zili Wang[2]([⊠]), and Kristin Yvonne Rozier[2]

[1] University of Michigan, Ann Arbor, MI 48109, USA
jelwing@umich.edu
[2] Iowa State University, Ames, IA 50011, USA
{lpgamboa,ziliw1,kyrozier}@iastate.edu
[3] University of Amsterdam, 1018, WV Amsterdam, Netherlands
jeremy.sorkin@student.uva.nl
[4] University of Wisconsin, Madison, WI 53715, USA
travesset@wisc.edu

Abstract. Mission-time Linear Temporal Logic (MLTL) represents the most practical fragment of Metric Temporal Logic; MLTL resembles the popular logic Linear Temporal Logic (LTL) with finite closed-interval integer bounds on the temporal operators. Increasingly, many tools reason over MLTL specifications, yet these tools are useful only when system designers can validate the input specifications. We design an automated characterization of the structure of the computations that satisfy a given MLTL formula using regular expressions. We prove soundness and completeness of our structure. We also give an algorithm for automated MLTL formula validation and analyze its complexity both theoretically and experimentally. Additionally, we generate a test suite using control flow diagrams to robustly test our implementation and release an open-source tool with a user-friendly graphical interface. The result of our contributions are improvements to existing algorithms for MLTL analysis, and are applicable to many other tools for automated, efficient MLTL formula validation. Our updated tool may be found at https://temporallogic.org/research/WEST.

Keywords: Mission-time Linear Temporal Logic (MLTL) · MLTL Validation · Temporal Logic Validation

1 Introduction

System specifications, such as aerospace operational concepts, often utilize timelines to express critical requirements. We can cite examples of this from NASA's

Work supported in part by NSF grant DMS-1950583 and NSF CAREER Award CNS-1552934.

J. Elwing, J. Sorkin, C. Travesset and Zili Wang—Contributed equally to this work.

Automated Airspace Concept [11], the U.S. Navy's Aircraft Carrier Deck Scheduler [33], the JAXA-NASA Global Precipitation Measurement (GPM) Observatory [10], and many others. Formal methods provide continuously advancing tools and techniques to rigorously analyze timelines expressed in the form of temporal logic requirements, from early design-time model checking and theorem proving to on-board runtime verification. The U. S. Federal Aviation Administration (FAA) even advocates the use of formal methods for flight certification of these critical systems [27–29]. Yet, a significant hurdle to the use of formal methods remains: how to convincingly demonstrate to the humans in the loop, from system designers to certifiers, that the analyzed formulas truly represent the system requirements [31]. We creatively address this validation question using regular expressions.

NASA, for example, has developed several tools that operate over temporal logic requirements, such as FRET [12], R2U2 [32], and a PVS library [7] for the logic MLTL (Mission-time Linear Temporal Logic) [19,30]. MLTL was the specification logic for NASA's Robonaut2 verification project [16] and is currently the specification logic for both design-time and runtime verification of the NASA Lunar Gateway Vehicle System Manager [8]. Other recent verification efforts involving MLTL include a JAXA autonomous satellite [24], a UAS Traffic Management (UTM) system involving Collins and Mosaic Aerospace [13], a sounding rocket [14], and multiple small satellites [2,20,21]. However, all of these successful verification efforts were carried out by groups specializing in formal methods research. To enable broader application of formal verification, and adoption across larger projects, we critically need better validation, e.g., so that analysis over MLTL-specified requirements can transparently contribute to flight certification.

Many specifications from case studies, in logics such as Metric Temporal Logic (MTL) [1] and Signal Temporal Logic (STL) [22], fall within the MLTL fragments of these logics. Variations on MTL such as MLTL have grown increasingly popular, in part due to their comparatively tractable complexity-to-expressibility trade-offs [25]. The model checker nuXmv encodes a popular subset of MLTL for use in symbolic model checking [17].

There exists a SAT solver for MLTL, MLTLSAT [19], but there are currently no tools for MLTL formula validation. This paper introduces the WEST tool [GitHub][1] repository, which produces a description of the set of all finite timelines (of a fixed length) that satisfy a given MLTL formula, similar to a truth table for propositional formulas. MLTL validation can be done by verifying that the output of the WEST program indeed matches the behaviour of the specification in question.

We show that our contributions not only fill a critical gap in temporal logic validation, but also directly connect to parallel developments to enable better temporal logic formula analysis, benchmark generation, proof generation (e.g., in ACL2), and synthesis of verified C++ code from temporal logic behavior descriptions.

---

[1] https://github.com/zwang271/WEST.

We structure the paper as follows. Section 2 builds on the semantics of MLTL to define a computation and its bit string representation. Section 3 recursively defines regular expressions encapsulating the satisfying computations of MLTL formulas. We provide a calculation for the minimum computation length required to describe all the satisfying computations of an MLTL formula that slightly improves upon existing calculations in the literature. Finally, we show an application of the regular expressions by using them to prove an MLTL rewriting theorem. We introduce the WEST tool that implements automated validation in Sect. 4 and calculate its space and time complexity, both theoretically and experimentally. Section 5 proves the correctness of WEST and provides a test suite to show correctness of implementation with high confidence. Intelligent fuzzing techniques contribute to test suite construction from a state diagram representing the control flow of WEST. We also verify the correctness of outputs of the WEST program against a naïve brute force implementation. Section 6 provides a combinatorial theorem for simplifying certain outputs of the WEST program to the trivial computation. Section 7 demonstrates a specific use case of the WEST tool and explores the currently supported features. Section 8 discusses impacts and future work.

2   Preliminaries: Mission-Time LTL and Bit String Computations

Mission-time Linear Temporal Logic (MLTL) [19] is a finite variation of LTL over bounded, closed, discrete intervals of the form $[a, b]$ where $a, b \in \mathbb{N}$ and $0 \leqslant a \leqslant b$. The syntax of MLTL formulas, φ and ψ over a (finite) set of atomic propositions $\mathcal{AP}$, where $p \in \mathcal{AP}$ is a propositional variable, is given by the following BNF grammar:

$$\varphi, \psi := \top \mid \bot \mid p \mid \neg\varphi \mid \varphi \wedge \psi \mid \varphi \vee \psi \mid \mathcal{F}_{[a,b]}\varphi \mid \mathcal{G}_{[a,b]}\varphi \mid \varphi\mathcal{U}_{[a,b]}\psi \mid \varphi\mathcal{R}_{[a,b]}\psi.$$

2

The symbols $\mathcal{F}, \mathcal{G}, \mathcal{U}, \mathcal{R}$ respectively denote the temporal operators Finally, Globally, Until, and Release. MLTL formulas can be interpreted using both finite and infinite "timelines" that are called *computations*, which represent a discrete sequence of time instances and the truth values for the propositional variables on each one of these. For the purpose of this paper, we are only going to deal with *finite* computations that represent only finitely many time steps.

Definition 1 (*Finite computations*). *A computation π of length m is a sequence*
$\{\pi[i]\}_{i=0}^{m-1}$ of sets of propositional variables, $\pi[i] \subseteq \mathcal{AP}$, where the ith set contains the propositional variables that are true at the ith time step. That is, a

---

² For simplicity, we do not include parentheses in the grammar, but the WEST program requires parentheses (see Sect. 4). We encode Release directly rather than as the dual of Until. Refer to the WEST Appendix(see footnote 5) for a straightforward proof of equivalence using the semantics.

propositional variable p is true at time step i if and only if $p \in \pi[i]$. We denote the suffix of π starting at i (including i) by π_i. Note that $\pi_0 = \pi$.

We provide the formal semantics for MLTL below. A computation π satisfies a given MLTL formula α, written $\pi \models \alpha$, in the following cases[3]:

$\pi \models p$ iff $p \in \pi[0]$ $\pi \models \neg\alpha$ iff $\pi \not\models \alpha$

$\pi \models \alpha \wedge \beta$ iff $\pi \models \alpha$ and $\pi \models \beta$ $\pi \models \alpha \vee \beta$ iff $\pi \models \alpha$ or $\pi \models \beta$

$\pi \models \mathcal{F}_{[a,b]}\alpha$ iff $|\pi| > a$ and $\exists i \in [a,b]$ such that $\pi_i \models \alpha$

$\pi \models \mathcal{G}_{[a,b]}\alpha$ iff $|\pi| \leq a$ or $\forall i \in [a,b]$ $\pi_i \models \alpha$

$\pi \models \alpha \, \mathcal{U}_{[a,b]}\beta$ iff $|\pi| > a$ and $\exists i \in [a,b]$ such that $\pi_i \models \beta$ and $\forall j \in [a, i-1]$ $\pi_j \models \alpha$

$\pi \models \alpha \, \mathcal{R}_{[a,b]}\beta$ iff $|\pi| \leq a$ or $\forall i \in [a,b]$ $\pi_i \models \beta$ or $\exists j \in [a, b-1]$ such that $\pi_j \models \alpha$
and $\forall a \leq k \leq j$ $\pi_k \models \beta$

Definition 2 (*Bit String Representation of a Computation*). *Let p_0, p_1, ..., p_{n-1} be propositional variables for a fixed $n \in \mathbb{N}$. We represent a (finite) computation π of length $m \in \mathbb{N}$ using a bit string representation as follows:*

- *Each time step $j \in [0, 1, \ldots, m-1]$ corresponds to a bit string of length n, where the kth bit represents the truth assignment of the proposition p_{k-1}.*
- *Each time step is separated by a comma and orders the time steps chronologically.*

Example 1. Suppose $n = 2$. The bit string $\pi = 10, 01$ represents a timeline on which p_0 is true and p_1 is false in the zeroth time step, whereas p_0 is false and p_1 true in the first time step.

3   MLTL Regular Expressions

We modify the standard definition of *Regular Expressions* (regex) to introduce notation that describes the satisfying computations of an MLTL formula. We begin by quoting the parts of the standard definition of a regex from [34] that we use to describe our computations:

Definition 3 (*Regular Expression*). *Let Σ denote an alphabet. We say that R is a regular expression if one of the following holds:*

- *$R = a$, for some $a \in \Sigma$.*
- *$R = \epsilon$, where ϵ is the language containing the empty string.*
- *$R = \varnothing$, the empty set.*

---

[3] We do not include the Next operator, which is often denoted $\mathcal{X}$, since it is equivalent to both $\mathcal{G}_{[1,1]}$ and $\mathcal{F}_{[1,1]}$.

- $R = (R_1 \vee R_2)$, where R_1, R_2 are regexes and $\vee$ denotes alternation; the set union of all the strings described by R_1 and R_2.
- $R = R_1 R_2$, which denotes concatenation, i.e., the set of strings obtained by concatenating any string generated by R_1 with any string generated by R_2, in that order.

Now we introduce the additions to the definition of a regex that we utilize to describe the computations. These additions allow us to write regexes of a known, finite, fixed length, which is required when describing the computations in MLTL.

Definition 4 (*Temporal Regular Expression*). *Let R and T denote regular expressions, and let S be an abbreviation for $(0 \vee 1)$. Let fixed $n \in \mathbb{N}$ denote the number of propositional variables in an MLTL formula. We use the following operations to describe the form of satisfying computations of the formula in the bit string representation:*

- *Pad(R, T) determines which regular expression is longer and concatenates $(, S^n)$ repeatedly to the end of the shorter regular expression until the two regular expressions are the same length. Note that in the bit string representation, $(, S^n)$ denotes a time step in which the truth values of all n propositional variables do not matter.*
- *$R \wedge T$ is the intersection of the sets of strings described by R and T. To perform this operation, we first use Pad(R, T), and then take the set intersection of the sets of strings described by the two regular expressions.*
- *R^i denotes regular expression consisting of R repeated i times for $i \geqslant 0$. $R^0 = \epsilon$.*

Note that our regular expressions do not use the Kleene star. This is because our computations are of a fixed, finite length.

Example 2. Let $n = 2$, and let $R = S1$ and $T = (1S, 1S) \vee (S1, S1)$. To compute $R \wedge T$ and $R \vee T$, we perform Pad(R,T). Since T is the longer regex by one time step, we extend R by one time step. Thus $T = (1S, 1S) \vee (S1, S1)$ and $R = S1, SS$. Now we can perform set intersection and alternation on the two regular expressions of equal length:

- $R \wedge T = (11, 1S) \vee (S1, S1)$
- $R \vee T = (S1, SS) \vee (1S, 1S) \vee (S1, S1) = (S1, SS) \vee (1S, 1S)$

Definition 5 (*MLTL Regular Expressions*). *Let $\Sigma = \{$"0", "1", ","$\}$ be the alphabet and define S as an abbreviation for $(0 \vee 1)$. Let φ and ψ be well-formed MLTL formulas in negation normal form (NNF[4]) containing the n propositional variables $p_0, p_1, ..., p_{n-1}$. We recursively define the regular expression of all satisfying computations for an MLTL formula as follows:*

$$reg(\top) = S^n \qquad\qquad reg(\bot) = \varnothing$$

$$reg(p_k) = S^k 1 S^{n-k-1} \qquad\qquad reg(\neg p_k) = S^k 0 S^{n-k-1}$$

$$reg(\varphi \vee \psi) = reg(\varphi) \vee reg(\psi) \qquad\qquad reg(\varphi \wedge \psi) = reg(\varphi) \wedge reg(\psi)$$

$$reg(\mathcal{G}_{[a,b]}\varphi) = \bigwedge_{i=a}^{b} (S^n,)^i reg(\varphi) \qquad\qquad reg(\mathcal{F}_{[a,b]}\varphi) = \bigvee_{i=a}^{b} (S^n,)^i reg(\varphi)$$

$$reg(\varphi \,\mathcal{U}_{[a,b]}\psi) = \bigvee_{i=a}^{b} reg\left(\mathcal{G}_{[a,i-1]}\varphi \wedge \mathcal{G}_{[i,i]}\psi\right)$$

$$reg(\varphi \mathcal{R}_{[a,b]}\psi) = reg\left(\mathcal{G}_{[a,b]}\psi\right) \vee \bigvee_{i=a}^{b-1} reg\left(\mathcal{G}_{[a,i]}\psi \wedge \mathcal{G}_{[i,i]}\varphi\right)$$

Definition 6 (*Computation Length*). *We recursively define the computation length* $cplen(\varphi)$ *of an MLTL formula φ:*

$$\text{cplen}(p_k) = \text{cplen}(\neg p_k) = 1,$$
$$\text{cplen}(\varphi \wedge \psi) = \text{cplen}(\varphi \vee \psi) = \max(\text{cplen}(\varphi), \text{cplen}(\psi)),$$
$$\text{cplen}(\mathcal{G}_{[a,b]}\varphi) = \text{cplen}(\mathcal{F}_{[a,b]}\varphi) = b + \text{cplen}(\varphi),$$
$$\text{cplen}(\varphi\mathcal{U}_{[a,b]}\psi) = \text{cplen}(\varphi\mathcal{R}_{[a,b]}\psi) = b + \max(\text{cplen}(\varphi) - 1, \text{cplen}(\psi)).$$

Here, $\text{cplen}(\varphi)$ is the minimum computation length required to ensure that none of the intervals in φ are out of bounds. A computation that is of length $\text{cplen}(\varphi)$ or greater will reach the end of every interval in φ. Our minimum computation length for Until and Release are slight optimizations of what was previously considered the minimum computation length in the literature. The previous bound in [16] was

$$\text{cplen}(\varphi\mathcal{U}_{[a,b]}\psi) = \text{cplen}(\varphi\mathcal{R}_{[a,b]}\psi) = b + \max(\text{cplen}(\varphi), \text{cplen}(\psi))$$

whereas Theorem 1 proves our minimum computation length for Until and Release is

$$\text{cplen}(\varphi\mathcal{U}_{[a,b]}\psi) = \text{cplen}(\varphi\mathcal{R}_{[a,b]}\psi) = b + \max(\text{cplen}(\varphi) - 1, \text{cplen}(\psi)).$$

---

[4] Note that any MLTL formula can easily be converted into NNF.

Theorem 1 (*Minimum Computation Length of Until and Release*). *Let $0 \leqslant a \leqslant b \in \mathbb{N}$ and let φ, ψ be well-formed MLTL formulas in NNF. The minimum computation length of $\mathcal{R}$ and $\mathcal{U}$ is given by $cplen(\varphi\mathcal{U}_{[a,b]}\psi) = cplen(\varphi\mathcal{R}_{[a,b]}\psi) = b + max(cplen(\varphi) - 1, cplen(\psi))$.*

The formulas for minimum computation length follow directly from the regular expressions for the satisfying computations for Until and Release and the minimum computation lengths for Finally, Globally, AND, and OR. See the WEST Appendix[5] for details of the proof.

We can reduce the minimum computation length of Until for the formula $\varphi\mathcal{U}_{[a,b]}\psi$ for the following reason: ψ must be assigned true at time step b if it has not been true at a prior time step by the semantics of $\mathcal{U}$, and thus the truth value of φ at time step b does not matter. Likewise for the formula $\varphi\mathcal{R}_{[a,b]}\psi$, if ψ is true from time step a to time step b, the computation satisfies the formula regardless of the value of φ at time step b.

Let $\mathscr{L}(reg(\varphi))$ denote the language of $reg(\varphi)$, i.e., the set of computations represented by the regular expression $reg(\varphi)$.

Theorem 2 (*Soundness and Completeness*). *For any well-formed MLTL formula φ in negation normal form, a computation π with $|\pi| = cplen(\varphi)$ satisfies φ if and only if $\pi \in \mathscr{L}(reg(\varphi))$.*

We omit the proof for this theorem since it follows straightforward by induction on the length of a formula. See the WEST Appendix (see footnote 5) for details of the proof. As an application of the regular expressions in the above theorem, we prove a previously known MLTL rewriting theorem. This demonstrates the utility of our regular expressions for theoretical analysis.

Theorem 3 (*Nested Until and Release Rewriting Theorem*). *Any MLTL formula using the Until or Release operator can be rewritten with right-nested subformulas. Let $a, b, c \in \mathbb{Z}_{\geqslant 0}, a \leqslant b$, and φ, ψ be well-formed MLTL formulas in NNF. Then*

$$\varphi\, \mathcal{U}_{[a,b+c]}\psi \equiv \varphi\, \mathcal{U}_{[a,b]}(\varphi\, \mathcal{U}_{[0,c]}\psi) \text{ and } \varphi\, \mathcal{R}_{[a,b+c]}\psi \equiv \varphi\, \mathcal{R}_{[a,b]}(\varphi\, \mathcal{R}_{[0,c]}\psi).$$

The proof is omitted here as it follows from the definition of regular expressions for MLTL. See the WEST Appendix(see footnote 5) for details of the proof.

4   WEST Algorithm and Analysis

Algorithm 1 (Fig. 1) recursively computes all satisfying temporal regular expressions to an input formula φ. We use sets to represent alternation of regular expressions; for n regular expressions $t_0, ..., t_{n-1}$, we write $\{t_0, ..., t_{n-1}\} = \bigcup_{i=0}^{n-1} t_i$. Additionally, we provide details for performing set intersection of temporal regular expressions, and the algorithms for the temporal operators $\mathcal{G}$ and $\mathcal{U}$.

---

[5] The Appendix for this paper can be found at https://temporallogic.org/research/WEST.

Note how `reg_U` parallels the regular expression defined for $\mathcal{U}$, and the algorithms (see WEST Appendix(see footnote 5)) for the other three temporal operators follow an identical structure.

For regular expressions w_0 and w_1, a useful reduction is that $\{w_0 1 w_1, w_0 0 w_1\} = \{w_0 s w_1\}$. Each time we perform set intersection, we greedily apply this reduction to all appropriate pairs of regular expressions in the set. This prevents repeated set intersection operations from blowing up exponentially most of the time, and drastically improves running time. We call this simple algorithm `simplify` and use it extensively throughout the WEST code.

4.1   Proof of Correctness of WEST

Theorem 4 (*Theoretical Correctness of WEST*).   *Given a well-formed MLTL formula, the WEST Algorithm outputs the regular expressions of the satisfying computations as described in Sect. 3.*

Proof. Correctness of the WEST algorithm is dependent on the correctness of subroutines `reg_prop_cons`, `reg_prop_var`, `join`, `set_intersect`, `reg_F`, `reg_G`, `reg_U`, and `reg_R`. The routines `reg_prop_cons` and `reg_prop_var` take as input an MLTL formula of the appropriate form and return the regular expression defined in Sect. 3.

The function `join` concatenates two sets of regular expressions R and T, which is equivalent to $\mathcal{L}(R) \cup \mathcal{L}(T)$. `set_intersect` takes as input two sets of regular expressions $R = \{r_0, ..., r_{a-1}\}$ and $T = \{t_0, ..., t_{b-1}\}$, such that each r_i and t_j are regular expressions over $\Sigma = \{\text{"0"}, \text{"1"}, \text{"S"}, \text{","}\}$. Without lost of generality, assume that all strings of regular expressions are right-padded to equal length. We show that $\mathcal{L}(\texttt{set\_intersect}(R,T)) = \mathcal{L}(R) \cap \mathcal{L}(T)$:

$$\mathcal{L}(R) \cap \mathcal{L}(T) = \left(\bigcup_{i=0}^{a-1} \mathcal{L}(r_i) \right) \cap \left(\bigcup_{j=0}^{b-1} \mathcal{L}(t_j) \right) = \bigcup_{i=0}^{a-1} \bigcup_{j=0}^{b-1} \left(\mathcal{L}(r_i) \cap \mathcal{L}(t_j) \right).$$

The loop in `set_intersect` computes the union of `bit_wise_and`(r_i, t_j) over all such pairs, and so it suffices to show $\mathcal{L}(\texttt{bit\_wise\_and}(r_i, t_j)) = \mathcal{L}(r_i) \cap \mathcal{L}(t_j)$. Given a computation π, $\pi \in \mathcal{L}(r_i) \cap \mathcal{L}(t_j)$ if and only if π matches every character of both r_i and t_j. `Bit_wise_and`(r_i, t_j) compares r_i and t_j character by character and computes their intersection, which is defined naturally: $0 \cap 1 = \varnothing$, $0 \cap S = 0$, $1 \cap S = 1$, $0 \cap 0 = 0$, $1 \cap 1 = 1$, and $S \cap S = S$. Note that this operation is commutative. This exhaustively captures all the cases for which π must match corresponding characters from r_i and t_j. Thus $\mathcal{L}(\texttt{bit\_wise\_and}(r_i, t_j)) = \mathcal{L}(r_i) \cap \mathcal{L}(t_j)$ and the claim holds.

The correctness for `reg_F`, `reg_G`, `reg_U`, `reg_R`, and `reg` is proven by induction on depth of recursion to `reg`. The depth of recursion is exactly the depth of the parse tree of the input formula. For the base case (depth 0), `reg_prop_var` and `reg_prop_cons` are called to handle input formulas that consist of a propositional variable, the negation of a propositional variable, or a propositional

Algorithm 1 WEST Algorithm

Inputs: φ - MLTL formula in NNF
φ_1 and φ_2 below are subformulas of φ
n - number of propositional variables
Output: set of REGEX satisfying φ

1: **procedure** REG(string φ, int n)
2:    **if** φ is $\top$ or $\bot$ **then**
3:       return reg_prop_const(φ, n)
4:    **if** φ is p_k or $\neg p_k$ **then**
5:       return reg_prop_var(φ, n)
6:    **if** $\varphi = \varphi_1 \wedge \varphi_2$ **then**
7:       return   set_intersect(reg(φ_1), reg(φ_2),   n)
8:    **if** $\varphi = \varphi_1 \vee \varphi_2$ **then**
9:       return join(reg(φ_1), reg(φ_2), n)
10:   **if** $\varphi = \mathcal{F}_{[a,b]}\varphi_1$ **then**
11:      return reg_F(reg(φ_1), a, b, n)
12:   **if** $\varphi = \mathcal{G}_{[a,b]}\varphi_1$ **then**
13:      return reg_G(reg(φ_1), a, b, n)
14:   **if** $\varphi = \varphi_1\mathcal{U}_{[a,b]}\varphi_2$ **then**
15:      return reg_U(reg(φ_1), reg(φ_2), a, b, n)
16:   **if** $\varphi = \varphi_1\mathcal{R}_{[a,b]}\varphi_2$ **then**
17:      return reg_R(reg(φ_1), reg(φ_2), a, b, n)

Algorithm 2 set_intersect

Inputs: R, T - two sets of REGEX
n - number of propositional variables
Output: set of REGEX equal to $R \wedge T$

1: **procedure** SET_INTERSECT(R, T, n)
2:    Pad(R, T, n), ret $\leftarrow$ {}
3:    **for** $(r,t) \in R \times T$ **do**
4:       add bit_wise_and(r, t) to ret
5:    return simplify(ret)

Algorithm 3 reg_G

Inputs: r_φ - set of REGEX for MLTL formula φ (after calling reg)
a, b - interval bounds
n - number of propositional variables
Output: set of REGEX for $G_{[a,b]}\varphi$

1: **procedure** REG_G(set r_φ, int a, int b, int n)
2:    pre $\leftarrow$ (('S')^n + ',')^a
3:    comp $\leftarrow r_\varphi$
4:    **if** $a > b$ **then return** $\{S^n\}$
5:    **for** $(1 \leqslant i \leqslant b - a)$ **do**
6:       temp$_\varphi \leftarrow$ (('S')^n + ',')^i + r_φ
7:       comp $\leftarrow$ set_intersect(comp, temp$_\varphi$, n)
8:    **return** pre + comp

Algorithm 4 reg_U

Inputs: r_φ, r_ψ - sets of REGEX for MLTL formulas φ and ψ (after calling reg)
a, b - integers representing interval bound
n - number of propositional variables
Output: set of REGEX for $\varphi\mathcal{U}_{[a,b]}\psi$

1: **procedure** REG_U(r_φ, r_ψ, a, b, n)
2:    comp $\leftarrow$ (('S')^n + ',')^a + r_ψ
3:    **if** $a > b$ **then return** {}
4:    **for** $(a \leqslant i \leqslant b - 1)$ **do**
5:       G1 $\leftarrow$ reg_G(r_φ, a, i, n)
6:       G2 $\leftarrow$ reg_G(r_ψ, i + 1, i + 1, n)
7:       temp_comp $\leftarrow$ set_intersect(G1, G2, n)
8:       comp $\leftarrow$ join(comp, temp_comp)
9:    **return** comp

Fig. 1. Pseudocode for WEST, set_intersect, reg_G, and reg_U. The pseudocode for all other algorithms referenced can be found in the WEST Appendix(see footnote 5).

constant. Then assume **reg** is correct on all formulas of depth at most d, for some integer $d \geqslant 0$. Let γ be an MLTL formula in negation normal form of depth $d + 1$. Then γ must be of the form $\varphi \vee \psi$, $\varphi \wedge \psi$, $\mathcal{G}_{[a,b]}\varphi$, $\mathcal{F}_{[a,b]}\varphi$, $\varphi\mathcal{U}_{[a,b]}\psi$, or $\varphi\mathcal{R}_{[a,b]}\psi$, for some formulas φ and ψ of depth at most d, and a pair of non-negative integers, a and b. Correctness of the first two cases have been proven. The proof for the four temporal cases are of similar structure, and it suffices to verify that the algorithms compute appropriate regular expressions correctly using `join` and `set_intersect`.

We give the explicit proof for the case $\gamma = \varphi \mathcal{U}_{[a,b]} \psi$ as an example. `reg_U` takes as input $r_\varphi = \text{reg}(\varphi)$ and $r_\psi = \text{reg}(\psi)$, which by the induction hypothesis are correctly computed. The regular expression for the Until operator may be rewritten as $\text{reg}(\varphi\, \mathcal{U}_{[a,b]} \psi) = \text{reg}\left(\mathcal{G}_{[a,a]} \psi\right) \vee \bigvee_{i=a}^{b-1} \text{reg}\left(\mathcal{G}_{[a,i]} \varphi \wedge \mathcal{G}_{[i+1,i+1]} \psi\right)$. In line 2 of `reg_U`, the variable `comp` is initialized to $(\text{``}S\text{''}^n + \text{``},\text{''})^a$ pre-concatenated to r_ψ, and is the regular expression for $\mathcal{G}_{[a,a]} \psi$. Next, the $\vee$ from $i = a$ to $b - 1$ is computed by the for loop in line 4. Lastly, lines 5 through 7 computes $\text{reg}\left(\mathcal{G}_{[a,i]} \varphi \wedge \mathcal{G}_{[i+1,i+1]} \psi\right)$. This shows correctness of `reg_U`; although, in a complete proof, correctness of `reg_G` needs to be shown first since lines 5 and 6 calls `reg_G`. Continuing in the same fashion to prove the other three cases, `reg` is correct on all depth $d + 1$ inputs, and thus `reg` is correct on all inputs by induction.

4.2 Theoretical Complexity

In order to reason about the complexity of our algorithms, we first introduce several assumptions about the input. Suppose that the lower and upper intervals of temporal operators are bounded by some constant $d \in \mathbb{N}$, and that the difference between any bound is less than some constant $\delta \in \mathbb{N}$. These are reasonable assumptions since MLTL turns into a finite temporal logic when a known mission end is given. We provide a summary of the complexity of each of the operators that contribute to the worst-case behavior of the final output.

For any function $f(\varphi)$ taking a string argument φ, we use $|\varphi|$ to denote the number of characters in φ and $S(f(\varphi))$ to denote the space complexity of f in terms of the number of characters in the output.

If φ is a propositional constant or variable, it is easy to see that $S(\text{reg}(\bot)) = 0$ since only the empty set is returned. By definition, $\text{reg}(\top) = S^n$, so we have that $S(\text{reg}(\top)) = n$. Similarly, $\text{reg}(p_k)$ and $\text{reg}(\neg p_k)$ both return strings of length n, whence $S(\text{reg}(p_k)) = S(\text{reg}(\neg p_k)) = S(\text{reg}(\top)) = n$.

If φ is "$\varphi_1 \vee \varphi_2$", we return $\text{join}(\text{reg}(\varphi_1), \text{reg}(\varphi_2))$, which simply computes the union of the two sets. Thus $S(\text{reg}(\varphi_1 \vee \varphi_2)) = S(\text{reg}(\varphi_1)) + S(\text{reg}(\varphi_2))$.

If φ is "$\varphi_1 \wedge \varphi_2$", $\text{set\_intersect}(\text{reg}(\varphi_1), \text{reg}(\varphi_2), n)$ returns a set of size $S(\text{reg}(\varphi_1)) \cdot S(\text{reg}(\varphi_2))$ in the worst case when no simplification can be made. Thus, our space complexity is $S(\text{reg}(\varphi_1 \wedge \varphi_2)) = S(\text{reg}(\varphi_1)) \cdot S(\text{reg}(\varphi_2))$.

For the next cases, we use these two bounds and define the constants $\mathcal{C}_G$ and $\mathcal{C}_F$:

$$\prod_{i=a}^{b} (n+1)i = (n+1)^{b-a} \cdot \frac{b!}{(a-1)!} \leqslant (n+1)^\delta b! \leqslant (n+1)^\delta d! = \mathcal{C}_G$$
$$\sum_{i=a}^{b} (n+1)i \leqslant (n+1)b\delta \leqslant (n+1)d\delta = \mathcal{C}_F$$

If φ is "$\mathcal{G}_{[a,b]} \varphi_1$", recall that $\text{reg}(\mathcal{G}_{[a,b]} \varphi_1) = \bigwedge_{i=a}^{b} (S^n,)^i \text{reg}(\varphi_1)$. From the analysis of `set_intersect`, worst-case space complexity is multiplicative. Thus

$S(\mathbf{reg}(\varphi)) = \prod_{i=a}^{b}(n+1)i \cdot S(\mathbf{reg}(\varphi_1)) < \mathcal{C}_G \cdot S(\mathbf{reg}(\varphi_1))^\delta$. In this calculation, $(n+1)i$ counts the concatenation of the padded components in the computation.

If φ is "$\mathcal{F}_{[a,b]}\varphi_1$", recall that $\mathbf{reg}(\mathcal{F}_{[a,b]}\varphi_1) = \bigvee_{i=a}^{b}(S^n,)^i\mathbf{reg}(\varphi_1)$. From the analysis of join, worst-case space complexity is additive, which implies that

$$S(\mathbf{reg}(\varphi)) = \sum_{i=a}^{b}(n+1)i \cdot S(\mathbf{reg}(\varphi_1)) < \mathcal{C}_F \cdot S(\mathbf{reg}(\varphi_1)).$$

If $\varphi = $ "$\varphi_1 \mathcal{U}_{[a,b]}\varphi_2$", then $\mathbf{reg}(\varphi_1 \mathcal{U}_{[a,b]}\varphi_2) = \bigvee_{i=a}^{b} \mathbf{reg}\left(\mathcal{G}_{[a,i-1]}\varphi_1 \wedge \mathcal{G}_{[i,i]}\varphi_2\right)$. We can bound $S(\mathbf{reg}(\mathcal{G}_{[i,i]}\varphi_2))$ by $(n+1) \cdot i \cdot S(\mathbf{reg}(\varphi_2))$ because the operation is equivalent to simply prepending $(S^n,)^i$. Thus, using our previous results for the $\mathcal{G}$, $\wedge$, and $\vee$ operators, we have that:

$$S(\mathbf{reg}(\varphi)) \leqslant \sum_{i=a}^{b}[\mathcal{C}_G S(\mathbf{reg}(\varphi_1))^\delta \cdot (n+1)iS(\mathbf{reg}(\varphi_2))]$$

$$\leqslant \delta[\mathcal{C}_G \cdot \delta(n+1)d \cdot S(\mathbf{reg}(\varphi_1))^\delta S(\mathbf{reg}(\varphi_2))]$$

$$= \mathcal{C}_U \cdot S(\mathbf{reg}(\varphi_1))^\delta S(\mathbf{reg}(\varphi_2))$$

where $\mathcal{C}_U = \mathcal{C}_G \delta(n+1)d$.

If $\varphi = $ "$\varphi_1 \mathcal{R}_{[a,b]}\varphi_2$", recall that

$\mathbf{reg}(\varphi_1 \mathcal{R}_{[a,b]}\varphi_2) = \mathbf{reg}\left(\mathcal{G}_{[a,b]}\varphi_2\right) \vee \bigvee_{i=a}^{b-1} \mathbf{reg}\left(\mathcal{G}_{[a,i]}\varphi_2 \wedge \mathcal{G}_{[i,i]}\varphi_1\right)$.
A similar argument to the $\mathcal{U}$ case shows

$$S(\mathbf{reg}(\varphi)) < \mathcal{C}_R \cdot S(\mathbf{reg}(\varphi_1)) \cdot S(\mathbf{reg}(\varphi_2))^\delta,$$

where $\mathcal{C}_R = \mathcal{C}_G \cdot (1 + \delta(n+1)d)$.

Theorem 5 (*Space Complexity*). *Given a well-formed MLTL formula φ, $\mathbf{reg}(\varphi)$ has worst-case space complexity that is $O(\mathcal{C}_R^{\delta^\ell} \cdot (\ell+1)^{\delta^{\ell+1}})$, where ℓ is the number of logical connectives in $\{\wedge, \vee, \mathcal{F}, \mathcal{G}, \mathcal{R}, \mathcal{U}\}$ that occurr in φ.*

Proof. To analyze worst-case complexity, it is clear from the analysis above that $\mathcal{U}$ and $\mathcal{R}$ give the worst complexity. In the previous analysis, we defined $\mathcal{C}_U = \mathcal{C}_G \delta(n+1)d$ and $\mathcal{C}_R = \mathcal{C}_G \cdot (1 + \delta(n+1)d)$. Observe that $\mathcal{C}_R > \mathcal{C}_U$, and so we analyze only repeated nesting of the operator $\mathcal{R}$.

However, notice that the structure of the parse tree is important. Formulas similar to $(p_3\mathcal{R}p_1)\mathcal{R}(p_1\mathcal{R}p_0)$ generate a balanced binary parse tree where the maximum depth of recursion is $O(\log \ell)$. However if the nesting is only from one side, such as formulas similar to $p_3\mathcal{R}(p_2\mathcal{R}(p1\mathcal{R}p_0))$, then the maximum depth of recursion is $O(\ell)$. Thus we focus on the formula

$$\varphi = p_\ell\mathcal{R}_{[a_\ell,b_\ell]}(p_{\ell-1}\mathcal{R}_{[a_{\ell-1},b_{\ell-1}]}...\mathcal{R}_{[a_3,b_3]}(p_2\mathcal{R}_{[a_2,b_2]}(p_1\mathcal{R}_{[a_1,b_1]}p_0))...)$$

where there are ℓ logical connectives $\mathcal{R}$ and $n = \ell + 1$ propositional variables.

We derive the complexity of $S(\mathbf{reg}(\varphi))$ by defining the sequence $\{s_k\}_{k=1}^{\ell}$ recursively as follows, $s_1 := S(\mathbf{reg}(p_1\mathcal{R}_{[a_1,b_1]}p_0))$ and $s_{k+1} := \mathcal{C}_R S(\mathbf{reg}(p_{k+1}))(s_k)^\delta$, for each $1 \leqslant k < \ell$. The recurrence relation captures an extra nesting of the $\mathcal{R}$ operator, based on the complexity of $\mathcal{R}$ defined above. We calculate $S(p_m) = n = \ell + 1$ for all m such that $0 \leqslant m \leqslant \ell$, thus $s_1 = \mathcal{C}_R(\ell+1)^{\delta+1}$ and $s_{k+1} = \mathcal{C}_R(\ell+1)(s_k)^\delta$.

The explicit formula is given by $s_k = \mathcal{C}_R^{\sum_{i=0}^{k-1}\delta^i} \cdot (\ell+1)^{\sum_{i=0}^{k}\delta^i}$. It is easy to check that the base case $k = 1$ holds, and we prove the claim by induction:

$$S_{k+1} = \mathcal{C}_R \left(\mathcal{C}_R^{\sum_{i=0}^{k-1}\delta^i} \cdot (\ell+1)^{\sum_{i=0}^{k}\delta^i} \right)^\delta \cdot (\ell+1)$$

$$= \mathcal{C}_R^{1+\sum_{i=0}^{k-1}\delta^{i+1}} \cdot (\ell+1)^{1+\sum_{i=0}^{k}\delta^{i+1}}$$

$$= \mathcal{C}_R^{\sum_{i=0}^{k}\delta^i} \cdot (\ell+1)^{\sum_{i=0}^{k+1}\delta^i}.$$

Thus we have that $S(\mathbf{reg}(\varphi)) = \mathcal{C}_R^{\sum_{i=0}^{\ell-1}\delta^i} \cdot (\ell+1)^{\sum_{i=0}^{\ell}\delta^i} = O(\mathcal{C}_R^{\delta^\ell} \cdot (\ell+1)^{\delta^{\ell+1}})$.

Through a similar analysis, we have found that the time complexities of all of the above functions is unsurprisingly the same as their space complexities.

Theorem 6 (*Time Complexity*).   *Given a well-formed MLTL formula φ,* **reg**(φ) *has worst-case time complexity that is $O(\mathcal{C}_R^{\delta^\ell} \cdot (\ell+1)^{\delta^{\ell+1}})$, where ℓ is the number of logical connectives in $\{\wedge, \vee, \mathcal{F}, \mathcal{G}, \mathcal{R}, \mathcal{U}\}$ that occurr in φ.*

If in the worst case no simplification occurs in any call of `set_intersect`, space complexity remains unchanged, but simplifying a set of regular expressions is cubic in input size. In practice, however, both time and space complexities are much more optimistic than worst-case estimates.

4.3   Experimental Benchmarking

We accompany theoretical space and time complexity with experimental evaluation of these complexities using randomly-generated MLTL formulas. What we observed from the simulations is that the worst-case complexity, both for space and time, is relatively rare, and that otherwise the program has good complexity. WEST ran in under 10 s for nearly all the inputted random formulas. The number of characters outputted was typically under 5000, and often less. This is approximately the length of a single paragraph. We also observe that these worst cases are extreme outliers and that in nearly every case, are examples of nested binary temporal operators. As seen in [2, 14, 16], and [13], nested binary temporal operators do not appear in any specifications, and thus are unlikely to appear both in the literature and in practical applications.

We ran these experiments on an Intel(R) Xeon(R) Gold 6140 CPU @ 2.30 GHz with 376 GB RAM. For each simulation, 1000 MLTL formulas were randomly generated using the parameters `delta`, `interval_max`, number of propositional variables, and number of iterations. Here, `delta` is the maximum length we allow for any interval, `interval_max` is the largest allowed upper bound for any interval, and Number of iterations is the level of nesting in the generated formulas. For example, $\mathcal{G}_{[0,2]}p_0$ is a formula generated with one iteration, while

$\mathcal{G}_{[0,2]}(p_0 \wedge p_1)$ is a formula generated with two iterations. We measure the number of characters in the output versus time in seconds taken to run the program. For the pseudocode of the program that generated the random formulas, we refer the reader to check the WEST Appendix (see footnote 5).

Simulation 1. For the first simulation, we consider 2 iterations, 5 propositional variables, `delta = 10`, and `interval_max = 10`. We obtain plots 2a and 2b.

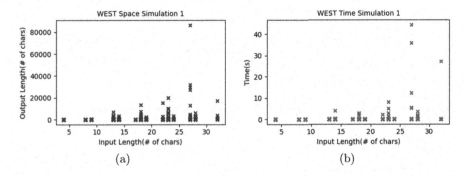

Fig. 2. $(p_0 = p_1)\mathcal{U}_{[2,9]}(p_1\mathcal{U}_{[7,9]}p_3)$ is an outlier in both. $(p_4 \rightarrow p_2)\mathcal{R}_{[1,8]}(p_3\mathcal{U}_{[3,4]}p_0)$ and $(p_3\mathcal{R}_{[2,7]}p_4)\mathcal{R}_{[1,9]}(p_4\mathcal{R}_{[4,9]}p_3)$ are outliers only in b.

Simulation 2. For the second simulation, we consider 1 iteration, 10 propositional variables, `delta = 20`, `interval_max = 20`. We obtain plots 3a and 3b.

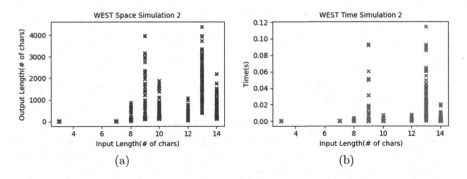

Fig. 3. We observe no outliers. The zero second runtimes are observed for MLTL formulas that consist of a single propositional variable or its negation.

Simulation 3. For the third simulation, we consider 2 iterations, 10 propositional variables, `delta` = 5, and `interval_max` = 10. We obtain plots 4a and 4b.

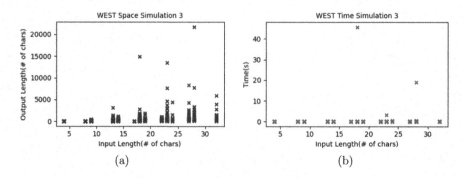

(a)   (b)

Fig. 4. $(p_7 \mathcal{U}_{[5,7]} p_9) \mathcal{U}_{[3,7]} (\mathcal{F}_{[1,4]} p_4)$ and $\mathcal{G}_{[3,7]} (p_9 \mathcal{U}_{[0,4]} p_0)$ are outliers in both. $\mathcal{G}_{[3,7]} (p_9 \mathcal{U}_{[0,4]} p_0)$ is an outlier in 4a only.

Simulation 4. For the fourth simulation, we consider 1 iteration, 5 propositional variables, `delta` = 10, `interval_max` = 10. We obtain plots 5a and 5b.

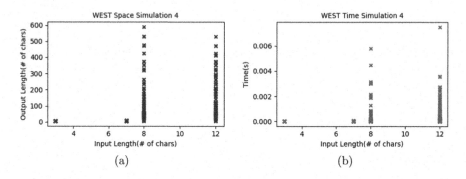

(a)   (b)

Fig. 5. We observe no outliers. The zero second runtimes are observed for MLTL formulas that consist of a single propositional variable or its negation.

We conclude from the simulations that for most practical purposes where nesting of binary temporal operators rarely occur, the WEST algorithm demonstrates good space and time complexity.

5   Correctness of WEST Tool Implementation

We accompany our proof of algorithmic correctness with a rigorous evaluation of implementation correctness, showing that our WEST tool correctly implements our WEST algorithm. Since our proof of algorithmic correctness is manual and our focus is on usability for validation by humans, we utilize more traditional techniques for robust software engineering with testing-based evaluation. The naïve approach is to test all inputs up to a certain size and verify the outputs, but this strategy would generate an unnecessarily large and redundant test suite. For instance, there is little sense in testing all MLTL formulas of the form $p_0 \mathcal{U}_{[0,t]} p_1$ for all t such that $0 \leqslant t \leqslant 99$; verification of a few should give sufficient confidence of correctness of the program. Instead, we test our implementation with a test suite that explores all possible sequences of lines of code that are executed (up to a certain depth).

5.1 Intelligent Fuzzing

Traditional black-box fuzzing is defined by Miller [23]: *"If we consider a program to be a complex finite state machine, then our testing strategy can be thought of as a random walk through the state space, searching for undefined states."*

Instead we utilize intelligent fuzzing, an alternate approach that leverages knowledge about program structure to generate valid inputs and increase coverage. Borrowing the words of Miller, our approach to testing the WEST program can be thought of as walking all possible paths up to a certain depth of the state space of our algorithm. We first outline our overall approach to intelligent fuzzing:

1. Construct a directed graph representation of our algorithm. The edges capture control flow of our algorithm, and vertices represent non-branching blocks of code.
2. Construct a test suite that explores all possible paths in the directed graph up to a certain depth. Run the WEST program on the test suite to produce a set of output files.
3. Run a naïve brute force generator of satisfying computations on the test suite and verify that both outputs match for all test cases.

State Diagram Construction. We can represent the state space of the WEST algorithm as a directed graph with the edges representing the control flow and vertices representing blocks of contiguous code without branching statements. The core of the WEST program lies in the recursive routine, `reg`, which calls the 8 different subroutines as shown in Fig. 6.

In order to construct the intelligent fuzzing test suite, we make the design choice to abstract away the eight subroutines in the overall state space diagram, despite the fact that they may have different possible execution paths within them. Without this abstraction, attempting to explore all execution paths in this finer graph is infeasible due to the explosion in the number of paths [26], some of which are provably impossible to construct a test input to explore.

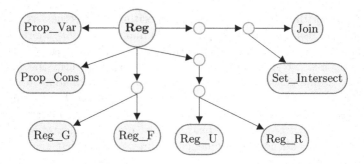

Fig. 6. Abstracted graph of the `reg` main routine. Red nodes signal recursive calls to `reg` on subformulas of the input formula.

Creating the Test Suite. To generate our intelligent fuzzing test suite, we first count the number of formulas $\varphi(d)$ to be generated as a function of the exact depth d of recursion desired. For $d = 0$, only the paths leading to `prop_var` and `prop_cons` can be explored, so $\varphi(0) = 2$. For $d \geqslant 1$, we recursively calculate $\varphi(d + 1) = 2\varphi(d) + 4\varphi(d)^2$; paths to `reg_G` and `reg_F` is counted by the linear term, and paths to `reg_U`, `reg_R`, `set_intersect`, and `join` is counted by the quadratic term. This gives $\varphi(1) = 20$, $\varphi(2) = 1640$, and $\varphi(3) = 10761680$, which tells us that $d = 3$ is computationally infeasible and $d = 1$ does not give us assurance about operators interacting with each other through nesting. Whence we select $d = 2$ as a happy medium. We generate the full test suite in a similar recursive manner. Firstly, the $d = 0$ test suite consists of two formulas: a propositional variable or its negation, and a propositional constant. Then for any $d \geqslant 1$, we iterate through all formulas in the depth $d-1$ test suite for `reg_G` and `reg_F`, and all pairs of formulas from the $d - 1$ test suite for the remaining four recursive paths. To ensure wider coverage, we randomly generate each of the propositional variables or their negation and propositional constants.

Verifying Against Naïve Brute Force. A relatively straightforward approach to generating the set of all satisfying computations of an MLTL formula φ over n variables, such that $m = \text{cplen}(\varphi)$, is to iterate over all $2^{m \cdot n}$ possible computations, which counts all possible length $m \cdot n$ bit strings. An interpreter function takes computation π and MLTL formula φ and determines if $\pi \models \varphi$ based purely on MLTL semantics. Our test program translates every first-order quantifier into a loop; then checking for satisfying conditions of the suffix of a computation naturally lends itself to recursion. The full implementation details are available in the WEST [Github](see footnote 1). On an Intel(R) Core(TM) i7-4770S CPU at 3.10GHz with 32gb RAM, the brute force program took nearly nine hours to execute the depth two test suite of 1640 formulas. For this test suite, we fixed the number of propositional variables at $n = 4$ and the largest computation length was $m = 5$, from formulas with doubly-nested temporal operators.

In comparison, the WEST program executed the same test suite in under thirty minutes on the same machine. Note that the brute force program outputs only computations of zeros and ones, and thus comparing the outputs of the WEST program requires expanding out the "S" characters in the regular expressions. It is important to state that although the full test suite matches between both implementations, absolute correctness on all inputs is not guaranteed for either program. However, the successful execution of the test suite gives us a much higher confidence in correctness of both the WEST program and the brute force program.

6 Regular Expression Simplification Theorem (REST)

As a final result, we provide a regular expression simplification theorem. This theorem describes the form of a set of MLTL regular expressions that simplify to all "S" characters. This theorem may help users identify tautologies, as the WEST program does not always output a string of all "S" characters when a formula holds true for every computation. We first define some vocabulary. We call an *arbitrary computation* any regular expression composed entirely of "S" characters and commas. For the purposes of the following theorem, we remove all commas from computations. We say a "0" or a "1" in a regular expression is a *fixed truth value*. We overload the definition of a matrix and say that a *matrix* is a representation of a union of regular expressions, where each row is a regular expression. This aids significantly in the description and proof of the theorem. Note that usual matrix algebra is not relevant to this definition.

Theorem 7 (*Regular Expression Simplification Theorem*). *Let M be an $(n+1) \times n$ matrix, where each of the $n+1$ rows represents a regular expression of length n with commas stripped. If each column has one "1", one "0", and $n-1$ "S" characters, then the union of this set of regular expressions can be simplified to S^n, the arbitrary computation of length n.*

The proof of REST follows from induction on the size of M and the pigeon hole principle. See the WEST Appendix(see footnote 5) for details of the proof.

This theorem gives us a sufficient but not a necessary condition for simplification to the arbitrary computation. One such example is the regular expression $(101) \vee (S1S) \vee (1S0) \vee (0SS)$, which fails the hypothesis of the simplification theorem but is still equivalent to SSS.

6.1 Theoretical Analysis of REST

We present an algorithm based on Theorem 7 for simplifying disjunctions of regular expressions and provide theoretical analysis, as well as experimental benchmarking. We determine that REST runs exponentially with respect to the length of the inputted regular expressions, both in the worst-case and average case. However, REST does not apply for many MLTL formulas, and WEST

Algorithm 5 Regular Expression Simplification Algorithm (REST)

Inputs: vector v of m regular expressions each of length n
Output: simplified set of equivalent regular expressions using Theorem 7

1: **procedure** REST(set v)
2: **for** $r \in [3, \min(m, n+1)]$ **do**
3:      **for** all vectors of regular expression $w \subseteq v$ s.t. $|v| = r$ **do**
4:          diff_cols ← indices of all columns of w that are not uniformly the same character
5:          **if** $|\text{diff\_cols}| = r - 1$ **then**
6:              $w' \leftarrow w$ containing only columns $\in$ diff_cols
7:              **if** w' satisfies Theorem 7 **then**
8:                  In w, replace all columns $\in$ diff_cols with s
9:                  $v \leftarrow$ remove_duplicates(v)
10:     return v

---

already demonstrates good time and space complexity in the average case without REST (see Sect. 4.3). Thus, the algorithmic complexity of REST is not of practical concern.

Theorem 8. *On input vector of regular expressions v of m strings each of length n, REST has a worst-case runtime of $O(n^2 2^m)$.*

Proof. We first analyze the statements in the innermost loop. In line 4, the construction of *diff_cols* can be done in $O(nr)$ time, by iteratively scanning the columns of w. In line 7, checking if w' satisfies the conditions of Theorem 7 is done in $O(r^2)$ time, by keeping a count of the number of $0, 1, S$ in each column. Thus, the innermost portion of the loop has runtime $O(nr + r^2) = O(n^2)$. The total runtime is bounded as follows:

$$\text{runtime}(\text{REST}(v)) = \sum_{r=3}^{min(m,n+1)} \binom{m}{r} O(n^2) = O(n^2 2^m).$$

6.2   Experimental Benchmarking of REST

We provide an experimental evaluation of the runtime of REST using randomly-generated sets of regular expressions satisfying the conditions of REST. Unfortunately, results suggest that the average case time complexity is of the worst case.

We generated 100 sets of regular expressions satisfying the REST conditions, with n between 10 and 25. We measured the amount of time in seconds taken to run the program. We ran these experiments on an Intel(R) Xeon(R) Gold 6140 CPU @ 2.30GHz with 376 GB RAM, taking over one hour. We conclude that REST is not advisable to use as a part of the WEST program because it is often too computationally expensive (Fig. 7).

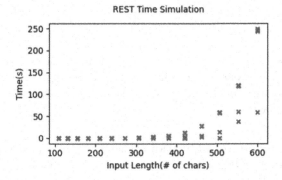

Fig. 7. For most inputs, REST's runtime is exponential with respect to the input length.

7   Using WEST: An Example

For this section, we include a Video tutorial[6] that demonstrates the use the WEST GUI program to explore specifications. The video uses the formula $(p_0 \wedge \mathcal{G}_{[0,3]}p_1) \rightarrow p_2$ from [16] as an example. The WEST program interface can aid a user in the process of MLTL formula validation by allowing them to explore the behavior of the formula and its subformulas.

The user can toggle the value of propositional variables at individual time steps to explore if the resulting computation satisfies the given formula. Additionally, the tool can randomly generate a satisfying computation that matches a specific regular expression, randomly generate an unsatisfying computation, and perform backbone analysis. All of these functionalities are immensely useful for allowing a user to validate that the formula they have written means what they think it means.

8   Closing Remarks

The primary goal of this work is to visually represent MLTL formulas to aid in debugging of MLTL specifications in industrial domains. We have accomplished this with our regular expressions framework, which captures many structural patterns of satisfying computations for a given MLTL formula. The tool itself has demonstratively reasonable runtime for most inputs, and the correctness of outputs has been verified to a high degree of confidence through intelligent fuzzing.

8.1   Future Work

The WEST algorithm and the release of our open-source tool open a multitude of different research directions.

---

[6] https://youtu.be/HoBJwdCq42c.

Similar Analysis of LTL. ω-regular expressions match only infinite words and can be used to describe satisfying computations of LTL formulas. Our work on validation for MLTL formulas lays the groundwork for future work on validation of the finite-trace logic LTLf [9] as well as LTL formulas. For the infinite-trace semantics of LTL, the particular difficulties revolve around the Kleene star operation, which behaves poorly due to computing infinite unions and intersections of regular expressions.

Regular Expression Simplification. Theorem 7 addresses a non-trivial situation in which a set of regular expressions may be simplified. A natural question to ask is what is the minimum number of regular expressions needed to represent a language of computations. However, such a minimal representation is not unique. For instance, $\{S1, 1S\} = \{S1, 10\} = \{01, 10, 11\}$. Other schemes may be needed to simplify any arbitrary union of regular expressions to a minimal representation.

Fuzzing General Recursive Algorithms. A tool to systematically convert a recursive algorithm into a directed graph representation of the state space would be a helpful aid for generating test suites. Additional care should be put into allowing for varying levels of abstractions of execution due to concerns of the path explosion problem. We note that such avenues for code-level verification will still be necessary even upon the completion of potential future work avenues like synthesizing the core implementation of the WEST algorithm from an interactive theorem prover. This is because the goal of explainability to humans will require at least some manual code authorship for the foreseeable future.

Code Synthesis from MLTL Specification. The truth tables generated by the WEST tool can now serve as input to a recently-published toolchain [3]. This newly-enabled workflow would produce encodings of the represented MLTL behavior for the interactive theorem prover ACL2, including automatically generating related properties of general interest such as unambiguousness [4,6,15]. Next, a synthesis pipeline consisting of a verified program transformation suite [18] along with a proof-generating C code generator [5] (both built on ACL2) generates verified software implementing the behaviors originally described in MLTL. By providing a new front-end for this tool chain, we have now enabled a path to generating provably correct software from validated MLTL formulas describing the desired behaviors of a system. Considering the rising popularity of MLTL for describing such behaviors, we expect this to be a rewarding avenue for future exploration.

Acknowledgements. This work was done as part of Iowa State University's Research Experience for Undergraduates funded by NSF grant DMS-1950583. We would like to thank Iowa State University and the NSF for this research opportunity. The assistance of our mentors Dr. Kristin Yvonne Rozier and Laura Gamboa Guzmán was invaluable and greatly appreciated. In addition, we thank Dr. Steve Butler and Dr. Bernard Lidický for their management of this program and organization of its funding. Finally, we want to thank Brian Kempa for his guidance and suggestions on the intelligent fuzzing portion of our research, Michael Q. Y. Chen for his guidance on the complexity analysis for the main algorithms, and Dr. Steve Butler for his intuition on the Regular Expression Simplification Theorem.

References

1. Alur, R., Henzinger, T.A.: Real-time logics: complexity and expressiveness. Inf. Comput. **104**(1), 35–77 (1993)
2. Aurandt, A., Jones, P.H., Rozier, K.Y.: Runtime verification triggers real-time, autonomous fault recovery on the CySat-I. In: Proceedings of the 13th NASA Formal Methods Symposium (NFM), pp. 816–825. LNCS, Springer International Publishing (2022). https://doi.org/10.1007/978-3-031-06773-0_45
3. Cofer, D., et al.: Flight test of a collision avoidance neural network with run-time assurance. In: 2022 IEEE/AIAA 41st Digital Avionics Systems Conference (DASC) (2022)
4. Coglio, A.: A complex java code generator for ACL2 based on a shallow embedding of ACL2 in java. In: Sumners, R., Chau, C. (eds.) Proceedings Seventeenth International Workshop on the ACL2 Theorem Prover and its Applications, Austin, Texas, USA, 26th-27th May 2022. EPTCS, vol. 359, pp. 168–184 (2022). https://doi.org/10.4204/EPTCS.359.14, https://doi.org/10.4204/EPTCS.359.14
5. Coglio, A.: A proof-generating C code generator for ACL2 based on a shallow embedding of C in ACL2. In: Sumners, R., Chau, C. (eds.) Proceedings Seventeenth International Workshop on the ACL2 Theorem Prover and its Applications, Austin, Texas, USA, 26th-27th May 2022. EPTCS, vol. 359, pp. 185–201 (2022). https://doi.org/10.4204/EPTCS.359.15, https://doi.org/10.4204/EPTCS.359.15
6. Community, T.A.: The acl2 theorem prover and community books: Documentation. https://www.cs.utexas.edu/~moore/acl2/manuals/current/manual/ Accessed 10 Sep 2022
7. Conrad, E., Titolo, L., Giannakopoulou, D., Pressburger, T., Dutle, A.: A compositional proof framework for FRETish requirements. In: Proceedings of the 11th ACM SIGPLAN International Conference on Certified Programs and Proofs, pp. 68–81 (2022)
8. Dabney, J.B., Badger, J.M., Rajagopal, P.: Adding a verification view for an autonomous real-time system architecture. In: AIAA Scitech 2021 Forum, p. 0566 (2021)
9. De Giacomo, G., Vardi, M.: Linear temporal logic and linear dynamic logic on finite traces. In: IJCAI, pp. 2000–2007. AAAI Press (2013)
10. Dion, S.: Global Precipitation Measurement (GPM) Safety Inhibit Timeline Tool. Tech. Rep. GSFC.ABS.7501.2012, NASA Goddard Space Flight Center, Greenbelt, MD, United States (2013). https://ntrs.nasa.gov/citations/20130000831

11. Erzberger, H., Heere, K.: Algorithm and operational concept for resolving short-range conflicts. Proc. IMechE G J. Aerosp. Eng. **224**(2), 225–243 (2010). https://doi.org/10.1243/09544100JAERO546, http://pig.sagepub.com/content/224/2/225.abstract

12. Giannakopoulou, D., Mavridou, A., Rhein, J., Pressburger, T., Schumann, J., Shi, N.: Formal requirements elicitation with fret. In: International Working Conference on Requirements Engineering: Foundation for Software Quality (REFSQ-2020). No. ARC-E-DAA-TN77785 in NTRS (2020)

13. Hammer, A., Cauwels, M., Hertz, B., Jones, P., Rozier, K.Y.: Integrating runtime verification into an automated UAs traffic management system. Innovations in Systems and Software Engineering: A NASA Journal (2021). https://doi.org/10.1007/s11334-021-00407-5

14. Hertz, B., Luppen, Z., Rozier, K.Y.: Integrating runtime verification into a sounding rocket control system. In: Proceedings of the 13th NASA Formal Methods Symposium (NFM 2021), pp. 151–159. LNCS, Springer International Publishing (2021). https://doi.org/10.1007/978-3-030-76384-8_10

15. Kaufmann, M., Moore, J.S.: The acl2 theorem prover: Website. https://www.cs.utexas.edu/users/moore/acl2/ Accessed 10 Sep 2022

16. Kempa, B., Zhang, P., Jones, P.H., Zambreno, J., Rozier, K.Y.: Embedding online runtime verification for fault disambiguation on robonaut2. In: Proceedings of the 18th International Conference on Formal Modeling and Analysis of Timed Systems (FORMATS). Lecture Notes in Computer Science (LNCS), vol. 12288, pp. 196–214. Springer, Vienna, Austria (2020). https://doi.org/10.1007/978-3-030-57628-8_12

17. Kessler, F.B.: nuXmv 1.1.0 (2016–05-10) Release Notes. https://es-static.fbk.eu/tools/nuxmv/downloads/NEWS.txt (2016)

18. Kestrel Institute: APT: Automated Program Transformations. https://www.kestrel.edu/home/projects/apt/ (2020)

19. Li, J., Vardi, M.Y., Rozier, K.Y.: Satisfiability checking for Mission-time LTL (MLTL). Inform. Comput. **289** 104923 (2022). https://doi.org/10.1016/j.ic.2022.104923

20. Luppen, Z., et al.: Elucidation and analysis of specification patterns in aerospace system telemetry. In: Proceedings of the 14th NASA Formal Methods Symposium (NFM 2022). Lecture Notes in Computer Science (LNCS), vol. 13260. Springer, Cham, Caltech, California, USA (2022). https://doi.org/10.1007/978-3-031-06773-0_28

21. Luppen, Z.A., Lee, D.Y., Rozier, K.Y.: A case study in formal specification and runtime verification of a cubesat communications system. In: SciTech. AIAA, Nashville, TN, USA (2021). https://doi.org/10.2514/6.2021-0997.c1

22. Maler, O., Nickovic, D.: Monitoring temporal properties of continuous signals. In: Lakhnech, Y., Yovine, S. (eds.) Formal Techniques, Modelling and Analysis of Timed and Fault-Tolerant Systems: Joint International Conferences on Formal Modeling and Analysis of Timed Systmes, FORMATS 2004, and Formal Techniques in Real-Time and Fault -Tolerant Systems, FTRTFT 2004, Grenoble, France, September 22-24, 2004. Proceedings, pp. 152–166. Springer Berlin Heidelberg, Berlin, Heidelberg (2004). https://doi.org/10.1007/978-3-540-30206-3_12

23. Miller, B.P., Fredriksen, L., So, B.: An empirical study of the reliability of UNIX utilities. Commun. ACM **33**(12), 32–44 (1990). https://doi.org/10.1145/96267.96279

24. Okubo, N.: Using R2U2 in JAXA program. Electronic correspondence (November-December 2020), series of emails and zoom call from JAXA with technical questions about embedding MLTL formula monitoring into an autonomous satellite mission with a provable memory bound of 200KB

25. Ouaknine, J., Worrell, J.: Some recent results in metric temporal logic. In: Cassez, F., Jard, C. (eds.) FORMATS 2008. LNCS, vol. 5215, pp. 1–13. Springer, Heidelberg (2008). https://doi.org/10.1007/978-3-540-85778-5_1

26. Pham, V.T., Böhme, M., Roychoudhury, A.: Model-based whitebox fuzzing for program binaries. In: Proceedings of the 31st IEEE/ACM International Conference on Automated Software Engineering. ACM (2016). https://doi.org/10.1145/2970276.2970316

27. Radio Technical Commission for Aeronautics: DO-333 - formal methods supplement to DO-178C and DO-278A (2011). https://www.rtca.org/content/standards-guidance-materials

28. Radio Technical Commission for Aeronautics: DO-178C/ED-12C - software considerations in airborne systems and equipment certification (2012). https://www.rtca.org/content/standards-guidance-materials

29. Radio Technical Commission for Aeronautics (RTCA): DO-254: Design assurance guidance for airborne electronic hardware (April 2000)

30. Reinbacher, T., Rozier, K.Y., Schumann, J.: Temporal-logic based runtime observer pairs for system health management of real-time systems. In: Ábrahám, E., Havelund, K. (eds.) TACAS 2014. LNCS, vol. 8413, pp. 357–372. Springer, Heidelberg (2014). https://doi.org/10.1007/978-3-642-54862-8_24

31. Rozier, K.Y.: Specification: the biggest bottleneck in formal methods and autonomy. In: Proceedings of 8th Working Conference on Verified Software: Theories, Tools, and Experiments (VSTTE 2016). LNCS, vol. 9971, pp. 1–19. Springer-Verlag, Toronto, ON, Canada (2016). https://doi.org/10.1007/978-3-319-48869-1_2

32. Rozier, K.Y., Schumann, J.: R2U2: tool overview. In: Proceedings of International Workshop on Competitions, Usability, Benchmarks, Evaluation, and Standardisation for Runtime Verification Tools (RV-CUBES). vol. 3, pp. 138–156. Kalpa Publications, Seattle, WA, USA (2017). https://doi.org/10.29007/5pch, https://easychair.org/publications/paper/Vncw

33. Ryan, J., Cummings, M., Roy, N., Banerjee, A., Schulte, A.: Designing an interactive local and global decision support system for aircraft carrier deck scheduling. In: Infotech@Aerospace. AIAA (2011)

34. Sipser, M.: Introduction to the theory of Computation. Course Technology (2020)

Symbolic Model Checking of Relative Safety LTL Properties

Alberto Bombardelli[(✉)] [iD], Alessandro Cimatti[iD], Stefano Tonetta[iD],
and Marco Zamboni

Fondazione Bruno Kessler, Via Sommarive, 18, 38123 Povo, TN, Italy
{abombardelli,cimatti,tonettas,mazamboni}@fbk.eu

Abstract. A well-known classification in formal methods distinguishes
between safety and liveness properties. A generalization of these concepts
defines safety and liveness relative to another property, usually considered an assumption on the traces of the language. Safety properties have
the advantage that their model checking problem can be reduced to simple reachability. However, the generalization of such reduction to the case
of relative safety has not yet been investigated.

In this paper, we study the problem of model checking relative safety
properties in the context of Linear-time Temporal Logic. We show that
the problem can be reduced to reachability when the system model is
free of livelocks related to the assumptions. More in general, we provide
an algorithm that removes such livelocks from the system model driven
by counterexamples to the relative safety property. We compare the approach with other reduction to safety algorithms on several benchmarks.

1 Introduction

The distinction between safety and liveness properties is very well known by
the formal methods community. It was first introduced by Lamport in [26] to
reason about the correctness of programs. Safety properties like mutual exclusion
demand that "bad things" never happen, while liveness properties like non-
starvation require that "good things" will eventually be achieved by the system.
Alpern and Schneider in [2] formalized the definitions in terms of languages
of infinite words. A safety property is a property whose counterexamples are
characterized by a prefix reaching a bad state, while a liveness property is a
property that can be fulfilled by extending any prefix to an infinite execution
with good states. The classification is complete in the sense that every omega-
regular language can be decomposed into a safety and a liveness property. As
proven by Alpern and Schneider in [3], model checking safety properties can be
reduced to checking an invariant.

In [24], Henzinger introduced the notion of relative safety and relative liveness, which extend the standard definitions considering an assumption property.
For example, a property φ is safety relative to an assumption α if any counterexample to φ satisfying α has a bad prefix. This is the case for example

P. Herber and A. Wijs (Eds.): iFM 2023, LNCS 14300, pp. 302–320, 2024.
https://doi.org/10.1007/978-3-031-47705-8_16

of a bounded response property that states that every request is followed by a response within δ time units: this property is safety relative to the assumption that requires δ time units to always eventually elapse (i.e., avoiding Zeno executions).

In this paper, we study the model checking problem of Linear-time Temporal Logic properties in the form $\alpha \rightarrow \phi$, where ϕ is safety. These properties are not usually safety, but are safety relative to α. We prove that if the system model M is live with respect to α, i.e., that prefixes of M can be extended to infinite executions satisfying α, then the model checking problem $M \models \alpha \rightarrow \phi$ can be reduced to an invariant check. More in general, we provide an algorithm that iteratively removes the states that are not live with respect to α (α-livelocks). These iterations are driven by (finite) counterexamples to ϕ.

We implemented the algorithm in the nuXmv [8] model checker on top of SMT-based symbolic model checking for finite and infinite-state systems. As additional contributions, we provide a symbolic compilation of SafetyLTL and a look-ahead heuristics that avoids deadlocks by requiring a bounded extension of finite counterexamples. We evaluated the algorithm on a number of benchmarks including assume-guarantee reasoning, bounded response properties assuming non-Zenoness, and asynchronous properties assuming a fair scheduling. The results show the benefit of reducing to invariants whenever the number of α-livelocks/iterations are limited.

Outline: The rest of the paper is organized as follows. Section 2, we provide some examples that motivates the form of properties addressed in this paper. In Sect. 3, we compare with other approaches based on reduction to safety. Section 4 gives basic definitions of safety, relative safety, and LTL. Section 5 details the compilation of SafetyLTL into symbolic transition systems. Section 6 provides the algorithms and proves their correctness and completeness. In Sect. 7, we describe the experimental evaluation and results. Finally, in Sect. 8, we draw some conclusions and directions for future works.

2   Motivating Examples

In this section, we give various examples where we are interested to prove properties of the form $\alpha \rightarrow \phi$ where ϕ is safety.

2.1   Bounded Response Example

The key observation of Henzinger in [24] was that some properties like bounded response in dense time are safety only restricting the language to non-Zeno paths. Although the contribution of this paper can be lifted to dense and super-dense models of time, we port the example to the discrete-time setting using an explicit real *time* variable. Therefore, let us consider the property:

$$\psi := G((p \wedge time = t) \rightarrow F(q \wedge time \leq t + \delta))$$

for some constant δ.

Let us assume that the values of $time$ are diverging over infinite execution traces, for example by posing the following constraints:

$$\alpha := G(next(time) \geq time) \wedge GF(next(time) - time > \zeta)$$

for some constant ζ.

Every trace π satisfying α and violating ψ will have a a state $\pi[i]$ in which p holds and $time$ has some value τ and a following state $\pi[j]$ with $j \geq i$ in which $time$ has a value greater than or equal to $\tau + \delta$ and for states between $\pi[i]$ and $\pi[j]$ q is false. Note that the assumption α is necessary to rule out counterexamples to ψ where $time$ is always less than $\tau + \delta$. The prefix of π up to $\pi[j]$ violates ψ for any possible suffix. Thus it is a finite trace witnessing the violation of ψ.

In fact, we can be prove that:

$$\alpha \rightarrow (\psi \leftrightarrow \phi)$$

where

$$\phi := G((p \wedge time = t) \rightarrow (time \leq t + \delta)W(q \wedge time \leq t + \delta))$$

which is safety. Thus, instead of $\alpha \rightarrow \psi$, we can prove $\alpha \rightarrow \phi$.

2.2 Safety Contracts

In contract-based design and assume-guarantee reasoning, the properties are often in the form $\alpha \rightarrow \phi$ with both α and ϕ safety. Consider for example the case in which $\alpha = Ga$ and $\phi = Gb$. In some frameworks (e.g., in AGREE [22]), this is interpreted as $G((Ha) \rightarrow b)$, meaning that if we find a violation of b we check that a is true in the past states, without caring about the future continuation. In a sense, we assume that the counterexample can be continued to satisfy Ga.

2.3 LTL Gp vs. Invariant

Similarly to the previous case, the LTL property Gp and an invariant property p are often considered interchangeably. However, they are not equivalent as the LTL is interpreted over infinite traces, while the invariant is violated by finite traces. Therefore, by reducing Gp to an invariant p, we are assuming that the counterexample violating p can be continued to an infinite trace.

3 Related Work

In [25], Kupferman and Vardi studied the verification of safety properties; they introduce the notion of informative path to formally denote a computation violating a safety property. That work also defines a PSPACE procedure to check whether a property is safety. Later, in [27], the same approach have been applied in a BDD-based algorithm. Another related work for the verification of safety property is [19]. In [19], LTL formulas are translated into circuits. If the property is syntactically safety, it is possible to reduce its verification to reachability checking; otherwise, the verification procedure involves also liveness checking. In all these works, the reduction to reachability is limited to safety properties, while relative safety is not considered.

The approach of AGREE [22] (see Sect. 2.2) proposes a semantics for contracts that can be seen as extension of the reduction for specific pattern of safety assumptions. However, such reductions assume implicitly the absence of deadlocks and livelocks. We are not aware of other approaches that use the assumptions explicitly and exploit the notation of relative safety for generic assumptions.

Other well-known reduction to safety are used to prove full LTL formulas. In [5], the approach duplicates the state variables and add monitoring constraints to look for a fair lasso. It works only for finite-state systems and the resulting reachability condition is related to the structure of the lasso-shaped counterexample. K-liveness [20] is more similar to our reduction as it counts and looks for a bound to the number of times the fairness condition of counterexamples can be visited. If the property is safety, the fairness cannot be reached or can be reached only once, depending on the actual construction. However, in the case of properties in the form $\alpha \to \phi$, the fairness conditions related to α are mixed with those of $\neg\phi$ in looking for a counterexample. So, in a sense, our approach gives more priority to look for a counterexample to ϕ, considering the fairness of α in a second step.

4   Notation and Preliminary Definitions

4.1   Notation for Sequences, Concatenation and Prefix

Given a sequence u and $i < |u|$, we denote by $u[i]$ the $i + 1$-th element of the sequence starting to count from 0 (thus, $u[0]$ is the first element), and by $u[i..]$ the suffix of u starting from $u[i]$. Given a finite sequence u and a finite or infinite sequence w, we denote by uw their concatenation. Given an infinite sequence, we denote by $Pref(\pi)$ the set of prefixes, i.e., $Pref(\pi) = \{u \in \Sigma^* \mid uw = \pi\}$.

4.2   Safety and Relative Safety

Given an alphabet Σ, a infinite/finite trace is an infinite/finite word over Σ, i.e., a sequence in Σ^ω or Σ^* respectively. A property is a subset of Σ^ω. A property is safety if nothing bad happens during an execution. If something bad happens, it occurs in a finite prefix of the execution. This is formalized as follows.

Definition 1. *Let P be a property. P is a safety property iff*

> *for all $\pi \in \Sigma^\omega$ s.t. $\pi \notin P$, there exists $\pi_f \in Pref(\pi)$ s.t.*
> *for all $\pi^\omega \in \Sigma^\omega : \pi_f \pi^\omega \notin P$*

Furthermore, we denote π_f as a bad prefix of P.

Definition 2. *Let P be a property. P is a liveness property iff*

for all $\pi \in \Sigma^\omega$, for all $\pi_f \in Pref(\pi)$, there exists $\pi^\omega \in \Sigma^\omega$ s.t. $\pi_f \pi^\omega \in P$

In [3], it was proved that for every omega-regular property P, there exists a safety property P_S and a liveness property P_L such that $P = P_S \cap P_L$.

Definition 3. *Let P and A be two properties. P is safety relative to A iff*

for all $\pi \in A$ s.t. $\pi \notin P$, there exists $\pi_f \in Pref(\pi)$ s.t.
for all $\pi^\omega \in \Sigma^\omega$: if $\pi_f \pi^\omega \in A$ then $\pi_f \pi^\omega \notin P$

In [24], it was proved that for every property P relative safety to A, there exists a safety property P_W such that $A \cap P = A \cap P_W$.

4.3   LTL and Safety Fragments

In this paper, we consider LTL [29] extended with past operators [28] as well as predicates, functions and the *next* operator. For simplicity we refer to it as LTL. We work in the setting of Satisfiability Modulo Theory (SMT) [4] and LTL Modulo Theory (see, e.g., [13]). First-order formulas are built as usual by proposition logic connectives, a given set of variables V and a first-order signature Σ, and are interpreted according to a given Σ-theory $\mathcal{T}$. We assume to be given the definition of $M, \mu \models_\mathcal{T} \varphi$ where M is a Σ-structure, μ is a value assignment to the variables in V, and φ is a formula. Whenever $\mathcal{T}$ and M are clear from contexts we omit them and simply write $\mu \models \varphi$.

LTL Syntax

Definition 4. *Given a signature Σ and a set of variables V, LTL formulas φ are defined by the following syntax:*

$$\varphi := \top \mid \bot \mid p(u_1, \ldots, u_n) \mid \neg\varphi \mid \varphi \wedge \varphi \mid X\varphi \mid \varphi U \varphi \mid Y\varphi \mid \varphi S\varphi$$
$$u := c \mid x \mid func(u, \ldots, u) \mid next(u)$$

where c, func, and p are respectively a constant, a function, and a predicate of the signature Σ and x is a variable in V.

LTL Semantics.
LTL formulas are interpreted over traces, i.e., infinite sequences of assignments to the variables in V. We denote by $\Pi(V)$ the set of all possible traces over the variable set V. Given a trace $\pi = s_0 s_1 \cdots \in \Pi(V)$ and a Σ-structure M, the semantics of a formula φ is defined as follows:

- $\pi, M, i \models \top$
- $\pi, M, i \not\models \bot$
- $\pi, M, i \models p(u_1, \ldots, u_n)$ iff $p^M(\pi^M(i)(u_1), \ldots, \pi^M(i)(u_n))$
- $\pi, M, i \models \varphi_1 \wedge \varphi_2$ iff $\pi, M, i \models \varphi_1$ and $\pi, M, i \models \varphi_2$

- $\pi, M, i \models \neg\varphi$ iff $\pi, M, i \not\models \varphi$
- $\pi, M, i \models \varphi_1 U \varphi_2$ iff there exists $k \geq i, \pi, M, k \models \varphi_2$ and for all $l, i \leq l < k, \pi, M, l \models \varphi_1$
- $\pi, M, i \models \varphi_1 S \varphi_2$ iff there exists $k \leq i, \pi, M, k \models \varphi_2$ and for all $l, k < l \leq i, \pi, M, l \models \varphi_1$
- $\pi, M, i \models X\varphi$ iff $\pi, M, i + 1 \models \varphi$
- $\pi, M, i \models Y\varphi$ iff $i > 0$ and $\pi, M, i - 1 \models \varphi$

where the interpretation of terms $\pi^M(i)$ is defined as follows:

- $\pi^M(i)(c) = c^M$
- $\pi^M(i)(x) = s_i(x)$ if $x \in V$
- $\pi^M(i)(func(u_1, \ldots, u_n)) = func^M(\pi^M(i)(u_1), \ldots, \pi^M(i)(u_n))$
- $\pi^M(i)(next(u)) = \pi^M(i + 1)(u)$

and the $p^M, func^M, c^M$ are the interpretation M of the symbols in Σ.

Finally, we have that $\pi, M \models \varphi$ iff $\pi, M, 0 \models \varphi$.

In the following, we assume to have a background theory such that the symbols in Σ are interpreted by an implicit structure M (e.g., theory of reals, integers, etc.). We therefore omit M to simplify the notation, writing $\pi, i \models \varphi$ and $\pi(i)(u)$ instead of respectively $\pi, M, i \models \varphi$ and $\pi^M(i)(u)$.

Moreover, we use the following standard abbreviations: $\varphi_1 \vee \varphi_2 := \neg(\neg\varphi_1 \wedge \neg\varphi_2)$, $\varphi_1 R \varphi_2 := \neg(\neg\varphi_1 U \neg\varphi_2)$ (φ_1 releases φ_2), $F\varphi := \top U\varphi$ (sometime in the future φ), $G\varphi := \neg F\neg\varphi$ (always in the future φ), $\varphi_1 T \varphi_2 := \neg(\neg\varphi_1 S \neg\varphi_2)$ (φ_1 is triggered by φ), $O\varphi := \top S\varphi$ (once in the past φ), $H\varphi := \neg O\neg\varphi$ (historically in the past φ), $Z\varphi := \neg Y\neg\varphi$ (yesterday φ or at initial state), $X^n\varphi := XX^{n-1}\varphi$ with $X^0\varphi := \varphi$, $Y^n\varphi := YY^{n-1}\varphi$ with $Y^0\varphi := \varphi$, $Z^n\varphi := ZZ^{n-1}\varphi$ with $Z^0\varphi := \varphi$.

Safety Fragments of LTL. SafetyLTL is a fragment of Linear Temporal Logic which disallows positive occurrence of until.

Definition 5. *The syntax of SafetyLTL is defined as follows:*

$$\varphi := \top \mid \bot \mid p(u, \ldots, u) \mid \neg p(u, \ldots, u) \mid \varphi \vee \varphi \mid \varphi \wedge \varphi \mid$$
$$\varphi R\varphi \mid X\varphi \mid Y\varphi \mid Z\varphi \mid \varphi S\varphi \mid \varphi T\varphi$$
$$u := c \mid x \mid func(u, \ldots, u) \mid next(u)$$

Note that we use include also past operators in SafetyLTL although this is typically defined only with the future ones.

Another safe fragment of LTL is full-past LTL. Although the syntax of the fragment is far stricter than SafetyLTL, the two logics have the same expressibility.

Definition 6. *The syntax of full-past LTL is of the form* $\phi := G\beta$ *where* β *is as follows:*

$$\beta := \beta \wedge \beta \mid \neg\beta \mid Y\beta \mid \beta S\beta \mid p(u, \ldots, u)$$
$$u := c \mid x \mid func(u, \ldots, u)$$

It was proved in [9] that both fragments, SafetyLTL (even without past operators) and full-past LTL express all and only the safety properties of LTL.

In [25], the authors introduce the notion of *informative* prefix. Informally, an *informative* prefix for an LTL property is a finite path that witnesses the violation of the formula. The formal definition introduces a mapping from the finite path to the sub-formulas of the property. The definition is as follows:

Definition 7 *[25]. Let ψ be an LTL formula in negative normal form, $Sub(\psi)$ be the set of sub-formulas of ψ and let π be a finite path of length n over the language of ψ. We say that π is informative for ψ iff there exists a mapping $L : \{0, \ldots, n\} \to 2^{Sub(\neg\psi)}$ such that:*

1. *$\neg\psi \in L(0)$.*
2. *$L(n) = \emptyset$.*
3. *For all $0 \leq i < n$, forall $\varphi \in L(i)$:*
    - *If φ is propositional, $\pi, i \models \varphi$.*
    - *If $\varphi = \varphi_1 \vee \varphi_2$, $\varphi_1 \in L(i)$ or $\varphi_2 \in L(i)$.*
    - *If $\varphi = \varphi_1 \wedge \varphi_2$, $\varphi_1 \in L(i)$ and $\varphi_2 \in L(i)$.*
    - *If $\varphi = X\varphi_1$, $\varphi_1 \in L(i+1)$*
    - *If $\varphi = \varphi_1 U\varphi_2$, $\varphi_2 \in L(i)$ or $[\varphi_1 \in L(i)$ and $\varphi_1 U\varphi_2 \in L(i+1)]$.*
    - *If $\varphi = \varphi_1 R\varphi_2$, $\varphi_2 \in L(i)$ and $[\varphi_1 \in L(i)$ or $\varphi_1 R\varphi_2 \in L(i+1)]$.*

4.4   Symbolic Transition System and Invariant Checking

A *Symbolic Transition System* (STS) M is a tuple $M = \langle V, I, T \rangle$ where V is a set of (state) variables, $I(V)$ is a formula representing the initial states, and $T(V, V')$ is a formula representing the transitions. A *state* of M is an assignment to the variables V. A [finite] *path* of M is an infinite sequence $s_0, s_1, \ldots$ [resp., finite sequence $s_0, s_1, \ldots, s_k$] of states such that $s_0 \models I$ and, for all $i \geq 0$ [resp., $0 \leq i < k$], $s_i, s'_{i+1} \models T$. Given two transitions systems $M_1 = \langle V_1, I_1, T_1 \rangle$ and $M_2 = \langle V_2, I_2, T_2 \rangle$, we denote with $M_1 \times M_2$ the synchronous product $\langle V_1 \cup V_2, I_1 \wedge I_2, T_1 \wedge T_2 \rangle$.

A property of $M = \langle V, I, T \rangle$ is specified over a set $V' \subseteq V$ of variables. The alphabet is therefore given by the set of assignments to V'. A finite or infinite path defines a corresponding trace given by restricting the assignments to V'.

An invariant property is a Boolean combination of predicates. Given an invariant property ϕ, the invariant model checking problem, denoted with $M \models_{inv} \phi$, is the problem to check if, for all finite paths $s_0, s_1, \ldots, s_k$ of M, for all i, $0 \leq i \leq k$, $s_i \models \phi$.

Given an LTL formula ϕ, the LTL model checking problem, denoted with $M \models \phi$, is the problem to check if, for all (infinite) paths π of M, $\pi \models \phi$.

The automata-based approach [30] to LTL model checking is to build an automaton (or in our case an STS) $M_{\neg\phi}$ with multiple fairness conditions $f^i_{\neg\phi}$ such that $M \models \phi$ iff $M \times M_{\neg\phi} \models \bigvee_i FG\neg f^i_{\neg\phi}$. This reduces to finding a counterexample as a fair path, i.e., a path of the system that visits each fairness condition $f^i_{\neg\phi}$ infinitely many times. In case of finite-state systems, if the property fails there is always a counterexample in a lasso-shape, i.e., formed by a prefix and a loop.

As anticipated in Sect. 2.3, given an invariant property ϕ, it may be the case that $M \models G\phi$ but $M \not\models_{inv} \phi$ because there is a finite path violating ϕ that cannot be extended to an infinite path. We thus introduce the notion of live system as follows.

Definition 8. *An STS $M = \langle V, I, T \rangle$ is live with respect to an LTL property α iff for every finite trace σ and finite path π of M over σ, if there exists a trace σ' such that $\sigma\sigma' \models \alpha$, then there exists an infinite path π^ω of M such that $\pi \in Pref(\pi^\omega)$ and $\pi^\omega \models \alpha$.*

Note that if $\alpha = \alpha_S \wedge \alpha_L$ where α_S is safety and α_L is liveness, then M is live w.r.t. α iff for every finite trace σ and finite path π of M over σ, if σ is not a bad prefix of α_S then there exists an infinite path π^ω of M such that $\pi \in Pref(\pi^\omega)$ and $\pi^\omega \models \alpha_L$ (and thus $\pi^\omega \models \alpha$). If such path does not exist, we call the states of π livelocks with respect to α.

4.5 Symbolic Techniques Reducing LTL Model Checking to Invariant Checking

SAT/SMT-based model checking techniques reduce full LTL model checking to invariant model checking. Such techniques typically apply a construction called *degeneralisation*, which is able to combine all the fairness conditions $f^i_{\neg\phi}$ into a single fairness condition f. For simplicity, in this section, we assume that the problem consists of a single fairness condition f.

Liveness to Safety. The *liveness-to-safety reduction* (L2S) [6] is a technique for reducing an LTL model checking problem on a finite-state transition system to an invariant model checking problem. The idea is to encode the absence of a lasso-shaped path violating the LTL property $FG\neg f$ as an invariant property.

The encoding is achieved by transforming the original STS S to the STS S_{L2S}, introducing a set $\overline{X}$ of variables containing a copy $\overline{x}$ for each state variable x of the original system, plus additional variables *seen*, *triggered* and *loop*. Let $S \doteq \langle X, I, T \rangle$. L2S transforms the STS in $S_{L2S} \doteq \langle X_{L2S}, I_{L2S}, T_{L2S} \rangle$ so that $S \models FG\neg f$ if and only if $S_{L2S} \models \neg bad_{L2S}$, where:

$$
\begin{aligned}
X_{L2S} &\doteq X \cup \overline{X} \cup \{seen, triggered, loop\} \\
I_{L2S} &\doteq I \wedge \neg seen \wedge \neg triggered \wedge \neg loop \\
T_{L2S} &\doteq T \wedge \left[\bigwedge_X \overline{x} \iff \overline{x}' \right] \\
&\quad \wedge \left[seen' \iff (seen \vee \bigwedge_X (x \iff \overline{x})) \right] \\
&\quad \wedge \left[triggered' \iff (triggered \vee (f \wedge seen')) \right] \\
&\quad \wedge \left[loop' \iff (triggered' \wedge \bigwedge_X (x' \iff \overline{x}')) \right] \\
bad_{L2S} &\doteq loop
\end{aligned}
$$

The variables $\overline{X}$ are used to non-deterministically guess a state of the system from which a reachable fair loop starts. The additional variables are used to remember that the guessed state was seen once and that the signal f was true at least once afterwards.

K-Liveness. K-liveness [20] is an algorithm that reduces symbolic LTL model checking to invariant checking. In order to prove the validity of an LTL formula ψ in an STS M, the algorithm count the occurrence of the fairness condition in the composed automaton $M \times M_{\neg\psi}$. If the algorithm is able to find a bound k such that the fairness condition f is visited at most k times, then the property is valid. It should be noted that the algorithm is not able to disprove the property; therefore, it is usually executed in lockstep with BMC.

The formal construction of the problem is as follows:

$$M_e = \langle V_\psi \cup \{c\}, I_\psi \wedge c = 0, T_\psi \wedge (f \to c' = c + 1) \wedge (\neg f \to c' = c) \rangle$$
$$M \times M_e \models c \leq k$$

where M_ψ is the automata construction of ψ, c is the counter variable, M_e is the automata of ψ extended with the fairness counter and k is a positive integer constant.

5   Symbolic Compilation of Safety LTL

5.1   Symbolic Compilation of Full LTL

Following [21], the encoding of an LTL formula ϕ over variables V into a transition system $M_{\neg\phi} = \langle V_{\neg\phi}, I_{\neg\phi}, T_{\neg\phi} \rangle$ with a set $F_{\neg\phi}$ of fairness conditions is defined as follows:

- $V_{\neg\phi} = V \cup \{v_{X\beta} \mid X\beta \in Sub(\phi)\} \cup \{v_{X(\beta_1 U \beta_2)} \mid \beta_1 U \beta_2 \in Sub(\phi)\} \cup \{v_{Y\beta} \mid Y\beta \in Sub(\phi)\} \cup \{v_{Y\beta_1 S\beta_2} \mid \beta_1 S \beta_2 \in Sub(\phi)\}$
- $I_{\neg\phi} = Enc(\neg\phi) \wedge \bigwedge_{v_{Y\beta} \in V_{\neg\phi}} \neg v_{Y\beta}$
- $T_{\neg\phi} = \bigwedge_{v_{X\beta} \in V_{\neg\phi}} v_{X\beta} \leftrightarrow Enc(\beta)' \wedge \bigwedge_{v_{Y\beta} \in V_{\neg\phi}} Enc(\beta) \leftrightarrow v'_{Y\beta}$
- $F_{\neg\phi} = \{Enc(\beta_1 U \beta_2 \to \beta_2) \mid \beta_1 U \beta_2 \in Sub(\phi)\}$

where Sub is a function that maps a formula ϕ to the set of its subformulas, and Enc is defined recursively as:

- $Enc(\top) = \top$
- $Enc(v) = v$
- $Enc(\phi_1 \wedge \phi_2) = Enc(\phi_1) \wedge Enc(\phi_2)$
- $Enc(\neg\phi_1) = \neg Enc(\phi_1)$
- $Enc(X\phi_1) = v_{X\phi_1}$
- $Enc(\phi_1 U \phi_2) = Enc(\phi_2) \vee (Enc(\phi_1) \wedge v_{X(\phi_1 U \phi_2)})$
- $Enc(Y\phi_1) = v_{Y\phi_1}$
- $Enc(\phi_1 S \phi_2) = Enc(\phi_2) \vee (Enc(\phi_1) \wedge v_{Y(\phi_1 S \phi_2)})$

This construction can be easily extended to reason about First-Order LTL defined in Sect. 4.3. The details can be found in [1].

5.2   Symbolic Compilation of SafetyLTL

We propose a novel symbolic compilation of SafetyLTL formulas into STSs, that enables the reduction of their model checking problem to reachability. The resulting algorithm follows the ideas already presented in [25,27]. However, the construction of the STS is aligned with the one of full LTL proposed in [21] and recalled in the previous section.

We denote such construction as *SafetyLTL2STS*. The construction of the STS is based on the construction of Sect. 5.1, the only differences are:

- $\neg\phi$ is rewritten in negative normal form (*nnf*) by pushing $\neg$ to the leafs. Since ϕ is a SafetyLTL formula, then the negative normal form of its negation does not contain the R operator.
- Since the construction is applied to the formula in *nnf*, the encoding *Enc* is extended to the derived operators in the straightforward way (e.g., $Enc(\phi_1 \vee \phi_2)$ is defined as $Enc(\phi_1) \vee Enc(\phi_2)$).
- Instead of constructing $T_{\neg\phi}$ using double implication for $v_{X\beta}$ and $v_{Y\beta}$ we use single implication i.e.

$$T_{\neg\phi} := \bigwedge_{v_{X\beta}\in V_{\neg\phi}} (v_{X\beta} \rightarrow Enc(\beta)') \wedge \bigwedge_{v_{Y\beta}\in V_{\neg\phi}} (v'_{Y\beta} \rightarrow Enc(\beta))$$

- Instead of using the set $F_{\neg\phi}$ of fairness conditions, we generate an invariant INV_ϕ defined as

$$INV_\phi := \neg(\bigwedge_{v_{X\beta}\in V_{\neg\phi}} \neg v_{X\beta})$$

Finally, we define $SafetyLTL2STS(\phi) := \langle M_{\neg\phi}^{saf}, INV_\phi\rangle$.

The idea behind this construction is to find a finite trace that witnesses $\neg\phi$. The variables of the form $v_{X\beta}$ are proof obligations for the next states. Thus, as before, the initial states of the automaton must contain the encoding of $\neg\phi$, initializing the proof obligations of the $v_{X\beta}$ variables. The transition condition propagates the needed proof obligations to the next state. Since $\neg\phi$ is co-safety, eventually a state is reached in which all $v_{X\beta}$ variables are false. This is equivalent to the algorithm in [25] for finding *informative prefixes* (see Definition 7). In fact, we can prove that any trace violating the invariant condition is informative for ϕ.

To clarify further, we provide an example considering the safety LTL formula $\psi_{ex} := G(a \rightarrow Xb)$. The construction of $M_{\neg\psi_{ex}}$ is as follows:

$$I_{\neg\psi_{ex}} :=(a \wedge v_{X\neg b}) \vee v_{XF(a\wedge X\neg b)}$$
$$T_{\neg\psi_{ex}} :=(v_{X\neg b} \rightarrow \neg b') \wedge (v_{XF(a\wedge X\neg b)} \rightarrow ((a \wedge X\neg b) \vee v'_{XF(a\wedge X\neg b)}))$$
$$INV_{\psi_{ex}} :=v_{Xb} \vee v_{XF(a\wedge X\neg b)}$$

To falsify ψ_{ex}, our counterexample π must satisfy $I_{\neg\psi_{ex}}$ at position 0; thus, π satisfies one of the two next variables and $INV_{\psi_{ex}}$ is true at the beginning. If b is true at the second step and at the initial step a and v_{Xb} were true, then we found a finite counterexample to the property $\pi = \{a\}\{\neg b\}$. Otherwise, we might continue for an arbitrary amount of steps in which $v_{XF(a \wedge X \neg b)}$ is true until we find a point i such that $\pi, i \models a \wedge v_{X \neg b}$ and $\pi, i+1 \models b \wedge \neg v_{X \neg b}$. If such a state is not reachable, then ψ_{ex} is valid.

Theorem 1. *Let M be an STS, ϕ be a SafetyLTL formula, $\langle M_{\neg\phi}^{saf}, INV_\phi \rangle = SafetyLTL2STS(\phi)$. Then, $M \models \phi$ iff $M \times M_{\neg\phi}^{saf} \models_{inv} INV_\phi$*

The proof can be find in [1].

5.3   Symbolic Construction of Live Systems

Note that the above constructions use in general prophecy variables that guess the future satisfaction of subformulas and may lead in general to systems that are not live. However, if α is in full-past LTL, then M_α in both constructions is live with respect to α. A live system can be built also for a SafetyLTL formula but with a more expensive BDD-based computation of the fair states (this is for example done for runtime verification of LTL properties, see, e.g., [17]).

6   Algorithm

In this section, we define a novel algorithm to verify relative safety properties. Section 6.1 defines a simple algorithm based on the SafetyLTL compilation to STS that verifies relative safety properties of the form $(\alpha_S \wedge \alpha_L) \rightarrow \varphi$. In Sect. 6.2, we extend that algorithm by iteratively blocking livelock counterexamples. Finally, in Sect. 6.3, we provide an optimization to reduce the amount of iteration required to verify relative safety properties.

6.1   Simple Algorithm Without Loops

```
1 Function verifyRelativeSafetyNoLoop(M, α, φ):
2 │    M' ← M × M_αS;
3 │    ⟨M_{¬φ}^{saf}, INV_φ⟩ ← SafetyLTL2STS(φ);
4 │    if M' × M_{¬φ}^{saf} ⊨_inv INV_φ then
5 │    │    return VALID
6 │    end
       /* π_f is a finite cex, try to extend it to α        */
7 │    if M' ⊨ α_L → G(¬l(π_f)) then
8 │    │    return UNKNOWN
9 │    end
10│    return INVALID
```
Algorithm 1: Algorithm to verify $\alpha \rightarrow \varphi$ without loops

Algorithm 1 verifies that an STS M satisfies $\alpha \to \varphi$, where φ is a SafetyLTL property and $\alpha = \alpha_S \wedge \alpha_L$ is an LTL property decomposed a safety part α_S and liveness one α_L.

The algorithm computes the STS satisfying α_S (i.e. M_{α_S}) using the construction of Sect. 5.1, it composes it with M into a new STS M'. It uses the construction of Sect. 5.2 to build an automaton $M_{\neg \phi}^{saf}$ and an invariant INV_φ such that $M' \models \varphi$ iff $M' \times M_{\neg \phi}^{saf} \models_{inv} INV_\varphi$. Then, if $M' \times M_{\neg \phi}^{saf} \models_{inv} INV_\varphi$, then $M \models \alpha \to \varphi$; otherwise, the algorithm provides finite counterexample π_f. However, as discussed in Sect. 2.3, a counterexample for an invariant might not be a real counterexample for φ due to livelocks in M', if M is not live w.r.t. α. Therefore, the algorithm checks if π_f is extensible to infinity through LTL model checking. If $M' \not\models \alpha_L \to G\neg l(\pi_f)$ (in which $l(\pi_f)$ denotes $\pi_f(|\pi_f| - 1)$), the trace has an infinite continuation that violates φ; on the other hand, if $\alpha_L \to G\neg l(\pi_f)$ is valid, we cannot determine whether or not $M \models \alpha \to \varphi$ because π_f contains a livelock with respect to α.

Theorem 2. *Algorithm 1 is sound.*

Proof. We consider the two VALID, INVALID cases:

If $M' \times M_{\neg \phi}^{saf} \models_{inv} INV_\varphi$, there is no finite trace of M' violating φ; Since φ is a safety property there is no infinite trace of M' that violates φ. Moreover, the finite traces of M' are the conjunctions of finite traces of M with the finite traces of α_S (due to the construction of M_{α_S}). Therefore, $M \models \alpha_S \to \varphi$, which entails that $M \models \alpha \to \varphi$.

If $M' \not\models \alpha_L \to G\neg l(\pi_f)$, then the finite counterexample π_f is a prefix of M' and can be extended by a suffix π^ω (which is part of the violation of $\alpha_L \to G\neg l(\pi_f)$) making $\pi = \pi_f \pi^\omega$ a trace of M' that satisfies α_L and, consequently, a trace of M and a trace of α. Therefore, since π_f is a bad prefix for φ, π is a trace of $\alpha \wedge \neg\varphi$ which is a legitimate counterexample of $\alpha \to \varphi$.

Theorem 3. *If LTL and invariant model checking terminate, α_S is a full-past LTL formula and M is live w.r.t. to α then Algorithm 1 is complete.*

Proof. It is sufficient to prove that Algorithm 1 does never return UNKNOWN. In fact, it can only return UNKNOWN when there is a counterexample π_f to $M' \times M_{\neg \phi}^{saf} \models_{inv} INV_\varphi$ and $M' \models \alpha_L \to G\neg l(\pi_f)$. Let σ be the trace of π_f. σ is a bad predix for φ and any extension violates φ. Moreover, α_L is liveness, thus σ can be extended to a trace σ^ω satisfying α_L. Since $M' = M \times M_{\alpha_S}$, $\sigma^\omega \models \alpha_S$ and thus $\sigma^\omega \models \alpha$. By assumption M is live with respect to α. Thus, there exists an infinite path π_M of M over σ^ω. Since α_S is full-past, the construction M_α is also live with respect to α and there exists a path π_α of M_α over σ^ω. Since the variables in common between M and M_α have the same value in π_M and in π_α because assigned by σ^ω, then their composition is a path of M' over the trace σ^ω. Thus, $M' \not\models \alpha_L \to G\neg l(\pi_f)$.

We observe that if M is a finite-state STS, then both invariant and LTL model checking terminates.

6.2   CEGAR Loop Algorithm

```
1 Function verifyRelativeSafety(M, α, φ):
2 |   M' ← M × M_α;
3 |   ⟨M^{saf}_{¬φ}, INV_φ⟩ ← SafetyLTL2STS(φ);
4 |   if M' × M^{saf}_{¬φ} ⊨_{inv} INV_φ then
5 |   |   return VALID
6 |   end
      /* π_f is a finite cex, try to extend it to α          */
7 |   if M' ⊨ ⋀_{f∈F_α}(GFf) → G(¬l(π_f)) then
8 |   |   M' ← ⟨V' ∪ V_{gen}, I', T' ∧ ¬last(π_f), F'⟩;
9 |   |   goto 4;
10|   end
11|   return INVALID
```

Algorithm 2: Algorithm to verify $\alpha \rightarrow \varphi$

Algorithm 2 generalises algorithm 1 to deal with α with a generic structure by introducing a loop to block livelock states w.r.t. α. The algorithm keeps looping until it either proves or disproves the property.

Theorem 4. *Algorithm 2 is sound.*

Proof. If $M' \times M^{saf}_{\neg\phi} \models_{inv} INV_\varphi$, then there is no finite trace of M' violating φ; therefore, since φ is a safety property there is no infinite trace violating φ that satisfies α without fairness and consequently α with fairness. If $M' \models \bigwedge_{f\in F_\alpha}(GFf) \rightarrow G\neg l(\pi_f)$, then $l(\pi_f)$ is a state in M' that cannot be extended visiting infinitely often F_α; thus, blocking it preserves satisfiability.

Finally, as for Algorithm 1, if $M' \nvDash \bigwedge_{f\in F_\alpha}(GFf) \rightarrow G\neg l(\pi_f)$, then the finite counterexample π_f is a prefix of M' and can be extended by a suffix π^ω (which is part of the violation of $GFf_\alpha \rightarrow G\neg l(\pi_f)$)making $\pi = \pi_f\pi^\omega$ a trace of M' and, consequently, a trace of M and a trace of α. Therefore, since π_f is a bad prefix for φ, π is a trace of $\alpha \wedge \neg\varphi$ which is a legitimate counterexample of $\alpha \rightarrow \varphi$.

Theorem 5. *If M is a finite state STS, Algorithm 2 is complete.*

Proof. We omit the proof for Line 4 and line 7 since they are identical to the proof of Algorithm 1. We only need to prove that at some point we stop blocking bad states. Since M is a finite state STS and M_α does not introduce infinite states, then the livelock states are finite and will eventually be all blocked forcing the algorithm to exit either with VALID or INVALID result.

6.3   Extending Algorithm with Lookahead

The main weakness of Algorithm 2 is the overhead given by the loop iterations for any found livelock. To face this issue, we introduce an optimization that computes a lookahead of length n on each invariant counterexample. The idea is that the invariant check must compute n successor states after the bad prefix of φ. The new construction is built on top of $SafetyLTL2STS$ as follows:

Definition 9. *We define* $Xdepth(\phi)$ *recursively as follows:*
(i) $Xdepth(p) = 0$ *(ii)* $Xdepth(\neg\phi) = Xdepth(\phi)$
(iii) $Xdepth(X\phi) = Xdepth(\phi) + 1$ *(iv)* $Xdepth(next(\phi)) = Xdepth(\phi) + 1$
(v) $Xdepth(\phi_1 \vee \phi_2) = max(Xdepth(\phi_1), Xdepth(\phi_2))$
(vi) $Xdepth(\phi_1 U \phi_2) = max(Xdepth(\phi_1), Xdepth(\phi_2))$.

We integrate this construction into Algorithm 2. At the first iteration parameter n is initialised heuristically to $Xdepth(\alpha) + 1$, then it is incremented by one at each step. Moreover, when we check that a finite counterexample is extensible, instead of considering the last state of π_f, we pick the last state of the violation of φ. We observe that all the states after the bad state in π_f are livelocks because otherwise our violation would be extensible. Therefore, we can safely block those states as well.

7   Experimental Evaluation

We evaluated the performances of our algorithm by comparing it to the other two well known algorithms used in the reduction of LTL to invariant model checking: k-liveness and liveness to safety (adapted for infinite state systems as proposed in [23]). All the algorithms are implemented inside the nuXmv symbolic model checker. Since the k-liveness algorithm is not able to disprove properties, it has been executed in lockstep with BMC. In our implementation, the algorithms are constructed on top of MathSAT5 [15] SMT-solver, which supports combinations of theories such as $\mathcal{LIA}$, $\mathcal{LRA}$ and $\mathcal{EUF}$. Moreover, k-liveness and the algorithms presented in this paper are built on top of an infinite state version of the IC3 algorithm [14].

The experiments[1] were run in parallel on a cluster with nodes with Intel Xeon CPU 6226R running at 2.9 GHz with 32CPU, 12 GB. The timeout for each run was one hour and the memory cap was set to 1 GB.

We carried out the experimental evaluation comparing the execution time of each algorithm on each instance. In the remainder of this section, we denote the relative safety algorithm with the lookahead construction as rels-la, the relative safety algorithm without lookahead construction as rels-no-la, the liveness to safety algorithm as l2s and kliveness algorithm as klive.

7.1   Benchmarks

The benchmarks have been taken from different sources: (i) Assume-guarantee contracts models of OCRA [10] representing a simplified Wheel Brake System,

---

[1] The results of the experimental evaluation can be found at https://es-static.fbk.eu/people/bombardelli/papers/ifm23/ifm23.tar.gz.

Redundant Sensors and other models. (ii) A subset of finite state models from NuSMV examples. (iii) Automatically discretized timed nuXmv benchmarks [12] such as the emergency diesel and a modified version of the Fischer algorithm. (iv) Handcrafted parametrized benchmarks to study the scalability of rels-la compared to kliveness and liveness to safety.

Overall, we collected roughly 850 formulas to be verified by each algorithm. The evaluation considered both valid and invalid properties. Regarding the structure of the formulas, we considered both pure safety properties (i.e. properties in which $\alpha := \top$) and relative safety properties (with the form $\alpha \rightarrow \varphi$). The structure of α was not limited as well, we considered cases in which α was pure safety, pure liveness and also a generic LTL property. Regarding the type of models, they are both from discrete and timed benchmarks, with variables ranging from *enumeratives, Booleans, integers* and *reals*.

In the following, we describe the handcrafted parameterised benchmarks.

Asynchronous Discrete Bounded Response: This benchmark considers the asynchronous composition of l bounded response components. Each component receives the same input *trig* and if it keeps receiving the input for n steps, then in m steps it set the variable *res* to *true*. When a component is not running it stutters i.e. it ignores inputs and its variable remain unchanged.

The property ψ in form $\alpha \rightarrow \varphi$ is as follows: α is a liveness property that guarantees that each component will be scheduled infinitely often i.e. $\alpha := GFrun_i$. φ asks that if a trigger remains true for g_n steps, then in g_m steps a variable result becomes true i.e. $\varphi := G(G_{[0,g_n]}trig \rightarrow F_{[0,g_m]}res)$. The parameters g_n and g_m depends on the parameters l, n and m. Each parameter n, m, l is instantiated with different values; moreover, the model gives different assignments to g_n and g_m to produce both valid and invalid properties.

Monitor Sensor: This benchmark is composed of a sensor and a monitor. The sensor reads a *real* input signal and, if there are no faults, it returns a signal with a perturbation bounded by a constant; otherwise, it replicates its last value forever. The monitor reads the sensor output every q time unit and if it reads the same value twice it raises an alarm.

The property to be verified is as follows. Assuming non-Zenoness of time, if there is a fault an alarm is raised in at most p time units. Parameters p, q are instantiated with different values and as both *integers* and *reals*. Depending on the assignments of p and q the property can be either valid or invalid. Moreover, we considered a variation of the model that introduces livelocks.

7.2   Experimental Results and Analysis

Figure 1 shows scatter plots comparing the rels-la algorithm with k-liveness, liveness to safety and rels-no-la in terms of execution time. The y-coordinate of each point represents the execution time of rels-la in that particular instance; conversely, the x-coordinate represents the execution time of the other algorithm. When a point is below the diagonal, it means that rels-la is faster on the given instance. When the point is above the diagonal the other algorithm is faster than rels-la.

Comparison with l2s and K-Liveness

Comparison with Liveness to Safety: Figure 1b and Fig. 1e highlight significant differences in the performance between l2s and rels-la. Although there are few instances that can be solved by l2s in a few seconds and are not solved by rels-la, the vast majority of the instances timed out with liveness to safety. This result is due to the weaknesses that liveness to safety has with infinite-state systems because it needs a finite-state abstraction.

Comparison with K-Liveness: As Fig. 1d shows, klive appears to be more performant than rels-la with invalid instances even though rels-la still outperforms klive in several invalid instances and overall is able to solve more invalid instances. We think that in many cases BMC, which runs in lockstep with klive, can be significantly faster in finding counterexample because rels-la has an overhead of time to check the extendibility of π_f and can still need multiple interactions to converge. On the other hand, when the liveness part of α is significant, rels-la outperforms klive.

Regarding the valid instances, Fig. 1a shows that rels-la outperforms in most cases klive. Few instances times out with rels-la while they are solved in a short time with the klive algorithm and rels-no-la. Apparently, in these instances, the lookahead counter prevents ic3 to converge. Moreover, we observed that with small variation over parameters of the monitor sensor models neither rels-la nor rels-no-la are able to converge. This result occurs because the algorithm keeps finding counterexamples in an unfair region and it is not able to generalise them. Moreover, the lookahead construction is not effective in this case because the trace extendibility depends on the assignment of two parameters. When livelocks are removed from the model the algorithm converges easily.

Relative safety algorithm performs significantly better than k-liveness with benchmarks from *Asynchronous discrete bounded response* and with the valid instances of *mutual exclusion* benchmarks. We think that the reasons why this happens are the following. In these benchmarks, φ is slightly complicated; this characteristic penalizes k-liveness because the construction of the model with the counter needs a degeneralization of $M_{\neg\varphi}$ to produce single fairness. This situation hinders ic3 in the process of inductive invariant construction. On the opposite side, the construction of *SafetyLTL2STS* is quite effective and does not suffer the overhead of the liveness conditions of α; therefore, invariant checking is significantly faster with our algorithm with these instances.

In many instances, the two algorithms appear to have comparable results. We observed that is often the case when φ and α are both simple safety properties, the model does not contain many livelocks and the fairness is either absent or simple. Our theory is that for such instances k-liveness construction is similar to ours and the counter does not provide an overhead with valid formulas. However, when the formulas are invalid, we observe that such instances are easier to verify with BMC, which runs in lockstep with klive.

Impact of Lookahead Construction: The lookahead construction forces each finite counterexample to be extended with n steps. As Fig. 1c and Fig. 1f shows, this optimization provide a significant performance boost. In particular with the instances that contain several deadlocks or livelocks in M'. The intuition behind this result is that with a lightweight overhead in the invariant verification, the algorithm is able to discard a potentially infinite amount of livelocks that could potentially block the algorithm forever. Moreover, the livelocks caused by prophecy variables for X are all discarded by a sufficiently large lookahead.

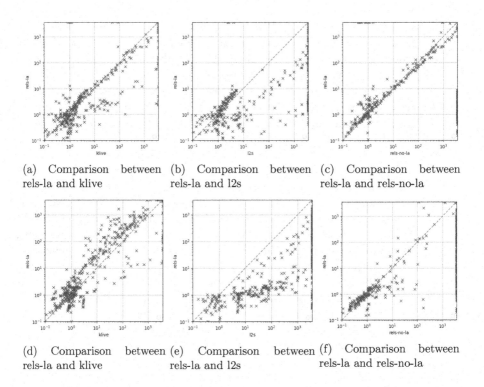

(a) Comparison between rels-la and klive

(b) Comparison between rels-la and l2s

(c) Comparison between rels-la and rels-no-la

(d) Comparison between rels-la and klive

(e) Comparison between rels-la and l2s

(f) Comparison between rels-la and rels-no-la

Fig. 1. Scatter plots comparing rels-la with the other algorithms. Plots with green crosses represent valid properties while red crosses represent invalid properties.

8   Conclusions and Future Work

In this work, we proposed an approach that extends the standard reduction to safety properties to invariants by exploiting the concept of relative safety. We thus focused on LTL properties of the form $\alpha \rightarrow \phi$ where ϕ is safety, providing various examples to motivate the choice. We proved that the reduction is complete when the system model is live with respect to the assumption α. We then provided a general algorithm that performs iteratively more than one invariant checking blocking at each time livelocks. We compared the approach to other techniques for generic LTL properties based on reduction to safety showing that is much more efficient in case of valid properties and complementary to BMC in finding counterexamples.

The directions for future work are many. In order to improve the efficiency of the approach we may consider various options: use BMC in parallel to the reduction to find counterexamples; explore incrementality in the different iteration of invariant model checking; investigate more efficient ways to generalize the livelocks to be blocked. In terms of directions for further extensions, we will apply the approach to contract-based compositional reasoning [18] and asynchronous composition of properties [7], we will consider other safety fragments such as the one defined in [11], and we will study the relation with assumption-based runtime verification [16].

References

1. Alberto Bombardelli, S.T., Cimatti, A., Zamboni, M.: Symbolic model checking of relative safety LTL properties - extended with proofs. https://es-static.fbk.eu/people/bombardelli/papers/ifm23/ifm23_ext.pdf
2. Alpern, B., Schneider, F.B.: Defining liveness. Inf. Process. Lett. **21**(4), 181–185 (1985)
3. Alpern, B., Schneider, F.B.: Recognizing safety and liveness. Distrib. Comput. **2**(3), 117–126 (1987)
4. Barrett, C.W., Sebastiani, R., Seshia, S.A., Tinelli, C.: Satisfiability modulo theories. In: Handbook of Satisfiability, Frontiers in Artificial Intelligence and Applications, vol. 336, pp. 1267–1329. IOS Press (2021)
5. Biere, A., Artho, C., Schuppan, V.: Liveness checking as safety checking. Electron. Notes Theor. Comput. Sci. **66**(2), 160–177 (2002)
6. Biere, A., Artho, C., Schuppan, V.: Liveness checking as safety checking. In: International Workshop on Formal Methods for Industrial Critical Systems (2002)
7. Bombardelli, A., Tonetta, S.: Asynchronous composition of local interface LTL properties. In: Deshmukh, J.V., Havelund, K., Perez, I. (eds.) NASA Formal Methods: 14th International Symposium, NFM 2022, Pasadena, 24–27 May 2022, Proceedings, pp. 508–526. Springer, Cham (2022). https://doi.org/10.1007/978-3-031-06773-0_27
8. Cavada, R., et al.: The NUXMV symbolic model checker. In: Biere, A., Bloem, R. (eds.) CAV 2014. LNCS, vol. 8559, pp. 334–342. Springer, Cham (2014). https://doi.org/10.1007/978-3-319-08867-9_22
9. Chang, E., Manna, Z., Pnueli, A.: Characterization of temporal property classes. In: Kuich, W. (ed.) ICALP 1992. LNCS, vol. 623, pp. 474–486. Springer, Heidelberg (1992). https://doi.org/10.1007/3-540-55719-9_97
10. Cimatti, A., Dorigatti, M., Tonetta, S.: Ocra: A Tool for Checking the Refinement of Temporal Contracts, pp 702–705 (2013)
11. Cimatti, A., Geatti, L., Gigante, N., Montanari, A., Tonetta, S.: Reactive synthesis from extended bounded response LTL specifications. In: FMCAD, pp. 83–92. IEEE (2020)

12. Cimatti, A., Griggio, A., Magnago, E., Roveri, M., Tonetta, S.: Extending nuxmv with timed transition systems and timed temporal properties. In: International Conference on Computer Aided Verification (2019)
13. Cimatti, A., Griggio, A., Magnago, E., Roveri, M., Tonetta, S.: SMT-based satisfiability of first-order LTL with event freezing functions and metric operators. Inf. Comput. **272**, 104502 (2020)
14. Cimatti, A., Griggio, A., Mover, S., Tonetta, S.: IC3 modulo theories via implicit predicate abstraction. In: Ábrahám, E., Havelund, K. (eds.) TACAS 2014. LNCS, vol. 8413, pp. 46–61. Springer, Heidelberg (2014). https://doi.org/10.1007/978-3-642-54862-8_4
15. Cimatti, A., Griggio, A., Schaafsma, B.J., Sebastiani, R.: The MathSAT 5 SMT Solver (2012)
16. Cimatti, A., Tian, C., Tonetta, S.: Assumption-based runtime verification with partial observability and resets. In: Finkbeiner, B., Mariani, L. (eds.) RV 2019. LNCS, vol. 11757, pp. 165–184. Springer, Cham (2019). https://doi.org/10.1007/978-3-030-32079-9_10
17. Cimatti, A., Tian, C., Tonetta, S.: Assumption-based runtime verification. Formal Methods Syst. Des. **60**(2), 277–324 (2022)
18. Cimatti, A., Tonetta, S.: Contracts-refinement proof system for component-based embedded systems. Sci. Comput. Program. **97**, 333–348 (2015)
19. Claessen, K., Eén, N., Sterin, B.: A circuit approach to LTL model checking. In: 2013 Formal Methods in Computer-Aided Design, pp. 53–60 (2013)
20. Claessen, K., Sörensson, N.: A liveness checking algorithm that counts. In: 2012 Formal Methods in Computer-Aided Design (FMCAD), pp. 52–59 (2012)
21. Clarke, E.M., Grumberg, O., Hamaguchi, K.: Another look at LTL model checking. Formal Methods Syst. Des. **10**, 47–71 (1994)
22. Cofer, D., Gacek, A., Miller, S., Whalen, M.W., LaValley, B., Sha, L.: Compositional verification of architectural models. In: Goodloe, A.E., Person, S. (eds.) NFM 2012. LNCS, vol. 7226, pp. 126–140. Springer, Heidelberg (2012). https://doi.org/10.1007/978-3-642-28891-3_13
23. Daniel, J., Cimatti, A., Griggio, A., Tonetta, S., Mover, S.: Infinite-state liveness-to-safety via implicit abstraction and well-founded relations. In: Chaudhuri, S., Farzan, A. (eds.) CAV 2016. LNCS, vol. 9779, pp. 271–291. Springer, Cham (2016). https://doi.org/10.1007/978-3-319-41528-4_15
24. Henzinger, T.A.: Sooner is safer than later. Inf. Process. Lett. **43**, 135–141 (1992)
25. Kupferman, O., Vardi, M.Y.: Model checking of safety properties. Formal Methods Syst. Des. **19**(3), 291–314 (2001)
26. Lamport, L.: Proving the correctness of multiprocess programs. IEEE Trans. Softw. Eng. **3**(2), 125–143 (1977)
27. Latvala, T.: Efficient model checking of safety properties. In: Ball, T., Rajamani, S.K. (eds.) SPIN 2003. LNCS, vol. 2648, pp. 74–88. Springer, Heidelberg (2003). https://doi.org/10.1007/3-540-44829-2_5
28. Lichtenstein, O., Pnueli, A., Zuck, L.: The glory of the past. In: Parikh, R. (ed.) Logic of Programs 1985. LNCS, vol. 193, pp. 196–218. Springer, Heidelberg (1985). https://doi.org/10.1007/3-540-15648-8_16
29. Pnueli, A.: The temporal logic of programs. In: FOCS, pp. 46–57. IEEE Computer Society (1977)
30. Vardi, M.Y., Wolper, P.: An automata-theoretic approach to automatic program verification. In: Proceedings of the First Symposium on Logic in Computer Science, pp. 322–331. IEEE Computer Society (1986)

Extending PlusCal for Modeling Distributed Algorithms

Horatiu Cirstea and Stephan Merz[✉]

University of Lorraine, CNRS, Inria, LORIA, Nancy, France

Abstract. PlusCal is a language for describing algorithms at a high level of abstraction. The PlusCal translator generates a TLA$^+$ specification that can be verified using the TLA$^+$ model checkers or proof assistant. We describe Distributed PlusCal, an extension of PlusCal that is intended to facilitate the description of distributed algorithms. Distributed PlusCal adds two orthogonal concepts to PlusCal: (i) processes can consist of several threads that share process-local variables, and (ii) Distributed PlusCal provides communication channels with associated primitives for sending and receiving messages. The existing PlusCal translator has been extended to support these concepts, and we report on initial experience with the use of Distributed PlusCal.

1 Introduction

Distributed systems and the algorithms that these systems implement are notoriously difficult to design and to verify. This is due to the high number of potential executions that interleave steps of system components (distributed nodes, threads, messaging subsystem) executing independently, leading to bugs that are difficult to reproduce. Formal verification techniques such as model checking or theorem proving help ensure correctness properties of algorithms and of programs. They can be applied at different levels of abstraction. In particular, verifying formal specifications of distributed algorithms at high levels of abstraction allows designers to identify errors that would be very costly to correct during later development stages.

However, languages used for formal modeling and verification are often substantially different from languages used in software development. For example, TLA$^+$ specifications [10] are formulas in a logical language that mixes mathematical set theory and temporal logic, which can be intimidating for system developers. It is therefore desirable to introduce front-end languages that are more familiar to system designers, while still enabling the use of formal verification techniques. In the context of TLA$^+$, PlusCal [11] is a language for describing sequential or concurrent algorithms at a high level of abstraction. PlusCal combines the "look and feel" of imperative pseudo-code with the power of mathematical set theory, used for modeling the data structures manipulated by the

P. Herber and A. Wijs (Eds.): iFM 2023, LNCS 14300, pp. 321–340, 2024.
https://doi.org/10.1007/978-3-031-47705-8_17

algorithm. The PlusCal translator generates a TLA$^+$ specification from a Plus-Cal algorithm, and this specification can be verified using the existing TLA$^+$ model checkers TLC [16] and Apalache [6] or the TLAPS proof assistant [2], thus allowing a system designer to obtain high confidence in the correctness of the algorithm.

However, PlusCal lacks certain constructs that would be useful for modeling distributed algorithms. In particular, it only offers top-level parallel processes, making it difficult to model distributed systems where nodes consist of several threads executing in parallel. In PlusCal, different threads of the same node must be modeled as individual processes, and variables shared by these threads must then be declared as global variables, obscuring the structure of the code. PlusCal also lacks primitives that support inter-process communication through message passing. Instead, such operations have to be described by defining global variables representing the channels and implementing the send/receive operations using low-level TLA$^+$ operators. Constructs similar to those missing in PlusCal can be found in several languages used for programming distributed systems. For example, lightweight threads exist in Ada [1] in the form of *tasks* and in Go [3] as *goroutines*. The latter also offers built-in channel primitives, which are also available in other programming languages including DistAlgo, MPI [13], and Erlang [17].

We propose an extension of PlusCal, that we call Distributed PlusCal, which allows users to specify multi-threaded processes and that provides built-in communication channels accessible with classical send/receive primitives. The syntax for threads is simple and intuitive and the translation to TLA$^+$ takes into account the possible interactions with other PlusCal features such as macros, procedures or fairness. Distributed PlusCal supports two types of channels that differ in whether they guarantee that messages are received in the order that they were sent or not. The operations on channels include standard send and receive, as well as a multicast operation that can be used to send a given message to several nodes simultaneously.

In the next section we briefly present TLA$^+$ and PlusCal. Section 3 describes the Distributed PlusCal language and the translation to TLA$^+$. In Sect. 4 we discuss the specification of two classical algorithms in Distributed PlusCal. We eventually conclude and discuss future work.

2   TLA$^+$ and PlusCal

2.1   The Specification Language TLA$^+$

TLA$^+$ [10] is a formalism for describing algorithms and systems at a high level of abstraction. It is based on mathematical set theory for representing data structures in terms of sets and functions, and on the Temporal Logic of Actions TLA for representing executions of systems. TLA$^+$ specifications usually have the form

$$Init \wedge \Box[Next]_v \wedge L$$

where *Init* is a predicate describing the possible initial states, *Next* is a predicate that represents the possible state transitions, v is a tuple containing all state variables that appear in the specification, and L is a liveness or fairness property expressed as a formula of temporal logic. Specifications are structured in modules; in particular, standard modules provide frequently used data structures such as integers, sequences or bags (multisets). A module may contain constant and variable declarations, statements of assumptions and theorems, and definitions of operators that are used in assembling the overall specification as well as correctness properties. Specifically, *state formulas* such as the initial condition or state invariants contain constant and variable symbols, where *actions* such as *Next* may also contain primed variable symbols, and *temporal formulas* additionally contain the operators $\Box$ ("always") and $\Diamond$ ("eventually") of linear-time temporal logic. State formulas are evaluated over individual states,[1] action formulas over pairs of states with unprimed variables denoting the value of the variable in the state before the transition and primed variables the value in the state after the transition. Temporal formulas are evaluated over infinite sequences of states.

As a concrete example, consider the specification

$$x \in Nat \land \Box[x' = x + 1]_{\langle x \rangle} \land \text{WF}_{\langle x \rangle}(x' = x + 1)$$

of a counter represented by the variable x. The state predicate $x \in Nat$ requires the initial value of x to be some natural number. The action $[x' = x + 1]_{\langle x \rangle}$ asserts that at every step, x either increments by 1 or remains unchanged,[2] and the temporal formula $\text{WF}_{\langle x \rangle}(x' = x + 1)$ states that the counter is incremented infinitely often. In general, the formula $\text{WF}_v(A)$ representing weak fairnes of action A abbreviates the temporal formula $\Box(\Box(\text{ENABLED } \langle A \rangle_v) \Rightarrow \Diamond \langle A \rangle_v)$ that asserts that whenever an A transition that changes the value of v is forever enabled, then such a transition must occur eventually. Replacing the subformula $\Box(\text{ENABLED } \langle A \rangle_v)$ with $\Box\Diamond(\text{ENABLED } \langle A \rangle_v)$, one obtains the definition of $\text{SF}_v(A)$ representing strong fairness of action A.

The formal verification of TLA$^+$ specifications is supported by the explicit-state model checker TLC [16], the SMT-based symbolic model checker Apalache [6], and the proof assistant TLAPS [2]. Konnov et al. [7] present an overview of the different verification tools applied to a common case study.

TLA$^+$ is an untyped language that provides a rich language of expressions. The expression $[x \in S \mapsto e]$ denotes the function with domain S such that every element x of S is mapped to the expression e (in which x may occur). This is reminiscent of a λ-expression while also introducing the domain of the function. Function application is written $f[x]$, and the expression $[f \text{ EXCEPT } ![v] = e]$ denotes the function that is similar to f, except that argument v is mapped to e. Within e, the symbol @ can be used to denote $f[v]$. A tuple $s = \langle e_1, \ldots, e_n \rangle$ is a function with domain $1 .. n$. In particular, $s[i]$ (for $i \in 1 .. n$) denotes e_i. Similarly,

---

[1] A state assigns a value to each variable.

[2] TLA$^+$ formulas are invariant under finite stuttering, and in particular specifications always allow for stuttering transitions.

a record such as $[foo \mapsto 42, bar \mapsto \text{FALSE}]$ is a function whose domain is the set of strings $\{\text{``}foo\text{''}, \text{``}bar\text{''}\}$; $r.foo$ is shorthand for $r[\text{``}foo\text{''}]$ and record update can be written $[r \text{ EXCEPT } !.foo = @ + 1]$.

```
algorithm <algorithm name>

(* Declaration section *)
variables <variable declarations>

(* Definition section *)
define <definition name> == <definition body>

(* Macro section *)
macro <name>(var1, ...)
  <macro body of statements>

(* Procedure section *)
procedure <name>(arg1, ...)
 variables <local variable declarations>
 <procedure body of statements>

(* Process section *)
process (<name> [=|\in] <expr>))
   variables <variable declarations>
   <process body of statements>
```

Fig. 1. General structure of a PlusCal algorithm.

2.2 The Algorithmic Langage PlusCal

PlusCal [11] was designed as a language for describing algorithms, providing a syntax that resembles imperative pseudo-code. PlusCal's expression language is TLA+, and this makes the language highly expressive, but also means that PlusCal algorithms are in general not executable. PlusCal algorithms are written inside a comment in a TLA+ module, using either a C-like syntax or the P-syntax closer to the Pascal programming language. The PlusCal translator generates a TLA+ specification from the algorithm and inserts it within the module containing the algorithm. Properties of algorithms are expressed as TLA+ formulas and are verified using the standard TLA+ tools. A central objective in designing PlusCal was to ensure a simple translation from PlusCal to TLA+, resulting in human-readable specifications.

The overall structure of a PlusCal algorithm is shown in Fig. 1. It is subdivided into several (possibly empty) sections that must appear in the given order. Global variables are declared first, followed by definitions of operators that may be used

```
--algorithm SemaphoreMutex {
  variables sem = 1;
  fair+ process (p \in 1..N) {
start:- while (TRUE) {
enter:     await sem > 0;
           sem := sem - 1;
cs:        skip;
exit:      sem := sem + 1;
} }      }
```

Fig. 2. Semaphore mutex example in PlusCal.

in the remainder of the algorithm and that may refer to the previously declared variables. Macros may contain PlusCal statements; their bodies are expanded at translation time, similarly to the expansion of macros in the C language. In contrast, procedures are invoked using the `call` statement of PlusCal. They may declare local variables and may themselves contain procedure calls, including recursive calls. Procedures do not return values but may modify global variables; the `return` statement transfers control back to the calling site.

The final section contains either process declarations as shown in Fig. 1 or a single body of statements for representing a sequential algorithm. Process declarations may introduce a single or a fixed number of instances of the process; the expression on the right-hand side must evaluate to a constant or to a finite set of constants that represent the process identities. Within the body of the process, the identity is denoted by `self`. Process declarations may be annotated by fairness conditions `fair` for weak fairness or `fair+` for strong fairness.

PlusCal statements include `skip` (which does nothing), assignments, conditional statements, while loops, and procedure calls. Processes may synchronize using `await` (or, synonymously, `when`) instructions that block until a predicate becomes true. PlusCal also includes two forms of non-deterministic control structures: `either` ... `or` ... can be used to introduce a choice between a fixed number of alternatives, whereas the statement `with` $x \in S$ expresses a choice among the values in a set S. In particular, combining `either` ... `or` and `when` provides guarded commands à la Dijkstra.

An important concern when describing concurrent algorithms is to model the "grain of atomicity", i.e., which statements are assumed to execute without interleaving with statements of other processes. PlusCal uses statement labels to this effect: all statements appearing between two labels are executed atomically. In addition, PlusCal imposes certain rules on the placement of labels. For example, every `while` statement must be labeled, and therefore processes may interleave between every iteration of the loop body. Labels may also take modifiers + or - that increase or decrease the fairness constraints with respect to that of the enclosing process.

As an example, Fig. 2 shows the PlusCal representation of a semaphore-based mutual exclusion algorithm between N processes where the constant N is declared in the enclosing TLA$^+$ module. In particular, the test and decrement of the semaphore are executed atomically since the instructions are not separated by a label, and strong fairness guarantees starvation freedom.

2.3   Translating PlusCal to TLA$^+$

Using the example of Fig. 2, we outline how the PlusCal translator generates the TLA$^+$ specification corresponding to an algorithm.

1. Generate TLA$^+$ variable declarations for all variables declared in the algorithm, regardless of their scope. The translator also declares the pc variable for tracking control flow, as well as a stack variable if the algorithm contains procedures. Define the tuple vars of all variables and the set ProcSet of all process identifiers.

```
VARIABLES sem, pc
vars == << sem, pc >>
ProcSet == (1..N)
```

2. Generate Init, the predicate that specifies the initial values of all the declared variables. Process-local variables (including pc) are represented as functions with domain ProcSet in order to distinguish the values corresponding to different instances of processes.

```
Init == /\ sem = 1
        /\ pc = [self \in ProcSet |-> "start"]
```

3. For each label appearing in the algorithm, generate a TLA$^+$ action that represents the effect of the statements following that label. In a multi-process algorithm, the definition takes the parameter self that stands for the identifier of the process instance executing the statements.

```
enter(self) == /\ pc[self] = "enter"
               /\ sem > 0
               /\ sem' = sem - 1
               /\ pc' = [pc EXCEPT ![self] = "cs" ]
```

4. For every process, generate a TLA$^+$ action that corresponds to the possible transitions of an instance of that process, as the disjunction of the actions generated for each label appearing in the process. Generate the action Next as the disjunction of the actions corresponding to each process, existentially quantified over its instances. In case control flow may reach the end of a process, Next contains an extra disjunct Terminating that requires all variables to remain unchanged. Finally, generate the overall specification Spec, including fairness conditions corresponding to the annotations in PlusCal.

```
p(self) == start(self) \/ enter(self) \/ cs(self) \/ exit(self)
Next == \E self \in 1..N: p(self)
Spec == /\ Init /\ [][Next]_vars
        /\ \A self \in 1..N: SF_vars(pc[self] # "start" /\ p(self))
```

3   Distributed PlusCal

Distributed PlusCal extends PlusCal with two independent features: it adds light-weight (sub-)processes, as well as communication channels with standard operations. Both of these features are available for the C-syntax and the P-syntax; we mainly use the former in this paper. These features are activated using the option -distpcal either on the command line or using the PlusCal options line in the enclosing TLA$^+$ module.

3.1   Sub-processes

A Distributed PlusCal process may have several sub-processes that we also call threads. When using the C-syntax, each thread appears within a pair of curly braces, a process with only one pair of braces corresponding to an ordinary PlusCal process. For P-syntax, threads are enclosed by **begin** and **end thread**. An example illustrating the declaration of threads using both syntaxes is given in Fig. 3. Threads cannot declare local variables but can access the local variables of the enclosing process as well as global variables. This corresponds to the intuition that in a distributed system, threads share local memory whereas nodes (represented by Distributed PlusCal processes) communicate via messages.

Translation to TLA$^+$. At every step in the algorithm, one of the threads performs a transition. Consequently, although the syntax additions for threads are quite minor compared to the single-threaded processes of PlusCal there are multiple aspects that have to be taken into account in the translation to TLA$^+$.

The VARIABLES declaration as well as vars and ProcSet are generated as for plain PlusCal. For Distributed PlusCal algorithms, the program counter progresses in each thread and thus, in order to distinguish the values corresponding to each thread, the pc variable is represented as a two-dimensional array indexed by the process identity and a thread index. The set SubProcSet of thread indexes depends on each process:

$$\text{SubProcSet}[p] = \{1, 2, \ldots, nt_p\}, p \in \text{ProcSet}$$

with nt_p the number of threads for process p. For the algorithm of Fig. 3, in TLA$^+$ this corresponds to:[3]

---

[3] The complete translation is presented in Fig. 4 at the end of this section.

```
1   --algorithm MyAlgo {              --algorithm MyAlgo
2     variables                         variables
3       tab = [ x \in 1..2 |-> 0 ];       tab = [ x \in 1..2 |-> 0 ];
4     process (pid = 3)                 process pid = 3
5     variables lv = 0;                 variables lv = 0;
6     {                                 begin
7   s1: lv := lv + 1;                 s1: lv := lv + 1;
8       tab[1] := tab[1] + lv;            tab[1] := tab[1] + lv;
9     }                                 end thread
10    {                                 begin
11  s2: lv := lv + 1;                 s2: lv := lv + 1;
12      tab[2] := tab[2] + lv;            tab[2] := tab[2] + lv;
13    }                                 end thread
14
15    process (qid \in 1..2)            process qid \in 1..2
16    variables t = 0;                  variables t = 0;
17    {                                 begin
18  rc: await tab[self] > 0;          rc: await tab[self] > 0;
19      t := tab[self];                   t := tab[self];
20  ut: t := t + 1;                   ut: t := t + 1;
21    }                                 end thread
22  }                                 end algorithm
```

Fig. 3. A Distributed PlusCal algorithm in which one process has two threads.

```
ProcSet == {3} \union (1..2)
SubProcSet == [self \in ProcSet |->  CASE self = 3 -> 1..2
                                     []   self \in 1..2 -> 1..1 ]
```

The pc of each thread is initialized to the label corresponding to its first action:

$$pc[p] = \langle l_1, l_2, \ldots, l_{nt_p} \rangle, \; p \in ProcSet$$

with l_i the label of the first action in the thread i of process p. If procedures are defined, they can be called from any thread and thus, the **stack** variable is also a two-dimensional array initialized to the empty record for each thread:

$$stack[p] = \langle \langle \rangle, \ldots, \langle \rangle \rangle, \; p \in ProcSet, \; size(stack[p]) = nt_p$$

For our example we have:

```
Init == ...
        /\ pc = [self \in ProcSet |-> CASE self = 3 -> <<"s1","s2">>
                                      [] self \in 1..2 -> <<"rc">>]
```

Then, the translation of each thread corresponds to the disjunction of all its atomic actions, and a process corresponds to the disjunction of all its threads.

Thus, for each $p \in$ ProcSet:

$$p = \bigvee_{i=1..nt_p} p_i \quad \text{with} \quad p_i = \bigvee_{l \in \mathcal{A}_{p,i}} l$$

where $\mathcal{A}_{p,i}$ denotes the set of (labeled) actions of the thread i in process p.

If p is a process template (specified with \in), the translation of p and of its threads takes the parameter self that stands, as in PlusCal, for the identifier of the process instance executing the statements.

The first process in our algorithm consists of two threads, translated respectively with the operators pid1 and pid2 which correspond to the PlusCal action translations but taking into account the fact that the pc variable depends not only on the process id (3 in this case) but on the thread as well.

```
1   s1 == /\ pc[3][1]  = "s1"
2         /\ lv' = lv + 1
3         /\ tab' = [tab EXCEPT ![1] = tab[1] + lv']
4         /\ pc' = [pc EXCEPT ![3][1] = "Done"]
5         /\ UNCHANGED << stack, y, lvp, t >>
6   pid1 == s1
7
8   s2 == /\ pc[3][2]  = "s2"
9         /\ ...
10  pid2 == s2
11
12  pid == pid1 \/ pid2
```

For the second process there is only one thread, and since this is a process template (qid \in 1..2), the translation uses a parameter self:

```
rc(self) == /\ pc[self][1]  = "rc"
            /\ ...
ut(self) == /\ pc[self][1]  = "ut"
            /\ ...
qid1(self) == rc(self) \/ ut(self)

qid(self) == qid1(self)
```

The Spec operator and in particular the Next operator are generated as for a single-threaded PlusCal specification, with the stuttering action Terminating adapted to activate only when all threads have terminated:

```
Terminating == /\ \A self \in ProcSet : \A sub \in SubProcSet[self]:
                  pc[self][sub] = "Done"
               /\ UNCHANGED vars
Next == pid \/ (\E self \in 1..2: qid(self)) \/ Terminating
```

Macros and Procedures. Macros can be used as in plain PlusCal and behave as textual substitutions. Procedures are also used similarly to PlusCal but some care has to be taken in the translation since a procedure can be called in any thread. First, as explained above, the **stack** variable is a two-dimensional array in Distributed PlusCal. For the same reasons, the TLA^{+} variable declarations corresponding to the procedure parameters and local variables are also two-dimensional arrays. Moreover, the operators corresponding to the procedure and to its actions are parameterized not only by a process, as in PlusCal, but also by a thread.

For example, consider the following procedure:

```
procedure foo(ind = 0, y = 0)
variables lvp = 0;
{
s:  lvp := lvp + y;
    tab[ind] := tab[ind] + lvp;
e:  return;
}
```

Three variable declarations corresponding to the parameters and to the local variable of the procedure are added to the **Init** operator:

```
/\ ind = [ self \in ProcSet |-> [ thd \in SubProcSet[self] |-> 0]]
/\ y = [ self \in ProcSet |-> [ thd \in SubProcSet[self] |-> 0]]
/\ lvp = [ self \in ProcSet |-> [ thd \in SubProcSet[self] |-> 0]]
```

and the following operator is generated for the action labeled **s**:

```
s(self, thd) ==
/\ pc[self][thd] = "s"
/\ lvp' = [lvp EXCEPT ![self][thd] = lvp[self][thd] + y[self][thd]]
/\ tab' = [tab EXCEPT ![ind[self][thd]] = tab[ind[self][thd]]
                                        + lvp'[self][thd]]
/\ pc' = [pc EXCEPT ![self][thd] = "e"]
/\ UNCHANGED << stack, ind, y, lv, t >>
```

The operator **e** is handled in a similar way and finally, an operator is generated for the whole procedure:

```
foo(self, thd) == s(self, thd) \/ e(self, thd)
```

One could use this procedure in the specification in Fig. 3 and replace the line 8 by call foo(1,lv) in which case the line 3 in the original translation of s1 becomes

```
/\ /\ stack' = [stack EXCEPT ![3][1] = << [ procedure |->  "foo",
                                            pc        |->  "Done",
                                            lvp       |->  lvp[3][1],
                                            ind       |->  ind[3][1],
                                            y         |->  y[3][1] ] >>
                                  \o stack[3][1]]
   /\ ind' = [ind EXCEPT ![3][1] = 1]
   /\ y' = [y EXCEPT ![3][1] = lv']
```

Fairness. As in PlusCal, fairness conditions can be attached to the algorithm, to process templates or to labels. When fairness is introduced at the top level with **fair algorithm**, we indicate that some statement must eventually be executed if the algorithm can take a step, and this corresponds to the condition WF_vars(Next) in the definition of Spec.

One can strengthen the condition to ensure that a process will eventually execute if it remains enabled by using the **fair** keyword at the process level. For Distributed PlusCal this corresponds to fairness for each thread of the respective process template. In our example, when writing **fair process (pid = 3)**, the following conditions are added to Spec:

```
/\ WF_vars(pid1)
/\ WF_vars(pid2)
```

As in PlusCal, we can strengthen even more the condition with **fair+** and in this case the condition SF_vars is used instead of WF_vars for all the threads.

The overall fairness requirement attached to a process can be modulated for individual actions and we can exclude a label from the fairness assumption using - or assume strong fairness using +. If, for the sake of the example, we change the specification of the first process to

```
fair process (pid = 3)
variables lv = 0;
{
s1a:+ lv := lv + 1;
s1b:- tab[1] := tab[1] + lv;
}
{
    // unchanged
}
```

then, the conditions added to Spec become

```
/\ WF_vars((pc[3][1] # "s1b") /\ pid1) /\ SF_vars(s1a)
/\ WF_vars(pid2)
```

PlusCal's **-termination** option can be used to generate a TLA$^+$ formula that asserts that all processes and threads will eventually terminate.

```
Spec == /\ Init /\ [][Next]_vars
        /\ WF_vars(pid1)
        /\ WF_vars(pid2)
        /\ \A self \in 1..2 : WF_vars(qid1(self))

Termination == <>(\A self \in ProcSet: \A sub \in SubProcSet[self] :
                   pc[self][sub] = "Done")
```

3.2   Communication Channels

In contrast to threads that communicate using shared variables, processes (or nodes) in distributed systems usually communicate by message passing. In a PlusCal algorithm, channels must be modeled explicitly using global variables, and operations on channels be defined using TLA$^+$ operators or macros.

Channels in Distributed PlusCal are built-in and can be declared just after the global variables of the algorithm. Channels that guarantee that messages are received in the order in which they are sent are declared using the keyword fifo whereas channels that do not offer such guarantees are declared as channel.[4] Channels are unbounded, meaning that there is no maximum capacity for the number of messages they can hold.

One can declare an N-dimensional matrix of unordered channels by writing

$$\texttt{channel } id[Expr_1][Expr_2]\ldots[Expr_N]$$

with id the name of the channel and $\langle Expr_i \rangle$, $i = 1..N$, the expressions defining the indexing sets; no set is specified for a simple 0-dimensional channel. Such a declaration gives rise in TLA$^+$ to the declaration of a variable named id and to an initialisation

$$id = [x_1 \in Expr_1, \ldots, x_N \in Expr_N \mapsto EmptyBag];$$

or just $id = EmptyBag$ for a simple channel, where $EmptyBag$ is the operator from module $Bags$ representing an empty bag (i.e., multi-set). More precisely, unordered channels are represented in TLA$^+$ using bags and ordered channels using sequences. Thus, if the channel were declared with fifo the initialisation would use the empty sequence $\langle \rangle$ instead of the empty bag.

The following initialization predicate is generated for the algorithm in Fig. 5:

```
Init == ...
        /\ ch = [ _n20 \in  Nodes |-> EmptyBag ]
```

with _n20 a freshly generated variable.

The following operations are supported on (unordered or ordered) channels:

---

[4] Following the PlusCal convention that the keyword variable can also be written variables, we also allow the plural forms for fifo and channel.

```
VARIABLES tab, pc, lv, t
vars == << tab, pc, lv, t >>

ProcSet == {3} \cup (1..2)
SubProcSet == [self \in ProcSet |->  CASE self = 3 -> 1..2
                                      []   self \in 1..2 -> 1..1 ]

Init == /\ tab = [ x \in 1..2 |-> 0 ]
        /\ lv = 0
        /\ t = [self \in 1..2 |-> 0]
        /\ pc = [self \in ProcSet |-> CASE self = 3 -> <<"s1","s2">>
                                      [] self \in 1..2 -> <<"rc">>]

s1 == /\ pc[3][1]  = "s1"
      /\ lv' = lv + 1
      /\ tab' = [tab EXCEPT ![1] = tab[1] + lv']
      /\ pc' = [pc EXCEPT ![3][1] = "Done"]
      /\ t' = t
pid1 == s1
s2 == /\ pc[3][2]  = "s2"
      /\ lv' = lv + 1
      /\ tab' = [tab EXCEPT ![2] = tab[2] + lv']
      /\ pc' = [pc EXCEPT ![3][2] = "Done"]
      /\ t' = t
pid2 == s2
pid == pid1 \/ pid2

rc(self) == /\ pc[self][1]  = "rc"
            /\ tab[self] > 0
            /\ t' = [t EXCEPT ![self] = tab[self]]
            /\ pc' = [pc EXCEPT ![self][1] = "ut"]
            /\ UNCHANGED << tab, lv >>
ut(self) == /\ pc[self][1]  = "ut"
            /\ t' = [t EXCEPT ![self] = t[self] + 1]
            /\ pc' = [pc EXCEPT ![self][1] = "Done"]
            /\ UNCHANGED << tab, lv >>
qid1(self) == rc(self) \/ ut(self)
qid(self) == qid1(self)

Terminating == /\ \A self \in ProcSet : \A thread \in SubProcSet[self]:
                     pc[self][thread] = "Done"
               /\ UNCHANGED vars

Next == pid \/ (\E self \in 1..2: qid(self)) \/ Terminating
Spec == Init /\ [][Next]_vars
```

Fig. 4. Translation in TLA$^+$ of the algorithm in Fig. 3.

```
--algorithm ChannelAlgo {
  variables s = 0;
  channels ch[Nodes];
  define {
      Nodes == 1..2
      Id == 3
  }


  process (pid = Id)                    process (qid \in Nodes)
  {                                     variables t = 0;
s1: send(ch[1],Id+1);                   {
  }                                     rcv: receive(ch[self],t);
  {                                     add: s := s + t;
s2: send(ch[2],Id+2);                   }
  }                                   }
```

Fig. 5. A PlusCal algorithm using channels.

- send(*chan, expr*): sends a message corresponding to the expression *expr* on channel *chan*;
- receive(*chan, var*): receives a message from channel *chan* and stores it in the variable *var*;
- multicast(*chanId*, $[i_1 \ op_1 \ expr_1, \ \ldots, \ i_N \ op_N \ expr_N \mapsto expr$): for an N-dimensional channel $(N > 0)$ named *chanId*, sends on all the channels whose indexes match $\langle expr_i \rangle$ with respect to op_i (with op_i either = or $\in$), the message corresponding to the expression *expr*.

Sending a message corresponds to adding the message to the bag (respectively, at the end of the sequence). For our example, this corresponds to the following statement added to the action labeled s1:

```
/\ ch' = [ch EXCEPT ![1] = @ (+) SetToBag({Id+1})]
```

where SetToBag is the operator for constructing a bag from a set and (+) denotes bag union. If ch had been declared as fifo, its new value would have been Append(@, Id+1).

The receive operation consists in checking the existence of a message in the channel, removing it and assigning it to the target variable. For our example, this corresponds to:

```
/\ \E __c1__ \in DOMAIN ch[self]:
    /\ ch' = [ch EXCEPT ![self] = @ (-) SetToBag({__c1__})]
    /\ t' = [t EXCEPT ![self] = __c1__]
```

For a fifo channel, the message at the head of the channel is received using a similar definition in terms of the standard operators Len, Tail and Head on sequences. Note that in both cases receive is a blocking operation that is enabled only if a message is present on the channel.

The process `pid` in the algorithm `ChannelAlgo` could be replaced by a single-threaded one consisting of a single multicast operation:

```
multicast(ch, [n \in Nodes |-> Id+n ] );
```

sending a message on `ch[1]` and `ch[2]`. In TLA$^+$ this corresponds to:

```
/\ ch' = [n \in DOMAIN ch |->  IF n \in Nodes
                               THEN ch[n] (+) SetToBag({Id+n})
                               ELSE ch[n]]
```

In this example, the domain of the multicast coincides with the domain of the channel but an expression restricting the domain such as Nodes \ {1}, can be used.

Macros handle channels as any other PlusCal object and, in particular, channels can be passed as arguments to macros. The broadcast of a message m on all the channels of an N-dimensional channel can be expressed using a macro:

```
macro broadcast(chan,m) {
    multicast(chan,[ag \in DOMAIN chan |-> m]);
}
```

Procedures are also compatible with channels. We should note however that, since the modifications performed in the procedure on its arguments are not persistent, passing as parameter a channel or the target variable for a receive operation is not really useful.

4   Evaluation

PlusCal and Distributed PlusCal are front-ends for writing TLA$^+$ specifications: they provide an input syntax that is more familiar to programmers than writing logical formulas, without giving up on a precise formal semantics. The main objective of Distributed PlusCal is to help the user express distributed algorithms in a more natural way than would be possible using regular PlusCal, while remaining backward compatible for algorithms that do not make use of the extensions.

The tool has been developed as a fork of the TLA$^+$ repository[5] and, in particular, extends the version 1.11 of PlusCal. The source code as well as some examples and a quite extensive test suite are publicly available.[6] A README file provides instructions on compiling the source code and using it (or the pre-compiled distribution available in the tlatools/dist directory) to translate Distributed PlusCal algorithms. The examples presented in this paper are available in the tlatools/examples-distpcal directory.

4.1   Two Distributed Algorithms Expressed in Distributed PlusCal

We briefly discuss our experience with modeling distributed algorithms using Distributed PlusCal. Figure 6 shows the distributed mutual-exclusion algorithm

---

[5] https://github.com/tlaplus/tlaplus.

[6] https://github.com/DistributedPlusCal/DistributedPlusCal.

```
------------------------ MODULE LamportMutex ------------------------
EXTENDS Naturals, Sequences, TLC
CONSTANT N
ASSUME N \in Nat
Nodes == 1 .. N
(* PlusCal options (-distpcal) *)
(**--algorithm LamportMutex {
   fifos network[Nodes, Nodes];
   define {
      Max(c,d) == IF c > d THEN c ELSE d
      Request(c) == [type |-> "request", clock |-> c]
      Release(c) == [type |-> "release", clock |-> c]
      Acknowledge(c) == [type |-> "ack", clock |-> c]
   }
   process(node \in Nodes)
      variables clock = 0, req = [n \in Nodes |-> 0],
                ack = {}, sndr = self, msg = Request(0);
   { \* thread executing the main algorithm
ncs: while (TRUE) {
      skip;  \* non-critical section
try:  clock := clock + 1; req[self] := clock; ack := {self};
      multicast(network, [m = self, n \in Nodes |-> Request(clock)]);
enter: await (ack = Nodes /\ \A n \in Nodes \ {self} :
                            \/ req[n] = 0
                            \/ req[self] < req[n]
                            \/ req[self] = req[n] /\ self < n);
cs:   skip;  \* critical section
exit: clock := clock + 1;
      multicast(network, [m = self, n \in Nodes \ {self} |->
                         Release(clock)]);
      } \* end while
   } { \* message handling thread
rcv:  while (TRUE) { with (n \in Nodes) {
          receive(network[n,self], msg); sndr := n;
          clock := Max(clock, msg.clock) + 1
      };
handle: if (msg.type = "request") {
          req[sndr] := msg.clock;
          send(network[self, sndr], Acknowledge(clock))
          }
        else if (msg.type = "ack") { ack := ack \cup {sndr}; }
        else if (msg.type = "release") { req[sndr] := 0; };
        msg := Request(0); sndr := self;
      } \* end while
   } \* end message handling thread
} **)
```

Fig. 6. Lamport's distributed mutual-exclusion algorithm.

from [8] written in Distributed PlusCal; the GitHub repository also contains a Distributed PlusCal expression of the Paxos consensus algorithm [9]. Both algorithms consist of N nodes, each of which has a main thread and a concurrently executing helper thread that handles messages received from other nodes. The distributed mutual-exclusion algorithm relies on FIFO communication between nodes, Paxos does not impose any ordering on messages. In both cases, the possibility of declaring multiple threads per node rather than having only top-level processes, makes expressing the algorithms more natural. In particular, the local scope of variables would be lost if the language did not provide threads. We believe that this observation explains why these algorithms are available from the collection of TLA^+ examples[7] only in the form of TLA^+ specifications rather than PlusCal algorithms.

The main safety properties of these algorithms are mutual exclusion (for LamportMutex) and agreement (for Paxos), expressed respectively as the TLA^+ formulas

$$Mutex \triangleq \forall m, n \in Nodes : m \neq n \Rightarrow \neg(pc[m] = \text{``cs''} \wedge pc[n] = \text{``cs''})$$
$$Agreement \triangleq \forall m, n \in Nodes : chosen[m] \neq None \wedge chosen[n] \neq None$$
$$\Rightarrow chosen[m] = chosen[n]$$

The TLC model checker is able to verify these properties for the specifications generated from our Distributed PlusCal algorithms.[8] For example, when `fifos` is replaced by `channels` in algorithm LamportMutex, TLC generates a counterexample that illustrates why FIFO channels are necessary for this algorithm. The size of the state space for LamportMutex matches that of the existing TLA^+ specification of this algorithm. For Paxos, the state space generated by the Distributed PlusCal version is larger than that of the existing TLA^+ specification, which makes a few shortcuts whereas we emphasized readability.

As for existing PlusCal algorithms, the interactive proof assistant TLAPS can also be used for reasoning about Distributed PlusCal algorithms. The use of the symbolic model checker Apalache requires type annotations for variables and operator definitions; just as for regular PlusCal these have to be added manually by the user. A future version of the translator could propagate type annotations at the Distributed PlusCal level to the generated TLA^+ specification.

4.2 Related Work

Modular PlusCal is a variant of PlusCal based on archetypes (similar to PlusCal's processes), mapping macros (a more disciplined form of macros avoiding side-effects), and distinguishes parameter passing by value or by reference. The PGo compiler [4] can generate either regular PlusCal algorithms or Go programs from Modular PlusCal algorithms. Just like PlusCal processes, archetypes in Modular

---

[7] https://github.com/tlaplus/Examples/tree/master/specifications.

[8] As is standard in finite-state model checking, finite bounds have to be introduced for variables that could grow indefinitely such as clocks or ballots.

PlusCal cannot contain multiple threads executing in parallel. Unlike Distributed PlusCal, Modular PlusCal is not backward compatible with ordinary PlusCal.

The DistAlgo language [12] is a domain-specific language, implemented in Python, for writing distributed programs. It provides primitives for interprocess communication through messages, including asynchronous message reception, and contains declarative constructs such as queries over the histories of sent and received messages. However, its focus is on execution rather than verification.

IronFleet [5] introduced a methodology for describing distributed algorithms as state machines, similar to TLA$^+$, in a form that was amenable to automated program verification with Dafny. Languages such as EventML [14] or Verdi [15] embed the semantics of distributed algorithms and systems in interactive proof assistants and therefore require familiarity with these frameworks for modeling and verification.

5   Conclusion

We presented an extension of the PlusCal algorithm language for describing distributed algorithms. Rather than introducing many new features that could break the design objectives of PlusCal being a lightweight front-end to writing TLA$^+$ specifications, our objective was to add few, orthogonal concepts while both remaining compatible with the existing language and keeping simple the generation of human-readable TLA$^+$ specifications. The added concepts are inspired from those found in distributed programming languages. Compared to the original PlusCal language, Distributed PlusCal allows processes to consist of multiple threads that communicate via process-local variables, and it introduces communication channels that can be declared as preserving FIFO order or not. Whereas PlusCal supports writing concurrent programs by providing a process abstraction, elevating threads to top-level processes requires all variables shared between threads to be declared as global variables, breaking locality. Moreover, PlusCal does not provide communication channels with corresponding operations. Although these can be represented using global variables and macros or operator definitions, this requires that users write low-level TLA$^+$ instead of expressing their algorithm in PlusCal.

We have illustrated Distributed PlusCal using two well-known algorithms and our preliminary findings indicate that the extensions provided by Distributed PlusCal help us express distributed algorithms in a natural way. Moreover, any overhead incurred in verification with respect to a specification written in TLA$^+$ is not different from that of ordinary PlusCal. However, more experience, including by users of Distributed PlusCal different from its authors, will be necessary for a more thorough evaluation of the language.

As for PlusCal, the semantics of the language is given by the translation towards TLA$^+$ and, in the future, we intend to give a formal description in order to compare it with semantics of distributed programming languages and eventually aim for a translation of some Distributed PlusCal specifications into distributed programs.

Currently, Distributed PlusCal supports a fixed number of distinct threads per process. It may be interesting to add replicated instances of threads, just as processes can be replicated in PlusCal. For example, such a feature could be used for modeling processors having multiple CPU and GPU cores. Distributed PlusCal does not currently allow threads to be nested inside another thread. Doing so would require maintaining a tree of control locations and would thus result in a more complicated translation to TLA$^+$.

Beyond providing just two types of FIFO and unordered channels, one could imagine providing a collection of user-extensible libraries for representing channels supporting different abstractions of causality in distributed systems.

Eventually, we aim at integrating Distributed PlusCal into the existing PlusCal translator.

Acknowledgments. We would like to thank several Master students, and in particular Heba Alkayed, who contributed to earlier versions of Distributed PlusCal.

References

1. Barnes, J.: Programming in Ada 2012. Cambridge University Press, USA (2014)
2. Cousineau, D., Doligez, D., Lamport, L., Merz, S., Ricketts, D., Vanzetto, H.: TLATLA$^+$ proofs. In: Giannakopoulou, D., Méry, D. (eds.) FM 2012. LNCS, vol. 7436, pp. 147–154. Springer, Heidelberg (2012). https://doi.org/10.1007/978-3-642-32759-9_14
3. Donovan, A.A.A., Kernighan, B.W.: The Go Programming Language. Addison-Wesley Professional, 1st edn. (2015)
4. Hackett, F., Hosseini, S., Costa, R., Do, M., Beschastnikh, I.: Compiling distributed system models with PGo. In: Aamodt, T.M., Enright Jerger, N.D., Swift, M.M. (eds.) Proceedings of 28th ACM International Conference on Architectural Support for Programming Languages and Operating Systems (ASPLOS), Vancouver, Canada, pp. 159–175. ACM (2023)
5. Hawblitzel, C. et al.: Ironfleet: proving practical distributed systems correct. In: Miller, E.L., Hand, S. (eds.), Proceedings of the 25th Symposium on Operating Systems Principles (SOSP), Monterey, CA, U.S.A., pp. 1–17, ACM (2015)
6. Konnov, I., Kukovec, J., Tran, T.-H.: TLA$^+$ model checking made symbolic. In: Proceedings of the ACM on Programming Languages, vol. 3(OOPSLA), pp. 123:1–123:30 (2019)
7. Konnov, I., Kuppe, M., Merz, S.: Specification and verification with the TLA$^+$ Trifecta: TLC, Apalache, and TLAPS. In: Margaria, T., Steffen, B. (eds.) 11th International Symposium On Leveraging Applications of Formal Methods, Verification and Validation (ISoLA 2022), Rhodes, Greece, vol. 13701. LNCS, pp. 88–105. Springer (2022). https://doi.org/10.1007/978-3-031-19849-6_6
8. Lamport, L.: Time, clocks, and the ordering of events in a distributed system. Commun. ACM **21**(7), 558–565 (1978)
9. Lamport, L.: The part-time parliament. ACM Trans. Comput. Syst. **16**(2), 133–169 (1998)
10. Lamport, L.: Specifying Systems: The TLA$^+$ Language and Tools for Hardware and Software Engineers. Addison-Wesley, USA (2002)

11. Lamport, L.: The PlusCal algorithm language. In: Leucker, M., Morgan, C. (eds.) ICTAC 2009. LNCS, vol. 5684, pp. 36–60. Springer, Heidelberg (2009). https://doi.org/10.1007/978-3-642-03466-4_2

12. Liu, Y.A., Stoller, S.D., Lin, B.: From clarity to efficiency for distributed algorithms. ACM Trans. Program. Lang. Syst., **39**(3), 12:1–12:41 (2017)

13. Message Passing Interface Forum. MPI: A Message-Passing Interface Standard Version 4.0 (June 2021)

14. Rahli, V., Guaspari, D., Bickford, M., Constable, R.L.: Eventml: specification, verification, and implementation of crash-tolerant state machine replication systems. Sci. Comput. Program. **148**, 26–48 (2017)

15. Wilcox, J.R., et al.: Verdi: a framework for implementing and formally verifying distributed systems. In: Grove, D., Blackburn, S.M. (eds.) 36th ACM SIGPLAN Conference on Programming Language Design and Implementation (PLDI), Portand, OR, U.S.A., pp. 357–368. ACM (2015)

16. Yu, Y., Manolios, P., Lamport, L.: Model checking TLA$^+$ specifications. In: Pierre, L., Kropf, T. (eds.) CHARME 1999. LNCS, vol. 1703, pp. 54–66. Springer, Heidelberg (1999). https://doi.org/10.1007/3-540-48153-2_6

17. Zeller, P., Bieniusa, A., Ferreira, C.: Teaching practical realistic verification of distributed algorithms in Erlang with TLA+. In: Bieniusa, A., Fördós, V. (eds.) Erlang Workshop, pp. 14–23. ACM (2020)

Autonomous Systems

Formal Modelling and Analysis of a Self-Adaptive Robotic System

Juliane Päßler[1]([✉])[ID], Maurice H. ter Beek[2][ID], Ferruccio Damiani[3][ID],
Silvia Lizeth Tapia Tarifa[1][ID], and Einar Broch Johnsen[1][ID]

[1] University of Oslo, Oslo, Norway
{julipas,sltarifa,einarj}@ifi.uio.no
[2] ISTI–CNR, Pisa, Italy
maurice.terbeek@isti.cnr.it
[3] University of Turin, Turin, Italy
ferruccio.damiani@unito.it

Abstract. Self-adaptation is a crucial feature of autonomous systems that must cope with uncertainties in, e.g., their environment and their internal state. Self-adaptive systems are often modelled as two-layered systems with a *managed* subsystem handling the domain concerns and a *managing* subsystem implementing the adaptation logic. We consider a case study of a self-adaptive robotic system; more concretely, an autonomous underwater vehicle (AUV) used for pipeline inspection. In this paper, we model and analyse it with the feature-aware probabilistic model checker ProFeat. The functionalities of the AUV are modelled in a feature model, capturing the AUV's variability. This allows us to model the managed subsystem of the AUV as a family of systems, where each family member corresponds to a valid feature configuration of the AUV. The managing subsystem of the AUV is modelled as a control layer capable of dynamically switching between such valid feature configurations, depending both on environmental and internal conditions. We use this model to analyse probabilistic reward and safety properties for the AUV.

Keywords: feature models · probabilistic model checking · self-adaptive systems · cyber-physical systems · robotics

1 Introduction

Many software systems are subject to different forms of uncertainty like changes in the surrounding environment, internal failures and varying user requirements. Often, manually maintaining and adapting these systems during runtime by a system operator is prohibitively expensive and error-prone. Enabling systems to adapt themselves provides several advantages. A system that is able to perform self-adaptation can also be deployed in environments where, e.g., communication between an operator and the system is very limited or impossible, like in space or under water. Thus, self-adaptation gives a system a higher level of autonomy.

© The Author(s), under exclusive license to Springer Nature Switzerland AG 2024
P. Herber and A. Wijs (Eds.): iFM 2023, LNCS 14300, pp. 343–363, 2024.
https://doi.org/10.1007/978-3-031-47705-8_18

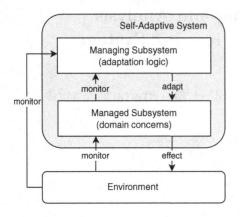

Fig. 1. Two-level SAS architecture

A self-adaptive system (SAS) can be implemented using a two-layered approach which decomposes the system into a *managed* and a *managing* subsystem [18], see Fig. 1. The *managed* subsystem deals with the domain concerns and tries to reach the goals set by the system's user, e.g., navigating a robot to a specific location. The *managing* subsystem handles the adaptation concerns and defines an adaptation logic that specifies a strategy on how the system can fulfil the goals under uncertainty [25], e.g., adapting to changing environmental conditions. While the managed subsystem may affect the environment via its actions, the managing subsystem monitors the environment and the internal state of the managed subsystem. By using the adaptation logic, the managing subsystem deduces whether and which reconfiguration is needed and adapts the managed subsystem accordingly.

This paper models and analyses the case study of a self-adaptive autonomous underwater vehicle (AUV) as a two-layered system based on Markov decision processes. The functionalities of the managed subsystem of the AUV are modelled in a feature model, making the dependencies and requirements between the components of the AUV explicit. The behaviour of the managed subsystem is modelled as a probabilistic transition system whose transitions may be equipped with feature guards, which only allow a transition to be taken if the feature guarding it is included in the current system configuration. Thus, it is modelled as a family of systems whose family members correspond to valid feature configurations. As the behaviour of the AUV depends on environmental and internal conditions, which are both hard to control, we opted for a probabilistic model in which uncontrolled events, like a thruster failure, occur with given probabilities. We model the behaviour of the managing subsystem as a control layer that switches between the feature configurations of the managed subsystem according to input from the probabilistic environment model and the managed subsystem. We consider a simplified version of an AUV, with limited features and variability, but there are many different possibilities to extend the model to a more realistic underwater robot.

The case study is modelled in ProFeat [8], a tool for probabilistic family-based model checking. Family-based model checking provides a means to simultaneously model check, in a single run, properties of a family of models, each representing a different configuration [23]. Analyses with ProFeat give system operators an estimate of mission duration and the AUV's energy consumption, as well as some safety guarantees.

The main contributions of this paper are as follows:

- A case study of an SAS from the underwater robotics domain, modelled
  as a probabilistic feature guarded transition system with dynamic feature
  switching;
- Automated verification of (quantitative) properties that are important for
  roboticists, using family-based analysis.

Outline. Section 2 presents the case study of pipeline inspection with an AUV.
Section 3 explains both the behaviour of the managed and managing subsystem
of the AUV and the environment, as well as their implementation in ProFeat.
Section 4 presents quantitative analyses conducted on the case study. Section 5
provides related work. Section 6 discusses our results and ideas for future work.

2   Case Study: Pipeline Inspection by AUV

In this section, we introduce our case study of an AUV used for pipeline inspection, which was inspired by the exemplar SUAVE [22].

An AUV has the mission to first find and then inspect a pipeline located
on a seabed. During system operation, the water visibility (i.e., the distance in
meters within which the AUV can perceive objects) might change (e.g., due to
currents that swirl up the seabed), while one or more of the AUV's thrusters
might fail and needs to be restarted before the mission can be continued.

The AUV can choose to operate at three different altitudes, *low*, *med* (for
medium) and *high*. A higher altitude allows the AUV to have a wider field of
view and thus increases its chances of finding the pipeline during its search. The
probability of a thruster failure is lower at a higher altitude because, e.g., seaweed
might wrap around the thrusters at a lower altitude. However, the altitude at
which the AUV can perceive the seabed depends on the water visibility. With
low water visibility, the AUV cannot perceive the seabed from a high or medium
altitude. Thus, it is not always possible to operate at a high or medium altitude,
and the altitude of the AUV needs to be changed during the search, depending
on the current environmental conditions. Once the pipeline is found, the AUV
will follow it at a low altitude to avoid costs for switching altitudes. In fact, once
found, a wider field of view provides no benefit. However, the AUV can also lose
the pipeline again (e.g., when the pipeline was partly covered by sand or the
AUV's thrusters failed for some time causing the AUV to drift off its path). In
this case, the AUV has to search the pipeline again, enabling all three altitudes.

Two-layered View of the AUV. Considering the AUV as a two-layered SAS, the
AUV's managed subsystem is responsible for the search for and inspection of
the pipeline. Depending on the current task and altitude of the AUV, a different
configuration of the managed subsystem must be chosen. Thus, the managed
subsystem can be seen as a family of systems where each family member corresponds to a valid configuration of the AUV. To do so, the different altitudes for
navigation (*low*, *med* and *high*) and the tasks *search* and *follow* can be seen as
features of the managed subsystem that adhere to the feature model in Fig. 2,

which models the dependencies and constraints among the features. Each configuration of the AUV contains exactly one feature for navigation and one for pipeline inspection, and feature *follow* requires feature *low*, yielding four different configurations of the managed subsystem of the AUV.

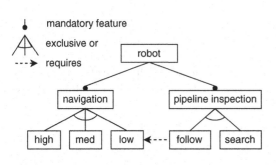

Fig. 2. Feature model of the case study

The managing subsystem of the case study switches between these configurations during runtime by activating and deactivating the subfeatures of *navigation* and *pipeline inspection*, while the resulting feature configuration has to adhere to the feature model in Fig. 2. The features *low*, *med* and *high* are activated and deactivated according to the current water visibility. If the water visibility is good, all three features can be activated; if the water visibility is average, *high* cannot be activated; and if the water visibility is poor, only *low* can be activated. The managing subsystem switches from the feature *search* to *follow* if the pipeline was found, and from *follow* to *search* if the pipeline was lost.

3   Modelling the AUV Case Study with ProFeat

In this section, we describe the behavioural model of the managed and managing subsytem and the environment and model the case study with the family-based model checker ProFeat[1] [8]. ProFeat provides a means to both specify probabilistic system families and perform family-based quantitative analysis on them. It extends the probabilistic model checker PRISM[2] [19] with functionalities such as family models, features and feature switches. Thereby, it enables family-based modelling and (quantitative) analysis of probabilistic systems in which feature configurations may dynamically change during runtime. The whole model can be analysed with probabilistic family-based model checking using PRISM. The probabilities used in our model are estimates and have not been validated by experiments, since in this paper our goal was not to make a model that is as realistic as possible, but rather to show the feasibility of our approach.

Similar to an SAS, a ProFeat model can be seen as a two-layered model, as illustrated in Fig. 1. The behaviour of a family of systems that differ in their features, such as the managed subsystem of an SAS, can be specified. Then a so-called *feature controller* can activate and deactivate the features during runtime, and thus change the behaviour of the system, such as the managing subsystem of an SAS that changes the configuration of the managed subsystem. Furthermore,

---

[1] https://pchrszon.github.io/profeat.
[2] https://www.prismmodelchecker.org/manual.

the environment can be specified as a separate module that interacts with the managed and managing subsystem. Thus, ProFeat is well suited to model and analyse the case study described in Sect. 2.

A ProFeat model consists of three parts: an obligatory feature model that specifies features and their relations and constraints, obligatory modules that specify the behaviour of the features, and an optional feature controller that activates or deactivates features. The pipeline inspection case study was modelled as a Markov decision process in ProFeat.[3] It consists of (i) the implementation of the feature model of Fig. 2; (ii) modules describing the behaviour of the managed subsystem of the AUV (see Fig. 3) and of the environment (see Fig. 4); and (iii) the feature controller that switches between features during runtime, corresponding to the managing subsystem of the AUV (see Fig. 5).

We start by explaining how the feature model was implemented in ProFeat in Sect. 3.1, then describe the behaviour and implementation of the managed and managing subsystem and of the environment in Sect. 3.2, 3.4, and 3.3 respectively.

3.1 The Feature Model

We first show how the feature model of the case study is expressed in ProFeat, including connections and constraints among features. Each feature is specified within a **feature** ... **endfeature** block, the declaration of the root feature is done in a **root feature** ... **endfeature** block.

The Root Feature. An excerpt of the implementation of the root feature of the pipeline inspection case study according to Fig. 2 is displayed in Listing 1.1. The root feature can be decomposed into subfeatures; in this case only one, the subfeature robot, see Line 2. The **all of** keyword indicates that all subfeatures have to be included in the feature configuration if the parent feature, in this case the root feature, is included. It is, e.g., also possible to use the **one of** keyword if exactly one subfeature has to be included, see Line 2 of Listing 1.2. The modules modelling the behaviour of the root feature are specified after the keyword **modules**. In this case study, the root feature is the only feature specifying modules, thus the behaviour of all features is modelled in the modules auv and environment described later.

Contrary to an ordinary feature model, ProFeat allows to specify feature-specific rewards in the declaration of a feature. Like costs, rewards are real values, but unlike costs (and although they may be interpreted as costs) rewards are meant to motivate rather than penalise the execution of transitions. Each reward is encapsulated in a **rewards** ... **endrewards** block. In the case study, we consider the rewards *time* and *energy*, see Lines 4–18 of Listing 1.1. During each transition the AUV module takes, the reward time is increased by 1; it is a transition-based reward, see Line 5. We assume that one time step corresponds to one minute, allowing us to compute an estimate of a mission's duration.

---

[3] The model is publicly available at [21].

The reward energy is a state-based reward and can be used to estimate the necessary battery level for a mission completion. If a thruster of the AUV failed and needs to be recovered, a reward of 2 is given, see, e.g., Line 9. The model also reflects that switching between the search altitudes requires significant energy. Since the altitude is switched if the AUV is in a search state and a navigation subfeature that does not correspond to the current search altitude is active, a higher energy reward is given in these states. If the AUV needs to switch between low and high altitude, as, e.g., in Line 13, an energy reward of 4 is given, while all other altitude switches receive a reward of 2, see, e.g., Line 14. Since the altitude must be changed to *low* once the pipeline is found, these cases also receive an energy reward as explained above, see Lines 15–16. All other states receive an energy reward of 1. We use the function active to determine which feature is active, i.e., included in the current feature configuration; given a feature, the function returns true if it is active and false otherwise. Note that both time and energy rewards are interpreted as costs.

```
1  root feature
2    all of robot;
3    modules auv, environment;
4    rewards "time"
5      [step] true : 1;
6    endrewards
7    rewards "energy"
8      // Costs for being in a recovery state
9      (s=recover_high) : 2;
10     // .. omitted code ..
11
12     // Costs for switching altitudes
13     (s=search_high) & active(low) : 4;
14     (s=search_high) & active(med) : 2;
15     (s=found) & active(high) : 4;
16     (s=found) & active(med) : 2;
17     // .. omitted code ..
18   endrewards
19 endfeature
```

Listing 1.1. An excerpt of the declaration of the root feature of the case study

Ordinary Features. The remainder of the feature model is implemented similar to the root feature, but the features do not contain feature-specific modules or rewards. The features are implemented and named according to the feature model in Fig. 2. To have only one initial state, we initialise the model with the features search and low active, using the keyword initial constraint, see Line 3 of Listing 1.2. As an example of the implementation of another feature, the declaration of the feature navigation can be seen in Listing 1.2.

```
1  feature navigation
2    one of low, med, high;
3    initial constraint active(low);
4  endfeature
```

Listing 1.2. The declaration of the navigation feature of the case study

3.2   The Managed Subsystem

The Behavioural Model of the Managed Subsystem. The behaviour of the managed subsystem of the AUV can be described by a probabilistic transition system equipped with features that guard transitions (a probabilistic featured transition system). Only if the feature guarding a transition is included in the current configuration of the managed subsystem of the AUV, the transition can be taken. This transition system adheres to the feature model in Fig. 2 and is depicted in Fig. 3, where a number of details have been omitted to avoid cluttering (in particular, all probabilities). The details can be obtained from the publicly available model in [21]. The probabilistic model allows to easily model the possibilities of, e.g., finding and losing the pipeline depending on the system configuration.

The transition system can roughly be divided into two parts, one concerning the search for and one the following of the pipeline, as shown by the grey boxes in Fig. 3. At deployment time, i.e., in state *start task*, the AUV can either immediately start following the pipeline if it was deployed above it, or start searching for it. During the search for the pipeline, i.e., when the AUV is in the grey area labelled *search*, the feature *search* should be active and remain active until the state *found* is reached. The managing subsystem can switch between the features *low*, *med* and *high* during every transition, depending on the water visibility as described in Sect. 2. Once the pipeline is found, the managing subsystem has to deactivate the feature *search* and activate the feature *follow*, which also implies activating the feature *low* and deactivating *med* and *high* due to the feature constraints in Fig. 2. We assume that the managing subsystem activates and deactivates features during transitions, so the features *follow* and *low* should be activated during the transition from the state *found* to the state *start task*. When the AUV is following the pipeline, i.e., in the grey area labelled *follow*, it can also lose the pipeline again, e.g., because of sand covering it or because it drifted off its path due to thruster failures. Then the managing subsystem has to activate the feature *search* during the transition from *lost pipe* to *start task*.

We distinguish two kinds of transitions: transitions that model the behaviour of a certain configuration of the managed subsystem (black transitions) and (featured) transitions that switch between configurations, enabled by the managing subsystem during runtime (blue transitions). The labels *search*, *follow*, *low*, *med* and *high* on the transitions represent the features that have to be active to execute the respective transition. The transitions between configurations (blue) implicitly carry the action to start the task or go to the altitude specified by the feature associated with the transition. For instance, the transitions from *search low* to *search medium* can be taken if the feature *med* is active because the transition has the guard *med*. When taking this transition, the AUV should perform the action of going to a medium altitude. The transitions inside a configuration (black) with a feature label contain the implicit action to stay at the current altitude because the navigation subfeature has not been changed during the previous transition.

Whether a transition inside the configuration or between configurations is executed in the search states *search low*, *search medium* and *search high* depends

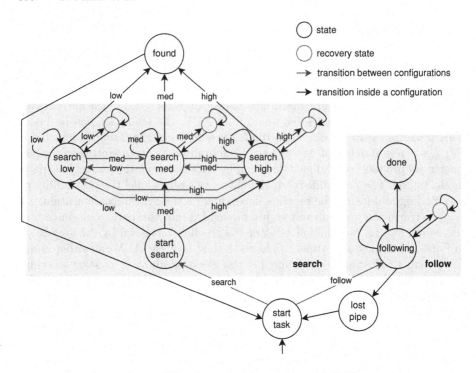

Fig. 3. The managed subsystem of the AUV

on the managing subsystem, i.e., the controller switching between features (see Sect. 3.4). If the managing subsystem switched between the features *low*, *med* and *high* during the last transition, a transition to the search state corresponding to the new feature will be executed, i.e., the configuration will be changed. Otherwise, a transition inside the configuration will be executed. For instance, consider the state *search low*. If the feature *low* is active, then a black transition will be executed. If, however, the managing subsystem deactivated the feature *low* during the last transition and activated either *med* or *high*, then the AUV will perform a transition to the state *search medium* or *search high*, respectively.

The ProFeat Implementation of the Managed Subsystem. The module auv models the behaviour of the managed subsystem of the AUV as displayed in Fig. 3, see Listing 1.3 for an excerpt of the model. As in Fig. 3, there are thirteen enumerated states in the ProFeat module with names that correspond to the state labels in the figure. The recovery states are named according to the state they are connected to (e.g., the recovery state connected to search_high is called recover_high). The variable s in Line 2 represents the current state of the AUV and is initialised using the keyword init with the state start_task. To record how many meters of the pipeline have already been inspected, the variable d_insp in Line 3 represents the distance the AUV has already inspected the pipeline, it is initialised with 0. The variable inspect represents the desired inspection length and can be set by the user during design time. Since the number of times a thruster failed impacts how much the AUV deviates from its path, the variable t_failed can be increased if a thruster fails while the AUV follows the pipeline. It is bounded by the influence a thruster failure can have on the system (infl_tf) that can be set by the user during design time.

```
1   module auv
2     s : [0..12] init start_task;
3     d_insp : [0..inspect] init 0;
4     t_failed : [0..infl_tf] init 0;
5
6     // To the correct task
7     [step] (s=start_task & active(search)) -> 1: (s'=start_search);
8     [step] (s=start_task & active(follow)) -> 1: (s'=following);
9
10    // .. omitted code ..
11    // From search state to another state
12    [step] (s=search_high & active(high))
13              -> 0.59:(s'=found)
14              + 0.4:(s'=search_high)
15              + 0.01:(s'=recover_high);
16    [step] (s=search_high & active(med)) -> 1:(s'=search_med);
17    [step] (s=search_high & active(low)) -> 1:(s'=search_low);
18    // .. omitted code ..
19
20    // Go to other task if pipeline is found
21    [step] (s=found) -> 1:(s'=start_task);
22
23    // Following the pipeline
24    [step] (s=following) & (d_insp<inspect) & (t_failed=0)
25              -> 0.92: (s'=following) & (d_insp'=d_insp+1)
26              + 0.05: (s'=lost_pipe)
27              + 0.03:(s'=recover_following)
28                  & (t_failed'=(t_failed<infl_tf? t_failed+1 : t_failed));
29    [step] (s=following) & (d_insp<inspect) & (t_failed>0)
30              -> 0.92*(1-t_failed/infl_tf): (s'=following)
31                  & (d_insp'=d_insp+1) & (t_failed'=t_failed-1)
32              + 0.05*(1+((0.92*t_failed)/(0.05*infl_tf))): (s'=lost_pipe)
33              + 0.03:(s'=recover_following)
34                  & (t_failed'=(t_failed<infl_tf? t_failed+1 : t_failed));
35    [step] (s=following) & (d_insp=inspect) -> (s'=done);
36
37    // Lost the pipeline
38    [step] (s=lost_pipe) -> 1: (s'=start_task) & (t_failed'=0);
39
40    // Recovery states
41    [step] (s=recover_high) ->0.5:(s'=recover_high)+0.5:(s'=search_high);
42    // .. omitted code ..
43  endmodule
```

Listing 1.3. An excerpt of the ProFeat AUV module of the case study

The behaviour of the module is specified with *guarded commands*, corresponding to possible, probabilistic transitions, of the following form.

$$[action] \text{ guard} -> prob\_1: update\_1 + \ldots + prob\_n: update\_n;$$

A command may have an optional label action to annotate it or to synchronise with other modules. In PRISM, the guard is a predicate over global and local variables of the model, which can also come from other modules. ProFeat extends the guards by, e.g., enabling the use of the function active. If the guard is true, then the system state is changed with probability prob_i using update_i for all i.

An update describes how the system should perform a transition by giving new values for variables, either directly or as a function using other variables.

For instance, consider the command in Lines 12–15, which can be read as follows. If the system is in state search_high and the feature high is active, then with a probability of 0.59, the system changes its state to found, with a probability of 0.4 it changes to search_high and with a probability of 0.01 it changes to recover_high. These are exactly the black transitions shown in Fig. 3 exiting from state *search high*. This command also has an action label, step. Using this action label, it synchronises with the environment module and the feature controller, as described later. The blue transitions exiting state *search high* in Fig. 3 are modelled in Lines 16–17. If the model is in state search_high, but the feature low or med is active, indicating that the AUV should go to the respective altitude, then the state is changed to the respective search state. The transitions exiting the states search_med and search_low are modelled similarly. However, the probability of going to the state found is highest from state search_high and lowest from search_low because the AUV has a wider field of view when performing the search at a higher altitude. Furthermore, the probability of a thruster failure, i.e., of going to the respective recover state, is highest in state search_low and lowest in state search_high because the probability of seaweed getting stuck in the thrusters is higher at a lower altitude. If the AUV found the pipeline, then a transition to start_task is taken, see Line 21.

From the state start_task, a transition to either start_search or following can be taken, depending on which subfeature of pipeline_inspection is currently active, see Lines 7–8.

From the following state, the transitions that can be taken depend on the variables d_insp and t_failed. Lines 24–28 consider the case where the distance of the pipeline that has already been inspected (d_insp) is less than the distance the pipeline should be inspected (inspect) and the variable t_failed is 0, indicating that there were no recent thruster failures. Then the AUV stays in the following state and inspects the pipeline one more meter, it loses the pipeline, or a thruster fails and it transitions to the failure state and increases t_failed if t_failed is not at its maximum. Lines 29–34 consider the case where d_insp is less than inspect and t_failed is greater than 0. In this case, the probabilities of following and of losing the pipeline depend on the value of t_failed. The bigger the value, the more likely it is to lose the pipeline because it indicates that the AUV's thrusters did not work for some time, causing it to drift off its path. If the already inspected distance is equal to the required inspection distance, the AUV transitions to the done state (see Line 35) and finishes the pipeline inspection. If the AUV lost the pipeline (see Line 38), then a transition to start_task is taken and the variable t_failed is set to 0 again.

When the AUV is in a recovery state, it can either stay there for another time step or exit it again to the state from where the recovery was triggered (see Line 41).

All commands in the module auv are labelled with step. Thus, every transition receives a time reward of 1, i.e., the time advances with every transition the AUV takes, see Lines 4–6 of Listing 1.1.

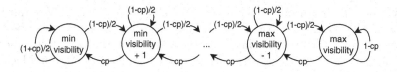

Fig. 4. The behaviour of the environment

3.3 The Environment

The Behavioural Model of the Environment. We assume that there is a minimum and a maximum visibility of the environment, depending on where the AUV is deployed and set by the user during design time. Furthermore, different environments also have different probabilities of currents that influence the water visibility. This can also be set during design time. The behaviour of the environment is then modelled as depicted in Fig. 4, where *cp* represents the *current probability*. With the probability of currents *cp*, the water visibility decreases by 1, while it stays the same or increases by 1 with probability $(1\text{-}cp)/2$. If the water visibility is already at minimum visibility, the water visibility stays the same with probability $(1\text{+}cp)/2$ and, at maximum visibility, it stays the same with probability $(1\text{-}cp)$.

The Implementation of the Environment in ProFeat. The environment is modelled in a separate environment module, see Listing 1.4. The variable water_visib in Line 2 reflects the current water visibility and is initialised parametrically, depending on the minimum and maximum visibility, see Line 3. The function round() is pre-implemented in the PRISM language and rounds to the nearest integer. The environment module synchronises with the AUV module via the label of its action, step. Since the guard of the only action in the environment module is true, the environment executes a transition every time the AUV module does. By decoupling the environment module from the AUV module, we obtain a separation of concerns which makes it easier to change the model of the environment if needed.

```
1  module environment
2    water_visib : [min_visib..max_visib]
3          init round((max_visib-min_visib)/2);
4    [step] true -> current_prob: (water_visib'= (water_visib=min_visib?
5          min_visib:water_visib-1)) + (1-current_prob)/2: (water_visib'=
6          (water_visib=max_visib? max_visib:water_visib+1))
7          + (1-current_prob)/2: true;
8  endmodule
```

Listing 1.4. The ProFeat environment module of the case study

3.4   The Managing Subsystem

The Behavioural Model of the Managing Subsystem. As described in Sect. 2, the managing subsystem of the AUV implements the AUV's adaptation logic, which corresponds to activating and deactivating the features of the managed subsystem. The behaviour of the managing subsystem of the AUV is displayed in Fig. 5. The grey area of the figure includes the transitions that can be taken during the search for the pipeline, and the white area the transitions once the pipeline has been found. Each transition contains a guard, written in black, and an action, written in grey after a vertical bar.

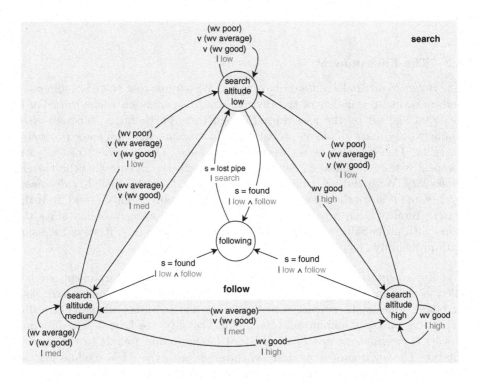

Fig. 5. The managing subsystem of the AUV

During the search for the pipeline, i.e., in the grey area of Fig. 5, the managing subsystem activates and deactivates the features *low*, *med* and *high* according to the current water visibility as described in Sect. 2. The activated feature is displayed in grey on the transition, implicitly the other two subfeatures of *navigation* are deactivated. Note that the transitions in the grey area implicitly carry the guard *s != found*, i.e., the AUV is not in the state *found*, because they represent the transitions during the search for the pipeline. This guard was omitted for better readability.

Once the pipeline has been found, i.e., the managed subsystem is in the state *found*, one of the transitions in the white area, guarded by $s = found$, is taken. These transitions include the action of activating *low* and *follow*, and thus deactivating *med*, *high* and *search*. When the AUV loses the pipeline, i.e., it is in the state *lost pipe*, the managing subsystem activates *search* and deactivates *follow*. Since the AUV is following the pipeline at a low altitude, the AUV will start searching at a low altitude.

```
1  formula med_visib = (max_visib−min_visib)/3;
2  formula high_visib = 2*(max_visib−min_visib)/3;
3
4  controller
5    // Change altitude depending on water visibility
6    [step] (s!=found) & active(search) & water_visib < med_visib
7           -> activate(low) & deactivate(high) & deactivate(med);
8    [step] (s!=found) & active(search)
9           & med_visib <= water_visib & water_visib < high_visib
10          -> activate(low) & deactivate(med) & deactivate(high);
11   [step] (s!=found) & active(search)
12          & med_visib <= water_visib & water_visib < high_visib
13          -> activate(med) & deactivate(low) & deactivate(high);
14   // .. omitted code ..
15
16   // Switch task from "search" to "follow"
17   [step] (s=found) & active(search)
18          -> deactivate(search) & activate(follow) & activate(low)
19          & deactivate(med) & deactivate(high);
20
21   // Switch task from "follow" to "search"
22   [step] (s=lost_pipe) & active(follow)
23          -> deactivate(follow) & activate(search);
24
25   // Enable transitions when following the pipeline
26   [step] (s!=lost_pipe) & active(follow) -> true;
27 endcontroller
```

Listing 1.5. An excerpt of the ProFeat feature controller of the case study

The Implementation of the Managing Subsystem in ProFeat. The managing subsystem of the AUV is implemented as a feature controller in ProFeat. The feature controller can also use *commands* to change the state of the system. Such commands are similar to those used in a module; they are mostly of the form [action] guard −> update. Each command can have an optional label action to synchronise with the modules, and its guard is a predicate of global and local variables of the model and can also contain the function active. In contrast to the commands in the modules, the feature controller can activate and deactivate features in the update of a command. Several features can be activated and deactivated at the same time, but this cannot be done probabilistically and the resulting feature configuration has to adhere to the feature model.

In the pipeline inspection case study, subfeatures of navigation (i.e., the different altitudes at which the AUV can operate) and subfeatures of pipeline_inspection (i.e., the tasks the robot has to fulfil) can be switched by the feature controller during runtime, see Listing 1.5.

When the feature search is active and the pipeline has not been found yet, the feature controller activates and deactivates the altitudes non-deterministically, but according to the current water visibility, as described before. The minimum and maximum water visibility can be set by the user during design time and influence the altitudes associated with the features low, med and high; i.e., it influences when the feature controller is able to switch features. To reflect this, the variables med_visib and high_visib are declared as in Lines 1–2 (a *formula* in PRISM and ProFeat can be used to assign an identifier to an expression). If the water visibility is less than med_visib, the feature controller activates the feature low (see Lines 6–7) because the AUV cannot perceive the seabed from a higher altitude. If the water visibility is between med_visib and high_visib, it chooses non-deterministically between low and med (see Lines 8–13), whereas it chooses non-deterministically between all three altitudes if the water visibility is above high_visib. Note that it is also possible to deactivate or activate a feature if it is already inactive or active, respectively.

When the pipeline is found, i.e., the AUV is in state found, the feature controller activates the feature follow and deactivates search, see Lines 17–19. Since the AUV should be at a low altitude while following the pipeline, the feature controller also deactivates the features high and med and activates low. If the AUV lost the pipeline, i.e., it is in state lost_pipe, the feature controller deactivates follow and activates search to start the search for the pipeline, see Lines 22–23.

The feature controller synchronises with the auv and environment modules via action label step. Since all transitions of the modules and feature controller have the same action label, they can only execute a transition if there is a transition with a guard evaluating to true in both modules and in the feature controller. Thus, the feature controller needs to include a transition doing nothing if the feature follow is active and the AUV is not in state lost_pipe, see Line 26.

4   Analysis

ProFeat automatically converts models to PRISM for probabilistic model checking. To analyse a PRISM model, properties can be specified in the PRISM property specification language, which includes several probabilistic temporal logics like PCTL, CSL and probabilistic LTL. For family-based analysis, ProFeat extends this specification language to include, e.g., the function active. (ProFeat constructs have to be specified in ${...}$ to be correctly translated to the PRISM property specification language.)

The operators used for analysis in this paper are P and R, which reason about probabilities of events and about expected rewards, respectively. Since we use Markov decision processes which involve non-determinism, these operators must be further specified to ask for the *minimum* or *maximum* probability and expected cost, respectively, for all possible resolutions of non-determinism.

The analysis of the model considered two different aspects. First, the rewards energy and time were used to compute some safety guarantees that can be used for the deployment of the AUV. Second, safety properties with regard to unsafe

Table 1. Two different scenarios used for analysis

Scenario	min_visib	max_visib	current_prob	inspect
1 (North Sea)	1	10	0.6	10
2 (Caribbean Sea)	3	20	0.3	30

states were analysed. Note that it is not necessary to analyse whether the model satisfies the constraints of the feature model because this is automatically ensured by ProFeat. Of course, in addition to that, more complex analysis can be done. In this paper, we just give a taste of possible analyses to demonstrate the feasibility of our approach.

We analysed two different scenarios; the values used in these scenarios are reported in Table 1. Scenario 1 is in the North Sea, where the minimum and maximum water visibility (in 0.5 m units) are relatively low and the probability of currents that decrease the water visibility is relatively high. In this case, only 10 m of the pipeline have to be inspected. Scenario 2 is in the Caribbean Sea, with a higher minimum and maximum visibility and a lower probability of currents compared to the North Sea, and 30 m of pipeline that have to be inspected. For both scenarios, we first analysed whether it is always possible to finish the pipeline inspection, i.e., reach the state done. This could be confirmed since the minimum probability for all resolutions of non-determinism of eventually reaching the state done is 1.0.

Reward Properties. The rewards time and energy were used to analyse some safety properties related to the execution of the AUV. Since the AUV only has a limited amount of battery, an estimation of the energy needed to complete the mission is required. This ensures that the AUV is only deployed for the mission if it has sufficient battery to complete it. The commands in Listing 1.6 were used to compute the minimum and maximum expected energy (for all resolutions of non-determinism) to complete the mission. Since the model includes two reward structures, the name of the reward has to be specified in {"..."} after the R operator. Similarly, the minimum and maximum expected time to complete the mission was analysed to give the system operators an estimate of how long the mission might take. The results for Scenarios 1 and 2 are reported in Table 2. It can be seen that the variation of the parameters in the two scenarios strongly influences the expected energy and time of the mission. It is interesting to see that the difference between minimum and maximum expected energy and minimum and maximum expected time for Scenario 2 are significantly bigger than for Scenario 1. In particular, the maximum expected energy and time are much higher for Scenario 2 than for Scenario 1. Further analysis in this direction could

Table 2. Expected min-/maximum rewards for completing the mission for both scenarios

Scenario	Energy		Time	
	min	max	min	max
1	24.78	44.39	23.66	32.40
2	59.08	4723.29	55.54	1315.58

investigate trade-offs between different scenarios and a better understanding of
the influence in the results for the different parameters.

```
1 R{"energy"}min=? [F ${s=done}];
2 R{"energy"}max=? [F ${s=done}];
```

Listing 1.6. Analysis using the rewards

```
1 label "unsafe" = s=recover_high | s=recover_med | s=recover_low
2            | s=recover_following;
3 label "safe" = s=start_task | s=lost_pipe | s=start_search
4 | s=search_high | s=search_med | s=search_low | s=found
5 | s=following |s=done;
6 Pmin=? [G "safe"];
7 filter(min, Pmin=? [ F<=k "safe" ], "unsafe");
8 filter(max, Pmax=? [ F<=k "unsafe" ], "safe");
9 filter(avg, Pmax=? [ F<=k "unsafe" ], "safe");
```

Listing 1.7. Analysis of unsafe states

Unsafe States. Thruster failures, although we assume that they can be repaired,
pose a threat to the AUV. Unforeseen events like strong currents might cause
the AUV to be damaged, e.g., by causing it to crash into a rock. To analyse this,
the state space was partitioned into two parts, *safe* and *unsafe* states. This was
achieved by using labels, see Lines 1–4 of Listing 1.7.

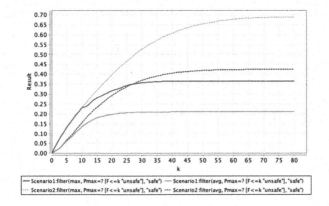

Fig. 6. Results for reaching an unsafe state from a safe state in k time steps

These labels were then used to calculate the probability of several properties.
The minimum probability of only taking safe states (see Line 6) was shown to
be 0.65 for Scenario 1 and 0.32 for Scenario 2. As expected, the probability
of only taking safe states is higher for a shorter pipeline inspection. It is also
important to ensure that a safe state will be reached from an unsafe state after
a short period of time, as, e.g., in Line 7, where k is an integer. For every unsafe
state, the minimum probability (for all possible resolutions of non-determinism)
of reaching a safe state within k time steps is calculated. Then the minimum

over all these probabilities is taken. Thus, it gives the minimum probability of reaching a safe state from an unsafe state in k time steps. PRISM experiments allow analysing this property automatically for a specified range of k. Using PRISM experiments, it was shown that in both scenarios the probability of reaching a safe state from an unsafe state is above 0.95 after 5 time steps and above 0.99 after 7 time steps.

The probability of going to an unsafe state from a safe state should be as small as possible. This is analysed with the properties in Lines 8–9. First, the maximum probability (over all possible resolutions of non-determinism) for reaching an unsafe state from a safe state is calculated, and then the maximum (or average) is taken. Again, PRISM experiments were used to analyse this, the plotted graphs for Scenarios 1 and 2 are displayed in Fig. 6. They show that the probability of reaching an unsafe state from a safe state increases with the number of considered time steps. Furthermore, the probability of reaching an unsafe state from a safe state stabilises much later and at a higher value in Scenario 2 than in Scenario 1. While the maximum probability of reaching an unsafe state from a safe state stabilises after about 42 time steps at ≈0.37 in Scenario 1, it stabilises after about 76 time steps at ≈0.69 in Scenario 2. Similar differences can be observed for the average probability.

5   Related Work

The analysis of behavioural requirements is often crucial when developing an SAS that operates in the uncertainty of a physical environment. These requirements often use quantitative metrics that change during runtime. Both rule-based and goal-based adaptation logics can be used to enable the SAS to meet its behavioural requirements. Many practitioners rely on formal methods to provide evidence for the system's compliance with such requirements [20,26], but many different methods are used [1,15]. We consider related work for family-based modelling and analysis approaches.

Family-based model checking of transition systems with features allows to model check properties of multiple behavioural models in a single run, following the seminal work by Classen et al. [10]. Such model-checking tools can be encoded in well-known classical model checkers like SPIN [17], NuSMV [9] or PRISM [19]. In this paper, we used ProFeat [8], a software tool built on top of PRISM for the analysis of feature-aware probabilistic models. Alternatively, QFLan [24] offers probabilistic simulations to yield statistical approximations, thus trading 100% precision for scalability. In [6,7], configurable systems are modelled and analysed as role-based systems, an extension of feature-oriented systems, with a focus on feature interaction; in contrast to our paper, they do not consider a separation between managed and managing subsystem.

Software product lines (SPLs) can be seen as families of (software product) models where feature selection yields variations in the products (configurations). SPLs have previously been proposed to model static variability, i.e., variability during design time, for robotic systems [12]. In [3] it is argued that most of the costs for robotic systems come from non-reusable software. A robotic system mostly contains software tailored to the specific application and embodiment of the robot, and often even software libraries for common robotic functionalities are not reusable. Therefore, they must be re-developed all the time. Thus, a new approach for the development of robotic software using SPLs is proposed in [3].

Finally, dynamic SPLs (DSPLs) [13,16] have been proposed to manage variability during runtime for self-adaptive robots [4]. There are several approaches that model, but do not analyse, SASs as DSPLs, e.g., [2,11,14]. For robotics, the authors in [12] propose the toolchain HyperFlex to model robotic systems as SPLs; it supports the design and reuse of reference architectures for robotic systems and was extended with the Robot Perception Specification Language for robotic perception systems in [5]. It allows to represent variability at different abstraction levels, and feature models from different parts of the system can be composed in several different ways. However, contrary to the approach used in this paper, HyperFlex only considers design time variability. Furthermore, it is only used for modelling robotic systems, not for analysing them.

6   Discussion and Future Work

In this paper, we used a feature model together with a probabilistic, feature guarded transition system to model the managed subsystem of an AUV used for pipeline inspection, and a controller switching between these features to model the managing subsystem of the AUV. This allowed modelling the managed subsystem of the AUV as a family of systems, where each family member corresponds to a valid feature configuration of the AUV. The managing subsystem could then be considered as a control layer capable of dynamically switching between these feature configurations depending on both environmental and internal conditions. The tool ProFeat was used for probabilistic family-based model checking, analysing reward and safety properties.

ProFeat allowed to model the two different layers of abstraction of an SAS, the managed and managing subsystem, which also makes it easier to understand the model and the adaptation logic. Furthermore, it makes analysing all configurations of the managed subsystem more efficient by enabling family-based model checking. However, it remains to be seen how this scales with larger models. We are unaware of other work that exploits the family-based modelling and analysis capabilities of ProFeat for SASs, but we believe this is a natural approach.

The case study in this paper is of course a highly simplified model of an AUV and its mission. However, we showed that it is feasible to model and analyse a two-layered self-adaptive cyber-physical system as a family of configurations with a controller switching between them. To analyse a real AUV, both the models of the AUV and the environment, and in particular the probabilities, have to be adapted to the robot and the environment with the help of real data and domain experts. We plan to investigate this together with an industrial partner of the MSCA network REMARO (Reliable AI for Marine Robotics).

In the future, we plan to investigate which kind of models can be modelled and analysed as we did with the case study to try to find a general methodology for modelling and analysing SASs as family-based systems. Furthermore, we plan to find optimal strategies for the managing subsystem, i.e., the controller switching between features, e.g., to minimise energy consumption. We would also like to find patterns between choosing a certain feature configuration and the effect of this on quality criteria of the system. Finding such control patterns could help to improve the adaptation logic of the managing subsystem to be more resilient towards faults.

Acknowledgments. We would like to thank Clemens Dubslaff for explaining Pro-Feat and its usage to us, and for answering numerous questions. Furthermore, we would like to thank Rudolf Schlatte for his help in preparing the artifact for the final artifact submission. This work was supported by the European Union's Horizon 2020 Framework Programme through the MSCA network REMARO (Grant Agreement No 956200), by the Italian project NODES (which has received funding from the MUR - M4C2 1.5 of PNRR with grant agreement no. ECS00000036) and by the Italian MUR PRIN 2020TL3X8X project T-LADIES (Typeful Language Adaptation for Dynamic, Interacting and Evolving Systems).

References

1. Araujo, H., Mousavi, M.R., Varshosaz, M.: Testing, validation, and verification of robotic and autonomous systems: a systematic review. ACM Trans. Softw. Eng. Methodol. **32**(2), 51:1–51:61 (2023). https://doi.org/10.1145/3542945
2. Bencomo, N., Sawyer, P., Blair, G.S., Grace, P.: Dynamically adaptive systems are product lines too: using model-driven techniques to capture dynamic variability of adaptive systems. In: Thiel, S., Pohl, K. (eds.) Proceedings of the 12th International Conference on Software Product Lines (SPLC 2008). vol. 2, pp. 23–32. University of Limerick, Lero (2008)
3. Brugali, D.: Software product line engineering for robotics. In: Cavalcanti, A., Dongol, B., Hierons, R., Timmis, J., Woodcock, J. (eds.) Software Engineering for Robotics, pp. 1–28. Springer, Cham (2021). https://doi.org/10.1007/978-3-030-66494-7_1
4. Brugali, D., Capilla, R., Hinchey, M.: Dynamic variability meets robotics. IEEE Comput. **48**(12), 94–97 (2015). https://doi.org/10.1109/MC.2015.354
5. Brugali, D., Hochgeschwender, N.: Managing the functional variability of robotic perception systems. In: Proceedings of the 1st International Conference on Robotic Computing (IRC 2017), pp. 277–283. IEEE (2017). https://doi.org/10.1109/IRC.2017.20
6. Chrszon, P., Baier, C., Dubslaff, C., Klüppelholz, S.: From features to roles. In: Proceedings of the 24th International Systems and Software Product Line Conference (SPLC 2020), pp. 19:1–19:11. ACM (2020). https://doi.org/10.1145/3382025.3414962
7. Chrszon, P., Baier, C., Dubslaff, C., Klüppelholz, S.: Interaction detection in configurable systems - a formal approach featuring roles. J. Syst. Softw. **196** (2023). https://doi.org/10.1016/j.jss.2022.111556
8. Chrszon, P., Dubslaff, C., Klüppelholz, S., Baier, C.: ProFeat: feature-oriented engineering for family-based probabilistic model checking. Formal Aspects Comput. **30**(1), 45–75 (2018). https://doi.org/10.1007/s00165-017-0432-4

9. Cimatti, A., et al.: NuSMV 2: an OpenSource tool for symbolic model checking. In: Brinksma, E., Larsen, K.G. (eds.) Proceedings of the 14th International Conference on Computer Aided Verification (CAV 2002). LNCS, vol. 2404, pp. 359–364. Springer, Heidelberg (2002). https://doi.org/10.1007/3-540-45657-0_29

10. Classen, A., Heymans, P., Schobbens, P.Y., Legay, A., Raskin, J.F.: Model checking lots of systems: efficient verification of temporal properties in software product lines. In: Proceedings of the 32nd International Conference on Software Engineering (ICSE 2010), pp. 335–344. ACM (2010). https://doi.org/10.1145/1806799.1806850

11. Dhungana, D., Grünbacher, P., Rabiser, R.: Domain-specific adaptations of product line variability modeling. In: Ralyté, J., Brinkkemper, S., Henderson-Sellers, B. (eds.) Situational Method Engineering: Fundamentals and Experiences. ME 2007. IFIP – The International Federation for Information Processing, ITIFIP, vol. 244, pp. 238–251. Springer, Boston, MA (2007). https://doi.org/10.1007/978-0-387-73947-2_19

12. Gherardi, L., Brugali, D.: Modeling and reusing robotic software architectures: the HyperFlex toolchain. In: Proceedings of the International Conference on Robotics and Automation (ICRA 2014), pp. 6414–6420. IEEE (2014). https://doi.org/10.1109/ICRA.2014.6907806

13. Hallsteinsen, S., Hinchey, M., Park, S., Schmid, K.: Dynamic software product lines. In: Capilla, R., Bosch, J., Kang, K.C. (eds.) Systems and Software Variability Management: Concepts, Tools and Experiences, pp. 253–260. Springer, Heidelberg (2013). https://doi.org/10.1007/978-3-642-36583-6_16

14. Hallsteinsen, S., Stav, E., Solberg, A., Floch, J.: Using product line techniques to build adaptive systems. In: Proceedings of the 10th International Software Product Line Conference (SPLC 2006), pp. 141–150. IEEE (2006). https://doi.org/10.1109/SPLINE.2006.1691586

15. Hezavehi, S.M., Weyns, D., Avgeriou, P., Calinescu, R., Mirandola, R., Perez-Palacin, D.: Uncertainty in self-adaptive systems: a research community perspective. ACM Trans. Auton. Adapt. Syst. 15(4), 10:1–10:36 (2021). https://doi.org/10.1145/3487921

16. Hinchey, M., Park, S., Schmid, K.: Building dynamic software product lines. IEEE Comput. 45(10), 22–26 (2012). https://doi.org/10.1109/MC.2012.332

17. Holzmann, G.J.: The SPIN Model Checker: Primer and Reference Manual. Addison-Wesley, Boston (2004)

18. Kephart, J.O., Chess, D.M.: The vision of autonomic computing. IEEE Comput. 36(1), 41–50 (2003). https://doi.org/10.1109/MC.2003.1160055

19. Kwiatkowska, M., Norman, G., Parker, D.: PRISM 4.0: verification of probabilistic real-time systems. In: Gopalakrishnan, G., Qadeer, S. (eds.) Proceedings of the 23rd International Conference on Computer Aided Verification (CAV 2011). LNCS, vol. 6806, pp. 585–591. Springer, Heidelberg (2011). https://doi.org/10.1007/978-3-642-22110-1_47

20. Luckcuck, M., Farrell, M., Dennis, L.A., Dixon, C., Fisher, M.: Formal specification and verification of autonomous robotic systems: a survey. ACM Comput. Surv. 52(5), 100:1–100:41 (2019). https://doi.org/10.1145/3342355

21. Päßler, J., ter Beek, M.H., Damiani, F., Tapia Tarifa, S.L., Johnsen, E.B.: Formal modelling and analysis of a self-adaptive robotic system (Artifact) (2023). https://doi.org/10.5281/zenodo.8275533

22. Rezende Silva, G., et al.: SUAVE: an exemplar for self-adaptive underwater vehicles. In: Proceedings of the 18th International Symposium on Software Engineering for Adaptive and Self-Managing Systems (SEAMS 2023), pp. 181–187. IEEE (2023). https://doi.org/10.1109/SEAMS59076.2023.00031

23. Thüm, T., Apel, S., Kästner, C., Schaefer, I., Saake, G.: A classification and survey of analysis strategies for software product lines. ACM Comput. Surv. **47**(1), 6:1–6:45 (2014). https://doi.org/10.1145/2580950

24. Vandin, A., ter Beek, M.H., Legay, A., Lluch Lafuente, A.: QFLan: a tool for the quantitative analysis of highly reconfigurable systems. In: Havelund, K., Peleska, J., Roscoe, B., de Vink, E. (eds.) Proceedings of the 22nd International Symposium on Formal Methods (FM 2018). LNCS, vol. 10951, pp. 329–337. Springer, Cham (2018). https://doi.org/10.1007/978-3-319-95582-7_19

25. Weyns, D.: An Introduction to Self-Adaptive Systems: A Contemporary Software Engineering Perspective. John Wiley & Sons, Hoboken (2020)

26. Weyns, D., Iftikhar, M.U., de la Iglesia, D.G., Ahmad, T.: A survey of formal methods in self-adaptive systems. In: Proceedings of the 5th International C* Conference on Computer Science and Software Engineering (C3S2E 2012), pp. 67–79. ACM (2012). https://doi.org/10.1145/2347583.2347592

CAN-VERIFY: A Verification Tool For BDI Agents

Mengwei Xu[1(✉)], Thibault Rivoalen[3], Blair Archibald[2], and Michele Sevegnani[2]

[1] Department of Computer Science, University of Manchester, Manchester, UK
mengwei.xu@manchester.ac.uk
[2] School of Computing Science, University of Glasgow, Glasgow, UK
[3] Ecole Nationale de L'Aviation Civile (ENAC), University of Toulouse, Toulouse, France

Abstract. CAN-VERIFY is an automated tool that aids the development, verification, and analysis of BDI agents written in the Conceptual Agent Notation (CAN) language. It does not require users to be familiar with verification techniques. CAN-VERIFY supports syntactic error checking, interpretation of programs (running agents), and exhaustive exploration of all possible executions (agent verification and analysis) to check against both generic agent requirements, such as if a task can be achieved successfully, and user-defined requirements, such as whether a certain belief eventually holds. Simple examples of Unmanned Aerial Vehicles (UAV) and autonomous patrol robots illustrate the tool in action.

1 Introduction

The BDI architecture, where agents are modelled based on their beliefs, desires, and intentions, is a practical approach to developing complex and autonomous systems. BDI agents make decisions based on their beliefs, which reflect their understanding of the world, their desires, which represent their goals, and their intentions, which are the plans they've committed to achieve those goals. The design of these agents is challenging because of the mixed nature of the goal: declarative (a description of the state sought) and procedural (a set of instructions to perform), failure handling, inherently interleaved concurrent behaviours, and ultimately the safety of these agents' employment.

There is a software collection to develop BDI agents including JACK [33], Jason [10], and Jadex [28]. These platforms focus on the simulations of BDI agents primarily programmed in variants of AgentSpeak [29], one of the most well-known BDI languages. Simulations cannot, by their nature, analyse all possible agent behaviours. As such, formal verification techniques [20] have been used to exhaustively assess whether agents will indeed behave as required. For example, the Model Checking Agent Programming Languages (MCAPL) framework [16] offers model checking for GWENDOLEN [15] programs (another variant of AgentSpeak).

P. Herber and A. Wijs (Eds.): iFM 2023, LNCS 14300, pp. 364–373, 2024.
https://doi.org/10.1007/978-3-031-47705-8_19

To widen access to formal methods, we present an automated tool, CAN-VERIFY, for BDI programmers to verify agents in the Conceptual Agent Notation (CAN) language. As a superset of AgentSpeak, CAN includes advanced behaviours *e.g.* declarative goals, concurrency, and failure recovery. In a nutshell, CAN-VERIFY takes as input CAN programs and supports the following features:

- static checking for a wide range of BDI program syntactic issues;
- support for BDI program interpretation;
- exhaustive exploration of BDI program executions;
- verification, through model checking, of agents against a set of built-in generic agent requirements and (optional) user-defined agent requirements that can be expressed in natural language;
- verification of BDI agents parameterised by their initial belief base to support analysis of agent behaviours under different initial environments.

This is the first tool to support reasoning about CAN programs without requiring users to have specialised knowledge of verification techniques and formal logics. CAN-VERIFY, and all examples shown in this work, are openly available [35].

Related Work. There is wide interest in applying formal verification to autonomous agents [7,12,25], but adoption has been limited mainly due to the complexities of formal verification tools [1]. This is also an issue in the broader Formal Method community for applicable formal methods [19]. Our tool allows agent programmers to benefit from verification without specialist knowledge.

Previous work on reasoning about BDI agents using automated techniques includes the MCAPL framework. MCAPL implements a BDI language in Java allowing it to be verified with the Java PathFinder [11] program model checker. While verifying an implementation tells you how the specific *system* will operate, it may not give insight into how the *language* semantics were meant to operate, especially if the implementation does not fully correspond. For example, GWENDOLEN (supported by MCAPL) only selects the first applicable plan, while language semantics usually allow *any* applicable plan to be chosen. Bordini et al. [9] translates a simplified AgentSpeak language into Promela [23] and verifies agents using the Spin model-checker [22]. Similarly, term-rewriting, specifically in Maude [14], has also been used to encode BDI agent languages, allowing verification of temporal properties with the Maude LTL model checker [17]. Recently, Jensen [24] applied the Isabelle/HOL proof assistant [27] to BDI programs. However, no tool is fully automated to relieve users from the error-prone translation and complex verification stages, whereas we streamline the BDI agent design, interpretation, and verification process, alleviating these burdens from users.

2 CAN—Overview

The Conceptual Agent Notation (CAN) [31] language formalises a classical BDI agent consisting of a belief base $\mathcal{B}$ and a plan library Π. The belief base $\mathcal{B}$ is a set

Listing 1.1. CAN agent for conference trip arrangement.

```
1 at_home  // Initial belief bases
2 travel   // External events
3 // Plan library
4 travel: own_car & driving_distance <- start_car; driving.
5 // Action descriptions
6 start_car: car_functional <- <{engine_off}, {engine_on}>
7 driving: engine_on <- <{not_at_venue}, {at_venue}>
```

of formulae encoding the current beliefs and has belief operators for entailment (*i.e.* $\mathcal{B} \models \varphi$), and belief atom addition (resp. deletion) $\mathcal{B} \cup \{b\}$ (resp. $\mathcal{B} \setminus \{b\}$). In this case, we assume propositional logic. A plan library Π is a collection of plans of the form $e : \varphi \leftarrow P$ with e the triggering event, φ the context condition, and P the plan-body. The triggering event e specifies why the plan is triggered, while the context condition φ determines if the plan-body P is able to handle the event. Events can either be external (*i.e.* from the environment) or internal (*i.e.* sub-goals that the agent itself tries to accomplish). The language used in the plan-body for agent programmers is $act \mid e \mid P_1; P_2 \mid P_1 \parallel P_2 \mid goal(\varphi_s, e, \varphi_f)$ where act is an action, e is a sub-event (*i.e.* internal event), composite programs $P_1; P_2$ (resp. $P_1 \parallel P_2$) for sequence (resp. concurrency), and $goal(\varphi_s, e, \varphi_f)$ a declarative goal program. Actions act take the form $act : \varphi \leftarrow \langle \phi^-, \phi^+ \rangle$, where φ is the pre-condition, and ϕ^- and ϕ^+ are the deletion and addition sets of belief atoms, *i.e.* a belief base $\mathcal{B}$ is revised to be $(\mathcal{B} \setminus \phi^-) \cup \phi^+$ when the action executes. Composite programs $P_1; P_2$ is for sequenced execution and $P_1 \parallel P_2$ for interleaved concurrency. A declarative goal program $goal(\varphi_s, e, \varphi_f)$ expresses that the declarative goal φ_s should be achieved through an event e, failing if φ_f becomes true, and retrying as long as neither φ_s nor φ_f is true. The full semantics of CAN can be found in [30,34].

The example in Listing 1.1 describes a fragment of agent arranging a conference trip [3]. An agent desires to travel, *i.e.* an external event travel (line 2) and believes it is at home initially, *i.e.* a belief at_home (line 1). In this fragment, the only plan (line 4) expresses that if the agent believes it owns a car (*i.e.* own_car holds) and the venue is in driving distance (*i.e.* driving_distance), it will start the car (start_car) and drive (driving) to the venue. Actions change beliefs, for example, start_car (line 6) says that if the car is functional (car_functional) then, after executing the action, the agent should believe the engine is on (engine_on) and remove the belief the engine is off (engine_off).

3   CAN-VERIFY Components and Features

Our tool is based on an executable semantics of CAN [3] enabled through an encoding into Milner's Bigraphs [26], a computational model based on graph-rewriting. The dataflow of the toolchain is in Fig. 1. Step ① translates input CAN programs into bigraphs expressed in the BigraphER [32] language. During the translation, static checks are performed and errors/warnings reported to users.

Listing 1.2. Built-in (lines 1-4) and user-defined (lines 5 and 6) agent requirements. Belief-lists have $\wedge$ semantics *i.e.* there is a state where all beliefs hold at the same time.

```
1 A [ F ("no_failure" & X ("empty_intention")) ];
2 E [ F ("no_failure" & X ("empty_intention")) ];
3 A [ F ("failure" & X ("empty_intention")) ];
4 E [ F ("failure" & X ("empty_intention")) ];
5 A [ F (<belief-list>) ];
6 E [ F (<belief-list>) ];
```

To verify an agent, the agent requirements in both built-in and user-defined requirements will be compiled as bigraph patterns for state predicate labelling (②) if the pattern matches the current state then the predicate is true. Step ③ combines bigraph models representing agent programs and CAN semantics [3], and asks BigraphER to explore all possible executions. The output of BigraphER (an explicit transition system with state predicate labels), and built-in and user-defined temporal logic formulae (complied from ④) are then verified by PRISM[1] (⑤). Next, we will go through the features of our tool in detail one by one.

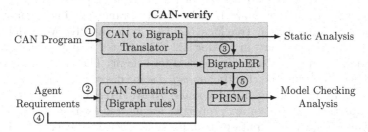

Fig. 1. Toolchain overview: ① agent program compilation to bigraphs, ② predicate labelling in bigraph model, ③ (exhaustive) execution of programs, ④ built-in and user-defined belief-based specification formalisation in CTL, ⑤ formal verification.

Static Analysis of BDI Programs. Our tool provides static checks of agent programs including reporting syntax errors, type errors *e.g.* when a plan is used where a belief is expected, and undefined errors *e.g.* when an actions is used but does not exist, or no plan is able to handle a defined event. We also support design aids as warnings, for example, reporting if (customisable) limits are violated such as the mininum/maximum number of plans for an event.

CAN Interpreter. As the bigraph model includes the semantics for the CAN language, given an initial state we can execute any CAN programs. Note: there is no support to actually execute actions, but only to record their outcomes.

---

[1] Any model checker supporting explicit model import would work. PRISM is chosen as BigraphER natively supports PRISM format, and as ongoing work we aim to allow probabilistic extensions and reasoning on CAN programs [2,5].

Listing 1.3. CAN agent for concurrent sensing in UAVs

```
1  ram_free, storage_free // Initial belief bases
2  sensing // External events
3  //Plan library
4  sensing: true <- dust || photo.
5  dust: ram_free & storage_free <- collect_dust; analyse; send_back.
6  photo: ram_free & storage_free <- focus_camera; save_shots; zip_shots.
7  // Actions description
8  collect_dust: ram_free <- <{ram_free}, {}>
9  analyse: true <- <{}, {}>
10 send_back: storage_free <- <{}, {ram_free,storage_free}>
11 focus_camera: true <- <{}, {}>
12 save_shots: storage_free <- <{storage_free}, {}>
13 zip_shots: ram_free <- <{}, {ram_free, storage_free}>
```

Model Checking of BDI Programs. Model checking is enabled by taking the executable model of the agent program and constructing a labelled transition system of the program's possible executions that allow checking agent requirements against this model. Built-in agent requirements for generic properties include determining if for some/all executions an event finishes with failure or success (these failure or success state are labelled using bigraph predicates [8] automatically). These requirements are translated into branching time temporal logic formulae *e.g.* Computation Tree logic (CTL) [13] for the PRISM model checker. Example requirements are in Listing 1.2. The first 4 requirements are built-in properties that will always be checked by default. The last 2 properties are user-defined requirements, checking on *e.g.* if some desired/avoided beliefs would hold true in all possible agent behaviours. To avoid requiring users to formalise these properties in CTL syntax, properties are instead expressed in natural language. For example, the input of "In all possible executions, eventually the belief at_venue holds"[2] equals to the CTL formula A [F ("at_venue")], checking eventually the agent of Listing 1.1 arrives at the venue. This translation is performed by the tool as well. Although current support from natural language to formal properties is limited, and an area of future work, we focus on this style of property specification as this is what non-expert users often encounter in practice. Finally, to verify BDI agents starting from different environmental conditions (*i.e.* different initial belief bases), our tool supports verification from parameterised initial belief bases defined in the CAN file. This is useful as the users do not have to run the agent with each initial belief manually, and, importantly, it facilitates a quick comparison of the results from different initial beliefs. Each initial belief set is numbered and the tool automatically runs multiple times to output a result for each initial belief base. For example, we can add another initial belief base *e.g.* at_shop in Listing 1.1 to analyse agent behaviours with the initial location at a shop.

4   Examples

We give two simple examples to show how our tool improves agent designs and guarantees correct agent behaviours. The aim is to relieve non-expert users from

---

[2] Parser requires exact natural language wording with user-defined strings as beliefs.

Listing 1.4. CAN agent for two-storey building patrol robot.

```
1  //Initial belief bases
2  at_F1, F1_dirty, F1_uninspected, F2_clean, F2_inspected
3  patrol // External events
4  // Plan library
5  patrol: true <- goal(F1_inspected & F2_inspected, check, false).
6  check: at_F1 <- goal(F1_clean, vacuum, false); goal(F1_inspected, inspect
       , false); go_to_F2.
7  check: at_F2 <- goal(F2_clean, vacuum, false); goal(F2_inspected, inspect
       , false); go_to_F1.
8  inspect: at_F1 & F1_uninspected <- inspect_F1.
9  inspect: at_F2 & F2_uninspected <- inspect_F2.
10 vacuum: at_F1 & F1_dirty <- clean_F1.
11 vacuum: at_F2 & F2_dirty <- clean_F2.
12 // Actions description
13 inspect_F1: at_F1 & F1_uninspected <- <{F1_uninspected}, {F1_inspected}>
14 inspect_F2: at_F2 & F2_uninspected <- <{F2_uninspected}, {F2_inspected}>
15 clean_F1: at_F1 & F1_dirty <- <{F1_dirty}, {F1_clean}>
16 clean_F2: at_F2 & F2_dirty <- <{F2_dirty}, {F2_clean}>
17 go_to_F2: at_F1 <- <{at_F1}, {at_F2}>
18 go_to_F1: at_F2 <- <{at_F2}, {at_F1}>
```

the underlying complex translation and verification process by supporting the users' workflow from agent design to agent behaviour analysis.

Concurrent Sensing. We consider a UAV that analyses dust particles and performs aerial photo collection *e.g.* for analysis of post volcanic eruptions. An agent design is in Listing 1.3 from [3]. The external event **sensing** (line 2) initiates the sensing mission, and the relevant plan (line 4) has concurrent (interleaved) tasks for dust monitoring (**dust**) and photo collection (**photo**). Onboard dust sensors require high-speed RAM to collect and analyse the data (**ram_free**), and, when the analysis is complete, results are written to storage (requiring **storage_free**), and sent back to control. Similarly, to collect aerial photos the UAV reserves and focuses the camera array (**focus_camera**), then camera shots are compressed (**zip_shots**), and sent back (where only relevant beliefs are specified in the addition/deletion set of each action (lines 8–13). Static analysis does not identify any issue, however, model checking shows **sensing** is not always completed successfully. A possible explanation is that interleaved concurrency introduces a race condition. To confirm, the agent programmer could replace **dust || photo** (line 4) with **dust; photo** and re-run the tool. The new result shows that the event is now always successful, giving feedback to the agent designer to fix the design through explicit sequencing of actions.

Multi-storey Building Patrol Robot. We consider an autonomous patrol robot that inspects/cleans all floors of a building. For simplicity, the design of two-storey building is given in Listing 1.4. The initial belief base (line 2) gives the location of the robot and the inspection and clean status of each floor. The external event **patrol** (line 3) initiates the patrol mission. The plan (line 5) addressing **patrol** has a true context (always applicable), and a declarative goal whose success condition shows that the event **check** will be pursued until every floor is inspected. To address the event `check`, plans (lines 6–7) instruct the robot to vacuum and inspect the floor if needed and move to the next higher floor or get to the bottom if the top floor is reached. Plans (lines 8–11) are for actually inspecting and vacuuming. There are no static analysis issues and model checking shows that the event `patrol` is always completed with success, confirming the robot can successfully achieve its task given the initial belief base. To provide an even stronger guarantee of successful cleaning no matter where the robot is initially located, we can parameterise the initial belief base by agent location, *e.g.* adding another initial belief base in which the belief atom `at_F1` changes to `at_F2`, and in each case, the agent exhibits the correct behaviours.

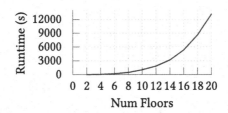

Fig. 2. Transition system construction time increases exponentially with floors.

To evaluate scalability, we increase the number of floors. The time to construct the model is in Fig. 2. As expected, there is an exponential increase in time from a couple of seconds to a couple of hours. As our tool is intended to be used at design time we do not believe this to be an issue in practice.

5   Discussion and Conclusion

CAN-VERIFY is motivated by the clear need for verification tools that are comprehensible and usable by non-experts. We streamlined the entire underlying process of formal modelling/encoding from BDI agents to Bigraphs, model execution in BigraphER, and model-checking with PRISM. CAN-VERIFY requires only one mandatory input of BDI programs written in the CAN languages and an additional user-defined requirement input file that can be expressed in natural language. The significance of this tool is to meet the growing demands for safe autonomy through formal verification, *e.g.* for early error detection and design improvement, without the costs of applying it *e.g.* formalisation effort.

Current research [4,6] employs the same Bigraph framework to show the use of PRISM and Storm [21] for strategy synthesis and verification of BDI agents and under dynamic environment. We anticipate a small software engineering effort to extend CAN-VERIFY to support both quantitative verification and strategy synthesis. Additionally, the current property specifications mechanism is limited, and we see the task of formalising complex and evolving agent requirements for analysis as a challenging but necessary area. A good starting point may be to integrate with our tool an existing property elicitation interface such as NASA's Formal Requirements Elicitation Tool (FRET) [18].

Acknowledgments. This work is supported by the Engineering and Physical Sciences Research Council, under grants EP/S035362/1, EP/W01081X/1, EP/V026801, and an Amazon Research Award on Automated Reasoning.

References

1. Arcaini, P., Bonfanti, S., Gargantini, A., Riccobene, E., Scandurra, P.: Addressing usability in a formal development environment. In: Sekerinski, E., et al. (eds.) FM 2019. LNCS, vol. 12232, pp. 61–76. Springer, Cham (2020). https://doi.org/10.1007/978-3-030-54994-7_6
2. Archibald, B., Calder, M., Sevegnani, M., Xu, M.: Probabilistic BDI agents: actions, plans, and intentions. In: Calinescu, R., Păsăreanu, C.S. (eds.) SEFM 2021. LNCS, vol. 13085, pp. 262–281. Springer, Cham (2021). https://doi.org/10.1007/978-3-030-92124-8_15
3. Archibald, B., Calder, M., Sevegnani, M., Xu, M.: Modelling and verifying BDI agents with bigraphs. Sci. Comput. Program. **215**, 102760 (2022)
4. Archibald, B., Calder, M., Sevegnani, M., Xu, M.: Verifying BDI agents in dynamic environments. In: Proceedings of the International Conference on Software Engineering and Knowledge Engineering, pp. 136–141 (2022)
5. Archibald, B., Calder, M., Sevegnani, M., Xu, M.: Quantitative modelling and analysis of BDI agents. Softw. Syst. Model. (2023). https://doi.org/10.1007/s10270-023-01121-5
6. Archibald, B., Calder, M., Sevegnani, M., Xu, M.: Quantitative verification and strategy synthesis for BDI agents. In: Rozier, K.Y., Chaudhuri, S. (eds.) NASA Formal Methods. NFM 2023. LNCS, vol. 13903, pp. 241–259. Springer, Cham (2023). https://doi.org/10.1007/978-3-031-33170-1_15
7. Bakar, N.A., Selamat, A.: Agent systems verification: systematic literature review and mapping. Appl. Intell. **48**(5), 1251–1274 (2018)
8. Benford, S., Calder, M., Rodden, T., Sevegnani, M.: On lions, impala, and bigraphs: modelling interactions in physical/virtual spaces. ACM Trans. Comput.-Hum. Interact. (TOCHI) **23**(2), 1–56 (2016)
9. Bordini, R.H., Fisher, M., Visser, W., Wooldridge, M.: Verifying multi-agent programs by model checking. Auton. Agent. Multi-Agent Syst. **12**, 239–256 (2006)
10. Bordini, R.H., et al.: Programming Multi-agent Systems in AgentSpeak using Jason. vol. 8. Wiley, New York (2007)
11. Brat, G., Havelund, K., Park, S., Visser, W.: Model checking programs. In: Proceedings of IEEE International Conference on Automated Software Engineering, pp. 3–11. IEEE (2000)
12. Cardoso, R.C., et al.: A review of verification and validation for space autonomous systems. Curr. Robot. Rep. **2**(3), 273–283 (2021)
13. Clarke, E.M., Emerson, E.A.: Design and synthesis of synchronization skeletons using branching time temporal logic. In: Proceedings of Workshop on Logic of Programs, pp. 52–71 (1981)
14. Clavel, M., et al.: Maude manual (version 3.0). SRI International (2020)
15. Dennis, L.A.: Gwendolen semantics: 2017 (2017)

16. Dennis, L.A., et al.: Model checking agent programming languages. Autom. Softw. Eng. **19**(1), 5–63 (2012)

17. Eker, S., Meseguer, J., Sridharanarayanan, A.: The Maude LTL model checker. Electron. Notes Theor. Comput. Sci. **71**, 162–187 (2004)

18. Farrell, M., Luckcuck, M., Sheridan, O., Monahan, R.: FRETting about requirements: formalised requirements for an aircraft engine controller. In: Gervasi, V., Vogelsang, A. (eds.) REFSQ 2022. LNCS, vol. 13216, pp. 96–111. Springer, Cham (2022). https://doi.org/10.1007/978-3-030-98464-9_9

19. Gleirscher, M., van de Pol, J., Woodcock, J.: A manifesto for applicable formal methods. arXiv preprint arXiv:2112.12758 (2021)

20. Hasan, O., Tahar, S.: Formal verification methods. In: Encyclopedia of Information Science and Technology, 3rd Edition, pp. 7162–7170. IGI Global (2015)

21. Hensel, C., Junges, S., Katoen, J.-P., Quatmann, T., Volk, M.: The probabilistic model checker STORM. Int. J. Softw. Tools Technol. Trans. 1–22 (2021). https://doi.org/10.1007/s10009-021-00633-z

22. Holzmann, G.J.: The model checker SPIN. IEEE Trans. Softw. Eng. **23**(5), 279–295 (1997)

23. Holzmann, G.J., Lieberman, W.S.: Design and Validation of Computer Protocols, vol. 512. Prentice hall Englewood Cliffs (1991)

24. Jensen, A.B.: Machine-checked verification of cognitive agents. In: Proceedings of the 14th International Conference on Agents and Artificial Intelligence, pp. 245–256 (2022)

25. Luckcuck, M., Farrell, M., Dennis, L.A., Dixon, C., Fisher, M.: Formal specification and verification of autonomous robotic systems: a survey. ACM Comput. Surv. (CSUR) **52**(5), 1–41 (2019)

26. Milner, R.: The Space and Motion of Communicating Agents. Cambridge University Press, Cambridge (2009)

27. Nipkow, T., Wenzel, M., Paulson, L.C. (eds.): : 5. the rules of the game. In: Isabelle/HOL. LNCS, vol. 2283, pp. 67–104. Springer, Heidelberg (2002). https://doi.org/10.1007/3-540-45949-9_5

28. Pokahr, A., Braubach, L., Jander, K.: The Jadex project: programming model. In: Ganzha, M., Jain, L. (eds.) Multiagent Systems and Applications. Intelligent Systems Reference Library, vol. 45, pp. 21–53. Springer, Berlin (2013). https://doi.org/10.1007/978-3-642-33323-1_2

29. Rao, A.S.: AgentSpeak(L): BDI agents speak out in a logical computable language. In: Van de Velde, W., Perram, J.W. (eds.) MAAMAW 1996. LNCS, vol. 1038, pp. 42–55. Springer, Heidelberg (1996). https://doi.org/10.1007/BFb0031845

30. Sardina, S., Padgham, L.: A BDI agent programming language with failure handling, declarative goals, and planning. Auton. Agent. Multi-Agent Syst. **23**(1), 18–70 (2011)

31. Sardina, S., Silva, L.D., Padgham, L.: Hierarchical planning in BDI agent programming languages: a formal approach. In: Proceedings of the International Joint Conference on Autonomous Agents and Multiagent Systems, pp. 1001–1008 (2006)

32. Sevegnani, M., Calder, M.: BigraphER: rewriting and analysis engine for bigraphs. In: Chaudhuri, S., Farzan, A. (eds.) CAV 2016. LNCS, vol. 9780, pp. 494–501. Springer, Cham (2016). https://doi.org/10.1007/978-3-319-41540-6_27

33. Winikoff, M.: Jack^{TM} intelligent agents: an industrial strength platform. In: Bordini, R.H., Dastani, M., Dix, J., El Fallah Seghrouchni, A. (eds.) Multi-Agent Programming. MSASSO, vol. 15, pp. 175–193. Springer, Boston, MA (2005). https://doi.org/10.1007/0-387-26350-0_7

34. Winikoff, M., Padgham, L., Harland, J., Thangarajah, J.: Declarative & procedural goals in intelligent agent systems. In: KR, vol. 2002, pp. 470–481 (2002)
35. Xu, M., Rivoalen, T., Archibald, B., Sevegnani, M.: CAN-verify source repository and models, September 2022. https://zenodo.org/record/8282684

PhD Symposium Presentations

Scalable and Precise Refinement Types for Imperative Languages

Florian Lanzinger[1(✉)], Joshua Bachmeier[2], Mattias Ulbrich[1],
and Werner Dietl[3]

[1] Karlsruhe Institute of Technology, Karlsruhe, Germany
`lanzinger@kit.edu`
[2] FZI Research Center for Information Technology, Karlsruhe, Germany
[3] University of Waterloo, Waterloo, Canada

Abstract. In formal verification, there is a dichotomy between tools which are scalable and easy to use but imprecise, like most pluggable type systems, and tools which are expressive and precise but badly scalable and difficult to use, like deductive verification. Our previous research to create a formal link between refinement types and deductive verification allows programmers to use a scalable type system for most of the program, while automatically generating specifications for a deductive verifier for the difficult-to-prove parts. However, this is currently limited to immutable objects. In this work, we thus present an approach which combines uniqueness and refinement type systems in an imperative language. Unlike existing similar approaches, which limit refinements such that they cannot contain any reference-typed program variables, our approach allows more general refinements, because even if a type constraint is not provable in the type system itself, it can be translated and proven by a deductive verifier.

Keywords: Pluggable type systems · Deductive verification ·
Refinement types · Ownership types

1 Introduction

There are many ways to prove a program's correctness, each with their own strengths and weaknesses. In deductive verification, a formal specification describing the expected behavior needs to be written and then proven using some partially interactive tool. Both the specification languages and the proof

F. Lanzinger—This work was supported by funding from the topic Engineering Secure Systems of the Helmholtz Association (HGF) and by KASTEL Security Research Labs. It was also supported by a Mitacs Globalink Research Award for the project "Scalable Verification of Imperative Programs."

W. Dietl—This work was supported by the KIT International Excellence Fellowships Program with funds granted to the University of Excellence concept of Karlsruhe Institute of Technology.

P. Herber and A. Wijs (Eds.): iFM 2023, LNCS 14300, pp. 377–383, 2024.
https://doi.org/10.1007/978-3-031-47705-8_20

tools are often difficult to use for non-experts. In addition, the approach is time-consuming and scales badly with program size and complexity. Pluggable type systems [2], which annotate variables and sub-programs with types that describe their expected values and behavior, offer a light-weight alternative. However, most of these type systems only check for a conservative approximation of the formal guarantee they are designed for.

In our previous research [8], we presented a bridge between the two methods to combine the advantages of both: The developer first uses pluggable type systems to establish formal guarantees. If the type checker cannot show the well-typedness of the complete program, it emits a translated program in which all unproven typing constraints are turned into formal specifications for a deductive verifier, while all proven constraints are turned into auxiliary assumptions. Unlike existing refinement type systems, this combined approach allows us to state and prove refinements beyond the capabilities of a type checker or SMT solver while still retaining the benefits of scalable type checking where possible.

However, this is so far limited to immutable objects. Here, we present an extension of the approach to mutable objects by leveraging a uniqueness type system to deal with aliasing. In addition to uniqueness types, we use a *packing type system* based on an approach by Leino and Müller [11] to allow consistent updates in the presence of dependent types. We have formalized the approach and are currently working on a proof and implementation. Similar combinations of ownership/uniqueness and refinement types in imperative languages exist [10, 12,15], but they limit refinements such that they cannot contain any reference-typed program variables. We can allow more general dependent refinements, because even if a type constraint cannot be shown to hold by the syntactic type rules, it can still be translated into a specification for the deductive verifier.

2   Combining Refinement Type Systems and Deductive Verification

```
boolean is_leq(@NonNull VarInfo v1, @NonNull VarInfo v2) {
  @Nullable Invariant inv = null; @Nullable Slice slice = null;
  slice = findSlice(v1, v2);
  if (slice != null) {
    inv = instantiate(slice);
  }
  if (inv != null) {
    boolean found = slice.is_inv_true(inv);
    return found;
  }
  return false;
}
```

Fig. 1. A false positive in the Nullness Checker.

```
//@ requires v1 != null && v2 != null;
boolean is_leq(VarInfo v1, VarInfo v2) {
  //@ assume v1 != null && v2 != null;
  Invariant inv = null; Slice slice = null;
  slice = findSlice(v1, v2);
  if (slice != null) {
    //@ assume slice != null;
    inv = instantiate(slice);
  }
  if (inv != null) {
    //@ assume inv != null;
    //@ assert slice != null;
    boolean found = slice.is_inv_true(inv);
    return found;
  }
  return false;
}
```

Fig. 2. JML translation of Fig. 1

This section summarizes our previous work [8]. Figure 1 is an example taken from that paper; it shows a slightly modified code snippet from the Daikon Invariant Generator [5], which uses the Nullness Checker of the Checker Framework [3], a framework for pluggable Java type systems. The checker detects a possible null-pointer exception for the method invocation on `slice`. This is a false positive because the implementation ensures that if `inv` is non-null, `slice` is also non-null. Our approach allows us to use a deductive verifier to avoid the false positive being reported: We associate each type qualifier with a *refinement*, a logical formula expressing its semantics. Here, `NonNull`'s refinement is `subject` $\neq$ `null`, where `subject` stands for the typed variable, and `Nullable`'s refinement is `true`. Since the former formula implies the latter, we are allowed to define the subtyping hierarchy `NonNull` $\preceq$ `Nullable`. We then translate the type constraints into specifications in the Java Modeling Language (JML) [9], as seen in Fig. 2. There, instead of working with the type qualifiers and their predefined hierarchy, we work directly with the underlying formulas. The type constraint that the checker was unable to show is turned into an assertion, while the other constraints are turned into assumptions. This JML translation can be given to a deductive verification tool like KeY [1]. If all assertions in the translated program are valid, then we know that the putative type error is indeed a false positive.

Using our approach, only the parts of a program's central logic which establish and change the type properties in complex ways have to be considered for deductive verification, while the high-level parts which mostly just preserve the properties or rely on lower-level methods can be discharged by the type checker, which significantly lowers the verification overhead [7,8].

3   Refinement Types for Mutable Objects

This section summarizes our current work on extending what was presented in Sect. 2 to work with mutable objects. The two main issues we must consider are aliasing, for which we introduce a uniqueness type system in Sect. 3.1, and consistent updates in the presence of dependent types, for which we introduce a packing type system in Sect. 3.2. In Sect. 3.3, we then state the basic ideas needed to formalize and prove our approach.

3.1   Combining Uniqueness and Refinement Types

```
@MinLength(5) List a; @MaxLength(5) List b;
@MinLength(b.length) List c;
void foo() { a.insert(42); }
```

Fig. 3. Aliasing issue with refinement types.

To be able to apply refinement types to mutable objects, we need some way to restrict reference aliasing. Consider the example in Fig. 3. It contains the type qualifiers MinLength(n) and MaxLength(n) with the refinements subject.length $\geq n$ and subject.length $\leq n$ respectively. The method call a.insert(42) seems to be well-typed if we only consider a's type; but if a and b are aliases, it violates b's type. In addition, it may violate c's dependent type.

There are many type systems we could use to alleviate this problem. We settled on a simple system with the hierarchy Unique $\preceq$ MaybeAliased $\preceq$ ReadOnly, where MaybeAliased references may have other MaybeAliased aliases, but Unique references can only have ReadOnly aliases, which can never be used to mutate the object and may never occur in a refinement. Our system also supports ownership transfer mechanisms such as borrowing: A method argument has both an input and an output type, so for example a method with the signature foo(@Unique -> @Unique List arg) receives a unique reference, but must preserve the uniqueness so it can later be returned to the caller.

This system is quite restrictive. For example, it is impossible to have a well-typed mutable cyclic list. However, this restrictiveness has one major advantage that will be explained in Sect. 3.2. In the future, we may investigate using a more powerful type system like Universe Types [4]. Another possible avenue is to do with uniqueness types what we did with refinement types, i.e., define a translation into a specification language for deductive verifiers, such that ownership structures too complex to be proven by the type system can still be verified. The RustBelt project [6] already does something similar for Rust's ownership types.

In any case, our uniqueness types solve the aliasing problem with refinement types, as long as we abide by the following restrictions: Refinements may only appear on unique references. A refinement may only depend on other unique references in the current scope. A reference may only be mutated or transferred if doing so cannot violate any refinement dependent on it. E.g., if we make every reference in Fig. 3 unique, the method call becomes well-typed: We know that a is unique and that no refinement in the current scope depends on it[1]; thus no other reference's type is violated.

3.2 Consistent Updates with Packing Types

```
class List {
  @NonNegative int length;
  @Unique @Length(this.length) Node head;
  public void insert(@Unique -> @Unique List this,
                     int newDatum) {
    head = new Node(newDatum, head); ++length; }
```

Fig. 4. Keeping the fields consistent is impossible.

However, Fig. 4 shows a problem with our approach so far. No matter in what order we execute the two statements in the insert method, we will temporarily violate **head**'s type!

To alleviate this, we use a variant of the approach by Leino and Müller [11]: For an object o that is *packed* up to the class τ, all fields defined in τ and its superclasses must respect their declared types. In addition, these fields are unassignable and immutable. Fields defined in subclasses of τ in contrast can be reassigned and mutated and need not respect their declared types. An object's packing state can be changed via statements of the form **pack** o **as** τ and **unpack** o **from** τ. Packing an object is only allowed if all involved fields respect their declared types. Unlike Leino and Müller, who use special run-time fields to remember an object's packing state, we use a pluggable type system, i.e., a reference is packed up to τ if it has the type qualifier **Packed**(τ). To ensure that every non-read-only reference to the same object has the same packing type (a read-only reference's packing type is irrelevant, as it cannot be mutated or appear in refinements anyway), we only allow (un-)packing unique references. This means that the packing type system now serves double duty as an immutability type system: Since maybe-aliased references cannot be (un-)packed, such references with type **Packed**(τ) are immutable up to τ; thus we can use their state up to τ in refinements.

The problem in our example can be solved by inserting **unpack this from List** at the beginning and **pack this as List** at the end of the insert method. That pack statement is well-typed if the type checker can show that every field respects its declared type at that point in the program. If it cannot, then, as

---

[1] Actually, we cannot know whether this is true in the presence of subclassing, but this is dealt with in the following section.

usual, an assertion to that effect can be inserted into the program to be shown by a deductive verifier.

But suppose that our list has additional fields (e.g., tail, cache, etc.). Then to show the well-typedness of the pack statement, we would have to prove that every single field respects its declared type, even though we have only changed two. This is where our restrictive uniqueness type system comes in useful: A unique reference that has not been transferred cannot have been mutated; thus it is still in the same state it was in when the receiver was unpacked.

This packing type system allows us to relax the restrictions on refinements from the preceding subsection. Now, the refinement of a field or local variable in a class τ is allowed to depend on the abstract state $A(\text{this}, \tau)$, which includes:

1. Every field declared in τ or a superclass.
2. For every Unique or MaybeAliased field f declared with type Packed(τ_f) in τ or a superclass: $A(\text{this}.f, \tau_f)$.

3.3   Formalization and Proof Idea

For the proof, we are considering an approach similar to the one by Timany et al. [14] who differentiate between *syntactically well-typed* and *semantically well-typed* statements: The former holds if the statement respects the syntactic typing rules. The latter holds if the statement preserves well-typed states (in our case, that it preserves all refinement formulas, as well as the uniqueness and packing properties), even if this cannot be shown by the syntactic type checker. This formal framework fits nicely with our approach of encoding properties that cannot be shown by the type checker as assertions.

4   Conclusion and Outlook

We presented an approach which combines the scalability of type systems with the precision of deductive verification by translating those type constraints which a type checker was unable to show into specifications for a deductive verifier. By leveraging additional guarantees given by a uniqueness and a packing type system, we can apply this approach to languages with mutable objects.

We have formalized the approach and are working on an implementation and proof. We will build on the implementation of our previous work [8], which used the Checker Framework [3] and KeY [1]. For the proof, we are considering either using the Iris framework by Timany et al. [14], or Steinhöfel's work on extending KeY with abstract programs [13], which has the advantage that KeY already contains a complete formalization of our target language Java, but the disadvantage that KeY's dynamic frames are much more cumbersome than Iris's separation logic to reason about ownership and framing properties. We also plan to evaluate the approach by using it to verify a piece of software that uses the Checker Framework: Using our approach, we should be able to discharge any suppressed warnings using KeY; also, our combined approach should be easier and faster than using KeY alone.

References

1. Ahrendt, W., Beckert, B., Bubel, R., Hähnle, R., Schmitt, P.H., Ulbrich, M. (eds.): Deductive Software Verification - The KeY Book - From Theory to Practice, Lecture Notes in Computer Science, vol. 10001. Springer, Heidelberg (2016). https://doi.org/10.1007/978-3-319-49812-6
2. Bracha, G.: Pluggable type systems. In: OOPSLA 2004 Workshop on Revival of Dynamic Languages (2004)
3. Dietl, W., Dietzel, S., Ernst, M.D., Muslu, K., Schiller, T.: Building and using pluggable type-checkers. In: Proceedings of the 33rd International Conference on Software Engineering, ICSE 2011, pp. 681–690. Association for Computing Machinery (2011). https://doi.org/10.1145/1985793.1985889
4. Dietl, W., Ernst, M.D., Müller, P.: Tunable static inference for generic universe types. In: Mezini, M. (ed.) ECOOP 2011. LNCS, vol. 6813, pp. 333–357. Springer, Heidelberg (2011). https://doi.org/10.1007/978-3-642-22655-7_16
5. Ernst, M.D., Perkins, J.H., Guo, P.J., McCamant, S., Pacheco, C., Tschantz, M.S., Xiao, C.: The Daikon system for dynamic detection of likely invariants. Sci. Comput. Program. 69(1–3), 35–45 (2007)
6. Jung, R., Jourdan, J.H., Krebbers, R., Dreyer, D.: RustBelt: securing the foundations of the rust programming language. Proc. ACM Program. Lang. 2(POPL), 1–34 (2017). https://doi.org/10.1145/3158154
7. Klamroth, J., Lanzinger, F., Pfeifer, W., Ulbrich, M.: The Karlsruhe java verification suite, pp. 290–312. Springer, Heidelberg (2022). https://doi.org/10.1007/978-3-031-08166-8_14
8. Lanzinger, F., Weigl, A., Ulbrich, M., Dietl, W.: Scalability and precision by combining expressive type systems and deductive verification. Proc. ACM Program. Lang. 5(OOPSLA), 1–29 (2021). https://doi.org/10.1145/3485520
9. Leavens, G.T.,et al.: JML reference manual (2013). http://www.eecs.ucf.edu/leavens/JML//refman/jmlrefman.pdf, revision 2344
10. Lehmann, N., Geller, A., Barthe, G., Vazou, N., Jhala, R.: Flux: liquid types for rust (2022). https://doi.org/10.48550/ARXIV.2207.04034
11. Leino, K.R.M., Müller, P.: Object invariants in dynamic contexts. In: Odersky, M. (ed.) ECOOP 2004. LNCS, vol. 3086, pp. 491–515. Springer, Heidelberg (2004). https://doi.org/10.1007/978-3-540-24851-4_22
12. Sammler, M., Lepigre, R., Krebbers, R., Memarian, K., Dreyer, D., Garg, D.: Refinedc: automating the foundational verification of C code with refined ownership types. In: Proceedings of the 42nd ACM SIGPLAN International Conference on Programming Language Design and Implementation, PLDI 2021, pp. 158–174. Association for Computing Machinery, New York (2021). https://doi.org/10.1145/3453483.3454036
13. Steinhöfel, D.: Abstract execution: automatically proving infinitely many programs. Ph.D. thesis, Technische Universität, Darmstadt (2020). https://doi.org/10.25534/tuprints-00008540. http://tuprints.ulb.tu-darmstadt.de/8540/
14. Timany, A., Krebbers, R., Dreyer, D., Birkedal, L.: A logical approach to type soundness (2022). https://iris-project.org/pdfs/2022-submitted-logical-type-soundness.pdf
15. Toman, J., Siqi, R., Suenaga, K., Igarashi, A., Kobayashi, N.: ConSORT: context- and flow-sensitive ownership refinement types for imperative programs. In: ESOP 2020. LNCS, vol. 12075, pp. 684–714. Springer, Cham (2020). https://doi.org/10.1007/978-3-030-44914-8_25

Shuffling Posets on Trajectories

Luc Edixhoven[1,2]([✉])([iD])

[1] Open University of the Netherlands, Heerlen, The Netherlands
luc.edixhoven@ou.nl
[2] Centrum Wiskunde & Informatica (CWI), Amsterdam, The Netherlands

Abstract. Choreographies describe possible sequences of interactions among a set of agents. We aim to join two lines of research on choreographies: the use of the shuffle on trajectories operator to design more expressive choreographic languages, and the use of models featuring partial orders, to compactly represent concurrency between agents. Specifically, in this paper, we explore the application of the shuffle on trajectories operator to individual posets, and we give a characterisation of shuffles of posets which again yield an individual poset.

Keywords: Posets · Shuffle on trajectories · Concurrency

1 Introduction

Distributed systems are becoming ever more important. However, designing and implementing them is difficult. The complexity resulting from concurrency and dependencies among agents makes the process error-prone and debugging non-trivial. As a consequence, much research has been dedicated to analysing communication patterns, or protocols, among sets of agents in distributed systems. Examples of such research goals are to show the presence or absence of certain safety properties in a given system, to automate such analysis, and to guarantee the presence of desirable properties by construction.

Part of this research deals with *choreographies*. Choreographies can be used as global specifications for asynchronously communicating agents, and contain certain safety properties by construction. As a drawback, choreographic languages typically have limitations on their expressiveness, since they rely on grammatical constructs for their safety properties, which exclude some communication patterns. We have recently shown that the *shuffle on trajectories* operator can be used to specify choreographies without compromising expressiveness [2]. Consequently, it could serve as a basis for more expressive choreographic languages.

Other recent work on choreographies includes the use of models featuring partial orders, such as event structures [1] and pomsets [3,6], to represent and analyse the behaviour of choreographies. By using a partial order to explicitly capture causal dependencies between pairs of actions, these models avoid the exponential blowup from, e.g., parallel composition of finite state machines.

© The Author(s), under exclusive license to Springer Nature Switzerland AG 2024
P. Herber and A. Wijs (Eds.): iFM 2023, LNCS 14300, pp. 384–390, 2024.
https://doi.org/10.1007/978-3-031-47705-8_21

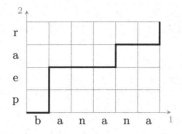

Fig. 1. The shuffle of 'banana' and 'pear' over a trajectory 1221112112: 'bpeanaanar'.

We aim to join these two lines of research by extending the shuffle on trajectories operator from words, i.e., totally ordered traces, and languages to partially ordered traces and sets thereof. In this paper, as a first step, we explore the application of the shuffle on trajectories operator to individual partially ordered sets, or posets. The main challenge is that the resulting behaviour cannot always be represented as one poset and may require a set of them. In particular, we give a characterisation of shuffles of posets which again yield an individual poset.

Outline. We recall the concept and definition of the shuffle on trajectories operator in Sect. 2. We briefly discuss posets in Sect. 3. In Sect. 4 we discuss how to apply the shuffle on trajectories operator to posets, and specifically which shuffles of posets will yield an individual poset as a result. Finally, we briefly discuss future work in Sect. 5.

The proofs of Proposition 1 and Lemma 1 can be found in a separate technical report on arXiv (https://arxiv.org/).

2   Shuffle on Trajectories

We recall the basic definitions from [2]. The shuffle on trajectories operator is a powerful variation of the traditional shuffle operator[1], which adds a control trajectory (or a set thereof) to restrict the permitted orders of interleaving. This allows for fine-grained control over orderings when shuffling words or languages. The binary operator was defined—and its properties thoroughly studied—by Mateescu et al. [4]; a multiary variant was introduced slightly later [5].

When defined on words, the shuffle on trajectories takes n words and a *trajectory*, which is a word over the alphabet $\{1, \ldots, n\}$. This trajectory specifies the exact order of interleaving of the shuffled words: in Fig. 1, the trajectory 1221112112 specifies that the result should first take a symbol from the first word, then from the second, then again from the second and so on.

---

[1] In concurrency theory, the shuffle operator is also known as free interleaving, non-communication merge, or parallel composition.

Formally, let $w_1, \ldots, w_n$ be finite words over some alphabet and let t be a finite word over the alphabet $\{1, \ldots, n\}$. Let ε be the empty word. Then:

$$\sqcup_t^n(w_1, \ldots, w_n) = \begin{cases} a \sqcup_{t'}^n (w_1, \ldots, w_i', \ldots, w_n) & \text{if } t = it' \text{ and } w_i = aw_i' \\ \varepsilon & \text{if } t = w_1 = \ldots = w_n = \varepsilon \end{cases}$$

We note that $\sqcup_t^n(w_1, \ldots, w_n)$ is only defined if the number of occurrences of i in t precisely matches the length of w_i for every i. We then say that t *fits* w_i.

Example 1.

– $\sqcup_{121332}^3(ab, cd, ef) = acbefd$, since 121332 fits every word.
– $\sqcup_{121}^2(ab, cd)$ is undefined, since 121 does not fit cd.

The shuffle on trajectories operator naturally generalises to languages: the shuffle of a number of languages on a set (i.e., a language) of trajectories is defined as the set of all valid shuffles of words in the languages for which the trajectory fits all the words. Formally:

$$\sqcup_T^n(L_1, \ldots, L_n) = \{\sqcup_t^n(w_1, \ldots, w_n) \mid t \in T, w_1 \in L_1, \ldots, w_n \in L_n\}$$

As the operator's arity is clear from its operands, we typically omit it.

3   Posets

Partially ordered sets, or posets for short, consist of a set of nodes E (events), and a partial order[2] $\leq$ defining dependencies between pairs of events—i.e., an event can only fire if all events preceding it in the partial order have already fired. We write $a < b$ to denote that $a \leq b$ and $a \neq b$. We write $a \geq b$ resp. $a > b$ to denote that $b \leq a$ resp. $b < a$. We write $a \not\leq b$ to denote that $a \not\leq b$ and $b \not\leq a$; we then say that a and b are *concurrent*. We occasionally write $E_P, \leq_P, <_P, \geq_P, >_P$ and $\not\leq_P$ to specify that the set of events or relation belongs to poset P, but where this is clear from context we typically omit the subscript.

The behaviour (or language) of a poset P, written $L(P)$, is the set of all maximal traces, i.e., maximal sequences of its events, that abide by $\leq$. In this sense, posets can be considered a generalisation of words with concurrency: they feature a fixed set of symbols (events)[3], but they can allow multiple orderings of them instead of only a single one. Concurrent events can happen in any order.

---

[2] Recall that a partial order is reflexive, transitive and antisymmetric.

[3] There is a difference between words and posets in the sense that the events in a poset must be unique, whereas a word may contain duplicate symbols. It would be more accurate to say that words generalise to *labelled* posets, or lposets, and from there to partially ordered *multisets*, or pomsets. However, in this paper we focus on posets, where all symbols are thus unique.

Consequently, all traces obtained from a trace in $L(P)$ by swapping adjacent concurrent events must also be in $L(P)$. In fact, any trace in $L(P)$ can be obtained from any other trace in $L(P)$ in this fashion.

Example 2. For poset P_{ex} in Fig. 2, $E = \{a, b, c, d\}$ and the partial order consists of $a \leq a$, $a \leq c$, $a \leq d$, $b \leq b$, $b \leq d$, $c \leq c$ and $d \leq d$. Its language $L(P_{ex})$ consists of the traces *abcd*, *abdc*, *acbd*, *bacd*, and *badc*.

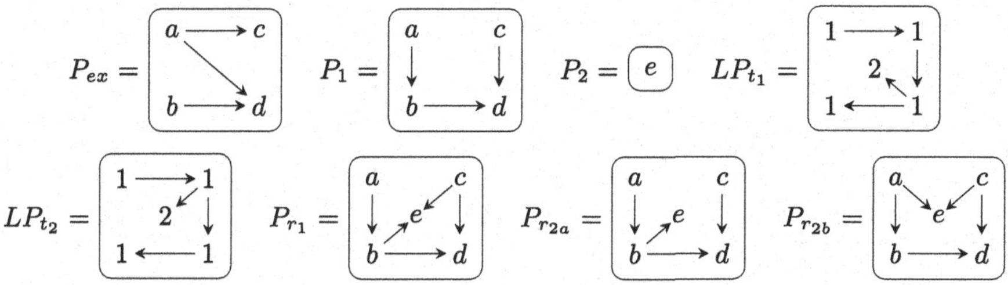

Fig. 2. Graphical representation of a number of posets and lposets, where an arrow from a to b should be read as $a \leq b$. The partial order is the reflexive and transitive closure of the dependencies depicted by the arrows. For the lposets, the labels are shown rather than their events.

We note that the dependencies in a poset can also be observed in its set of traces. For example, if $a < b$ then a will precede b in every trace, and if $a \not\geq b$ then there will both be traces where a precedes b and traces where b precedes a. Formally, we can extract the following relation $\leq_L$ from a set of traces $L \subseteq E^*$:

$$\frac{\exists x, y, z \in E^* : xaybz \in L \qquad \forall \hat{x}, \hat{y}, \hat{z} \in E^* : \hat{x}b\hat{y}a\hat{z} \notin L}{a \leq_L b} \qquad \frac{}{a \leq_L a} \qquad \frac{a \leq_L b \leq_L c}{a \leq_L c}$$

We then propose the following:

Proposition 1. *Let* $P = \langle E_P, \leq_P \rangle$ *be a poset. Then* $\leq_{L(P)} = \leq_P$.

To model trajectories, which require duplicate symbols, we must also introduce *labelled* posets, or *lposets*. In these, every event is assigned a label, which is not necessarily unique. Its traces then use these labels instead of the events.

4 Shuffling Posets

As a first step towards shuffling posets, we first reinterpret shuffles on words as posets. In other words: we consider the case where all posets, including the trajectory, are totally ordered and thus consist of a single trace. This is shown in Fig. 3, which features the shuffle from Fig. 1 interpreted as a poset. The traces 'banana' and 'pear' are present as totally ordered parts of the poset, and the trajectory adds additional dependencies between the two, as shown by the vertical (and diagonal) arrows.

Generalising this to arbitrary posets and lposets is not trivial, but we have some knowledge to assist us. Crucially, since we can determine the language of a poset, it must be so that the result of shuffling posets yields the same language as the shuffle of the languages of these posets, which is defined in Sect. 2:

$$L(\sqcup_{P_t}(P_1, \ldots, P_n)) = \sqcup_{L(P_t)}(L(P_1), \ldots, L(P_n))$$

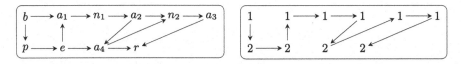

Fig. 3. The figure on the left shows the shuffle from Fig. 1 interpreted as a shuffle of posets. Indices have been added to duplicate symbols to make them unique. Some of the arrows are redundant but are kept to illustrate the general idea. The figure on the right shows the trajectory, 1221112112, as an lposet.

If the result is an individual poset, by Proposition 1 it must then be:

$$\sqcup_{P_t}(P_1, \ldots, P_n) = \langle E_{P_1} \cup \ldots \cup E_{P_n}, \leq_{\sqcup_{L(P_t)}(L(P_1), \ldots, L(P_n))} \rangle$$

For example, consider $\sqcup_{LP_{t_1}}(P_1, P_2)$, with LP_{t_1}, P_1 and P_2 as in Fig. 2. LP_{t_1} has traces 1121 and 1112, P_1 has traces $abcd$, $acbd$ and $cabd$, and P_2 has a single trace e. Shuffling these languages yields $L_1 = \{abced, acbed, cabed, abcde, acbde, cabde\}$. From this we extract $\leq_{L_1}$, which contains all the dependencies present in P_1 and P_2 and, additionally, $a \leq_{L_1} e$, $b \leq_{L_1} e$ and $c \leq_{L_1} e$. This corresponds to poset P_{r_1} in Fig. 2, which indeed yields the language L_1.

However, now consider $\sqcup_{LP_{t_2}}(P_1, P_2)$, again as in Fig. 2. LP_{t_2} has traces 1211, 1121 and 1112, which yields $L_2 = L_1 \cup \{abecd, acebd, caebd\}$. From this we extract $\leq_{L_2}$, which still contains all the dependencies in P_1 and P_2, but otherwise only $a \leq_{L_2} e$: the traces $abecd$ and $acebd$ imply that b and c are concurrent with e. However, then the trace $aebcd$ should also be in L_2, which it is not. We can then conclude from Proposition 1 that there exists no poset P such that $L(P) = L_2$. In fact, L_2 corresponds to a set of two posets, namely $P_{r_{2a}}$ and $P_{r_{2b}}$ in Fig. 2.

We proceed by giving a characterisation of shuffles of posets for which the result corresponds to an individual poset. A key insight is that, if the result must correspond to an individual poset, then any two events which are concurrent in one of the operands of the shuffle must, in the resulting poset, have the same relation ($<$, $>$ or $\nleq$) to any third event originating from another operand:

Lemma 1. *Let LP_t be an lposet and $P_1, \ldots, P_n, P$ posets such that $L(\sqcup\!\sqcup_{LP_t}(P_1, \ldots, P_n)) = L(P)$ and $L(P) \neq \emptyset$. If $a, b \in E_{P_i}$ such that $a \not\geq_{P_i} b$ and $c \in E_{P_j}$ with $i \neq j$, then either $a, b <_P c$, or $a, b >_P c$, or $a, b \not\geq_P c$.*

We can then group the events in every P_i according to the reflexive and transitive closure of the concurrency relation $\not\geq_{P_i}$; two events which are related in this closure then belong to the same group. Note that, while the events in a group are partially ordered, the groups of every P_i are, by construction, totally ordered. It follows from Lemma 1 that two events in the same group, even when not concurrent, must have the same relation to any event outside of their group in P. This in turn implies a similar condition on the trajectory lposet: any two i-labelled events in LP_t that can match two events from the same group of P_i must have the same relation to any j-labelled event in LP_t (where j is not necessarily unequal to i) that can match an event outside of their group.

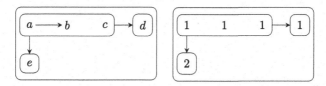

Fig. 4. The figure on the left shows P_{r_1}, corresponding to $\sqcup\!\sqcup_{LP_{t_1}}(P_1, P_2)$ (see Fig. 2), restructured to show the groups of P_1 and P_2. An arrow from one group of events to another should be read as an arrow from all events in the originating group to all events in the target group. The figure on the right shows the restructured LP_{t_1}; the dependencies within groups in LP_{t_1} are irrelevant for the resulting traces.

Figure 4 shows P_{r_1}, corresponding to $\sqcup\!\sqcup_{LP_{t_1}}(P_1, P_2)$, and LP_{t_1} (from Fig. 2), both restructured to show the groups of P_1 and P_2. This demonstrates an interesting parallel with Fig. 3: both feature horizontal traces with additional arrows specifying dependencies between components of these traces. However, in Fig. 3 the components consist of individual events, whereas in Fig. 4 the components consist of posets. In this sense, shuffles resulting in individual posets generalise shuffles on traces.

Concluding, we can then characterise shuffles on posets which result in individual posets as those where the trajectory lposet is structured along the operand posets' groups, as in Fig. 4, possibly with dependencies between different operands' groups.

5   Future Work

Now that we have studied shuffles of posets resulting in individual posets, there are two evident avenues for future work: (1) shuffles of lposets, where one label may occur multiple times rather than just considering orderings of unique events and (2) shuffles of posets resulting in sets of posets and shuffles of sets of posets, where the main challenge may be to minimise the resulting number of posets.

References

1. Castellani, I., Dezani-Ciancaglini, M., Giannini, P.: Event structure semantics for multiparty sessions. J. Log. Algebraic Methods Program. **131**, 100844 (2023)
2. Edixhoven, L., Jongmans, S.: Balanced-by-construction regular and ω-regular languages. Int. J. Found. Comput. Sci. **34**(2&3), 117–144 (2023)
3. Edixhoven, L., Jongmans, S., Proença, J., Cledou, G.: Branching pomsets for choreographies. In: ICE. EPTCS, vol. 365, pp. 37–52 (2022)
4. Mateescu, A., Rozenberg, G., Salomaa, A.: Shuffle on trajectories: syntactic constraints. Theor. Comput. Sci. **197**(1–2), 1–56 (1998)
5. Mateescu, A., Salomaa, K., Yu, S.: On fairness of many-dimensional trajectories. J. Autom. Lang. Comb. **5**(2), 145–157 (2000)
6. Tuosto, E., Guanciale, R.: Semantics of global view of choreographies. J. Log. Algebraic Methods Program. **95**, 17–40 (2018)

A Framework for Verifying the Collision Freeness of Collaborative Robots (Work in Progress)

Artur Graczyk[✉], Marialena Hadjikosti, and Andrei Popescu

University of Sheffield, Sheffield, UK
{apgraczyk1,mhadjicosti1,a.popescu}@sheffield.ac.uk

Abstract. Collision avoidance is a major problem when robotic devices are being deployed to perform complex collaborative tasks. We present a vision for a framework that makes it convenient to program collaborative robots and to verify that their behaviour is collision-free. It consists of a domain-specific language that is shallowly embedded in the ROS (Robot Operating System) framework and a translation into a programming language that is deeply embedded in the Isabelle/HOL theorem prover.

1 Vision

Our research targets collaborative tasks involving the movement of robots (mobile platforms or robotic arms). Such tasks are naturally expressed as controlled sequences of commands requesting the movement of robots to specific locations where to perform specific activities.

Collisions between two robots can occur in several scenarios, including:

Scenario 1. Two robots must visit the same location during a task. E.g., one robot brings an item to a location, from where another robot picks it up.

Scenario 2. While moving between two locations, the trajectories of two robots intersect. E.g., two robots need to enter an enclosure through the same gate.

Scenario 3. The trajectory of one robot touches the location where another robot performs a task. E.g., the second robot does a repairing job at the gate through which the first robot must enter.

Each scenario above suggests a possible collision point in space, i.e., a point that each of the two robots need to visit. Communication with the robots and subsequent synchronization can avoid such collisions, for example:

- In Scenario 1, the program can ask the second robot to wait at a safe distance until the first robot has successfully delivered the object to the given location and has moved away from that location.
- In Scenario 2, one can implement a mutual exclusion protocol whereby the first robot who announces its intention to go through the gate makes any other robot who wants to enter, pause and wait.

© The Author(s), under exclusive license to Springer Nature Switzerland AG 2024
P. Herber and A. Wijs (Eds.): iFM 2023, LNCS 14300, pp. 391–397, 2024.
https://doi.org/10.1007/978-3-031-47705-8_22

– In Scenario 3, the robot needing to pass through the gate could wait for the repairer robot to finish; or one might implement a more involved protocol whereby, depending on the urgency of the task, the repairer robot could pause its activity and move aside to let the other robot pass.

What all the discussed scenarios have in common is that they are fairly abstract: we can understand the collision problems that they raise in terms of the coordinates of the targeted locations and (a conservative over-approximation of) the sizes of the robots. And the solutions we discussed for these problems are equally abstract; indeed, they can be expressed in a high-level robot command language that tells the robots *what* movements to make, and in which sequence and under which conditions—but does not indicate *how* they should move from one location to another. In short, under this abstract view, both the collision problems and their solutions refer to the *what* but not to the *how*. This abstract view enables the following fruitful analogy: *Robot Collisions* $\simeq$ *Data Races*.

Of course, for collisions we are not talking about the usual data races, which take place in the digital space, but about *races in the physical space*. However, the ideas are essentially the same: While in concurrency one requests that the executions of two processes (or threads) never enter certain critical sections of their code at the same time, with collisions one requests that, during a collaborative task, the trajectories of two robots are never crossing each other. Moreover, it is in principle possible for robot programs to "internalize" the information about collision, in that the avoidance of collision can be mapped to the execution of certain critical sections, just like in concurrency. This has an important methodological consequence: *Verification and analysis techniques from concurrency can be adapted to produce collision avoidance guarantees for collaborating robots.* In this ongoing work, we are bringing to fruition some of the consequences of this analogy with concurrent programming:

– developing a formal semantics of a robot programming language and a property specification language that regard collisions as a form of data races, and
– performing an encoding of collisions as actual data races whose absence can be proved using concurrency verification and analysis tools.

2   Achieving the Vision

Achieving this vision requires the following:

– choosing and adapting a robot programming environment (discussed in Sect. 2.1),
– setting up a formal verification framework (discussed in Sect. 2.2), and
– building the infrastructure for protected navigation, including a path analysis tool for computing safe corridors (not detailed in this paper).

Importantly, it also requires connecting these three components, which must exchange data between each other in order to achieve overall *strong collision freeness guarantees covering both fundamental and incidental collision hazards*. This will happen through the following tools:

- a code generator connecting the verification framework with the robotic programming environment,
- a tool for automatically transporting information from within the verification framework to a navigation path analysis tool, and
- a tool for plugging the computed corridors into the ROS run-time environment, to change the way robots view the physical space for navigation purposes.

Of course, there will be some assumptions about the robot environment and the navigation system in order for the formally proved guarantees to hold; for example, it will be assumed that the navigation system keeps the robot within the limits of the computed corridors (which in turn relies on the correctness of certain navigation algorithms).

2.1   Robot Programming Environment

Our goal is to have a practical programming environment, in which we can easily program collaborative robotic tasks in a transparent fashion, suitable for verification. Because of the practicality desideratum, we have chosen the ROS system as implemented in Python via the *rospy* library—which is widely used by robot practitioners.

However, at its core the ROS framework employs a model of communication (based on topics and/or services) that is very versatile but somewhat bureaucratic. For this reason, we implemented, on top of ROS, an API for enabling more direct communication with the robotic devices (Sect. 2.1.1). The user of the API does not need to explicitly create, use or subscribe to topics or services. Rather, the creation of these entities happens behind the scenes, and the API allows one to issue direct movement commands to the robots, and send inquiries to them about their status.

The API thus abstracts away from the communication complexity, allowing one to focus on programming the movements of the robots, which makes the programs more amenable to collision-freeness verification. As it will be sketched in Sect. 2.2, the functions of the API have been not only implemented in Python, but have also been given a formal semantics in our verification framework—for the purpose of connecting the programming and verification platforms. In addition to the API, the connection between the two platforms also requires an identification of a domain-specific language (DSL), covered by a formal semantics. Our DSL is a Turing-complete multi-threaded fragment of Python featuring calls to the API as atomic statements (Sect. 2.1.2).

2.1.1   ROS-Based API

The API consists of functions for initializing, moving and sending inquiries to the robots for various pieces of information. More precisely, we have the following functions, with the following behaviors:

- initRobot: Takes a robot ID and the coordinates of a desired initial position and initializes a robot at the given position.

- moveTo: Takes a robot ID and a target position and issues a command to the indicated robot for moving to the indicated position.
- getSuccessStatus: Takes a robot ID and sends an inquiry to the given robot on whether the last attempted action was completed successfully.
- getMovingStatus: Takes a robot ID and determines whether the robot is currently moving.
- getPosition: Takes a robot ID and returns the robot's current position.

These functions were chosen to have a simple and intuitive semantics, and to allow the programming of interesting examples.

2.1.2 Python/ROS-Based DSL
Below is the syntax of our domain-specific language:

$$
\begin{array}{ll}
\text{Lit} & ::= \text{IntLit} \mid \text{RealLit} \mid \text{BoolLit} \mid \text{StringLit} \\
\text{Op}_1 & ::= - \mid \text{not} \\
\text{Op}_2 & ::= + \mid - \mid * \mid \% \mid = \mid \text{and} \mid \text{or} \\
\text{RobotID} & ::= \text{StringLit} \\
\text{Exp} & ::= \text{Var} \mid \text{Lit} \mid \text{Op}_1 \text{ Exp} \mid \text{Exp Op}_2 \text{ Exp} \mid \\
& \quad \text{getSuccessStatus (RobotID)} \mid \\
& \quad \text{getMovingStatus (RobotID)} \mid \\
& \quad \text{getPosition (RobotID)}
\end{array}
$$

$$
\begin{array}{ll}
\text{Coord} & ::= (\text{RealLit}, \text{RealLit}) \qquad \text{for now, two dimensions only} \\
\text{ACom} & ::= \text{skip} \mid \text{Var} = \text{Exp}; \mid \text{moveTo (RobotID, Coord)}; \\
\text{InitGV} & ::= \text{initGlobalVar(Var, Exp)} \\
\text{RobotInfo} & ::= \ldots \\
\text{InitR} & ::= \text{initRobot(RobotID, RobotInfo)} \\
\text{ISec} & ::= \text{InitGV}^* \text{ InitR}^* \\
\text{Com} & ::= \text{ACom} \mid \\
& \quad \text{Com Com} \mid \\
& \quad \text{if (Exp) \{Com\} else \{Com\}} \mid \\
& \quad \text{while (Exp) \{Com\}} \\
\text{Thread} & ::= \text{ISec Com} \\
\text{Prog} & ::= \text{Thread}^*
\end{array}
$$

We have the usual real, integer, boolean and strings expressions (built from literals and operators—logical, arithmetical, etc.), as well as calls to our API observation functions (in blue), which take robot IDs parameters (string literals). Only well-typed programs are accepted, but we omit the obvious typing.

The atomic commands are skip (i.e., "do nothing"), assignments of expressions to variables, and calls to the robot moving function of our API. The moving function takes a robot ID and a coordinate. For now, coordinates are just pairs of numbers, since initially we focus on two-dimensional moves—but both the verification and the programming frameworks have been built in such a way that an upgrade to three dimensions can be made without much rewriting.

Finally, programs consist of multiple threads. We opted for a multi-threaded DSL (using the multi-threading facilities of Python) because this makes it easier to program collaborative tasks. Usually there is one thread dedicated to each participating robot, but our framework does not impose that—indeed, any thread can issue commands to any robot.

A thread consists of an initialization section (ISec) and a compound command (Com). In the initialization section, the global variables (visible in all the threads hence usable for inter-thread communication) are initialized with expressions, and the robots are initialized with "robot info" that has a format specific to each type of robot (e.g., various types of robotic arms or mobile platforms). Any variable that is not initialized as global is assumed to be local. The compound command is the actual code of the thread, written in a while language defined on top of the atomic commands.

This DSL, which (as mentioned) was implemented in Python on top of ROS, has the runtime behavior that one might expect. Thus, unless the code contains synchronization logic (e.g., waiting for a global flag to become true), the threads' commands are executed concurrently, so any ordering between the commands in different threads is possible. When a robot is asked for some information (via an API call in an expression), we can assume it will answer in a certain amount of time, so not necessarily instantly—any collaborative task program should take this into account, for example, the implemented protocol should take into consideration that a response to getPosition may become outdated. Similarly, when a "move to" command is issued (as discussed in Sect. 2.1.1) the robot will put this command in its queue and will get to it when it finishes the other commands from the queue (which it has received before).

The language does not contain timed commands. Moreover, we have no information about the speed with which a robot performs its tasks; but can only learn of the current status if we ask for it. These design decisions are intentional, since we aim for *collision-freeness gurantees that do not rely on time*.

2.2 Verification and Analysis Infrastructure

We have chosen the theorem prover Isabelle as the primary host of our verification infrastructure, because of its versatility and expressiveness. To enable verification, we will connect our programming environment with Isabelle. The identification of a suitable API and DSL for programming robot behaviors in a hassle-free manner (discussed in Sect. 2.1) has been a major step towards achieving this connection. Indeed, by isolating a relatively small fragment of Python and defining a simple interface to ROS-managed robots has created a manageable formalization task.

We have already specified a formal semantics of our API and DSL in Isabelle. To connect the Python/ROS DSL implementation with the Isabelle counterpart, we are implementing a translation (a code generator) between the two. This way, for example, the robot programmer can use the DSL to program the desired robot behavior, then the verification expert can employ the Python-to-Isabelle translation to obtain a copy of the program in Isabelle, where collision-freeness can be verified. This translation will be part of the trusted code base, and we will validate its soundness via testing.

From a formal perspective, collision freeness is a safety property ("something bad never happens") and has been defined as such in Isabelle. The formal semantics represents, in addition to the usual state containing values for the global and local variables, a "robot store" that keeps the status of each robot involved in the program—indicating whether the robot is currently stalling or moving between two waypoints, and the queue of tasks for which the robot has already received commands. In this context, collision freeness is formulated as follows: It is never the case that two robots are at the same time engaged in trajectories (i.e., pairs of waypoints) that can collide. The "can collide" predicate, which takes two trajectories (i.e., two pairs of positions) and returns true or false, is currently left generic in Isabelle. It will be instantiated to suitable concrete predicates based on domain-specific knowledge (obtained with the help of robot experts) about the type of the robot and its spatial and moving characteristics, and the known obstacles at the site. For example, if we have a room with only one gate and two trajectories whose start locations are outside the room and whose target locations are inside the room, then the "can collide" predicate will return true. Note that the "can collide" predicate will also be able to accommodate properties such as "physical" starvation, when two robots both need to enter some space but neither are ever able to.

3   (Very Rough Summary of) Related Work

The general area of robotic system safety assurance and verification is a large and rapidly growing area.[1] Important subareas include the verification of autonomous robotic systems [1,4] and of industrial collaborative robots [2] using methods such as theorem proving, model checking and safety controller synthesis and monitoring. The employed formal models include timed automata [3] and process algebras [5]. Our work will mostly apply to robotic systems that are involved in pre-determined and largely pre-scripted collaborative tasks.

Acknowledgment. We thank the three anonymous reviewers for their valuable comments and suggestions, which led to the improvement of the presentation.

References

1. Dixon, C.: Verifying autonomous robots: challenges and reflections (invited talk). In: Muñoz-Velasco, E., Ozaki, A., Theobald, M. (eds.) TIME 2020, vol. 178 LIPIcs, pp. 1:1–1:4 (2020)
2. Douthwaite, J.A.: A modular digital twinning framework for safety assurance of collaborative robotics. Front. Robot. AI **8**, 758099 (2021)

---

[1] See https://www.andreipopescu.uk/litrev.pdf for a detailed literature review, including the connection with major verification projects such as those pursued at the RoboStar* center (https://robostar.cs.york.ac.uk).

3. Halder, R., Proença, J., Macedo, N., Santos, A.: Formal verification of ros-based robotic applications using timed-automata. In: FormaliSE, pp. 44–50 (2017)
4. Luckcuck, M., Farrell, M., Dennis, L., Dixon, C., Fisher, M.: Formal specification and verification of autonomous robotic systems: a survey. ACM Comput. Surv. **52**(5), Sept. 2019
5. O'Brien, M., Arkin, R.C., Harrington, D., Lyons, D., Jiang, S.: Automatic verification of autonomous robot missions. In Simulation, Modeling, and Programming for Autonomous Robots, pp. 462–473, Cham (2014)

Correction to: Integrated Formal Methods

Paula Herber and Anton Wijs

Correction to:
P. Herber and A. Wijs (Eds.): *Integrated Formal Methods*,
LNCS 14300, https://doi.org/10.1007/978-3-031-47705-8

In the original version of this book the main and subtitle was not correct. This was corrected.

The updated version of this book can be found at
https://doi.org/10.1007/978-3-031-47705-8

P. Herber and A. Wijs (Eds.): IFM 2023, LNCS 14300, p. C1, 2024.
https://doi.org/10.1007/978-3-031-47705-8_23

Author Index

P. Herber and A. Wijs (Eds.): iFM 2023, LNCS 14300, pp. 399–400, 2024.
https://doi.org/10.1007/978-3-031-47705-8

Printed in the United States
by Baker & Taylor Publisher Services